PREFACE

The history of our county is best told in a record of the lives of its people. We have gone to the people, the men and women who have, by their enterprise and industry, made this county the success it is today, so that Lake Couty is second to none in this great Hoosier State and noble Nation!

No more interesting or instructive matter could be presented to an intelligent public. In this volume will be found a record of many whose lives are worthy of imitation by coming generations. In every life there is a lesson that should not be lost upon those who follow afterward. Coming generations will appreciate this work and preserve it as a sacred trust, from the mere fact that it contains so much that would never find its way into public print or would otherwise be lost to future generations.

The faces of some and the life stories of many will be missed in this volume. Most did not have the proper conception of the project; some refused to give the information necessary to compile their story; while many others were indifferent. Some family members would oppose the project and on that account, support and interest was withheld.

If this history project is ever completed and printed it will be because the community became involved in the project to preserve our story, our heritage. No one person could ever complete the story of our complex county!

A good history is more than a record of things past; it's a record of things people felt to be important to preserve. The more Lake County people who share some part of their story, the better, more complete glimpse it will be when viewed by future generations.

So I salute those who have taken the time to become involved in this project — it matters not if your kin have lived here before this area became Lake County, or if you and your family have lived here a short while — thanks for sharing and preserving your story and leaving a record of yourself, your family and/or business on the pages of history.

Our Lake County Heritage is worthwhile to preserve!

> Steven Yaros, Jr.
> Project Director
> December 12, 1988

[Mr. Yaros resigned as project director in 1988]

LAKE COUNTY HERITAGE

Ann Weitgenant
Project Director

Supported by The Friends of the
Lake County Public Library

ISBN: 0-88107-170-6

Copyright Curtis Media Corporation — 1990

TABLE OF CONTENTS

TOWNS AND PLACES 1

TRANSPORTATION 7

SCHOOLS AND EDUCATION 13

CHURCHES 27

ORGANIZATIONS 35

MISCELLANEOUS 41

FAMILY STORIES 47

BUSINESS STORIES 201

INDEX 219

Printed and published in the United States by Curtis Media Corporation, Dallas, Texas. All rights reserved. No part of this work covered by the copyright may be reproduced or copied in any form or by any means — graphic, electronic or mechanical, including photo-copying, recording, taping, or information and retrieval systems — without written permission from the publishers. The materials were compiled and produced using available information; the publishers regret they cannot assume liability for errors or omissions.

iii

THE HISTORY OF LAKE COUNTY

Lake County was first settled at its highest point of altitude on the little Fancher Lake, which is now the center of the Lake County Fair Grounds, near Crown Point. This was in 1834. Almost simultaneously the "Yankee" or West Creek settlement was started, a few miles west of Lowell. The first families were the Fancher, Wilson, Horner, Robinson, Childers, Clark and others. The first Court of Justice in Lake County was organized in 1836. The town of Liverpool became its first County Seat, but existed only on paper. The same year the first post office was established at Lake Court House, in the store of Solon Robinson, the first store in the county. The proceeds of the post office for the first three months were $15.00, at 25 cents per letter. It all went to paying the postmaster and mail carrier vested in one man, Solon Robinson.

The county was organized in March, 1837. Its first officers were: Henry Wells, Sheriff; Solon Robinson, Clerk; William Holton, Recorder; William Crooks and William Clark, Judges; Amasi Ball, Thomas Wells and Stringham were its first Commissioners. The first regular physician of Lake County was Dr. H.D. Palmer. Religious services were first held at Solon Robinson's home. The first church buildings erected in the county were the M.E. Church in West Creek, and the Roman Catholic at St. John, in 1843. The first formal organization on record in the county was the Methodist class at Pleasant Grove. In 1838 Congress established two mail routes through the county — from Laporte to Joliet through Lake Court, now Crown Point. The first sawmills were built by Walton, Wood, Dustin and Taylor. The northern end of the county furnished much of the pine to build Chicago, by being stolen.

Bridge building began in 1838 over West Creek and Cedar Creek; five were built that year for $1,500. In 1839 the County Seat became located at Crown Point where it has been ever since. The population of the county was then 1,463. In 1843 the scarlet fever entered Crown Point, and brought about the selection of a special ground for the first cemetery of the county.

In 1844 the first Presbyterian Church was organized at Crown Point with eighteen members. Two years later, the Methodists and Presbyterians both erected their first brick church.

In 1847, thirteen years after its first settlement, Lake County had seven post offices, five sawmills, two grist-mills, five church buildings, five stores, about fifty frame houses, and many more less pretentious log houses. There were two lawyers, seven physicians, fifteen justices of the peace, five local ministers, one circuit preacher and one Presbyterian preacher. The first railroad to enter Lake County was the Michigan Central, in 1851.

Achievements

Lake County has now a population of about 75,000. It has twenty-two railroads passing within its boundaries, with a total mileage of about 350 miles of main track and 200 miles of side track — more than any other county in the state. These railroads are assessed at $20,000 per mile of roadbed.

There are about $1,000,000 worth of graveled road in the county. There are sixty-six church buildings, and about the same number of ministers and priests; one hundred and twenty schoolhouses, two hundred teachers, one hundred physicians, fifty attorneys and fourteen banks.

Lake County has a taxable property of $34,000,000; the appropriation for the running expenses for 1907 is $90,000. It stands at the head of all the counties in the state in manufacturing and railroads, two-thirds of its taxes being derived from these sources. The northern portion of the county is best located for manufactures, and the southern portion is finest for agriculture.

The early history of Lake County owes much to the quality of its immigrants from New England, for its thrift and intelligence. Later on have come other nationalities — German, Bohemian, Irish, Swedes, Norweigians, Poles — which by admixture have strengthened, enriched and varied the population.

Some Notable Features of Lake County

Lake County has the largest printing and book-binding establishment in the world — the Conkey plant at Hammond; the largest surgical instrument manufacturing establishment in the world — the Betz plant at Hammond; the largest oil refinery in the world — the Standard Oil refinery at Whiting; the largest steel plant in the world; the two smallest men in the world — the dwarfs exhibited by Mr. Rossow, and the best equipped distillery in the United States, with a capacity of 25,000 gallons, located in Hammond. It has the longest mileage of railroads of any county in the state; the only self-supporting Poor Farm in the state; the largest porous tile (terra cotta) factory in the state, if not in the country. It has the greatest variety and number of manufacturing plants of any county in the state, Marion not included. It has the most lake coast, and the best harbor of any county in the state. It is the longest county in the state, though Vermilion, Knox and Jasper rank close with it in this respect. It has one of the largest and most varied foreign-born populations of any county in the state. It is the nearest to Chicago of any county in the state.

Lake County Poor Farm

No condition of life appeals more strongly to the heart of humanity than, when, the strength of life having been spent in its battles for sustenance and position, life's evening shadows at last creep around the combatant, desolate forsaken and homeless. It is to prevent, or at least to ameliorate, such conditions that County Poor Farms have been established by statute, and they they are supported by the contributions of common citizenship, through taxation.

Yet the thing that is meant in good, and is the child of noble impulse, has been made to result in much evil in practce, and to become father to crying abuses. Newspapers, reformers and men of honor, heart and courage in high places, have exposed and rebuked the abuses that had grown in connnection with the management of Poor Farms. They have told how in almost every county in our fair state old people were treated neglectfully and shamefully.

This happily cannot be said of Lake County's Poor Farm. Especially during the present administration, which dates from 1898, the Farm has made a splendid record, thanks to the humane, sympathetic, vigilant and business-like management of the big-hearted superintendent, Erehart Bixenman, and his noble wife.

There are at present writing, 44 inmates in the Lake County Poor Farm, ranging in age from 48 to 95, six of them being women. The fine farm of 310 acres is located four miles directly east of Crown Point, on a good gravel road. It has seventy acres of good timber, 120 under profitable cultivation; the rest in pasture and pleasure or ornamental grounds. It is kept strictly neat and productive, and is so well managed that it pays its expenses. This can scarcely be said of any other Poor Farm in the state. The residence for inmates was erected in 1884; it costs $5,000 per year for maintenance. It is thoroughly modernized in construction, and two men and two women are employed to keep it in attractive order. There are extensive barns, horse and cattle sheds all kept with the same systematic care, Mr. Bixenman being himself the hardest worker of all.

The inmates are greatly attracted to their "home." The eldest, 95, has it for her routne to set the table for the inmates, and is as jealous and proud of her care as if she were appointed first maid in the White House. Mr. Bixenman is as attentive and courteous to visitors as he is considerate to inmates, and faithful to his public trust.

First School House of Lake County

This school house was built in the early spring of 1838, in the dawn of the history of Lake County. It was located near the west bank of Cedar Creek, on the old Ditmar farm. At the last account it served the less dignified purpose of housing horses. Two other school houses were built that year in Lake County that dispute its right to priority. Hewn logs were its masonry; the puncheon floor, the split log bench against the walls, a slanting board for a teacher's desk, a large, smoking chimney, and a screeching door constituted its outfit of furniture. Its library consisted principally of blue-back spelling books, some worn readers, a dull geography recited in chanted lessons, an incomprehensible grammar, and a few broken slates. Its first teacher was Mrs. J.A. Ball, mother of Rev. T.H. Ball, who despite the care of her home and her own family of five children, found time to instruct the budding generation of early Lake County.

This was before the days of elaborate equipments. There were no teachers' institute or licenses then; no dreaded examinations for children or teachers. The curriculum consisted chiefly of the three R's — Readin', Ritin' and 'Rithmetic, to the Rule of Three. The graduating exercises were a "spell-down" exercise of the whole school or quitting by the boys in order to husk corn.

Out of these primitive schools came those who have attained to fame, to greatness, and to true goodness of citizenship.

(Compiled from the Souvenir Album of Lake County, Indiana, Crown Point-Lowell, June 18-19, 1909)

CROWN POINT—INDIANA

OFFICE OF THE
CROWN POINT REGISTER,
SAM B. DAY, Editor and Proprietor.
☆Oldest☆ Established☆ and ☆Best☆ Advertising ☆Medium☆in☆
Subscription, $1.00 in Advance; $1.50 if Paid at end of Year.
Lake County
Tasty Job Work a Specialty.

Crown Point, Ind. Feb. 19th 1890

S of V Order
To Sam B. Day Dr.
To printing 100 half-sheet bills and
500 dodgers $6.00

Rec'd Payment,
Sam B. Day.

OFFICE OF LAKE COUNTY STAR
J. J. WHEELER, Editor and Publisher.
CROWN POINT, IND. Feb. 21 ——— 1890
JOB WORK A Specialty.

Sons of Veterans   Dr.
To
Lake County Star for
Advertising and job work
for dance and enter-
tainment — Nine and
Fifty-one hundredths dollars
($9.50)

Rec'd Payment in
full   J. J. Wheeler
                    Pr. Smith

To all whom it may concern.
This may certify that Lydia Swick is a member
of good standing in the First Baptist Church
of Twenty Mile Prairie, and as such we would
cheerfully reccommend her to any sister church of
the same faith and order. And when united to
them shall consider her dismissed from us.

This 15th day of Nov. 1851.
S Sawyer. C.C. Protem.

TOWNS AND PLACES

FOUNDING OF WINFIELD TOWNSHIP
T1

A Birds Eye View

Jeremy Hixon first permanent settler in this area located his claim in April 1835.

At this time there were only country paths for travel. Here he and his family camped in a wagon, while cutting trees and building his log house. It was nearly five years before there were neighbors who came to camp close by.

Gradually more came to the area and it was decided they needed a name for the settlement.

Winfield Township was named by Jeremy Hixon in honor of General Winfield Scott born in 1786. He was general in Chief of the Army of the United States for over 20 years. He was a War Hero of two Wars in his own right, of Mexican War Fame. He insisted on tight security in Washington D.C. to safeguard President Lincoln's life at the time of his first inauguration.

On the last day of October 1861 General Winfield Scott sent President Lincoln his resignation of Military Services. He was seventy-five years old at this time. He died in 1866 at the age of eighty years.

Winfield Township was formed in 1843 from part of Center Township. In 1844 sections were put back in Center Township, and later certain sections were put in Eagle Creek. In March 1844 it was ordered that Winfield Township be divided in two road districts by an East and West line down through centers of section 19-20-21 of Town 34 North Range 8 West. All that part of Township lying north of said line shall be known as road district #9. All that part lying south of said line to be known as road district #24.

The Sioux Indians roamed the area for a short period of time. The Pottowatomie Indians stayed for several years after the first settlement. Then they too left this area.

The nearest trading point in 1835 was Michigan City. The nearest mill was Scott's five miles past Michigan City.

The Pioneers were sturdy, sociably, highly intelligent, religious people. Most of the homes were made of logs and agriculture was their principal occupation.

In 1836 the first death of a child belonged to a Mr. Higby who was buried in the fork of a fallen tree. The County Home Cemetery is located in Winfield Township, earliest burial 1884, last recorded 1908. One cemetery in Deer Creek and one in Hickory Point.

There has been schools, churches, blacksmith shops, post offices, stores, shoemakers, a weighing scale, creamery, tannery, two pipe lines one in 1891, and one in 1914. A telegraph line in 1914 and telephone in 1890. First set of railroad tracks laid 1882, second set of tracks laid 1915. A depot 1882, and a milk station. The people in Winfield say they could set their clocks by the train whistle at 7:15 A.M. each day.

One old timer coming as a child in 1885 to the area told how was a child he used to hide along the road at night to watch the unclaimed bodies from the County Home being taken by horse and wagon to the Valparaiso University Medical College.

Information: History of Lake County, Ind., Vol. XI; Centennial Edition, Star Press 1934; The Lincoln Reader 1947; People of Winfield

by Mrs. Thomas W. Haney

NOSTALGIA ABOUT LOWELL
T2

Is it nostalgia – or was it a better time, when Lowell was incorporated in October 1868?

The board of commissioners of the County of Lake, Indiana passed the articles of incorporation at the September term September 1868 and notice of election to be held Nov. 30, in the schoolhouse. Prior to this action the settlement was called Outlet, on County Line road. The elected trustees were Lewis Westerman, president, P.A. McNay, C.M. Blachley and clerk Daniel Fry.

Our first ordinance? "Be it ordained that it shall be unlawful to let run at large within the corporation any horses, cattle, sheep or hogs. Anyone permitting horses, cattle, sheep or hogs to do so shall be fined in any sum not to exceed five dollars, for each offense. Provided, however, this shall not be construed as to prohibit horses or cattle from running at large during the daytime between April first and December." An addendum was added, "A pound shall be built and owners notified. If not claimed in twenty four hours, owners shall pay a fine of one dollar and thirty five cents for catching them."

Ordinance #2

Any saloonkeeper who sells less than a quart of whiskey to a customer must pay $30.00 a year tax." Followed this addition, "This means all intoxicating liquors."

The church we were taken to for Sunday school still stands with the rectory, between Union and Castle streets, the original structure remains, but is now covered with stucco. We twins yearned to be old enough to sit in the choir loft with our older friends, but when this occurred we found the winters comfortable but the summers were stifling hot and the nave was always comfortable. The one who suffered most was the boy who pumped the organ with a long handle, and no rest between hymns.

Following is another ordinance passed November 30, 1880

"Property owners on Clarke street shall build a sidewalk commencing at H.B. (Horatio) Nichols' gate, then running to George Death's lot, to the north east corner of the public square to William Hills' lot near the town well." Those sidewalks were of "good lumber, four feet wide with three stringers, and substantially nailed". They were undoubtedly the first sidewalks in Lowell.

Here is another ordinance dated June 5th, 1871, that I cannot resist recording here.

"It shall be unlawful to go, swimming in a state of nudity in daylight. A fine of three dollars shall be levied, if caught."

On the same date our town board the following law was adopted,

"It shall be unlawful to ride or drive on any street or alley at a gate faster than six miles per hour."

My twin and I were born on the property which lies between what are now named Center and Prairie. At that time they were two dirt cow paths. The west trail led to Adam Ebert's property on the west and our home at Prairie and Commercial. Everyone on the east side of town owned a cow, pasture, and a running spring for them to drink from.

Colonel Manning's property was across the street from our home, and owned the spring most often recalled. Enclosed in a four sided spring house with a steepled roof and handsome flagpole. A wooden seat ran around the interior and the spring which was rising in the center was enclosed in a deep stone basin. It never froze, was very cold and clear. That is where we cooled watermelons during the season.

I remember Col. Manning who practiced law in Chicago and came to Lowell on the five o'clock train each Friday afternoon. To us he was a very awesome gentleman in his Prince Albert coat, high silk hat, gold topped cane, white hair and full beard, as he walked by our house. In 1903 there was no public transportation.

by Alice Ruley

EARLY HISTORY OF CEDAR LAKE
T3

It is not generally known that the first settlers in Lake County established claims on the east and west banks of Cedar Lake, consequently we can establish a fascinating and exciting history for our town.

The first white settlers arrived in the early 1830's. Previously, the area was the territory of the Potawotomie Indians and a summer camp was established on the Lake of the Red Cedars.

Of greatest importance from a historical viewpoint was the Cedar Lake and or Potawotomie Indian Trail. This trail crossed the Kankakee river near what is now Momence, Illinois, traveled northeast to Cedar Lake, then called "The Lake of the Red Cedars," traversing the bluffs on the west and north end of what is now Lake Shore Drive.

Timothy Horton Ball, son of Harvey Ball, wrote, "Along the north and west side of the lake, the feet of the children of the prairie and the forest wild, the native red children of America, often passed, for the first white settlers found a well trodden pathway along the bank of the shore height, where the waters never reached . . . They were Potawotomies."

The Potawotomie Indians were a branch of the Algonquin, people of the place of the fire. In 1774, a map drawn in Paris of our territory (Charelvoux-Bellen Map) shows a village of the Potawotomie Indians at the foot of Lake Michigan near the Calumet River.

The Potawotomies were gradually driven westward. The 1832 Treaty of Tippecanoe abolished Indian title to all of Lake County with the exception of 10,000 acres reserved for eighteen Potawotomie chiefs.

Timothy Ball in his book, *The Lake of the Red Cedars*, published in 1880 said of Cedar Lake; "A few miles southwest of the center of the county (Lake) is the Lake of the Red Cedars. Westward and southward as far from the lake shores the eye can see, extends a beautiful stretch of level and the rolling land known as Lake Prairie. Parts of it are as beautiful, as gently undulating, and as fertile, as can be found in any of the western states. It has become the home of a number of New England families. This little lake, from which the prairie takes its name, as viewed on a summer day, from some prairie height, with the blue sky above, is beautiful beyond the art of painters to represent, because nature in sunny loveliness reflects light from the crystal water, and varying hues from the trees that skirt its bank, and from the green herbage, and from the sunlit sky. The glory of such a scene, in "the leafy month of June," the blue dome above, the sparkling, cooling water, the green-robed oaks, and the flowery meads, and above all the sunshine, painters may in colors bright and in fair outline represent, but can not equal. There are many lakes in this great lake region of America, with grander outlines and with more majestic surroundings. There can be none in June more sunny, there can be few more lovely."

Joseph Bailey established Baileytown, 12 miles east of Gary, in 1822, four years before the government started purchasing land in northwest Indiana from the Indians. The first settlers in Lake County established their claims on land surrounding Cedar Lake.

The Ball estate was established in 1834. It appears that Charles Wilson made a claim in section 27 on the west side of Cedar Lake. This passed into the possession of Jacob L. Brown. From his it was sold to Hervey Ball for $300.00.

In June of 1834, William S. Thornburg, Thomas Thornburgh, William Crooks, and Samuel Miller settled and established claims. William S. Thornburg lived in the Cedar Lake area for he is shown as the Inspector of the first two elections held in Lake County. In both cases, he was the Inspector for the polling place held in the home of Amsi L. Ball. William Crooks and Samuel Miller established a timber and mill seat in section 35.

Other known Cedar Lake early settlers were David Horne, Doctor Galvin Lilley, Horace Edgartown, and Adjonidah and Horace Taylor. They came here between 1835 to 1837.

Obadiah Taylor, Revolutionary War veteran buried in Cedar Lake came from Massachusetts in 1836. He is buried at West Point Cemetery on Fairbanks Street.

Dr. Calvin Lilley settled on the east side of Cedar Lake in 1835. He sold to Benjamin McCarty who established the town of West Point on this property with the thought in mind of it becoming the County Seat. Lake Court House (Crown Point) was chosen; however, over the bids of West Point and Liverpool.

Lewis Warriner, from West Springfield, Massachusetts, settled on the east side in November, 1837 with his wife, Sabra. Lewis was elected in 1839 to the Indiana Legislature representing Lake and Porter Counties.

Hervey Ball and family took possession of much government land in 1837.

Lake County was legally established by an enactment of the State Legislature that Lake should be an independent county after February 15, 1837. On March 28, 1837, the first election of Lake County officials was held. Solon Robinson, who established Crown Point, and came to Lake County in 1834, became the first Clerk of the Circuit Court. Amsi L. Ball of the Cedar Lake area became one of the first County Commissioners, with William B. Crooks elected one of the first Associate Judges.

Previous to this in 1836 an election was held of interest to the citizens of the Cedar Lake area. On April 30th a Justice of the Peace was elected for Ross township. A polling place in Cedar Lake area at the home of Amsi L. Ball with William S. Thornburg and W.B. Crooks as clerks of election, Amsi L. Ball was elected Justice of the Peace. Those voting were R.T. Tozier, Jesse Pierce, Henry Biddle, William B. Crooks and William S. Thornburg. Amsi L. Ball, as a candidate, did not vote. He received 5 votes.

In the March 28, 1837 election, there were three precincts in Lake County: the House of Russel Eddy with William Clark, inspector, the house of Samuel D. Bryant with E.W. Bryant, inspector, and the house of Amsi L. Ball with William S. Thornburg, inspector. The results were:

Clerk of Circuit Court: Solon Robinson 38, D.Y. Bond 21, L.A. Fowler 17.

County Recorder: Wm. A.W. Holton 50, J.V. Johns 22.

Two Associate Judges: Wm. B. Crooks 51, William Clark 50, Samuel D. Bryant 28, Horace Taylor 1.

Three County Commissioners: Amsi L. Ball 78, S.D. Stringham 59, Thomas Wiles 59.

In October, 1835, the Hornor "settlement" was established on the lands to west of Cedar Lake in what is now Hanover Township. The Hornor family together with other settlers from the Wabash Region of Indiana established claims. Thomas Hornor located on Section 28, David Hornor on Section 29, Aaron Cox had a claim in Section 22, and Jacob L. Brown's claim was on the west shore of Cedar Lake on Section 27.

The first school house in Lake County was Ball Log School built in the summer of 1838 on property donated by Hervey Ball. Hervey also paid for most of the expense of erection of the large hewed-log schoolhouse. Others involved were Aaron Cox, John Hornor and John Geisen. In June of 1839 Mrs. Jane A.H. Ball, wife of Hervey, commenced teaching a boarding school. Records indicate that in addition to the three R's, painting, botany, philosophy, algebra, penmanship, Latin and Greek were taught. Hervey Ball assisted in the teaching. The school continued until 1855.

Vignettes of Some Cedar Lake Pioneers

Benjamin McCarty – His background is unknown except that he came from LaPorte County where he was an acting sheriff and probate judge. He located in Porter County, then brought his large family to Cedar Lake where he had purchased the Lilley place. Benjamin platted a town and named it West Point. This was on the east side of Cedar Lake. In 1840, he attempted to have West Point named as the County Seat. He also succeeded but the legislature selected Solon Robinson and his Crown Point area on the premise that it was nearest the geographical center of the county. One can only ponder what Cedar Lake would be like today, had West Point been chosen. The home at West Point in 1840 was a center for religious meetings. A literary society was established there. Benjamin had six sons and two daughters. It is known that some of his sons became school teachers.

Hervey Ball – A descendant of the pioneer Massachusetts distinguished Ball family of early 1600 origin, he was born October 16, 1794 in West Springfield, Mass. In 1818, he graduated from Middlebury College in Vermont and became a lawyer. He practiced law in Georgia until 1834. In 1837, he brought his family to City West in Porter County. He purchased a claim at Red Cedar Lake in Lake County and by the end of the year, he and his family were fully established on the farm where he lived until his death on October 13, 1868. His home was a literary, educational, religious and social center for the people around Cedar Lake and its environs.

Timothy Horton Ball – Timothy (T.H.) was an integral part of the family that homesteaded on the shore of Cedar Lake in 1837. He was one of the sons of Judge Hervey Ball and Jane A. Horton Ball. Jane was the product of an extensive education in New England schools. She was an extremely proficient teacher, also versed in fine arts and medicine. She was the teacher for the log cabin school built on the Ball property. She taught her students in primary, secondary and academic education. One of her superior pupils was her son, Timothy. He was graded "excellent" in Latin, Greek and Science. At an early age, he entered Franklin College, Indiana of which his father was a Trustee, where he earned his B.A. and M.A. After teaching in Indiana, he entered in 1860 the Newton Theological Institute in Boston. He became a Baptist pastor in Crown Point in 1863. T.H. Ball's greatest fame is as the *Historian of Lake County*. Preacher, teacher, poet and historian.

by Charles C. Thornburg

THE LAND OF THE RED CEDARS

T4

Our Cedar Lake history is unique inasmuch as it was originally not man's idea.

It began as an 805 acre body of water, the result of a melting glacier that left a clay-lined depression with depths of 6-19 feet. A government land survey named it Clear Lake. It's native inhabitants were the Pottowatomi Indians.

It's only natural that in 1834, earliest pioneers chose the shore of Cedar Lake and Francher Lake. Named now for it's red cedar trees, it was appreciated as a place to live and thrive, on protective forests, wild game and fish.

In time, pioneer families platted small towns – by 1840 West Point, 1854 Fairport and by 1870 a Handle factory seed, the Village of Armour Town.

Schools were seriously dealt with. We can claim Lake County's first public school – the Ball School in 1838; then followed the Red Cedar School and many others. Also, a post office in 1870 was named "The Cedar Lake Post Office."

As early as 1858 boat builders were here. City folks, vacationing here were living in tents under trees and along the lake shores. We were being discovered by the lovers of the great outdoors.

Another era had set in by 1882, when the Monon Railroad was laid along Cedar Lake's western shores.

Swiftly we became an industrial region as trains, by the carload, hauled both people and most of life's necessities.

Along came hotels, taverns, general and grocery stores, ice farming and more boat building, churches and parks.

This all led to the next era in approximately 1914.

Now came the subdividers.

We acquired cottages by the hundreds, excursion trains and boats, lake piers, water toboggans and chicken dinner signs, as people packed our hotels and swarmed over our parks.

In the course of time we record over 50 hotels and inns, ranging from 25 rooms to over 100 rooms in size. The old style saloon was usually located within the larger hotels.

Local citizens voiced a need for control and tried in 1914, 1933 and 1950 to incorporate.

After much vehement opposition, court hassles and expense, loyal citizens made it happen in 1967. Cedar Lake became a Town.

Our population in 1984 numbers 8,900.

For our long 150 years of Cedar Lake history, our water sources have been natural springs and private wells.

Because nature still governs our town with a powerful lake, inlets, outlets, swamps and ditches, we always will be unique and singular in our needs.

Because of Cedar Lake's natural beauty, it behooves us to keep it looking like a treasured park worthy of everyone's pride and attention.

by Beatrice Horner

AN EARLY DYER, INDIANA SIGN
T5

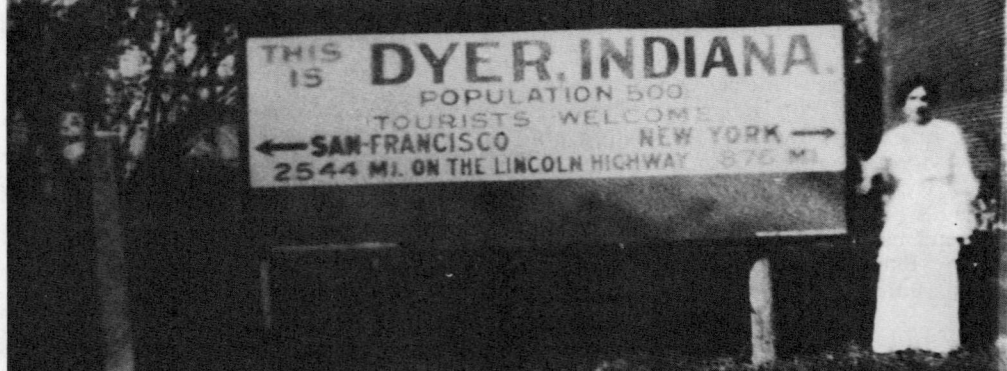

One of Dyer's new signs in 1916

by Mrs. Ralph Oldendorf

THE TOWN OF BEMIS
T6

The small town of Bemis sprang up on the property of Conrad Oldendorf Sr. It was located on the corner of Bemis Road and State Line Road; on both sides of the State Line. The town consisted of a shoe store and repair shop, dairy, store and Post Office.

In 1885, William and Mary (Saller) Hartman built a store with living quarters and Post Office in Bemis. (William later owned and operated stores at Woodworth, Crete and Steger, Illinois. The Steger store still stands.) On a slope, near a ravine west of the store, he built a barn with a loft for their horse, buggy and Conestoga wagon. He used the wagon to haul supplies to stock the store. They retained the store for 27 years.

During June 1891, local farmers in a co-op fashion, erected the Interstate Creamery Company. Farmers from both sides of the State Line brought their milk to the dairy to be made into butter. Ice was cut in winter from the pond beyond the dairy and hauled to the ice house. The ice house was located south of town at the edge of State Line Road on the Indiana side, along Conrad Oldendorf Sr.'s driveway. This was convenient and out of the way for the teams of horses and wagons that came and went from the dairy. The ice was a necessity to keep milk cool. The ice didn't melt because the icehouse was built strongly with double walls. (It was moved from its original location and is used as a grain bin on the Oldendorf farm.)

Soon after the dairy was established, minutes of the Board meetings and elections were recorded. Anton Buehler, who was single, was the first Interstate Creamery Company buttermaker. He roomed at the Louis Guritz home until Sam Grimm became the buttermaker. After Sam took the job, a well built home was erected at a cost of $55.00 for Sam, his wife and their seven children.

In 1894, William Claus (or Klaus) rented a room at Sam Grimm's home until his shoestore and repair shop was built. (After the shoe store was built, a house was built for him and a barn for his horse, mangers and buggy with a loft for hay.) The tack room was located in the back of the store. The show room was the full width of the store room. It was stocked with all the necessities in a neat and orderly way. William stocked the shelves with new shoes. He sold and repaired them for everyone in the area. Folks would say that when you entered the store, William always looked down at your feet and if the shoes were not from his store, he would smile, shake his head, and then turn around and get what was requested. (William later drove one of the first pick-up trucks to get supplies.) His widowed mother came to live with him, and did the housework. After she died, his sisters came and baked bread, coffee cakes and cookies, as well as took care of the housekeeping. He lived there until he died on July 1, 1929.

There were several families, whose homes clustered in the area of Bemis. To the east of Bemis stood the Louis Guritz family farm. Louis was a Board Member and Director of the Creamery. Fred Claus (or Klaus), a brother of William's, and wife Mina bought one acre of woodland pasture (in Illinois) from Conrad Jr. during September 1893. They built a home and other buildings on the property, which was located ¼ mile west of Bemis. This is where Fred continued his carpenter trade. Lizzette Behrens, widow of Christ, and her family purchased the old Brands School from ¼ mile

William Claus as a young man in 1894, owner of the shoe store and repair shop that stood in IN, where W 117th meets on State Line Road.

north of 121st on the east side of Calumet Avenue. She moved it northwest to Bemis and used it as a home for her and her family. William Oldendorf (Conrad Jr.'s son) and his wife Louise (Schrage) and daughter Florence lived on their farm ¼ mile west of Bemis in 1903. (They completely remodeled their home in 1916.)

South of Bemis was the retirement home of Conrad Oldendorf Sr. and his second wife Dorothea (Matthias). Conrad Jr. and his wife and children built and lived in the larger house next door. Although retired, Conrad Sr. helped at the dairy until his death on September 14, 1894.

Bemis was a midpoint between Crown Point, Dyer and Klassville Indiana and Crete, Illinois. It was a convenient location. As times progressed, and cars and trucks became more available; the dairy became outmoded. Eventually the Hartman Store was moved to a site southwest of the Oldendorf home and became the home for the widow, Mrs. Batterman. Later, it became the Fred Wassman home. The buttermaker's home was moved and added to the August Piepho family home on 113th and Calumet Avenue. The dairy stood empty from December 12, 1918 until it was taken down in May 1925. The William Claus home was moved to Brunswick, Indiana. The shoe store was moved to the Louis Guritz farm and was used as a garage. The front of the store was replaced with double sliding doors, which changed its appearance. When Henry, Louis Guritz's son died in 1969 the building was still in mint condition, it has since fell to disrepair. The town of Bemis (1885-1938) is now a dim memory.

by Mrs. Ralph Oldendorf

(Top left): Hartman Store 1885. (Bottom left) Buttermaker, Sam Grimm Family 1891. (Top right) Interstate Creamery Co., June 1891. (Bottom right) Wm. Claus Shoestore 1894, in sketch.

TRANSPORTATION

AN UNKNOWN RAILROAD

Although its location is unknown, it is very possible that the brick railroad depot shown here is still standing. Also unknown are the names of all except one of the men who posed for this interesting photograph which was taken about 1869. The boss of this motley crew was sitting in the center of the front row, and he was wearing a necktie, perhaps as a symbol of his position. He was James Nathaniel Moore, master carpenter, and he had a contract with the Union Pacific railroad to build depots such as this one, beginning in the late 1860's. The depots were to be built along the first transcontinental railroad line from Omaha, Nebraska to Promontory, Utah Territory.

According to family tradition, J.N. Moore was at the ceremonies which celebrated the joining of the Union Pacific with the Central Pacific and the driving in of the last, golden spike in 1869. His contract began prior to that year and it is known that he was still gone from his wife and children in 1870. He and his wife Mary Ault Moore lived in Lowell, Lake County, Indiana from the time he enlisted to fight for the Union in the Civil War until their deaths in 1913 and 1921 respectively.

Upon his return from the Western frontier, he related that he and his crew had one memorable skirmish with unfriendly Indians, and he was also bitten once by a rattlesnake. His companion used a knife to cause the wound to bleed, then sucked out the venom.

This photo was submitted by a great-granddaughter, Dorothy Jean Schroeder of Quincy, Washington, whose maternal grandmother was J.N. Moore's daughter Daisy. Since photos such as this were unusual for that period in history, she wonders if perhaps the completion of this particular depot held some special significance. Could it have been the last depot built on the Union Pacific line?

by Dorothy Jean Schroeder

MODES OF TRANSPORTATION TO SCHOOLS IN LAKE COUNTY INDIANA

by Mrs. Ralph Oldendorf

Top left: Echterling Bus. Bottom left: St. John Train was a bus for those who had to come 8-10 miles to get to and from school. Top right: Krietzburg Bus. Bottom Right: Schererville Bus.

WE HAVE THE POWER TO MOVE YOU

Chicago South Shore and South Bend Railroad

While its proud tradition of serving Lake Michigan's southern shore with dependable, efficient rail transportation dates back to 1908, the Chicago South Shore & South Bend Railroad has risen to new levels of service success since September 1984.

It was at this time, after years of absentee ownership, that the South Shore Line was returned to local proprietorship with a renewed commitment to service excellence and new business development. With innovative marketing concepts and new and well-maintained operating freight and passenger fleets, the "new" Chicago South Shore & South Bend Railroad has quickly become one of the most personalized and customer-oriented short lines in the nation.

A new excitement is evident all along the 90-mile railway system. Passengers on the country's last inter-urban electric railroad enjoy the new, stainless-steel trains that run daily between downtown Chicago and South Bend, Indiana. And, with a strong marketing team working aggressively to solve customer problems, freight traffic managers are finding that where there is a way, the Chicago South Shore will find a means to solve shipper needs.

The boss of this motley crew, James Nathaniel Moore, was a master carpenter, and he had a contract with the Union Pacific railroad to build depots such as this one, beginning in the late 1860's.

1982 emergency repairs were made to prevent further deterioration with permanent restoration work beginning in early 1983 and proceedings as funds allow.

The excellent progress of the Save Our Station project would not have been possible without the interest Hobart has shown or the contributions of funds and services that have been made. Among the many valued contributors, the Hobart Industrial and Commercial Foundation and the Office of the Hobart Township Trustee provided major financial support.

In addition, the citizens who have given their valuable time to the S.O.S. Committee deserve recognition. They include: Dorothy Ballantyne, Anthony Cefali, Elin Christianson, Virginia Curtis, Jim Finan, Chuck Flick, Cal Green, Mary Glynn, Richard Harrigan, David Katz, Bob Krull, Jerry Pavese, Ed Prentiss, Vic Sable, Dick Shaw and Brook Sonnicksen.

THE HISTORY OF THE LINCOLN HIGHWAY
T12

Presented by Tony Vorsten, Vice President of Iowa Highway 30 Association at the 1974 Annual Meeting

During the early frontier days, seven trails crossed the country, winding their dusty and hazardous trails across desert and mountain, over plain and through forest, between the precipitous walls of cliffs and canyons and along the banks of many rivers. None of these is richer in picturesque legends than the Old Salt Lake Trail, known now as the Lincoln Highway. Fremont and other intrepid explorers followed this trail into the Indian country; the Mormons made their weary pilgrimage along this route to Salt Lake City; innumerable trains of covered wagons plodded across vast expanse, carrying the pioneers who were to bring civilization to the West; and this was the gold rush route in 1849. In 1860 the Pony Express traveling east out of Sacramento, California, made its first trip using the route that is now the Lincoln Highway.

Carl G. Fisher had an idea. One was desolving calcium-carbide slowly with water. The result — a good light to enable cars to be driven more safely at night. This was the start of the Prestolite Co. Another idea of his was the Indianapolis Speedway. This enabled auto manufacturers and tire companies to test and show off their products.

But the main idea referred to here is one to build a highway across the United States from east to west. In 1912, Mr. Fisher presented it to an astonished assembly of leaders of the infant automobile industry. Regardless of the skepticism, he was able to obtain pledges of $4 million for this project. Canal building in the 1830's and the extensive railroad building which followed, had monopolized the public's attention up to this time.

Of 48 states at this time, only 28 spent anything on roads. In the decade that followed, the United States was to spend $2 billion for roads, and still lacked a national system of highway transportation. Road signs were a rarity. Carl Fisher's idea — that which later became the famous Lincoln Highway.

On July 1, 1913, a group of organizers met to form the Lincoln Highway Association as a legal entity. Some of the persons who were so active in forming the Lincoln Highway Association were, along with Mr. Fisher, R.A. Alger, A.J. Beveridge, R.D. Chapin, E.W. Clark, P.H. Deming, A.Y. Gowen, Henry B. Joy, A.R. Pardington, F.A. Seiberling and John N. Willys.

On September 10, 1913 the group issued a proclamation, as follows: The Lincoln Highway — Whereas: The purpose of this Association is to immediately promote and procure the establishment of a continuous improved highway from the Atlantic to the Pacific, open to traffic of all descriptions, without toll charges and to be of concrete whenever practicable. This highway is to be known, in memory of Abraham Lincoln, as "The Lincoln Highway."

There was some difficulty in selecting the route of the highway, but the definite plan was to select the best and shortest route across the United States, and not to let pressure groups persuade them to vary from this direct route. The route of travel selected after much investigation, travel and discussion was first offered to the governors of the states through which it would pass, for approval and endorsement by them and who would start the new road off with a backing and influence obtainable in no other way. New York was chosen as the eastern terminal and San Francisco was chosen as the western terminal.

A plan that did much to promote the laying of a concrete roadway along the route was to construct "Seedling Miles" of roadway in Illinois, Iowa, Nebraska, Wyoming, Utah and Nevada. These Seedling Miles proved the value of concrete as an all weather road. The first Seedling Miles were constructed in Illinois in 1914. In Nebraska in 1915 and in Iowa in Linn County in 1918. By 1919 this had proved its value and long stretches of concrete were being laid.

At the beginning of 1916 a new source of revenue was devised: Sustaining Memberships. For a contribution of $5.00 or more annually, an emblem was presented which could be attached to the radiator of a car. This emblem was porcelain in red, white and blue, with Lincoln Highway and a large L in Blue on the white field.

Active persons along the route of the highway in the cities and town were named to help get publicity, and to raise funds for the Association. They were listed as consuls. Some of the 42 consuls in Iowa were Parley Sheldon of Ames, J.B. McHose of Boone, Edward Killion of Cedar Rapids, A.A. Daehler of Clinton, E.B. Wilson of Jefferson, J.E. Moss of Scranton and M.M. Mackey of Carroll.

Automobile, tire and cement companies contributed heavily to the project of developing the Lincoln Highway. Contributions ranged as high as $130,000.00 from a single company.

As early as 1913, a group of highway minded men prepared to take a tour to the west coast to prove that it could be done. The automobiles, all of which finished the trip, were a Marmon, 2 Marions, 1 Pilot 60, 2 Haynes, 2 Americans, 1 McFarland, 2 Appersons, 2 Hendersons, 1 Empire, 2 Premiers, 1 Pathfinder, 1 Brown Truck and 1 Premier Truck, which carried camp equipment, repair parts, supplies and extra tires. Equipment specified to be carried on each car included one pick, one sledge, one steel stake 3 feet long, one pair of tackle blocks, 600 feet of ¾ inch rope, one lantern, 12 mud-hooks, one set of tire chains, four African water bags, one envelope type tent and chocolate bars in cans, beans, canned goods.

The tourists started from Indianapolis, Inc. at 2 P.M. on July 1, 1913, and had traveled only 50 miles when they realized the enormity of the amount of work which still had to be done on the route, even though nearly every mile of the road had been scraped, dragged, graded or otherwise improved for the use of the tour. The tour invoked tremendous publicity and interest so that the group had difficulty to make a moderate schedule of 150 miles per day because of the many banquet and speech making stops which were requested.

The increase in auto travel over long distances meant that highway route marking was essential. In 1916 it consisted mainly of red, white and blue colors painted on poles, fence posts, stakes or on rocks. In 1920 this was upgraded by painted metal or porcelain signs in red, white and blue with the words Lincoln Highway and a large letter L in the white field. In 1927 better and more durable signing was needed because many of the markers were missing or had been destroyed by hunters' bullets.

The Boy Scouts were well organized by this time and were eagerly looking for a project to carry out. So Secretary Hoag, Vice-President Bement and Colonel Waldon worked out a design of a concrete post, reinforced with four steel bars, bearing the Lincoln Highway insignia and a bronze medallion of Lincoln on the front and an arrow giving direction of travel on the side. The wording "This highway dedicated to Abraham Lincoln" was on the medallion. Much effort was expended to have the markers placed at the correct locations and the Boy Scouts dug the holes ahead of time, and on September 1, 1928, placed nearly all of the markers on the first day. These markers stood for many years because they were so durable, well made and attractive. Had the Association been willing to commercialize its markers, it could have had an elaborate system, but all such offers were rejected. The Association had to rely quite a lot on donations to defray the cost of the great number of road markers needed. The permanence and the value placed on the attractive concrete markers by the public and the state highway departments, is evidenced by the fact that less than 5% had been destroyed or removed after six years of service.

In addition to the concrete highway markers, many memorials have been placed along the Lincoln Highway. One noteworthy memorial was erected beside the road at Clinton, Iowa by the citizens in memory of W.F. Coan, Iowa's first state consul. J.E. Moss of Scranton, Iowa erected two handsome ones bearing the busts of the Emancipator at either end of an important curve on the route. Mr. and Mrs. E.B. Wilson of Jefferson, erected on the court house grounds there the finest of them all, a standing figure of Lincoln in bronze, mounted on a granite pedestal with a bronze tablet.

Motorists placed great reliance on the Lincoln Highway markers. To protect the design, the Association copyrighted its official tricolored marker and its name and also registered them in each state. The example set by the Lincoln Highway Association in its successive efforts to establish and sustain an adequate road marking system, stimulated widespread marking by other highway organizations. One 1500 mile stretch in the west was included in no less than fifteen of these named trails, each sponsored by different promoters. This condi-

U.S. STEEL SHELTERS SOUTH SHORE CARS
T10

Historians consider the Chicago, South Shore and South Bend Railroad to be the last operating electric interurban railroad in the United States. It is a link to an era when the electric interurban railroads were a major mode of transportation, connecting cities and towns and enabling our society to become more mobile.

In an effort to preserve the history of the South Shore and its role in the history of Northwest Indiana, Indiana Dunes National Lakeshore has acquired 19 of the railroad's recently retired vintage passenger cars.

Most of the cars, which were manufactured in the mid-1920's by the Pullman and Standard Car Companies of Chicago, were donated to the Lakeshore by the Northern Indiana Commuter Transportation District. According to Superintendent Dale Engquist, the Lakeshore's recently completed Transportation Study recommended that the Park Service restore some of the cars as exhibits interpreting the history of transportation in Northwest Indiana.

It has also been proposed that a number of the cars might in the future be used for transportation of visitors to and within the Lakeshore; the South Shore railroad runs the length of the 35 mile-long Lakeshore, and stops serve most of the major visitor facilities. A local private group, the Friends of the South Shore, is working closely with the Lakeshore staff in these preservation efforts.

Funding for the storage, maintenance and restoration of the cars has been appropriated by Congress specifically for the project. One car is currently being restored at the Indiana Transportation Museum with an additional car being made available to the museum for parts and material. A second car is programmed to be restored in 1985.

Locating a storage facility to house the remaining 17 cars proved to be a challenge. The cars' wood and canvas roofs would deteriorate rapidly if left to sit outdoors exposed to the elements and to potential vandalism. Several nearby industries that had enough indoor trackage and storage space were solicited through the Lakeshore's recently published gift catalog. The U.S. Steel Corporation responded by donating indoor storage space in an idled Gary works building, the 12 inch, No. 5 bar mill.

The Baltimore and Ohio Railroad, Chessie System and the Elgin, Joliet and Eastern Railway Company agreed to move the cars to the storage site at no charge to the Park Service.

The donation of storage space and movement of the cars will save the park $20,000 in fiscal 1985, which can be directed towards the restoration of a car. Superintendent Engquist said: "This was the largest contribution to the park since officials began soliciting assistance through the gift catalog. We are pleased that these corporations share our concern for preserving the railroad cars and the history they reflect."

The South Shore Railroad has been serving the citizens of Indiana and Illinois since 1903. Earlier in this century, riding the South Shore was *the* way to visit the Dunes. Today many visitors to Indiana Dunes still ride the South Shore to the Lakeshore to enjoy the beauty of the forests, dunes and beaches. It is only fitting that the history of this last electric interurban railroad be preserved.

by Warren Snyder

DEPOT HISTORY
T11

Hobart's Pennsy Depot

The Pennsy Depot is the third Pennsy station building to serve Hobart. Two earlier station buildings were of frame construction.

Railroad companies provided depots for the comfort of passengers and the protection of freight. Early stations tended to be wooden sheds. Beginning in the late 19th century, many states established railroad regulatory commissions whose functions included setting requirements for better station facilities. An attractive depot was important to the community image so architectural style was a matter of great interest. The railroad companies had to balance these factors with the demands of business.

Beginning in the 1880s, the Pennsylvania Railroad adopted standard plans for its depots west of Pittsburgh. The size and features of the depot plans varied, depending on the volume of business. It is probable that Hobart's depot was built from one of the standard plans in use in 1911.

The architects were Price and McDanahan of Philadelphia. The cost was $25,000. Work began in July 1911 and the new Pennsy depot was opened in January 1912. The depot served Hobart for over 60 years until it was closed in the early 1970s.

Hobart's depot is a combination station, accommodating passengers, freight and office under one roof. It does not have a bay for train control as many stations do. The Pennsylvania Railroad frequently used separate control towers when a high volume of business and/or dense traffic movements existed. This is the case in Hobart where the control tower is located along the track south of the depot.

The depot is a one-story building, 25'x65'. The central waiting room is 20'x25' with a freight room of the same size on one end and an office and ladies' waiting room on the other. There is a basement under the freight room.

The exterior is of pressed brick with ceramic tile inserts set in the brick gap border below the roof and in the pediments on the main entries. The roof, now shingled, was originally slate with tile caps and copper gutters.

The most noticeable alteration is that the freight room floor and dock have been raised with changes in windows and doors to the new level. However, the original high arched ceiling in the waiting room and many other interior features are still in place.

Why Save Our Station?

Hobart's Pennsy Depot, located beside the Pennsy (now CONRAIL) tracks at Lillian and Illinois streets, is a local landmark. For many local people it holds fond memories.

It is important as a symbol of the first railroad through Hobart, a turning point in history, which brought the area out of the pioneer age and put the settlers in close contact with the outside world. Thus, the Pennsy Depot is also a link to the history of our nation which experienced similar great change as the rails pushed their way across the continent.

By saving and restoring the Pennsy Depot, we can show that we need not destroy the past to build the future. Instead, we can link past and future by preserving the best of one and adapting it to the needs of the other.

Finally, the most important reason to save the Pennsy Station is because the community is interested and supports its preservation. The donated services, muscle and time; the financial support, and the messages of encouragement — in short, the responses to the Pennsy Depot S.O.S. show that Hobart believes the Pennsy Depot should be saved.

Buying the Depot for Hobart

On February 23, 1983, ownership of the Pennsy Depot was transferred to the Save Our Station Committee of the Hobart Historical Society in an ancient ceremony based on English common law.

S.O.S. Chairman Ed Prentiss, Society President Elin Christianson and Attorney Anthony Cefali met with CONRAIL's representative on the Depot property. Cefali picked up a twig, broke it in half and handed one piece to the seller, thus binding the sale according to ancient English tradition.

Earlier, in more ordinary surroundings, the modern exchange of deed and check had taken place.

Efforts to purchase the Pennsy Depot began early in 1982 when the late Congressman Adam Benjamin, Jr. learned that it be be available. Mayor Calvin Green and Robert Krull pursued Benjamin's lead and invited interested citizens to meet with CONRAIL personnel in late April. At that time CONRAIL offered the property at $6,000 to a non-profit organization with a public service intent.

Realizing that they must act quickly, the citizens went to work and, within a month, had formed the Save Our Station Committee under the sponsorship of the Hobart Historical Society which had the necessary legal status.

First efforts were concentrated on fund-raising and initial restoration work. In the fall of

tion was highly confusing to the traveler. Clarification of the system was needed.

In May of 1925, a joint meeting of state and federal highway officials in Washington, D.C. approved a plan of numbers for roads designated as U.S. Highways and uniformly marked. Some of the Highway organizers battled vigorously against this idea; others, including the Lincoln Highway Association sought to have their markers retained along with the numbers. Thus the concrete markers remained along the Lincoln Highway, now marked as U.S. 30 for many years. Some highway departments, upon reconstruction of the road, would remove and store the markers and then replace them upon completion of the road.

The men who founded the Lincoln Highway Association and those who carried on its work, have all had full and busy lives. The names of its leaders stand high in many fields of endeavor. There were among them no little men, no pettifoggers, no seekers of personal gain. They took broad views, and they held high standards of accomplishment by which to judge. They knew well what is worthy and what is not. Mr. Henry Joy, in 1933, spoke for all of them when, looking back over his rich career, he said: "I consider the Lincoln Highway as the greatest thing I ever did in my life."

In 1931, an organization called the Lincoln Highway Bureau was founded to perpetuate the ideals of the founders of the Lincoln Highway, to encourage traffic thereon and to assure the motorist fair dealing and courteous treatment throughout his journey on the Main Street of the Nation.

Throughout the years following, the Lincoln Highway was nearly always represented by a group of men, interested in promoting travel along the route. Various folders were printed and widely distributed. Some of the state organizations had signs erected extolling the directness of the route.

With the advent of the opening of the Interstate System across Iowa in about 1965, the Iowa Association lost a lot of its financial support as the various businesses along the route felt the effects of the loss of heavy traffic, and decided to disband, since all debts were paid at this time and to wait until there was more interest in new promotions.

In March, of 1971, Dr. J.K. Johnson and several other Jefferson men sparked a general meeting in Ames to reorganize the Association. This meeting marked the rebirth of the Lincoln Highway Association. At this meeting, Dr. J.K. Johnson was elected president, A.J. Tony Vorsten of Carroll was elected vice-president and George Sparks of Nevada was elected secretary. Directors were appointed from each of the counties through which the highway passes. The group has printed a full color folder depicting a showcase of what one can expect to see along the 30 mile corridor that is along U.S. 30 through Iowa. The group has a 25 year plan of improvements, and co-operates closely with the Iowa Highway Commission, the Iowa Development Commission and the Iowa Conservation Commission to help in the accomplishment of its goals.

by Tony Vorsten

SCHOOLS AND EDUCATION

EARLY TEACHING IN LAKE COUNTY 1928
T13

My home was two miles west of Crown Point. Before I was 16 I dared to think I was armed to teach, because I had an 18 months license to show. With the same in my hand I walked to the little frame building on the east side of Cedar Lake, called the Binyon school.

The furnishing of that small room was very scant. The old box-stove had but three legs of its own, the other a brick caused it to rest on its side many times. The stove pipe was rotten and often smoked, so we could hardly see. Each patron delivered a large load of wood sometime during the winter. The boys cut it into stove-lengths, and the girls would carry it into the schoolhouse.

The plank seats were without backs, and so high that only the older pupils could rest their feet on the floor. They were made of hewn logs, and held numerous slivers for the unshod feet. We had a small blackboard 3 feet x 4 feet made by the older boys.

Our greatest handicap was lack of books to study the lessons. Some parents were too poor to buy the needed textbooks, and thought the teacher would manage until times were better.

Our water supply the first years was carried from the outlet of the lake and contained real live specimens of nature. The children would laugh and say, "Oh throw it out, we'll try again." In our second year a hole was dug below the hill and covered with logs, but it was never bricked in.

I had thirty six pupils, aged from five years to twenty three years. I boarded around one week for each child, starting on Monday night and remaining until Friday noon. My salary was $14.00 per month. The people were poor; there had been a crop failure. Several families from other states moved in to start new homes, but all were kind and hopeful. During my second year three families had pulled out by covered wagon route for Kansas, the land of promise. Later they sent letters home saying that grasshoppers and drought had taken their crops. Cedar Lake friends sent them dried apples, corn and blackberries and all the clothing they could spare. Our school gave a little play; charged ten cents admission; the house was crowded. Lawyer Fancher brought his school from Brunswick. Some came up from Lowell to help in the good cause; many had to stay outside, but the ten cents was sent in. This money bought shoes for the Kansas children, so that they were able to attend school. I will only speak of this, my first school. Many of you will remember my six years in the Crown Point 8th grade work and the same number of years in Lowell school. I must mention three of the pupils in that first school: Martha Binyon, a successful writer of short stories and two books; Will Haan, who became a Major General in our army; Barbara Craft, who died last year at Monon. All business in that city was stopped during the funeral, to honor the woman who had done so much for the poor.

How different to the school life of children 63 years ago; at the time of this writing! This was given to the Historical Society in 1928 by Mrs. J.L. Hill.

Taken from "History of Lake County Vol. X," page 122. This is believed to have been the first school building in Lake County.

by Mrs. J.L. Hill

BRANDS SCHOOL CLASS 1910
T14

This schoolhouse was used until mid 1912 when the large brick two-classroom school, with a full basement, was ready at the end of 1912. The old one was moved to west of the state line to become the home of Mrs. Liz Behrens, widow of Christ, and her family. It has since been enlarged several times over the years.

by Mrs. Ralph Oldendorf

Teacher, Miss Nell Cosgrove. (Back Row) Art Claus, Marie Schoenbeck, Ida Russell, Lydia Russell, Martin Bauermeister, Alvin Russel, Harold Brands, Ray Seegers. (Front Row) Ben Russel, Alma Russel, Henrietta Brands, Alma Hitzeman, Alfreida Claus and Erna Claus.

The Brands Schoolhouse in 1910.

BRANDT SCHOOL PICNIC 1895

T15

The Brandt School Picnic, June 22, 1895; Teacher: Minnie Kobelin, photo taken by Vilmer Studio. This school was located in West Creek Township, Lake County, Indiana, west of Lowell, and one mile east of the state line. It stood at the end of Klassville Rd. across from the Ed Meyer farm and also across from the Fred Kohlsheen farm. It was known to be east of the Sutton Mill farm, and the time it was known as District No. 1.

by Mrs. Ralph Oldendorf

CENTER SCHOOL

T16

Center School, in the center of the twp., is still in existence, although it is scheduled to be abandoned by 1990, now that a new area elementary school has been proposed on the 20 A. site on S. Burr St. in Lowell, next to the Tri-Creek School Adm. Offices. In 1979, Ball State U. did a study on the Tri-Creek Schools. At that time, they called Center School "antiquated," classrooms too small, special programs being held in gym, hallways or cafeteria, lack of a "materials" space. The Tri-Creek School system covers 168 sq. miles. The Tri-Creek School Corp. was formed 7-1-65. The South Creek School Bldg. Corp. organized 10-13-66; the new Lowell High School Bldg. was built and was dedicated 3-8-70. The "old" H.S. Bldg. then became the Jr. High.

In an earlier History of Lake Co. book by Bowers, Taylor, Woods of 1929, it stated: Center School (all brick, 4 classrooms, full basement, modern) built in 1926 by F.E. Muzzal & Sons, at a cost of $40,000.00. Winifred Bryant was Trustee then.

Center School in Eagle Creek Township.

Brandt School District No. 1 School Picnic. Teacher, Minnie Kobelin, June 22, 1895. These were the children enrolled that year, listed by family: Guritz, August: Lena, Mary, Herman, August, Ida, Gusta, Emma, Minnie. Guritz, Henry: Rosa, August, Friedrich, Mary, Louisa. Meyer, Henry: Emil, Harry. Heusman, Antone: Mary, Antone, Joseph, Bennie. Brandt, Henry: Ernest, Alice, George. Monix, Bernard: Bernard, Jr. Berg, Frank: Rosa, Helen, Bennie. Miller, Peter: Albert, Mary, Charles. Kohlscheen, Fred: Herman, Dorothy, Emma, Frieda, William.

Center School is located on Range Line Rd. (Clay St.) north of St. Rd. #2. It opened for school students in Sept. 1927. The first teachers were: Bertha Garriott, 1st & 2nd grade; Mildred Sparling, 3rd & 4th grades; Elizabeth Bradford, 5th & 6th grades; Hubert Long (principal), 7th & 8th grades. Grace McPhearson was the music teacher (later becoming Mrs. Klein). The first bus drivers were: Martin Fisher, Clayton Bryant and Albert Schilling. (Later Eliz. Bradford became Mrs. Martin Fisher.) Ray Rinkenberger was a 1st grader in the new school and supplied the above information.

Thomas K. Fisher became Twp. Trustee in 1931, and held that position for 16 years. Ted Van Swearingen was custodian for many years. In the spring of 1934, the school grounds were landscaped by the community. All the labor was donated. (No funds were in the budget.) The Monon Rwy. Co., which owned the abandoned Gifford Rwy. property, donated the limestone which was used for the new retaining wall around the playground area. The Pennsy. Rwy. that ran through LeRoy, donated a carload of cinders to cover the parking lot for the school. Purdue U. sent specialists to landscape. All native shrubbery was used, dug up from the woods, fields and roadsides in Eagle Creek Twp. A beautiful job! Dec. 23, 1938, some parents started serving hot lunches to the school children. They were indeed welcomed.

During the mid to late '30's, the following teachers were remembered: Dorothy Turner (soon became Mrs. Oehmich), Helen Sparling, Helen A. Shew, Anna Weiland, Geneva McCammon, Clara Knarr, Charlotte Knarr, Prin. Byron McCammon, Prin. Merle Allyn, Prin. C.A. Anderson.

Other later ones incl. Prin. Kenneth Wright, Dorothy Hewitt who taught for 16 years from 1942-1958, Ila Jean Heckel, Margaret Wright, Elizabeth Fisher, Carol Bryant, Mary Childress, Bonita Schrag, Vernice Hough and Prin. Mr. Smead.

After reorganization took place, there are records of who taught at Center. Kindergarten teachers were: Virginia Jerzyk, Hermia Wilson, Karla Crewes, Janet Gray, Jean Schaffer, and Kathy Bryant. 1st grade teachers were: Bonita Schragg, Wanda Frank, Judy Rieke, Linda Fox, Rose Huber, Marilyn Marr. 2nd grade teachers were: Margaret Coffman, Sally Blend, Shirley Angelidis. 3rd grade teachers were: Shirley Angelidis, Mary Bush and Stephanie Werner. 4th grade teachers were: Stan Hurst, Denny Miller, Judy Keithley, Jane Gorbal, Russ Hodges, Duane Aiken, Joyce Milakovic. 5th grade was Joyce Milakovic. Principals were: Stan Hurst, Doug Wiseman, Jim Cooper and Jack Foss. The above list is not in perfect order, and perhaps some names have been omitted over the years. (The writer apologizes to anyone missed.)

Eagle Creek residents will miss their elementary school when it closes; but memories will linger for those who were privileged to gain their early education within its walls.

by Dorothy Sorensen

HANOVER TOWNSHIP DISTRICT NO. 6

T17

1905-1906

In school records of 1905-1906, District No. 6 was listed under Glade School, Brands School was District No. 9 that year. It stood on the southeast side of the Glade Farm, as it was known then, located just ¼ mile south of 113th and Calumet Avenue, among a group of maple trees.

The following year, District No. 6 was recorded as the Seehausen School, which was located, some say, on the NE corner of the former Road 8, now 231, and Calumet Avenue. Others claim it was on the SE corner of that road, which would have been Piepho property. It was even-

Hanover Township Dist. No. 6. Back Row: Unknown, Ed Segert, Herman Piepho, Ben Reichert, Elmer Piepho, Emma Piepho, Doris Wood, Edna Piepho, unknown, Hitzeman girl, Ora Piepho, Caroline Seehausen, unknown. Middle Row: Art Grosse, Theodore Piepho, Ben Hitzeman, John Haake, unknown, unknown, Fred Grosse, unknown, unknown, Ida Piepho, Louise Piepho, Ella Seehausen, unknown. Forefront: Harry Seehausen, unknown, Segert Boy, Arnold and Rose Piepho, Dora Grosse, Lydia Haake, Haake Boy, small child unknown.

tually moved to SE of the Piepho home, later known as the Gilbert Piepho farm. After standing empty a number of years, it was dismantled and believed to be reconstructed elsewhere in Indiana.

A small frame house was built, but not immediately. In 1864 District 6 was built at a cost of $244.77. The first schoolhouse in that district.

by Mrs. Ralph Oldendorf

by Mrs. Ralph Oldendorf

DISTRICT NO. 6, MAY 24, 1899

T18

In July, 1957, the following citizens in the school district north of Brunswick at the time signed a petition for a schoolhouse in Section 12, range 10, the building to be 20 x 24 feet: Athanasius Hepp, Frederick Hue, Christoph Wassmann, William Noehren, Frederick Ohlerkent, Conrad Ohlendorf, Gottlieb Burtle, William Bauermeister, George Leseman, Antoine Griss, Fred Batterman and Charles Hitzeman.

Mrs. Groman (left), Mr. Ed Echterling (right). Brunswick Dr.'s wife. Back Row: Dick Oldendorf, Liz Paul, Laura Hitzeman, Herman Piepho, unknown, Hy/Wm Segert, unknown, Christ Brands, Fred Segert, Minnie Becker. Row 2: Ed Oldendorf, Elsie Haake, Otto Russel, Lydia Russel, Rose Russel, August Seegers, Louise Segert, Emma Russel. Row 3: Willie Russel, Emilie Oldendorf, Edna Piepho, unknown, Rose Seehausen, Emma Hitzeman, Emma Piepho, Ben Piepho, Dora Piepho, Carrie Becker, Ed Haake. Bottom Row: Herman Russel, unknown, Alma Russel, Elsie Haake, Emma Borger, Harry Russell, unknown, unknown, John Haake.

LIBERTY SCHOOL
T19

During this century, Eagle Creek Twp. had two brick schoolhouses, up until around 1940, when Liberty School, in the southern part of the township, was demolished. The last classes were held there in 1937-1938.

In an earlier "History of Lake Co." book by Bowers, Taylor, Woods of 1929, it stated: Liberty School (all brick, 2 classrooms, full basement, modern) built in 1920 by F.E. Muzzal & Sons for $16,000.00. Jay M. Pearce was Trustee at that time.

Co. and Twp. records have been destroyed when the Co. Courthouse was moved to the new Gov. Center north of Crown Point. So a complete list of teachers and trustees is no longer available. What information is listed on the two schools has been derived from individuals who had attended these schools.

Liberty teachers in 1921-22 were Paul Sheehan for upper grades and Mary Fisher in the lower grades. 1923-24 was Smith V. Glass, with Grace Hathaway as Music Supervisor, W.A. Bryant was Twp. Trustee and A.E. Condon was Co. Sup't. Students then in the upper grades were: 5th grade: Roy Solomon, Edna Solomon, Clark Appleton, Laura Herron, Irene Jurs, Violet Hessling, Magdalena Kretz. 6th grade: Marion Iliff, Joe Hessling, Alice Reed, Ophelia Winkler, Lorena Hillyer. 7th grade: Wesley Jurs, Gladys Sutton, Cecil Sutton, Elmer Solomon. 8th grade: Ruby Herron, Ruth Meadows, Opal Meadows, Fred Solomon, Harvey Hillyer, Daniel Solomon. Edwin Hough and Zora Busselberg, also Martha DeKock taught in 1925-26. Hubert Long became principal, Lena Bryant, Mildred Sparling and Lois Berdine taught in 1926-27. Ann DeKock and Mildred Sparling taught in 1927-28. Then a period without available information. — During the winter, when mud roads became almost impassable, Wm. Amey drove a horse-drawn wagon to get the children to school, probably around 1934-35-36. Doris Morrow and Frances Fry also were teachers at Liberty in the late '30's. Laureva Sloan was a teacher there in 1937-38. John Amey was a bus driver in 1937-38 (later these two were married). Spring of 1938 was the last time Liberty was used as a school. Those students were bused to Center School after that, and a year or so later, the old Liberty School Bldg. was demolished.

by Dorothy Sorensen

NEW ELLIOTT SCHOOL CLASS
T20

Prior to 1927

Miss Ida Piepho taught at this New Elliott School before her marriage on June 12, 1927. She became Mrs. Carl Pfau, whose husband was born in Keokuk, Iowa, but eventually settled near Grant Park, Illinois.

After farming in several nearby areas, they settled on a farm three miles north of Brunswick, Indiana, next to Schiller School. This was across to the east of her homeplace, a daughter of August and Dorathea (Wille) Piepho. Her sisters, Ora and Dora, were also teachers in the area; another sister Emma was a home nurse; Herman, a postal clerk, and Elmer farmed the home place.

In the 1930's, Ida Rosalinda taught at the St. John Township School in Dyer, Indiana. Later, this was known as the Dyer High School, and then Kahler School in more recent years. She taught at various other schools in the area over the years, then part-time, and finally as a substitute up through the mid 1950's. After they sold their farm, they retired in their own home in Lowell, Indiana. He passed away on December 23, 1966, and Ida Rosalinda on June 25, 1978. There were no children.

by Mrs. Ralph Oldendorf

The New Elliott School Class, prior to 1927.

THE NEW ELLIOTT SCHOOLHOUSE Prior to 1927
T21

The New Elliott Schoolhouse prior to 1927 at the time Ms. Ida R. Piepho taught there. [Photo courtesy of Mrs. Ralph Oldendorf]

THE 1919 SECOND GRADE CLASS OF THE OLD MILLER SCHOOL
T22

Pictured here is a second grade class in 1919. The group is standing at the entrance to the old Miller school on Lake St., four miles east of downtown Gary. The building was erected in 1810. One of the first teachers was George Peterson, of Miller. At the time Miller was sparsely settled, mostly by Swedish and Irish immigrants. The teacher pictured here was Miss Minnie Carlson, second grade teacher. First grade teacher was Clara Peterson. Both of these young ladies had to relinquish their duties because they had tuberculosis, and died shortly thereafter. The city of Gary annexed the town of Miller about 1920. The school was taken into the Gary school corporation. W.A. Wirt, superintendent, established the Work-Study-Play system in the Gary schools about that time. Students pictured in this second grade class were:

Virginia Hamilton Kaiser, Iva Phillips Newman, Julia Sloan Strom, Ethel Bowgreen, Esther Carlson, Eleanor Nelson, Rose Matson, Aldean Myers, Charlene Bailey, Caroline Quantz, Celia Crisman, Ruth Domberg, Harriott Lundstrom, Eileen Bond, Helen Cramer Cummins, Paige Berger, Vivian Micheal, Clifford Anderson, Clifford Hayes, Arthur Mattis, Eric Lindstrom, Carl Gross, Rinehardt Johnson, Clinton Erlandson, Carl Olander, Kenneth Lemert, Cecil Crisman, George Lemon, Clarence Berg, Ethel Babcock, Harry Huff, Howard Bokich, and Alwood Eng.

by Virginia Kaiser

THE ORCHARD GROVE SCHOOL
T23

Another of the early schools was the one at Orchard Grove. It served a long, useful life — longer than many early schools. It was housed in 4 different buildings. It is a tribute to our forefathers that one of their first projects was always a school.

Though I have not been able to find a date for the first Orchard Grove School, it must have been in the 1840's. It was a log structure built in a woods on a slope, which was south and across the road from the present Carlton Ebert Jr. home — or just north of the Orchard Grove Cemetery. It was on Warner land at that time. Hazelnut brush and shrubbery grew thick in front of the school. Many deer lived in this brush and could be seen coming and going most any time. Its patrons were Kenneys, Vander-Cars, Warners, and Handleys. Orlando Beebee was its first teacher. John Dwyer and Harrison Ragon also taught in this log building.

The second building was located southwest from the log structure. Grant Street now goes past the spot. This land was given by James Woodruff to the township for school purposes. It faced east and often housed as many as 70 students. During the winter months all the local boys attended school but when spring opened up the farm work there was a great falling off in attendance as the boys were expected to help on the farms.

This building burned during a school term so another was hurriedly built to meet the emergency. It faced north and was somewhat east of the other building. Its construction was so poor that it was condemned and torn down, then rebuilt during the summer. The third and last was built in 1898 while James Black was trustee. Thomas Grant was the contractor. The last school closed in 1927 when the children were bused to Lowell. This school district had served the children for about 80 years.

It became the community center when the children were taken into Lowell and was the social heart of the neighborhood. From the earliest times, Sunday School and church were held in the schoolhouse. Through the years it has been used for funerals, for the early

Old Miller School's second grade class in 1919.

"literaries," family reunions. It has been a center for community meetings, Farm Bureau, Grange women's clubs, parties, entertainment, 4H meetings, conservation, and other civic groups. Thus its influence reached far and many people. The township (Cedar Lake) sold the land and building at public auction in 1952. It was bought by Ernest Ebert, whose land surrounded it, then was torn down to be used in other buildings.

Carl Miller was the last teacher. An incomplete list of other teachers: Jim Westbay, Libbie Kenney, Alice Robbins, Billy Northrup, Luella Fuller, Fred Ewer, Hattie Sanger, Starr Brownell, Minnie Ebert, John Buckley, Bessie Purdy, Roy Daum, Gretna Norton, Ruth Brownell, Ben Lynch, Judson Sanger, Mildred Surprise, Lois Metcalf, Ruby Nichols, Julia Stenerson, Ethel Burroughs, Rachel Dodge, Herbert Prage.

by Bessie Kenney

THE EARLY RILEY SCHOOL
T24

The early Riley School of Cedar Creek Township, rural Crown Point, IN. Miss Crawford was the teacher on the far right. The only ones known in the photo are Olga and Mary Rust, daughters of Sophia (Borchers) and Henry Rust. This school burned down and later a new one was built.

by Mrs. Ralph Oldendorf

ST. JOHN TOWNSHIP SCHOOL IN DYER
Clsss of 1924-1925
T25

(Back Row) Charles Taylor, Lillian Russel, Roy Helmer, Mildred Brands, Hazel De Mik, Robert Galbreath, Willard Russel. (Middle Row) Lucille De Mik, Bunkowfst girl, Leona Brands, Evelyn Dust, Bunkowfst girl, Nick Thiery, Annette Bush, Norman Taylor, Andrew De Mik, Phillips boy. (Bottom Row) Robert Bolt, Norbert Seehausen, Grace Lambert, Dorothy Seehausen. [Photo courtesy of Mrs. Ralph Oldendorf]

ST. JOHN TOWNSHIP SCHOOL IN DYER
T26

HISTORY OF ST. MICHAEL SCHOOL
T27

In 1886, when St. Michael's Parish was hardly more than ten years old one of the greatest desires of the people of the parish, that of establishing a school, became a reality.

At this time many of the children had to attend the local village school. Others living on outlying farms went to small schools closer to their homes.

In 1886, Father Berg, St. Michael's pastor at the time, obtained two Franciscan Sisters of the Sacred Heart to teach in the village school lower grades. Sister Elizabeth and Sister Josephine were housed in two rented rooms in the home of Nicolaus Scherer. Later, church members converted a 16 x 20 foot barn into the first Sister's house. This enlarged building served as their home until their present residence was built in 1914.

In 1893, the parish purchased a 20 x 24 foot section of the old public (village) school and moved it north of the cemetery. The Sisters utilized this one room building for religious instruction only. St. Michael's children who were attending the village school now came up from the public school after lunch for one hour religion classes and then returned to the public school. Children who attended small outlying schools came on Sunday afternoon for religious instructions in church.

In June of 1900, the pastor at St. Michael's announced to the congregation that the time had come for a parochial school which would offer all subjects. In spite of hard times the people of St. Michael's sacrificed and an addition expanded the one room school to two.

On Sept. 15, 1900, the building was blessed and the school year began. St. Michael's school opened as what we know as a high school. And two years later expanded into a full elementary school. With an ever increasing enrollment two additional classrooms were added in 1908. These children, our ancestors, played under the same old oak tree in the front of the school, as we do today.

Classes continued in this four-roomed school until 1916, when a new brick school was erected. St. Michael's parishioners were very proud of their new school and they grew and prospered. In 1925, St. Michael8's School offered 9th and 10th grades allowing the students to receive ten years of formal Catholic education. This continued for eight years until 1933. Many of our grandparents graduated from St. Michael's during this time and reminisce with great pride.

St. Michael's continued to grow. Enrollment at this time was 70 boys and 54 girls. Only 4 pupils of the parish attended public grade school. One of the highlights of the schools extracurricular events was the annual "Thanksgiving Parade." Led by two older pupils holding prize turkeys, the children marched up and down the streets of Schererville, each carrying a gift of food to be presented to the Sisters and the Priest.

By 1950, St. Michael's School was bulging with children. Many of these children are your moms and dads today. A survey in 1953-54 revealed that not enough classroom space was available to accommodate the following year's enrollment. Therefore the ground was broken for the school addition July 1954. February 1955, the new addition was opened. This addition housed Miss Schiesser's third grade, Sis-

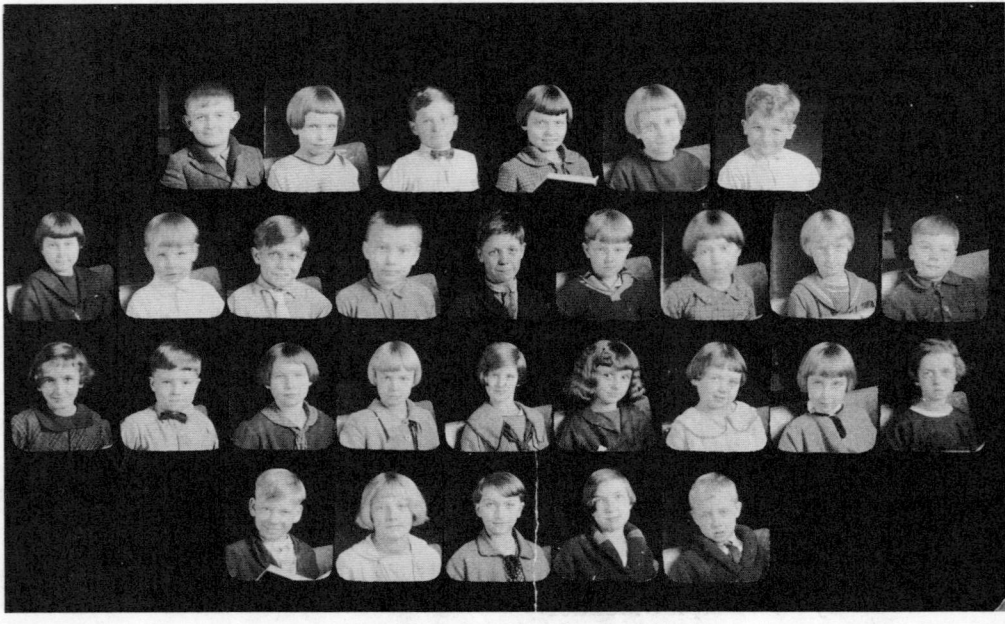

St. John Township School in Dyer, Indiana 19—. Top Row: Andrew De Mik, unknown, Norbert Seehausen, Lucille De Mik, Della Russel, unknown. Row 2: Ella Brands, unknown, Oliver Kaiser, unknown, Raymond Kammer, unknown, Griner girl, Elsie Dust, Hearne boy. Row 3: Evelyn Dust, Robert Hearne, Evelyn Russel, unknown, Amy Cassill, Helen Litwa, Rilla Griner, Genevieve Zeck, Dorothy Thiery. Row 4: Orin Lambert, Elizabeth Bush, June Good, Clarabelle Schroeder, Ray Zeck. [Photo courtesy of Mrs. Ralph Oldendorf]

ter Theresa Clare's first grade, Sister Elizabeth Anne's third/fourth grades and Sister Lorita's second grade today.

Enrollment continued to increase and there were no longer sufficient Sisters to staff the entire school, thus the first lay teacher was employed for the 1954-55 school year.

St. Michael School continued to prosper and

grow, still more classrooms were needed. After about a year of construction our beautiful new Junior High wing was completed and dedicated in 1970.

The dedication plaque reads: "This building is dedicated to the Glory of God; to the Christian education of His children; to the unity of the parish family; in memory of the loyal benefactors through whose generosity our parish plant and this addition have been provided. May many loving servants be their reward."

Enrollment at St. Michael's at the present time is 373, 184 girls and 189 boys. Our faculty consists of seven lay teachers and six Franciscan Sisters.

St. Michael's parishioners have always had a special pride in their school. We are fortunate to be able to say, "I am a Catholic, and I go to St. Michael's School."

by Wilma Jansen

Schiller School, early years.

HISTORY OF SCHILLER SCHOOL
T28

room. In the late 1930's, when children were bused from different areas of Hanover Township to Schiller, it again became a two room school.

In 1960 or 1961, Schiller was closed and then torn down. The land on which the school stood reverted back to the Christ Brands family since they had donated the ground for the school to be built on.

by Mrs. Walter Karstensen

Schiller School

There were small one room schoolhouses north of Brunswick in Hanover Township which were replaced by a two room brick school in 1912 known as Schiller. This school was called the "big" school. Later it was used as a one room school, with all eight grades in one

Early year school bus for Hanover Township Schiller School.

SCHILLER SCHOOL CLASSROOM 1917-1918
T29

(Teachers) left, Ed Echterling, (far right) Ora Piepho. (Back Row) Henry Piepho, unknown, Arnold Piepho, Dora Hitzeman, unknown, unknown. Row 2: Lyla Oberloh, Alma Hitzeman, Bernice Helmer, Alma Russel, Lydia Oberloh, unknown, unknown, Dora Piepho. Row 3: Ray Seegers, Hilda Hitzeman, Mildred Claus, Rose Brands, unknown, Lenore Claus, unknown, Margaret Wassmann. (Front Row) John Schoenbeck, Ben Claus, Walter Piepho, Albert Russel, Wm. Brands, Otto Paul, Ben Piepho. [Photo courtesy of Mrs. Ralph Oldendorf]

TWO CLASSES, SCHILLER SCHOOL 1927
T30

Schiller School was named after a German poet. The school was located at ¼ mile north of 121st and the east side of Calumet Avenue, or 2 ¼ miles north of Brunswick, Indiana.

by Mrs. Ralph Oldendorf

Teachers: Irma Hall and Dora Piepho. (Top Row) Clara Brands, Clara & Marie Wassman (twins), Gilbert Piepho, Edna Reichert, Mildred Brands, Lydia Stolzenbach. (Row 1) Leona Brands, Ruby Asche, Milford Kohlscheen, Lillian Piepho, Elwood Meier, Mabel Seegers, Paul Bloesch, Edwin Segert, Lorena Stolzenbach, Lester Hitzeman. (Row 2) Mary Ketwig, Harriet Oldendorf, Laverne Seehausen, Lucille Wassman, Naomi Borger, Ella Brands, Ray Segert, Leonard Fricke, Ralph Oldendorf. (Row 4) Walter Segert, Albert Brands, Wilbert Seehausen, Henry Ketwig, Ervin Reichert, Walter Bloesch, Ray Brands.

TWO CLASSES, SCHILLER SCHOOL 1928-1929
T31

Teachers: Irma Hall, Dora Piepho. (Top Row) Wilbert Seehausen, Edwin Segert, Arnold Segert, Ray Brands, Albert Brands. (Row 2) Selma Dust, Lillian Piepho, Mabel Seegers, Leona Brands, Ruby Asche, Lorraine Stolzenbach, Ella Brands. (Row 3) Mary Ketwig, Harriet Oldendorf, Walter Bloesch, Leonard Fricke, Walter Segert, Henry Ketwig. (Row 4) Dorothy Brands, Naomi Borger, Ray Segert, Herbert Reichert, Anna Ketwig, Laverne Seehausen, Ralph Oldendorf. [Photo courtesy of Mrs. Ralph Oldendorf]

SCHILLER SCHOOL CLASS OF 1934-1935
T32

SHERIDAN SCHOOL
T33

Schoolhouses of yesteryear are disappearing, both physically and educationally. They were important centers of learning. It is sad that they disappear so completely, when no one is left that remembers. I wish to refresh the image of the one I attended 5 years. This story takes place in 3 different buildings.

When my family moved in the spring of 1912, I had a different school. It was a one room wooden structure, 45 or 50 years old, known as the Bixeman School. It was about 3½ miles west of Creston in West Creek Township. Mr. Dunkleberger was the teacher. I was in 4th grade. By fall a new two room, brick school, renamed Sheridan, was ready to use.

The wooden building and a half acre of land had been sold to the Gleaner organization. Its usefulness continued, as it served as the Gleaner Hall, and for other social functions of the neighborhood. Farmer's Institutes were held two or three times a year. What interesting, educational programs for the farmers — the overflowing basket dinners — baking and serving contests for ladies and young people. That was my first taste of fame — I had a first prize loaf of bread! The school children always attended. The hall also served as a regular polling place.

The new school had an entrance hall across the front with steps going down either side to the basement which served as a play area. The wide steps in the center went up to the classrooms with a cloak hall for each room. Each room was heated by a large furnace type stove. There was a small room at the rear between the two rooms containing library books and supplies. If we had a good record we could go in there sometimes when we were finished with our work; some browsed among the books, others ate the paste. Ernie Gragg and Lucille Doris were teachers. One year there were so few pupils that we were all taught in one room by Sadie Morey. Then back to two room; our teacher, Ernie. Both boys and girls were supposed to play ball recesses and noons when Gragg was teacher (no objections from the boys). There was a huge black locust tree near the road. Walking was the transportation. The teachers drove; the horses were put in the barn. A bus began about 1914. There was a delightful woods west. What a heyday when Mr. Gragg took us there on field trips even if we had to write compositions on which side of the tree moss grew!

One sad morning Sheridan was gone. Burned. Signs indicated a tramp had slept in, burning books for warmth. Classes moved back into Gleaner Hall while another school was built. When schools were consolidated, Sheridan was disbanded and sold. Vandalism was becoming a factor, so the Gleaner Hall was sold and torn down. Empty space but now Sheridan Acres — full of homes.

by Bessie Kenney

(L to R) Laverna Thoms, Laverne Seehausen, Norbert Segert, Ray Segert, Ralph Oldendorf, Margaret Reichert, Evelyn Klemme, Erna Segert, Marcella Piepho, Dorothy Brands. (Seated, Row 2) Leland Schoenbeck, Virginia Schoenbeck, Roger Meyer. (Seated, Row 3) Arlene Rehborg, Albert Seehausen, Mildred Stolzenbach, Viola Thoms. (Seated, Front Row) Adeline Klemme, Arlene Fricke, Dale Whittle, Virgil Schoenbeck. [Photo courtesy of Mrs. Ralph Oldendorf]

EARLY PHOTO OF ZION CHURCH SCHOOL CLASS
T34

Rev. H.E. Blum. (Back Row) Ernest Riechert, Ray Seegers, Frieda Rickenberger, Dora Piepho, Alfrieda Claus. (Middle Row) Harold Brands, Mathilda Ohlendorf, Alice Guritz, Henrietta Brands, Alma Russel. (Front Row) Harold Brands, Harvey Hahn, Elmer Klemme, Ed Bremer, Henry Klemme, Art Hartman.

Oct. 1966 and at present the old Zion German Ev. School.

A pencil sketch from memory of the Zion German Ev. Schoolhouse, built shortly after June 1873.

The Zion German Evangelical Church School Class began at first under this early name. In June of 1873, it was decided to teach German on Monday and Thursday each week. Later, when students became of Confirmation age at 12, 13, 14 years, they left public school to attend a full day, two year term. Upon completion, they resumed their public school education from where they left off. Either they completed 8th grade already or continued on, went on to high school, or joined the working force. This came to an end around 1919.

The building was then used for other purposes until 1948, when Mrs. Alma Seehausen purchased it for a retirement home. It was moved to the northeast corner of the Seehausen farm at Kreitzburg, Indiana, where it remains a home in use at the present time.

by Mrs. Ralph Oldendorf

OLD ZION GERMAN EVANGELICAL SCHOOLHOUSE
T35

by Mrs. Ralph Oldendorf

The Old Zion German Ev. Schoolhouse, remodeled into a home by Mrs. Alma Seehausen on the NE corner of the farm place near Kreitzburg in 1948.

LAFAYETTE SCHOOL
T36

Lafayette School, Hammond, Indiana.

by Mrs. Ralph Oldendorf

25

CHURCHES

FIRST BAPTIST CHURCH

T37

Of Hammond

A Look at the Past & Present First Baptist Church

The town directory reads: The First Baptist Church of Hammond was organized November, 1887, under the labors of Rev. Allen Hill, home missionary, with eleven constituent members. For a time the congregation met in the garrett (attic) of the Morton House. (The Morton House was on Willow Court, one block west of Hohman, on the south side of the street.) The Rev. B.P. Hewitt settled as pastor the first of April, 1888, holding services in the Hohman Opera House (located at State and Hohman, where the Army Surplus Store is) until November, when the present commodious chapel on Sibley Street was dedicated (located at about the center of parking lot across the street from the present church auditorium), costing about $2,000. $2,358 was raised by the members. The church membership at the last annual meeting was thirty-two. A prosperous Sunday school with an average attendance of 50. An active Ladies' Home Worker's Society. Preaching services held every Lord's Day at 10:30 a.m. and 7:30 plm., Sunday School at 12:00 noon. A weekly prayer meeting on Tuesday evening.

The First Baptist Church was organized November, 1887, under the labors of Rev. Allen Hill, home missionary, with eleven constituent members. They first met in the garrett (attic) of the Morton House Hotel in Hammond, Indiana. The hotel was steam heated and had electric lights and electric bells.

The Hohman Opera House, located at State Street and Hohman Avenue (where the Army Navy War Surplus Store is located), was the meeting place for the First Baptist Church from January, 1888 – November, 1888. Rev. B.P. Hewitt was the Pastor of the church at that time.

The First Baptist Church dedicated their new chapel on Sibley Street (located about the center of the parking lot across the street from the Educational Building) in 1888. Thirty-two members raised $2,358.00 to pay for the building. The Sunday school average attendance was 50.

In 1901 the First Baptist Church outgrew their little chapel on Sibley Street. Under the direction of Pastor Edward T. Carter the chapel was rebuilt and enlarged with used lumber from a fire at the G.H. Hammond Meat Packing Company. This building was used for 12 years and then sold to the Knights of Columbus. We redeemed this buillding in 1964 after our fire and used it for Sunday school departments and adult clasrooms.

The First Baptist Church sold their first church building at 526 Sibley Street to the Knights of Columbus. Then the church rented a hall, which they called "Baptist Hall" on the second floor of the old Lion Store on Hohman Avenue. (The "new" Lion Store, which we know as the Goldblatt's Building, was constructed in 1927.) They met in "Baptist Hall" for 14 months until the new church building at 523 Sibley Street was ready for occupancy.

The new church building at 523 Sibley Street was dedicated on November 27, 1914. It was the largest auditorium in the city, therefore, it was used for high school commencements and similar meetings. The basement was the first fully equipped gymnasium, complete with locker and showers, in Hammond. For several years it was used by the public schools of Hammond.

With the coming of Pastor Owen L. Miller in 1947, our Sunday school attendance rose from 600 to 1000. Sunday school space became a serious problem. A three-story addition on the east side of the church building was built; this was dedicated in 1951. The overhanging eaves were removed from the original building at this time because of a problem with the roosting pigeons.

The dedication of our auditorium on Sunday, April 5, 1964, was an exciting time for us at First Baptist Church of Hammond. We had 2,374 in Sunday School. Then at 3:00 p.m. a special Service of Dedication for the Auditorium was held: The keys to the auditorium were presented to Pastor Hyles; Deacon Chairman Ed Rausch prayed a prayer of dedication; sister churches of the area sent words of congratulations; and Brother Hyles preached, "Upon This Rock." During the 7 o'clock evening service, Dr. G. Beauchamp Vick, Pastor of the then World's Largest Church, preached the dedicatorial sermon.

When the 1975 church auditorium construction was being planned, Bro. Hyles suggested that a facade be added across the front of the church buildings. This wall not only created a hallway around the auditorium and added a few extra rooms, but it also unified Miller Hall, dedicated in 1951, and the Educational Building, in 1967, with the expanded Auditorium.

An arsonist set fire to two of our buildings, the Youth Center and the 1914 "Church with the Dome," during the night of June 4, 1964. The alarm was turned in at 1:15 a.m. Friday, June 5. The fire burned for 30 hours, completely destroying these two buildings and causing smoke and water damage to Miller Hall and to our two-month-old auditorium. All day Saturday, June 6, hundreds of our people worked round the clock to get the auditorium ready for the Sunday services. (It would be days before Miller Hall cooled down enough for anyone to be allowed inside to steam-clean the walls, get the water out of the basement, etc.) On Sunday, June 7, the Calumet Region was shocked that we held our regularly scheduled Sunday services! The Junior I Department met across the street on the parking lot; the nursery for babies birth-3 years of age was set up in a rented room next to the poultry shop. We praised the Lord that the new auditorium had been spared: We had a place to meet and meet we did!

On Sunday, June 18, 1967, our new four-story Educational Building was completed and ready for use. This building was built on the site of the old auditorium which burned. The ribbon-cutting ceremony was held at 9:30 a.m. Open house was from 5:00-7:00 p.m., and refreshments were served. Dr. John R. Rice brought the dedicatorial message at the 7:30 p.m. service.

The interior of our church building which was dedicated in 1914 was as elegant as the building itself. The beautiful dark oak floors, pews and pulpit furniture were complemented by the brass organ pipes which were above the choir loft. The stars on the servicemen's flag which hung over the choir loft represented the young men from our church who were serving in the armed services.

In 1962 it became apparent that we needed further seating; a new auditorium was a necessity, and plans were begun to provide twice the seating capacity of the old auditorium with the dome. The Men's Brotherhood Class building and the two-story frame flat which were located on the west side of the church building came down to allow room for the new construction. During 1963, the period of planning, sacrificial giving and extra labor, the church added 1400 members, bringing the total membership to 4,000. The new auditorium seated 2,000 and was dedicated April 5, 1964; we had 2,374 in

The First Baptist Church of Hammond in 1975.

The dedication of the auditorium on Sunday, April 5, 1964.

Sunday school!

On October 5, 1974, the Hammond Civic Center became our "home away from home" for four months, while our present auditorium was under construction to double the seating capacity to 5,000. (Since that time we have added the mezzanine, extended the side balconies, etc., to accommodate, 6,800 people.) While at the Civic Center the Pathfinders, Sunbeams, Nursery Departments and the "B," "C" and "D" Sunday School Departments met in their regular places on the church properties. The Beginner Departments met in separate rooms at the Civic Center, children primary age and older met in assigned sections of the balcony, and the adults met on the main floor where we had a combined two-hour morning service. We baptized our converts in the swimming pool. On February 19, 1975, Dr. R.G. Lee, the great orator-preacher of our day, brought the dedicatorial message in our new church auditorium.

by Tom McKinney

HISTORY OF FIRST BAPTIST CHURCH – HOBART
T38

First Baptist Church – Hobart

November, 1934 – The First Baptist Church of Hobart is a reality today because a group of Christians felt the need in their community for a Bible-preaching church. Dr. R.T. Ketcham, pastor of Central Baptist Church of Gary was asked to help form a mission in Hobart, Indiana. The first prayer meeting was held in the home of E.J. Harris.

February, 1935 – The mission rented the Episcopal Church located at Fourth and Main Streets. Harold E. Cole became the first pastor.

March 21, 1937 – The mission rented a large hall upstairs in the Stratton Building, known as the "Grand Duke's Opera House", located at Third and Main Streets.

October, 1937 – A constitution was adopted.

November 29, 1937 – The mission became an independent church and became recognized as First Baptist Church of Hobart, Indiana.

November, 1941 – Pastor Arlin Halvorsen became the second pastor. The Stratton Building lacked adequate space so the church moved to the Wilde Building at 619 East Third Street.

October, 1943 – Pastor Robert Johnson was called to this ministry as the third pastor after Pastor Halvorsen resigned to enter the military service as a Chaplain.

September, 1945 – The Wilde Building was purchased.

September, 1946 – The educational outreach of the church expanded with a day school kindergarten: Mrs. Robert Johnson and Mrs. Albert Haynes, teachers.

January 1, 1948 – Pastor Kenneth McQuere began his ministry.

July 30, 1950 – Six lots at First and Pennsylvania Streets were purchased and a building program was begun.

June, 1951 – Ground was broken for the first unit of the present building.

September 27, 1951 – The cornerstone was laid. Construction began.

September 7, 1952 – The completed church building was dedicated to the Lord.

Spring, 1954 – Construction started on the second unit which contained classrooms and larger offices.

September 2, 1956 – Dedication services were held upon completion of the second unit. The congregation was able to burn the mortgage on the entire building.

November, 1959 – The church observed its 25th anniversary. The anniversary theme was "To God Be The Glory".

September, 1961 – John and Alice Barcus, our missionaries from Africa, returned and John Barcus served as interim pastor.

April, 1962 – Pastor Max E. Tucker accepted the church's call to the pastorate.

Winter, 1963 – Plans were begun for the construction of the third unit: a larger auditorium, more room and better facilities for the expanding ministry of the church.

May 13, 1964 – Dedication services were held for the third unit.

January, 1966 – Pastor Donald Wallace was extended a call to become pastor of First Baptist. The church's outreach in missions and the Baptist Children's Home, Kouts, Indiana, were expanded at this time.

November 16, 1969 – Thirty-fifth anniversary was celebrated with joy.

September, 1970 – Pastor McQuere accepted the responsibility of interim pastor.

March 17, 1971 – Pastor Charles R. Wood began his ministry. There was growth in many areas, one being the purchase of several buses and a bus barn.

1973 – An educational unit was planned and work was completed within the next year, 1974.

September, 1975 – A Christian Elementary School was established, which continues today.

December, 1976 – Pastor LoTurco accepted a call to the ministry and pastorate of the church.

August, 1983 – Pastor G.C. Martin became interim pastor.

February 1, 1984 – Pastor Dick Brown of Marathon, New York, was called to the pastorate.

November, 1984 – Our 50th Anniversary was celebrated. God has laid the chief cornerstone.

by Juanita R. Tucker

LOWELL FIRST UNITED METHODIST CHURCH
T39

Lowell 1837-1987

In the summer of 1837 the Methodists organized a class in the vicinity where Lowell now stands. Rev. Colclasier was the minister who first preached to this small group. The service were held at the home of the settlers, Wayne Bryant, Robert Hyde, John Kitchel, Mrs. Henry Sanger and Mrs. John Sanger. The church was a mission until 1841 when it became a circuit.

In 1849 a log cabin was built a mile and three quarters east of Lowell, in a place called Pleasant Grove. It stood until 1869.

The society next came to Lowell. Services were held in a little brick school house, erected in 1852 near the junction of Clark and Commercial Ave. In 1858 some of the members drew off to attend services at Orchard Grove. September 1870 the Lowell congregation erected a red brick church, the first Methodist church.

The Ladies Aid was organized about 1890. It met in homes until 1903. The Woman's Foreign Mission Society was organized November 1912. The Young Woman's Missionary Society was organized October 1924.

Construction on the present church began in May 1924. The congregation moved into the new church on January 18, 1925. The old brick church, at the corner of Main St. and Burnham St., was sold to the Lutherans. This church stood until 1962 when it was torn down. The West Creek Methodist church, in 1925, decided to merge with the Lowell Methodist church.

In 1940 there was a revision and unification of the Methodist church and at this time the world "Episcopal" was dropped and the church became "The First Methodist Church of Lowell. Also in 1940 The Woman's Society of Christian Service was formed.

September 1946 a new pipe organ was dedicated. December 1946 Memorial Chimes were dedicated. In 1957 The Methodist Youth Fellowship was organized. In 1948 The Methodist's Men Club was organized. In 1953 the Lowell Methodist ceased to be a circuit, the Creston Church was served by the Cedar Lake minister. In 1954 the Clara Pixley scholarship loan fund was established. In 1954 additions were begun on the church. In 1958 The Methodist Messenger began. Its aim was to bring news and information to all members of the congregation. In 1959 an Accumulative Memorial Fund was adopted. In 1962 further additions were made on the church. - up to its present size and design.

In 1967 the church became active in church wide support of Spanish-Americans. At this time a new parsonage was built. The old parsonage, known as the Sanger home, was sold and moved to Viant Street where it is now a private home.

In 1969 The Methodist Church merged with the United Brethern Church. Hence the Lowell church became The First United Methodist Church. In 1971 a Carillion was given to the church. In 1972 The Woman's Society of Christian Service was Changed to the United Methodist Woman.

Periodically the church publishes a pictorial

directory. The church is active in sponsoring Cub Scout and Boy Scout troops. It also serves as a center for AA and ALNON. Also being used as a Learning Center for those working toward a General Education Diploma and those with reading problems.

In 1987 the church purchased three properties to the south with future growth in mind.

As of 1988 The First United Methodist Church of Lowell is a growing, active organization. It is looking forward to many, many more years of active service to the community of Lowell.

by Thomas I. Stuart

FRANCISCAN SISTERS 100 YEARS IN AMERICA
T40

1876-1976

One hundred ten years ago the congregation of the Franciscan Sisters of the Sacred Heart was founded in southern Germany by a parish priest, Rev. William Berger. Father Berger's purpose in establishing this religious congregation was to provide care for the sick, the aged, and the homeless in his parish, and to accommodate those young women who expressed a desire to live a religious life. His aim was to incorporate in the spirit of this young group the joy of St. Francis of Assisi and the mercy of St. Vincent de Paul.

Persecution followed the new community. The Sisters were forbidden by law to call their home a "Motherhouse." It was also forbidden that they wear a religious habit. Again "verboten" was the use of the name "Sister" when referring to each of the members.

In spite of the ill will of the German government the "Sisters" continued to nurse the sick, house the orphans, and teach the children in the surrounding area. They felt it their "call" to help in whatever capacity they were needed. The Sisters received the "Iron Cross," a mark of distinction, for their work among the sick and dying on the battlefields of the Franco-Prussian War.

Ten years after the community's inception Bismarck, the Iron Chancellor, enacted the May Laws. Religious congregations were suppressed and exiled. Parish priests and their bishops were forbidden under penalty of fine, loss of income, and imprisonment to minister to their flocks.

The Franciscan Sisters of the Sacred Heart received the order to disband. On February 23, 1876, the ministerial order from the government was delivered: "The Community of Sisters at Trettenhof is suspected of working against the laws of Baden, as of October 9, 1860."

A number of Sisters chose to remain in Germany and wait until Bismarck's iniquitous laws were repealed. Twenty-seven chose to sail to a new home in America.

On February 23, 1976, the Franciscan Sisters of the Sacred Heart will open the celebration of their centennial year in the United States of America.

Rejoice with us that God has found us fit instruments for the accomplishment of some of His work on earth.

Pray for us that we may continue to enjoy the favor of God's grace.

Pray also for your parish and your families that St. Michael Parish may be richly blessed with vocations to the priesthood and religious life.

Sister Rosemarie

by January 1976 Issue of the *Mike*

HISTORY OF GRACE REFORMED CHURCH, U. C. C.
T41

Grace Reformed Church (UCC) at 1300 Jackson Street

The First Hungarian Evangelical and Reformed Church began with a few devoted Hungarian pioneers of Gary as early as 1907. They first gathered in homes and later in Gary's Neighborhood House. Early records indicate only 10 to 12 families were meeting together to share the word of our Lord. There are no written records of the beginning. However, the treasurer's ledger of 1913 reads that there was an income of $246.69, and expenses of $143.59. In 1914, records indicate expenses of $18.15. There are no records available for the year of 1915. In 1916, we find that the congregation was worshiping in the English Reformed Church at 23rd and Washington Street; Gary, Indiana. In this year, the Home Mission Board of the Reformed Church of the United States accepted our church under its' jurisdiction and the first consistory was elected. Prior to these years, area Magyar immigrants were meeting to worship in their mother language in an empty store on the southside of Chicago.

In July of 1918, the congregation had obtained land from the Gary Land Company for property at 1300 Jackson Street. The small group pledged $5.00 a month for the building of the sanctuary and parsonage. By 1920, the first minister and family moved into the parsonage and Hungarian services were held on Christmas Day. Dedication took place on May 29, 1921. Both structures were built at a cost of $65,000.

The congregation continued to grow along with the City of Gary, as the steel mills attracted many to the area. English speaking services soon were instituted and both languages are heard in the church services today.

In the years that followed, various organizations and clubs were formed: The Ladies Aid, Sunday School, Hungarian Summer School, Christian Endeavor, Magyar A.C., Dart Ball, Choir and Youth Group, Martha Club, Friendship Circle, Hungarian Dance Group and Fellowship Circle.

On April 28, 1959, the First Hungarian Evangelical and Reformed Church was struck by lightning and the 39-year-old structure was totally destroyed. The Hungarian and English congregation remained faithful to the strong foundation which they had established and undertook the task of relocating their house of worship.

As the city grew, families began to move to the Gary suburbs. The present site was considered as a central location for all. Ground breaking took place on December 4, 1960, at 5160 Georgia Street, Gary. Rev. Frank A. Endrie was serving the congregation at that time.

The building was designed by Coole and Borre, Park Ridge, Illinois. Church seating capacity is 250 plus a 35 member choir arrangement. The pastor's office and library rooms are located in the ediface. The Christian educational wing has 3 separate classrooms, complete kitchen facilities and a fellowship-banquet hall.

In the interim, the name was changed to the Grace Reformed Church, United Church of Christ. Our church is affiliated with the Western Classis of the Calvin Synod, U.C.C.

Rev. Frank Endrei officiated at the cornerstone laying on May 13, 1961. The cornerstone was a gift from Mrs. Theresa Bogyo.

The Fellowship Hall was available for Sunday School and Church services on August 27, 1961. On September 9, 1961, our beautiful new sanctuary was dedicated to the Glory of God.

The congregation, led by Rev. Joseph Benedek, gathered in thanksgiving to celebrate the burning of the mortgage on April 24, 1977.

The church bell in the foyer is the original bell from the 13th Avenue Church. The Hungarian flag in the social hall was also salvaged from the fire, as were the lovely crocheted church linens.

Pastors who have served our congregation: Rev. Endre Kiss, Rev. Aladar Jezerniczky, Rev. Eugene Vecsey, Rev. Alexander Ludman, Rev. Steven Virag, Rev. Aladar Tomcsanyi, Rev. Arpad Bakay, Rev. John Szeghy, Rev. Eugene Boros, Rev. Alexander Mircse, Rev. Bela Bertok, Rev. Michael Kovacs, Rev. Arpad Bakay, Rev. Bela Bacso, Rev. Leslie Kecskemethy, Rev. Bertalan Szathmary, Rev. Joseph Rasky, Rev. Louis Molnar, Louis Kajatin (student), Rev. Frank Endrei, Dr. Charles Szabo, Rev. Carolyn Medyesy, Dr. Laszlo Kovacs, Rev. Orval Yover, Dr. Marion Hathaway, Rev. Joseph Benedek, Rev. Zsolt Takacs.

The church groups sponsor several annual events, with the help of our church "family"! They are widely known for their preparation of Hungarian sausage (Kolbasz), Chicken Paprikas (Csirke Paprikas), Stuffed Cabbage (Toltott Kaposta), and different kinds of noodles, including Csiga.

Our world-famous "Magyar Magic" cookbook contains many family favorites plus excellent Hungarian recipes.

by Barbara Brkovich

THE MERRILLVILLE TRINITY FREE METHODIST CHURCH
T42

The Merrillville Trinity Free Methodist Church

The Free Methodist Church denomination was organized by B.T. Roberts in Pekin, New York in 1860. The Free Methodist Church separated from the Methodist and took the name "Free" because of a strong belief in freedom to personally accept the work of the Holy Spirit in the individual life, to have freedom from slavery, and to have free pews rather than the current pew rental system which favored wealthy people.

Twenty-seven years later, Bishop B.T. Roberts organized the North Indiana Conference, in Knox, Indiana, on October 27, 1887. The Conference consisted of two districts, the Knox District with six churches and the Fort Wayne District with five churches. The Knox District churches were Crown Point, San Pierre, Knox, (Elkhart, Mishawaka, Springville, LaPorte were one circuit), Kewanna and Indian Point.

In 1919, members from the Crown Point church helped to organize a Gary Mission at Ninth and Washington. In 1923 the congregation moved to a small storeroom on East 7th Avenue where Memorial Auditorium was later located. On March 8, 1925, the Hosford Park Sunday School was organized at the Hosford Park School.

In 1926, the Gary mission was organized into the Gary Free Methodist Church. Property at 4931 Massachusetts was purchased. A small building on this property was used both as a church and as a parsonage. Later it was used as a garage. When the parsonage was completed, the services were held on the second floor.

In 1929, by the time the church was completed, there were eighteen members.

A branch Sunday school was organized at the Godair School in 1938 and continued until the school burned in 1944. A Gary Railways bus was then hired to bring the Sunday School members to the Church. Because of the needed Sunday School room, the church basement was excavated in 1945.

In 1953, anticipating the need of a new church, three pieces of property south of the church were purchased. In 1957, a ground breaking ceremony was held for the new church building and an additional piece of property was purchased. The first service in the new church was held on June 29, 1958.

In 1960, the North Indiana Conference merged with the Wabash Conference and the Gary Church became a part of the Wabash conference.

In September of 1964 ground was broken for the educational addition to the church. In 1965 the addition was completed with the installation of the cross on the church steeple and a large lighted cross on the front wall in the chancel. (The cross now hangs in the present church sanctuary)

In 1967, property across the street from the church was purchased and plans were made for building a new parsonage on the purchased property. Instead, in 1969, a six room brick house at 4970 Massachusetts was purchased.

On October 19, 1969, the dedication of the educational unit of the church and the parsonage was held. The mortgages for the entire church and educational unit were burned at this dedication.

In 1970 a teen center was created in the old parsonage.

In 1975 the society voted to demolish the old church and parsonage (teen center).

In May of 1976, the old church and parsonage were both demolished. The building had been used only as a social hall for several years. The garage, the original Gary Free Methodist church, was also leveled at this time.

Always a church with a vision, a new vision was caught for the South Lake area. In 1977, ten acres were purchased on Grand Boulevard in Merrillville where new housing was just beginning to develop.

By fall of 1978, a beautiful new parsonage had been completed on the ten acres.

The opportunity came to sell the present church to another church group. The closing service was held on April 1, 1979. For the following year, the United Methodist Church on Delaware Street was rented each Sunday.

By August of 1979, ground was broken for a new church. The church was completed at the close of March 1980, and the first service was held Easter Sunday, April 6, 1980. A dedication service for the new church was held on May 4, 1980.

Thirty-two senior adults were honored on October 30. They were "Grands and Greats" who had given many years of service to the church in various capacities.

Many working organizational arms of the church have existed during the past years. The organizations are the Women's Missionary Fellowship, the Light and Life Men's Fellowship, the Free Methodist Youth, the Christian Youth Crusaders, Christian Youth in Missions, Junior Church, and the Church Choir. Many other programs have contributed to the success of the church. These include the Sunday School, the Vacation Bible School, and the many special days programs and activities such as Christmas programs, Rally Day, Enlargement Campaigns, Children's Day, Mother and Daughter Banquets, and many church Fellowship Dinners.

Many individuals have personally contributed hours of their time and dollars from their pockets to the advancement of God's work. Maintainence skills, the bus driving, food preparation and serving, teaching, home visitation, music, bulletins and newsletters, and consistency in doing whatever needed to be done were talents freely given.

It is the earnest prayer of the congregation of the Trinity Free Methodist Church to continue its service to God and to the people of the community.

by Alma Meyer and Sharon Crist

TRINITY MEMORIAL LUTHERAN CHURCH
T43

Independence Hill (Merrillville)

In January, 1940, a canvass was conducted by the Rev. Wm. J. Schepman, pastor of Trinity Lutheran Church, Crown Point. The first session of Sunday School was held in a pool room next to a filling station, located in the 7800 block of Taft St., on February 4, 1940. The first teachers were: Edith (Struebig) Steinmann, Vivian Nielson, Norma (Hack) Meyer, and Harvey Vandersee. On April 28, 1940 the first preaching service was held in the first chapel at 7715 Independence Street which was built by members of Trinity, Crown Point for $755.00. It was dedicated on June 28, 1940.

On April 11, 1944, an informal organization meeting was held. Those present were: Mr. and Mrs. Julius Wentland, Gus Frank, Mrs. Dorothy Jacobus, Mr. and Mrs. Charles M. Kaiser, Mrs. Emma Makus, Mr. Edwin Patz, Mr. & Mrs. Leslie Davis, and Mr. & Mrs. Charles Yester. On August 13, 1944, the first pastor, Rev. J.K. Muhlenbruch was installed. The first baptisms were Alan Roberts, son of Mr. & Mrs. Leroy Roberts and Carol McLean, daughter of Mr. & Mrs. John McLean. At this time the congregation began receiving a subsidy from Central District Mission Board, the Lutheran Church-Missouri Synod.

On March 20, 1946, the first parsonage at 7526 Independence Street was purchased.

On July 20, 1948, the original land of the present church on Marshall St. (185' by 225') was purchased for $1800. On April 27, 1952 the church was dedicated; and in June, Rev. Muhlenbruch accepted a call. The first confirmand in the new church was Gwyneth Klipp, daughter of Mr. & Mrs. Alvin Klipp.

In September 1952, the Rev. Robert Rippe, institutional missionary for the Calumet region served Trinity Memorial until he accepted a call to Colorado Springs.

In September, 1955, a kindergarten was started with Mrs. Vernon Heintz as the teacher and Mrs. Clarabell Brunmeier and Mrs. Leo Brunmeier as helpers.

In December, 1956, the congregation voted to become self-supporting. July 21, 1957, a Seminary graduate Rev. Allen A. Gartner was installed.

On June 6, 1960, 6.7. acres of adjoining land was purchased from Mr. and Mrs. Henry P. Fieler for $14,740.00. The debt on the property was retired in February, 1962. On April 29, 1962, the tenth anniversary of the dedication of the church on Marshall Street was observed with mortgage burning and ground breaking ceremonies.

On November 11, 1962, the enlarged sanctuary was dedicated to the glory of the Triune God for the salvation of men.

In June 1964, Rev. Gartner accepted a call to Holy Cross Lutheran Church in Minneapolis, Minnesota and on December 19, 1964, Rev. Gerard E. Isenberg, the present pastor, was installed.

In late 1965, a new parsonage was built on land adjoining the church. September 10,

31

1978, a new educational wing and narthex added to the church were dedicated.

by Members of Trinity Memorial Lutheran Church

RANGE LINE PRESBYTERIAN CHURCH
T44

Old Range line Church. Was built in 1910 for $600

The history of the Range Line Presbyterian Church goes back to the year 1912. (The church is located in Eagle Creek Twp.)

Mrs. Wm. Bigger, saw the need for religious training for the children of the community and started a Sunday School in her home. The number of children attending, gradually increased to 30. Permission was obtained from the Twp. Trustee for use of the Range Line Schoolhouse. A Free Methodist Minister by the name of Mr. Mitchell held church services for a while. Then for a time non-demoninational services were held. Charter members of the Range Line Church were: Mrs. Jessie Bigger, Wm. Orsburn, Mrs. Etta Orsburn, Mrs. Lizzie Solomon, F.B. Van Swearingen, Mr. & Mrs. Wm. Amey, Mrs. Mary Solomon, Mrs. Nellie Walker, Ora Winkler, Mrs. Luda Winkler, John Bigger, Linda Bigger, Martha Bigger, Mrs. Zetta Cook, Clem & Charlotte Fifield, Mrs. May VanSwearingen, Mrs. Mary Garvey, Irene Garvey, Claude Osburn, Mrs. Vessie Osburn, Roy Osburn, Mrs. Alice Osburn, Presley Simms, Bessie Whicker, Mrs. Daniel Whicker, Cloyd Walker, Lawrence & Lorena Winkler, Ophelia Winkler, Ruby Herron, Lawerence Herron, Hubert Herron.

Around 1915, a Mr. Hill of the Presby. Board of Nat'l. Missions was in Thayer organizing a Sunday School. He came and helped organize Range Line. A Mr. B.J. Day was Sun. School Sup't. A Presby. Minister, Rev. I.M. Houser conducted preaching Services. June 21, 1920, the Congregation met with the committee on Nat'l. Missions of the Logansport Presbytery. The first elected Elders were: Clem H. Fifield, Claude C. Osburn, Ora Winkler, & F.G. VanSwearingen. Trustees elected were: E.P. Williams, Wm. Orsburn, Roy Osburn & Cloyd Walker. Later the Pulpit was supplied by ministerial students who came from McCormick Theological Seminary, on weekends. The first wedding in the old Range line Church was Wilford Tuttle to Bessie Whicker 4/17/22. During the Depression yr's, of the mid thirties, it was really hard to raise the money to pay the preacher. (he was sometimes pd. w/farm produce) Attendance was low, the sm. group carried on until 1942, when new life began to assert itself under the leadership of Rev. W.D. Williams, a retired minister from Chicago, who had moved to Hebron, (he was eager to get back into harness again!) Under his leadership, the Bldg. exterior was painted, a new roof was added & grounds beautified, he himself helping with the labor. A Belfry was erected and a bell now sounded throughout the area ea. Sun. morning. The Sunday School grew to near 100, so add'tl. classrooms were needed. In 1947, a wing was built onto the original one-room schoolhouse. This add'tl. room also became a pleasant meeting place for the church groups — The Women's Ass'n, the Men's Club and the Youth Fellowship. In 1951, the idea of a new church building was in the minds of some of the members. Plans began to take shape and the project was underway. A gift of land from the Jay M. Pearce family settled the question of the building site, just ¼ mi. South of St. Rd. #2 on Range Line Rd. After much discussion a decision was made to build the Manse first. This was done in '53. On Apr. 9, '53, ground was broken for a new church bldg. Much of the work of building both the Manse & the Church was done by members of the congregation, & friends of the community. The Bldg. Comm. for the Manse was: Harold Wilson & Wayne Hofferth. The Bldg. Comm. for the Church was: Wayne Hofferth, Jas. McNeill, & Richard Ellis. Trustee's who served during the planning & building were: Vernon Childress, Warren Schoon, Harold Wilson, Ray Zanders, John Jurs, Wayne Hofferth & Glen Hartz. Elders who served during this era were: Jas. McNeill, Mary Childress, Tom K. Fisher, Richard Ellis, Eleanor Little, John Jurs & Laureva Amey. The last wedding in the old church was 11/28/53 – Jas. Holding to Barbara Hofferth.

On Feb. 13, '55, the closing services were held in the building that had served as Sun. School 7 Church in the Range Line Community for more that 40 yrs! On Feb. 20, 1955, the first service was held in the new bldg. The first wedding in the new bldg. was Arthur Close to Dorothy Osburn – 7/16/55. Another happy occasion was the burning of the mortgage on 4/28/57.

The Range Line Community Presbyterian Church now operates with a full-time pastor and growing membership. All former Pastors were: I.M. Houser – 6/21/20 – May '21; B.C. Stuart – student supply – 9/4/21 – 3/1/22. Ernest L. Yorger, *s.s. student supply – 3/5/22 – 7/29/23. Richard Archer *s.s. – 3/30/23 – 9/1/24. A.W. Wilson *s.s. – 9/1/24 – 2/15/25. Kenneth E. Wells *s.s. – 2/22/25 – 3/1/26. E.W. Johnson *s.s. – Mar. '25 – Apr. '27. Thomas Smart *s.s. – May '27 – May '28. John J. Meyer *s.s. – May '28 – Apr. '29. Henry Bonnema – Pastor – 1932-1936. Ernest Armstrong – Pastor – May '36 – Oct. '36. Roy Brumbaugh – Pastor – June '37 – June '42. W.D. Williams – stated supply – July '42 – June '50. Malcolm Nygren – Kouts/Range Line Pastor – Nov. '50 – June '52. Paul Chalfant – student supply – July '52 – Nov. '52. Milton Nolan – student supply – Summer '53. Otis McMullen – Pastor – Sept. '53 – Sept. '55. Darrell Parker – Pastor – Jan. 1, '57 – June '59. David Frye – student supply – June '59 – June '60. Frank M. Elliott – Pastor – June '60 – June '64. Vernon DeVries – Pastor – Jan. '65 – June '67. Edward Leigh – Pastor – Dec. '67 – Aug. '70. Charles Gordon – stated supply – Jan. 1, '71 – July '76. Daniel Patterson – Pastor – July '76 – June '86. Roger Reaber – Pastor – July '87 – now serving.

by Dorothy Sorensen

ST. MARY'S CAPUCHIN SEMINARY
T45

A Short History

In 1953, seeking to establish themselves near Chicago, the Province of St. Joseph purchased a portion of the Willard Burge farm near Schererville, Indiana. At that time it was not determined what use was to be made of the wooded plot with its seven acre lake. The greatest need was for an enlarged philosophy house. Other projects forced themselves into

Present Range line Church

prominence, and it was not until 1956 that preliminary planning was begun on St. Mary's Seminary. Late in 1957, Most Reverend Andrew G. Grutka, D.D., Bishop of Gary, blessed the site and Very Reverend Gerald Walker, O.F.M. Cap., Provincial Superior broke ground for the new building.

August 24, 1958, saw a happy gathering at the building site. Monsignor Francis Jansen, P.A., a "young" prelate at 80-plus years, set the cornerstone for the new Seminary. In his pocket this grand old friend of the Capuchins carried a rosary as he had done with pride for more than half a century. This rosary was presented to him while he was still a student at St. Lawrence Seminary, Mr. Calvary, Wis., by Father Francis Haas, co-founder of the Province.

On this day the sandaled feet of 50 Capuchin seminarians brushed over acorns newly fallen on the site. Representing the new life of the Province, these young men had come from St. Felix Friary in Huntington, Indiana, to mingle for the day with their new neighbors. This was the first sight of the bearded and brown robed friars in the area. It was a foretaste of what would become a familiar sight in June of 1959.

The friar students who have moved into the new seminary have the thrill of occupying the newest and largest Capuchin house of studies. The bright and airy rooms and corridors plainly speak of modern architectural design. Yet, the simple Capuchin tradition is maintained in the brick walls, the plain concrete floors and the lack of adornment. All of this keeps before the friars the example of the Little Poor Man of Assisi who chose to imitate Christ.

ZION UNITED CHURCH OF CHRIST

T46

The New Zion United church of Christ

Zion United Church of Christ, Dyer, Indiana (Hanover Prairie), had its beginning when late in 1858, twenty-three families living on both sides of the Indiana-Illinois state line met to discuss the establishment of a church on Evangelical principles.

The congregation was officially organized on August 31, 1859. The church was then named Deutsche Ver. Evangelische Zions Kirche (German United Evangelical Zion Church).

Otto Buehre, a local farmer, sold a five acre plot of land to them for $50.00 upon which to build the church. The building measured 40' 30' which included living quarters for the pastor.

In October 1859, a well, 45 feet deep, was dug at a cost of $38.00. In the spring, a road was made and sand placed around the church. In September of 1860, a cellar measuring 8' x 10' was added at a cost of $80.00. In March, 1863, a horse barn was built at a cost of $16.50.

Several important "firsts" for Zion include: the first baptism, July 3, 1859, was Friedrich, Wilhelm, Heinrich, Albert, Karl, born April 7, 1859. His parents were Christian and Sophie Klemme; the first marriage was Heinrich Bahlman and Engel Marie Dorothea Harsten on April 1, 1860; the first death on January 26, 1860 was Heinrich Otto Schoenbeck who was born December 31, 1859; the first confirmands in 1860 were: Friedrich Leseman, Heinrich Leseman, Friedrich Geweke, Christoph Geweke, Karoline Leseman, Luise Glade, Luise Simon, Dorothea Seehausen, Karoline Brenker.

In January, 1865 a meeting was held relative to building a parsonage. The response was favorable and it was completed in 1866. This three room structure is still part of the present parsonage. A deeper well was dug in 1870 and a basement was added later. On May 7th, 1872 a cornerstone was laid for a new church. In 1882 the congregation either built or enlarged a school building, the record being unclear.

On April 15, 1882, the Articles of Association were written and signed. The object of the association was the organization and legal perpetuation of a Church. The congregation confessed itself a member of the Evangelical Church and was a member of the German Evangelical Synod of North America. The members that signed the Articles of Association were: Diedrich Haake, Carl Hitzeman, Fredrick Bremer, Christ Klemme, Friedrich Glade, Frederick Batterman, Henry Heisterberg, Christian Brands, Henry Glade, Christoph Piepho, William Russell, Christoph Boecker, Heinrid Huper, Heinrich Glade, Christoph Russell, Christoph Seegers, Joseph Reichert, Henrich Claus, Henry Klemme, Henry Becker, J.H. Huper, and Henry Claus.

Sometime between 1899-1907 the first choir of the church was organized. During this time, stained glass windows were installed at a cost of $170.00.

The Ladies Aid (Women's Guild) was organized on January 26, 1902. The first officers were Maria Seehausen, President; Wilhelmine Klemme, Secretary; and Mathilde Ohlendorf, Treasurer. Our present officers are: Carole Gilbert, president; Karen Bowyer, Vice President; Janise Voll, Secretary; and Bernetta Kretz, Treasurer.

In 1920, the church was remodeled and enlarged to almost double its original size. Furnaces were installed, new pews put in, new chancel furniture bought and a pipe organ was purchased by the Women's Guild.

Over the years many improvements have been made and extensive remodeling done to beautify the sanctuary. In 1954 a new four-rank Kilgen pipe-organ was installed at a cost of $6,000.

In 1961, ground breaking ceremonies were held for an Educational Building. In May, 1964, the building was dedicated. Many people have come through its doors, and the teaching and Christian fellowship that were the intent of the planners has continued.

In 1934 the Evangelical denomination merged with the Reformed Church and became Evangelical and Reformed. Zion Evangelical Church then became known as Zion Evangelical and Reformed Church. In 1957, the Evangelical and Reformed denomination merged with the Congregational Christian Church and Zion Evangelical and Reformed Church became Zion United Church of Christ.

For many years the church participated with other area churches of the same denomination in special services called Mission Festivals. There would be morning and afternoon ser-

The Old Zion United Church of Christ

vices with guest speakers. There would always be a noon meal served by the women of the church.

In 1946 the project of having a harvest dinner was started. The church women cooked and served the meal. It was a time for fellowship and a fund raiser for special programs of the Women's Guild. This dinner was served annually for over 30 years.

In 1954 a pancake and sausage supper was started by the Men's Brotherhood. It is still an annual project of the entire congregation, which takes place on Shrove Tuesday.

During Zion's lifetime there have been nine members that entered the ministry. These are the Reverends Henry Noehren, August Glade, Fred Klemme, Herman Klemme, W. Hattendorf, Herbert Bloesch, Paul Bloesch, Walter Bloesch and Herbert Reichert. Zion also sponsored the ordination of then – student pastor David Voll in 1988.

A cemetery is connected with the church and maintained by the congregation. Since the establishment of the church, there have been burials in this cemetery. There is a partial record of these early burials. Between twelve and fifteen veterans are buried here. Each year a Memorial Day service is presented by the American Legion, and Zion's pastor.

Pastors who have served the church are the Reverends Peter Lehman (1859-1868), Jacob Furrer (1868-1872), Robert Rugg (1872-1876), C. August Kitterer (1876-1881), Wilhelm Wahl (1881-1884), Gottfried Emil Dahler (1884-1885), H. Christian Friedrich Schmidt (1885-1899), Friedrich Grosse (1899-1907), T. Blum (1908-1918), E. Bloesch (1918-1942), H.J. Meier (1943-1952), George W. Knapp (1952-1965), Einar Greenholt (1965-1970), John C. David (1970-1975), Kenneth G. Hendrix (1976-1980), Clifford Voll (1980-1981) as interim pastor, Clifford Voll and David Voll (1981-1982) as co-pastors, and David Voll (1982-?).

by Mrs. Walter Karstensen

ORGANIZATIONS

LAKE COUNTY HISTORICAL SOCIETY
T47

In the year 1875 a group of Lake County pioneers and old settlers met at the Lake County Courthouse on July 24 and decided to form The Old Settlers Association of Lake County and to hold yearly meetings to renew old acquaintances and to recount pioneer experiences.

The first yearly meeting was held September 25, 1875 at the fairgrounds and after eating heartily of the sumptuous dinner, which had been spread in Floral Hall, the meeting was called to order by W.A. Clark and prayer was offered by Rev. T.H. Ball. After a few opening remarks by the chairman an old song, entitled *The Indian Captive*, was sung by Dr. Wood.

Reminiscences of old times were delivered by G. Hurlburt, R. Fancher, H. Wells, W.W.W. Holton, Amos Horner, J.H. Luther and others. Two long letters were read, one from Solon Robinson, who had gone to Tennessee for his health, and the other from Joseph Jackson of Wapello, Iowa.

It was decided that all who had come to the county prior to 1840, should be entitled to the distinction of being pioneers, while those who had come after 1840, and previous to 25 years ago, should be known as old settlers.

The objects of the Association are to renew old associations, to recover old events and to enjoy a few pleasant hours together. Meetings are to be held annually, subject to the call of the president.

The first permanent officers were: W.A. Clark, president; Oscar Dinwiddie, secretary; Rev. T.H. Ball, historical secretary; J.H. Luther, treasurer.

This fine association continues unbroken today and is known as The Lake County Historical Society.

Below are listed its past presidents: 1875-1881, Wellington A. Clark; 1881-1891, Bartlett Woods; 1891-1899, Wellington A. Clark; 1899-1908, Oscar Dinwiddie; 1908-1910, Sam B. Woods; 1910-1912, Mrs. J.S. Crawford; 1912-1914, Lewis Little; 1914-1916, M. Elmer Dinwiddie; 1916-1920, Oscar Dinwiddie; 1920-1922, Mrs. LeGrand T. Meyer; 1922-1923, Col. LeGrand T. Meyer; 1923-1924, A.W. Stommel; 1924-1925, A.J. Smith, 1925-1926, Albert Foster; 1926-1927, J.O. Bowers, 1927-1928, S.C. Dwyer, 1928-1929, J.B. Peterson,1929-1930, Jesse E. Wilson, 1930-1931, Claude Allman, 1931-1932, Arthur G. Taylor, 1932-1934, Matthew J. Brown, 1934-1936, Jesse Little, 1936-1940, Frank Borman, 1940-1941, Fred W. Schmal, 1941-1942, Herbert E. Graham.

Also 1942-1943, Frank Borman; 1943-1944, Dr. William Weis; 1944-1945, Dr. H.C. Groman; 1945-1946, Fred W. Schmall; 1946-1947, Otto J. Dahl; 1947-1948, Earl J. Bailey; 1948-1949, Thomas K. Fisher; 1949-1950, Paul W. Knight; 1950-1951, Roy W. Hack; 1951-1953, Dr. John W. Iddings; 1953-1954, Andrew J. Krieter; 1954-1955, Alice Mundell Demmon; 1955-1957, Fred Homfeld; 1957-1959, Joseph E. Brown; 1959-1961, Chester A. Clark; 1961-1963, Miss Rena Dahl, 1963-1966, Mrs. Thomas Haney; 1966-1967, Chester Crisler; 1967-1969, Walter Gard; 1969-1972, Miss Cerilla Saylor; 1972-1974, Miss Ijunia Ball; 1974-1975, Steven J. Yaros Jr.; 1975-1977, Bruce Woods; 1977 to the present.

by Steven Yaros

HOBART HISTORICAL SOCIETY AND MUSEUM
T48

The Hobart Historical Society Museum is located in the former Hobart Public Library building which was constructed in 1914-15 through the efforts of the Hobart Women's Reading Club and the aid of a Carnegie grant. Dedicated February 11, 1915, it served generations of Hobart citizens until 1968 when the Hobart Public Library moved to a new building.

The building is in English Renaissance style with nine colors of brick and a slate roof. The bay windows are of leaded glass and feature stained glass medallions. The main floor interior retains the original library plan and many of the original fittings. The building has been designated an Indiana Historic Landmark and has applied for National Historic Landmark status.

Exhibits

Main floor exhibits focus on the history of the Hobart area and home life in the late 19th and early 20th centuries. Objects and exhibits date from fossils and ice age objects through Indian artifacts, and furnishings brought to Hobart by covered wagon in the 1830s.

A large area is devoted to a home exhibit of furniture, clothing, linens and utensils of the period 1890-1920. A recent major acquisition is a 1967 aerial photo of Hobart.

Ballantyne Gallery

Built as a memorial to Donald Ballantyne, whose interest in the early craftsmen of the area brought to the museum its fine collection of wheelwright and woodworking tools, the Gallery includes full replicas of a blacksmith shop, a wheelmaking and woodworking shop and an operating letterpress shop. A street scene setting features shop window displays. Early agricultural implements are found "in the alley".

Mariam J. Pleak Library And Archive

The library and archive was established in memory of Miriam J. Pleak, founder and first president of the Society, who collected many of the books and materials. The library focuses on U.S., state and local history and related subjects. It includes books, magazines, a resource file and local materials arranged under more than 300 subjects, a genealogy file of Hobart families; Hobart newspapers from 1890 to date; federal census for Lake County; pictures; maps, and archives of Hobart organizations. A special favorite of many members if the "Old Favorites" collection of early 20th century popular fiction.

The Library is open to all users. Members have borrowing privileges.

Museum Services

Each year almost 4,000 visitors call at the Museum, individually, in families, or as members of the many groups who tour the Museum. Heavily used by Hobart and area schools, many young people visit the Museum with their schools and Scout troops. The Museum is a "must" for foreign exchange students.

Research is a fast growing service as increasing numbers of genealogical and local history researchers visit or write the Museum to use the Society's resources.

Other services include: Tours, during Museum hours or other times by appointment. Speakers service on various history topics. Publishing program on Hobart history. Small shop for local commemorative items. Traveling exhibits available for display at other locations. Programs on subjects of interest — recent ones have included speakers on old tools, woven coverlets, and electric railways.

HAMMOND HISTORICAL SOCIETY
T49

The Hammond Historical Society held its first organizational meeting on June 16, 1959, at the Harrison Park Branch of the Hammond Public Library with John F. Wilhelm, Hammond banker, presiding. Mr. Wilhelm, along with Edward B. Hayward, Director of the Library, and Warren A. Reeder, Hammond realtor and well-known local historian, had long voiced a need for a local historical society, and this meeting was the beginning of the realization of their hope. Twenty-three interested citizens attended, including Norris B. Coambs, President of the Duneland Historical Society in Chesterton and Walter Pickart, president of the Gary Historical Society and also serving as a representative of the Indiana State Historical Society, both offering their help in the formation of the new society.

The second meeting followed on September 22, 1959, to hear the reading of a constitution written by Mr. Wilhelm and Mr. Reeder. The twenty-five people present were also urged to get as many signatures as possible on sheets of incorporation by an October 15th deadline. Mr. Wilhelm was elected temporary president by acclamation.

At the third meeting on March 1, 1960, Mr. Wilhelm appointed the first officers to serve until the first annual meeting and election of officers would take place in May, a procedure still followed today. They were: 1st Vice-President – Warren Reeder; 2nd Vice-President – Mrs. Henry Eggers; 3rd Vice-President – Edward Hayward; 4th Vice-President – John Wamsher; 5th Vice-President – Mrs. Eleanor Brusel; Secretary – Miss Marjorie Sohl; Treasurer – Mrs. William Cook. Mr. Wilhelm also appointed an honorary Board of Directors and a Nominating Committee to prepare a slate of officers. Attendance was again twenty-five, and the first speaker to address the new society was Dr. Powell A. Moore, Professor of History at Indiana University Northwest. He spoke about his newly-published book, *The Calumet Region: Indiana's Last Frontier*.

On March 22, 1960, the first Board of Directors' meeting was held to confirm the final details of organization, such as dues, meeting places, number of meetings per year and types of programs. Each director was also assigned the task of writing an autobiography of 300-500 words to begin a membership genealogical file. Plans were also made for the collection of historical materials to be built up by the new society.

According to the Articles of Incorporation, the purposes of the Hammond Historical Society, Inc. are: 1 – To collect and preserve materials of history, art, education, and industry. 2 – To promote education of both young and old toward historical inquiry. 3 – To establish and maintain a historical collection. 4 – To publish and spread historical information with reference to Hammond and Lake County, Indiana. 5 – To promote a wider acquaintance and closer relationship among its members. 6 – To provide a means through which those engaged in building prestige and business for the city may assist each other through interchange of ideas. Membership is open to individuals, civic organizations, and business firms, and charter members are those signing the Articles of Incorporation.

Today the Hammond Historical Society has its home in the Hammond Public Library's Calumet Room, which houses the collection begun 28 years ago. The room is open to the public on Mondays and Wednesdays from noon till 4:00 p.m. with one part-time librarian. Meetings are held on the third Sunday of each month from September to April except in December, with the Annual Meeting and Election of Officers still a May dinner meeting in a local church. Twenty-six presidents have served the Society, Averill C. Colby II being the current officer. Except for one term as president, Marjorie Sohl remains as secretary and 1988 membership stands at 275.

G.F.W.C. ST. JOHN FEDERATED WOMAN'S CLUB
T50

The St. John General Federation Woman's Club received its charter in February of 1960. It was the year St. John Junior G.F.W.C. was also chartered. Because of age restrictions, a number of St. John women were not eligible to be members of that club, so with enthusiasm and leadership Virginia DuChene became the found of the St. John G.F.W.C.

There were seventeen charter members of whom five are still active members: the current president, Violet Bryant, Sylvia (Hal) Foltz, Edna (Fred) Malsch, Jean Mathews and Pearl Paulauski. There are presently 23 active members.

For years the club met regularly in the St. John Town Hall on the fourth Monday of the Months September through May. Since the remodeling of the Town Hall, our club meetings are held in the St. John Public Library.

The annual budget for community projects including a scholarship is in the area of $900.00 to $1,000.00. The membership works at various projects to raise funds such as: bake sales, farmers market, chili suppers, auctions, arts and crafts fairs and others.

A continuing project, after purchase of a flag pole for the St. John Public Library, is providing our nations' flags as needed.

Social activities include teas, dinners, potlucks, picnics, theater parties, and just getting together with a friendly group of women.

In February of 1985, the Club's 25th Anniversary was celebrated with most of its former presidents and founder, Virginia DuChene, as guests at a local restaurant. Past presidents include Caryl Juergens, Elinor Smith, Josephine Boyer, Pearl Paulauski, Mary Ellen Arndt, Margaret Holmes, Nell Thiery, Sylvia Foltz, Jean Mathews, Leila Boller, Lena Rayner, Fanella Clark, Pauline Strickland and Arlene Brumbaugh. Myrtle Ward presided as these gals recalled activities and accomplishments of former years.

Women in the area interested in contributing to the betterment of our community and at the same time enlarging their circle of friends should consider membership in the St. John G.F.W.C.

The Motto of our Club is: "Together with God we serve".

by Helen Mercier and Violet A. Bryant

LOWELL, INDIANA FEDERATED WOMANS CLUB
T51

The Lowell Womans Club was officially organized in 1916 by fifteen women who drew up the Constitution and bylaws and at their first meeting elected eleven other interested women to membership. Officers elected to serve during the first year were: President – Mrs. S.A. Brownell, Vice President – Mrs. Howard Slocomb, Secretary – Mrs. Sylvia Dwyer, Treasurer – Mrs. Hattie McNay. The Lowell Club was affiliated with Federation in 1916. In 1917, they went in with the Lake County Organization and in 1925 joined the General Federation, and have been very happy ever since.

Some of the programs in the early years were: Laws of Indians, American poets, Current Events, Review of Late Books, Current Day Industries, Great Men of the United States, American Literature, and Out Island Possessions just to name a few. Through the years, our way of living, our ideas, and our programs have changed considerably.

The Club initiated Lowell's first clean up day; sponsored the supplying of milk in the schools for underprivileged children; and, assisted in many fund contributions and war drives during the World War I period.

When the need for practical nurses became known in the 1950's, the Club decided to sponsor an interested local woman for practical nurses training. The first to accept this privilege was Lily Juuti; and she finished her studies in January, 1959. In September, 1958, Margret Caster started the study and finished in Sept., 1959. Each student took a twelve month course, the first four months were spent in classroom instruction and Purdue University Calumet Center, five days a week. The next eight months were spent in class work and nurses training at four hospitals; two months each at St. Catherines in East Chicago, St. Margrets in Hammond, St. Marys and Methodist Hospitals in Gary. If they successfully completed the twelve month course, they were eligible to practice as licensed practical nurses.

Back in 1957 & 58, as part of their community service projects, they started making cancer pads that were needed by South County cancer patients. They asked for help from the folks in town for clean, well pressed, worn out sheets and pillow cases either white or pastels. That was one of the projects the year Mrs. Glen Clark was president.

Looking back in our history, when Mrs. Lena Van Nada was president, in 1941 it was first mentioned that for quite some years before, the Woman's Club had been presenting two prizes; first – $5.00 and second – $2.50, to the Freshman and Sophomore classes in recognition of Better Oral English. The winners were selected by the faculty. Through the years, it has changed. We still give a prize, but now it is a $50.00 government bond to the most outstanding senior in English Literature for creative writing. The student is chosen by the English Lit. Department.

1932 & 33 was the first year the General Federation President, the Indiana Federation of Officers, Tenth District Officers, and the Lake County officers were added to our year books.

In 1937 & 38 selling Blind Goods was brought in as a club project.

In years back, a lot of work and help was given to the Red Cross, but since World War II our work and help has been given to the Salvation Army because of the many reports brought back by our men who served overseas.

In the 1970's the Town Hall was going to make the land, the Senior Citizens Park is located on, into a parking lot. One of our charter members seemed to recall that when the land was donated to the town that if it was used for anything other than park-like facilities the land was to revert back to the original owners. The Womans Club did the research and found that to be true. Thus, our beautiful Senior Citizen's Park. They also won $400.00 first prize for it's conception, beauty, and conservation.

We have worked on the Heart Drive — on M.S. — Cancer and Blood Drives. The Club has worked as a whole on many projects and given many volunteer hours. We have worked from the beginning with the Friends of the Library on the Arts & Crafts Fair. We have also worked with the Womans Association of the Northwest Indiana Sympathy for the last five years. For many years, we had hot coffee and donuts for the early folks at the Labor Day Parade.

The years have been a joy and have gone by fast; as I read back over our history, I wonder if those ladies who started all of this would be pleased. We've gone a long way ladies.

by Bette Lunn

CROWN POINT CENTER CLIMBER 4-H CLUB
T52

Secretary Books, Center Climbers' September 1955 – September 1968 "Junior Leader 4-H Club Reports Filed" papers through 1978.

At one time, clubs often had the name of their school district. In 1954, Mary Ann Wirtz and Clara Zieseniss enrolled in the Washington Workers 4-H Club in the Washington School District. 1955 leaders, Mrs. Nickolas

37

Wirtz & Mrs. Al Zieseniss believed smaller clubs provided more officers and personal growth opportunities. Agent Love, members, parents, and leaders met in the Zieseniss home on September 6, 1957 to form a club that would expand itself beyond the district. It was named 'Center Climbers'. Charter members and officers were. President, Barbara Bieker; Vice President, Frances Bieker; Secretary & Treasurer, Claudia Schmidt; Publicity, Clara Zieseniss; Safety, Linda Houk; Health, Linda Zieseniss; Song Leader, Eileen Zieseniss; Recreation, Vivan Bieker. The Washington Workers gave the Center Climbers $2.50 to start their treasury. Their Leaders were Mrs. Albert Zieseniss and Mrs. Glenn Zieseniss.

The Washington Home Demonstration Club sponsored both clubs by helping with county activities as judging events & achievement programs. All members performed in some matter during the Achievement Program. They enjoyed being hostesses, giving style shows, demonstrating, exhibiting homemade articles, or leading songs. That year they completed 29 articles, 26 garments, baked 92 products, prepared and served 132 meals and 222 other dishes. Four gave "How to Use & Care For an Electric Sewing Machine" demonstrations during the Lake County Fair. Seven received A's or B's in Dress Review and one a Baking County Champion ribbon. Mrs. Lucille Smith was Home Demonstration Agent.

In 1958 Center Climber Junior Leaders and Mrs. Frances Zieseniss served as teacher, guides, and cabin counselors during Dunes State Park summer camp. Entry to the park was 20 cents per person plus 20 cents per car. Activities each day were swimming, crafts, hikes, games, and vesper services.

In 1959, the camp was moved to Camp Limberlost on Oliver Lake, La Grange, Indiana. $35 for seven glorious days of swimming, crafts, skits, games, boating, fishing, photography, recreation and song.

4-H years began in September with displays in merchants' windows inviting students to become members. In 1960, Home Demonstration Agent Mary Rosenthal held Officers Training with group singing. The Center Climbers received an Award for 100 percent attendance yearly. Photography and Electric projects were born. Louise Dillbaugh's new waffle iron was used by the girls for waffle making, the care of electric cords, and how to clean an electric appliance. Feather ticks gave way to firm mattresses. The girls were proud to make beds with hospital square corners with tightness that would bounce a quarter. That was the years folks ask "In what food group are Pastas? Linda Houk held a Home & Farm Hazard Hunt. It became a yearly Center Climber event. This year the members welcomed Susan Turner and Judith Ross.

1961 Center Climbers participated in the 1st Annual 4-H Show held in years at the Lake County Fair. On stage were the 4-H King and Queen and their Court. There were three Share The Fun acts and a parade of Project Champions. 2 of our girls won County Achievement medals of Honor. Silver Key Awards and camp pins were won by Center Climbers.

The 1962 enrollment included: Peggy Dillabaugh, Kathy Jones, Lu Ann Hill, Mary Holtz, Marcia Odle, Kathy Luers, Karen Luers, Jan Luers, & Lottie Zieseniss. Mrs. A.D. Luers was Conservation leader. Lottie Zieseniss, historian. The club now reflected township growth. 5 members were urban, 4 from rural non farm homes, and the rest from farm homes. The girls spent hours with memory books, new projects, and community services and became recipients of Bronze, Silver, and Gold Key awards.

In 1963, George Zieseniss was the 1st lad to give a County Food Demonstration. The phase 'regardless of sex, race, creed, or color' was added to our constitution. 'Table grace & Devotion Leader' elited. It was the 1st year to have dues, ($1.50). Janet Adams, Gloria Randolph, Pauline Rzepski, William and George Zieseniss were new members.

Many members now carried seven projects, in 1964, so each Junior Leader became a project leader, Mrs. J. Rzespki assisted, Mrs. A. Zieseniss, Leader. John Rzeseki, Theresa Schafer, Eddie Stewart, and Harry Zieseniss were the 1st to receive an informal invitation.

1965 membership fell with the ruling 'enrollment age 9-18! Mrs. John Rzespki was a leader and Mrs. Albert Zieseniss became the project leader.

Eight new projects were born in 1966. All members enrolled in machinery, animals, or crops transferred to the Washington Workers 4-H Club. Gloria Randolph & Theresa Schafer transferred to Washington Workers 4-H club that led projects of their choice. Our club welcomed Kathi Rooker, Karen Strong, Romoma Ann Vogrig, & Bonnie Willy. Under Mrs. John Rzespki leadership, girls excelled in etiquette. They prepared and gracefully served Buffet meals. They received 'A-Honor' in county table setting. Mrs. Zieseniss gave an interesting account of Washington D.C. trip. The girls toured the Museum of Science & Industry. They accompanied Clubs United to Riverview Park. Spray cans appeared in 1967. Demonstrations were: "Spray can safety." How to spray can dust." Spray can a hair style." How to fill out & use a Emergency Phone Card."

1968 Officers elected were: President, Terri Einsphar; Vice President, Gale Gregory; Sec., Vickie Clark; Treas. Robecca Sons; Reporter & Historian Lottie Zieseniss; Songs, Iza Zieseniss; Health, Theresa Sark; Safety, Sue Lee; Recreation, Barbara Willy & Judy Gregory. Mrs. L. Sons served as assistant Leader. Jan. 1969 the club name was changed to "Center Charmers." March 1969, Mrs. Leslie Gregory became it's leader. Mrs. Albert Zieseniss retired as project leader in 1979.

In 1974 the club name was changed to "Center Charmers and Farmers".

by Frances Zieseniss

CROWN POINT GARDEN CLUB
T53

The Crown Point Garden Club was organized Aug. 13, 1929 and federated in 1933. First year book is dated Jan. 30, 1930 listing the following charter members: Mrs. John Iddings, Mrs. Delia Burge, Mrs. G.D. Clark, Mrs. William De Reamer, Mrs. Elmer Dinwiddie, Mrs. Otto Fifield, Mrs. J.M. Geiser, Miss Nellie Griesel, Mrs. John Gunder, Mrs. Pete Hard, Miss Cora Horst, Mrs. John Horst, Mrs. John Lehman, Mrs. Albert Mack, Miss Josephine Meeker, Mrs. J.W. Ott, Mrs. Virgil Place, Mrs. Julius Rockwell, Mrs. Clayton Root, Mrs. Martin Rudolph, Mrs. L.A. Salisbury, Mrs. E.L. Shortridge, Mrs. Martin Smith, Mrs. Wm. Thompson, Mrs. Wm. Upham, Mrs. Wm. Whitaker and Mrs. John Donnaha. Mrs. Iddings who was the first president, lovingly and untiringly brought together those friends who loved flowers and gardening and the study of their culture. Her own daughter, Mrs. Paul Brown was an active member and loyal supporter for many years.

Miss Josephine Meeker, a local nursery owner and member, recorded the club pledge "To take a personal interest in gardening and do something for the improvement of home and public grounds" and it is still used for monthly meetings.

In 1954 several charter members and guests gathered at the Presbyterian Church to celebrate the 25th anniversary. Among those present were Mrs. Florence (Glover) Thomas, president who poured for tea, also Mrs. Gunder, Mrs. Whitaker, Mrs. Geiser, Miss Meeker, Miss Griesel, Mrs. Delia Burge, Mrs. Fifield, Mrs. Horse and Mrs. De Reamer.

Mrs. Fred Mabrey made the arrangement placing chrysanthemums, carnations, rose buds, and snapdragons in compotes simulating a 4-tiered cake in white flowers.

The first flower show was held at the community building Aug. 1930, admission 25 cents. The club sponsored numerous bus trips to the Chicago Flower Show at Navy Pier.

May Day meant "May Baskets" time when members decorated baskets of fresh flowers and delivered them to shut-ins. Miss Meeker organized the project in 1948 and in later years they have also added "Meals on Wheels" trays.

One of the many town and country shows was held in 1957 including some of the oldest gardens. The general chairman was Mrs. C. Clarence Ensweiler and some of the homes and gardens were of Mrs. Roy Holley, Mrs. Geo, Knopf, also the Hanslik, Rippy, Wm. and Otto Fifield, J.B. and Burt Hawley, Loyd Cutler and Paul Brown homes.

In order to beautify the city, in 1962 the first skeleton planting of fourteen trees in the Court House lawn were to replace the Dutch elm diseased trees removed. The plan used was drawn by Purdue specialist H.W. Gilbert and was spearheaded by the Crown Point Garden Club, Mrs. Paul Brown, President and the Kiwanis Club, Mr. Roger Schnurlein, President of that club. More plantings were added at a later date. Some individuals and some clubs in town helped to pay for them. The Garden club from then on took the responsibility for their maintenance.

Petunia beds were planted for many years around the Court House and cared for by members, until the shade interfered and then within a few years geranium beds were put in and are as of this date still being enjoyed by passers by.

The 50th anniversary of the club was celebrated 1979 at Carnegie Library with floral art displays represented in wreaths, plaques, swags and cone trees. A tea table was centered with a silver five tier candelabra and white roses, fern and babysbreath. General chairman was Mrs. Paul Trulley, Mrs. Charles Bates, Pres., Mrs. C. Clarence Ensweiler, Mrs. Paul Brown, Mrs. Dorothy Sorenson, Mrs. John Simonetto, Mrs. Lillian Wood, Mrs. Armantrout, Mrs. Naomi Dikert, Mrs. Kay Latz and Mrs. Robert Stewart, Mrs. Verla Morrison, Mrs. Vivian Kelby, Mrs. Irene Homfeld, Mrs. Virginia Johnson and Mrs. Emily Akey.

Mrs. Wilbur Heidbreder and Mrs. Charles Bishop had charge of the wreath area and dried arrangements. Also helping were Mrs. Pony Kyle, Mrs. Barbara Metz and Mrs. Anne Berge. Others helping in various ways were Mrs.

Bothwell, and Mrs. Schlemmer, Miss Thelma Johnston, Miss Marie Saylor, Miss Edith Wallace and Mrs. Frances Graper. making fresh flower arrangements were Mrs. Brannock and Mrs. Ellicott, Mrs. Zury, Mrs. Harry Classen, Jr. and Mary May.

Officers of the year were Mrs. Bates, Pres., Mrs. Clade Morrison, Vice-Pres. Mrs. Harold Sorenson, Se'cy. and Mrs. Clayton Watkins, Treas. Many meetings are held in the homes and the club promotes the culture of vegetables, herbs, flowers and decorative grasses and has programs on wild life, birds and preservation activities.

In 1976 a bicentennial tour of homes and gardens benefited the restoration of the Old Lake Court House on the square in Crown Point with a monetary gift.

The club furnished many potted pink petunias for the steps of the Court House when the wedding was held there during the 150th celebration of Crown Point. They cooperated with other phases of the 150th as well as sponsoring a girl in the queen contest.

Six dozen geraniums are planted in front of the shop signs each May and watered, fertilized, weeded and cultivated throughout the summer months. This is one of the club's civic projects and they contributed $200.00 toward a tree planting by the city when needed in 1987. 36 inch wreaths are purchased every holiday season and hung on the east and west entrances.

The group belongs to the N.W. District, State of Indiana and National Council of State Garden clubs. District chairmen have been Mrs. Geo. Sherman, Mrs. Robert Stewart, Mrs. Robert Brannock and Mrs. Byron Williams. Mrs. Charles Bishop and Mrs. Paul Brown both served on the state board several. Mrs. Steven Zury is a National Life Member and a Master Judge for flower shows. She has done a great deal of judging and demonstrations in flower arranging.

Members who have been active in the club for 20 years or more are: Nina Heidbreder, Emily Akey, Jean Brown, Mary May, Margaret Schlemmer, Lois Trulley, Alice Watkins, Mary Jane Ensweiler, Gladys Gillogly, Jean Williams, Grace Zury, Lelia Bothwell, Marie Saylor.

by Nina Adank Heidbreder

LAKESHORE BUSINESS & PROFESSIONAL WOMEN'S CLUB
T54

Of Gary, Indiana

On March 11, 1921, a group of Gary business women met to form a club. On November 3, 1920, Mrs. William F. Hodges, then president of the Gary Y.W.C.A., appointed Miss Ina Martin as chairman to organize a Business and Professional Women's Committee of the Y.W.C.A. As a result of this appointment, on March 11, 1921, twenty-five young women met for the purpose of forming this club, objectives were to enable business women to know one another, learn how to increase efficiency in their work, take an interest in community affairs and events that pertain to their advancement.

March 24, 1921, the Gary Business and Professional Women's Club was formally organized with Miss Katherine Lynch, Board of Children's Guardian, elected as its first president. All areas of business, professions and civic service were represented among its twenty-five members. The meeting took place in the Club Rooms of the Gary Public Library. In one month, by April 21, 1921, its membership had grown to forty-six members. On October 21, 1925, the club became affiliated with the Indiana Federation of Business and Professional Women's Clubs. On June 17, 1926, it became affiliated with the National Federation. Miss Emma E. Claus, then president of the Gary Club, attended the founding of the International Federation at Geneva, Switzerland, in 1930.

National Objectives of the Business and Professional Women's Clubs are as follows: (1). To elevate the standards for women in business and professions. (2). To promote the interest of business and professional women. (3). To bring about a spirit of cooperation among the business and professional women of the United States. (4). To extend opportunities to business and professional women through education along the lines of industrial, scientific and vocational activities. On July 20, 1976, the name of the Gary B.P.W. Club became the Lakeshore Business and Professional Women's Club of Gary, Indiana. The decision for the name change was based on the fact that so many of its members now lived and worked outside the city of Gary.

During 1950 and 1960, the club joined with the Gary's Woman's Club and Association of University Women for outstanding speakers. Examples were Gaylord Hauser, Lowell Thomas, Jr. and Marlin Perkins. In July, 1930, the club was host to the Northern Central Regional Conference. Over five hundred delegates from Indiana, Illinois, Michigan, Wisconsin, Minnesota and Iowa attended. Highlight of the conference was an International Pageant on the Lake Front Park Lagoon, in which seventeen different nationalities were represented. From 1942-46, the war years, the program as set up by National Federation was followed. In the Victory Loan Drive, $90,726.75 in bonds were sold by our members. The club sponsored many programs such as Career Advancement Day for high school students from 1945-1973, Individual Development Programs for members, enabling them to learn more about B.P.W. and become more proficient at public speaking, work towards the passage of ERA in Indiana, and conducting seminars dealing with subjects of interest to working women. Each year we select a "Young Career Woman" for contests held on the District and State levels, honor a "Woman of the Year" and recently, "Outstanding Working Woman".

Two of our members have served as state presidents: Mary Louise Jessee and Helen Blaker. Vera Helmerick has also served on the state level as recording secretary and corresponding secretary. Isabelle Jones served as State Parliamentarian in 1945-46.

Meetings are held the third Tuesday of each month and are dinner meetings.

by Helen F. Marks

DAUGHTERS OF UNION VETERANS OF THE CIVIL WAR
T55

Elizabeth Hodson Tent #41, Hammond, Indiana

Five school girls of Massillon, Ohio as they watched members of the Grand Army of the Republic, pay tribute to the Nation's war dead on Memorial Day, in 1885, conceived the idea to band together in an organization to serve and perform patriotic duties. After three meetings with fourteen girls present, they became the original organizers of the Daughters of Union Veterans and were mustered in by James N. Mervin, of the Sons of Veterans.

Their object was to assist and perpetuate the memories of their fathers, and spread widely the teachings of Patriotism. On July 25th, it was voted to establish other branches in other cities and in September, the first badge was proposed which became official until 1927.

A committee to draw up a constitution, ritual and bylaws, was assisted by members from Hart Post #144, G.A.R. Major Wm. McKinley, later U.S. President, rendered advice and obtained incorporation under laws of Ohio, and under the name of "National Alliance of Daughters of Veterans. That name was changed at the National Convention held in Grand Rapids, Mich., in September, 1925, to the present name of Daughters of Union veterans of the Civil War, 1861-1865.

The first National Convention was held in Quincy, Ill., in June, 1890. The first Tent in Indiana was organized on March 9, 1915, at Peru. The Indiana Dept. was organized September 20, 1915 at Fort Wayne, with the first Dept., convention held in 1916. The Indianapolis Tent was formed in September 18, 1920, and first National Convention held in Indiana was held in the city shortly thereafter.

This is how our great Organization was begun. In two more years from now it will be one hundred years since the beginning of a dream of Those Five School Girls from Massillon, Ohio, to keep alive the memory of the men who fought and served in the Grand Army of the Republic.

The Birth Of Our Tent

It all began in April 1933, when the "Mother of our Tent", Sister Alice Hedges, of Gary Tent #6, with the assistance of Sister Matilda Roberts, also of Clara Barton tent #6, Gary, and who was the National Jr. Vice President at that time, began to hold meetings, made many trips to Hammond, and through advertising in the *Hammond Times*, kept notifying the interested to attend the meetings.

At the first called meeting on September 12th, everything was about ready and it was decided to proceed with the institution at that time. A name was needed, and Sister Ruth Merrill, after checking on the history of many Civil War nurses from Indiana, selected the name "Elizabeth Hodson" and the Dept. President Sister Bernice Hecht, from Elkhart, gave the number 41. On October 2nd, plans were completed for a public installation, and on October 12th, all gathered at the Hammond Women's Club to proceed with elections, appointments and finally the installation of the First Officers of the Tent.

Sister Hecht was the installing officer, assisted by Sister Matilda Roberts, and other members of Gary Tent #6. There were over a hundred persons to view the activities, and among the honored guests was Comrade John R. Taylor grandfather of new member Sister Mildred Harder. Sister Bliss Brown of Gary Tent presented Sister Alice Hedges with a gold membership pin. Many other gifts were given to members and guests.

A string orchestra led by Sister Ethel Holway, the tent's first musician, furnished the music for the entertainment. A Mrs. Godwin gave several readings, which helped complete a beautiful installation ceremony.

by Lillian Schafer

DEEP RIVER PARK
T56

The Deep River Park was dedicated as part of the bicentennial on October 10, 1976 with a large crowd of 300 to 400 in attendance.

Several Girl Scout troops participated in the presentation and retirement of colors.

The Invocation was presented by Reverend Arthur Wilkerson of Deep River Church. Paul Wharton Lake County Parks and Recreation Board President gave the welcome and A.D. Luers a past Lake County Park Board President was the dedication speaker.

The ceremony which followed was a brief history of John Wood and the mill. There was an introduction of the descendants from this area and Michigan and recognition of several prominent people responsible for the culmination of this project.

On Saturday, May 28, 1977 there was A Deep River County Park Dedication Celebration. The Ross Township Historical Society and arts and crafts exhibitors set up their wares on the grounds and in the mill. At noon a parade came from the park manager's home on county line past the mill to Old Mill Manor. It was probably one of the only parades to come to this area. It consisted of; Color Guard – 4th Battery Light Artillery, 1st Indiana Brigade, Crown Point; Fort Tassinong Muzzle Loaders, of Hebron; the La Salle Expedition; Canoe Livery/Barber Shop Quartet; Elbert Webb's Horse Drawn Wagon/Ross Township Historical Society; Bill Remus's Horse Drawn Wagon, Calumet Council Boy Scouts Order of the Arrow; Old Mill Riders Pony Club and the Lake County Sheriff's Posse.

Following the parade the dedication ceremonies featured speakers; James R. Whitehouse superintendent, Indiana Dunes National Lakeshore: Indiana State Senator Ernie Niemeyer of Lowell, and Charles Swisher of Crown Point, who read his poem *On The Bank of Old Deep River*.

One of the first antiques, a wicker rocker, was donated to the Mill from Jack and Mildred Hutchison, and a grain cradle from Robert Baker.

Ross Township Historical Society loaned several other antiques over the years.

The Indiana Arts Commission worked to bring Arts to the Park. A gallery on the third floor of The Mill was established and periodically displays artwork.

Rug Weaving and Grain Grinding, (corn, wheat, rice, and rye) are several of the products from the past that are demonstrated and available for purchase today.

In April 1979, Volunteers in the Park, was formed. The intent of VIPS is to train volunteers who will support the John Wood's Old Mill, commitment to interpreting the History of the facility and the Deep River County Park.

Quilting Bees were held with volunteers donating quilt blocks and quilting under the shade of the trees on warm summer days. The result of this fellowship is a collection of many Friendship Quilts displayed in the Mill.

The restored boiler house, on the North West corner of the Mill, was used as a blacksmith shop/potter's shed and opened on May '79. The Potter made stoneware from clay using a foot powered wheel as done in the 18th and 19th centuries. Also, a strolling violinist roamed the park site.

Deep River offered canoeing on weekends, during spring, and cross country skiing in the winter.

In June 1980, the sounds of pop and jazz could be heard by such performers as Corkey Seigel, the Afro-Jazz Quintet, Research, and the Northwest Indiana Symphony. In September Woods' Mill Faire was an opportunity for artists to display their fine arts, and antique auto owners to exhibit their old machines and performers from theatre companies to perform for everyone's enjoyment. Puppet shows, hayrides, and a mini-bluegrass festival were just a few additional attractions.

In 1981, more musical concerts were presented for the enjoyment of picnicers on Sunday afternoons, along with the Memories of Yesteryear, which consists of: the Liars Club, Square Dancers, old time photographs, cooking in the Old Mill kitchen, and featuring many more craftsmen, artists, and historians.

Also the blacksmith shop was developed and demonstrations were held frequently. Maple Syrup Days started by tapping the local maple trees, boiling the tap down from forty gallons to one gallon of maple syrup. The temporary sugar shack, at the north end, aided in this attempt to make quality maple syrup. The new shack will be at the south end of the park.

The Nature Center was developed and opened in the Church building, and featured a 10,000 year old mastodon skull, which was found in a farmer's field in South County near Crown Point. There was a living bee hive, snakes, and fish.

Many Girl Scouts and Boy scouts took advantage of the park's facilities, including hikes and lectures, to earn badges in wildlife, ecology, forestry, and geology. They gave service projects to the park in return.

The kid's Corner was initiated to introduce how to make kites, draw, and to teach about the bald eagle, birds, night sounds, solar cooking, and many more "nature crafts for nuts."

Midsummer's Knight Faire was introduced June 27, 1982 with Maypole dancing, court dancing, jousting, quintaine and rings, music, food and festivities enjoyed by King Traboh, Queen Drasan and Princess Trillium. Madrigals were on hand to add to the enjoyment of all the Lords and Barons.

Through out the years many workshops were presented such as; woodworking, chair caning, costume making with fashion show of the 1830's, blacksmithing, weaving, tatting, dutch oven cooking, spinning, soap making, basket making, marquetry, china painting and many more skills were demonstrated.

Many interesting events over the years directly and indirectly effected the mill, like the tornado which came thru the area, raised the roof and set it back down on the mill in March 1976. In July of 1983 we had 6 inches of rain which flooded Deep River and washed out the Grand Trunk road bed causing a 21 car freight train derailment, down the 70 foot embankment at the north end of the park.

Each year new programs are presented such as Apple Days, Pumpkin Days, Special Event Saturdays, Old Fashion 4th of July with watermelon eating contests.

Recently the gift shop moved into the visitors center in the church completely. Most of the nature items were moved to Gibson Woods.

A new bridge was put in Spring 1988, so the newly acquired property east of the mill on county line could be reached thru the park. The new saw mill will soon be built there. The New Gazebo is completed and the many weddings performed in the park can take advantage of it.

by Theresa Weber

MISCELLANEOUS

THE UNDERGROUND RAILROAD
T57

A small view of what was seen through the cracks of the wagon along the way on the Old Post Road.

Lake County, Indiana had an important role in the Underground Railroad prior to and during the Civil War. Slaves were brought from Kentucky and Ohio through Crown Point on their way to freedom. Folks in the area talked of a "way station" right on the "line" (the Indiana/Illinois State Line).

The slaves were transported both to and from Crown Point, west on a route through, or near Kritzburg over the State Line, via Exchange Road, to Klemme Road (in Crete, Illinois). They proceeded north along a heavily wooded area on the winding old Post Road and crossed what is now known as I-394 and went west onto Richton Road. They went past a creamery (what was once a cheese factory) adjacent to the Meier farm, to the next farm on the south side of the road. Once there, they were hastily hid in the attic of the home on the farm of Sam Cushing. His brother was a deacon in the Crete area and was know to have lived in Dyer on Route 30 and Sauk Trail at one time.

When Sam felt it was safe, he took the slaves in a false-bottom wagon loaded with, depending on the season, either cornstalks, straw or hay under the pretense of hauling it to the markets in either Blue Island or Chicago, Illinois. When they arrived, deacons Temple and Johnson would receive them. Volunteer lookouts would take them to a place along the Lake Michigan shore onto a boat or steamer (usually free passage) which would take them to safety in Canada. In some writing, it reads that the slaves would dress up like women and march down the street in broad daylight and get on board ship, and sail off to freedom.

In one account, fifty slaves had been freed, and no passengers had been "lost". Neighbors, who at one time refused to assist, responded quickly to their aid, once shown the condition that the slaves were in. There were many secret trails, and no one would write about them for fear of being caught.

Evidently deacon Cushing was caught once and taken to the Joliet Court House. However, he had such a large following of supporters that the court let him go without conviction.

by Mrs. Ralph Oldendorf

MARCH OF THE INDIANS
T58

The most famous Indian trail in the Calumet is the present route of Dunes Highway. One of the pioneer women of the area, Sister Mary Joseph, was a guest at the Bailey Homestead when thousands of Indians on the march to one of their historic encampments passed by in silent review. Of this stirring scene she wrote:

"There was the Indian trail, a deep, wide rut, made by centuries of pacing feet, which the traveling Indians never forsook for the white man's roads, but always used in their comings and goings.

"The warriors of a tribe in full force, in stately single file procession, always made a showing pageant, but the most brilliant array of savage glory ever witnessed here or perhaps anywhere, was on an occasion when all Wisconsin and Minnesota Indians passed by arrayed for battle, on the way to a general encampment near Detroit.

"First came the Menominees, then the Winnebagoes, and then the Foxes, divided into bands according to their totems and attired in all their bravery.

"The single file passed on in perfect silence and unbroken order, not looking either to the right or to the left; one uniform steady stride not varying an inch from one another.

"This part of the procession the family viewed from the verandah without the slightest fear; but, when the servants whispered to Joseph Bailey, 'These are the last band of Foxes; the Decotahs are next,' the ladies stepped quietly into the house where the heavy shutters already were closed and bolted, the window shades of threaded rushes in the second story lowered.

"For the Decotahs, as Seuks were called by other Indians, were tribes which had no respect for women.

"In this way, they differed from the eastern Indian who might murder women, but never wrong them.

"The Decotahs, however, formed the grandest part of the pageant; their paint was more brilliant, their war bonnets more expansive, and their display of arms more unique.

"Feminine curiosity peered through the crevices in the window shades at the fine stalwart figures, tall, lithe, athletic warriors of most commanding appearance. Each warrior's elegant blanket hung from the shoulder, bows and arrows hung at their backs, while right arms balanced rifles slung over the shoulder."

by Hammond Historical Society

RADIO HISTORY MADE IN LAKE COUNTY
T59

In 1933 the present site of South Lake Mall was open farm land. The road that is now busy 4 lane U.S. 30 was a mere dirt track, all but impassable in the winter months. Steam trains were a common sight on the nearby C&O railroad, television and computers were unknown and the DC-3 was the utmost in air travel. In this rural setting the Mackay Radio division of I.T.&T. built a state of the art short wave receiving station. The isolated location was chosen to avoid problems with motor car ignition noise in the sensitive receiving circuits. A companion transmitting station was built on land to the west of U.S. 41, near the present location of Lake Central high school.

The stations were built to provide a high speed telegraph service between the metropolitan centers of Chicago, New York and San Francisco, and augmented the existing wire telegraph services. RCA Communications soon followed the lead of Mackay and built two stations in Lake County: A receiving station near Leroy and a transmitting station near Creston. The rural Indiana stations were con-

Mackay Radio shortwave transmitting station near St. John, Lake Co. Indiana. Sent telegraph message from Chicago to New York and San Francisco 1933-1942.

nected by wire lines to the operating centers in Chicago, where operators sent and received messages on automatic equipment capable of speeds up to 200 words per minute.

Similar schemes had been tried 20 years earlier, but the technology of that time did not provide reliable communication over the distances involved. The Lake County stations of 1933 employed the same techniques used in international communications and were reliable and profitable from the start.

In 1933, researchers were starting to think about the possibility of space travel. One of the problems was that no one then knew whether radio signals would penetrate into outer space. Early investigations involved the launching of high altitude, unmanned balloons from the so-called "strato-bowl" in South Dakota. Radio stations all over the world listened for the radio beacons carried aloft by the balloons. The Mackay station at Merrillville was one of those cooperating in these experiments that helped solve the mysteries of space.

The stations were closed by government order in June 1942 as war time censorship of radio communication made it impractical to continue operation. The stations were operated for military purposes by the U.S. Signal Corps until October 1943; then they were closed and dismantled. The 1943 merger of Postal Telegraph and Western Union had ended the possibility of competition in the domestic telegraph industry and the depression born domestic radio service was never resumed after World War II.

by Lewis Coe

THE HISTORICAL QUILT STORY
T60

Last summer during a meeting of Court House Foundation Volunteers, their director, Janet Holley, asked the women to suggest a fund-raising project. The group, numbering about forty, is working for the renovation and preservation of the Lake County Courthouse on the square, and have accomplished a great deal in their endeavors. The only idea considered was one presented by Virginia Kaiser. She suggested they make an historical quilt, each person contributing an appliqued and embroidered twelve-inch square patch, representing an event, building, or memento of the past. Further discussion revealed that not many of the group were adept at this kind of handiwork. One member didn't know the difference between percale and reep, but the enthusiasm of Janet and some of the others inspired Virginia to go forward with the idea. She volunteered to do the graphic work, designing, cutting and assembling of the quilt.

The Court House Volunteers that contributed patches were: Marie Olson, Effie Laney, Janet Holley, Martha Maki, Ruth Mader, Evelyne Radzwill and Virginia Kaiser. Planning on thirty-three squares for the ninety-square-inch quilt prompted Virginia to recruit some of her friends to help. Many of them gladly participated, some doing more than one patch, others doing detailed work on commenced work.

Now that the quilt is finished the women are very pleased and quite proud of their handiwork. With one exception, the women are of retirement age.

This quilt was raffled off to benefit the Lake Court House Foundation. Patches or squares were embroidered by Ann Klaas, Effie Laney, Lillian Holley, former L.C. Sheriff, Leone Van Koten, Ruth Mader, Alberta Haberichter, Elaine Englebright, Mary Kucia, Garner Barmore, Margaret Brueckman, Virginia Kaiser, Evelyn Heinzman, Mary Rehm, Evelyn Radzwell, Ida Krieter, Marie Olson, Ruth Hoffman, Mary Angela Pavlish, Janet Holley, and Kay Latz.

The ideas portrayed on this work of art includes local and county points of interest. The center, and largest square, pictures the old Court House at sundown, with pigeons flying around the roof. County places represented vary greatly. One site, the Buckley farm, in Lowell, was done by Mary Rehm. A snapshot of the farm was provided by Pat Hall, of the Lake County Parks Department. Mary also did a LaSalle portrayal. The statue of Father Marquette at Marquette Park was the copy work of Ellen Stewart, the Kankakee River by Leone Van Koten, a county map by Ruth Mader, and Ruth also did the covered bridge at the fairgrounds. Elaine Englebright contributed the sand dunes with Lake Michigan in the background; Ruth Hoffman, a view of the steel mills, and another of a winter pastoral. Ruth and Margaret Hoffman had two sisters, Thelma Guthrie and Bernice, now deceased. They lived on North Main Street for many years, their father and mother having been born in Crown Point in 1872. Evelyne Radzwill worked on a copy of Woods' Mill at Deep River; Roberta Haberichter, a South Shore train leaving the Gary depot. Evelyn Heinzman worked on a forest scene of cedars at Cedar Lake, with sailboats on the lake. Effie Laney depicted Washington school, where she had served as a teacher and acting principal. Garnet Barmore designed and embroidered the view of the old log cabin church, the first church in Lake County. It now stands in St. John facing Route 41, its new home since being moved from the fairgrounds. Virginia Kaiser embroidered a pheasant, a memento of the prairies of the past and present-day cornfields, to call attention to the establishment of the county seat in Liverpool in 1839. In the same year, the political structure moved the county seat, establishing it in Crown Point. A view of the old Brewery on the northwest side of Crown Point was done by Lillian Holley who is 93 years young. She served as Lake County Sheriff. A story is told about the Brewery, that one of the contributing factors to their moving out of Crown Point, was the probability of their polluting Beaver Dam Ditch. Other local mementoes of the past that are pictured are the Old Homestead on South Court Street, done by Janet Holley. Martha Maki and her husband, Gunnar, are avid supporters of the old Court House, so Martha worked on two squares – the fairgrounds grandstand with polka dots resembling the people sitting there – and the Sowash grain elevator that stood on the northeast side of town. The elevator was destroyed by fire about twenty-five years ago. The capacity of the elevator was forty thousand bushels. Mrs. Christine Sowash McMichael provided the picture to be copied. Kay Latz lent her talents by an embroidery of traffic on Industrial Highway, a main artery in Lake County. Virginia Kaiser depicted a cobblestone path that leads one to a P.W.A. project, an airconditioned back yard unit, decorated with a crescent, and surrounded by the usual hollyhocks. Ida Krieter embroidered a resemblance of the concrete dog in Lamson's front yard, which is a landmark. St. Mary's Church, pictured as it was many years ago, was captured from a picture loaned by Betty Trulley. She and her husband, former residents, reside in Greendale, Wisconsin. It was aptly done by Mary Angela Wise Pavlish. Mary Angela's family have lived in Crown Point many years. When she was a child, her father was proprietor of a grocery store on East Goldsborough Street, now the site of Weaver's Way. The northeast side of town was the Mecca of business before the turn of the century. It was known as "Bridgeport", and still retains the name. Streets there, such as Jackson, Grant, Sherman and Sheridan, were named to honor Civil War generals.

Marie Olson worked on a patch picturing two Pottawatomie Indians, hunched over a dying fire, smoking their pipes, wigwam in the background. This was Pottawatomie turf before early settlers came here about one hundred and fifty years ago. Margaret Brueckman did a patch featuring the building on the corner across from the theatre. It was built for Hugo Brueckman to house his butcher shop. Margaret is married to his son, Hugo. He is owner of Hugo's Augo Repair Service on Grant Street. His son and grandson are employed there. He has two sisters, Agnes Making and Gussie. Margaret's family were old timers here, too. Her father was Ed Franz. Other then Margie, his descendants are Mrs. Warner (Edith) Besse, and her sons, John and Mark; also Pat and Jim Donley and their families, Gemma Brandt, and Ambrose Franz of Hebron, and his family. Ed Franz was one of the first streetcar conductors on the Crown Point-Gary line. A street car is pictured on another patch, as it traveled down the center of Main Street. That line was discontinued over forty years ago. Mayor James Forsythe provided a street car picture. His father had been a streetcar conductor on the Crown Point line. Virginia Kaiser worked on a patch showing Eva Kaiser standing in front of her candy store. She bought the property with her husband, Pete, in 1892. It was located at 311 N. Jackson Street, the family homeplace until recently. Eva's local descendants are: Margaret Kaiser, Mrs. John (Grace) Malayter, Mrs. Curtis, (Phyliss) Stockwell, and her family, Clayton Kaiser and his family, and Carl J. "Cuney" Kaiser, a third

43

generation city fireman, and his family. Carl is owner of Cuney's Printing on Grant Street, located a block from his great-grandmother's former candy store. Virginia Kaiser and Olga Kaiser are granddaughters-in-law of Eva Kaiser. Olga and husband, Charles "Dutch" Kaiser, now deceased, gave the city of Crown Point five acres of land on South Main Street, to be used as a park. The city has buried a huge reserve water tank there. Pictured on another patch is a horse and dairy wagon owned by Oscar Adank. The dairy was located on Grant Street. Adah Letz Mueller loaned a brochure which advertised Letz Farm Feeders. Letz, a world renown manufacturer of farm equipment, employed many townspeople. Bringing back memories for some is an ice truck. Ice was cut from Fancher Lake, stored, and delivered by horse and wagon, and in later years, delivered by truck. It was delivered to customers that had placed a large card in their windows, denoting how many pounds of ice they wanted. That patch was done by Mary Kucia. In the past Crown Point was nicknamed "Gretna Green", named after a small village in Scotland where young couples went to get married, avoiding the stringent marriage laws in England. Couples from all over our country came here to be married because it was so convenient, no medical examinations or waiting being required. Many notables came here to "tie the knot" making Crown Point romantically famous. A patch denotes that period of our history. An even more historical event is related in a patch showing a lovely gift, given to all of us, mentioned in our Bibles, in John, Chapter Three, verse Sixteen. Thanks to God is certainly due Him, and also for the privilege of living and raising our children in this community of friendship and love. Maxine Radu and Bea Taylor helped in finishing work.

by Virginia Kaiser

HORNER ESTABLISHES CEDAR LAKE HISTORY CENTER
T61

Cedar Lake — Cedar Lake became a town in 1967.

Its early government locations were in small rented buildings.

Despite those adjustments, by 1971, the town board decided to provide a protective area for their region's unique history.

It was thought best to set up quarters where a telephone, copy machine, and materials could be provided. Also, a place where communications and trust would be available to the public.

Beatrice Horner was invited by the town board to establish this History Center, and it is now apparent that the archives have proved to be a very strong undertaking.

Out of this effort came recorded interviews of old times, store photographs, abstracts, maps, memorabilia, artifacts, as well as filed current events.

Help has been available to students, "Root" hunters landowners and private citizens as Mrs. Horner meets those needs and demands successfully.

Beatrice Horner

She claims no expertise but relies on innovation, intense interest and a willingness to contribute her time.

Beatrice Horner is nonpolitical and has volunteered her work under several town boards for these past 14 years.

She was a native of this region and is a D.A.R. member and takes pride in descending from a Mohawk Indian Chief and a Tishi Mingo Tribe, both of Eastern Canada and New York.

She has also traced her Dutch, French and English ancestry, making this Cedar Lake Town Historian a likely one to peer into the past and use such information to bolster our present and future.

Mrs. Horner was also selected to serve as a Historian by the Cedar Lake Historical Association since its inception in 1978. – The Oracle –

by Beatrice Horner

LUTHERAN RETIREMENT VILLAGE
T62

Health Care Center at the Lutheran Retirement Village, Crown Point, IN.

Lutheran Retirement Village, located on 35 beautiful acres in southeast Crown Point, is a developing and growing multi-service community planned for persons age 60 and over. As of publication date of this book, Lutheran Retirement Village is comprised of: (1) health care center which serves up to 175 residents, providing residential and intermediate nursing care; and (2) thirty-six apartments designed for independent retirement living.

The genesis of this organization came in 1970. A committee, formed by Lutheran clergy and laymen, began to investigate the possibility of starting up a continuing care community. This community was to be located in northwest Indiana and offer a distinct Lutheran heritage.

In 1971, a group of Lutheran congregations in Northwest Indiana formed an association, known as the Lutheran Home Association, to sponsor a nursing home. Also in 1971, Lutheran Retirement Village was incorporated as a not-for-profit corporation with this stated general purpose; to provide assistance, aid, care and treatment for the moral, social, mental and physical betterment of elderly persons. Later that year, a set of bylaws was adopted, which detailed organizational structure.

The original Board of Directors, elected in 1971, included: Herbert F. Borman, President; Harold J. Helbling, Vice President; Clarence J. LeVoy, Treasurer; Betty Mulholland, Secretary; William J. Harder; Rev. Thomas Mroch. Other individuals who have served on the Board of Directors include: Luther G. Bloomberg; Wilbur Heidbrder; Howard Jennings; Clark Johnson; Rev. Dr. Julius W. Acker; Raymond D. Kickbush; Rev. William R. Timmer; Rev. Marvin Rastl; Dr. Robert Kelsey; Jake Mabry; J. George Schiller; Donald R. O'Dell; Anton H. Hoeppner; Robert C. Anderson; Rev. John L. Telloni; William F. Gernand; Jerry Sykora; Dale L. Money; Rev. Bohuslav D. Tuhy; Harold F. Oman; Rev. Karl R. Davies; Hugh M. Bell; Ronald N. Schultz; Rev. Milton Beer; Vernon Vierk.

Long-term planning conceived Lutheran Retirement Village as a community offering a continuum of care, from apartments designed for independent retirement living to skilled nursing care. Favored as the first phase of this long-term development plan was a health care center licensed for intermediate-level nursing care.

Personal contacts, established by the Board of Directors and special committee members, played a significant role in fostering momentum needed to make Lutheran Retirement Village a reality. A turning point came in 1972 when Mr. Charles Blume, a resident of Crown Point, bequeathed $100,000 for the purpose of building a home for the aged in the Calumet area. This money was available to any group that would start building within five years of his death.

The Lutheran Home Association and Lutheran Retirement Village took advantage of this bequest to get the health care center project started. Mr. Frank Elmore was hired on June 1, 1973 to serve as Executive Director for developing Lutheran Retirement Village.

During the years 1973-76 fund raising became the major emphasis. Important to this fund raising was that more Lutheran congregations joined the Lutheran Home Association. In 1974, a 21-acre tract of land was purchased, part of which would eventually become the site for the health care center.

The mid-1970's also saw the Board of Directors deeply involved in getting all necessary governmental approvals to build a health care center licensed for intermediate nursing care.

On March 16, 1977 ground was broken to begin construction of a 175-bed health care center. Dedication of this facility took place on May 21, 1978 and the first residents were welcomed into the health care center on June

12, 1978.

An additional five cares of land was purchased in the Autumn of 1978. The following year this land was put to use as Lutheran Retirement Village began building apartments. 1979 witnessed the construction of the first quadruplex (four-unit apartment building) designed for independent retirement living. Additional quadruplexes were completed in 1980-82 and 1984-86. As of publication date, there were nine "independent-living" quadruplexes (total of 36 apartments).

Ten more acres were purchased in 1982 with an eye towards long-term development of "congregate care" apartments designed for assisted living. Congregate care will likely offer such services as housekeeping, centralized dining and laundry service to apartment residents who otherwise live independently.

In 1987, a Director of Pastoral Care was hired to enhance the spiritual care/guidance of residents and employees. As of publication date, Lutheran Retirement Village's resident population totaled approximately 230 (175 in health care center, 55 in apartments). Since the doors first opened in 1978, over 750 residents have been served. In the process of serving these many residents, we have also provided important service to many relatives and friends of residents.

Lutheran Retirement Village's future development goals include: (1) establishing skilled nursing care; (2) adding another wing to health care center; (3) building a chapel/auditorium; (4) building "congregate care" apartments designed for assisted living; (5) starting up an adult day care program with possible satellite operations strategically located throughout our service area; and (6) addition of recreational amenities such as nature walks, putting greens, tennis courts, clubhouse with indoor/outdoor swimming pool, etc.

We pray that God's blessings be upon us as we strive to serve persons of retirement age for generations to come.

by Henry Rohling

HISTORY OF ST. MARGARET HOSPITAL
T63

The First Hospital In Lake County

Before this area was known as the Calumet Region, or even Northwest Indiana, Saint Margaret Hospital was caring for patients. The hospital was an expression of love and commitment made by the Sisters of Saint Francis of Perpetual Adoration. At the invitation of the city fathers, they came to Hammond in 1898 and established Saint Margaret, the first hospital in Lake County. Ever since, they have cared for all who came to their doors.

As the area grew, so did the hospital, not only in the number of beds, but with the latest equipment and a growing staff of medical personnel. In 1915, the hospital installed one of Indiana's first x-ray units; in 1918, we opened the area's first clinical laboratory; the following year, we started our own school of nursing, to ensure the quality of care our patients deserve.

More recently, we opened (in 1959) one of the state's first Inhalation Therapy departments (now Cardiopulmonary Services); and in 1961 we pioneered Intensive Care in this area. Every new instrument, every employee, every new procedure, was added for one reason — to care for the ill and injured.

And our growth to provide the best quality health care continues. Our new 50-bed Critical Care Pavilion will open later this year, housing intensive care, coronary care and intermediate care beds. There patients will receive the latest, most sophisticated medical treatment available. The monitoring and therapeutic instruments will be matched by the most capable, skilled and compassionate staff anywhere. All for one reason: to bring the best possible care to the patient.

by *Post-Tribune* – Feb. 14, 1982

WINFIELD TOWNSHIP CEMETERY'S
T64

Hickory Point Cemetery is located 8.8 miles from the South East corner of the Court House square or intersection of Joliet and Main St. Crown Point, Ind.

Take R.R. #8 East to 145th St. turn North then East to Union St. the Cemetery is at the bend. It was once owned by the Ward family, and is Ninety by thirty feet in size. There are two Pine Trees, and under growth of blackberry bushes, Sumac and brush trees, which the boy Scouts cleared so one could see the graves.

The Cemetery is small, but is the oldest in the Township. Not only a sadly neglected Cemetery, but there are very few Head Stones left to mark this Settlements remains. The graves have oft times been vandalized with the stones taken and left in the front yard of the homes in the area. The earliest burial we found was William and P. Nichols Son, Silas G. who died April 20th, 1837 age 5 years, 9 days. The latest was the Daughter of David and Mary McFarland who died October 18th, 1877 age 3 years 3 months, 7 days.

The County Home Cemetery is not in use for many years, has only twelve (12) graves, as we could determine, there were no Head Stones, only indentations in the ground.

The Deer Creek Cemetery located on Grand Blvd. and 109th, Ave. due to road name changes, is also an old Cemetery, The earliest burial being Alice Abdill, June 6, 1859 age 1 mo. 26 days. It has been fairly kept, and is still being used, but not often.

Many stones of the 1840's and 1850's and 60's have definite characteristics. Markers of this period have usually been made of white marble and approximately two feet (2ft) high, Twenty two (22) inches across and two and one half to three (2½ to 3) inches thick.

There are certain decorations on these Stones, For example we found that a Bird carved in a circle or an Angel in this circle is the marker of a child.

Other symbols found are hands folded as in Prayer, or a fist with the index finger pointing toward Heaven or Hands Clasped.

In the 1880's there were ornately carved Stones, these were discovered to be mostly the work of a Hoosier group of Stone carvers from Bedford, Indiana, There is carved Bibles, open Bibles, Vines, Leaves, Tree Trunks and Figurines. Some of the Head Stones have oblong dome picture frames placed for a picture of the deceased.

Information: Cemeteries of Lake County Prior to 1880. 75th. Anniversary Centennial Paper.

by Mrs. Thomas W. Haney

FAMILY STORIES

AKEN, CHARLES ALBERT
F1

Charlie Aken's ditching machine working in a field between Hebron and Leroy, Indiana. The two men working on the front wheel are unknown. The man to the extreme right is Charlie Aken.

Pioneer Vision

My Father, Charles Albert Aken, was a man of vision. This article is about how he fit into the development of Northwest Indiana and why many farmers are still reaping the benefits made possible by his vision and hard labor.

My Father was born in Martinsville, Illinois on April 9, 1871. He became a farmer like his father, only he always thought big and had a sideline which eventually took all of his time. He sold fertilizer to other farmers, because he recognized the farmland had become famished of nutrients that make good crops flourish.

He worked his way to Monon, Indiana where he was a tenant farmer showing what fertilizer can do for rocky, stony, sandy soil. His business took him to Francesville, Indiana, and he gave up farming.

This was the time when the great Kankakee River was being straightened and dredged. This project was called the Cady Ditch project. My Dad understood the potential good that this project would bring about to the landowners. The Ditch made it possible to reclaim much of the land that had been flooded each year. But, it still needed additional help to make it good farming land.

While in Francesville, Dad met a man named Charlie Hewitt. Together, the two men had vision and foresight of what could happen to the lowland on either side of the Kankakee River, after the Cady Ditch was completed. The flood plains that existed at that time could be made into the very best farmland. The naturally rich soil left by the annual flooding and the manure left by the huge flocks of migrating birds had formed some of the richest soil in America. My Dad and Mr. Hewitt set out to sell the idea to the farmers who were barely making ends meet. Their land consisted of sloughs, fens and swamps.

These farsighted men mortgaged their souls and bought a steam powered ditching machine. The first one burned wood to make the steam to power the big shovels. They would dig a deep center ditch through the field and smaller laterals that were tailored to the land in these wet soggy fields. They laid tile of appropriate size and covered the tile with the dirt that had been dug out. These tiles would drain into a master open ditch that would carry the water to the Kankakee River. They had to survey the land to make the precise calculations of how deep and what the proper slope would need to be. They worked their way from farm to farm from Francesville to Leroy, Indiana. Each farm would be a better producing property because of this tiling to improve it. They were using horses and carts to get to and from their work.

By 1916, my family had moved to Leroy where there were many fens and swamps. The partnership worked there for five or six years and then moved to Crown Point. During the Leroy years, a new ditching machine was purchased. It was much larger and it was fueled by oil to make the steam. This machine was capable of digging a deeper ditch for the main line. They still used the small machine for the laterals. It had been converted to oil for a long time.

I was born in Leroy and remember my older sisters showing me the Will-O-The-Wisp that sometimes glowed over the swamp that was due west of our house. The weather conditions had to be just right for this phenomenon to occur.

Both partners moved to Crown Point and soon Mr. Hewitt died. This ended the partnership, and my Dad continued to work alone. I remember Dad working on payroll at our dining room table at night. Most men received a dollar a day for their hard work. They always had to work and wait until a job would be completed to get their wages.

My Dad had an eighth grade education and never stopped reading and learning. He was a brilliant man. He understood the work he was doing and could work out the mathematical problems each field presented. In those days, this work had to be done in the seasons with no frost or freezing. They used every bit of sunlight that was available. There were good times and hard times. In the winter, he would pick up jobs. He helped cut and store ice for the summer.

He did several farms around Crown Point and then started doing drainage tiles for new roads being built. His last job was the drainage for US 12 from Gary to Benton Harbor, Michigan. Occasionally, he would take one of us kids along with him for a day. I remember walking with the tape line when he would survey. I had no idea what I was doing at the time, but it must have been according to his wishes, because he always said, "Good Work". There are farms along US 421 and US 53 that have the original tile fields laid by my Dad and his men. He believed in education and hard work. He made dreams come true for many men by his work and foresight. He really was a man of vision.

by Lloyde (Mickie) Aken Louis

ANSBRO, JAMES H.
F2

An Early Settler in Lake County, Indiana and His Descendants

The following information pertains to an early settler of Lake County, Indiana, James H. Ansbro. The source of this data is a book "Counties of Porter and Lake" published by F.A. Battey & Co. 1882. Edited by Weston A. Goodspeed, biographical editor, Charles Blanchar. More up-to-date information was supplied by Virginia Kaiser, Crown Point, Indiana. As recorded in the book, it states that in a treaty made with the Pottawatomies in 1828, a strip of land along the northern border of Indiana was acquired by the United States government. In 1832 the remainder of Lake County was acquired. No white man up to this time, except for traders, and the soldiers at Fort Dearborn had been there. A route for travel was immediately opened along the beach of Lake Michigan. Three men, Hart, Steele, and Sprague started a coach line from Detroit to Fort Dearborn, (now known as Chicago), in 1833. One of the early settlers of this area along northern Lake County was James H. Ansbro, an immigrant from Ireland. He was a son of Michael and Anna Hughes Ansbro of Ireland, where he was born on July 28, 1829. When he was ten months old his parents left him with his grandmother and they came to America. His grandmother was not willing to allow them to take so young a child across the ocean. When about six years old, he commenced school, and continued until about seventeen years of age. After which he taught school for about two years. On July 10, 1848 he came to America, and located in Wyandot County, Ohio. He went to work for a railroad for some eight months, then to Sandusky City, where he taught school for some time. From there he went to work on the Kentucky Central Railroad, from there to the New Albany and Salem Railroad, as a foreman. He went back to Kentucky Central Railroad for two years. While there, on Sept. 19, 1853, he was married to Catherine Pendergast, daughter of Patrick and Bridget Matthews Pendergast. Nine children have been born to them. Three boys and six girls. John, born Sept. 6, 1854 died Dec. 10, 1854. Ann J. born Dec. 8, 1855. Catherine B. born July 1, 1857. Margaret A. born Aug. 24, 1858. Mary A. born July 15, 1860. Jane E. born April 13, 1862. James F. born Feb. 18, 1865. Bridget A. born July 18, 1869. John, born April 10, 1877.

In December of 1855, Mr. Ansbro came to Porter County, Indiana, and worked on the railroad until 1863. From there he went to Miller's Station, Indiana, bought eighty acres of land in section eight. He then went to railroading as a telegrapher for the railroad. He and his family were members of Saint Patrick's Catholic Church in Chesterton, Indiana. The property in the Miller section of Gary was bequeathed the Catholic Church by James H. Ansbro. St. Mary's of the Lake Church has been established there. He died in 1915, and was buried in Chesterton alongside of his wife and some of his children. His son, John, was married to Isabel Kelly, they had five children. John, James, Cecilia, who married Albert Quigley; Pigeon married Lawrence Gray, and Vivian, married Ed Stark. Mr. Ansbro's son, James, married a lady named Hattie from Garret, Indiana. They had one daughter, Phillipine who left no descendants. Mr. Ansbro's daughter Catherine was married to Thomas Walton. Their three children were Richard, and Kate Boyd who left no descendants, Margaret married James F. Hamilton, they had three children. Virginia married Carl H. Kaiser, who had one son, Carl J., who married Frances Kucia. They had two children, Carl S., and Sherri Lynn. Sherri Lynn married Michael Ham. As of July 1989, they have one son, Jordan Michael Ham. Carl S. married Sue Geis.

Hamilton's daughter Blanche, married Francis Carrigan, they have to sons, John and Pat. Pat married a lady named Jo, they had two children, named Gena Jo and Carmen. The son of Hamilton's was James Jr., he married Janyce Renyard. They have one child, Janyce. Mary was another daughter of James H. Ansbro. She married John Ryan, four children were born to them, James, John, Joseph and Mary. Bridget Ansbro married Michael Stack. Their children were Mary, married to Arthur Steward, Bernard, James, Desmond, Eugene, Harold and Lawrence. Another daughter of James H. Ansbro, Annie, married a Mr. Sperb. Two of their children were named William and Mamie. There are many other descendants not mentioned here.

by Virginia Kaiser

BACON, DR. RALPH
F3

Dr. Ralph Bacon came to Lowell about 1870. He was enlisted in the Union Army Medical Corps during the Civil War, serving in the Tennessee area.

He started one of the first drugstores soon after his arrival, located in the present Masonic building. He married Martha Sanger, only daughter of James Sanger Sr. He was finishing his medical training at the Chicago Medical College at the time of the Great Chicago Fire. He said "the scene resembled a huge burning brick yard with its street all aglow like the door of a brick kiln."

At first, he had his office in his drug store. When he built his house near his business, on the corner of Commercial and Freemont, he moved his office there. This house became one of Lowell's showplaces and continues to be a historic landmark. It was protected from Lowell's Great Fire in 1890 "by spouting water from the hoselines from his underground residential water facilities, fed from his windmill tower tank, the town having no organized volunteer fire department." A town water works and fire department were soon created after the fire had shown the need for such.

Dr. Bacon's practice extended many miles in all directions. To be equipped to meet the demands of his profession, he kept several good driving horses in his two barns, with a steady hostler in attendance. The renowned Kent family of Kentland were among his patients. Even travel trials didn't keep him from being good natured. His patients declared that his presence did them as much good as his medicine.

His concern for his patients was always dominant. If dangerous cases came up, he sometimes drove nearly to Lockport, Ill. for a consultation with his doctor brother. His reputation spread. An eczema case came from Peotone, Ill. Another patient came from Chicago with blood poisoning who said he could get better treatment here than Chicago.

Dr. Bacon worked closely with another of Lowell's doctors who came to town about the same time. Dr. J.E. Davis had an office across the street from Dr. Bacon and the men held many consultations, as doctors of a clinic do today. These two men established a liquorcuring place in Lowell in the 1890's.

Dr. Bacon was a public spirited man. He purchased a large tank of Big Mouthed Bass minnows from the Fish Commission in 1901 to stock Lafler Lake.

He died in 1906 at the age of 66.

by Bessie Kenney

BALL, TIMOTHY HORTON
F4

Timothy Horton Ball – Baptist minister and historian, born at Agawam, Hampden County, Mass. February 16, 1826, and died November 8, 1913 at Crown Point, Ind.; son of Hervey and Jane Ayrault (Horton) Ball, of Holyoke and Agawam, Mass.; grandson of Charles and Merab (Miller) Ball and of Dr. Timothy and Elizabeth (Hanner) Horton of Agawam, Mass. Col. Hervey Ball was an officer of militia in Georgia and later probate judge of Lake County, Ind. Lieut. Charles Ball, son of Charles Ball, Sr. was a representative in the Massachusetts legislature for nine years. Francis Ball, the original ancestor came from Wiltshire, England, and settled at Springfield, Mass. in 1640. Timothy H. Ball's early education was secured at Franklin College, Ind. from which he graduated with degree of A.B. 1850, and received the A.M. in 1853. He graduated from the Newton theological institution in 1863. His first work, which was as a teacher, was at Franklin Springs, in 1851. This point, now absolutely deserted, was at that time a fashionable watering place. He began preaching here a short while later. Much of his life was spent in Clarke County, but at the time of his death, his pastoral relation was in Lake County, Ind. He was a Mason. Author: "Lake County, Indiana, from 1834 to 1872"; "The Lake of the Red Cedars, or will it live?"; "A Glance into the great Southeast or Clarke County, Ala., and its surroundings from 1540 to 1877," 1882; "Northwestern Indiana from 1800 to 1900"; "The Creek War" (in collaboration with Henry S. Halbert), 1895; "Notes on St. Luke's Gospel"; "Poems and Hymns"; "Annie B."; "Immorality of Human Soul"; and numerous others. Martha Caroline, daughter of Rev. Hiram and Mary (Thomas) Creighton, who lived near Grove Hill, the former a Baptist minister, son of John Creighton, who came to Clarke County, were Scotch Presbyterians who came to South Carolina in 1800. Children: 1. Herbert Laurin, St. Maries, Idaho; 2. Georgietta Ethberta, m. Rev. Isaac Walter Martin, Sheffield. Last Residence: Crown, Point, Ind.

BALLANTYNE, DOROTHY DUNNING
F5

Dorothy Dunning Ballantyne, museum worker, retired educator; born Aetna, Indiana, March 17, 1910; daughter of Harry Leland and Ella L. (Larson) Dunning; married Donald Bock Ballantyne (Deceased June, 1973); children — Elin Christianson, Dorothy Eastwood, Brianne Lowery, Alexander. Student of Indiana University. Newspaper editor of the Hobart Gazette, Indiana, 1929-32; clerk at Home Owners Loan Federal Government, Hammond, Indiana, 1932; deputy auditor of Lake County, Crown Point, Indiana, 1932-36; substitute teacher at Hobart Schools, Indiana, 1954-65, special education teacher, 1965-72; volunteer director of the Hobart Historical Society Museum, Indiana, 1970 –. Contributor of articles to professional journals. Author of pamphlets for the Hobart Historical Society Members advisory commission. Hobart School Board, 1980 –, Hobart PTA. Recipient of the Distinguished Service award from the West Hobart Civic Club, 1970; named one of the 12 most valuable women in the country by Trade Winds, Lake County, Indiana, 1978. Member of the Indiana Historical Society, Hobart Historical Society (president, 1970-76), Mensa, Hobart Jaycees (Laura Bracken Woman of the Year award, 1968), League of Women Voters (president). Lodge: Order Eastern Star (worthy matron 1938, distribution department 1940). Home: 121 South Ash Street, Hobart, IN 46342. Office: Hobart Historical Society Museum, Box 24, Hobart IN 46342.
(From the 1986-87 "Who's Who in the Midwest")

BASSETT, CHARLES AND MARY
F6

When Charles Hall Bassett and Mary Ann Kyger were married in Brookville, Indiana, on August 25, 1863, they brought together families that had been part of the earliest settlements along the Whitewater River valley in Southeastern Indiana. The children of this marriage were to participate in the building of a new settlement in northern Lake County named Gary. The seven children of Charles and Mary were:
Leora T. (1865-1922) m. Daniel Havens (known to all as Lola and Doc) Ch. Mabel, Georgia, C. Howard, Madeleine
Lewis W. (1869-1873)
A. Gertrude (1872-1959) m. Frank O. Hodson Ch. Ralph
Grace (1876-1961) m. Charles Allison Ch. Vivian L.
Orris W. (1878-1966) m. Mary Emma Hains Ch. Maxine
Harry H. (1880-1893)
Walter S. (1884-1908) m. Golda Tegarden. Ch. Mary, Robert, Virginia

About 1893 the family moved to Elwood, Indiana, where the oldest daughter had gone to live with her husband. As the children married and established their own homes, they either lived nearby or made the weekly trek to spend Sunday with Charles and Mary. Charles had been a brick layer but joined his son, Orris, in the plumbing business in Elwood.

Gertrude was the first of the Bassett brothers and sisters to move to Gary where she and her husband, Frank Hodson, became socially prominent community leaders. Encouraged by the Hodsons and the opportunity offered in this budding city, one by one the other family members made the move. The Allisons and Havens had moved to Indianapolis, but both families were in Gary by 1920 with daughters Vivian Allison and Madeleine Havens enrolled in Emerson High School. About 1920 Charles and Mary also moved to Gary and were joined by Orris in 1925. When first arriving in Gary the families usually lived with or near one another — often renting a house from the Hodsons. The addresses include 521 Monroe,

221 W. 6th Ave., 525 and 527 Jackson. Walter was the only Bassett off-spring to resist Gary. He and his family moved frequently and to several different states, but resided for a number of years at 1473 Davis Ave. in Munster. Distance, however, seldom prevented them from joining in family gatherings.

An appreciation of and talent for art and music was evinced in several family members. Lola taught art for a time in the Gary Schools and Gertrude's hand painted china is still admired by family members. Ralph Hodson and his daughter, Sally, were both singers and lent their voices to most of the family weddings. Walter's pumpkin carvings were an annual art event for the family.

Charles had served in the Union Army during the Civil War and was one of the 14 charter members of the William A. Ketcham Post of the Grand Army of the Republic which was organized in Gary in 1923 — believed to be the last post to be organized. In 1926, at age 86, he became Commander of the post.

In their final years, Charles and Mary lived with the Hodsons at their home at 1516 W. 6th Ave. where the regular Sunday gathering of the clan took place.

Charles and Mary each died in 1929 but their children, grandchildren, and great-grandchildren still assembled with some regularity. They were a fun loving group, able to create their own entertainment or adopt the latest game craze. There were beach parties at Wells Street and "10-cent" Christmas parties at the home of Frank or Ralph Hodson or at Walter Bassett's home in Munster, where Walter was the first family member to discover that a basement could be converted to a "rec-room". The younger children often produced a play for the Christmas gathering. All of the youngsters have fond memories of special times at the Hodson's Long Beach summer cottage. In later years, the family gathered at Joe and Madeleine (Havens) Wildermuth's beach home or at their farm near Leroy, Indiana.

In 1989 the descendants of Charles and Mary Bassett are far flung and see one another only rarely. Yet each holds a special place in his childhood memory of the Bassett family gatherings.

by Dorothy Wildermuth Vekasi

BAUERMEISTER, WILLIAM FAMILY
F7

William Bauermeister, Sr. was born April 2, 1824 in Mesmarode, HessenSchaumburg, Hannover, Germany. He was married to Dorothea (Rohe) who was born on February 15, 1834 in Mesmarode, a province of Hannover, Germany.

Together they journeyed to Indiana to purchase land in Hanover Township in Lake County in Section 13 and Section 17. (Later their son John and his wife Bertha (Engel) resided on the land owned in Section 17.).

On June 29, 1855, William's first land claim was filed on Section 13. This land was located south of 121st Avenue at State Line Road, and is where they made their home. Their property located in Section 13 contained some swamp land, which needed an unusually large amount of drainage tile. The farm became quite productive after the tile was installed.

The William Bauermeister Home built in 1879, with William Bauermeister standing on the left, his sister and husband; Mary, wife of William, Jr., and a nephew, Harry of Iowa.

Their children were: Henry who married Sophia Heisterberg of the Kreitzburg area; William who married Mary Oltrogge the daughter of Conrad and Mary (Blume) Oltrogge; John who married Bertha (Engel), they resided in Crown Point and later in Hammond; Dorothy who married Nickels Nielsen of Watseka Illinois, they resided in Crown Point; Herman who married Louise Grabe of Brunswick and resided in Iowa; Caroline who married Adolph Russell and they resided in Kreitzburg; Fred who married Sophia Grabe of Brunswick, and resided in Iowa; Amanda who married William Paul of Brunswick. (Henry Bauermeister, a relative, possibly William's brother, married Maria Schmidt and settled in Yellowhead Township in Kankakee, Illinois.)

John, one of William Sr.'s sons had three children: Lydia (Prevo) and her husband operated the Prevo Grocery Business for many years in Hammond; Reverend John (Jr.) of Lancaster, California; and Walter and his wife Pauline of Hammond. (Walter's son, Robert and his wife Pauline, resided in Redlands, California. A grandson, Fred Bauermeister is of Smi Valley, CA.)

William Jr. was born on January 19, 1857. He purchased the farm from his father William Sr. on December 11, 1883. William Jr. and some of his brothers and hired men farmed the 217 acres. Twenty additional acres were added making the farm total 237 acres. This was considered a large farm at the time.

On April 13, 1903, William, Jr. married Mary Oltrogge. At this time, one of the nephews, Harry, from Iowa came to live with William Jr. and Mary. Harry attended Brands School before the new Schiller School was erected in 1912. (Schiller School was located 2 1/4 miles north of Brunswick, on Calumet Avenue.)

In 1893, William Jr.'s barn was struck by lightning and destroyed by fire. Carpenters were kept busy constructing a large, new barn, which still stands today.

William Jr. and Mary's children include: William III, born May 18, 1904; Martin, born on June 27, 1905; and Walter born on September 15, 1907 died on October 6, 1907.

Martin married Elnora (Kiedaisch) of Washington Township, Will County Illinois on December 18, 1938. Elnora, the daughter of George and Laura (Heller) Kiedaisch, was born on July 3, 1907. Martin and Elnora lived in the farm house. Rooms in the upper portion of the home were converted into an apartment for Martin's parents and his brother William III. Martin and brother William III continued farming. William III remained single; and rather enjoyed keeping the machinery in top shape, repairing buildings and maintaining the property.

Martin and Elnora's daughter, Joann, grew up on the farm, attended Schiller School and graduated from Dyer High School. She was employed by the Nutt Insurance Agency until her marriage September 5, 1961, to Arnold "Bud" Schutz, son of Clarence and Emma Schutz of Dyer, Indiana.

A new home was built just east of the farm home where Joann and Bud raised their daughter Cindy. They sold the home and the farm and later they moved to a Wheatfield, Indiana farm. (After graduating from Hanover Central High School, Cindy Schutz attended Indiana University.)

by Mrs. Ralph Oldendorf

BAZIN, JOHN AND BARBARA
F8

John Bazin wrote his own story in the family Bible, "I, John Bazin, came to America, state of Pennsylvania on May 15, 1901. From there I moved to Gary, Indiana, on January 1, 1915. First we lived at 26 Jefferson St., and moved again to 1620 Delaware Street. I built the house at 1924 Adams Street. I started with the store in 1918 on March first. I bought the lot . . . for $775.00;; the cost of the house was 1500.00 and the building of the store was 6,000 dollars." (Translated from Hungarian)

John was born in the township of Jabloncza, County of Abauj-Torna, Hungary (now part of Czechoslovakia) on Tuesday, March 22, 1877, to Stephen and Julianne (Matyus) Bazin. In 1922 when John wrote in the family Bible about his parents and brothers and sisters, he prophetically concluded with "May those mentioned above for a long time stay alive and their descendants may multiply, thus they may carry their beautiful name among the living."

In 1900, when John was drafted by the Hungarian army, his occupation was given as a farmer. The following year he immigrated to America. John returned to Jabloncza to marry Barbara Papp on June 29, 1903, "in the presence of many beautiful people" — according to his own written words. His bride was born on June 30, 1884, in Jabloncza which was also the birthplace of their first child. Returning to Pennsylvania, John and his family lived in Johnstown, then briefly in Twin Rocks before responding to the opportunities offered by the young city of Gary, Indiana. The family continued to grow and in 1922 the family was complete with eight of his ten children living:

Elizabeth (1902-1970) m. Michael Vekasi Ch: Michael E. and Linda

John Jr. (1908-1975) m. Lydia Holas Ch: John III, Bonita and Cynthia

Barbara (1910-1974) m. John Bencie Ch: Charles and Barbara Ann

Helen b. 1912 m. Alex Nestor Ch: Ronald and Nancy

Steven b. 1914 m. Helen Ch: Steven John and Robert

Mary b. 1917 m. Nicholas Kokinda Ch: Dorothy, Dennis and Diana.

Daniel (1919-1987) m. Ernesta Putti Ch: Mary J., Kathleen and Daniel

Joseph (1922-1973) m. Helen Gersack Ch: Sharon and Jo Ellen

When John first moved to Gary, he worked in the steel mill but later took great pride in the neighborhood grocery store he established, not retiring until he was 78 years old. The family lived in the house behind the store and two boarders lived in basement rooms. In the European tradition, John was the patriarch of the family. The older children helped in the store before quitting school to get jobs. Before marriage, the older girls were store clerks. Elizabeth worked at Levin Brothers, then Broadway Style Shop; Barbara worked at Sam Mayo & Co., then Nick S. Kencoff. John Jr. followed his father's footsteps in the grocery business; after working with his father a few years, he had his own store in East Gary. Steve made his life work in the steel mill and became a leader in the Union. Mary was the first to finish high school. Dan became a fireman and Joe drove a truck for the city.

The family belonged to the First Hungarian Evangelical and Reformed Church (later known as Grace Reformed Church) where, in the early days, the charm and excitement of the old Hungarian traditions were preserved. The women prepared food as they had learned from their mothers and church members would don traditional costumes to celebrate festivals in the manner of the old country.

John died March 10, 1957, preceded by his wife by ten years. They are both buried at Oak Hill Cemetery in Gary. John's wish that the descendants multiply and carry their beautiful name among the living has come to pass. Among his grandchildren and great-grandchildren are doctors, lawyers, university professors, engineers, businessmen, etc. They are spread over many states, universally doing credit to their names.

by Dorothy Wildermuth Vekasi

BECKMANN, BERNARD THEODORE
F9

Bernard and Johanna Beckmann in front of their retirement home in Bradenton, FL about 1950.

Early Resident of Lowell, Indiana

Bernard T. Beckmann and his wife Johanna Mary nee Hessling settled in Lowell, Indiana in 1913 after moving several times around Indiana and Illinois. They decided Lowell was a good place to raise their family. Their new residence was at 213 No. Halstead St., a white framed double story home.

Bernard was the son of Bernhardt von Beckmann and Katherine nee Beaumkamp. His father immigrated from Ahaus, Germany in 1867 and settled in Libertyville, IL. His family farmed and raised their children: Henry b. 1868; Mary (1870-1958); Christina b. 1872; Bernadina (1874-1942); George (1876-1944); Bernard (1879-1958); and Catherine (1882-1968).

Bernard was born on a farm east of Libertyville, IL on the 25 of Feb. 1879 and died in Gary, IN on July 10, 1958. Johanna Mary nee Hessing was born May 26, 1880 in Huizen, Holland. She was adopted by John Hessling after his marriage to her mother. Johanna died on June 28, 1959 in Bradenton, Florida. They are both buried in St. Mary's Cemetery in Crown Point, Indiana.

Bernard, a well known Lowell businessman and civic leader, was a blacksmith by trade. He was an apprentice in the area of the Chicago Stockyards at the young age of twelve. He had formal schooling for five years and was able to read and write in English and German. Bernard owned and operated a blacksmith shop in Lowell, IN at 225 W. Washington St. It was a gathering place for the town residents and farmers, who discussed current events. Bernard was voted the town board president for fourteen years and a member for eighteen years, from 1923 to 1941 the year that he retired. At this time voters chose their candidates by their good names and not by party lines. Bernard usually voted Republican. He influenced the development and future of the town. Improvements in the water and sewer system, a new town hall and a modern fire department were some of his accomplishments. Along with George Hoevet, he built the town's main garage located on 210 E. Commercial Ave., about 1912.

Bernard was also active in St. Edwards Catholic Church, practicing his faith and singing in the Adult Choir. He assisted in the founding of the new school and church in 1915 after the infamous fire of 1915. It was located at 255 Burnham St.

Bernard and Johanna were married at St. Margarets of Scotland in Blue Island, IL. They parented eleven children:

Bernard Joseph (1900-1983) married Inez Finney, resided in Washington, D.C. Edward John (1902-1981) married Sabena E. Berg and lived in Gary, Indiana. George Harold (1904-1983) married Thelma Roy and lived in Lowell, Indiana. Leo Aloyious (1905-1982) married Dorothea Schmelter and lived in Crown Point, Indiana. Reverend John Nicholas b. 1907, was ordained a Roman Catholic Priest on June 10, 1933 and retired from the Diocese of Gary, IN on August 17, 1971 to Sarasota, Florida.

Mary Louise b. 1909 married Eugene Erlenbach and lived in Crown Point, IN. Gertrude Henrietta b. 1911 married Harry Fiske and lives in Sarasota, FL. Henry Arthur b. 1912 married Marion Sebben and lives in Crown Point, IN. Mildred Agnes (1914-1985) married Ralph Geisen and lived in Crown Point, Indiana. Irene Anna b. 1916 married Henry F. Ross and lives in San Diego, California. Vincent Paul b. 1919 married Elizabeth Murdock and lives in Edgewater, Florida.

by Mary L. Davis

BELL, ROBERT T.
F10

Eleanor Nissen was born in 1925 on a farm in southwest Iowa. She attended a country school until 7th grade and then attended the public school in the town of Walnut. Upon graduation from high school she went to the

Bob and Eleanor Bell on Caribbean cruise 1987, taken on board ship Carla Costa.

University of Iowa in Iowa City and graduated with a major in Sociology in 1948.

Bob Bell was born in 1924 in Council Bluffs, Iowa. He was the son of a plumber. He went to grade school and high school in Council Bluffs and then went to college at the University of Iowa. He graduated in 1947 with a degree in Civil Engineering.

Bob and Eleanor met on a blind date their freshman year of college and went together off and on the next four years. Eleanor and Bob got engaged in the spring before Bob graduated. Bob went to work as an engineer for the Standard Oil refinery in Whiting, IN.

When Eleanor graduated she took a job as a social worker for the Indiana Department of Public Welfare in Hammond, Indiana. Bob and Eleanor were married Dec. 19, 1948 in Council Bluffs, Iowa. They rented the front part of a home on Atchison Ave. in Whiting for three months and then moved to an upstairs apartment on Superior St.

After a year and a half with the Welfare Dept., Eleanor quit and stayed home a year. She then went to work for the Ind. Employment Bureau in Hammond. Bob worked for 4½ years as an engineer, then in 1952 he was promoted to a supervisory position in the plant. Since their first child was to arrive, the couple needed more space and moved to a garage apartment behind a home on Indianapolis Blvd. near the Community Center.

Son, Bill, was born on Feb. 18, 1952 and twenty-two months later a daughter, Kathleen Joan was born on November 17, 1953.

As the children grew they needed more space, so the family moved to a rented house on Columbia Ave. in Hammond. After six months of renting they purchased a small home on White Oak Ave. near the Calumet River on the southern border of Hammond. They lived in this house for 7½ years. The children attended Riley Elementary School.

As the children got older, still more room was needed, so the family built a quad-level home on Melbrook Dr. in Munster. They moved in in April 1962.

The children attended the public schools in Munster. Bill went to Drake University in Des Moines, Iowa for four years and then got a Masters and Ph.D. in Statistics at the University of Wisconsin in Madison, Wisc. He went to work for the Census Bureau in Wash. D.C. and was married in 1986.

Kathy attended Indiana University, graduating in 1976 with a major in Physical Therapy. She worked in hospitals in Indianapolis, New Hampshire and now is employed in a large hospital in Boise, Idaho.

Bob has been active in Lion's Club activities in Whiting and Munster. He held several offices, including the presidency, and was chosen Lion of the Year by the Munster Club. He enjoys playing golf in the summer.

Eleanor worked part time as a Welcome Wagon hostess in Dyer, and taught beginning piano students in her home for 10 years. She then went to work part time at a nursery school in Highland for 6 years. Her activities included Newcomers Club. She was President of the parent club and the alum club. She joined a music teacher group which she also served as president and secretary. She was active in the Alpha Xi Delta Alumnae Chapter and held several offices and was president of this group. She also belonged to P.E.O. and played in several bridge groups.

Bob retired from Amoco in 1984 after 36 years. He held many supervisory positions.

When he retired, he was manager of Blending, Packaging and Shipping in the Heavy Oils Department. Eleanor retired from her part time job at the nursery school.

The Bells spend time traveling in their retirement.

by Robert Bell

BERQUIST, ARTHUR VICTOR
F11

Arthur Victor (Bjorkquist) Berquist was born in Ludington, Mich. on April 3, 1893 to Anders Victor of Kronoby, Finland and Anna Josephine (nee Strandberg) of Fjaras, Sweden. He was raised in Ludington and as a young man worked in the lumber camps in northern Wisconsin at Ashland and Odanah, with his father. While working in Odanah he lived on an Indian Reservation for two years and mastered the tribal language. He later attended Valparaiso University majoring in business. He was employed as traveling auditor for the Erie Railroad and while at the Erie office in Palmer, Indiana met his fate in the person of Gertrude Margaret Lewis, daughter of Albert and Lydia Maria Lewis (nee Hutton) and granddaughter of Levi and Gertrude Hutton (nee Fieler). They were married in the Methodist parsonage in Crown Point on April 28, 1917. They lived in Reading, Penn. until May, 1920. Arthur accepted a position as Safety Director in the safety department of Youngstown Sheet and Tube of America, Indiana Harbor. In 1922 he was appointed Chief Safety Inspector of the Harbor and South Chicago Works.

Born to this union were Vivian Marjorie (Spencer) on May 31, 1918 and Lyle Levi (Alyce) on November 11, 1922. Arthur had two brothers, Runger Sigurd and Walter Raymond and one sister, Lillian Josephine.

Arthur Berquist was well known in many parts of the United ates due to his activities in the Metals Section of the National Safety Council. He passed away February 14, 1936.

by Gerald Born

BERQUIST, VIVIAN MARJORIE
F12

Vivian Marjorie Berquist was born in Porter Memorial Hospital on May 31, 1918 in Valparaiso, Indiana to Arthur Victor Berquist and Gertrude Margaret (Lewis) Berquist.

Raised in East Chicago, Indiana, attended Harrison and McKinley grade schools and graduated from Roosevelt High School in the Class of 1936. She was a member of the In and About Chicago High School Chorus and Farrar Choral Club of East Chicago. Attended Gary Business College and St. Catherine's School of X-Ray.

Married Max J. Spencer November 25, 1939, had two children, Brian Arthur born Feb. 22, 1942 in St. Catherine's Hospital, East Chicago, IN, and Susan Christine born July 2, 1945 at Illinois Central Hospital, Chicago, IL. The family moved to Crown Point in 1945.

Vivian's first full-time employment was with Edward Valve's Manufacturing Plant in East Chicago. She was Crown Point's Welcome Wagon Hostess for two years. Was employed by the Lake County Tuberculosis Association as medical secretary from 1952 to 1961, was then employed by the Crown Point Community School Corporation from 1961 to 1982 serving as financial secretary at Crown Point High School for twelve years and secretary at Solon Robinson Elementary School for nine years.

Vivian was president of Crown Point Mother's Club, Junior Women's Club and Playcrafters, worked as secretary for Well's Corporation during building fund drive for the United Methodist Church, was Sunday School teacher, and chairman of Wesley Circle of United Methodist Women. She was a member of the General Federation of Women's Club Chorus of Crown Point, Order of the Eastern Star, South Ward PTA, Crown Point Garden Club, Christianheirs of First Methodist Church and Recamier Pinochle Club (with girlhood friends of East Chicago).

by Gerald Born

BLACK – HOMFELD – SORENSEN – BELL
F13

1890 Homfeld home with Queen Anne turret.

John Ernst (Schwartz) 1832-1924 came to America from Germany in 1854. He anglicized his name to Black (Schwartz means Black in German), so Black is the name on his citizenship papers. In 1857, he married Caroline Marie Peters, also a German immigrant (1839-1917). To this union were born: Henry Frederick, William Ernst, Annie Louisa, Charles Edward, Carrie Amelia, Ella Elvina, Hannah Christine and John Matthew.

Wm. Ernst Black of Eagle Creek married Emaline Massey, a schoolteacher of Hebron on Feb. 15, 1888. They began farming on one of his father's farms in Eagle Creek Twp. They purchased some of the land and built a large beautiful Queen Anne style 10 room home with a turret and large front porch. A daughter Mamie Irene was born Sept. 6, 1892. A new barn was built in 1900.

Irene tells of neighbors banning together, going to Cedar Lake or the Kankakee River to cut ice in the winter, hauling it to their ice houses and enjoying it most of the summer. Also, of cutting logs along the Kankakee for winter fuel, hauling on bob-sleds. On these outings, their lunches would be frozen by noontime. Those fabulous Threshermen's Dinners, but oh so much work over a hot cook stove in very hot weather!

Irene attended South Eagle Creek School, sitting around the pot-bellied stove to eat lunch. A water pail and dipper in the hall (no one worried about germs). Spelling bees and box socials were highlights in those years. Later, Irene attended St. Joseph's Seminary in Kankakee and Dixon College in Dixon, Ill., studying piano and art. Painted still life in water colors, also did some China painting. After graduation, she taught private piano lessons in Eagle Creek Twp. On Mar. 12, 1919, she married Frederick Wilhelm Homfeld of Valparaiso. They went by train from Hebron to Chicago for their honeymoon. They began farming the Black farm, her parents Will and Em Black built a home in Crown Point and moved there, as Wm. Black was Lake Co. Assessor from 1906-1930. Emma Black died 11/16/46 and Wm. Black died 2/19/49.

Fred and Irene Homfeld were fortunate to have running water, a bathroom and furnace heat, also soon added a Delco plant which furnished electricity for the house and barn. They had a daughter Dorothy Jean, born 10/15/24. In the wintertime, all the neighbors would help "shovel" the road open to Rt. #53, south of Hebron (4 mi.). St. Rd. #2 was paved in 1930. Rural electrification came in 1936. (Some old records stated that in 1925, farmland was valued at $125.00 per acre.)

During the Depression, tramps were numerous. Irene always gave them a sandwich and a glass of milk. They were coming so often, that Fred started looking for a "tramp sign" and found a pile of stones near the driveway. People told him that was a sign for "food here."

The Homfelds always raised about 500 chickens each year and sold fryers and eggs. Dorothy Jean attended Center School 1930-1938 and Lowell High School 1938-1942. She raised Hampshire Hogs among her various 4-H Club projects, attended Purdue U. and Valparaiso U., then became a bookkeeper-parts lady at the International Harvester Farm Equip. Agency in Lowell. On Feb. 6, 1944, she married her boss, Harold Julion Sorensen of Lowell. On Oct. 29, 1948, they had a daughter, Sue Ann. Harold also had two daughters by a previous marriage. Agnes Ruth, now Mrs. Arthur Studer of Lake Village, and Evelyn June, now Mrs. Leeon Davis of San Antonio, Texas.

Sue Ann attended Oakland School southwest of Lowell, then the implement dealership was sold in 1951. In 1957, the Sorensens built a new home near Lake Village in Newton Co., where Harold was sub-dividing and building homes in a wooded area. Sue attended Lake Village school, then the family moved over along the Tippecanoe River near Argos, In. Sue attended Talma School in Fulton Co., while Harold Sorensen was sub-dividing along the river there. In early 1961, they moved back to Lake Co. to the old Queen Anne family home. The Homfelds had built a new brick home (ranch style), nearby. Sue finished 8th grade at Center School in Eagle Creek Twp., then attended Hebron High School 1962-1966. The Sorenson family built a new brick home across the road in 1963.

In 1951, Fred Homfeld built a private lake and picnic shelter. It's a busy place in summer. Area church, club and reunion groups schedule picnics there, plus youngsters skate and play hockey in winter. In Aug. 1962, Fred joined a People-to-People tour group and flew to Russia, Poland, Hungary and Germany. He took many photos on the trip and later became a popular entertainer for church and community groups in the area, showing his slides and telling of his experiences. Fred Homfeld passed away suddenly on Mar. 8, 1969, just a few days before they would have celebrated their Golden Anniversary.

Dorothy's husband, Harold Sorensen passed away 5/7/77. Dorothy and her daughter, Sue, who worked at a Crown Point bank for 15 years, built an A-frame house on the farm. Sue had an upstairs apartment. Sue Ann Sorensen married Donald Eugene Bell of Hebron on 6/6/81. (Both are avid square dancers, that is how they met.) Don began farming the Homfeld-Sorensen land in the fall of 1981. Mrs. Homfeld moved into the Sorensen A-frame upstairs apartment, and the Bells occupied her ranch-style brick home. In the fall of 1984, the old Queen Anne farmhouse was moved across the field to a new location on the corner of Range Line Rd. and St. Rd. #2. Tragically, an arsonist destroyed it on Feb. 8, 1985! (The beloved birthplace of both Irene and Dorothy.) A new home for the Bells had been planned at the farmstead location. A lovely log home was completed in June 1985.

The Bells now live in the log home at the west end of the lake, and Mrs. Sorensen and her mother, Mrs. Homfeld occupy the brick ranch-style home at the east end of the lake. Mrs. Sorensen sold the A-frame home nearby.

On May 7, 1986, Irene Homfeld was awarded the Hoosier Homestead Award by Gov. Orr of Indiana in a formal ceremony at the Statehouse in Indianapolis. John Black purchased the original farm on Feb. 8, 1886. Part of the land was purchased from him by his son, Wm. Ernst Black, and part was later inherited. Then Irene Black Homfeld eventually inherited the family farm, the only heir. The farm had been in the same family for 100 years!

Mrs. Homfeld will be 96 years old on Sept. 6, 1988. She enjoys crocheting, watching game shows on T.V. and attending various club meetings.

The three generations enjoy many good times together on the old homestead.

by Dorothy Sorensen

BLOESCH, REV. ERNEST AND MARGARET STURM
F14

Ernest Bloesch was born in Switzerland, 1/27/1864, second of eleven children, near Bern. While apprenticing as a commercial gardener, he became converted and entered the theological seminary, graduated and was ordained into the Christian ministry. He came to the United States and served churches in Des Plaines, Ill. (1892) and Freeport, Illinois before coming to Zion Evangelical church in Hanover Township (Dyer, Indiana) in 1917, serving that congregation until his death in 1943.

At the age of 28 he married Margaret Sturm (b. 9/23/1875 – d. 9/20/42), who served with him in church work for 50 years. Rev. & Mrs. Bloesch were parents to 4 boys and 5 girls.

Edward Bloesch (b. 12/28/1893 – d. 2/13), grew up in Freeport, Illinois, attended Elmhurst College to prepare for the ministry at the age of 20. He died shortly before his mother gave birth to their son, Paul.

Also growing up in Freeport, Ill., was son Herbert J. Bloesch (b. 8/30/1898). He also became a minister, serving churches in Seattle, Wash., Bremen, Ind., Monee, Ill., and Chicago – also serving as administrator of St. Paul's House – a retirement home in Chicago. While in Chicago he received an honorary doctors degree from Elmhurst College. In 1928 he married Adele Silberman of Homewood, Ill. Two sons are Dr. Donald Bloesch, theology professor at Dubuque, Iowa, and Dr. Richard Bloesch, head of the choral department at the University of Iowa.

Esther Caroline Bloesch was their first daughter (b. 8/7/1896 – d. 1/5/1990). Married Joseph Riechert of Hanover Township, Ind. in the 1920s. This union was blessed with 2 children, Rev. Herbert Reichert, hospital chaplain in Cleveland, Ohio, and Margaret Reichert Brink of Park Forest, Ill. In 1952 Esther married Arthur Wallmeyer, a cartographer from Chicago.

Lydia Emma Bloesch (b. 1/29/1901) in Freeport, Ill. married August Rinkenberger, a farmer of Dyer, Indiana. They had one daughter Betty Lou Rinkenberger Slack (b. 12/23/27). In 1950 Lydia married Wilhelm Kramer of Brunswick, Indiana, a cabinet maker with the Steel Company in Gary.

Marie Magdeline Bloesch (b. 1/4/1903 – d. 5/1986). Marie taught school in the Schiller School before her marriage to Raymond Seegers of Hanover Township in 1927. Their children, Paul Seegers, President of Centex Corp. of Dallas, Texas – Gerald Geegers, executive with Waste Management of Oak Brook, Ill, and Nancy Seegers Bruich of Libertyville, Ill.

Ruth Grace Bloesch (b. 1/20/1909 – d. 4/1973), worked in the County Extension Office for Lloyd Cutler (agent) until her marriage to Adjutant Russell Webster of the Salvation Army. Their children are Lt. Col. Russell Webster of the U.S. Air Force, Marjorie Webster Geer and Cathy Webster Patterson, both of Valparaiso, Ind.

Margaret Erna Bloesch (b. 12/10/11 – d. 10/85) trained as a nurse at the Evangelical Hospital of Chicago. She married Dr. William Walton, an osteopath in Chicago Heights. Their children, Dr. Mark Walton, practicing in New York City; Steve Walton, a computer programer in Lake Station, Ind., Judy Walton Kinder of Wakeman, Ohio; Bitsy Walton of Chicago Heights, Ill.

Paul Calvin Bloesch (b. 1/13/14) attended Schiller School and High School in Dyer, Ind., Elmhurst College, Eden Theological Seminary and was ordained a minister in the United Church of Christ. Rev. Paul served churches in Minnesota, Oak Park, Ill., and St. John's United Church of Christ in Crown Point, Ind. He is married to Lillian Keller Bloesch from Webster Groves, Missouri. Their children include Cynthia Boester of Westport, Conn., Asst. Executive Director of the Bronx Hospital in New York; Julia Bloesch Wadle, an art teacher in Denver, Colorado; Mary Cusack, Health Store owner in Hot Springs S. Dakota, and Rev. Calvin Bloesch, minister in Marine, Ill.

Walter William Bloesch, (b. 10/17/16 – d. 5/69) also grew up in Hanover Township. Attended Schiller School and Dyer High School, went on to Elmhurst College and Eden Theological Seminary and was also ordained a minister in the United Church of Christ. He served churches in Kansas City, Monee, Ill, and Crystal Lake, Ill. until his death in 1969. He was married to Margaret Davis, a missionary

1921 — Twelve ministers: Paul Mauer; Herbert Bloesch, on the occasion of their ordination. Rev. Silberman; Rev. E. Bloesch, Synod representative; Rev. Gebhardt; Rev. Sam Press; Rev. Hotz; Rev. Gabe; Rev. Horst; Rev. Kurt Seidenberg; Rev. Stommel.

daughter. They have two children — Gail Ossowski, an artist in Portland, Oregon, and Rev. Daniel Bloesch, minister in Round Lake, Ill.

BOHLING, JOHN
F15

John Bohling, well known in the early settlement of Lake County, Indiana, was born in Germany, November 26, 1823, and was reared there to the age of fifteen, when he was brought by his father, Andrew, to America in 1839. (The spelling of the German surname has been found spelt: Bolig, Bolin, Bolen and Bohlin. It was changed to "Bohling" some time after the family's arrival in the new country.)

The Bohlings lived in Joliet, Illinois, for about two years, and in 1841, came to Lake County. It was here as a young man that John met and later married Miss Anna Mary Schillo of Turkey Creek, in Ross Township; oftentimes walking there from St. John Township to visit and court her. Miss Schillo was also born in Germany, and came to America in 1842. They were married February 29, 1844.

John Bohling had bought from the U.S. Government, adjoining land in St. John and Center Townships, and the couple then located on this tract of unimproved land and he gave his attention to it's improvement and cultivation for many decades. John and Anna Mary Bohling had seven children, only four of which lived to maturity:

Magdalen (Bart Schaefer); Susanna (Nicholas Klassen) (Nicholas Maginot Jr.); Joseph (Elizabeth Jourdain); and John George (Lillosa Schmal) (Mary Jourdain).

Over the years Mr. Bohling continued purchasing Lake County land from the Government and his neighboring farmers, increasing his homestead to well over 300 acres. The house and buildings were originally located on John's acreage in Center Township, but later, wanting to reside in St. John Township, the Bohlings built a new house and barns around 1848, across the township line, north of the old Jackson Highway (101st Street). (It is thought that their first home was a log cabin.)

There were also 21 acres of non-adjacent wooded land a mile or so north of the farm, on Bohling Road; the trees of which were frequently cut down to supply firewood to heat their home in the cold months, and also for cooking purposes year round.

Periodically, John and some of the farmers in the area drove their cattle to the stock yards in Chicago, Illinois, following the "Joliet Road" west to Joliet, Illinois, and then continuing north to Chicago. Walking there and back, a journey which has been reported to have taken two weeks to complete.

In 1894, Mr. Bohling deeded a half acre of his farmland, north of the house and barnyard, to St. John Township for the purpose of education — with the stipulation that when the real estate was no longer used for school intent it was to be returned to the family. A one room school house was constructed on the site and continued to be in use until the early 1920's. (John Bohling's grandchildren would later receive part of their education attending this school on their family homestead.)

In their later years John and his wife resided on the Bohling farm with their son John George and his family. John, naturalized in 1847, lived past eighty years of age. Anna Mary died at the age of seventy.

From the 1904 History of Lake County, Indiana, by T.H. Ball. Additional information: Jim Stephen 1989

by Jim Stephen

BOHLING, JOHN GEORGE
F16

John George Bohling (1855-1936)

John George Bohling, a prominent farmer of St. John Township, resided in Lake County, Indiana, all his life and carried on his extensive agriculture operations on the same farm on which he was born, and which his father settled in the early days of the county's existence. He was born October 11, 1855, son of John Bohling and Anna Mary (Schillo) Bohling, and received his early education in the schools of St. John Township.

Mr. Bohling first married on April 27, 1880, to Miss Lillosa Schmal, who was born in the village of St. John, Lake County, February 4, 1857, a daughter of Adam and Margaret Schmal; and a granddaughter of Joseph and Catherine Schmal, who were one of four families that immigrated together from Germany, and settled in St. John Township in September of 1838. Five children were born to John and Lillie Bohling: Clara, 1881-1959 (Frank Bieker); William, 1883-1969 (Agnes Kleine); Eleanor, 1885-1942 (John Hoffman); Norbert, 1888-1954 (Carrie Schaefer); and Joseph, who died as a child. In the mid 1890's, Lillie died at an early age, when the children were still young.

Years later, John married Miss Mary Jourdain, daughter of John Jourdain and Johanna (Klassen) Jourdain, born March 5, 1866. They were united in marriage June 30, 1908.

On his fine farm of one hundred and sixty acres John raised general crops and stock, and was able to extract more than a good living from his fertile soil, so that he ranked among the progressive and representative farmers of the township.

In the early 1900's, John and Mary moved from the Bohling farm to a home in the town of St. John, located on Joliet Street. John's son Norbert, newly married, took over the homestead.

It was at this time that John George Bohling became actively involved in politics and held the position of St. John Township Assessor a number of years. Mr. Bohling entered politics as a Democrat and won the election. Later when he was defeated on the Democratic ticket by an opposing candidate, John then ran for Township Assessor on the opposite ticket, and once again won the election — that time as a Republican.

Mr. Bohling was also a key figure in aiding the community of St. John to be incorporated, and was a member of it's first town board, being selected as the Clerk-Treasurer. He held the office from 1911 to 1914, when he then served on the town of St. John's newly formed school board.

Always known among his neighbors and fellow-citizens as a man of ability and energy and progressive spirit, John so managed his affairs as to gain a substantial place in the world and surround himself with comfortable circumstances.

John George Bohling died in his early eighties, April 16, 1936. Mary died the same year on January 13th. They are buried in the St. John the Evangelist Cemetery, St. John, Indiana.

From the 1904 History of Lake County, Indiana, by T.H. Ball. Additional information: Jim Stephen 1989.

by Jim Stephen

BOHLING, NORBERT
F17

Norbert (1888-1954) and Carrie (1890-1977) (Schaefer) Bohling.

Norbert Frank Bohling tilled the soil of the Bohling farm in St. John Township, Lake County, Indiana, like his father and his grandfather. The staunch German-American was born April 8, 1888, the fourth child of John George and Lillosa (Schmal) Bohling. Being reared on the family farm, he spent his youth in Lake County, and received his education attending the local schools where he was taught the German language as well as English.

As a young man he dated and married Miss Caroline Schaefer, the daughter of a farmer in the town of St. John, Indiana. She was born October 2, 1890, to John Schaefer and Susan (Jourdain) Schaefer. For a number of years when they were children, Carrie and Norbert were neighbors. This was when the John Schaefer family lived on their farm west of the Beaver Dam, land adjoining the Bohling homestead.

Norbert and Carrie were married May 3, 1911, and settled on the Bohling farm. Through the years they had eight children, all born on their one hundred and sixty acre homestead: Adeline (1912), (Harold Weiler); Lawrence (1913), (Alice Keilman); Teresa (1916), (Joseph Stephen); Arnold (1918-1975), (Thelma Granger Knesek); Dorothy (1919), (Clarence Wirtz); Marie (1924), (Paul Coleman); Norbert (1927), (Nell Hogan); and Marjorie (1929), (Loron Carmicheal).

Norbert had a fine herd of dairy cattle. He worked his fields with a steel wheeled "Titan" International Harvester tractor, and later bought a McCormick-Deering, which also had steel wheels. Before mechanized horse-power Norbert plowed the fields like his ancestors with teams of horses, four of which were "Dick" and "Dan," and "Flory" and "Nance."

While Norbert was occupied in the barn or in the fields, Mother Bohling was kept busy with the children and the housekeeping, performing the domestic chores, but she still found time for crocheting and quilting, a couple of diversions she thoroughly enjoyed. Carrie also sewed much of the clothing for the eight children on her pedal-driven "White" sewing machine, a wedding gift from Norbert. As the children became older they joined in the work of the farm, feeding the chickens, milking the cows, pitching the hay, carrying in the woods, gathering the eggs, etc. In the late afternoons when Norbert and the children were "milking," they could be heard singing many a cheerful song all the way out into the barnyard!

From 1915 to 1918, Norbert played the tuba in the St. John Band which gave concerts on Saturdays. He also performed years later in uniform at the Lake County Courthouse Square, Friday and Saturday evenings, and on the 4th of July, at the Fair Grounds.

The head of a happy home, Norbert continued the work of cultivation until 1938, when he sold the farm and moved the family to the town of Crown Point, Indiana. The first few years there the Bohlings rented a house of Pettibone Avenue, and Norbert was a janitor for St. Mary's School. About three years later they relocated across town to Hoffman Street where they bought a home. Through the next decade and into the 1950's, Norbert worked for the Indiana Farm Bureau Co-Op, driving a petroleum truck, and being a pleasant person, he was very much liked and was quite well known in the county.

With the sons and daughters marrying, the Norbert Bohling family continued to grow, and there was quite a houseful when the children and the grandchildren gathered together for the holidays and other occasions.

Norbert enjoyed his favorite sport of fishing as often as he could find some free time to get away to one of the few spots in the area he preferred. Throughout his life he enjoyed in large measure the respect and confidence of his fellow-man. Norbert died at the age of sixty-five in 1954. Carrie lived to be eighty-six years old. She died in 1977. Norbert and Carrie Bohling are buried in St. Mary's Cemetery, Crown Point, Indiana.

by Jim Stephen

BOONE, DAVID
F18

Whether David Boone, the prosecuting attorney of Lake and Porter Counties, is a descendant of Daniel Boone, the courageous Kentuckian, we do not know; but certain it is that he has the same kind of grit and courage possessed by Daniel in his younger days, when the Indians and wolves were howling around. David Boone is a resident of Hammond, and until he was elected, two years ago, to his present office, he practiced law. He is an eloquent pleader before a court. His promise to the people of the two counties, when he was asking them for their suffrage, that should he be elected he would be the prosecutor in reality as well as in name, and that lawbreakers would have to hunt their holes or get nipped, has been made good. He personally conducts all important cases, especially murder cases. So vigorously did he prosecute the murderer, Donahue, that a verdict of murder in the first degree was rendered, and he was sentenced to hang. Governor Hanly commuted the sentence to life imprisonment. A bitter feeling was engendered against Mr. Boone on the part of Donahue's friends, and after receiving a number of threatening letters an unsuccessful attempt was made to blow his house up with dynamite. Mr. Boone is the most tireless, energetic and willing Republican worker in Lake County. He is an eloquent, forceful and logical political speaker.

(Compiled from the Souvenir Album of Lake Co. Ind., Crown Point-Lowell, June 18-19, 1909.)

BORCHERS, HENRY FAMILY
F19

Henry Borchers, the son of John Borchers Sr., was born on March 3, 1832. Henry came to America from Ohndorf, HessenSchaumburg, Hannover, Germany. He married Maria Sophia Jordening on November 19, 1854. She was born on November 26, 1830 to the Phillipp Jordenings of Grossen, Endorf, Hessen-Schaumburg, Germany.

They purchased their first parcel of land, as early as May 21, 1849, for their home and farm on the corner curve, one mile east and immediately south of Kreitzburg, Indiana, on 101st and Calumet Avenue in Section 6. (The buildings stand at present.) On April 15, 1852, they added land to the farm. His brother John Borchers had joined him in this venture.

Henry and Maria's children include: Mary, John III, Phillip, William, Fred, Herman, Sophia, Caroline and Wilhelmina.

Maria married Henry Oldendorf, son of Conrad Oldendorf Sr., on April 8, 1875. (Henry and Maria had no children.) They made their home on the Oldendorf farm on Route 55 (the "Nine Mile Stretch"), midway between Lowell and Crown Point Indiana, directly west of his sister Caroline and her husband August Fischer, Sr.'s farm. (There was a provision for a strip of land so that there was an access drive from one farm to another.) Their neighbors to the north and east, adjoining the farm, was the August and Mayme (Fiegle) Fischer, Jr. farm (the corner of 145th avenue and Grant Street.)

The Henry Borchers family lined up, the barn in the background. Henry Rust is on the left, Maria and daughter, Sophia, wife of Henry Rust, Henry, Sr., and Fred on the mules, and Herman standing in the wagon with the team of horses in 1907.

Henry and Maria sold the farm on November 27, 1897 to her sister Sophia and her husband, Henry Rust, of the Rust Nursery farm of Cedar Creek Twp of Lake County, Indiana.

Fred married Wilhelmina Batterman.

Sophia married Henry Rust on August 29, 1895. Henry and his brother, George Rust Sr., operated the Rust Nursery on Route 55 on the "Nine Mile Stretch." Later, George Sr.'s sons (Bill and Jim) carried on the business.

Caroline Borchers married Conrad Hecht on July 19, 1884.

Herman, who was born December 13, 1870, married Caroline Oldendorf on February 16, 1896. (Caroline, the daughter of Conrad Oldendorf Jr., was born March 17, 1870.) Herman continued to farm on his father's farm. They had three children: Alvina died as an infant on June 3, 1898; Ella was born October 15, 1899; and Emilie was born on August 18, 1902.

Ella (Herman and Caroline's daughter) married Otto Marquardt and resided on Wallace Avenue in Steger, Illinois. His widowed mother lived with them for a time. They owned a gas station and paint store there. There were no children. In later years, Ella and Otto sold their home and business and resided in St. Petersburg, Florida.

Emilie (Herman and Caroline's daughter) married Henry Bohn, and they went on to farm a Thompson farm northwest of Monee, Illinois until their retirement and then resided in her parents home, as Caroline died November 13, 1948 and Herman on December 8, 1955. Later, Emilie and Henry moved to St. Petersburg, Florida and lived several blocks from Ella and Otto. Henry resides there at present. The children of Emilie and Henry include: Gerhardt, Irene and Herman. Gerhardt married Jenette Schlagel and have two daughters, Sharon and Carol. Irene died at age seventeen of polio. Herman (who was named after his grandfather) married Karen and along with two sons, Terry and Mark, lived in Steger. Herman later resided in Florida.

by Mrs. Ralph Oldendorf

BORN, GERALD M.
F20

Gerald M. Born

Gerald Malcolm Born, born May 16, 1936, at St. Margaret's Hospital, Hammond, spent his childhood and school years at Morocco, graduating from high school in 1954. He is the son of John and Gay (Nichols) Born and the grandson of Roscoe and Ella (Stowell) Born and John and Maude (Graves) Nichols. He attended Purdue, Butler and Indiana Universities, having received degrees from Butler (B.A. in history and political science, and religion) and Indiana University (M.A. in library science and history of fine arts).

While still in college he preached in Christian churches at Alaska and Crown Center, Indiana. His first library job was at Columbus, Indiana where he reorganized the Bartholomew County Library and planned a new library building, designed by the world famous architect, I.M. Pei, raising over two million dollars for its construction.

Next he went to the Illinois State Library, Springfield, where he was consultant on new library construction and administered a $2,000,000 a year federal grant that stimulated over 18 million dollars in new library buildings. From there he went to the North Suburban Library System, where he coordinated programs of collection development, audio-visual services and a union catalog. In 1970 he was appointed Executive Secretary of the Public Library Association and the Association of State Library Agencies, two divisions of the American Library Association (ALA) and for the next seven years he was at the decision making center of the library world, administering federal grants for a major survey of public libraries and developing new measures for assessing the use and effectiveness of public libraries.

In 1976 he went on his own as a library consultant. He has done projects for the Oak Forest, Park Forest, Oak Park, and South Stickney Library District. In 1977 he started his own business, Celadon Press, and in 1984 published his own book, *Chinese Jade: An Annotated Bibliography*, which he has sold to research libraries around the world.

Recently, he, with his business partner, Dale A. Nelson, opened an antique shop in Morocco, Indiana. He also does restoration of oil paintings and fine furniture. He is also widely recognized as an astrologer, maintaining one of the largest astrology libraries in the midwest. He has lectured on both coasts and in the South on the subject and uses it in counseling people who are in life-crisis situations. When his friend, Judith Bennett, was killed in an air crash at O'Hare in 1979, he with a group of her friends finished a book she was writing, *Sex Signs, Every Woman's Astrological Guide to Love, Men, Sex, Anger and Personal Power*, which was published by St. Martin's Press, New York in 1980 and since then has been translated into German, French, Italian and Japanese, as well as being serialized in Australia. In 1984 he ran for state representative and lost, but found the political scene fascinating.

His hobby is genealogy and he has traveled to many of the countries of his origins. In 1967 he went to Quantock, County Somerset, England to visit the Stowell house, the Manor of Cothelstone, which came into possession of the Stowells in 1066. He also followed the trail taken by another of his ancestors, Thomas Trowbridge, a wool merchant, who was knighted by Henry VIII for establishing a safe route for bringing wool from the Scottish highlands to Exeter for export. He and his wife lie buried under the floor of the Exeter Cathedral.

The Born family has Swiss roots, having come from the village of Niederbipp, Canton Bern, where records have been found that go back to 1492. Family tradition traces the origins of the family before Switzerland to France and a man by the name of Bertran de Born, a troubadour of the 12th century, who had a reputation for keeping things stirred up between King Henry and his sons. Bertran de Born was a chatelaine from the bishopric of Perigord, lord of a castle called Autafort. He was always at war with his neighbors, the County of Perigord, the Viscount of Limoges, his own brother Constantin, and Richard the Lionhearted when he was Count of Poitiers. He was a good knight, a good warrior, a good courtier of women, a good troubadour, knowledgeable and clever of speech; and he was a man who knew how to make the best of any situation. Whenever he so wished, he could dominate King Henry and his sons, but he always wanted them to be a war with one another — father, son and brother. And he always wanted the kings of France and England to be at war with each other.

Bertrand de Born was born around 1140 and had two brothers, Itier and Constantin, was twice married and had at least five children. His datable poems fall between 1181 and 1197. Richard the Lionhearted was made Count of Poiteirs and Duke of Aquitaine in 1169 and was one of the three oldest sons of Henry II and Eleanor of Aquitaine. The others were Henry the Young King and Geoffrey of Brittany. For his political stirring of the emotions of these leaders, he won the enmity of his arch enemy, Dante Alighieri (1265-1321), who a hundred years later assigned him to the lowest depth of hell for being a sower of discord between the sons of King Henry II in the *Divine Comedy*. He died about 1215 after entering the monastery of Dalon in the order of Citeaux.

The English branch of the family spells the name Bourne, the Scandinavian, Bjorn, while the French still keep the de Born.

by Gerald M. Born

BORN, DR. GORDON AND SUE
F21

Dr. Gordon Stuart Born, born April 26, 1933, Hammond, Indiana spent his formative years at Morocco, graduating from high school in 1951. He is the son of John and Gay (Nichols) Born. He attended Purdue University receiving three degrees, B.S. in Pharmacy, a Masters in Environmental Toxology, and a PhD. in Health Physics.

He married October 5, 1957 at Morocco, Sue Carolyn Cole, who was born March 18, 1933 at Trimble, Tennessee, the daughter of Leeman and Lois (Kelly) Cole. She lived at Gary during her childhood and attended Purdue University where she received her B.A. in Home Economics. After teaching several years at Hobart, she returned for her Masters in Library Science (Indiana University, Bloomington). They have one son, John Erick Born, born April 2, 1968 at Lafayette, who is a senior in the School of Pharmacy at Purdue.

Dr. Born's first job as a Registered Pharmacist was in a pharmacy in Munster, Indiana and later at a medical clinic in Gary. He served on active duty as Detachment Commander of the 395th Evacuation Hospital during the Berlin Crisis and was stationed at El Paso, Texas at William Beaumont General Hospital. He was promoted to the rank of Captain and after discharge returned to Purdue for his advanced degrees. He had taught at Purdue from 1966 to the present, becoming a full professor in 1973, and had been actively engaged in research, using radioactive isotopes to trace the utilization of drugs in the human body. He is the author of over 50 scholarly papers and is now the Radiological Control Officer overseeing the use of radioactive substances in all fields of Purdue's research and the removal of toxic wastes. As a member of the American Pharmaceutical Association, he has gained national recognition for his contributions to nuclear medicine and nuclear pharmacy.

His wife, Sue, is the school librarian at the Murdock Elementary School and has been involved in redesigning the library and installing computers. She is an excellent seamstress and a gourmet cook.

The Borns trace their origins back to Neiderbipp, Canton Bern, Switzerland, where records of the family have been found as far back as 1490. Jacob C. Born (1809-1875), the immigrant ancestor, came to this country about 1833 and went to Fairfield County, Ohio where he married Elizabeth Shoup. He was a mason and all of his sons went into the construction business.

Their son, Emanuel Born (1838-1889), a plasterer, fought in the Civil War and was discharged in 1865. He was born March 17, 1838 in Fairfield, Ohio and on June 27, 1871 married Phoebe M. Gordon at Hardin County, Ohio. She was born May 23, 1849 in Ohio and died September 4, 1883 in Hardin County. They had three children, who survived them, Clinton Born, b. July 12, 1874, Roscoe Conklin Born b. September 19, 1877 and Oscar Born b. June 22, 1882. All of their children were born at Kenton, Hardin County, Ohio. Clinton married May 16, 1900 Myrtle Kudasill and had eight children, Grace, who married Willard Handenshield, Marian, who married Russell Tarlton, Ruth, who married Lester Ledman, all of whom lived at Kenton and a daughter, who married Karl Miller and lived at Byhalia. Besides Roscoe, who is mentioned elsewhere, Oscar Born married Ethel and resided at Belshaw, Indiana, where he was station agent.

The Gordon family for whom Gordon Born was named, trace their beginnings to Joseph Gordon, who was born in Pennsylvania. Sometime before 1820 he moved to Ohio and married Mary Davis of Virginia, who was living in Champaign County at the time. Shortly thereafter they moved to Bellefountaine, Logan County, where Joseph erected one of the earliest, if not the very earliest, buildings. This was a round log cabin on the rear of the lot upon which Boyd's Grocery later stood, and still later a two-story brick building. Gordon occupied this house a little while, and then built the hewed log house on the corner of Cincinnati and Chillicothe streets which remains to this day, in part, covered within and without with dressed boards, and used as a general grocery story. While occupying this building as a residence, Mr. Gordon made use of his first cabin as a stable. He soon parted with the second house, for we find Anthony Ballard occupying it as a place of public entertainment and resort as early as 1822. Gordon then built another log house on the premises, which he sold in a few years to Reuben Arnold. Joseph Gordon was an important local character during the War of 1812. He was a mail carrier. He was faithful, daring and energetic. He sought no shelter, but rode and slept in the forest swarming with hostile Indians, and carried news and information from post to post, and from army to army, his life always fluttering in his hand from the beginning to the end of the war. Such was Joe Gordon, a small, slim, active man, whom pioneers knew well and trusted.

For his acts of courage and daring Joseph Gordon was immortalized in stone, a statue of him on his white horse being carved for display in the Nation's Capitol. His son, Oliver P. Gordon was born ca. 1813-14 in Ohio and married Catherine Beam (Boehme) a native of Maryland, who died April 1, 1894, aged 79y, 11m, 18d. They were married at Tymochtee, Wyandot County, Ohio on July 15, 1838 and had seven children, Nelson V. Mary, Amanda, Joseph, Phoebe M., John and Elizabeth.

by Gerald Born

BORN, JOHN AND GAY
F22

John Born and Gay (Nichols) Born on their wedding day.

John Warren Born was the third child born to Roscoe Conklin and Ella Almeda (Stowell) Born at Rose Lawn, Indiana on November 29, 1904. His father, a telegrapher, worked as station agent for the Monon Railroad at the time. In the fall of 1910 the family moved to Conrad, Indiana, a town built and operated by Jennie M. Conrad, Indiana's richest woman, much as a feudal fifedom on her 5,000 acre ranch. They lived in the newly constructed hotel, which Ella managed and "Ross" was station agent of the new depot on the C.A.S. line (later the New York Central), which was built by Jennie M. Conrad to ship her cattle and the products of her cement block factory to Chicago and the East.

About 1915 the family moved to Raub where John completed his schooling in the country schools of that period. In 1927 he married Sarah Gay Nichols, the daughter of John Livingstone and Clara Maude (Graves) Nichols, with whom he had attended school at Conrad. Her father owned 120 acres just east of town.

In the same year, John, in partnership with Jerry Turner, operated a grocery store at Schererville and in 1928 they moved the store to Griffith, which was starting to grow. During the first days of opening the store they gave away six different patterns of carnival glass dishes, which filled two barrels as premiums. This partnership did not last long and John and Gay, who had been living above the store, felt the effects of the great crash of '29, as did the whole country, and moved into a house at Schneider owned by her parents and John started working at the lumber yard. Gay was in delicate health, a result of the influenza epidemic of 1917-18 and decided in 1931 that California's climate might help her condition and went by train to stay with relatives at Pomona for a few months. John drove his "Model T" Ford to California for her return trip and had 16 flat tires on the round trip. Gay's health improved markedly.

While working at a gas station at Schneider, John met some truckers with the Dealer's Transport Company, who told him of the advantages of their job. Ever restless, he applied to the company and for the next two years drove transport trucks, hauling automobiles to distant points across the country. Their first son, Gordon Stuart Born, was born at St. Margaret's hospital, Hammond, on April 24, 1933.

John rose quickly in the company and soon entered the office force and became general manager of Dealer's Transport. This entailed his traveling a great deal, so Gay and Gordon moved in with her widowed mother, who was living in Mrs. Yott's house at Lake Village, Indiana in 1935. By this time Gay was expecting her second child and after Gerald Malcolm's birth on May 16, 1936 at St. Margaret's Hospital, she moved the family to Morocco, which was the home of her mother's family.

With the advent of World War II, John expected to serve in the army, but his job was adjudged critical to the war effort as the company was transporting war materials. He took an apartment not far from his work and as time and rations allowed spent time with his family living at Morocco.

When Preston T. Tucker organized Tucker Corporation in 1945 to produce the Tucker "Torpedo," a car that was 25 years ahead of its time, John, along with Mr. Bender and Mr. Massey bought stock in the company in hopes of winning a piece of the action. Unfortunately, the major car companies blocked the new venture at every turn, as is so graphically portrayed in the movie, *Tucker*, and they all lost a large sum of money.

Soon after this financial reversal, another event happened that changed John Born's life. His sister, Mary's husband, Cecil, or "Dolly" Minninger, was killed in an auto accident. She requested that he come and run their general store. So he left his job and moved to Schneider to manage the IGA General Store. An experienced meat cutter in his younger days he quickly adapted to the needs of the community. He was quick to extend credit, for he knew how difficult life was in that railroad community. It is a tribute to both him and the people of the community that when he sold the business all but a few dollars of the $10,000 owed him was collected.

Also being near the Kankakee River allowed him to indulge in his favorite hobby, as he was an avid hunter and fisherman. He was also a dedicated card player, pinochle and buck euchre being his favorite games. Gordon worked in the store at one time or another during these years. When John sold the business to Ed LaCroix, he and Johnny Hartwick formed a partnership and ran a store next door for awhile.

When a fishing resort on Mission Lake near his brother, Robert's, tavern and gift shop at Ossippi, Minnesota became available in 1952, he purchased it and moved there and for the next decade did what he most enjoyed, fished and hunted. With failing health it became apparent that he could not continue, so he sold the resort and his properties on Mission and Edwards lakes and returned to Indiana. He died of a heart attack at Brook, Indiana where he had been helping his friend, Ed Pasel, in his grocery store on May 17, 1963, only 58 years of age.

by Gerald M. Born

BORN, ROSCOE AND ELLA
F23

Roscoe Conklin Born was born at Kenton, Hardin County, Ohio September 19, 1877, the son of Emanuel and Phoebe (Gordon) Born, both natives of Ohio. His grandfather, Jacob C. Born (b 1809) emmigrated to this country about 1832 from Niederbipp, Canton Bern, Switzerland where he had been a mason. He settled first in Fairfield County, Ohio, where he married Elizabeth Shoub on September 3, 1835. By 1850 he lived in Kenton Township, Hardin County where he and his wife had the following children, Henry (b 1836), Emanuel (b 1838), Jacob (b 1840), Mary Ann (b 1841), Samuel (b 1842), Caroline (b 1844), Melinda (b 1845), Elizabeth (b 1847), Emily (b 1847), Sarah (b 1848), and Joseph (b 1849). Jacob's will was probated Oct. 1, 1875.

Emanuel Born, born March 17, 1838 took up the building trade, and became a plasterer. He answered the call during the Civil War and was enrolled in Capt. Powell's Company B of the 82nd Regiment of the Ohio Volunteer Infantry on November 11, 1861 and was discharged at Columbus, Ohio on July 30, 1865. At Savannah, Georgia on January 1, 1865 he was struck with a chronic disease, which ultimately resulted in an early death.

After the war Emanuel Born married Phoebe M. Gordon, the daughter of Oliver P. and Catherine A. (Beam/Boehme) Gordon, who was born May 23, 1849 at Logan County Ohio on June 27, 1871 at Kenton, Hardin County, Ohio. They were the parents of five children, all born at Kenton, Jennie (b & d 1872), Clinton (b 1874), Roscoe (b 1877), Halley (b & d 1881), and Oscar (b 1882). Clinton married Myrtle Rudasill and many of his six children stayed around Kenton, Ohio.

Phoebe's father, Oliver B. Gordon was a stage coach driver and caught Catherine Beam's attention by driving his coach into the Beam yard when he was delivering mail. He had the honor of driving Charles Dickens in his coach, when that noted British author made his well publicized trip to the United States, and later became his book agent. Oliver Gordon's father was Joseph Gordon, who gained recognition in the War of 1812 by taking teams of horses to Ft. Meigs and carrying mail and messages through enemy lines while also acting as a spy. A statue of him on his white horse still stands in the Nation's Capitol. Joseph Gordon married Mary Davis of Virginia at Champaign County, Ohio on Jan. 14, 1811.

Phoebe (Gordon) Born died September 4, 1887 at Kenton leaving Emanuel with the three surviving children. Then, he too, died on January 13, 1889 at Kenton. For awhile the children were under the guardianship of their grandfather, Oliver P. Gordon. After his death, they were placed in an orphanage for awhile until Oscar and Roscoe went to live with their aunt, Amanda (Gordon) Rosebrook at Rushsylvania, Ohio and soon Roscoe went to study telegraphy with his uncle, Billy Beam, a son of Obediah and Ann (Bassett) Beam, who lived at Rensselaer, Indiana. William or "Billy" Beam married Katherine Wright and had three boys and three girls, Merle, Madge, Gladys, Hurley, Don and Paul. Roscoe learned a great deal from his uncle and soon was ready for his first job with the Monon Railroad, locating at Rose Lawn, Indiana to be their agent.

While staying with the Stewart Stowell family at Shelby he met his future wife, Ella Almeda Stowell, who had been living with relatives in and around Lowell after the death of her mother, Lestina (Sutzer) Stowell. They were married January 3, 1901 in Lake County, Indiana. They lived at Rose Lawn when three of their four children were born, Mary Martha (b 1902), Myron Emanuel (b 1903), John Warren (b 1904). While at Rose Lawn he handled the shipping of cattle for Jennie M. Conrad, Indiana's richest woman, who was

Mary Born and parents Roscoe Born and Ella (Stowell) Born.

building a new town on what would later be the New York Central line. She persuaded him to come work for her and to occupy the new depot that she had recently constructed. She also provided him a place to live in her new 14-room motel, provided that his wife would manage it and also teach Sunday School. The family moved to Conrad about 1910, and stayed until their oldest son, Myron, was ready for high school and then moved to Raub to be station agent there where Myron could attend Ambia High School. Their youngest son, Robert Oliver, was born at Conrad in 1910.

The family moved to Schneider, Indiana before the Second World War and Roscoe, or "Shorty" or "Ross" as they called him worked in the switch tower. Ella (Stowell) Born died August 30, 1926 in Lake County. "Ross" Born then married Mary Mitchum, who lived at Ambia, and he died there on September 10, 1942. Both Ross and Ella are buried not far from her parents in the Sanders Cemetery, West Creek Township.

Mary M. Born married Cecil Earl or "Dolly" Minninger on May 15, 1926 and they operated a general store and post office at Schneider until his accidental death in 1947, when the car in which members of the volunteer fire department were riding was hit by a train. John Born married Sarah Gay Nichols on July 11, 1927. He was working for the Dealer's Transport Company as their manager when "Dolly" Minninger was killed. Soon after John came to Schneider to operate the store. Myron or "Mike" Born married Lydia Cora Kuhn on June 17, 1925 and they lived at Chicago, where he was a steel salesman. Robert or "Tuffy" Born served on the Italian front during World War II and married Florence Kuhn, a niece of Lydia, and operated a tavern and gift shop near Deerfield Minnesota.

by Gerald M. Born

BOWSER, ARTHUR J.
F24

Arthur J. Bowser was born at Valparaiso in 1862. He was educated at St. Paul's Academy, Valparaiso High School and Valparaiso Normal. He learned the printers' trade and newspaper business in Springfield, Ill., and in Grand Rapids, Mich. He engaged at once in his chosen profession, and started Valparaiso's first daily in 1882 — the *Daily Advertiser*. He started the *Vidette* in 1883, and the *Chesterton Tribune* in 1884, of which he is still the progressive editor and genial proprietor. In 1893-4 he was receiver for the Porter Land Company and American Brass Company, with the Chicago offices, and paid out dollar for dollar from what had been considered hopeless assets. He was made reading clerk of the Indiana Senate in 1889, an office which Senator Beveridge had held ten years before, and from which he was elected U.S. Senator. Mr. Bowser served four years in the county council. During his term in this office Porter County's tax was reduced twenty-five cents lower than ever before. His public career has been clean throughout. He is now candidate for Joint Representative of Porter and Lake Counties on the Republican ticket. He was married in 1882 to Nettie Drago, by whom he is the happy father of three bright children: Theresa, Frances and Arthur J., Jr.

(Compiled from the Souvenir Album of Lake Co. Inc., Crown Point-Lowell, June 18-19, 1909.)

BRIDGE, W. F.
F25

W.F. Bridge, surveyor of Lake County, living at Hammond, Ind., was born in Carroll County in 1884. After graduation from high school he attended Wabash College. He spent four years in the State of Colorado making land surveys, platting towns, and being engaged in mining engineering; then came back, and located in Hammond in 1890, where he has been active in his chosen line ever since. He has served a number of years as city engineer for Hammond and has done a large share of the work in laying out the neighbor cities of East Chicago and Whiting. He was one of the board of police commissioners of Hammond appointed by Governor Durbin and served in this capacity from 1901 to 1903, when he resigned. He has been secretary of the Commercial Club of Hammond and one of its directors since its organization. He is affiliated with the following orders: Masons, K. of P., Elks and National Union.

(Compiled from the Souvenir Album of Lake Co. Ind., Crown Point-Lowell, June 18-19, 1909.)

BROWN FAMILY
F26

The Jeremiah Brown family (Picture taken about 1902 or 1904). Jeremiah Frank, Sarah Jane, Everett, John, Frank William, Edward, Lotis, Charlie and baby's name Pearl or Anna.

Jeremiah Brown was born October 22, 1817 in Indiana. His parents came from North Carolina. He was a farmer and lived his life in Washington County, Indiana. He married Susannah Jones September 21, 1837 who was born March 22, 1815. Their children were: Hannah 1838, Sarah 1841, Mary 1843, Infant son 1845, Michael 1845, Wylie 1846, Henry 1848, William Marion 1850, Amanda W. 1852, and Susannah 1854, Jeremiah Franklin 1857. Jeremiah died February 26, 1888 and Susannah August 4, 1879, buried in the Curtis-Morgan Cemetery in South Boston, Washington County, Indiana.

Jeremiah Franklin born August 8, 1857 Washington County, Indiana married Anna Moore Hardy December 10, 1891 Washington County, Indiana. She was born in 1860 and died from a horse accident January 25, 1892. Jeremiah Franklin then married his wife's daughter Sarah Jane Moore March 6, 1892, she was born April 2, 1877 and died November 13, 1940, Jeffersonville, Clark County, Indiana. Jeremiah Franklin died December 22, 1905. From this marriage 8 children were born: Everett May 1893, Lotus July 1894, John E., February 1896, Frank William, May 28, 1897, Edward Lee, October 1898, Charlie, May 7, 1900, Daughter (Pearl)? 1902, Anna Belle, February 16, 1904. After Jeremiah Franklin died Sarah Jane married William Schellers April 5, 1909 Clark County, Indiana, two daughters from this family: Clara Elizabeth, August 1, 1910 and Olive May, April 1, 1914. The boys were put in a Jeffersonville, In. orphanage. A Mr. William Haymond brought Frank William from the orphanage to Valparaiso to work on the farm. When he was older Frank William was in the Service, Co. L in Valparaiso (42nd Batt. Michigan). September 28, 1921 he married Ruth Clara Spohn born June 27, 1900, died January 9, 1936 and buried in Ridge Lawn Cemetery in Gary, In. Frank and Ruth had 7 children: Katherine, Frank William Jr., Alvin, Harry, Doris, Donna, and Carroll. Lived in East Chicago, Gary, Hessville, Hobart, Wheeler. Frank William worked for Youngstown Sheet and Tube Co. Retired and moved to Otisco, Indiana. Died in Jeffersonville, Indiana January 28, 1968 and buried in Walnut Hill Cemetery, Jeffersonville, Indiana. (See Spohn-Brown)

by Lois Brown

BROWN, ASA PACE
F27

Asa Pace Brown was born March 2, 1834 in Monroe Township, Luzerne County, Pennsylvania, a son of Severn and Elizabeth (Pace) Brown. This family left Pennsylvania and came to Indiana, where Nancy P. Brown (1836-1930), a daughter of Severn and Elizabeth, was married to John D. Wilson (1829-1895) in Lake County December 11, 1853. To their union were born six children: Edmund L., a clerk of Porter County, and later contractor, builder, with his brother J.H. Wilson, of the Central school; Rachel, Mrs. E.F. Van Ness; John Hilen, who was Deputy County Clerk; Emma J., Mrs. Charles E. McKeehan; William; and Frank S. who died in infancy. John D. Wilson was the general contractor on the Porter County court house at the time of its erection in 1883-4.

Asa P. Brown was married in Valparaiso, Indiana December 5, 1865 to Jane M. Maxwell, who was born March 3, 1848 in Centerville, Lake County, Ohio, on the banks of Lake Erie. Asa and Jane lived in Hobart, Lake County, Indiana for four years. They then moved to Chetopa, Labette County, Kansas, remaining there for ten years. They left Kansas in 1880, driving 30 head of cattle to Colorado and up back of Pikes Peak to Four Mile, then later to Fountain Creek, Colorado. They were living in Colorado City in 1880, in Fountain, Colorado in

59

1882, later in Delta and Brookside, and Canon City, Colorado, in 1895, before eventually reaching Seattle, Washington, and later California.

Asa and Jane Brown had four children: (1) Netta Permelia was born September 14, 1866 in Hobart, Lake County, Indiana. Her first marriage was to Robert Koppe on February 19, 1886. This marriage ended in divorce and Netta married a second time to Jacob Frederic Schaufele on May 27, 1910; (2) Willard W. was born in Hobart on June 7, 1868 and died January 20, 1895 at Canon City, Colorado; (3) Franklin Grant born August 20, 1870 at Chetopa, Labette County, Kansas married Emma Lewetta Ward on July 3, 1912. Franklin died May 14, 1959; (4) Mary Grace born December 15, 1882 at Fountain, El Paso County, Colorado married first to John Wise Siefert on December 15, 1904, and second to William Andrew McBeth. Mary died September 29, 1976.

Asa Pace Brown served during the Civil war in Company "E" 9th Regiment of Indiana Infantry Volunteers, for which he later received a pension. Asa died January 9, 1913 at Pasadena, Los Angeles County, California.

The last two years of her life Jane lived in the home of her granddaughter, Mrs. Clara M. Dutton. Clara took care of her grandmother at her residence in Placentia, California, where Jane died on February 15, 1929.

by Betty L. Williams

BROWN, CARROLL AND LOIS JEAN
F28

Carroll Gene Brown born November 19, 1934 Hobart, Indiana to Frank William Brown and Ruth Clara Spohn. Frank's parents, Jeremiah Frank Brown and Sara Jane Moore of Washington County, Indiana. Ruth's parents Sylvan Sinclair Spohn and Minnie Warren Miller of Adams County, Ohio and Valparaiso, Indiana. Carroll had three brothers and three sisters: Katherine, Frank Jr., Alvin, Harry, Doris, and Donna. At the age of thirteen months his mother died and when he was about two years old his Aunt (sister of his father) Anna Belle and her husband Horace G. Burger of Indianapolis raised him and a son of their own Horace Jr. Carroll graduated from Ben Davis High School in 1955. On June 30, 1956 he married Lois Jean Helms born June 26, 1938 Indianapolis, Indiana. Her parents Cash Lawson Helms and Mary Elizabeth Cobb, sister Linda Kay and brothers Gerald William and Larry Lawson. Graduated from Lawrence High School, Lawrence, Indiana in 1956. Married in the East 38th Street Christian Church in Indianapolis. Moved to Gary, Indiana in 1956, also lived in Hammond and Whiting. Worked at East Chicago National Bank. Carroll worked for the steel mills, Youngstown Sheet and Tube Company. Moved back to Indianapolis in 1959. Carroll works for Indianapolis Power and Light Company and Lois works for Sears Roebuck. Two children: Natalie Sue born January 21, 1960 and Lance William born February 6, 1962. Natalie married Marshall Aldwin Day III, one daughter Gretchen Michelle born April 11, 1982, San Antonio, Texas. Lance married August 23, 1986 Mary Adele Lobraico born September 24, 1958 and lives in Indianapolis.

by Lois Brown

BROWN, JOHN
F29

John Brown, 5th Indiana Cavalry (Courtesy Court House Museum, Crown Point).

John Brown was born in Lake County in 1840. He was one of the first babies born to settlers, who had emigrated from Schenectady, New York. Young John was named for a grandfather who had served as a Major in the War of 1812. The name was prophetic, for John turned out to be quite a warrior himself.

When he was nine a runaway horse and wagon killed his father who left a widow and five children. John was the eldest boy.

John farmed until September, 1862 when he enlisted in Company I of the Fifth Indiana Cavalry as a Private. He was tall for the time, just under six feet, with auburn colored hair according to the records.

That winter the company from Lake County was sent to Rising Sun, Indiana, ostensibly to prevent Confederate raids across the Ohio River. Since there weren't any raids at the time, and since much of southern Indiana sympathized with the Confederate cause, the northern Hoosiers began persecuting their southern leaning brethren, and before long . . . "almost anyone else in the region."

Soon the regiment was united and waged warfare in middle Kentucky where they were ably led and most effective.

Confederate General John Morgan raided through Indiana and Ohio in the summer of 1863, and the Fifth was sent after him on July Fourth, the same day John Brown was promoted to Sergeant.

Morgan was finally chased down in Ohio at Buffington Island while trying to ford his army over the Ohio River. Although many units of the Union Army had congregated upon Morgan, it was Company I of the Fifth Indiana that attacked and struck the first blow at Buffington Island.

The next campaign was for Knoxville and East Tennessee. The Fifth was the first regiment to ride triumphantly into Knoxville amid the cheers of the population, for many of its citizens were of the Union persuasion. Campaigning in East Tennessee was arduous, however. When it was finally over that winter, they withdrew across the mountains back into Kentucky. Many of their horses were dead or played out and more than a few men were barefoot, and ragged as they subsisted on quarter rations in the long trek through the snow-covered mountains.

The next summer the Fifth was sent into Georgia in the campaign for Atlanta. They operated most effectively and sustained surprisingly few casualties. A dispatch from an Inspector General mentions them as an elite unit.

General George Stoneman led his whole calvary division deep into Georgia that summer on a raid to disrupt communications and free the Union prisoners at the Prisoner-of-war camp at Andersonville. While somewhat successful wrecking railroad and supply depots, Stoneman rode into a trap at a place called Sunshine Church. The Fifth Indiana held off the enemy while the remainder of Stoneman's force fled. Eventually, when they were down to their last bullets, Stoneman ordered them to surrender. Colonel Thomas Butler, who led the Fifth, proposed that they cut their way out of the encirclement with "Cold steel". (Sabers) Stoneman's will was broken, however, and the entire regiment went into captivity.

John Brown spent the remainder of the war under deplorable conditions at Andersonville.

Home after the war John successfully ran for Treasurer of Lake County. He also served as Auditor, and helped found the First National Bank of Crown Point, later serving as president.

John Brown died in 1924 at the age of eighty-four, one of the most respected men in the county.

by Mr. John R. Sickles

The Brown's – Carroll, Lois, Lance William and Natalie Sue

BUCKLEY FAMILY
F30

Irish immigrants Dennis and Catherine Buckley, along with their five children, fled the Potatoe Famine in the mid-1800's. The Buckley children were William, John, Patrick, an infant son who died on the trip coming over, and a daughter, Julia. The Buckley family entered the U.S. at Ellis Island, in upper New York Bay, and traveled to the Lowell area to be near friends and relatives, the Driscoll family.

Dennis Buckley purchased the original 80 acre homestead for 50¢ per acre from soldiers who had received land grants after the war. Dennis built his cabin just west of the present home on the Buckley farm. Thrilled about being a landowner, Dennis worked hard on his land, and probably died from overwork, for he died in 1851 at the age of 45. Catherine Fleming Buckley, born in 1804, died in 1858.

The oldest Buckley son, William, was born in 1828. William worked by the month as a farm hand and also as a builder for Mr. Halsted, the founder of Lowell.

When his father died, William became the head of the family, ruled with a heavy hand, and divided the land among his brothers and sister. His mother lived with him on the farm west of the homestead. William suggested to his mother that she donate land for a school house and soon the Buckley School was erected, before 1858.

For several years William farmed with his brothers John and Patrick, and for sometime engaged in farming alone. In 1897, he retired from farming and moved into Lowell.

Patrick Buckley, born in 1841, was 8 years old when the family arrived in the U.S. He was a soldier in the Civil War, serving with the Indiana Volunteers from November 1864 to the end of the war in 1865. Patrick was a progressive and successful farmer. Patrick and his wife farmed just north of the Homestead with their home at the corner of Hendricks Street and State Route 2.

Julia, the only Buckley daughter was born in 1831. She married Patrick Feeley, who was a farmer in Cedar Creek Township. The Feeley farm was south of the Buckley Homestead. Julia died in 1915.

John Buckley was born in 1835. He died in 1918. He farmed with his brothers, then later bought them out. In the early 1850's, he built the house on the Buckley Homestead.

John married Harriet Dewitt and they became the parents of four daughters and one son. John raised beef cattle and grain on the old homestead. About 1894 John moved to Lowell and his son Charles took over the Homestead raising Holstein cattle and sending the milk to Chicago. The large white pine on the lawn in front of the house was planted by Harriet Buckley, John's wife, soon after the house was built.

Charles married Alta M. Garrison in 1861 and they became the parents of five children: Irene, Gladys, Rose, Archie, and Gerald. None of these children had any children of their own.

When the last three children were living, they decided to donate 160 acres of the homestead to the Lake County Park and Recreation Department. Rose made the actual donation in 1977. The farm is now a living history farm open to the public for all to enjoy.

BUEHRE, OTTO FAMILY
F31

Otto Buehre, born January 20, 1825 in Riepen, Rodenburg, Churhessen, Germany along with his wife Wilhelmine (who was born August 9, 1834 in Idensen, a Province of Hannover, Germany) arrived in New York on May 12, 1851 on the *Bark Emma*. Also on the voyage were Wilhelmine's parents, Conrad and Engel Maria (Wassmann) Oldendorf Sr.; her grandmother Katharine Oldendorf (widowed); and her uncle (Engle Maria's brother) Henry Wassman and his family.

Otto and Wilhelmina settled in Hanover Township in Lake County Indiana. They filed their first land claim in 1851. On November 11, 1853, they filed their second claim for land they purchased from Fred Norton. Both claims were filed for land in Section 12. Their property was located on the north side of 113th Avenue. (In 1859, the Zion United Church of Christ, known then as the Zion Evangelical and Reformed Church and often referred to as the Hanover Prairie Church, was built to the east of the Buehre home on a five acre corner of property obtained from the Buehre's.)

Otto and Wilhelmine's children include: Otto Jr. who was born on August 20, 1860; Maria who was born in 1863; Wilhelmina who was born on July 23, 1865; Henry who was born on October 13, 1867; John who was born in 1870; and Louise who was born on June 15, 1873. Several more died in infancy. Otto died in 1895 and Mina died in 1901. They are buried at the Zion United Church of Christ cemetery.

Most of the family members decided to move to the west near Wells, Minnesota; to follow other relatives already established there. In the meantime, John, Otto and Wilhelmine's son, and his wife Mary (Bock) continued to farm the Buehre farm until 1923, when they moved near Wells, Minnesota to live near their relatives. They are buried there. None of their three children survived. Sylvia, born December 31, 1894 was two and one-half years old when she died; Bernard, born in 1901, was three and one-half years old when he died; and Johannes, born in 1906, died an infant.

Louise Buehre married Theodore Elting on March 3, 1892. Their children included: Albert who was born May 18, 1902 and died at 2 months; Carl who was born on March 10, 1896 and died on January 24, 1911; August who was born on June 1, 1893; and Edwin who was born on March 20, 1897.

Theodore Elting's grandfather was Gerhardt Elting who was born February 1, 1794 in the province of Hannover, Germany. John Elting, Theodore's father, and his wife Dorothy had four children: Anna, Henry, Louise, and Theodore. John and Dorothy purchased land in Hanover Township in Lake County Indiana as early as 1853. The corner of White Oak Avenue on Road 8, known now as Route 231 remained in the Elting family until they left to farm in Nebraska.

In 1986, Orval and Don Elting from Davenport, Nebraska, two brothers who are descendants of the Elting family, visited relatives, obtained photos and information on the family, and also gathered souvenirs of the remaining foundations. (They said that many Elting families reside in the area around Davenport, Nebraska and that they themselves, at the time, farm 2,000 acres in that area.)

The Elting farm was later owned and rented out by Ben Maas, who lived in Grant Park, Illinois, and then by Alfred Monix. The barn burned through vandalism and the rest of the buildings removed for the growth spread of home building south west of St. John, Indiana.

by Mrs. Oldendorf

Otto and Wilhelmina (Oldendorf) Buehre standing in front of their home. Circa 1885.

BURCH, MARY (KLEINER)   F32

Mary Anna "Mamie" (Kleiner) Burch

My mother Mary Anna Walburga ("Mamie," "Mame," or "May") Kleiner was born 22 July 1883 in Chicago. She lived in many different Chicago neighborhoods, in Hegewisch, IL, and briefly in Passaic, NJ before moving to East Chicago.

She was the elder of 2 children of Benedikt Kleiner, an immigrant from Germany, and Caroline Mathy Kleiner. Benedikt died of typhoid fever when mother was 8. Her mother then supported the family by operating a candy store. When my mother was 12, her mother married Henry Jaik, also a German immigrant.

Caroline and Henry had 3 daughters, whom my mother loved and cared for as if they were her own sister. She worked as a clerk in stores in the Loop and as a hired girl, which was the term used to denote a cook and housekeeper. She could earn a larger salary working in a store but had expenses, such as streetcar fare, that she didn't have while working and living in someone's home. She also worked as a cook in a boarding house in Hegewisch owned by R.H. and Julia Alexander.

In 1914, she was working in a grocery and butcher shop operated by two of her cousins. My mother witnessed an accident in which one cousin was injured and the other possibly at fault. In order not to be forced to testify on either cousin's behalf against the other, she went to Passaic, NJ with a friend who obtained a job for her with friends of his. She was highly respected by the couple and loved by the children. We visited the family 30 years later, and she was welcomed as a dear friend.

In 1916, she returned home and began working for the Alexanders again, this time in the Reiland Hotel in East Chicago. She was chief cook and baker with 2 or 3 immigrant girls working under her. She baked enough bread and pies to use a barrel of flour each week. The hotel had about 35 residents, but over 100 men ate there each day. These men came to East Chicago without their families to work in the new mills. They ate breakfast and were given a lunch to take with them to work and then came back for supper.

Mamie was about 35 at this time. Groceries for the boarding house were delivered from W.R. Diamond's store by Bert Burch, a widower of 52, who had 2 teenage daughters. These brief and practical meetings over groceries led to friendship, courtship, and marriage.

Mamie and Bert were married on 20 June 1918. About 3 years later, Bert went to work for the Sinclair Refinery on Indianapolis Blvd. They were childless until 4 May 1923 when my sister Margaret Helen was born. I was born 7 November 1924. My sister and I attended Harrison Elementary School and Roosevelt High School. She later married Peter Michael Kelly of Chicago and moved to Hinsdale, IL.

My father died in 1953 at age 86, but my mother lived until 1964, dying at 81. She was a vigorous, kind, generous, and humorous woman, always interested in current events, the arts, and her family and neighbors. She was independent in her thinking and did not necessarily follow the crowd.

During World War II, for example, she attended a ladies club meeting during which the other women said that life was cheap among the Japanese and mothers didn't care if their sons were killed in the war. My mother disagreed, saying, "They care. A mother is a mother."

When there was a death in the neighborhood, other women would take a cake to the bereaved family. My mother would take a big pot of stew to them. My mother and her sisters were great story tellers. She told us many incidents of her working days, many anecdotes beginning "When I was in Passaic, NJ," and stories of problem-solving. Recalling her independent thinking, her attitudes toward women and men, and her pride in being able to vote has made me realize that she was a feminist long before my generation started a new wave of feminism.

I stayed at home with my mother until her death and then began a teaching career that lasted until 1982. I earned a Bachelor's degree from Calumet College in 1964 and a Master's in English from DePaul in 1967. After teaching at Calumet College from 1964 to 1967, I taught at the College of New England in Biddeford, ME for one year.

In 1968, I went to the University of Minnesota to get a doctorate in American Studies, and I have lived in MN since except for one school year in Ashland, WI. In 1981, I joined the staff of the Minnesota Legislature as a media writer. I retired from the Legislature in 1988 and now engage in volunteer activities and research and writing in women's history, immigration history, and family history.

by Betty Ann Burch

BURCH, NATHAN ALBERTUS "BERT"   F33

Nathan Albertus (Bert) Burch, 1866-1953.

My father Nathan Albertus "Bert" Burch lived in East Chicago about 45 years. He was born 26 December 1866 in Marshall County, IN. He farmed and later worked for a general store. His work included selling groceries from a wagon.

15 March 1896, he married Mamie Pogue in Moreland, GA. He brought his bride back to Marshall County. They had 2 children while living there. Thelma was born on 6 April 1897 and Lora on 17 October 1899. Bert and his family moved to East Chicago ca. 1906. He worked for W.R. Diamond as a grocery clerk. Diamond's store on Chicago Avenue was either the first or second grocery store in East Chicago. W.R. "Will" Diamond was the husband of Elsie Maxey, my father's cousin. In those days, and up until the 30s, a person could phone a grocery store, give an order, and have it delivered. Delivering those orders was part of my father's job.

Another son, William Cecil, was born in East Chicago on 25 May 1909. In August 1911, Mamie became ill and went to Plymouth, IN with the children to stay with her mother. She died in Plymouth the following January 28. Bert let Mamie's sister Minnie and her husband William Reiter adopt William on 27 February 1912. He was always known as William Burch Reiter. My father later regretted his hasty decision to allow his son to be adopted.

Bert's grocery route in East Chicago included the Reiland Hotel, a small hotel and boarding house at Chicago Avenue and Olcott, owned by Robert H. and Julia Alexander. The chief cook was Mary Anna "Mamie" Kleiner. Bert and Mamie became acquainted, dated, and were married on 20 January 1918. By this time, both of Bert's daughters had returned to East Chicago. Thelma had married Raymond

M. Jones, who was serving in the U.S. Army. Lora was working as a stenographer at Central High School. Lora later married Robert Stirling and in the early 30s moved to Washington, D.C. They had 3 children, Dean, Mary Jane, and Lora May. Thelma and R.M. Jones later lived in Whiting with their sons, John Calvin "Jack" who died in 1968 and Charles Richard "Dick" who lives in the Washington area. I was born on 4 May 1923, and my sister Betty Ann was born on 7 November 1924.

In about 1921, my father began working as a pumper at the Sinclair Oil Refinery on Indianapolis Blvd. During the Depression, my father never lost his job, although his work days were cut to 4 days one week and 3 the next. Sinclair kept its men on in this way rather than laying off some and keeping others on full time. About 1931 or 1932, Bert became ill and was home and on a special diet for about 9 months. Sinclair paid his wages for a few weeks and then stopped but promised he could return to work when able.

We knew people who went on welfare and received flour, rice, and other foodstuffs. Our family did not go on welfare, so we ran up bills at two grocery stores and the East Chicago Dairy. Art Schaler had taken over Diamond's store, where we continued to trade, and we also traded at Peterson's grocery. My mother borrowed money from Ray Jones and her youngest sister. When my father returned to work, my mother paid the bills first and then repaid family members who had helped us.

My father occupied himself with carpentry, home repairs, lawn care, and gardening. He renewed his early interest in photography when my sister and I took up photography in our teen years. He built a darkroom for us in the basement, which we made great use of while we were in high school. I graduated from Roosevelt High School in 1941 at which time my father retired at age 75.

In late summer 1941, I went to work as a bookkeeper for John F. Rahn, Inc., a building contractor at 500 W. 150th St. I worked there until shortly before the birth of my first child.

I married Peter Michael Kelly of Chicago on 21 August 1948 and later moved to Hinsdale, IL, where I still live. I have 6 children. Michael Burch Kelly lives in Libertyville, IL with his wife and 4 children. Donald, founding member, Boston Haiku Society, lives in Boston. Margaret Ann "Peggy" Kelly, a graphic artist, lives in Chicago. Kevin, an attorney, lives in Independence, MO with his wife Cindy Edwards, also an attorney. Kathleen, researcher in an executive search firm, lives in Minneapolis, MN. Sharon recently graduated from Southern Illinois University and also lives in Minneapolis.

My father lived for 12 years after his retirement. He died 22 January 1953, age 86. He is buried in Oak Hill Cemetery, Plymouth, IN next to his first wife, Mamie Pogue.

by Margaret Burch Kelly

CAMPBELL, DORRIS W.
F34

The first known ancestor of Dorris W. Campbell to arrive in America was Archibald Campbell, who came from Scotland and arrived in Lancaster County, Pennsylvania in 1700. He died there in 1738. Archibald's son Malcolm, moved south to Big Lick, Virginia (Roanoke) and lived there until he and his eldest son Archie were killed by Indians in 1763. Another son, William married Elizabeth McPheeters and produced 7 children. They gave their second eldest son William four hundred acres of land in the western country. Young William married Susannah in 1795 and they moved south from Big Lick through Cumberland Gap to their inherited land in Clark County, Kentucky. They traveled on horseback as there were no wagon roads through the Gap. William and Susannah had 6 children. In 1806 they moved by covered wagon to Gassaway, Tennessee. When William was 77 years old, Susannah had passed away previously, he married Susan Pelham age 32. His children objected to the marriage and tried to have him declared insane and committed to the asylum. The case was taken to the Tennessee Supreme Court and William won. He left all his property to his wife and at her death to the Methodist Church; he died in 1859 at the age of 85. William's grandson Robert Nathaniel Campbell fought for the Confederacy during the Civil War. Samuel L. George, my maternal great grandfather fought for the Union. After the Civil War ended hard feelings slowly died away with each generation until in May, 1928 Medford D. Campbell married Nina B. George. Medford was number 12 of the 21 children of Daniel S. and Minnie (Parker) Campbell. Medford and Nina had 9 children, 3 died shortly after birth. There were very few jobs during the depression so Medford worked at whatever was available, mostly farming. When World War II started war workers were in great demand and everyone said "Go to Hammond or East Chicago, Indiana." So, Medford, 5 of his brothers, 1 sister, his inlaws and their families moved to Hammond in 1942. They worked at several war plants: Metals Refinery, LaSalle Steel, Graver Tank, Superheater, Inland & Republic Steel and Pullman Standard were some of the more vital. After the war ended the factories converted to peace time operations and there were plenty of jobs, so everyone stayed in the area.

Dorris W. Campbell, second son of Medford and Nina Campbell, was born June 10, 1930 in Gassaway, Tennessee. He attended school in Tennessee until 1942 when the family moved to Hammond. Attended Lincoln Elementary, Washington Irving and graduated from Hammond Technical Vocational High School in 1948. He married Betty Louise Hlatko, daughter of Joseph and Gertrude Hlatko, on August 12, 1950. Betty attended school at Riverside, Columbia and Hammond Tech. She was born October 27, 1933 in Whiting, Indiana and moved to Hammond when she was 2 years old. She lived in Hammond until 1969 and then moved to Dyer, Indiana. Dorris and Betty have 4 children: Gail Diane, born September 8, 1952, attended school at Wilson, Edison and Gavit in Hammond and Lake Central High School in St. John, then Purdue University in Hammond. She married John Lesniewski of Schererville and they have four sons: Christopher John, Scott Joseph, Ryan Daniel and Cory Andrew. They live in Crown Point, Indiana. Daniel Keith, born September 5, 1955, attended school at Wilson and Gavit in Hammond, and Kahler in Dyer and Lake Central. He married Linda Howard of St. John and they have 2 sons: Daniel Christopher and Shawn Michael. They live in Green Acres, Florida. Cynthia Sue, born February 14, 1959, attended school at Wilson in Hammond, Kolling in St. John, Kahler and Lake Central. She married Samuel Calabrese Jr. of Hammond and had 2 sons: Samuel Anthony III and Brandon Michael. Cynthia and sons live in Dyer, Indiana. David Joseph, born April 20, 1964, attended school at Kolling, Grimmer, and Lake Central. David is unmarried and lives in Dyer, IN. Dorris started work for the Erie Railroad in 1950 and continued there until the Erie became part of Conrail on April 1, 1976. All the Erie trackage in Lake County was abandoned at that time and traffic was diverted over the former Penn Central tracks near the lake front.

by Dorris W. Campbell

CANINO, CARMELLO AND LOUISE
F35

Carmello and Louise with daughter Josephine

Early Residents

Louise Abasta was born on August 12, 1871, in Calabria, Italy. She married Carmello (Charles) Canino and with their oldest child, Josephine, immigrated to the United States. The family took up residence in New Orleans, where they established a grocery store on the corner of Fern and Olive Streets in the heart of the city. Carmello and Louise had eleven children.

Josephine Canino was born on December 24, 1890, in Calabria, Italy. Family legend says that Josephine was a delightful toddler on the ship to America, romping playfully on the deck. Josephine completed grammar school in New Orleans.

The other Canino children were born in New Orleans. Rose Canino was born on June 22, 1898; she married and moved to Portland Oregon where she spent the remainder of her life. A son, Paul E. Lybarger, currently resides in Portland. Rose died on March 9, 1971.

Anthony Canino was born on March 21,

Pictured: Four Generations of Daughters: Louise Canino, Josephine Centanni, Lillian Schulties and Charlotte Schulties.

1902. He married Bessie Nitchman. They had one son, Robert Canino, who currently resides in California. Anthony was a Bantam weight Prize Fighter who was known as "Jack Kennedy" throughout the Lake County, Indiana area. Anthony died on July 30, 1953, in Allens Park, Colorado.

Marie Canino was born on June 26, 1909. She was married to Michael Furtek (b. 1906) until his death on August 9, 1979. She then married Louis Signorini (b. 12-26-1898) of Pistoia, Italy. She had no children.

Charles Canino was born in 1911; he and his wife currently live in Beaver Dam, Wisconsin. Louie Canino was born on July 4, 1898, and died in Chicago. Katherine Canino was born on April 28, 1904 (See additional family history).

Carmello Canino died in 1915. Louise then married her second husband, Jake Lacatesa (AKA Lokatesa). One child was born to this union: Antoinette, born August 7, 1917, in New Orleans. Antoinette married Frank Faga (b. Nov., 1904) and adopted one child, Cynthia. Antoinette currently lives in Deltona, Florida.

Louise and her children came to the Gary area after Jake's death in New Orleans. Anthony and Louie had come earlier to live with Josephine and her husband, Sam Centanni. Sam worked at the Industrial Lumber Yard at 21st and Mass. St. and helped Anthony and Louie obtain employment there. Folks said that Sam knew everyone in Gary – "Gary was only sand dunes and everyone was building . . . and Sam delivered the lumber."

Louise married her third husband, James DeMaria in Lake County. Mr. DeMaria owned and operated a shoe shop in Gary. No children were born to this union.

Louise died on May 4, 1953, in Gary, and is buried in the Evergreen Cemetery in Hobart, Indiana.

by Joanne C. Clark

CASTLE, DR. FREDERIC
F36

Dr. Frederic Castle is an old resident of Lowell. He has devoted fifty years to the study of violin tone-problems — the philosophy of violin peculiarities, excellencies and defects. Violins come to him from various parts of the country for test, valuation or reformation. His interesting experiences and valuable conclusions to violin students, as to production, modification and preservation of violin tones, are set forth in his unique way of lectures to a mythical club, and published in his book, "Violin Tone Peculiarities," from which the doctor derives both deserved reputation and revenue.

(Compiled from the Souvenir Album of Lake Co. Ind., Crown Point-Lowell, June 18-19, 1909.)

CENTANNI, JOSEPH AND ANNE
F37

Joseph Peter Centanni was born on October 15, 1913, in Gary, Indiana, to Samuel and Josephine Centanni. He graduated from Emerson High School in 1931, as an outstanding R.O.T.C. student. As a youth, Joseph played the saxophone in a local band. He married Anne Czapko on June 3, 1939, in Gary, Indiana.

Joseph was a First Lieutenant in the United States Army and a weapons instructor – including the 57 mm anti-tank gun. He also served in the occupation of Japan. Upon his return he became reemployed at U.S. Steel and began attending Purdue University from which he later earned an A.A. degree. Joseph was em-

Joseph and Anne Centanni – 1988

Joanne and Leigh Clark with sons David and Steve.

ployed as a General Foreman in the 80" Hot Strip Division upon his retirement in 1971.

Anne Czapko Centanni was born to George and Anna Czapko of Gary, on December 28, 1912. She graduated from Froebel High School and Gary Business College before becoming employed by Kresge's as a Head Cashier for 10 years. Anne has also been an active member of St. Mary's Eastern Orthodox Church. The couple made their home in Glen Park. They recently celebrated their Golden Anniversary

64

and are currently residing in Schererville, Indiana.

Joseph and Anne had four children who were born and raised in Gary: Joanne Carole Centanni, born January 23, 1943; Joseph Robert Centanni, born April 12, 1946; Joyce Ann Centanni, born January 11, 1950; and Janet Ellen Centanni, born March 20, 1957. All four children are graduates of Lew Wallace High School.

Joanne Carole Centanni received a B.A. from Purdue University and a M.A. from the University of Chicago. She married Leigh Howard Clark (b. 9-18-46) of Houston, Texas on September 9, 1972, in Gary, Indiana. Leigh Clark attended Texas Technical University, received a B.A. from the University of Oklahoma and received a B.S.E. from Purdue University. He is employed by Amoco Pipeline Company. Leigh and Joanne have two children born in Hinsdale, Illinois: David Lee Clark, born January 24, 1977, and Stephen Howard Clark, born August 26, 1978. They have made their home in Peotone, Illinois.

Joseph Robert Centanni received an A.A. from Purdue University and is attending Elmhurst College. He is currently employed by Trans Union Credit Corporation. He married Shirley Marie Mihal, a Merrillville High School graduate, on August 26, 1967, in Merrillville, Indiana. They have three children: Joseph Edward Centanni, born June 10, 1969, in Gary, Indiana; Jason Michael Centanni, born July 14, 1972, in Gary, Indiana; and Jeremy Peter Centanni, born August 25, 1976, in Merrillville, Indiana. They have made their home in Schererville, Indiana.

Joyce Ann Centanni has been employed by Rockwell International for 16 years. She received an A.A. degree from Kirkland College and is currently a student at Mercer University. She has made her home in Lawrenceville, Georgia.

Janet Ellen Centanni has attended Purdue University and has been employed in the food service industries. She currently resides in Lynwood, Illinois.

Joseph Edward Centanni, grandson of Joseph and Anne Centanni, married Jodie Irene Concialde, (b. 7-1-65) of Griffith, Indiana on September 17, 1988, in Griffith, Indiana. They have one son, Ryan Edward, born March 19, 1989, in Hammond, Indiana. Joseph Edward is currently a student at Purdue University. They reside in Griffith, Indiana.

by Joanne C. Clark

CENTANNI, ROSS AND HELEN
F38

Ross Dominic Centanni was born on April 28, 1908, in New Orleans, Louisiana, the oldest child of Samuel and Josephine Centanni. As a young man he was active as a baseball and basketball coach at the Froebel Friendship House.

Ross was married to Helen Albina Petraitis on August 17, 1937, in Gary, Indiana. Their plans to marry were complicated by the amputation of Ross' right arm – the result of a mill accident. They overcame this difficulty, however and went on to live productive lives in the Gary area. Ross enjoyed dabbling in politics in Lake County and was supportive of the Democratic Party. Ross was employed by U.S. Steel for 28 years in the Sheet and Tin Division. He died on August 2, 1966, in Gary, Indiana.

Helen Petraitis Centanni, a graduate of Froebel High School was employed at the Lake County Treasurer's Office for 14 years and the Lake County Assessor's Office for 14 years, performing clerical work in both occupations. She was also a Glen Park Precinct Committeewoman for 14 years. Mrs. Centanni also held various offices in the Glen Park-Merrillville Professional Business Women's Club in which she was active for 12 years. Currently, she is an active participant in the Senior Citizen's Harvest Club. Ross and Helen made their family home in Glen Park.

Ross and Helen had two children who were born and raised in Gary, and graduated from Lew Wallace High School. Geraldine Ross Centanni, born March 30, 1939, and Ross George Centanni, born March 7, 1944.

Geraldine married Henry Harmon (b. 11-24-36) of Chicago on January 20, 1966, in Gary, Indiana. Two children were born to this union: Helen Marie Harmon, born June 9, 1967, in Des Moines, Iowa; and Stephen Henry Harmon, born April 3, 1970, in Gary, Indiana. Henry Harmon received a B.A. from DePaul University and has taught English in the Gary Public School System. He has also been extensively employed in the broadcasting business and is currently with Station WWJY in Crown Point, Indiana. Geraldine attended Gary Business College and was then employed by the Northern Indiana Public Service Company. Henry and Geraldine Harmon have made their family home in the Crown Point area.

Ross George Centanni married Gloria Jean O'Brien (b. 7-20-46) of Gary, on May 20, 1967, in Merrillville, Indiana. Two children were born to this union: Jeffrey Robert Centanni, born January 12, 1971, in Chicago Heights, Illinois; and David Ross Centanni, born April 24, 1974, in Valparaiso, Indiana. Ross George completed a B.A. at St. Joseph's College. He is currently employed by Inland Steel. Gloria graduated from Andrean High School in Merrillville. They have made their home in Merrillville.

by Joanne C. Clark

Ross and Helen Centanni with daughter Geraldine

CENTANNI, SAMUEL AND JOSEPHINE
F39

Samuel Centanni, Charlie Centanni and Charlie's son, Louis Centanni.

Early Residents

Rosario Centanni was born on May 31, 1843, in Alia, Sicily, Italy and married Lillian Constanza. Samuel (Salvatore) was born on December 12, 1879, in Alia, Sicily, as were his siblings. He was the third of five children born to this union: Charles, born May, 1873; Ross, born May 15, 1876; Theresa, born November 14, 1889; and Mary, who died in her youth.

Sam and his family reportedly arrived in Brooklyn, New York, in 1884. However, they returned to Alia, Sicily, in 1891, after the death of their natural mother, Lillian. They remained in Italy until Charles and Ross had completed their time in the Italian Army. The family immigrated again, settling in New Orleans. Sam helped his father and brothers establish a prosperous truck farming business.

Sam married Josephine Canino on April 7, 1907, in New Orleans, where they had two children: Ross Dominic Centanni, born April 28, 1908, and Lillian Antoinette Centanni, born November 15, 1909. In the meantime, Charles established the first barber shop in Glen Park, "Charlie's Barber Shop"; Ross established the first greenhouse, "Centenne's Greenhouse" at 4740 Broadway.

Sam was then persuaded to come to Gary where he obtained employment in the construction industries. He was one of the first members of the newly formed AFL Union. Sam soon saved enough to build his own home in the Lincoln Park area of Gary "high off the ground . . . since the Little Calumet River had flooded the surrounding territory." He later built a second home in Glen Park.

Their father, Rosario Centanni remained in New Orleans, where he remarried. He died on January 20, 1921, and is buried in Metairic, Louisiana.

In Gary, six additional children were born to Sam and Josephine: Joseph Peter Centanni,

Rosario Centanni and wife, Lillian (nee Constanza) with children: Charlie, Ross, Samuel, Theresa, and Mary – circa 1890.

born October 15, 1912; Carmello Centanni, born November 25, 1911; Louis Centanni, born July 25, 1920; Louise Marie Centanni, born October 7, 1916; Theresa Marietta Centanni, born August 2, 1924; and Ann Rose Centanni, born June 6, 1929. Louis died from diphtheria on March 19, 1925, and Carmello died in 1921 from an abscessed tooth.

Samuel Centanni petitioned and was admitted as a United States citizen on January 6, 1921, by the Lake County Superior Court. He died on Feb. 1, 1966, in Gary. Josephine died on January 5, 1972 in Gary. Both were members of St. Joseph's Church and are buried at Calvary Cemetery.

by Joanne C. Clark

CHRISTENSON, WARNER
F40

Some people who knew Griffith earlier would say, "Warner Christenson built Griffith." Not *all* of Griffith, but a good portion of homes and public buildings, at one time, felt his touch. But that's a little ahead of the story.

This Christenson family came from Lake Village in south Lake County where some of the ten children, seven girls and three boys,

Warner and Frieda Christenson wedding picture, 1917.

were born. But, before 1893, when Warner Paul was born, the family moved to a farm on what is now Old 330 in Merrillville. When Warner was twelve years old, his father passed away, and Warner quit school to work and help support this large family. However, at least one of the older sisters had already married and gone out west to live. Within a few years this sister's husband passed away, and she returned to the farm with four small children, enlarging the already bursting household.

When Warner was 23 years old, he left the farm and took a job on the Erie Railroad as a car repairman at Griffith, being promoted to inspector six months later. This job he held for two and one-half years, at which time he quit railroading and entered the trucking, hay and grain business, branching out into building construction and becoming one of Lake County's largest and most progressive building contractors. He was recognized as an authority on real estate valuations by several courts in Lake and Porter Counties, and served as appraiser for various banks, building and loan associations. His building was not just confined to homes in Griffith, but he also built many business buildings and schools in surrounding communities. His construction crews built houses that were sturdy and built to last.

Warner was also a very generous person and wanted to help young couples in whatever way he could. Many young married couples just starting out purchased their first home from him with little or no down payment, and rarely did Warner make a mistake in judgment. These deals were always well honored by both parties.

Sometime after Warner left the farm, he met Frieda Penning, the youngest daughter of Carl and Matilda Penning. The Pennings, a family of German background, had lived in Hammond but when the children were young moved to Griffith where Frieda attended elementary school on Junction St., now Broad St. She went to high school in Hammond, taking the train from Griffith. From high school, Frieda went on to attend Valparaiso University for two years to become a teacher. (While there, Frieda roomed with Constance Gustafson who became the wife of Axel Gustafson, another "old-time family" of Griffith.) After graduation, Frieda taught school in Black Oak until she met and married Warner in 1917. She had one sister, Emma Todd, and two brothers, William and Adolph Penning. Adolph, who was Griffith town clerk for many years, still lives in Griffith. At this writing he is in his nineties.

The family first lived in a house in the 200 block of south Griffith Blvd. and later built and moved into a house in the 200 block of North Griffith Blvd. which is, at this writing, the Fagen-Miller Funeral Home. Seven children were born, six boys and one girl: Roy, Arthur, Dale, Milford, Lela, Billy and Ervy.

Frieda was his helpmate and ran the office for Warner during the construction days and after the hardware store was opened. But, she was always conscious of her role as a parent. The children were always uppermost in her mind, and when the opportunity came for them to have a hot lunch at Beiriger's Tavern across the street from the small office she and Warner worked in, she made arrangements for them to enter the Family Entrance where Mrs. Beiriger made sure the children sat in the dining area as far away from the drinking area as possible.

Soon a furniture store was built next to the hardware store with an opening between the two. After W.W. II, Warner phased out the construction business, added fuel oil to his previous businesses — he was still selling coal, but not the hay and feed.

In 1944 Frieda became ill and passed away in March. Five of the sons were involved in various services of our country, and after they came home, three of them joined Roy who had not been eligible for the service, and they all took an active part in the business with their father.

In November 1951, the opportunity came to purchase the Chevrolet Agency that was located at the corner of Broad and Main Sts. in Griffith. Warner, being the forward-looking businessman he was, along with the boys, did purchase the agency. In 1963 Christenson Chevrolet was relocated in Highland, IN. Little by little the other businesses in Griffith were sold, but still are there on Broad St. By this time Warner was ready to retire and let the boys take over. His daughter also works at the agency.

Mr. Christenson served as a trustee on the Town Board of Griffith continuously from 1923 to 1940. He was president of the board for eight years, building a reputation for administration of town affairs, equal to the best in the state of Indiana. Warner was a man of many interests and abilities which this story shows — being interested in the administration of the town in which he lived as well as the people who lived there. He moved to Florida in his retirement, but made frequent trips back home to be sure things were going well. He passed away in Florida in 1970. In case the spelling of the name does not show it, these Christensons are of Danish ancestry. Warner's parents were Neils Peter Christenson from Denmark and Eliza Ann Butts.

by Margaret M. Christenson

CHRISTIANSON, ELIN BALLANTYNE
F41

Elin Ballantyne Christianson, librarian, civic worker; born Gary, Indiana, November 11, 1936; daughter of Donald B. and Dorothy May (Dunning) Ballantyne; B.A., University of Chicago, 1958, M.A., 1961, certificate advanced studies, 1974; married Stanley David Christianson, July 25, 1959; children — Erica and David. Assistant librarian, then librarian at J. Walter Thompson Co., Chicago, 1959-68; library consultant, 1968 –; part-time lecturer at the Graduate Library School, University of Chicago, 1981 –; School of Library and Information Sciences, Indiana University, 1982 –. Chairman of the Hobart American Revolution Bicentennial Commission, 1974-1976; board of directors of the Hobart Historical Society, 1973 –, president, 1980 –, president of the League of Women Voters, Hobart, 1977-79. Recipient of the Laura Bracken award from the Hobart Jaycees, 1976; certificate of achievement from the Indiana American Revolution Bicentennial Commission, 1975; Woman of the Year award by the Hobart Business and Professional Women, 1985. Member of the American Association of Information Sciences, American Library Association, Indiana Library Association, Special Libraries Association (chairman of the advertising and marketing division, 1967-68), English Special Libraries Association, Association of Library and Information Sciences Education, American Association of University Women (president of the Hobart Branch, 1975-77), University of Chicago Graduate Library School Alumni Association (vice-president 1971-74, 76-77, president 1977-79). Unitarian. Author: Non-Professional and Paraprofessional Staff in Special Libraries, 1973; Directory of Library Resources in Northwest Indiana, 1976; Old Settlers Cemetery, 1976; New Special Libraries: A Summary of Research, 1980; Daniel Nash Handy and the Special Library Movement, 1980; co-author: Subject Headings in Advertising, Marketing and Communications Media, 1964; Special Libraries: A Guide for Management, 1981. Address: 141 Beverly Blvd., Hobart, IN 46342.

(From the 1986-87 "Who's Who in the Midwest")

COOK, BENSON E.
F42

Benson E. Cook born November 16, 1871, in Marshall County, Indiana, came to Gary, Indiana, in April of 1907. He married Anna Louise Case born December 2, 1877, in Valparaiso, Indiana, on August 24, 1910 in Ft. Wayne, Indiana. They had three children, Margaret Louise born August 23, 1911, John Benson born July 16, 1913, and Edward Andrew born February 10, 1919. They were all born in Gary.

Benson's parents were James Weltner Cook, born February 22, 1845, and Margaret Rupe, born February 5, 1846, both in St. Joseph County, Indiana. James W. Cook's parents were Rev. Elias Benson Cook, born November 28, 1818, in Saratoga County, New York. He was a Methodist Circuit Rider in early northern Indiana. His mother was Sophia Eberhart born March 8, 1821, in Pennsylvania. The Eberhart family were early settlers of Mishawaka, Indiana, and established the Red Ball Boot Factory there. Margaret Rupe's parents were Daniel Rupe born December, 1816, and Martha Stull born January 27, 1820, both in St. Joseph County, Indiana. The Stull family were early settlers of South Bend. Mary Jane Stull, sister to Martha, married John Mohler Studebaker of the Studebaker brothers.

Rev. Elias Cook's father was Arthur Cook, born August 14, 1793, in Saratoga County, New York. He fought in the War of 1812. His mother was Abigail Smith born May 7, 1799, also in Saratoga County. They moved to Mishawaka, Indiana, in the early 1800's.

Sophia Eberhart's father was Frederick George Eberhart, born March 30, 1797, in Greensburg, Pennsylvania. Her mother was Elizabeth Weltner, born September 25, 1800, in Fayette County, Pennsylvania. They moved to Mishawaka, Indiana in the early 1800's also.

Daniel Rupe's father was Jacob Rupe and his mother was Susanna Long of Virginia.

Martha Stull's father was Henry Stull, born November 2, 1778 in Fayette County, Pennsylvania. Her mother was Rebecca Hughes born December 25, 1799, in South Carolina. They lived in St. Joseph County, Indiana.

Arthur Cook's father was Asher Cook, born October 5, 1756, in Freehold, N.J. His mother was Helena Barcalow, born September 9, 1758.

Abigail Smith's father was Elias Smith, born January 1, 1766.

Her mother was Pruella Holmes, born October 9, 1769. They moved from Freehold, New Jersey to Charlton, New York, then to Indiana.

Frederick George Eberhart's father was Adolphus Eberhart born January 4, 1760, in Wurtenburg, Germany. His mother was Sophia Spellman, born February 7, 1770. Adolphus Eberhart fought in the Revolutionary War.

Going back to the female side of Margaret Cook's history, her mother, Anna Case's father was Andrew Joseph Case, born May 18, 1847, in McGraw, New York. He attended Normal in Cortland, N.Y., and came to Indiana in 1868, a youth of 21. He was a pioneer Hoosier School Master teaching in one room school houses around Valparaiso, Indiana.

Different families in the area furnished a school house built on a corner of their property. Andrew never knew where he was to spend the night until one of the students brought a note from home telling him he was to stay at their house that night. He wrote in his daily diary where they were and how good or bad they were. His favorite place to stay was Dr. Andrew Barrett Price's home where Abigail Price, a curly haired girl lived. She eventually became his wife. His diaries have been preserved. They begin in 1869, and record the weather of each day, how many pupils he had and how they behaved. He was a lonely young man and confided everything to his diary, even his courtship with Abigail. He recorded his expenditures, his social life and things as they were at that time. There is one for each year from 1869 to 1905, which is in Margaret Cook Seeley's possession.

Andrew Joseph Case's father was Joseph Case, born 1812 in Rehoboth, Massachusetts. He married Catherine Goetcheus, born in 1817 in East Homer, Massachusetts. They lived in McGraw, N.Y., away from the sea coast so their offspring wouldn't go to sea.

Dr. Andrew Barrett Price born September 24, 1807, in Centerville, Ohio. He came to Indiana in the early 1800's to be a physician in and around Valparaiso. His second wife was Louise McDowell Dye, a widow with one son, Vincent. She was born October 3, 1823, in Pennsylvania.

Joseph Case's father was William Case, born March 11, 1785, in Rehoboth, Massachusetts. His mother was Rebecca Pierce born in 1785, also in Rehoboth, Massachusetts. The Case family began life in America in the early 1700's in Rhode Island.

Dr. Andrew Barret Price's father was John Price born 1763, in Delaware. His mother was Hannah Hatfield Davis. The first records are found in Delaware.

Margaret Cook married Clayton Barron Seeley, born September 25, 1903, in Hammond. Clayton attended the Chicago Conservatory of Music studying piano and eventually had his own little jazz band playing in the Lake County area. He was Safety Director of National Tube Company, Gary, Indiana. Margaret taught school in the Gary Public Schools. Clayton and Margaret had two sons, Mark, two taught school in Gary and worked in the United States Steel Company. He never married. Scott worked for I.B.E.W. in St. Croix, U.S. Virgin Islands, and in Birmingham, Alabama. He married Debra Sue Eiweglelben of Hobart, Indiana. They have one son, Matthew.

John B. Cook married Merel Brittain of Birmingham, Alabama. They have three sons, George, James and Thomas. Jack worked for U.S.S.

Edward A. Cook married Margaret Mary McLaughlin of Gary. They have one son, Timothy, and three daughters, Sheilah, Susan and Joan.

by Margaret Seeley

COOK, BENSON E. FAMILY
F43

The Benson E. Cook Family in Gary, Indiana

Gary, Indiana, in 1907, was a challenge to a young man's sense of adventure. A new city with a tremendous future was being built from scratch. Benson Elias Cook thought it was just that. He was born on a farm near Walkerton, Indiana, a son of James Weltner Cook and Margaret Rupe Cook. Benson left the farm to work on the Union Pacific R.R. out west. He came to Gary in 1907, to live in a tent on the sand hills at the foot of Lake Michigan. United States Steel was in the process of being built and needed men. Benson went to work as a police officer.

The sand hills were leveled to make way for the town. Benson bought one of the first houses built on the east side of Broadway. He also bought property on the west side of Broadway at 21st. The thinking was that the town would be away from the mills there. But the U.S.S. subsidiary, the Gary Land Company, bought up the land near the mills and built houses there for their employees. So the 21st Ave. property became less valuable.

On August 24, 1910, Benson married Anna Louise Case of Valparaiso, Indiana. Her parents were Andrew Joseph Case and Abigail Price Case. Abigail's father was a pioneer Hoosier Schoolmaster, her mother was the daughter of Dr. Andrew Barrett Price. Benson and Anna went to housekeeping in an apartment on Adams Street. Dr. Evans lived downstairs, and the Ewings lived across from them.

Margaret Louise Cook was born August 23, 1911, daughter of Benson and Anna. John Benson Cook was born July 16, 1913, and Edward Andrew Cook was born February 10, 1919. The family moved to 558 Connecticut Street, and later to 812 Rhode Island Street.

Anna Case Cook became very active in the United Presbyterian church located on the corner of 7th and Pennsylvania Street. Benson now worked on the E.J.&E. R.R. The children attended Emerson School.

Emerson School was built in 1906, probably the most modern school of its time. It went from kindergarten through high school. Its plant held an indoor swimming pool, a chemistry lab, a physics lab, a mechanical drawing room, a foundry, a wood shop, a machine shop, a boys' gymn and a girls' gymn, an auditorium, a cafeteria which included space for cooking and sewing, a biology room with an outdoor zoo with native animals, a music room, a band and orchestra room, and outdoors there was a well equipped playground, tennis courts and sports fields.

Emerson also had a nurse's office. Gary Public Schools were among the first to have a health program and supervision. It was supervised by Dr. Otis Nesbit. Dental services were also provided. Dr. William A. Wirt was superintendent of schools and originated the "Work-Study Play" plan. Part of the day, which went from 8:15 A.M. to 4:15 P.M., was given to work, part to study and part to play. He wanted the children to be occupied and not run the streets. There was Saturday school for make-up time, summer school for make-up and get-ahead time. Some churches used the school plant on Sundays until they could build. On Thursday evenings it was community time. Programs were given by classes and movies were shown all for the price of a dime for adults. There were night classes for the people who wanted to learn to read and write English, and other subjects.

Teachers were hired as specialists in their field. A Math teacher taught Math to six classes a day. She had one hour for lunch and one hour for preparation. It was a long day. If she got married she was automatically dismissed. Dr. Wirt wanted complete dedication. The children moved from classroom to classroom every hour. Soon after Dr. Wirt died in 1938, his "Work, Study, Play" plan was dispensed with and was replaced by the old fashioned one room, one teacher teaching all subjects except specials such as music, art, nature study etc.

Children from Scotland and England began to enroll in 1926. Their fathers were brought to Gary to run National Tube Company, a subsidiary of U.S.S. Children from more eastern European countries began to enroll as United States Steel needed more men. There was only a tiny settlement of Blacks on the south side of the Indiana Harbor Belt Line R.R. on Carolina Street and thereabouts. It was isolated territory.

As Gary grew more schools were needed. Froebel School was opened in 1912, and Roosevelt School in 1930, Horace Mann graduated its first class in 1929. Memorial Auditorium at 7th and Massachusetts was built 1925. It served for sports events, concerts and dramas. Many great artists performed there. Among them were Mme. Schumann-Heinck, John McCormick, Fritz Kreisler, Sergei Rachmaninoff, the Army and Navy bands, at various times different ethnic singing and dancing groups. Gary had a modern public library on 5th and Adams, with several satellite branches. High School football was played at Gleason Park, 1st and Virginia. Basketball was played in the Memorial Auditorium.

Chicago was close and provided many advantages. Plays, concerts, art exhibits, zoos, the planetarium and museums were attended. We walked down Michigan Boulevard, shopped on State Street. It was only a short ride on the South Shore R.R. Gary was a thriving city until around 1956, when people began to move to the surrounding suburbs.

by Margaret Cook Seeley

COVAULT, BEN AND IDA
F44

Early Residents of Hammond

Ben and Ida Covault came to Hammond in 1922 from Wapakoneta, Auglaize Co., Ohio where Ida was born 8 June 1889. Ida Ovadell Vorhees was the daughter of Robert B. Vorhees and Sarah Ella Ritchie. Benjamin Adalbert Covault was born 5 Jan. 1883 in Salem Twp., Shelby Co., Ohio. He was the last of 10 children

Benjamin A. Covault – probably taken in the 1940's

Ida O. (Vorhees) Covault. Taken in 1969.

of Robert I. Covault and Mary Partington. Ben and Ida were married 5 June 1909 in Wapakoneta.

At age 16 Ben worked in a broom factory carrying heavy loads which caused a hunched shoulder and curvature of the spine which crippled him for the rest of his life. Ben and his brother John were said to have started the first motion picture house in Wapakoneta. Later he worked in a carriage shop and painted milk trucks for the dairy. When they were married he was a painter and she was a waitress, probably at the Koneta Hotel. They worked together doing wall papering and varnishing for awhile and during World War I he worked at the Garford Motor Truck Co. in Lima, Ohio where they built troop carriers. Ben was a member of the Moose and Eagles Lodges in Wapakoneta.

In 1922 they went to Hammond, Ind. to visit her sister Edna and her husband George Poland. George worked in this brother's auto refinishing shop and while they were there Roy Poland offered Ben a job refinishing cars for $100 a week. They returned to Ohio for their belongings and moved to Hammond before school started and Ben started working at the Auto Craft Shop.

When they moved to Hammond they had 2 sons: Clarence Robert, born 3 Nov. 1909 and Charles Bernard, born 10 April 1912. A third son, George Frederick, was stillborn on 5 Nov. 1919. They had 4 children born in Hammond. Richard Earl was born 28 Mar. 1923. Betty Jean was born 20 Sept. 1925. Dorothy Ellen was born 22 Feb. 1928, and William Vorhees was born 26 Sept. 1929. They lived in Bieker's flat at 442 Indiana St. when Dick, Betty and Dot were born. Bill was born at 910 Eaton St. and they lived at 6220 Monroe St. in 1930. About 1932 they moved to 855 Indiana St. where Ida lived until 1953.

Ben worked for Roy Poland for a couple of years and then he and George Alan started their own auto paint shop on Indianapolis Blvd. in East Chicago where they used the new method of spray painting cars. This business lasted from 1924 to 1927 when Ben became very ill with stomach ulcers and had to have extensive surgery to remove almost half of his stomach. At some time he painted Pages and Jewett cars at O'Neals Auto Sales and painted striping on cars at Fred Lute's Studebaker dealership. During the depression Ida baked bread and coffee cakes which she sold to earn more money.

About 1933 they started decorating for the Metropolitan Insurance Co. which owned many repossessed houses and the Atlas Apartments north of the City Hall in East Chicago. Bud and Clarence also worked along with them at times. After Ben and Ida separated in 1936 Bud continued to decorate with his mother until 1940.

Neither Ben nor Ida ever remarried after their divorce in 1940. He worked for a time at the Dooling-Etter dry cleaning plant in Hammond and at the Lake Hills Country Club in St. John. He lived in downtown Hammond. Ben died at age 64 on 29 Oct. 1948 at 502-148th St. in East Chicago of a coronary occlusion. He was buried in Elmwood Cemetery in Hammond.

Ida continued to live at 855 Indiana St. and her daughter Dorothy continued to live with her after her marriage. In 1953 her son Richard purchased a new home for her across the Ill. state line in Lansing. Later she lived with Dorothy in Lansing. She died at age 89 on 17 June 1977, following several months of failing health, at the Homestead Convalescent Home in Burnham, Ill. She was buried beside Ben in Elmwood Cemetery.

Clarence Covault married Dorothy E. Blume on 23 Aug. 1930. He retired from the Hammond Police Department in 1961 after 21 years of service. They had 1 son, Clarence Robert, Jr. who lives in Highland. Clarence and Dorothy live in Highland too and have 4 grandchildren and 11 great-grandchildren.

Charles/Bud married Thelma W. Bivens on 12 April 1946 in Hobart, Ind. They lived in Michigan where he was a machinist until his retirement when they moved to Deming New Mexico for his health. They had no children. Bud died on 23 Jan. 1989 of emphysema.

Richard/Dick married Hope Harder in Springfield, Mass. on 30 Sept. 1961. They have one daughter, Carolyn, who is a lawyer for Texaco. Dick is retired from the Air Force and teaches in the Business Education Dept. at Hollywood High School. They reside in San Marino, Cal.

Betty and Harold R. Mason were married 3 Sept. 1949 in Hammond. He was retired from the Air Force and she was a retired Civil Service worker. Harold died at Fairborn, Ohio in 1979 and about 1984 Betty moved back to Hammond to be near her family. She had severe arthritis and was an invalid. She died on 6 Dec. 1986 at age 61 and was buried in Valley City, North Dakota beside her husband.

Dorothy/Dot and her husband Donald E. Eggebrecht were married 11 June 1950 in Hammond. They have 3 children: Donald R. of Florida; Christie L. (Mrs. James Saulters) of Highland; and Kimberly A. (Mrs. David Crawford) of Beecher, Ill. Don is retired and they live in Lansing, Ill. They have 3 grandchildren now and 2 more on the way.

William/Bill married Erma J. Roach on 16 Feb. 1952 in Gary. They live in rural Hebron, Ind. now. They had 3 children: Thomas William Covault, D.V.M. of Hebron; Jerry Jay who passed away at age 15 months in 1957 while they lived in Gary; and Cathleen Louise (Mrs. Kenneth Seramur) of rural Hebron. They have 3 grandchildren.

by Mrs. Erma J. Covault

COVAULT, WILLIAM AND ERMA ROACH
F45

Of Hammond and Gary

William, better known as Bill, Covault was born on 26 Sept. 1929 in Hammond, Ind. He was the youngest child of Benjamin A. and Ida O. (Vorhees) Covault who came to Hammond in 1922 from Wapakoneta, Auglaize Co., Ohio. He grew up at 855 Indiana St. and was baptized at the Christian Church on Calumet Ave. He attended Riverside and Columbia Elementary Schools and Hammond Technical Vocational School. His first job was at Waltz' Bicycle Shop on State Street. Later he delivered newspapers, was an usher at the Parthenon Theatre, and worked at House of Mirth Drive-In Restaurant, Northern Indiana Frozen Foods, Kenwood Grocery and Swift and Co. in Hammond; Jannsen's I.G.A. in Robertsdale; and Pre-Cast Concrete in Miller. After he met Erma in 1949 he went to work for her father at Roach's Service on Broadway in Gary.

Erma Jane Roach was born in Gary on 27 Sept. 1931 and lived at 336 Hayes St. until she was married. Her parents were Paris A. and Edna L. (Tucker) Roach. As a young girl she joined the First Presbyterian Church at 6th & Monroe St. She attended grades K to 12 at

Tom Covault's Family. (L to R) Lindsay, Jackie and Eric. Taken August 1988

William Covault Family. (L to R) Tom, Erma, Cathy and Bill. Taken at Cathy's wedding Dec. 3, 1983

(L to R) Kenny, Katie and Cathy Seramur, taken November 1988

Horace Mann School. Evenings after school she worked at Reliable Cleaners on 10th & Broadway. After graduation she was a telephone switchboard operator at Lou Ehlers Ford on West 5th Ave. and later worked at the Bader Corp. Office on Broadway as a typist.

Bill and Erma were married 16 Feb. 1952 at the First Presbyterian Church and Bill joined the church, too. They purchased their first home at 270 Johnson St., just 3 blocks from where Erma grew up, in 1953. In 1965 they moved across the Lake-Porter County line to their present home on 4½ acres in rural Hebron. Later they joined the Presbyterian Church in Valparaiso. Bill is a member of McKinley Lodge #712 F.&A.M. in Hammond, Oak Shrine and Scottish Rite of South Bend. Besides being a homemaker and mother Erma was a 4-H Club leader in Porter Co. for 5 years and was a charter member and past-president of Country Neighbors Extension Homemakers Club. She worked for several years as a Kindergarten teacher's aide at Boone Grove School. For the last 10 years she has been researching their family histories. Bill's hobby is woodworking and he is enjoying making toys and furniture for their grandchildren.

In 1953 Bill started working as a carpenter apprentice in the shop at Gary Lumber Co. on 10th & Madison St. in Gary. Later he worked as a carpenter at Hannah's Building Center in Merrillville. After moving to Porter Co. he worked for General Construction Co. in Valparaiso remodeling houses and in new home construction with J.D. Williams Construction Co. in rural Hebron.

In 1973 he changed careers again. After building the new offices for Metachem Laboratories in Valparaiso he assembled their new equipment for making copper powder and took over the operation of it. Metachem later moved to Schererville and in 1981 was sold to a company in Ill. He commuted to Downers Grove, Ill. for 4 years before deciding to start his own business in Valparaiso. On 1 Feb. 1985 Bill and Erma had incorporated and started their own business named Meta-Braze, Inc. which is located at 2705 LaPorte Ave. the last 4 years Bill has spent developing the business which manufactures custom brazing paste for production line brazing and Erma is Office Manager.

Bill and Erma had 3 children, all born in Gary Methodist Hospital. The oldest, Thomas William, was born 22 Oct. 1954 and attended John H. Vohr Elementary School through 5th grade. He completed grades 6 to 12 at Boone Grove School after they moved to the country in 1965 when he was 11. He earned a degree in Industrial Management at Purdue University Northwest and worked as an insurance auditor for a couple of years and as a carpenter for a couple years. After he was married he returned to Purdue to fulfill his lifelong desire to become a veterinarian. After receiving his degree in Veterinary Medicine in 1987 he worked in practices in Auburn, Ind. and Valparaiso for awhile. In March 1989 he joined Dr. Roger Casbon in his practice at Morthland Animal Clinic in Valparaiso. On 19 July 1980, at Queen of All Saints Church in Michigan City he married Jacquelyn Marie Ream. She is the daughter of Robert G. and Alice (Nowfel) Ream of Michigan City. Jackie is an elementary school teacher in Hebron. They reside in Hebron with their 2 children: Lindsey Ream Covault, born 12 July 1983 in Valparaiso; and Eric Thomas Covault, born 9 Dec. 1987 in Auburn, Ind.

The second child of Bill and Erma was Jerry Jay Covault, born 1 Aug. 1956. At age 15 months he was stricken with meningitis and died suddenly on 29 Oct. 1957. He was buried in the family plot at Calumet Park Cemetery in Merrillville.

Cathleen Louise Covault, the youngest child of Bill and Erma, was born on her Mother's birthday, 27 Sept. 1958. She attended grades K and 1 at John H. Vohr School in Gary and completed her education at Boone Grove School. She attended Don Roberts Beauty School in Valparaiso and is a licensed beautician. She works part time as a beautician in her home and part time in the office at Meta-Braze, Inc. On 3 Dec. 1983, at the Presbyterian Church in Valparaiso, she married Kenneth Edward Seramur, son of Donald (and Char) Seramur of Lowell, Ind. and June (and James) Steffel of Hebron. They have a daughter Kate Elizabeth, born 13 May 1987 in Valparaiso. Ken is a union ironworker. They live in rural Hebron, near her parents.

by Mrs. Erma J. Covault

COX, LAWRENCE
F46

Lawrence Cox, candidate for sheriff of Lake County, has been a resident of Lake County for a number of years, and has all through these years been a consistent and zealous Republican. After acting as deputy sheriff under George Lawrence, he filled the office of chief of police in Hammond, and has proved a firm, shrewd, vigilant and efficient officer. He is well known and liked through the entire county.

(Compiled from the Souvenir Album of Lake Co. Ind., Crown Point-Lowell, June 18-19, 1909.)

CRAMER, LEITH AND GERALDINE
F47

Leith M. Cramer and Geraldine (Shisler) Cramer

In August of 1953, Geraldine (Shisler) McKindley decided to make a trip to Chicago to visit her brother Vaughn. She meant to stay for the weekend but ended up staying for the next 36 years. Geraldine was born and raised in the St. Louis, Missouri area. She was born on May 5, 1918 to James and Stella (Allen) Shisler. Her only sibling is her older brother Lloyd Vaughn. While growing up around St. Louis she attended Sutten Grade School and was a graduate of Maplewood High School in 1936. Five years later WWII began and Geraldine had three wartime jobs which included working in a general goods store in Williamsburg, VA., working at McQuay Norris making airplane carburetors and lastly working as a collector for the St. Louis Credit Bureau. After the war she opened her own business, a lingerie and hosiery store in St. Louis. But in 1953 she decided to make that fateful trip to Chicago where she was introduced to Leith Cramer. It was very much "love at first sight" because they were married less than two months later on October 3, 1953 in Evergreen Park, IL. They settled in the south side of Chicago and on October 5, 1955 their only child was born, Nancy Ann Cramer. Geraldine had previously been married to Hugh McKindley but there were no children from that marriage.

As Geraldine was growing up in St. Louis, Leith Cramer was busy growing up on the south side of Chicago. On February 16, 1914, Benjamin and Minnie (Siebrandt) Cramer gave birth to their fourth child and named him Leith, after a river in Scotland. Benjamin and Minnie went on to have eight children altogether. While in school, Leith attended Sherman Grade School and graduated from eighth grade at Oliver Wendell Holmes Grade School in 1928. He was in his second year of high school at Tilden Technical when the Depression hit and he was forced to quit school and get a job to help support his family. He found his first job at the Belt Railroad as a machine apprentice. He was soon laid off and went to work for a jigsaw puzzle company. But in 1933 he began a job with a company called Air Reduction (later shortened to Airco), which turned into a 44 year career. His career was interrupted during the WWII years. He voluntarily joined the Army and found himself on the Pacific side of the war as an Amphibian. He was stationed in the Philippines, New Guinea, New Britain and Japan. The battles and campaigns he was involved in were, New Guinea, Bismark Archipelago, Southern Philippines and Luzon. He was discharged in 1945 as a PFC.

In 1940, before the war, he married Eileen Powers and their marriage produced a daughter, Judith Ann Cramer, born on March 20, 1941. However, their marriage ended in divorce shortly after the war. But luckily, Leith had a good friend named Lorraine Byrnes who introduced him to a friend visiting from St. Louis. And, of course, that friend became his wife shortly thereafter.

In 1964, Leith and Gerry decided to move to the south suburbs and they settled in Blue Island for the next eleven years. After their daughter grew up and went away to college Leith and Gerry left Blue Island for Glenwood where they purchased a house and lived there until 1980. Leith decided to retire in 1977 because he was suffering from emphysema. Then in 1979, Gerry retired to stay home and help her husband. They moved to Schererville, IN. in 1982 to be close to their daughter who was living in Dyer. On July 8, 1988 Leith passed away in Our Lady of Mercy Hospital in Dyer. He is buried in Mt. Auburn Cemetery in Stickney, IL.

Leith and Geraldine have four grandchildren and presently Geraldine resides in Hobart as does Nancy and her family.

by Nancy A. Dowdle

CRAVEN, JOE
F48

Joe Craven is a name that is synonymous with involvement whether it be parish involvement, community involvement or family involvement. It is the proper time of the year, with this being the Christmas issue of The Mike, to focus in on Joe and his part of Schererville and St. Michael's history.

Joe was born in New Hope, Kentucky on March 30, 1941 to Joseph and Elenor Craven. They moved to Schererville while Joe was in fifth grade. Joe graduated from St. Mike's in 1955. In 1959 he graduated from Bishop Noll. He has also attended St. Joseph's and Purdue.

Joe began working for Ford in 1962. But prior to that he married a gal with a well-known Schererville name, Sharron Keilman. The daughter of Vic and Marie Keilman and Joe exchanged vows at St. Michael's on June 9, 1962. Joe and Sharron have four boys; Joe, John, Jeff, and Jerry.

Joe's list of involvement in parish and civic activities is extensive. He is an active member of Holy Name, past Secretary of Holy Name, collection accountant, usher, commentator, MC of a number of the St. Michael's Sports Banquets, and was the key speaker in the St. Michael's Time and Talent search a few years ago.

Joe has served as a coach in the Schererville Town League from 1962 through 1965, has served on Schererville's Park Board, and is a member of the Police Commission.

One of his most extensive lists of accomplishments is with the JC's. He was a charter member of the Schererville chapter in 1966. He was named Key Man of the JC's in 1968. He served as President of Schererville JC's from 1969-70 and was named one out of five Outstanding Local Presidents of Indiana. In 1970-71 he served the area as Region Vice President. He then served as a national director and was ranked number 13 out of 400 in the United States. The following year he served as State Vice President. In May of 1973 he was elected President of Indiana JC's. He especially enjoyed traveling and meeting people such as the one familiar face in one of the pictures. In 1974 he was appointed National Chaplain.

One of his most extensive lists of accomplishments is with the JC's. Joe was a charter member of the Schererville chapter 1966. His chronological list that follows speaks of his involvement and commitment.

1968 – Was named Key Man of Schererville JC's.

1969-1970 – Was President of Schererville JC's – Named 1 of 5 Outstanding Local Presidents of Indiana at the State Convention and Schererville was 1 of 5 outstanding chapters.

1970-71 – Served area JC's as Region Vice President.

1971-72 – Served state as National Director where he ranked #1 of 8 in Indiana and #13 of about 400 in the United States JC organization.

1972-73 – Served as State Vice President.

May 12, 1973 – Elected President of Indiana JCs. During that year Joe met President Nixon in the Oval Office – had picture taken. Made several trips to Tulsa – headquarters for the US JC's – he and Sharron attended an International meeting in Nice, France. They traveled to San Diego for National Convention in 1974 where Joe was appointed National Chaplain.

1974-75 – Served as National Chaplain for US JC's. Trips included for Joe and Sharron were a prayer breakfast with Ford and Rockefeller in Washington, D.C., and a retreat in the Bahamas.

Joe currently is employed by Farm Bureau Insurance, Highland office, as a Sales Representative.

Supporting Joe in his many endeavors are his wife and family. Certainly the name of Craven has earned the respect that it has.

CRUMPACKER, HON. EDGAR DEAN
F49

Hon. Edgar Dean Crumpacker was born on a farm in Laporte County, Indiana, and was educated in the public schools and in the Male and Female College of Valparaiso. When twenty-two years of age, he left the farm to enter upon the study of law in Valparaiso, and took the senior year in the department of the State University. He began the practice of law in Valparaiso in 1879, was elected prosecuting attorney for the Thirty-first Judicial District in 1884 and 1886, was appointed one of the first judges of the appellate court by Governor Hovey in March, 1891, and served upon that bench for about two years. In 1896 he was elected to Congress for the Tenth District and has been reelected from time to time ever since, and is now a candidate upon the Republican ticket for a sixth term.

During the years of his service in Congress many questions of unusual importance have been up for consideration. He was actively identified with all these important measures and particularly with the constructive legislation for the government of Puerto Rico and the Philippine Islands. He is now chairman of the Committee on Census in the House and the ranking member of the Committee on Insular Affairs. The Congressional Record shows the character and extent of the work he has done since he has been a member of the National legislature. During the recent session of Congress he took an active part in all the important measures that were up for consideration, and presided over the House at the designation of the Speaker more than any other member of that body aside from the Speaker himself.

Congressman Crumpacker's recent renomination by enthusiastic acclamation speaks loudly what his supporters think of him. He lives in the heart of the people he represents, because they and their interest lie in his heart. He is a broad, conservative, judicious statesman, possessing eminently the qualities of pleader and jurist; an exceptionally pure public man, moving in an atmosphere far above political corruption and removed from petty quarreling; a conscientious, painstaking and industrious worker for the public good, with the gift of mastery of subjects in the public eye. He belongs to the sort of men the country always needs and always will insist on having at the front and top.

(Compiled from the Souvenir Album of Lake Co. Ind., Crown Point-Lowell, June 18-19, 1909.)

CULVER FAMILY
F50

On August 6, 1942 in San Diego, San Diego County, CA, Marion Harlan Culver (b 6 Mar 1919 Carroll Cty, MO) and Marjorie Loreta Brown (b 17 Apr 1926 Putnam County, MO) were married. After World War II was over and Marion was honorably discharged from the U.S. Marine Corp., they lived in Unionville, Putnam County, MO.

On September 10, 1945, Jan Darlene was born. She lived in Unionville, MO until she was 1 ½ years old when her parents moved to Gary, Lake County, IN. When she was 2 ½ they moved south of Griffith, IN to an area called New Elliot. She attended local Lake County public schools and graduated from Dyer Central High School in June 1963. She lived in Unionville, MO until 1964, then moved to Kansas City, MO where she met and married Arthur F. Wagner on July 2, 1966. She has 2 daughters, Lisa Marie born 7 Feb 1967 in Raytown, MO. She now resides in Minneapolis, MN. Teresa was born 26 Oct 1968 in Raytown, MO. She now resides in Bemidji, MN with her son Blake born 30 January 1989. Jan Darlene has worked selling and managing real estate for several years and now resides near Sedona, Arizona, where she is studying the ways of the Indians of that area.

On September 15, 1948, Lyn Ray was born in Unionville, Putnam County, MO. He attended local Lake County, Indiana public schools and graduated from Dyer Central in June 1966. On July 22, 1966, he married Sandra Roe in Lake County, IN. They had two children, Matthew E. born 23 May 1967 who now resides in Dyer, IN and Rachel born 12 June 1973 who now lives in Schererville and attends Lake Central High School. Lyn Ray is employed at Amoco Refinery in Whiting, IN as a pipefitter. His hobbies include reading and bicycling. He resides in Schererville, Lake County, IN.

Jil Marie was born on July 3, 1958 in Gary, Lake County, IN. She attended local schools and graduated as a member of the National

Back Row (L to R) Joy Lee Culver Staff, Jean Arlene Culver Ferestad, Lee Frederick Culver. Front Row (L to R) Lyn Ray Culver, Jan Darlene Culver Wagner and Jil Marie Culver Cannon. Picture taken August 4, 1978.

Honor Society in June, 1969 from Lake Central High School. She married Felix P. Cannon on September 19, 1970 in Lake County, IN. They have two children, Jennifer M. born 30 March 1971 and Felix P., Jr. born 17 April 1976 and attends North Newton High School in Newton County, IN. Jil is employed at St. Mary Medical Center, Hobart, Indiana as a medical transcriptionist, her husband Felix is an independent truck driver. Her hobbies are reading, visiting with friends and gardening. They reside in Roselawn, Newton County, IN.

Joy Lee was born 10 Feb 1953 in Gary, Lake County, IN. She attended local schools and graduated from Lake Central High School in June, 1973. She married Michael Staff on October 19, 1974. Mike resides in Crown Point, IN. She is employed by Pruzin Funeral Home, Lake County, Indiana and attends Indiana University, Gary, Indiana. Her hobbies are sewing, reading, bicycling and photography. She resides in the New Elliot area of Griffith, Lake County, IN.

Jean Arlene was born 28 June 1957 in Gary, Lake County, Indiana. She attended local schools and graduated from Lake Central High School in June 1975. Jean married Martin W. Ferestad (b 10 Apr 1955 Kirkwood, MO) on August 5, 1978 in LaPorte County, Michigan City, Indiana. They have 2 children, Teva Meredith born 18 December 1981 and Adam Jason born 4 February 1985. Jean is employed by Edinger Plumbing & Htg, Inc. in Munster, Indiana as an executive secretary. Her husband Martin is employed as a repairman for Hoosier Overdoors, Inc., Dyer, IN. Her hobbies are reading, writing poetry, genealogy, gardening and inventing. She is the leader for Troop #206 Girl Scouts of the U.S.A. They reside in Schererville, Lake County, IN.

Lee Frederick was born 10 June 1963 in Gary, Lake County, IN. He attended local schools and graduated from Lake Central High School in June 1981. Lee married Lisa Powell on October 29, 1983, Lake County, IN. Lee is a union plumber currently working for Edinger Plumbing & Htg, Inc., Munster, IN. Lisa works for Bank One, Merrillville, IN. Lee excels at his hobby of woodworking and designing and remodeling his home. They reside in Crown Point, Indiana.

That's it for the Culver Clan from New Elliot, Lake County, Indiana.

by Jean A. Ferestad

CULVER, MARION H.
F51

Marion Harlan Culver, March 1983.

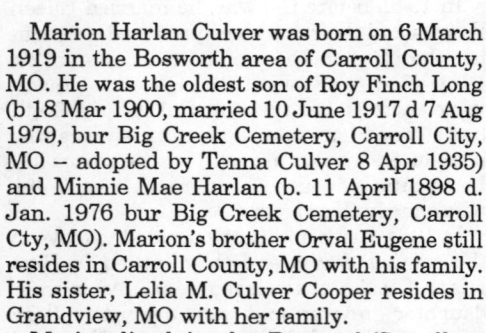

My Dad

Marion Harlan Culver was born on 6 March 1919 in the Bosworth area of Carroll County, MO. He was the oldest son of Roy Finch Long (b 18 Mar 1900, married 10 June 1917 d 7 Aug 1979, bur Big Creek Cemetery, Carroll City, MO – adopted by Tenna Culver 8 Apr 1935) and Minnie Mae Harlan (b. 11 April 1898 d. Jan. 1976 bur Big Creek Cemetery, Carroll Cty, MO). Marion's brother Orval Eugene still resides in Carroll County, MO with his family. His sister, Lelia M. Culver Cooper resides in Grandview, MO with her family.

Marion lived in the Bosworth/Carrollton area of Carroll County, MO until the age of 23. He had an early avid interest in electricity and its uses, which served him well in later years.

In the spring of 1941, he met Marjorie Loreta Brown of Putnam County, MO at a carnival in Unionville, MO. After courting for 1½ years, World War II began and on August 6, 1942, they were married in San Diego County, San Diego, California. He joined the United States Marine Corp. on March 18, 1942 and was placed with Signal Battalion MTC at Camp LeJeune, North Carolina. He served in the defense of the Russell Islands and Enawetok Atoll from 23 August 1942 to 2 September 1944 as a Radar Technician and electronic technician. He was honorably discharged on June 12, 1945 as a Master Technical Sergeant at Camp Lejeune, North Carolina. At the time of his discharge, he had earned the special qualifications of Radar Technician, Electronic Technician and qualified swimmer. He served his country well in a time of great need. After serving during the war, he returned to Unionville, Putnam County, MO and owned and operated Unionville Electronics for 1 ½ years.

In the following 18 years, 6 children were born to him and his wife Marjorie: Jan Darlene, Lyn Ray, Jil Marie, Joy Lee, Jean Arlene and Lee Frederick. The first two were born in Putnam County, MO. The last 4 were born in Gary, Lake County, IN.

He came to Gary, Lake County, Indiana on January 27, 1947 to accept a job at United States Steel, Gary Sheet & Tin. He worked as an instrument repairman for the company for 35 years.

During March, 1948, he and his family moved "south to the Boondocks." There was not much north of them except a small town named Griffith and definitely not much to the south all the way to Crown Point. They moved to one of the first houses in the still unincorporated area of St. John Township called "New Elliot." He lived there with his family and his dog "Snoopy" enjoying his "boondocks" and watching the area fill in around him with houses and towns.

He obtained his ham radio license in 1941 and his First Class Radio Operator's license with a Radar Endorsement in the 1970's from the Federal Communications Commission and operated with the call letters W9OFD or W9 "Old Fuddy Duddy" as he used to say. Although never commercially involved, he was always on the cutting edge of new technology. He also enjoyed metal working, woodworking, astronomy and his "ham" radio conversations around the world. On his vacations, he and his family traveled around the states and visited 45 of them and one other country.

He retired from United States Steel in July 1982 after suffering a stroke. He continued some of his hobbies and made a trip to Hawaii (where he spent some time as a serviceman) with his wife and granddaughter Jennifer in July 1983. He died on July 18, 1984 at St. Mary Medical Center, Hobart, Indiana from diabetes complications and is buried in the Friendship-Brown Cemetery in Putnam County, Missouri.

Marion H. Culver, my dad, passed on to his family a great many things. He is thought of often.

by Jean A. Ferestad

CULVER, MARJORIE L. BROWN
F52

Marjorie Culver, 9-81.

My Mom

Marjorie Loreta Brown was born on 17 Apr 1926 in the Mendota area of Putnam County, MO. She was the youngest child of Fred Obadiah Brown (b 11 Dec 1891 Putnam Cty, IN married 1 Apr 1913 d 19 Feb 1971; bur Friendship-Brown Cemetery, Putnam Cty, MO) and Icey Fern Allen (b 15 Apr 1896, d 31 Oct 1988; bur Friendship-Brown Cemetery, Putnam Cty, MO). Her oldest brother Darrel Obadiah (b 10 Mar 1914) died of pneumonia on 14 Mar 1943. Lloyd Allen (b 5 Feb 1924) resides in Enid, OK with his family.

She attended rural Putnam County schools until 1935 at which time the family moved to Unionville. She was a waitress at a place on Rte 5 owned and operated by her parents called Brown's Truck Stop. That place served the best pies in 5 counties!

In the spring of 1941, she met Marion H. Culver of Carroll Cty, MO at a carnival in Unionville, MO. After courting for 1½ years, World War II began and Marion joined the U.S. Marine Corp. They were married in San Diego County, San Diego, California on August 6, 1942.

While awaiting Marion's return, Marjorie returned to Unionville and completed high school at Unionville High. Her letters from the south seas and her husband, due to his position in the service, were highly censored by his superiors and she very often received them with areas clipped out.

After his return to the states in 1944, they lived on base at Camp Lejeune, North Carolina for a year awaiting his discharge.

She returned to Unionville, MO and made a home for her husband and her daughter, Jan Darlene. She remained in Unionville, MO until March, 1947, when she joined Marion in Gary, Lake County, Indiana. Her son, Lyn Ray was born in Unionville, MO.

In March, 1948, she moved with her family "south to the Boondocks." There was not much north of them except a small town named Griffith and definitely not much to the south of them all the way to Crown Point. They moved to one of the first houses in the still unincorporated area of St. John Township called "New Elliot." Her last 4 children were born in Lake County, Indiana: Jil Marie, Joy Lee, Jean Arlene and Lee Frederick. She is hoping to write down the history of the New Elliot area and the interesting people who have lived there thru the years.

She excels in sewing, often creating items for others. Her other hobbies include woodworking, birdwatching and gardening. She is a genealogist and the "Keeper of the Stories." Her mother having passed on the histories in great detail during her declining years. She has traveled for years and has visited 45 states and 2 countries. She resides in the New Elliot area of Griffith, Lake County, Indiana with her dog Gracie.

by Jean A. Ferestad

CZAPKO, GEORGE AND ANNA
F53

George Czapko was born on April 5, 1883, in Czechoslovakia. His parents reportedly died during the Bubonic Plague at the end of the nineteenth century, leaving George homeless. He apparently wandered and worked in Europe until he met a compassionate American businessman who paid his passage to the United States. The identity of this man has always been unknown.

George arrived in the United States at the age of 16 years through Chesepeake Bay in Baltimore, Maryland. He went to Pennsylvania and worked in the coal mines near Pittsburg.

George married Anna Chundoga on May 29, 1906, in Carnegie, Pennsylvania, after a one week courtship. They lived in Gary, Indiana, in search of financial success in 1911. George became employed at U.S. Steel where he worked until 1947. He attended night school in the Gary Public School System and became a naturalized citizen on May 9, 1921, in Lake Superior Court.

George owned an apartment building in Gary which had one of the first automated coal feeding devices available – a real treat from shoveling! He later owned his home in Glen Park.

Anna Chundoga (aka Hundaga, Chundago) was born on March 7, 1887, to Simko and Anna (nee Hajducok) Chundago in Vysny, Komornik, Czechoslovakia. The family had five children: Mike, Mary, John, Anna, and Theresa. The three eldest children had already immigrated to the United States, leaving Anna and Theresa behind.

Theresa, who was fatally ill, requested a pear which was unaffordable. Anna went about town pleading with neighbors for a pear for her dying sister. In the process, Anna realized her impoverishment and decided to come to America, also. A cousin, John Boby, gave her the money. Apparently, John financed many relatives in their immigration to the United States, making several trips to Europe.

Anna lived with her sister Mary (nee Chundoga) and Michael Zapotacky in Pennsylvania. Michael worked in the same coal mine as George Czapko and told him about his pretty red-headed sister-in-law. It was love at first sight, and they married one week later.

George and Anna had five children: John Czapko, born March 30, 1907, in Barnesboro, Pennsylvania; Ann Czapko, born in 1909; Mary Czapko, born October 3, 1910, in Morrisdale, Pennsylvania; Anne Czapko, born December 28, 1912; and Helen Czpako, born January 19, 1919, in Gary, Indiana. All of their children were raised in Gary. Ann Czapko, the second child died when she was two years old from an infection that began with an inflamed boil.

George died on June 9, 1965, in Gary, Indiana, and Anna died on December 7, 1969. They were both founding members of St. Mary's Eastern Orthodox Church and residents of Gary for 58 years.

by Joanne C. Clark

CZAPKO, JOHN
F54

John Czapko was born on March 30, 1907, in Barnesboro, Pennsylvania. He was the oldest child of George and Anna Czapko. He married Sophie (nee Sonja Nepsa, aka Nepsha) of Gary, on November 11, 1933, in Gary, Indiana. John was employed by U.S. Steel for 42 years.

Two children were born to this marriage: John Johnson Czapko, born February 28, 1936: and George John Czapko, born October 8, 1937. John and Sophie divorced in 1945. Both

George and Anna Czapko

73

Children of John and Elizabeth Czapko: Cindy and Betty Czapko, Patrick and Michael Dacey

John Czapko and sons John and George.

children continued to be raised in the Gary area, and both children are graduates of Lew Wallace High School.

George John Czapko married Barbara Kapella (b. 6-3-35) of Gary, on October 12, 1957, in Gary. George was employed by U.S. Steel for 31 years. Barbara, a Lew Wallace graduate, was employed by U.S. Steel for 34 years and a member of the U.S. Steel Choir. Both are members of the Gary Works Supervisor's Club. They retired in 1987, and have made their home in Bradenton, Florida. They have one daughter, Denise Lynn Czapko, born October 7, 1958, in Gary. Denise graduated from Andrean High School.

John Johnson Czapko married Mary Millicent Hilton (b. 4-5-36) of Gary on July 12, 1958, in Gary. John served in the United States Navy. Four children were born to this union: John Jr., Jean, Laura, and Daniel.

John Czapko (b. 3-30-07) was then married to Frieda Evans for a short time. Their divorce coincided with the loss of John's right leg due to medical incompetency.

John married a third time to Elizabeth Ann (Latieak) Dacey (b. 5-15-17) of Chicago, Illinois, on October 14, 1952, in Chicago. Elizabeth is a high school graduate and has been employed continually in the food service industries. Two children were born in Gary, Indiana, to this union: Cindy Czapko, born September 22, 1953; and Betty Ann Czapko, born October 8, 1954. The family of John and Elizabeth Czapko included two children from a previous marriage: Patrick James Dacey, born July 1, 1948, and Michael Timothy Dacey, born December 16, 1950.

Cindy graduated from Wirt High School in Miller and attended Indiana University for three years. Betty married Garth Grisby (b. 6-30-51) of Kentucky, on July 1, 1972, in Gary, Indiana. Betty and Garth have two children: Lisa Ann Grisby, born February 16, 1973, in Gary; and Chad Grisby, born February 6, 1978, in Wolcott, Indiana.

by Joanne C. Clark

DANIELS, RALPH
F55

I, Ralph Daniels, was an orphan at ten and then I spent the next five years in a number of homes where it seemed they needed an extra hand. I have a picture of my family that was taken a short time before the death of my father. Not only did my parents pass away at an early age but now all of my brothers and sisters have passed away. There were ten of us. My mother Alice, my dad John, and my five brothers Clifford (1896-1968), Clarence (1898-1976), Cary (1901-1970), Clay (1903-1980), and John Jr. (1910-1960). My youngest sister Marie and I were in the orphan's home in Bluffton, Indiana when we graduated from the eighth grade. She passed away at the age of thirty. My oldest sister passed away in 1981. She lived the longest.

I came to Gary when I was 15 or 16. I stayed with my brother and his wife until Ruth and I were married in 1929. We have two daughters, fourteen grandchildren, and five great-grandchildren.

When I first came to Gary, I worked in a number of places. Then, at the age of seventeen, I went to work for the Illinois Bell Telephone Company where I worked until my retirement some forty-two years later. I retired at the age of sixty. In my retirement, I have to thank my family and friends for making this the most enjoyable time of my life.

I have to thank my wife Ruth and our daughters Joyce Haskett and Jean Szymanski and their families for all the happiness I have today. I have found trying to write poetry and helping out at the local golf course, Oak Knoll, takes up most of my time. I have made many friends that have helped me make my later years truly a time of happiness.

[Mr. Daniels' poetry has been likened to American poet John Greenleaf Whittier (1807-1892). Like Whittier, Daniels' poems reflect his beliefs in family, American life, and religious faith.]

DAVIS, BASIL
F56

Basil and Martha Davis ready to leave for a party in the 1950's. Photo taken 800 block of Grant St., Gary.

Around 1887, Frank Divis (1846-1910), his wife, Elizabeth Konopa (1849-1892) and their children, Mary, Katerina, Terezie, Frank, and John came to America from Budejovice, Czechoslovakia.

Little is known of their trip nor of the reasons they went to the Braidwood area of Illinois, southwest of Joliet, but it is likely that a substantial settlement of fellow Bohemians attracted them. There were jobs to be had in the local coal mines, and inexpensive farmland could be purchased in the vicinity. They settled in Coal City.

Because Divis is similar to Davis, a common Welsh name, it seems that the Welsh paymasters at the mines changed the family name.

Basil Davis, youngest child of Elizabeth, was born in 1892, but she died soon after, and Frank then married a widow, Veronica Silhavy, who had two children of her own. But she passed away in 1897, leaving Basil and the younger boys in the care of their older sisters.

Life in those times were harsh; at a young age, Basil joined his older brothers in the coal mines, having had little chance to attend school beyond the elementary grades. As coal was mined only in the winter months, Basil and his brothers would leave the family home in Coal City during the wheat harvesting season and ride freight trains to Minnesota and the Dakotas, where they could earn badly needed money and enjoy the bountiful meals set out for the harvest workers.

The excitement of travel must have been an added zest, for all of the brothers had a taste for touring. John once built a boat and he and Basil traveled down the nearby Illinois River.

Basil and John served in World War I. Basil trained at Key West, Florida, and then became a truck driver in France. The skills learned in the Army led him to a new field of work, driving trucks for the telephone company, at that time establishing the basic telephone networks in the Chicago area. Working in Hammond, Indiana, he was introduced to Martha Lauerman, daughter of Mathias Lauerman, whose forebears were Lake County pioneers. Marriage followed in 1925, and after living for a time in Aurora, Illinois, they moved to a home on Arthur Street in Tolleston, and then to 10th Place. When it was time for Paul, their oldest child, to begin school, they bought a home at 829 Grant Street, also convenient to the Illinois Bell Telephone Company garage on 9th Avenue, Basil's job headquarters.

The children attended Holy Angels School and then Horace Mann High School, from which all were graduated. Paul (b. 1928) attended Gary Business College, worked at Kensington Steel Company in Chicago, then took a secretarial position at the Anderson Company in Gary, where he worked directly for its founder, John W. Anderson. Drafted into the Army in 1951, and earning a commission as an officer in the Signal Corps, Paul won the Bronze Star in Korea. Attendance on the campus of Indiana University in Bloomington followed, and Paul earned his B.S. in education, followed in 1957 by his M.A.T. in English. At that time he moved to California where he retired in 1987 after thirty years of teaching, most of them in the Downey Unified School District.

Jane (b. 1930) worked as a secretary for seven years at Mercy Hospital in Gary and then became registrar of Loyola University School of Law in Chicago; she was awarded her B.A. in English in1977. She is married to William L. Lamey, former dean of the School of Law. They live in Glenview, Illinois.

Jerome, youngest of the family, (1932) was active in the Horace Mann Band as a trombonist, but his adult hobbies include wood-carving and hiking in the Indiana Dunes, not far from his home in Chesterton. He has been employed for his entire career by the E.J. & E. Railroad and is now chief clerk at Kirk Yard in Gary.

He married Mary Lucille Beckman (b. 1934) who is a descendant of a Lowell pioneer family but a Gary native, graduate of Lew Wallace High School. She became a Registered Nurse after training at St. Mary Mercy School of Nursing in 1955 and was awarded a B.A. in psychology at Indiana University Northwest in 1988.

They have seven children: Loretta (Frank Mikels) is an attorney and lives in Springfield, Illinois; Julie (Ron Olthoff) is co-owner of Accent on Advertising in Crown Point; Audrey and Carl Worthington, her husband, are the parents of Alan, the only grandchild to date, and live in West Chicago, Illinois; Joseph is employed by Jewel Foods and lives in Crown Point; Philip is a draftsman in Chicago; Teresa (Tim Sullivan) is a computer analyst at Whiteco Industries; and Pauline is a student at Indiana University Northwest.

After 40 years of service, Basil retired in 1957 and was honored with life membership in the Telephone Pioneers of America, Theodore N. Vail Chapter. He and Martha sold their home and moved to an apartment near Merrillville in 1971, enjoying visits with their grandchildren.

Basil passed away in 1974; Martha in 1981. They are buried at Calumet Park Cemetery.

by Paul A. Davis

DAVIS, NANCY LEE FRANKLIN
F57

Last Thoughts

I cling to the memories of other days as I sit in my cottage and watch the leaves blow on the trees and watch the coming and going of my neighbors.

Oh! Days of the happy long ago!

How wonderful to open memories doors and visit with you again.

Childhood and loving parents. How pleasant are the thoughts with which I recall you.

The old homestead with it's many memories is rich food for these days of utter loneliness.

And then girlhood, love and romance.

I look back upon you with much gladness.

Life was then so full of vigor.

Joy in every morning sunrise, hope and promise when the western sun went down.

Then the stepping over girlhood's borderland into the marriage life.

I recall you all, days of my early marriage.

The little soft bodies of children born. The love of companion and the struggle for a living.

Then dark clouds, death, hardships, loneliness and the struggle of a woman battling the world for her children.

Was that woman I? I can so well see her in memories, as she toiled, schemed and planned.

Keen-minded, quick-motioned – she wrestled with and conquered an existence when many strong-bodied men failed.

The early memory picture fades.

The children are grown, they marry. My heart bleeds as I see them in suffering and trouble.

Again, in middle life, I find contentment and satisfaction in marriage.

A kind husband who respects me and gives me freedom to work, plan, and live my life unhampered.

We shall see each other again in the great days of the tomorrow.

And, last pleasure of life, my little grandson.

I loved him with a great love. We conquered life and loneliness together.

God bless the little man-child who made for me in old age a task to keep my heart young.

But as he went out in the field of life, to garner what it had to offer him, so went out the joy and contentment of a full life.

And so I sit and think of other days that are gone.

I believe I will see my friends and loved ones just over the borderland.

The great day for me is not many years hence and I walk toward it unerringly, in expectancy in the full belief that all the promises are true and that I shall know again a great happiness in tomorrow's world.

I shall go to sleep. I shall awake to whatever God has prepared for those who have walked uprightly.

Dear ones, friends, past joys, with all be forgotten in tomorrow's land of promise.

And my cottage sanctuary gives me shelter, and my pension gives me daily comforts. So I wait – I await the Master's call.

Nancy Davis to Jack
Nancy Lee (Springs) Franklin Davis
Date of Birth: July 23, 1849
Died in 1938 at 89 years old
(These last thoughts were written around 1935 – 2-3 years before she died)

by Nancy Lee Franklin Davis

DEMMON, ALICE ISABEL MUNDELL
F58

Alice Isabel Mundell Demmon

She was born 7/21/1889, daughter of Elmore Hart and Harriet Wilson Mundell and granddaughter of Hobart's original settler, Samuel Sigler. Raised on the family farm in west Hobart, she became a teacher and for seventeen years taught in Lake Station and Merrillville. She married Floyd Earl Demmon of Merrillville and had two children, Floyd Earl Jr. and William. In later years, she served as case work reviewer for the Lake Co. Dept. of Public Welfare, retiring in 1959. An avid genealogist, she not only traced her families but served for many years as historian of the Lake Co. Historical Society, and coauthored the *Centennial History Of Lake Co.* She was a member of the Order of the Eastern Star for over fifty years, serving as worthy matron. Both she and her mother were active members of the Hobart First Methodist Church. She was a member of Potowatomie Chapter, National Society Of Daughters of the American Revolution, and active in many civic organizations such as P.T.A., Band Mothers, etc. Alice died 12/23/1969 at age 80 and is buried with her parents in the Old Hobart Cemetery.

Her husband Floyd was born 7/12/1890 in Merrillville and practiced law in Hobart for many years, serving as City Attorney for a time. He delivered the paper on Ross Township prepared by Hattie Palmer, daughter of Lake County's first doctor in 1933 at the Lake County Centennial celebration. He predeceased Alice on 8/6/1955 and is buried at Calumet Park Cemetery.

by Ruth Demmon

DEMMON, MR. AND MRS. FLOYD EARL JR.
F59

Mr. & Mrs. Floyd Earl Demmon Jr. and daughter Kristina Lynn.

He was born 1/30/1926, son of Floyd Earl and Alice Mundell Demmon and great grandson of Hobart's first settler, Samuel Sigler. He is also a great-great-great grandson of Merrillville Revolutionary soldier Stephen Wilcox, a great-great grandson of early Ross township settler Benjamin Demmon, and great-great grandson of Elizabeth Owens who gave the cemetery land, Pleasant View, where so many of his people are buried. Educated in Hobart school systems, he graduated from Purdue University in chemical engineering after serving as an officer in the U.S. Navy during World War II. He has worked over forty years in area steel mills, first USX and for the last 32 years Inland Steel. A member of The Iron And Steel Engineers, Instrument Society Senior member, and a fellow member of Purdue's President's Council, he is currently at this writing senior staff engineer in Inland's Energy Management and Planning Department. He has authored one U.S. Patent. His civic activities include serving on the Hobart City Council and as Precinct Committeeman, ten years as Scoutmaster of Troop 42 as well as Scoutmaster of a council troop at the 1969 National Jamboree, treasurer of his church for ten years as well as organ and finance committee chairman, president of both elementary and junior high PTA's, several times delegate to his party's state convention, lecturer on colonial history and the U.S. constitution, and numerous others. Married to Ruth Ellen Rosenbaum, the Demmons have sons Floyd Earl III and Randolph Alan as well as daughter Kristina Lynn.

Ruth Ellen Rosenbaum Demmon, daughter of Elmer and Helen Thompson Rosenbaum, was born 4/28/1926 and also attended Trinity Lutheran and Hobart schools. Member of an instrumental group in her youth, she played extensively before local organizations. She is an avid genealogist and registrar of Meshowke-To-Quah Chapter of the Daughters of the American Revolution. She, too, is active in her church and serves many hours in the office there. Expert at many crafts such as macreme, stained glass, sewing, crocheting, knitting, etc., she is much in demand for church and other organization projects. Her besetting hobby is collecting Barbie Dolls, of which she has very many, and is a member of the Valparaiso Dolls and Friends Club.

The Demmons are campers and have progressed from tent campers through large trailers to their present 34 ft. motor home. They enjoy classic music, travelling, their summer home in Michigan, and most of all their children and the latter's families. They look forward to his impending retirement and even greater travel opportunities.

by Ruth Demmon

DEMMON, JULIUS ALONZO
F60

Julius was born 7/24/1821 near Bolton, VT, the son of Benjamin and Betsy Morse Demmon and grandson of Revolutionary soldiers Amos Demmon and Daniel Morse. In the 1830s he emigrated with his father to Lake Co., IN, settling near Merrillville, and marrying Nancy Harriet Wilcox, granddaughter of Revolutionary soldier Stephen Wilcox. Their children were Clarissa, Charles, Clinton, John, Ann, Mary Jane, Eliza, Martha, Daniel, George, William, and Alice. It is an interesting insight into the sparsely settled county that three of his twelve children married members of the Owens family while two others married Burges. Julius was a careful man with money, plowing it back into land until at his death he owned over 2,000 acres and was the wealthiest landowner in the township. His holdings were amidst the present malls along U.S. 30. He died 10/16/1898 at home and is buried with his ancestors in Pleasant View Cemetery west of Merrillville. The funeral was conducted by Rev. Timothy Ball, author of the famous area histories. Following the funeral, the sons and daughters gathered at the old farm and without benefit of lawyers divided his vast holdings among themselves. His funeral was attended by his twelve children, their spouses, and 61 grandchildren!

Nancy Wilcox Demmon was born 1/23/1833 and died 3/9/1902, being buried with her husband in Pleasant View Cemetery. As with her husband, the Rev. Timothy Ball officiated.

Benjamin Demmon was born in 1786 near Bolton, VT., and emigrated to Lake Co., IN, in 1837. Unfortunately, he was a victim of drought and sickness that ravaged the early settlers here in the summer of 1838, dying in August of that year and being laid to rest in Pleasant View Cemetery. His widow, Betsy Morse Demmon, took up a claim three miles west of Merrillville with her children Almira, Melissa, Caroline, Loretta, and Julius. Another child, Alma, remained in VT and never came west.

Betsy Morse Demmon, born in 1787, came here with her husband. There is a tradition that, during the Revolution, her mother, Polly Gibbs Morse, overheard British officers tell their plans to her uncle who was a Tory. Getting a horse, she rode through the night to give the news to American troops in the area. Betsy passed away in March of 1868 and is buried also in the Pleasant View Cemetery near Merrillville.

by Ruth Demmon

DILLABAUGH, ELLIS G. FAMILY
F61

Ellis Dillabaugh was born July 12, 1893 in Crown Point, In. to Charles G. Dillabaugh and Emma Wemple Dillabaugh. In early years he formed a boyhood friendship with Fred Wise that they both maintained and enjoyed until Ellis's death October 20, 1975.

His marriage to Hazel Fisher of Hobart produced a son Grant, who married Lena Blackman of Valparaiso and Shirley, who married Eugene Magner of Chicago, Ill. The marriage ended in divorce. After a few years of farming in Colorado, Ellis returned to Crown Point and on April 16, 1923 he married Lora (Lorraine) Shay of Hessville, In. Four children were born to the marriage, Donald Gene on May 16, 1924, who married Joyce Stoner of Valparaiso, In.; Ellison William born on July 9, 1925, who married Louise Alexander of Merrillville; Phyllis Elaine on June 8, 1927, who married Donald J. Ross of Crown Point, and Howard Lynn on December 16, 1928 who married Marge Ready of Griffith.

Ellis bought the house moving business from his father, Charles and operated the business on Indiana Avenue in Crown Point, until 1937. In the throws of the comeback from the depression and in need of more room to expand his business, he sold his home and moved the family and business to Center Township on East State Road 8, a seven acre piece of the Murray Zieseniss farm. On that seven acres the family planted a fruit orchard and asparagus patch, raised pigs, chickens and cows and built the house moving business into a flourishing business. The business was subsequently operated by sons Ellison and Howard and at this time by Howard, after Ellisons retirement. Ellison remains on the home place, Grant is retired and lives in Butler, Pa. Donald is retired and lives in East Grandby, Ct., Shirley lives in LaPorte, In.; Phyllis lives in Center Township and Howard Lynn in Hebron, Ind.

by Donald J. Ross

DONCH, JOHN
F62

Just like most people residing in Lake County at the start of the Civil War, John Donch was originally from somewhere else. He'd been born in Germany in 1824, had served

John Donch, 7th Indiana Cavalry. (Courtesy Court House Museum, Crown Point).

five years in the German Army, and had prospected gold in California before coming to Lake County and settling in Lowell in 1853.

Donch joined the Thirteenth Illinois Cavalry in 1861 and rose steadily in the ranks to Second Lieutenant. He resigned in January, 1863 and eventually enlisted in the Seventh Indiana Cavalry when it formed in late 1863. Although he joined as a Private he was rapidly promoted, even receiving two promotions in one month.

The Seventh had a tough first winter which included fording ice-clogged rivers and much battle action.

Donch was wounded twice on a raid deep behind enemy lines in Mississippi and slid off his horse unconscious. He was left on the field, supposed dead. He awakened during the night and made his way to a nearby log cabin. There rebel soldiers robbed him and placed him under guard. When the Confederate Surgeon began treating his wounds, some of the soldiers suggested that he amputate Donch's hand, but the Surgeon declined.

For nine weeks Donch lay in an enemy hospital near death. Finally he recovered and served time in a number of prison camps before being sent to Charleston, South Carolina.

The Union gunboats were shelling Charleston and Donch, along with other Northern officers were compelled to stand exposed to their own navy's gunfire in a desperate Southern ploy to stop the bombardment. Conditions were terrible. His clothes were worn out and his only comfort was a horse blanket. His cavalry boots served as a pillow on the bare ground where he made his bed.

Finally in mid-December, 1864 he was exchanged. He was sent to Washington and eventually home. Upon arriving he was shocked to learn that he'd been presumed dead and all of his affairs had been neatly settled.

Donch ultimately rejoined his regiment in Louisiana and later served in Texas, where he was promoted to Captain.

After the war Donch was elected Sheriff of Lake County twice, but died in office.

by Mr. John R. Sickles

DOWDLE, KEVIN
F63

Kevin Dowdle, taken summer of 1985.

In the spring of 1980 Kevin Dowdle and Nancy (Cramer) Medeiros were searching for a place of their own so they could be married and start their family. Both Kevin and Nancy were from Glenwood, Illinois but they were lured over the Indiana border by the lower cost of living. In May of 1980 they moved into their first home together in Dyer. They were already a family of three because Nancy had a one year old son, Nicholas, from her first marriage to Darrel Medeiros. By June of 1984 Darrel had resettled in Fresno, California so Kevin went to court and officially adopted Nicholas as his own son. Kevin and Nancy were married on May 1, 1982 by Judge Bielek in Crown Point, Indiana. By now they are a family of six. Their four children are: Nicholas James, born April 19, 1979 in Olympia Fields, IL; Megan Maureen, born December 9, 1982 in Munster, IN; Ashley Diana, born December 9, 1986 in Munster, IN; Patrick Kevin, born April 14, 1988 in Munster, IN.

Currently Nicholas is in the 4th grade and Megan is in kindergarten at Hammond Baptist Grade School in Schererville. The school is associated with their church, First Baptist of Hammond. However, when they first moved to Indiana they were Catholic and were members of St. Michael's parish in Schererville. They changed churches in October of 1983.

Kevin Thomas Dowdle was born on September 29, 1955 in Evergreen Park, Illinois to Richard and Lucille (Costigan) Dowdle. He has one brother, Richard, who is nine years older. He grew up in an area of Chicago called South Chicago and lived only a couple blocks away from the nurses's apartments where Richard Speck committed his infamous brutal murders and terrified the nation in July of 1966. Kevin attended Our Lady Gate of Heaven grade school and then attended St. Leo High School until his family moved to Glenwood in 1970. In 1973 he graduated from Bloom High School in Chicago Heights. He went on to get a college degree in business from Prairie State College in 1975. He is currently the credit manager in the corporate office for Armstrong's Diamond Center. In his spare time he enjoys golf, fishing, computers and genealogy.

Nancy Ann Cramer was born on October 5, 1955 in Chicago, Illinois to Leith and Geraldine (Shisler) Cramer. As the only child she enjoyed a childhood of plenty which included many different types of music lessons and also some dancing and acting. From her father she has a half-sister, fourteen years her senior, named Judy. Judy's whereabouts are unknown but some think she might have ended up in Texas. Nancy spent most of her childhood in Blue Island, Illinois where she attended grade school and graduated from Eisenhower High School in 1973. It was that year when she got a job as a nurses' aid at St. Francis Hospital in Blue Island that she immediately knew that a career in some field of medicine was the choice for her. In 1976 she received her college degree in Medical Technology from Moraine Valley Community College. Later that year, in September, she left for Hawaii to live with a family and help them start their own business. It was there that she met her first husband Darrel. They were married on August 14, 1977 in Honolulu and in October they chose to come back to Chicago hoping to launch Darrel's career as a professional trumpeter. That failed and Darrel decided to follow his dream and in September of 1979 he left. Eventually he ended up in Fresno, CA. Nancy's life decidedly improved after that for shortly thereafter she met Kevin. Nancy has been employed by Our Lady of Mercy Hospital in Dyer as a Medical Technologist since February 1983. Before that she worked at Community Hospital in Munster but was laid off in 1982 while on a maternity leave of absence. Her hobbies include genealogy, computers and reading. She is currently a member of Mensa, National Genealogical Society and a prospective member of the Daughters of the American Revolution.

by Nancy A. Dowdle

DWYER, HON. SCHUYLER COLFAX
F64

Hon. Schuyler Colfax Dwyer was born in Washington, D.C., July 22, 1869. He was named for that eminent Indiana statesman, Schuyler Colfax, of whom he still treasures a photograph with autograph. At an early age Schuyler's parents moved to Lake County, Ind., where he received most of his early schooling in Crown Point and Lowell. He pursued the preparatory course at Depauw, and the high school course at Washington City, where his father held a government position. Here he was a member of the famous Cadet Corps. He taught one term of school in Lake County, and returning to Washington, took the first year of his law course at Georgetown University. There he had the inestimable privilege of studying law in the office of Mr. Barnard, now one of the District Court judges in Washington. Mr. Dwyer completed his college and law course at Depauw University in 1889. In 1890 he was married to Miss Sylvia Bacon. Two daughters, Portia and Helen, grace this union. He has been engaged in the practice of law since his graduation. In 1893 he located in Lowell, where he enjoys a pleasant and lucrative business and a comfortable home. He is the recipient of the unanimous nomination on the Republican ticket for Joint Representative for Lake and Newton Counties. Mr. Dwyer is physically, intellectually, morally and socially equipped for exacting public service. He is well known among the fraternal orders, especially the Knights of Pythias and Odd Fellows. He is respected for his ability and fairness at the bar and for his public spirit in his own town.

(Compiled from the Souvenir Album of Lake Co. Ind., Crown Point-Lowell, June 18-19, 1909.)

ENGELMAN FAMILY
F65

The Engelman Family in Hammond: 1920-46

My father, George T. Engelman, was born in 1882, and raised in the southern Illinois village of Hamel, Madison County, across from St. Louis, Missouri.

Helen Wood, my mother, was the youngest of three sisters in the family of Henry and Eleanor Oxman Wood, of Albion, Edwards County, having descended from the early English immigrants who settled in this southern Illinois area around 1815.

My father was a grandson of Augustus Engelmann, who came to Cape Girardeau County, Missouri, with his family in October, 1845. They left relatives in the village (now a city of 30,000) of Northeim, Germany — located about 75 miles southeast of Hannover.

My grandfather Wood moved his little family to East St. Louis, IL in the early 1900s, searching for more work in his trade — that of cabinet making. He was a Sergeant in Company H, 136th Regiment, Illinois Volunteers during the Civil War, and his honorable discharge proudly hangs in my study.

It was on 21 October 1911 that my parents were married in St. Louis by a retired Lutheran minister who had baptized my father many years before. It was in 1911 that my father began working for the American Steel Foundries at the Granite City, IL. plant. I first saw the light of day on 11 November 1919 — being elivered at home where my folks lived in Granite City.

In rapid-fire succession, my father was sent as a troubleshooter to Alliance, Ohio; Sharon, Pennsylvania, and Hammond, Indiana. Maybe the firm thought our little family had had enough moving, so it was in 1920 that we settled down in Hammond, and my father took on the responsibilities of purchasing agent for the ASF Hammond Works. He held that job until he was forced to retire because of poor health in 1944, and he and mother moved from Hammond to Albion, IL, my mother's original hometown. There they raised chickens and garden produce, and enjoyed visiting my mother's relatives. Unfortunately, he didn't live long to savor the fun they were having in that small county-seat town. He passed away in August, 1946, at the age of 63. Mother was with us when she died at our Gloversville, N.Y. hospital in June, 1984, two months short of being 95 years old.

Let's jump back to October 1920, when our family of three moved into a brand new house at 1234 Jackson Street in Hammond. We hated to lose that easy-to-remember number when Hammond renumbered its streets, and our 1234 became 6410 Jackson Avenue.

Some names of neighbors I can recall in that block between Cleveland and 165th were: Franks, Beville, Spohn, Coleman, Seddlemeyer, Mishrock, MacDermid, Lockman, Erdman, Huntington, Green, Swingendorf and McCartney. I'm sorry I can't remember them all. I can see faces, but not the names.

We were in the Wallace School District, and well do I remember our excellent teachers and especially Principal Blanche Nixon. Lots of common sense and firm discipline ran Wallace School in those days before WWII. Parents backed the teachers and Miss Nixon 100%! And that's a condition you don't find often enough these days.

And then there was Boy Scout Troop 37 which met at Hyde Park Methodist Church at the corner of Harrison and Cleveland. This was a neighborhood troop, drawing boys from many blocks around the church. Troop 37 was known for its many campouts on weekends at various parks in the area — Wicker Park and the Forest Preserve in Calumet City are two that I remember.

I attended Washington School for 8th grade, and then went to Hammond High — graduating with the Class of '37. Boy! It makes you feel the years when your 50th Class Reunion is held. It's great to look at the group photo of that Class of 1937 and bring back many fond remembrances.

Then came Hitler, Tojo and WWII. With four years at Indiana University under my belt, I changed from civvies to olive drab. In September 1943 it was marriage for Irene Avery of Webb City, MO, and me — just weeks before I shipped out of New York City harbor on the USS Rocky Mount, to spend almost two years in the Central and Southwest Pacific areas. Christmas morning 1945 saw me struggling with overstuffed duffle bags up the Carroll Street apartment stairs to greet my wife after long months of separation. Shortly after my return from service, we moved to Bloomington, IN, and a new life.

by George T. Engelman, Jr.

ENGELMAN, GEORGE
F66

The Engelman Family in Hammond, 1920-46

My father, George T. Engelman, was born in 1882, and raised in the southern Illinois village of Hamel, Madison County, across from St. Louis, Missouri.

Helen Wood, my mother, was the youngest of three sisters in the family of Henry and Eleanor Oxman Wood, of Albion, Edwards County, having descended from the early English immigrants who settled in this southern Illinois area around 1815.

My father was a grandson of Augustus Engelmann, who came to Cape Girardeau County, Missouri with his family in October 1845. They left relatives in the village (now a city of 30,000) of Northeim, Germany, located about 75 miles southeast of Hannover.

My grandfather Wood moved his little family to East St. Louis, IL in the early 1900s, searching for more work in his trade – that of cabinet making. He was a Sergeant in Company H, 136th Regiment, Illinois Volunteers during the Civil War, and his honorable discharge proudly hangs in my study.

It was on 21 October 1911 that my parents were married in St. Louis by a retired Lutheran minister who had baptized my father many years before. It was in 1911 that my father began working for the American Steel Foundries at the Granite City, IL plant. I first saw the light of day on 11 November 1919 – being delivered at home where my folks lived in Granite City.

In rapid-fire succession, my father was sent as a trouble shooter to Alliance, Ohio; Sharon, Pennsylvania and Hammond, Indiana. Maybe the firm thought our little family had had enough moving, so it was in 1920 that we settled down in Hammond, and my father took on the responsibilities of purchasing agent for the ASF Hammond Works. He held that job until he was forced to retire because of poor health in 1944, and he and mother moved from Hammond to Albion, IL, my mother's original hometown. There they raised chickens and garden produce, and enjoyed visiting my mother's relatives. Unfortunately, he didn't live long to savor the fun they were having in that small county-seat town. He passed away in August 1946 at the age of 63. Mother was with us when she died at our Gloversville, NY hospital in June 1984, two months short of being 95 years old.

Let's jump back to October 1920, when our family of three moved into a brand new house at 1234 Jackson Street in Hammond. We hated to lose that easy-to-remember number when Hammond renumbered its streets, and our 1234 became 6410 Jackson Avenue.

Some names of neighbors I can recall in that block between Cleveland and 165th were: Franks, Beville, Spohn, Coleman, Seddelmeyer, Mishrock, MacDermid, Lockman, Erdman, Huntington, Green, Swingendorf McCartney. I'm sorry I can't remember them all. I can see faces, but not the names.

We were in the Wallace School District, and well do I remember our excellent teachers and especially Principal Blanche Nixon. Lots of common sense and firm discipline ran Wallace School in those days before WW II. Parents backed the teachers and Miss Nixon 100 percent! And that's a condition you don't find often enough these days.

And when there was Boy Scout Troop 37 which met at Hyde Park Methodist Church at the corner of Harrison and Cleveland. This was a neighborhood troop, drawing boys from many blocks around the church. Troop 37 was known for its many campouts on weekends at various parks in the area – Wicker Park and the Forest Preserve in Calumet City are two that I remember.

I attended Washington School for 8th grade, and then went to Hammond High, graduating with the Class of '37. Boy! It makes you feel the years when your 50th Class Reunion is held. It's great to look at the group photo of that Class of 1937 and bring back many fond remembrances.

Then came Hitler, Tojo and WW II. With four years at Indiana University under my belt, I changed from civvies to olive drab. In September 1943 it was marriage for Irene Avery of Webb City, MO and me – just weeks before I shipped out of New York City harbor on the USS Rocky Mount, to spend almost two years in the Central and Southwest Pacific areas. Christmas morning 1945 saw me struggling with overstuffed duffle bags up the Carroll Street apartment stairs to greet my wife after long months of separation. Shortly after my return from service, we moved to Bloomington, IN and a new life.

by George T. Engelman, Jr.

FAGEN FAMILY
F67

Anthony Fuegen (Fagen) married Catherine Fritchen in Frier, Germany in 1853. Came to America with other German families arriving in Indiana around 1854 and settled in Turkey Creek (Merrillville).

Anthony (July 7, 1826-Jan 1, 1891) and Catherine Dec. 19, 1829-Oct 30, 1904 had nine children.

John (Sept 10, 1854) left home as a young man to seek his fortune out west. Got as far as Iowa. Met and married Mary Holms. Settled in Iowa and raised 8 children, Frank, Ressa, Anthony, Walter, Mabel, Lyla, Blanch and Howard.

Michael (Oct 26, 1856/May 2, 1929) m Anna Lillig (July 19, 1865/Feb 23, 1943) on Nov 24, 1885 in Clear Creek Iowa. They had 3 children, Anthony, Nicholas and Marie. Adopted Eugene Geiger Dec 1886.

Margaret (Oct 26, 1858/Nov 4, 1858)

Mary (Sept 11, 1859) (shown 6 mos old in 1860 census, no other information)

Magdalena (Nov 19, 1861) m Peter Schneider, 3 children Anthony, John and Mary.

Margaret (Oct 18, 1864/Nov 17, 1881)

Peter G. (Sept 21, 1865/Jan 7, 1957) m Hannah Mangold June 17, 1897, 1 son Ray.

Nicholas (Feb 4, 1868/Nov 14, 1934) m Elizabeth Simon May 20, 1896. 7 children, Catherine m Wm Smith, Michael m Cora Demon, Margaret never married, Helen m John Wishtoski, Hugo m Eunice Long, Fred married Marie Henderlong.

Peter Stephen (Mar 12, 1870/Apr 15, 1872)

by Maureen Miller

FAGEN, MICHAEL FAMILY
F68

Anna Mary Lillig (Bohrofen) 3-19-1832 to 3-25-1922, married John Lillig. She was born in Tuensdorf, Germany.

Anthony (Foegen) Fagen and Catherine (Fritchen) Fagen.

Anna Lillig 7-19-1865 to 2-23-1943 married Michael Fagen 10-26-1956 to 5-2-1929. Wedding picture taken 11-24-1885 in Cedar Creek.

Michael, while visiting his brother in Iowa, met Anna at a dance. Anna Lillig's parents were Anna Mary Bohrofen born March 19, 1832 in Tuensdorf, Germany, (died March 25, 1922 in Keota, Iowa), and John Lillig. Anna was born in Linsdorf, Germany July 19, 1865. Mike and Anna were married in Iowa on November 24, 1885 and moved to Dyer, Indiana. They brought to the union a capacity for hard work and religious fervor (especially Anna), sternness and friendliness (especially Mike). Anna by nature was a kindly, motherly soul and did much to assist her fellow townsmen when there was sickness in a family, a new baby, etc. They adopted a ten year old boy, Eugene Geiger in December of 1886. On August 11, 1887 Anthony was born.

They had several business ventures before opening the original funeral parlor. They opened a meat market (did the butchering also). Later they added a bakery. In 1893 they ran a

Homestead, Turkey Creek, 61st and Broadway. Pictured (L to R) Peter Fagen, Mike, Roy, (seated) Mrs. A. Catherine, Catherine, Mary Schnieder Francee, baby Margaret, Eli, Nick and Aunt Hanna.

79

restaurant along side the railroad in Griffith serving the train passengers who were traveling to and from the World Columbian Expo in Chicago. They made money in that venture. Moved to Crown Point and opened a saloon. Their second son Nicholas was born August 19, 1894 in Crown Point.

They moved back to Dyer in 1896 and opened the funeral parlor which burned down shortly after. Nick was showing friends his brother's fireworks which were stored under their bed — he lit a match so they could see. Soon everything was gone. Townspeople banded together and rebuilt the house and funeral home on the opposite side of Adeway Road (Hart Street). The building still stands. Marie was born June 24, 1898.

In 1910 Dyer was incorporated and Michael was elected trustee, an office he held until his death in 1929.

Eugene (4-22-1876/5-6-51) m Barbara Ech (10-17-1880/2-2-68).

Anthony (8-11-1887/6-6-66) m Louise Schaller (1-25/1891/6-11-46) and their family of 9 children grew up at 2125 Hart St. Dyer. The house still stands. Rosemary 1911-1988, Joseph, Frances 1915, Dolores 1918, Mary Ann 1920-1941, Raymond 1922-59, Doris 1928, Donald 1932 and Daniel 1933. Dan and his family live south of Dyer.

Nicholas (8-19-1894/7-22-1977) m Eva Turner Aug. 14, 1929; 3 children Maureen 1930, Donna 1933 and Michael 1935.

Marie married Roy Hilbrich from Schererville. In 1932 they built a home at 2152 Nondrof Street. They had three children. Jim and Tom and their families still reside in Dyer. Patricia (John) Rosinko moved south of Dyer with her family (see Hilbrich family).

by Maureen Miller

FAGEN, NICHOLAS FAMILY
F69

Nick spent most of his childhood picking bugs off potato plants and tending the garden. He also walked pigs to the slaughter house in Chicago.

As Nick grew older, he would help his mother and father in the funeral business. The weather could be freezing, but when a call came they went as far as Merrillville or Crown Point sometimes with only a blanket and lantern for warmth. In 1910 Dyer was incorporated. Michael Fagen was on Dyer's first Board of Trustees representing the First Ward. Salary received was $30 annually. He held this position until his death in 1929 when Nick took over his seat.

The children attended St. Joseph Grade School. When Nick finished ninth grade at St. John Township High School (located on Route 30 near the Monon tracks), he quit school and immediately went to work in the brickyards north of town. In 1910, then 16, he left for Chicago to serve as an apprentice in a funeral home on the "Gold Coast." In early 1918 he and his cousin Frank Lillig joined the Marines.

The two were allowed to be together during their hitch. They were in the 13th regiment going to Europe. There were 13 ships in the convoy. Their ship was hit 13 times (and stayed afloat). They landed on the 13th of November — the war had ended. Thirteen became Nick's lucky number.

Nick attended Indiana Mortuary School in Indianapolis, graduated, and was licensed in 1922. Returned to the family home and went to work as a dispatcher for the Monon. At the same time was a deputy coroner and helping at the funeral parlor. Eva Turner graduated from Valparaiso University and came to Dyer to teach the primary classes at St. John Township School located on Route 30 near the Monon crossing. She roomed at the Fagen's where she met Nick. Mike Fagen became ill and died in 1929.

Eva, 26, and Nick, 35, were married on August 14, 1929 in the St. Joseph Church rectory. They bought the business from Anna, who then lived with her daughter Marie until her death on February 23, 1942. Nick and Eva had three children: Maureen, Donna and Mike. Eva became a licensed funeral director and helped at the funeral home. She played the organ for funerals and at Sunday School in the Methodist Church, which she was a charter member. She was active in the American Legion Auxiliary Post 66 in Griffith. She gave book reviews at club meetings and over the radio. As a member of the Legion, she was chairman of the committee who compiled pictures and information on the servicemen from Dyer, Schererville, Griffith and St. John serving in World War II.

In 1941, Nick opened a branch establishment in Highland where he developed a perpetual memorial to his parents, consisting of a rock garden casket setting. At the time, he received recognition in his professional circles. In addition to his enviable professional reputation, he became quite prominent for his work with youth of the district, having been the first Boy Scout Master in Lake County south of Hammond. He was also a member of the Munster Lions Club, American Legion Post 66, VFW and served as Deputy Coroner for 15 years.

Maureen was born Dec. 5, 1930 m. Robert Miller May 29, 1951. Four children, Larry, Jerry, Terri and Gary.

Donna Jean May 29, 1933 m. Julian Nichols 6-4-60. Three children: Brian, Bradley, and Lori Ann.

Michael 11-17-35 m. Catherine Rascher 10-5-57. Seven children: Patrick, Margaret, Catherine, Michael, Sheila, Nora and Daniel.

by Maureen Miller

FANCHER, RICHARD
F70

Ventures in Wild Lake County

The Fanchers were of French descent, coming to this country around 1700. They quickly figured in the histories of New Jersey, New York and Connecticut. The name Fancher or Faucher often appears as F-A-N-S-H-E-R in some early records.

The first Fancher to gain fame was Captain Richard Fancher of the Philadelphia Militia who was born in 1731. He is listed as Fancher number six in William Hoyt Fancher's book "The Fancher Family," which is part of the Indiana State Archives Collection.

Captain Fancher had seven children, among them a son named Ephraim, who later became the father of Richard Fancher who Fancher Lake at the County Fairgrounds is named after. His mother's name was the same as my mother's, Margret (Nitzer) Fancher. Richard had two brothers and two sisters.

Many of the current day Fanchers that are now living in Kentucky, Tennessee, Gary and Valparaiso can be traced directly through this line (through Richard's brother David). David and his family appear in many old records in Southern Indiana and Kentucky.

The first Fancher to come to Crown Point was Richard, who was the fourth person in this family with the same first name. At one time there were two Richard Fancher's living in Indiana, which made research confusing. One stayed in Southern Indiana, while our Richard came north. He was born in Pennsylvania Nov. 10, 1799, and died at the age of 94 July 19,

Nick and Eva Fagen

1893. He seems to follow the typical migration pattern of the early settlers from the east, coming through Ohio, then to Southern Indiana before dispersing elsewhere.

Richard is listed as a landowner around 1820 in Clairmont County, Ohio. Land in this area was awarded to soldiers in the Revolutionary War by the U.S. government, sometimes in lieu of pay. Richard probably inherited the land. Between 1822-1834 Richard shows up as a landowner in Bartholomew and Fountain Counties, Ind. He married a Presbyterian woman named Mariah Hulich, March 29, 1822. Mariah later sponsored religious meetings in Crown Point's first Courthouse.

In all Richard and Mariah later had six daughters, and one son. By 1834, the family was on the move, finally arriving in Crown Point from Attica by 1835. In the previous year, Richard had ventured into wild lake County and set his claim at Fancher Lake. While returning with his family to what would later be the Lake County Fairgrounds, he and his family had a "close encounter" with the Potawatomi Indians. Timothy Ball writes that tensions were eased after Fancher sold the Indians some well-watered whiskey, in exchange for furs at a reduced rate.

During this time the Potawatomis were being forced from their lands by white man settlements. Soon President Andrew Jackson stepped in and carved Lake County into homesteads and Indian Reservations. All of section 17 which today includes the fairgrounds, Luke's, Taft School and back north to South Street was turned over to Mis-Sink-Gu-Guah, an Indian squaw. Her name translated means goddess of war.

About this time the famous "squatters union" was created. Written by Solon Robinson and Richard Fancher, the document petitioned then President Jackson to allow the settlers to stay on land that now belonged to the Indians. I have looked through the Squatters Union Book several times, and have never found Fancher's name in it, but Ball says that he signed it. The book is currently kept in an air-conditioned vault at First National Bank.

Anyway, the settlers were denied rights to the Indian property and were forced to leave. Crown Point resident Catherine Madison called the settlers "a bunch of claim jumpers" foiled in their attempt to upset the President's Proclamation in favor of the Indians.

Later we find that Fancher gave up his claim at the lake, and purchased 40 acres of land in Hanover Township from the Winamac Land Office. This land today belongs to Mary Pavelchak, and is known as the Maplecroft Farm. This land was also the Henry Von Hollen Homestead. Fancher sold Von Hollen the property in 1857 for $300. An old home weathered, defeated by dry rot and held together with pegs was recently torn down on this site.

It is not known if Fancher ever farmed the property. Census records of 1840 show that he moved into Crown Point, which was then called Lake Courthouse. Also at this time Cedar Lake was known as The Lake of the Red Cedars. Freeport was a little settlement on Cedar Lake. And a town known as Clark bounded by today's Clark Street was beginning to grow on the north side of the Square.

About 1844, Fancher's wife Mariah filed one of the earliest divorces in Lake County history. In many books, the family members are referred to as Presbyterians, excluding Richard. The divorce records indicate the two were constantly feuding, which may or may not have had a religious tone.

At this point Mariah disappeared from county records, and Richard and his family moved in with one of his son-in-laws, wealthy landowner James C. Nicholson, who had married Richard's daughter Margret Ann. Between 1840 and 1860 the rest of his daughters marry. Sarah marries Sanford Clark, Mary Ellen weds Harry Church. Maria marries James Clingan, a well-decorated soldier and Elizabeth ties the knot with Walter Alton. Richard's only son, age 10 and a sixth daughter, age seven died in 1846 and were buried in Crown Point's first cemetery which is located on the north side of the hill overlooking Lake Seven. This property was owned by the Wheeler family for many years.

About 1880, Fancher sold the other portion of the Mills property west of the high school to James Nicholson, and then moved in with another son-in-law, James Clingan.

At this time, Fancher is 60 years old. An old issue of the Crown Point Register lists him as one of the first petit jurors in the town. He also served as constable of Clark, which now has become part of Center Township. At this time Richard Fancher owns 5 acres on the west side of what is today Crown Point High School. A house built in 1929 belonging to Dr. Koscielniak sets on the property today. This property for many years before was owned by Ephraim Sowash, and his two daughters Georgianna Sprinkle, and Christine McMichael. Fancher also owned a third of an acre on the southwest corner of West Joliet Street and West Street. On this property today is Ray Handley's Hastee-Freeze, and a home at 119 S. West St., owned by Sheldon Making.

According to Center Township Assessor Oliver H. Cooper and his deputy Sue Landske, this home was built in 1874. Fancher bought this property from Celista Mills in 1849 for $50.

Mrs. Mills began unloading many properties owned by her late husband Michael Mills about this time. She later married John Luther (Luther's Grove) who bought the rest of her late husband's interests, and paid off all his debts. Mills at this time, owned all the property where Crown Point High School sets today, and the south side of the square as well. Fancher sold this house and property to his daughter Mary Church who in turn sold the property to Fanchers other son-in-law James Nicholson.

Since this time other familiar names who have owned property adjacent in this block of West Street have been the Parry's, Stone's, Bob Casda, Herman Jebens the iceman, the Lauerman's, Batterman's, Holton's, Niksch family, John B. Kolling, Brasnuban's, George Vinnedge, Bruckman's, Sikora's, Blankenship's, Davis, Tracy, Rosenbower's, Connell's, and a large brickhouse belonging to the Weinbergs once stood where the bus barn is today. The famous Wise brickyard was on West Walnut Street nearby. On just about every abstract for these properties lists Solon Robinson as one of the first owners.

by John R. Ghrist

FANCHER, RICHARD
F71

Richard Fancher's Life after 1880

About 1880, Crown Point pioneer settler Richard Fancher sold part of his Mills property west of the high school to James Nicholson and moved in with son-in-law, James Clingan.

The Clingan home, according to 1880 Lake County assessment records, was on a 4½ acre tract near the corner of Wirtz Road and North Street.

In 1930, an account was read by Jessie Hill recalling early homes and real estate in the area at a meeting of the old settlers reunion. The story gives a rundown of some early families on the west side of the Square, mentioning the James Clingan home, Laws, Taylors, Thomas, Hardings; the Ruschlis, who lived at the bottom of the hill on West Joliet Street, and the Hoffman House with its many corners. (It may be one of two houses south of the Phillips 66 station.) The Wirtz's house, and the Hubers' house and new grist mill are included.

The Huber home still stands today.

The article also mentions Luther's Grove, Crown Point's second cemetery, located where the Crown Point High School track is today. The Ruschlis, about 1871, donated a large tract of land which became Crown Point's third cemetery next to Maplewood on south Indiana 55.

Incidentally at this time, Joliet Street was called the Logansport-Joliet State Road.

Crown Point's first opera house was located on West Joliet Street, according to Adelbert and Charlotte Wheeler Verplank. James Clingan is buried in Maplewood Cemetery; his land was later subdivided. Today, it includes several homes that were built about 1947.

Another interesting item came from the Presbyterian Church records which listed clerk Harry Church and his wife Mary Ellen (Fancher) as being dismissed from the church for joining the Plymouth Brethren Church. While we're on the subject of religion, Cedar Lake resident David Howkinson recently showed me an old book, "The Life of Jesus Christ," that he purchased in an antique sale. The book has Maria Fancher's name in the front. The book also contained a newspaper clipping announcing her marriage plans. The book is over 100 years old.

Another fact I don't think that we will ever understand why Richard Fancher sold (quit deed) the entire section of 17 acres some 50 years after he had lost his claim to the fairgrounds property. Fancher sold the property to a neighbor, Eliza M. Thomas about 1860. The account of this transaction is mentioned in part one of my report. Thomas was taken to court, and his claim was declared null and void by the Court of Common Pleas. Heirs had purchased the fairground property from the Indians.

Still living with the Clingans in 1890, "The Lake County Star" article mentions Richard Fancher this way: "Although now 90 years old, he is still seen quite regularly walking around town." Fancher, known as Uncle Dick to everyone who knew him, died July 19, 1893, at the Clingan home. Geisen's Funeral Home conducted the service the next day. Geisen's also handled the funerals of Sean Fancher in 1885, and John Fancher in 1878. These could have been two of Uncle Dick's children.

The real mystery now is where Richard

81

Fancher is buried.

He is not listed in any of the county cemetery records compiled some time ago by Avis Brown, Mary Lou Vanderlaan and Frances McBride. "The Crown Point Register" carried a front page story on his death, mentioning his passing, because of old age, at the Clingan home.

We have already concluded that the Clingans lived in Crown Point. His final remains could have been buried near Lake Seven with his younger children.

He could have also been buried at Luther's Grove. Luther's Grove, according to Crown Point resident Vernon Heintz, was located near the high school football field. The bones of the dead in this area were removed shortly before the high school was built, and re-interred in the Crown Point Cemetery, or Maplewood. Mrs. Vanderlaan said she still recalls seeing bones and human remains on that property when heavy equipment began to level the land. Fancher could have been missed, and his remains scattered under Crown Point High School.

Fancher could also have been buried in one of those graves that existed on the top of Buck Hill. Again, Ben Brown recalls seeing markers and stones there as late as the 1940's.

Richard Fancher could have been buried on his property as some people were in those days. One Crown Point resident reported recently that while completing an addition to his garage, part of a skeleton was discovered next to his foundation, about four feet under ground.

The most popular explanation of this mystery is shared by Bert Verplank former publisher of The Lake County Star and Crown Point resident Catherine Madison. Verplank suggests that Fancher was indeed buried in the Crown Point-Maplewood Cemetery. His marker possibly was lost, broken, or stolen.

Meanwhile Mrs. Madison suggests that the Fanchers were too well-known and affluent to allow his body to be buried just anywhere. Each daughter married successful businessmen, who could have easily paid for a dignified funeral.

It is, however, a shame that after all the work members of the DAR have done in collecting data on old area residents, that this one should escape them. The information is also lost because of two fires which destroyed records. And still too, Fancher's grave could have long been lost, even before the DAR began its intensive work.

Timothy Ball writing in the 1895 "Old Settler Reports" sums it up this way . . . "Some of us have not done all that we could have done in preserving from desecration and oblivion the resting places of our pioneer dead." So Richard Fancher who had been in the county 58 years, the oldest settler, is laid to rest, and no man knoweth where.

In another line of the Fancher family comes a string of wealthy lawyers and landowners. These are uncles and grandparents of my mother. They are not directly related to the late Richard Fancher. A common mistake is to acquaint Fancer Lake with the modern day Fanchers, like Reuben, Thaddeus, Thad and William Fancher. The truth is that all of these Fanchers came to, or were born in Crown Point some 50 years after Uncle Dick had set his claim at the fairgrounds. The last names were the same, so the Lake stayed named Fancher Lake. As a young child coming to the fair each year, I thought that the lake was named after grandpa.

There were a number of Richard Fanchers who made following the family line difficult; there were four people named Thaddeus Fancher. The first born in England in 1777 came from England to Ulster County, New York. Several Fanchers were alredy here at this time, and were instrumental in the settling of several towns in New York, Connecticut and New Jersey.

The first Thaddeus married Sarah Mead, the daughter of General Mead, a Revolutionary War hero. They had 12 children. One of those children was also named Thaddeus who spent most of his life on a farm in Huron County, Ohio.

The second Thaddeus married a Connecticut woman, Amy Chapman. They had 10 children, and once more one of the children was named Thaddeus. This Thaddeus also was known as Thaddeus Seymour, or T.S. as he was later called. He became one of the most successful lawyers in Lake County history. Born in 1845 in Ohio, he attended college in Indiana and Michigan, before coming to Crown Point in 1868. T.S. was the seventh child of Thaddeus the Second. Meanwhile the oldest child of the family and T.S.'s brother Reuben Fancher also ventured to Crown Point.

Reuben first lived in a log cabin, near Leroy, known now as the Rosey Rainer Farm, near the Dillabaugh estate. Both Reuben and T.S. owned vast amounts of real estate in Lake County. On an 1880 map of Crown Point, supplied by Crown Point resident Walter Breyfogle, it shows the Fancher property on the northside of East Joliet Street, and east of Ridge Street.

Reuben married Mary Hawkins in 1857. They had four children: Flora, who died as an infant, William R., Mary and Grace who never married. Mary, known to many folks as May Fancher, married well-known contractor E.H. Cowell. Crowell built many fine buildings and bridges around Lake County.

May and E.H. had two daughters, Essa and Cecil. Essa married attorney Edwin Knight. Cecil married John R. Krost. Krost was the Center Township Justice of the Peace for 20 years. Cecil served two terms as Eagle Creek Justice of the Peace, until the office was replaced by the small claims court a few years ago.

The Reuben Fanchers moved from Leroy to Crown Point, and purchased about 20 acres near the intersection of Indiana Avenue and East Joliet Street. The 1909 city directory lists the family at 630 E. Joliet. But today the Fancher mansion has the address of 928 E. Joliet. The family was routed once by fire, but returned home after repairs were completed. The family also lived at 428 S. Main St. about 1909.

Reuben served as deputy sheriff, and for a short time lived in the jail where his son William Reuben was born.

Reuben's name appears on a plaque in the old Courthouse. He and his son also operated a well-drilling and tin smith business. Reuben died in 1909 and is buried at Maplewood.

Reuben's son William Reuben probably invented the practical joke. Great grandpa Will, as he was called, capitalized on the fact that he was born in the jail building, by telling everyone, "not to expect much from him."

Vernon Heintz, a former clerk at the Letz factory, tells us that Will used to work at the old Fogli Hotel. The hotel today sets on the Kankakee River just south of Shelby. The Lake County Star correspondent Pat Tilton said the hotel was a favorite lodge for people from as far away as England. Many hunters and trappers stayed there, while they explored the wilds of the Kankakee River. The hotel is now the home of Jack and Edith Lessie, and has been renamed Camelot.

Back in the early 20's, trappers and fishermen would be served their main meal at suppertime. And Will would be cooking 'possum for the boys.

One night the meal was through, some of the men wanted second helpings. When Will Fancher went back into the kitchen, he didn't have any more food. So, he snatched up the hotel pet, a large stringy alley cat, and prepared it.

After the meal, compliments for the dinner were passed around. Then the men, who usually played and teased the cat after dinner, inquired about the whereabouts of the cat. It was at this point, that old great grandpa Will informed them that they had just eaten it.

Sometimes Will would put up children to perform some of his stunts. One time he dragged an outhouse into the Crown Point Square and placed a prominent businessman's shingle in front of it.

Other stories still abound about his mischief. His antics, however, were not amusing to his wife Myrtle Ennis who soon left him. Myrtle was a first cousin to Father Boney, a well-known priest from Lowell.

My grandpa Bill (Will's son) also liked to tease. He used to call me "Pieface." His favorite remark was, "I'll hurry up and eat my dessert and help you eat yours."

I cringed when I used to see him remove all the pickles from a jar and then drink the juice that remained.

Grandpa Bill was married three times. He had three daughters, my mother, Marge Ghrist of South Holland, Ill., Enid Eisele, now living in Florida, and Genevive, who died very young.

Bill Fancher left Crown Point sometime in the 1920's, and finally settled in South Holland, Ill. For some 60 years, he ran a successful printing business that still carries the Fancher name today.

He died in 1968.

by John R. Ghrist

FEDORCHAK, PAUL
F72

Brief History and Genealogy

An ethnical mix of Hungarians, Czechs, and Slovaks entered the United States from the Austria/Hungarian empire in the late 1880's and early 1920's and became known as "Slavs." They settled in the cities of Scraton, Pennsylvania, Pittsburgh, Pennsylvania, and Gary, Indiana. They became the backbone of labor for the steel and iron and coal mines of this country.

Paul Fedorchak was a member of this ethnic group. Paul Fedorchak was the son of Micklus Fedorchak and Sanna Bandura. Paul was born in Maskovce, Slovakia on March 15, 1891 in the district of Humenne in the northeastern part of Slovakia. Paul was the youngest of three brothers. The oldest was Michael Fedorchak. He married Anna Yacos and settled in Scraton, Pennsylvania. The second brother was John B. Fedorchak. He married Suzanna Dranchak and also settled in Scraton, Pennsylvania, and later moved to Gary, Indiana. The third brother was George Fedorchak. He married Mary Bonko. They settled in Gary, Indiana.

Paul was an orphan at the age of ten or eleven years old and was raised by Creek Catholic priests in his home town of Maskovce, Slovakia. Paul's brothers sent for him when he was 17 years old. Paul came to the United States in 1908 to live with his oldest brother Michael in Scraton, Pennsylvania. Paul left Scraton to visit his cousin John Fedorchak and Anna Mantic who came to the United States in 1896 and were living in Tolleston, later a part of Gary, Indiana. Paul came to find work in the steel mills that were being built in Gary.

Paul married Anna Richolka. Anna was the daughter of John Richolka and Barbara Koicordakora. Anna was born on August 9, 1891 in Niza Jablonka, Slovakia in the district of Humenne, northeastern part of Slovakia. Paul and Anna married September 1, 1913 at Saint Michaels Church at 12th Avenue and Madison street in Gary, Indiana. Paul and Anna lived at 1560 McKinley Street (Tolleston). Paul and Anna had three sons and two daughters. They were blessed with their first son, Michael on October 8, 1914 (at home). They were blessed with their second son, Joseph, born September 20, 1917 (at home). Their third blessing was a third son, Albert, who was born October 20, 1919 (at home). Paul and Anna had a home built at 554 Georgia Street in Gary, Indiana (east side). Their fourth blessing was the birth of their first daughter, Margaret. She was born May 20, 1925 at 554 Georgia Street (in the back bedroom on the first floor). Their fifth blessing was their second daughter, Betty, born on April 18, 1928 at 554 Georgia (at home).

Michael and Joseph attended Beverdge School (Tolleston). Later, after moving to 554 Georgia, all of their children attended Emerson School at 6th Avenue and Carolina street in Gary. Paul and Anna had a small grocery store at 39th Avenue and Maryland Streets (in Glen Park on the northeast corner of 39th Avenue and Maryland Street). Michael, the oldest son learned the meat cutters trade there. Paul also had a plumbing shop in a three car garage at his home at 554 Georgia Street. During the "Great Depression" of the thirties Paul lost his grocery and plumbing business and returned to United States Steel Corporation to work as a pipefitter until he retired. Anna had a stroke in 1964 and was bedridden for 12 years. She was cared for by her husband Paul and daughter Margaret.

Anna Fedorchak (Richolka) passed away July 30, 1976, of heart failure (at home). Her husband Paul Fedorchak passed away February 22, 1979 (at home) of heart failure. Paul and Anna were interred in Calumet Park Cemetery, Merrillville, Indiana.

Paul and Anna Fedorchak had five children, as listed, along with their offspring.

1. Michael Fedorchak, b. 10-5-1914, d. 8-25-1969, married Marie V. Janiga, b. 1-18-1919, d. 2-20-1983. They had two sons: 1. Gerald Fedorchak, married Rose A. Pampalone. They had two children: Gerald Jr. and Annette Fedorchak. 2. James J. Fedorchak, married Regina Herndon.

2. Joseph Fedorchak, b. 9-20-1917, d. unknown, married Violet L. Grant, b. 8-28-1920, d. 9-25-1985. They had three children: 1. Richard L. Fedorchak, married Suzanna Jarosak. They had two twin boys, Richard and Jeffery Fedorchak. 2. Ronald P. Fedorchak, b. 4-18-1946. 3. Rae Anne Fedorchak, b. 9-18-1954, married John C. Cogley Jr. They had three daughters, Heather, Hillary, and Tiffany Cogley.

3. Albert Fedorchak, b. 8-20-1925, d. unknown, married Doris Powers. They had one son, Albert Fedorchak Jr.

4. Margaret Fedorchak, b. 5-20-1925, d. unknown, married Harry C. Kukelka. They had one son, Charles M. Kukelka, married Lorrie Martin. They had two sons, Christopher and Bryan Kukelka.

5. Betty Fedorchak, b. 4-18-1928, d. unknown, married Dehlbert Peters, b. 6-2-1929. They had three children: 1. Lynn M. Peters, married James Dayhuff. They had two children, Michael and Rebecca Dayhuff. 2. Laura J. Peters, married Srbislav Brasovan. They had three sons, Nicholas, Phillip, and Peter Brasovan. 3. Dehlbert Peters Jr. married Sonya Ackerman. They had two daughters, Jennifer and Jessica Peters.

by Harry C. Kukelka

FERESTAD FAMILY
F73

Kevin Leslie Ferestad, Dorene Esther Ferestad Germain and Martin Wayne Ferestad, 1988.

On December 29, 1951, John Dale Ferestad, originally of Chicago, Cook County, IL and Georgianna Hills, originally of Van Buren County, MI were married in Van Buren County, MI. After returning to Eureka College in Eureka, IL and completing their degrees, they lived in the St. Louis, MO area.

On Easter day, April 10, 1955, their first son Martin Wayne was born at Kirkwood MO hospital. When Martin was three, they moved to Schererville, Lake County, IN. He attended the Schererville School Corporation schools, then the Lake Central School Corporation merge occurred and he continued his schooling. He was a member of Boy Scouts of America Troop #529. He graduated from Lake Central High School in June, 1974. He attended Nichols Engineering School of Technology, Sept. 1974 to May 1975. He graduated with a degree in mechanical repairs. On August 5, 1978, he married Jean Arlene Culver (born 28 June 1957, Gary, Lake Cty, IN) in Michigan City, LaPorte County, IN. They have two children, Teva Meredith born 18 Dec. 1981 and Adam Jason, born 4 Feb 1985. He is employed as a repairman with Hoosier Overdoors, Inc. His hobbies include any and all electronics and computers, traveling, woodworking and inventing.

On January 16, 1958, Kevin Leslie was born in Lake County, Indiana. He attended the local schools and was a member of Boy Scouts of America. Kevin graduated from Lake Central High School June 1976. He enlisted in the U.S. Marine Corps in September, 1977 and was stationed at Camp Pendleton, San Diego, California. He returned to Schererville, Lake County, Indiana in 1980 and continued his employ with Continental Baking Corp. of Hammond. In 1984, he transferred to another facility north of Chicago, IL. On August 10, 1986, he married Andrea Zimmerman (b. 15 Mar 1961, Waukegan, IL) in DuPage County, IL. On November 23, 1989, their daughter Rachel Victoria was born in DuPage County, IL. Kevin is employed with Remi Foods, Division of Borden Foods, Elk Grove, IL. He excels in his hobbies of woodworking and fishing. He resides in Streamwood, Cook County, IL with his family.

On December 26, 1960, their daughter Dorene Esther was born. She attended local schools and was a member of the Girl Scouts of the U.S.A. She married Louis Germain of Cook County, IL on March 3, 1979 in Schererville, Lake County, IN. She graduated from Lake Central High School in June 1979. They have two children Jeremy Louis born September 1, 1979 and Stacey Ann born November 3, 1982, both born in Lake County, Indiana. She is employed by the Tri-Creek School Corp. and resides in Schneider, Indiana. Her hobbies include being a Girl Scout Troop Co-Leader and room mother for her children's rooms.

by Jean A. Ferestad

FERESTAD, GEORGIANNA HILLS
F74

A Michigan Transplant

Georgianna Hills was born 10 June 1931 in Van Buren County, Michigan. She was the first daughter of Bertram Albert Hills (b 16 Jan 1895 M 2nd wife 24 June 1929) and Mary Esther Perry (b June 1897 Lowell, Ionia Cty, MI).

She has an older half brother named Burton F. Hills who resides in Van Buren County, MI. Her two sisters are Barbara Hills Putman of Oxnard, CA and Alice Hills Efting of Van Buren Cty, MI.

She attended Van Buren County schools and graduated from Bangor High School in June, 1948. She attended Eureka College, Eureka, IL from 1948 to 1952 where she met John Dale Ferestad, originally of Chicago, Cook County, IL. Dale and she were married 29 Dec 1951 in Van Buren Cty, MI. She graduated from Eureka College in 1952 with a Bachelor degree.

Her first son Martin Wayne was born 10 April 1955 in Kirkwood, MO. The family moved to Lake County, Indiana in 1958 at which time, her second son, Kevin Leslie was born on January 16. On December 26, 1960, her daughter Dorene Esther was born.

She was a Den Mother for Troop #529 Boy Scouts of America from 1963 to 1968. She was active in the Schererville School Corporation PTA (before it was merged into the Lake Central School Corp). She was a room mother for her children's classes and was active with the Girl Scouts during her daughter's young years. She ran for Schererville Town Board and was a Vice President Precinct Committeewoman.

A family gathering, Christmas 1988. Schneider, IN. (Back) Kevin Leslie Ferestad, Martin Wayne Ferestad; (front) Dorene Esther Ferestad Germain and Georgiana Hills Ferestad.

Georgianna spends time now visiting her children and their families, her parents in Michigan and friends. She now resides in Gary, Lake County, IN. and is an independent saleswoman for House of Lloyd's Home Decorating Company.

by Jean A. Ferestad

FERESTAD, J. DALE
F75

John Dale Ferestad was born 19 Feb 1929 in Cook County, Chicago, IL. He was the only child of Arnold Ferestad (b 25 Sept. 1903 M 1927 N. Dakota d Nov. 1979 bur Hot Springs Arkansas) and Victoria E. Trotter (b 30 June 1905 Minto D. Dakota).

He attended Chicago Public Schools until he joined the United States Marine Corp. on August 5, 1956 and spent boot camp on Paris Island, South Carolina. He was a member of the Headquarter Fleet Marine Force stationed at Camp Catlin, Oahu, Hawaii Islands until 1948 at which time he was put on reserve status. In 1950, while attending Eureka College in Eureka, IL he met Georgianna Hills originally from Van Buren County, MI. He maintained reserve status during the Korean War and in 1951 served in North Carolina for 1 year. On December 29, 1951, he and Georgianna Hills were married in Van Buren Cty, MI.

He attended Eureka College, Eureka, Illinois and graduated with a business degree in 1953.

His first son Martin Wayne was born 10 April 1955 in Kirkwood, MO. The family moved to the Lake County, IN area in 1958 at which time their 2nd son, Kevin Leslie was born on January 16.

In December, 1959, he began a job with the Chicago office of U.S. Borax. During his 6½ years with the company, he was introduced to a spokesperson and host for the show sponsored by his company called Death Valley Days. That spokesperson was Ronald Reagan. A picture was taken at that meeting and remains a family "talkabout."

John Dale Ferestad, 1949.

On 26 Dec 1960, his daughter Dorene Esther was born in Lake County, Indiana. He began working for Inlander Steindler Paper Company in May 1967 and has been with the company for the past 23 years.

He was active in Schererville politics in the 1960's and spent time as a Precinct Committeeman. His hobbies include reading, woodworking and travel. Dale currently resides in Lake Village, Newton Cty, IN.

by Jean A. Ferestad

FERESTAD, MARTIN WAYNE AND JEAN ARLENE CULVER
F76

Back Row: Jean Arlene Culver Ferestad and Martin Wayne Ferestad. Front Row: Adam Jason Ferestad, 4½ years old and Teva Meredith Ferestad, 8 years old. Photo taken December 1989.

The Meeting & After

On November 20, 1975, while on an outing with a friend, Jean Arlene Culver (born 28 June 1957 Lk Cty, IN) was setting alone in a car at the Blue Top Restaurant in Highland, Indiana awaiting her friends return. The side door of the car opened and an unfamiliar male sat down and leaned his head into her lap. He proceeded to, while laying in her lap, repair her friends Citizens Band radio. After finishing the job, he realized there was another person in the car. By that time, she was over her shock and was questioning the situation.

Less than 3 days later, they were an item around town. His name was Martin Wayne Ferestad (born 10 April 1955, Kirkwood, MO) and on August 5, 1978, they had a beautiful garden wedding at the International Friendship Gardens, Michigan City, LaPorte County, Indiana.

Jean and Marty resided in the downtown area of Griffith from August, 1978 to Sept. 1979. They moved to the New Elliot area of

Griffith and remained there until June 1981. She was employed with various banks in the area and he with auto repair shops.

On December 18, 1981, their daughter Teva Meredith was born in Munster, Lake County, Indiana. She was less than 5 lbs at birth and was the apple of their eye, their own Christmas miracle. She attends school at Homan in the Lake Central School Corporation and is a member of Troop #206 of the Girl Scouts of the U.S.A. She is loved for her ready smile and her openness and easiness with life. She enjoys art work, music and is an inventor at heart.

Martin attended Indiana Vocational Technical Institute in Gary, Indiana and during that time, worked as an auto mechanic in Lake County, Indiana during 1981-1982.

On February 4, 1985, their son Adam Jason was born in Munster, Lake County, Indiana. He was their immediately active and vocal son. He is an active member of the family and is loved for his frankness and indomitable spirit. He is an amateur inventor and takes after his dad in the area of curiosity and love of life.

Jean is employed by Edinger Plumbing & Htg, Inc. (Oct. 1987) in Munster, Indiana. She enjoys being the leader of Troop #206, Girl Scouts of the U.S.A. She's an avid reader, enjoys woodworking and all activities out of doors. She loves to travel and she's next in line in her family for "keeper of the stories" and is a genealogist. She's traced not only her own family lines but her husbands as well. She is writing a book to place in the libraries of the areas where the families have lived. She hopes to be a published fiction writer soon and is working on inventions of her own.

Martin is employed by Hoosier Overdoors, Inc. since October 1985 as a repairman. He enjoys all electronics, computers and woodworking. He repairs anything and everything not nailed down and enjoys traveling. He is working on a science fiction book, several inventions to help others and is active in the Cook County Computer Club. He also attends Inventor's Club meetings at Purdue University.

They reside in Schererville, Indiana and lead active, busy lives.

by Jean A. Ferestad

GALLAGHER, ALBERT OWEN
F77

Albert Owen Gallagher was born in Lake County on December 18, 1904 to Irish parents. His grandparents, Peter Gallagher and Mary Sullivan, came from Ireland during the potato famine and settled in Boston. In the mid 1860's, they came to Indiana looking for work and for rich soil for farming.

Albert's parents, Peter W. and his wife Mildred Long lived at Berry Lake in Whiting. Peter W. found work at Standard Oil, in part, helping to drain the land, and to construct the plant. He worked 12 hour days and was paid $1.00 per day. About 1900, Peter rented a farm near Palmer where the family lived for a number of years. Bert, as Albert was called in his early years, was the first boy born after three girls. In all, there were four girls and two boys. Besides helping with the usual farm chores, Bert learned to hunt and trap animals for food and also for the fur. He used the money he earned from the furs to buy himself a bike,

Albert O. and Margaret (Miller) Gallagher.

as there was no way the family could afford to buy him one. Before he got his bike, Bert had an "experience" with a trapped skunk, which he remembered all his life, and for good reason. This "experience" required that all the clothes he was wearing be burned and that he be scrubbed down with lye soap and a scrub brush. In addition, he was not allowed in the house for three days. After Bert got his bike, he used it to deliver papers, groceries, and about any other errand that needed doing.

Around 1919, the family moved to Hammond. At the same time, Al as he was then known, had saved enough money to buy a used pickup truck. He worked as a truck driver delivering ice and coal for a number of years. He met his wife, Margaret Miller, in 1926, at a dance in Chicago. They both loved to dance and would frequently go to the Treanon Ball Room at 63rd and Cottage Grove Ave. in Chicago. In 1927, Al and Margaret (Marge) entered and won a dance contest. The prize was a new Cadillac. This got Al started as a chauffeur, and then later as a jitney driver. He would take passengers from downtown Hammond to the South Shore station or back for five cents a ride.

Al and Marge were married on April 7, 1928 in Crown Point. They had one child, a girl, Marjorie, born March 21, 1931. Soon after they were married, they started the Hammond Yellow and Checker Cab Co. They then rented the four story Bunnell building at 5036 Hohman Ave., Hammond, which they later purchased. Marge worked alongside Al for the next forty-five years. They sold the cab business in 1952, after running it for almost 25 years. Besides owning the cab business, the Gallaghers were also agents for the Trailways Bus Company. In 1948, they became the first licensee of the Hertz Car and truck rental agency in the area. They sold their interest in Hertz in 1962. They also owned Gallagher Boat Sales, selling boats, motors, trailers, and accessories. They ran the boat sales from 1950, until Al's death on February 4, 1975.

The four story Bunnell building was built in 1920 for $150,000.00. This building had 2 foot thick walls on ground level and 18 inch thick walls at the upper levels. It had a foundation to hold an 8 story building. It was designated a bomb shelter in the 1960's. It was one of the first buildings to have a sprinkler system on all floors.

by Marge Mills

GEISEN FAMILY
F78

Bob Geisen

Among first families who came seeking the new life of freedom in America were many of German descent. Geisen was one family making its way to northwest Indiana well over a century ago and still remaining as one of Crown Point's prominent business families.

Robert Geisen, current co-owner of Geisen Funeral Home, represents the fourth generation of the business in Crown Point.

Early records reveal Bob's great-great-grandfather, Matthias Geisen, and wife, Hana, to be the immigrant ancestors coming over from Germany and becoming large landowners in the Cook area. As an original land donor for St. Martin's Church, now Holy Name Church, he later added enough land for a cemetery (known as God's Acre) and other buildings, for a total of four and one-half acres.

Matthias, a retired silversmith whose specialty has been casting bells, further proved his generosity to the church by having three bells cast in his hometown, Rappweiler, Germany. They were brought across the Atlantic from Hamburg by ship. When they arrived from the bellcasters, it was found "Matthias Geisen Benefactor" was inscribed on each bell.

The church steeple's eventual condemnation made disposition of the heavy bells necessary. One of them can be seen on the grounds of Geisen Funeral Home, 109 N. East Street, Crown Point.

Peter A. Geisen was one of 10 children of Matthias and Hana, and one who chose to locate in Crown Point and begin what was to be a lasting contribution to the city. With his first wife, Clara Scherer, there were two daughters,

85

Henrietta Huber and Frances Kilroy. In 1867 he established a furniture and undertaking business on North Main Street, now the location of Epperson's Furniture. A newspaper advertisement, dated July 14, 1877, announced his opening a new cabinet shop in his new building, where he expected to keep constantly on hand a good assortment of all kinds of furniture and coffins of all sizes — all handcrafted items.

From Peter's second marriage to Caroline Giegel there were nine children, three sons and six daughters. In 1872 the family moved into what became the Geisen homestead at 105 N. East Street, now occupied by great-grandson Bob, wife Marilyn and children, Cathy, Nancy, and Larry.

F. Charles Geisen, one of the sons of Peter A. and Caroline, took his state board examination at the first Indiana State Board of Embalmers in 1901 and joined his father in the business. Likewise his brother L. Edward, youngest of the family, continued the tradition by attending Askin College of Embalming, Indianapolis, also joining the business, which then became Geisen and Sons. Another son, Henry, was with the firm about a year, later locating in Hammond.

1900 marked the beginning of F. Charles Geisen's partnership in the family business and his marriage to Miss Lena Fiegle. Their children included Clarence (deceased) who had a long affiliation with First National Bank, Crown Point; Walter, Elmhurst, Illinois; George (deceased) formerly of Chicago, Raymond, Joliet, Illinois; Herbert, Gary; Vernon, Florida; Ralph (deceased); Harold, Crown Point; and Norbert, Merrillville. A single daughter, Mildred Geisen Huseman, resides in Cook. All are well remembered during their growing-up days in Crown Point.

When Peter A. Geisen retired, the business became known as the P. Geisen and Sons Furniture and Undertaking. In 1929, son Edward took over operation of the furniture store, then called Geisen Furniture Store. Edward subsequently sold the furniture business on North Main Street to Jack Kennedy.

Charles took charge of the newly-erected funeral home adjacent to the family home, 109 N. East Street. Built then at a cost of $20,000, it furnished the area with one of the most complete, modern funeral homes in this part of the state.

In 1932, Charles started a funeral business in Glen Park, purchased then in 1940 by son Herbert and wife Edna, still in operation. The business on N. East Street was purchased by son Ralph and wife, the former Mildred Beckman, who undertook extensive remodeling in 1945. Norbert started working for brother Ralph at the Crown Point location in 1941; in 1963, he joined the Gary firm. Norbert now operates a recently completed funeral home at 7905 Broadway, Merrillville.

William Geisen, son of Herbert and Edna, became associated in the Glen Park business in 1965.

In 1955 Charles was presented a certificate of honor by the Indiana Funeral Directors' Association for having served his profession for over 55 years.

Robert, son of Ralph and Mildred, became associated in the Crown Point business in 1958, and since his father's death in 1972 has managed the business. A second extensive addition was annexed to the north, featuring a modern chapel with 125 seating capacity, lounge area and other facilities.

The funeral business has been in the Geisen family since 1867, the oldest in Lake County, now over 108 years under the same family name.

by Violet Irvin

GIBBS, HARVEY FAMILY
F79

Harvey Gibbs, son of Hiram Gibbs and Elizabeth (Shanks) Gibbs, was born in Athens, Ohio, on October 14, 1842.

On September 5, 1861, while living at Hickory Point in Lake County, he was mustered into Co. H of the 9th Regiment during the Civil War. He was almost 19 years of age at that time. He was mustered out on September 28, 1865. His brother, Hamilton Gibbs, a recruit in Co. H 9th Infantry Volunteers, joined the army during the Civil War on August 14, 1862, and died January 24, 1863, of dysentery. There was also a brother, William.

On November 5, 1868, he married Hannah Jane Carson, daughter of Matthew and Margaret Carson. The Carsons had come to Indiana from near Canton, Ohio, in the spring of 1863, during the Civil War and settled at Hickory Point. They moved into a brick building that was partly a store and a dwelling place. Hannah waited on trade in the store, did sewing for the family, and taught school at Dublin School the winter of 1864 and 1865 after the war was over. For teaching school she received $3 a week in summer and $4 in winter. She would board with various families while teaching.

Following their marriage in 1868 they moved to a place called Wards Hill.

To this union were born seven children: Adda (Addie) May Gibbs was born October 4, 1869, and married Peter Kitwood Love on April 25, 1889; Alvah Hamilton Gibbs was born June 30, 1872, and married Alice Knarr on June 17, 1903; Maggie Jane Gibbs was born October 26, 1873, and died October 1, 1874; Maude Adelle Gibbs was born February 2, 1876, and married Moses Henderson on February 2, 1898; Nellie Mabel (affectionately known as Mamie) Gibbs was born on January 16, 1879, and married Christopher Nethery on March 14, 1901. There were also twin sons that died shortly after birth.

Harvey and Hannah lived in a log cabin across the road from what is now the Byron Henderson home on Montgomery Street. It was one large room, and when overnight guests came, sheets were hung from the ceiling to make separate rooms. After retiring from farming, they moved to Leroy and lived in the first house south of the Leroy Methodist Church. Their daughter and son-in-law, Addie and Peter Love, lived across the street.

When Hannah first came to Hickory Point, there were no railroads and mail was brought from Valparaiso twice a week. They stopped at Hickory Point and then went on to Lowell.

The Pennsylvania Railroad was built the summer of 1863, and while living at Wards Hill they heard that a town was going to be built close to the John Ross farm. During the summer of 1869 they could see a store building going up. That was the first building erected in the town of Leroy.

Hannah died on February 24, 1925, and Harvey on March 10, 1926. Both are buried at Salem Cemetery.

by Margaret V. Schlemmer

GOLD, ROSALIE DAVICH
F80

Robert, Gail, Rosalie and Steve Gold at family wedding in 1976.

I was born on November 30, 1939 in the small mining town of Lowesville, West Virginia, next to the Monongahelia River. Our town had approximately one hundred and twenty people. There was only one store, a combination grocery, liquor, and general store with gas pumps. Later they added a separate building for appliances. I had a brother and two sisters, with me being the third born. In order we were Mary Ann, John (Bucky), myself and Philomena (Penny).

My father, John Evan Davich, was born in Yugoslavia on February 27, 1894 to Jandre Devcic, a sailor, and Ika Bacic, a farmer. They immigrated to the United States when my father was about seven years old.

My mother Martha Agnes Marko was born in Bertha Hill, West Virginia on July 27, 1918 to Rok Markov and Anna Loscovitch, who had immigrated to the states from Czechoslovakia. Anna Loscovitch died on June 21, 1927 when my mother was eight years old. Rok Marko died in 1943. After my grandmother died, mother lived with foster parents that ran a boarding house, in which working miners roomed. My father was living there when they met. He liked my mother and told her foster parents he would take good care of her. She was only sixteen when they got married and my father was forty.

I remember when I was little we had a coal and wood burning cook stove, and we used to slice apples and potatoes, and brown them on the grates. In 1949, when I was ten years old, my mother left my father and moved to Lake County, Indiana with us three girls, leaving behind my brother, who wouldn't leave because of his love of hunting and fishing.

My father later remarried and had six more children, Anthony, Martha, Nancy, Jerry, Randy, and Robert. Dad died of a stroke on November 2, 1966. My mother married Leroy Wayne Sills, and had my younger sister Debbie, and my brother Roger. Mother died of a massive heart attack on July 21, 1976.

In May of 1958 when I was eighteen, a girlfriend and I went to a country music show at the Hammond Civic Center. There I saw this very handsome guy and knew right away he was the one for me. There were empty seats all around him and his friend, so I asked if we could sit there. He said "there's empty seats all over, sit anywhere you want." That was the start of our relationship that has lasted since. We made a date for him to come to my house the following Tuesday. When Steve came over my mother gave him a cup of coffee, a little later she had a cup and asked him if his coffee tasted funny. He said yes, but he drank it anyway. My little brother had put salt in the sugar bowl earlier.

Steven Douglas Gold was born in Kewanee, Illinois, the first of five living children born to Lee Robert Gold and Viola Katherine Swearingen. The children were, in order, Steve, Sharon, Gary, Richard, and Sandra.

Steve and I were married on September 22, 1959. He had gone into the construction trade as a laborer. In November of that year he went to Greenland to work. He signed a contract to stay for three months, and the company would pay his air fare, but he missed home and came back in two months. We were living in a basement apartment then on Adams St. near 38th Ave. (Ridge Rd.) I was working in a grocery store named Five Star in Merrillville on Broadway and 73rd Ave. where Albert Slater Furniture is now. During the winter months we moved to a rented house on Marshall St. at 38th. That's where our son Robert Lee was born on March 23, 1960. The summer after our son was born we moved to an apartment at 2911 W. 40th Ave., that's where our daughter Gail Renee was born on June 22, 1961.

We bought our first house in 1962, at 5966 Minnesota St. in Hobart, at a cost of $11,500.00. It was Ross Township at that time, now that north side of 61st Ave. is Hobart City limits. In June of 1965 we bought our second house at 6105 Minnesota St. Hobart (Ross Twp.) at a cost of $17,500.00. This is where we raised our children. They went to Fieler Elementary School, then to Harrison Junior High and on to Merrillville High. After our children were raised and gone from home, we built the house we now live in. On August 31, 1981 we moved into that house at 2963 E. 62nd Pl. Hobart, Ind. (Ross Twp.).

Our son married the former Brigit Lynn Marcoff on January 27, 1979, and they had two children, Brandon Robert, born April 4, 1981, and Amber Rose born July 7, 1982. Robert and Brigit were divorced on September 17, 1986. On Christmas day of that same year Robert died as a result of a single car accident on Route 41 the evening of December 24th.

Our daughter Gail is married to William Ryan Dykstra and they live in Sumerduck, Virginia with their four children. Gail had three daughters, Jamie Leigh, whose father Jeffrey Alan Monzulla was killed in a truck accident in Houston, Texas, on August 6, 1987, and Danielle Renee, and Amanda Rose Komenda, whose father Daniel Micah Komenda resides in Lake Station. Bill had two sons, Ryan Michael who lives with them and a son William Daniel who lives with his mother in Indiana.

In 1972 I started driving a school bus for Merrillville and I'm still with that same job. And Steve, a retired millwright, started driving for the same school system in January of this year.

by Rosalie Gold

GOLDIE, WILLIAM AND MARY
F81

Bill Goldie, wife Mary and son Billie — 1951

Mary Czapko was born on October 3, 1910, in Morrisdale, Pennsylvania, to George and Anna Czapko. She married Metro Popik and had one son, George Eugene Popik, born on November 8, 1932, in Cleveland, Ohio. This marriage was dissolved, and Mary then married William Andrew Goldie (b. 12-15-1909) of Glasgow, Scotland. They married on December 5, 1933, in Valparaiso, Indiana. William Goldie then adopted George as his own son. William Reid Goldie was born on July 18, 1940, in Gary, Indiana.

William Andrew and Mary made their home in the Glen Park area of Gary. William was employed by U.S. Steel until his retirement. He died on October 8, 1969, in Gary, Indiana. Mary was a member of St. Mary's Eastern Orthodox Church. She died on September 24, 1985, in Hobart, Indiana.

George Eugene Goldie married Sharol Lynn Redmond (b. 3-26-38 in Watertown, S. Dakota) of Gary, Indiana, on November 4, 1958, in Munich, Germany. George was a career soldier

George and Sharol Goldie on November 4, 1958

in the United States Army, having served in Korea, Germany, and Vietnam. He obtained his G.E.D. while in the service. He was a Sergeant when he retired in 1971. George has been employed in Plant Protection at U.S. Steel since his return. Sharol Goldie is a graduate of Lew Wallace High School. The family now resides in Valparaiso, Indiana.

Two children were born to George and Sharol: David Andrew Goldie, born March 2, 1959, in Munich, Germany; and William Keith Goldie, born September 15, 1960, also in Munich, Germany. David recently married Kelly Lake (b. 8-15-62) of Hobart, Indiana, on June 30, 1984, in Chesterton, Indiana. Two children were born to this union: Jacob Andrew Goldie, born April 6, 1985, in Valparaiso, Indiana, and Kaitlyn Ann Goldie, born October 26, 1988, in Valparaiso, Indiana. David graduated from Portage High School and is employed at Shafer Olds in Valparaiso. William Keith graduated from Portage High School and works at Pyro, Inc., in Portage, Indiana.

William Reid Goldie married Shirley Mae (nee Miley) Hirlston (b. 6-17-38) of Calumet City, Illinois, on November 9, 1964, in Hammond, Indiana. William graduated from Lew Wallace High School and was a Specialist 5th Class in the United States Army. He was employed in Plant Protection at U.S. Steel for 25 years and currently manages the Roadway Truck Plaza Restaurant at Burns Harbor, Indiana. Shirley Mae graduated from Calumet City High School and has worked intermittently in the food service industries. William describes himself as being "tall, handsome, and witty."

One child was born to William and Shirley: Julie Ann Goldie, born July 4, 1966, in Gary, Indiana. She graduated from Portage High School. Shirley had a child from her previous marriage, Dino Stanton Hirlston, born February 28, 1964, in Hammond, Indiana, who was adopted by William Reid Goldie. Dino also

87

graduated from Portage High School. The family resides in Valparaiso, Indiana.

by Joanne C. Clark

GOOD, ANDREW FRANKLIN FAMILY
F82

Andrew Franklin Good was born in Stafford Township, Greene County, IN on July 24, 1923. He is the son of Charles Vergil and Ruby Emma (Lacy) Good, and is the grandson of Charles Franklin and Sarah Jane (Moore) Good.

Andrew attended grade school in a one room schoolhouse, called Hopewell, located near his home. After leaving Hopewell School he attended school at Marco, IN and graduated in 1940. During his teens he helped his father and grandfather on the farm.

He moved to Hammond, IN in 1940 and was employed by the Riverdale Products Company in Calumet City, IL. He continued his work there until he went into the United States Army.

Andrew fell in love with his classmate Bonnie Louise Taylor. They were married on September 29, 1941 by Horace Hines, a minister for the Church of Christ, in Switz City, Indiana. Bonnie is the daughter of Louis Anderson and Edith (Givens) Taylor, and was born on January 27, 1923.

Andy and Bonnie's first child, Donald Gene, was born on February 3, 1943. A month later, Andy was drafted into the United States Army. He served in Patton's 3rd Army, 80th Infantry Division, in Europe, during World War II, where he served as a Sergeant. He was wounded three different times during the war, for which he received the Purple Heart ribbons. He received other ribbons during his stay with the Army and was given an honorable discharge in October 1945.

Upon returning home, after the war, he worked at LaSalle Steel Company until the summer of 1947.

In the meantime, while living in Hammond, IN, Bonnie gave birth to a set of twins, Jerry Wayne and Judith Ann, born on December 12, 1946.

In 1947, Andy and Bonnie moved to Sandborn, Knox County, IN, where Andy found employment at the Crane Ammunitional Depot. Later he began working for the Peabody Coal Co. driving a big dump truck from the mine to the processing unit, which was 42 feet from bumper to bumper.

Donald attended elementary school in Sandborn until the coal mine closed and the family returned to Lake County, where they purchased a home on Lindbergh Street, Griffith, IN, in August 1952.

Andy was able to obtain employment with Continental Steel, which in later years became known as Blaw Knox Steel, where he continued to work until he passed away.

Their children attended Griffith Public Elementary, Junior and Senior High Schools, graduating from Griffith High School. Donald Gene married Gwendolyn Mae Davis, of Highland, on January 5, 1963, and they have two children Kimberly Ann and Pamela Jean. Kimberly is married to Dave Coleman and they have three children. Donald and Gwendolyn live in Lake County near the Lake and Porter Counties line.

Judith Ann married Richard Lee Sheppard, of Griffith, on December 24, 1965 and they live near Knox, IN. They have six children: Darla Ann, Darla is married to James Granger; Tamara Sue, Wendi Lee, Amy Lynn, Angela Leann and Kathi Diane. Jerry Wayne married Sandi Pressley, of Hammond, on August 15, 1970. To this wedlock, two children were born: Matthew Wayne and Melissa Lynn. Jerry and Sandi live in Merrillville.

In 1958 Andy and Bonnie sold their home on Lindbergh Street and purchased a home on West Ash Street in Griffith.

Andy passed away on July 6, 1980 and was buried at the Calumet Park Cemetery in Merrillville.

Bonnie retired from Sears in 1988, after 18 years of service and still lives in Griffith.

by Paul W. Good

GOOD, CHARLES VERGIL FAMILY
F83

Charles Vergil Good was born in Stafford Township, Greene County, IN on Oct. 14, 1901, and was the son of Charles Franklin and Sarah Jane (Moore) Good. His grandparents were Jacob and Mary Jane (Ramsey) Good and his great-grandparents were George Washington and Judith (Garrett) Good.

After finishing his schooling on May 10, 1916, in Greene County, IN, he became a farmer as was his father and grandparents. When he was 19, he married Ruby Emma Lacy on Mar. 29, 1921. They were married in Sullivan County, IN by Justice of Peace, John T. Watson. She was born on Oct. 23, 1903 in Jackson County, IN and was the daughter of Charles Edward and Jessie Bell (Cohoun) Lacy. Ruby moved with her mother to Sullivan County when she was in her teens. She attended public school in Pleasantville, IN.

They purchased one acre of land from Vergil's maternal grandfather, Jessie Grundy Moore, on Feb. 7, 1922, at the cost of $125.00, where they built their home during the first year they were married. Ruby mixed all of the plaster by hand for the small three room house. On July 27, 1928, they purchased 18 acres of adjoining land for $1100.00, giving them a few acres to farm, raise chickens, pigs and have a garden.

Vergil and Ruby had five children: Andrew Franklin, July 24, 1923, m. Bonnie Louise Taylor, Sept. 29, 1941; Mildred Lagatha, Oct. 27, 1925, m. Opel Maurice Gilmore, Aug. 19, 1944; Robert Gene, Nov. 24, 1927, m. (1) Wilma Jean Core, Oct. 3, 1947, (2) Helen Lucille Sullivan Priddy, June 24, 1972; Wilma June, b & d June 13, 1933; and Paul Wayne, Jan. 22, 1936, m. Margaret Brown, Mar. 16, 1962.

When Vergil was fourteen years old, he became a member of the Marco Church of Christ. In 1925 he moved his membership to the Shiloh Church of Christ, where he was appointed as an elder in 1937. Ruby became a member of the Shiloh Church of Christ in 1923. Vergil and Ruby remained members of that church until they moved to Lake County, IN in 1953.

Vergil accepted employment as a truck driver for the Central Indiana Coal Company, Oct. 1, 1924. He continued to farm and work for the mine until he became disabled in an accident at the mine in May 1945, and due to his illness was terminated Jan. 7, 1948. From the time of the accident, he was unable to do any physical work until 1950. At that time he became an enumerator for the government for the 1950 Census.

In the fall of 1950, he purchased a hardware store in Pleasantville, IN, which he was forced to close in 1953 due to the lack of productivity in the coal mines, causing many to move away.

Vergil moved to Griffith, IN in July of 1953, where he obtained employment as a mold assembler for the Mapes Consolidated Manufacturing Company in Griffith. Ruby and Paul joined Vergil in Griffith a month later. Vergil and Ruby's oldest son, Andrew with his wife, Bonnie and children Donald Gene, Jerry Wayne and Judith Ann, had moved to Griffith in July of 1952.

After their move, Vergil, Ruby and Paul became members of the Hessville Church of Christ, in Hammond, IN. Paul obtained employment at the Stop and Shop Grocery Store on Main Street in Griffith, where he remained employed until August 1955, when he was old enough to be employed at Inland Steel Company in East Chicago, IN. Ruby worked at Harvey's Dime Store in Griffith.

Vergil was stricken with cancer in 1957 and passed away on May 1, 1958 at his home at 139 Lindbergh Ave., Griffith. His body was returned to Stafford Township, Greene County, IN for burial. Ruby passed away on Sep. 29, 1962 at the home of her son, Paul. She was laid to rest beside her husband and daughter, Wilma June, in Greene County, IN.

by Paul W. Good

GOOD, PAUL WAYNE FAMILY
F84

It was a cold wintery day when Paul W. Good was born in Stafford Township, Greene County, IN on January 22, 1936. He is the son of Charles Vergil and Ruby Emma (Lacy) Good, and is the grandson of Charles Franklin and Sarah Jane (Moore) Good.

Paul attended his twelve years of schooling at Marco, IN and graduated in 1953. During his Junior and Senior years, he worked on a farm for James Harris of Sandborn, IN.

Paul moved with his parents to Griffith, Lake County, IN, on August 3, 1953. He began working for the Stop and Shop Grocery Store the following day, and continued there for two years. He changed employment to Inland Steel Company on August 25, 1955, continuing until the present.

Paul's father passed away on May 1, 1958, leaving him to care for the bills for his mother and himself. In November he purchased a house at 118 Lindbergh, Griffith.

On Paul's twenty third birthday, January 22, 1959, he received a notice to report to Uncle Sam for Army duty. He was sent to Fort Leonard Wood, MO, for basic and advanced army training. In July he was shipped to Darmstadt, Germany, where he served as a Security Control Specialist. He travelled in six different countries while in Europe: Germany, France, Italy, Austria, Holland and Switzerland.

While in the Army, Paul's mother, Ruby,

agreed to allow the Griffith Church of Christ to meet in their home for Wednesday evening Bible Study, until the church could purchase a building suitable for holding worship services. Paul and his mother were charter members of that church.

In November 1960, Paul met Margaret Brown, from Albuquerque, NM while Margaret was visiting her sister whose husband was a preacher of the Gospel near Paris, France. Paul returned to the States in January, 1961 and continued to correspond with Margaret, who had in the meantime obtained employment with the United States Civil Service in Wiesbaden, Germany. After eight months she returned to the United States and made her home in Griffith, IN, while working for Graver Tank and later Sinclair Refinery in East Chicago, IN.

Paul and Margaret were married on March 16, 1962 by Horace Hines, minister for the Church of Christ, in Terre Haute, IN. After a short honeymoon in Indiana, Kentucky and Tennessee, they made their home in Griffith. Margaret is the daughter of Claude and Bertha Emeline (Crider) Brown, Mountainair, NM and granddaughter of Edward Ulysses Redmond and Amy Adeline (Kent) Brown. Margaret was born in the Estancia Valley, Torrance County, NM on February 4, 1933.

Three children were born to this wedlock: Dena Sue, April 21, 1963; Edward Franklin, June 23, 1965; and Steven Wayne, August 26, 1967.

The children attended and graduated from the Griffith Public Schools, and Florida College in Temple Terrace, FL. (near Tampa) where all three graduated with an Associate Arts degree. The children were members of the Griffith Grinners 4-H Club and held various offices during their tenures.

Dena met Mark David Roberts while attending Florida College and they were married on December 31, 1983. Mark is the son of Thomas David and Irene (Epp) Roberts of Longview, TX. They have one daughter, Rebecca Elizabeth, born September 6, 1989. Edward is employed with the Woodmar Church of Christ as an evangelist trainee. Steven is attending Purdue Calumet and will graduate in the spring of 1990.

Margaret is employed at the Methodist Hospital in Gary, where she works as an Inventory Control Clerk.

Paul, Margaret, Edward and Steven are members of the Woodmar Church of Christ, Hammond, IN. Paul was appointed as an elder of the church in August 1989.

Paul and Margaret began searching their ancestors in 1980. They have found that their grandparents lived in Jackson County, IN. The Browns and the Lacys lived only six miles apart. Records show they traded at the same store in Jackson County, which no doubt means they knew each other. It certainly is a small world. Paul is related to Nancy (Hanks) Lincoln and Margaret is related to the Lee family of VA.

by Paul W. Good

GOVERT FAMILY
F85

Family Contribution Recognized by Town

Community participation is a 74-year-old tradition in the civic-minded Govert family whose contributions to Schererville were recognized in a historic resolution adopted at the Town Board meeting. At the last session to be attended by Clerk-Treasurer Alice A. (Govert) Siebert before she leaves office, trustees adopted Resolution 1000. That resolution number was reserved to honor the family's contributions to their hometown. Wording of Resolution 1000 is based on family history compiled by Assistant Town Administrator Glen Eberly during a recent videotaped interview with Siebert and her relatives.

Siebert is the youngest of the seven children of William M. and Susan C. Govert who both were Schererville clerk-treasurers as was their son and her brother, Alfred B. Govert.

Altogether, a Govert family member has held the clerk-treasurer's post for 48 of the 76 years since Schererville was incorporated in 1911.

Ever since their patriarch, William M. Govert, took that office in 1913, one or more members of the immediate family has headed a town department.

In fact, Schererville's first clerk-treasurer, Peter Grimmer, who served from 1912-13, became a family member by marriage when years later his daughter, Sally, married William M. Govert, Schererville Street and Sanitation superintendent for the 25 years ending in 1985.

William J. Govert remained in office for 26 years until his death in 1938 when his wife was appointed to complete the term, serving through 1939. That year their son, Alfred, was elected and filled his parents' post from 1940-43.

In addition, the Goverts' daughter, Mary Kaiser, was Schererville Postmistress for 30 years ending in 1971. Her son, Edward "Beau" Kaiser and his cousin, Joseph Govert, Alfred's son, have alternated the position of chief of the Schererville Volunteer Fire Department for years. Kaiser, the present chief, is also fire inspector and the only full-time fire department employee.

The fire department roster also includes Gus and Herbert "Buddy" Govert, whose father, Herbert, another of the seven Govert children, completed 25 years service as a fireman here.

Although the Goverts were not among the early settlers of Schererville, the family roots in town go back to 1876 when blacksmith John L. Thiel, father of Susan, the future Mrs. William M. Govert, moved his family here from Crown Point. "A Century at the Crossroads," a local history booklet published in connection with the 1966 town centennial celebration, reports that move took place by sled because of deep snow although the date was April 7.

Thiel became the village smithy with a shop on Joliet Street where the Post Office stands today. The family home was across the street.

Govert, a Griffith native, moved here in 1906 when he married Susan Thiel. Their home was a 8 E. Joliet, next door to the house the Sieberts occupy today.

The Govert family was also honored by the Schererville Chamber of Commerce at a banquet where the four surviving children of William and Susan were honored guests. Those guests include the present clerk-treasurer, her brother Herbert and sisters Frances Peifer and Dorothy Schiesser, whose married names also are well known in Schererville history and local government.

by Eleanor Meyer

GRANT, THOMAS
F86

Thomas Grant, of the mercantile firm of Grant Brothers, of Lowell, is one of the prominent representative citizens of his home community, in a business, political and social way. He is also prominent in the affairs of the south part of Lake County and is well known over the entire county. He was born in Lowell on the 13th day of September, 1865, and is the son of Mr. and Mrs. Thomas Grant, the elder Grant being born in Scotland, and coming to this country, located in Chicago, but in 1860 he came to Lowell, where he identified himself with the building interests. He died in the South when his son Thomas was only nine years old, leaving a mother and a number of other children to be cared for. Being thrown upon his own resources, young Grant went to work on a farm and later worked on the Monon railroad as a section hand. By energy, honesty and economy he forged ahead, took a business course at Valparaiso University and became a contracting carpenter, which he followed until seven years ago, when he and his brother James opened their big mercantile establishment. He served four years as trustee of Cedar Creek township, during which time he brought about great improvements in the way of good roads and bridges. He is an ardent Republican and a splendid party worker. He was a candidate for the nomination of sheriff at the spring convention, but was defeated by Mr. Lawrence Cox. In 1893 Mr. Grant was united in marriage to Miss Grace Nichols, daughter of William C. and Mary Nichols. To this union one son was born, named Byrl. Mr. Grant is a member of the Knights of Pythias, Masonic and Odd Fellow lodges and takes an active interest in fraternal work.

(Compiled from the Souvenir Album of Lake Co. Ind., Crown Point-Lowell, June 18-19, 1909.)

GRIMMER, MICHAEL
F87

Michael Grimmer was born in Turkey Creek, (Ross Township) Indiana on July 18, 1853. His parents came to America from Alsace – Lorraine in about 1841 and made his way to Chicago. In France his father (also named Michael) was a Captain in the French Army and served under Napoleon Bonaparte.

In 1849 his father moved to Lake County, Indiana and was one of the pioneers of this Northwest corner of the state and devoted his energies to farming until his death, which occurred in 1843 when his son Michael was but eight weeks old.

He left his widow and two daughters and two sons, the eldest being just over twelve years of age.

Some years after his father's death, his mother married John P. Redar of St. John Township and this is where Michael grew up.

Michael Grimmer remained at home and worked on the family farm until about sixteen years of age.

He then struck out on his own, and though he had but limited school privileges to equip him for the duties of the business world he possessed energy, determination and resolved to win advancement. And by working as a farm hand he earned the money that enabled him to attend school in the winter months, and later he began teaching in the districts schools, being connected with that profession for ten years.

In 1879, Mr. Grimmer was united in marriage to Helena Neuman, a daughter of Joseph and Mary Neuman from Schererville and were married at St. Michael's Catholic Church in Schererville in August of that year.

In 1880, he embarked in general merchandising at Schererville, where he continued for seventeen years. His business was capably conducted, and his enterprise and fair dealing formed the substantial foundation upon which he built his success.

The general merchandising store was operated in partnership with his step-brother Peter F. Redar. After several years of this partnership, Grimmer purchased Mr. Redar's interest and became the sole owner. He acquired title for the real estate and erected a building and for many years this was the Post Office in Schererville with Mr. Grimmer being Post Master and later his wife was appointed Post Mistress for many years.

In the meantime Mr. Grimmer had been called to public office and as a staunch Republican, he took an active interest in the work of the party. While engaged in merchandising, he served eight years as a trustee of St. John Township, and in 1897, he was elected Auditor of Lake County, serving so faithfully, during the succeeding three years that in 1900 he was re-elected to a second term of office.

Upon assuming his duties as County Auditor he sold his merchandising business, creamery and ice business to John Weis and John Rietman as partners.

After concluding his term of office a County Auditor, Mr. Grimmer served two terms as a member of the House of Representatives in the Indiana General Assembly.

Mr. Grimmer died in his home in Crown Point in 1926. His widow died in 1934 and both are buried in St. Michael's Cemetery in Schererville.

In 1975, Michael Grimmer Middle School in Schererville was dedicated as fitting memorial to his memory. He has commanded the respect and esteem of people throughout Lake County and the entire state over the record of his private life. During his public career, he has been most loyal to his duties of friendship and of citizenship, and his history well deserves a place in the annals of his native land.

by Steven Yaros, Jr.

GURITZ FAMILY
F'88

Herman and Wilhelmina (Einspahr) Guritz farmed in West Creek Township, Lake County, Indiana, located on the east side of State Line Rd., Sec 24 (platt map), and north of 145th Av.

William and Mary (Schaper) Guritz 1899.

Minnie, as she was known, was born on September 8, 1884 at Lowell, Indiana; the daughter of Fred and Dorothea (Frederick) Einspahr. Minnie and Herman were married on December 9, 1908. Their children were: Irvin, single, born November 24, 1909, deceased in 1989. Edward, single, born May 22, 1911, died December 7, 1982, and Violet, single, who survives and resides at Lowell, Indiana. Their farm has been in the family since 1868, and is now farmed by a renter and his family.

Herman, born on January 3, 1885, was the son of August Guritz, born February 22, 1856 and wife, Dorothea Ohlenkamp, who was born October 3, 1855. His dad acquired the farm from his father, William, Sr., which were certain parcels added in later years. August and Dorothea's children were: Emma, wife of Edward Wille, and their children: Harold, Edward, Raymond, August, and Ray; Lena, wife of Emil Kiedaisch, whose children were: Mildred, Arthur, Dorothy, Carol, and Walter. Mary, wife of William Hamann, no children; Herman married Minnie Einspahr, whose children were: Irvin, Edward, and Violet; August married Hulda Bredemeier. No children; he remarried a Nancy Clayhorn; Ida, wife of Ed Albers, whose children were Florence and Myron. After Ida died, he married Dora Riechers; William married Ella Selk, whose children were: Vernon, Ruby, Ferne, and Orville; Dora married William Reichers, whose children were: Lorena, Norman, Lester, Wendell, and Eunice. After William died, she married Ed Albers.

August's father, and Herman's grandfather, William Guritz, Sr., who originally purchased the land, invented a reaper. In those days, it was used to cut the growing grain into bundles. They were then picked up with pitchforks, onto wagons to be hauled to the barnsite. There the grain would be separated from the straw, either flailed with a flailing fork or by early types of machines. This made work much easier than doing it all by hand. During the winter, when work was slack, the grandfather would weave all types of baskets; mainly, heavy duty ones for around the farmplaces.

Herman's grandparents were William Guritz, Sr., born July 8, 1824, near Nurnberg, Germany and Caroline Herran (or sometimes spelled Harren; even Herre) born November 2, 1830, in Grossen Nenndorf, Germany. Amalie (Egger) Herren married to Fred Herren went to Green Garden Township, Il. to farm, and descendants Peter and Mollie (Guritz) Lorenzen have continued on until the present time. But William, Sr. and Caroline then moved to the west side of the state line; the second farm south of Creamburg, Illinois at that time. This was another settlement evolving around a dairy there at the corner of Indiana Avenue and State Line Rd.

The children of William and Caroline (Herren) Guritz were: William, who married Catharine Ziegler; Henry married Auguste Voshage; Friederika married Fred Wehrman; August married Dorothea Ohlenkamp; Mollie wife of Peter Lorenzen, Christian married Amelia Tramm; Herman married Emma Voshage; Fred married Feernie Waits, later, Sarah Hanson; Caroline wife of Ernest Bergmeier of Mn; Peter, died age 4 mo. on 2-14-71, his mother Carolline Herren on November 2, 1870, shortly after his birth.

William, Sr. then married Widow Mary (Schaper) Miller, wife of Simon, who was born at Grossen Nenndorf, Germany. Her young baby son died soon after the father. Their marriage took place on April 4, 1871. Their children were Mary, wife of Fred Foy; Sophia wife of Frank Rudolph; Louise, single, died at age thirty years; John married Martha Tatge; Emma, wife of Henry Haseman; Louis married Emma Wehrman; Bertha wife of William Wilkening; George married Ella Lindeman.

August Guritz was a brother of William, and a sister, Wilhelmina, who married William Frobose, August married Caroline Schumacher. Their children were: Caroline Tatge; Henry married Mina Tatge; William married Bertha Ohlendorf; Louis married Mathilda Ohlendorf. The John and George Guritz families resided on farms on the Lake County side of the State Line Road.

Minnie Guritz's mother, Dorothea Frederick was born near Blue Island, Il. on August 17, 1859 and came to Dyer, Indiana. On November 17, 1878, Dorothea married Fred Einspahr and their children were: Christena Avis, Peter, Hammond, IN., Wilhelmina, Fred J., Odebolt, IA., Laura, Cedar Lake, IN., Anna Collins, Lowell, IN., Clara Herlitz, Cedar Lake, IN., Irvin, and Martha Haseman, Spencer, IN., Minnie's brothers were: John, Peter; four sisters: Mrs. Joseph Sons, Mrs. John Harms, of Dolton, Florida, Mrs. Albert Gerritsen, and Mrs. William Einspahr.

Minnie's father, Fred was born August 25, 1852, the son of Fred and Anna (Claussen) Einspahr from Schleswig-Holstein, Germany. His father Fred was born there March 13, 1816 and died October 26, 1876; a tailor by trade. His mother was born March 2, 1817 at Neuminster, SchleswigHolstein, married Fred I on June 7, 1842. In 1853, they came to America on a sailing vessel from Hamburg, Germany by way of England. After ninety days, landed at Quebec, Canada. From there they stayed in Blue Island, Il. a few years.

In 1867, the family came to West Creek Twp. Lake Co. In., and purchased 85 acres. The first few years, the log cabin was their home until the house and other buildings were erected. The farm became well established and progressive, an additional 80 acres were purchased. Fred being an experienced coachman, accompanied grain wagons to Chicago, Illinois, every two weeks during the season.

He had come along way from purchasing the first tract of land from heirs. He had been a road superintendent on and again years. Mrs. Einspahr succumbed on February 10, 1903 at the home of her son Fred.

by Mrs. Ralph Oldendorf

GURITZ, LOUIS FAMILY
F89

Louis Ludwig Guritz was born on December 11, 1870. He was a brother to August, William, Fred, Carl and Wilhelmina. On October 5, 1893, he married Mathilda Ohlendorf. Mathilda was born on December 12, 1873 to Christoph and Wilhelmina (Seegers) of Washington Township in Will County Illinois.

Louis and Mathilda acquired the Conrad Schweer farm on the corner of 117th and State Line Road. The farm had land on both sides of the Illinois/Indiana State Line, which made it an interstate farm. The front entrance to the farm home had a double-doored porch, known as "coffin doors" at the time. These doors opened up to an elaborate open stairway in the entry hallway.

The old timers used to joke that Louis didn't have much faith in banks, especially when they were failing, and as a result, kept his money hidden in various places around the property. "He didn't want to put all his eggs in one basket," they'd chuckle.

Louis Ludwig Guritz was very involved in the Interstate Creamery Company which stood on the corner of Bemis Road and the State Line. He was the final Board of Directors Secretary. He wrote minutes of the final Board of Directors meeting at the closing of the Interstate Creamery Company, on December 11, 1918. One of the original butter makers, Anton Buehler from Germany, stayed with the Louis Guritz family until Sam Grimm took over the job. (Sam's home was built just south of the dairy.)

Louis and Mathilda had three children: Mathilda who was born on October 17, 1894 and died on March 7, 1900; Henry Max was born July 28, 1898; and Alice was born May 9, 1904. Henry and Alice were both educated at the Brands School, which was located along the east side of Calumet Avenue, three miles north of Brunswick, Indiana; and the German Evangelical school of the Zion Evangelical and Reformed Church, also referred to as "Hanover Prairie."

Henry married Henrietta Meier. She was born on August 14, 1903, to the Henry Meier's of Washington Township. Henry and Henrietta's son, Doran, was born on February 6, 1931, but did not survive. Henrietta died shortly thereafter on April 1, 1931 due to complications stemming from Doran's birth.

Several years later, Henry married a young widow from Dyer, Indiana. Her name was Laura (Kloss) Dumsky. Laura was born December 23, 1899. Her first husband died of spinal meningitis. His illness resulted from being caught in a sudden, heavy rainstorm, after a long heat spell, during the oat harvest. Her daughter Wilneta married Melvin Tatge a son of the Henry and Anna (Sennholz) Tatge's who farmed on Indiana Avenue, near Beecher, Illinois. Wilneta and Melvin had one son named Kenneth, their daughter Ruth Ann died in infancy. His family includes his wife Bonnie Swinford and their children Dawn, Kenneth Jr., and James. They reside in Griffith, Indiana.

Wilneta Tatge later remarried. She and her second husband, Peter O'loughlin, lived in Dyer, Indiana. They had five children: James, who died an infant in the 1960's; Michael, John, and the twins Bob and Paul. At one time, the family moved to Phoenix, Arizona. Some of the children have since returned to the Lake County area.

Alice Guritz was born on May 9, 1904. She married Lawrence Dohmeyer, a resident of Crete Illinois, on December 14, 1924. Lawrence was born August 6, 1901. They raised two sons, Ralph and Warren. Warren died, at the time, of an unknown illness leaving a young widow and son.

by Mrs. Ralph Oldendorf

HACK, JACK
F90

Early Settlers

Early in the history of the settlement of Lake County, one finds a great many pioneers and settlers coming from the Great German Empire to live in Lake County especially in Prairie West.

Prominent among them of course, was John Hack, who founded St. John and built the Pioneer Catholic Church there.

In 1838, the following families settled near the Hacks, Joseph Schmal, Peter Orte, Michael Adler and Matthias Reder.

Two German Lutherans who came in 1838 were Henry Sasse Sr. and Henry Von Hollen.

Another early German settler was Herman Doescher who came in 1842 with his son and daughters and moved into the west part of Hanover Township.

Three Germans who became early Lake County Officials were J.C. Sauerman who was elected County Treasurer in 1875, John Krost elected County Treasurer in 1862 and County Auditor in 1868, and Michael Grimmer who served as St. John Township trustee and in 1897 was elected to Lake County Auditor.

Jacob Fieler came into the county in the year of 1854 and bought a farm in Ross Township. Balzer Franz was also an early Ross Township farmer.

John L. Keilman was one of the early businessmen of Dyer being a general merchant and director of the First National Bank of Dyer.

John G. Bohling was an early prominent farmer of St.John Township as was Jacob Schaefer.

The St. John village blacksmith was John M. Thiel and the Crown Point Brewing Company foreman was August Koehle who later operated the Spring Hill resort in St. John.

Michael Gerlach taught school for a time and was assessor of his township. Andrew Kammer also taught school and in 1887 he was appointed to the office of Postmaster of St. John.

Jacob Rimbach was an early prominent citizen of Hammond and was a section foreman on the Michigan Central Railroad for many, many years.

In 1894 Henry C. Batterman established a livery business in Dyer and later opened machine and blacksmith shops and owned stock in the Dyer creamery.

This article has just touched on the many, many early settlers of German lineage who lived in and contributed to Lake County, but no research into this would be complete without mention of the founder of Schererville, Nicholas Scherer who recognized his duty and opportunity in this new land of freedom and helped contribute to it's development and improvement. His name as is all those mentioned above, are interwoven into our Lake County heritage.

by Steven Yaros, Jr.

HACK, JOHN
F91

John Hack was born November 18th, 1788, in Nunhirchen, Prussia — a Rhine province in the Alsace-Lorraine region that some time before had passed from French possession into Prussian control. His parents were Monsieur Pierre Hack and Lady Johanna (Ross) Hack. John Hack was a farmer by profession, and a Government Real Estate Appraiser in the vicinity of Niederlosheim, Prussia, who on the 4th of August, 1807, married Miss Johanna ("Hanna") Schneider, an embroider. Hanna was also born in Nunhirchen, on September 7,

The Louis and Mathilda (Ohlendorf) Guritz farm home. The double doors to the front entry are obscured by the tree trunks. The snow white building, 2nd from left, is the old Bemis shoestore which moved there in 1938.

John Hack (1788-1856)

Hanna Hack (1787-1853)

1787, the daughter of Mayor Monsieur Joseph Schneider — mayor of Tanner, Prussia — and Lady Johanna (Klaeser) Schneider. Their wedding was performed in the community of Nunhiechen, by the assistant to the Mayor of Weierweiler.

John and Hanna had eleven children, six sons and five daughters: John, 1809 (Mary Scherer); Angeline, 1810 (Peter Gard); Elizabeth, 1812 (John Klassen); Johanna, 1814 (Peter Thielen); Mathias, 1816 (Barbara Thiel) (Angelina Schmal); Suzanne, 1818 (Vincent Sauter); Catherine, 1820 (John Seberger); Peter, 1822 (Helen Classen) (Verena Bury); Joseph, 1825 (Catherine Leinen); Mathias, 1826 (Eve Heiser); and Nicholas, 1828.

John Hack lived the majority of his life in Europe and was close to 50 years of age when he came to America and landed in Lake County, Indiana, September 17th, 1837. The event took place after this area was surveyed, and the Government opened it up to settlers at a very low cost. A time when land was abundant and there were still a few roving Indians in the county, although most of them were located on the banks of the Kankakee and the Calumet Rivers. Hack, and those who followed, most likely immigrated as they were farm laborers in the densely populated districts of Prussia, and owned no land. They worked for large landowners in their Fatherland and did not earn much pay; nor did they spend much, and so were able to save most of the meager income they received. In America was the opportunity to own land and build their own homes.

Mr. Hack was an experienced farmer, an honored, respected and peace-loving citizen, an outstanding and exemplary father. He reared his children in the Christian faith with big ideals, and hoped through the combined efforts of the entire family to establish a home and eventually to purchase a tract of land large enough to amply support himself and his family.

Upon his arrival locally in 1837, accompanied by his wife, Hanna, and many of their children, he immediately settled on a forty acre piece of land and established a home on the western limit of what was called "Prairie West." The homestead was located approximately one half mile east of present Route 41, and south of Joliet Street in St. John, on a small knoll overlooking the surrounding countryside. Here on this first piece of land in the township purchased from the Department of the Interior, John Hack built a cabin and a blacksmith shop, and so far as known, he was the first German immigrant to settle in the area.

Reputedly a man of far-sighted vision and considerable leadership ability, Hack was instrumental in bringing many of his countrymen to this country. He welcomed these immigrants who settled nearby shortly after his arrival, and foresaw the establishment of a flourishing and prosperous community here. The result was that St. John Township was very rapidly settled by hardy and industrious natives of the Fatherland. These pioneers cleared and plowed the fields with oxen, and it is said they used plows made of huge limbs; and that their wheat was delivered to Chicago, Illinois, in oxen driven wagons. For entertainment on summer evenings they would gather together around an out-of-doors fire, the smoke of which would keep off the mosquitoes, and sing the songs of their far away native Rhine region, presenting a scene reportedly to have been picturesque and impressive.

Not much else is known of these early Prairie West settlers, as they were kept far too busy performing the daily routine of hard work to have any time left for writing down a record, or of keeping a journal of any kind.

The town of St. John, Indiana, is named after its first settler. The prefix "St." was added to Hack's name for euphony, and was originally known as "St. Johns." The letter "s" was attached to "John" and continued to appear when the town was laid out in late 1881, but was dropped when it was incorporated in 1911. Upon establishment of a post office, after reaching agreement on the name for the community in 1846, Hack was appointed the first keeper, as the postmaster was then called, and held the position until 1854.

John Hack was tall and dignified in person, patriarchal in manner, clean and keen in intellect, and was well fitted to be a leader and a pioneer. He had large views of government and looked closely into the genius of our institutions.

Over the years Mr. Hack continued to add to his homestead until he owned 300 acres of well-improved land. In 1853, John and Hanna left this farm to reside with their son Joseph.

Jack Hack died at the age of 69, November 21st, 1856, and was buried alongside his wife, who had died three years earlier on August 2nd, 1853. John and Hanna Hack are at rest in the Hack Cemetery, the family burial site, St. John, Indiana.

There are only a few graves identifiable in the Hack Cemetery today, as most of the markers were made of wood and were destroyed, largely due to jumping sparks from railroad engines that passed nearby.

From writings and local history books

by Jim Stephen

HALL, ARCHIE E.
F92

Archie Eugene Hall, the son of John Abraham Hall and Alice Lillian McColley (daugh. of Hugh McColley and Jane Everett) was born in Crown Point June 30, 1904. He was also a grandson of John Hall and Catherine M. (Loucks) Hall. He married first wife Lillian and they had one daughter Ruby. Married second wife Lola May Mooney Nov. 1938.

Archie was a steelworker most of his working life. He first appears in the 1922 Gary City Directory a a patcher for Illinois Steel located at the foot of Broadway. He continued working there as a patcher and then inspector. Later on he went to work for Youngstown Sheet and Tube in East Chicago where he became a foreman and he received several safety awards. He was employed at Youngstown for twenty-three years.

He was a member of the Loyal Order of Moose and active in local politics. He really was a Lake County resident, having been born in Crown Point, lived in Gary, East Chicago, Hammond and Cedar Lake, where he died at age 56 in 1960.

His wife Lola was born 1916 in New Boston, Illinois. Lola was daugh. of Harry E. Mooney and Lula Myrtle Haynes. She came to Lake County about 1920 with her mother and stepfather. She lived a good number of years in Gary. She held several jobs, including being the first woman school crossing guard for the City of Hammond, and she was the first woman crossing guard in Lake County. This position was formerly held by police officers. She held this position until the move to Cedar Lake in 1958.

Upon the death of Archie, Lola entered Purdue University Nursing and became a Licensed Practical Nurse. She was employed at Our Lady of Mercy Hospital until she retired in 1976. She died in 1980 a resident of Crown Point.

Archie and Lola were the parents of 3 children: Ronald Byron b. 1939 m. Mary Louise Fox (daugh. of Robert Fox and Elenaor Hale) in 1963. Ron and Mary have two children: Deanna Marie b. Sept. 1964 m. Anthony Bielak Dec. 1983 they have one daughter Nicole Marie. Robert Byron b. March 1973. Carol Jean b. 1943. Geraldine Louise b. 1946 m. Roy B. Cook of Kentucky in 1964 no children of this marriage. #2 James M. Borden. Four boys were born of this marriage: Ronald Bruce b. 1972,

Thomas Eugene and Paul Wayne (twins) b. 1975, and David Owen b. 1977.

by Carol Jean Hall

HALL, GEORGE FRANKLIN
F93

George Franklin Hall son of John Hall and Catherine Melissa (Loucks) was born Oct. 10, 1875. He was their 4th child and first son. He married Ida Mae Warchus (daughter of George Warchus and Mary Rosina Esch) on March 11, 1896.

George and Ida became the parents of 13 children; they are:

1. Golda Alvina b. 1896 m. William Herman Pfaff in 1917. #2 was Frank Cook. Golda died in June 1972 a resident of California.

2. Mabel Vivian b. 1899 m. Charles Forsythe in 1918, died May 1980.

3. Leslie Raymond b. and died in 1901.

4. Edith Carribelle b. 1902 m. Frederick C. Murray 1920, m. #2 Herbert Leon Jones in July 1945 in Los Angeles, Calif. Edith died April 1980, a resident of Crown Point.

5. Gertrude Isabel b. 1904 m. Frank Timothy Murray Sept. 1923 died Aug. 1983.

6. Fred Franklin b. 1907 m. Mary Frances Anduski Nov. 1933. Fred died Feb. 1958.

7. Florence Helen b. April 1908 m. Alvin L. Rosenbower 1938. Died June 27, 1985.

8. Mary Katherine b. 1909 m. Cherril L. Dibble in 1931.

9. Dora Celia b. 1910 died Sept. 1921.

10. Arthur born and died Feb. 1912.

11. Esther Mae b. 1913, m. 31 – Reel #2 Martin Schuster 1941. She died Oct. 28, 1983.

12. Unnamed daughter born and died July 1915.

13. Raymond born and died 1917.

George and Ida lived most of their married life at 702 N. Grant St. Crown Point. George for many years was employed by Jay S. Crawford and Jay J. Baldwin in the flour and feed business, then he opened a junkyard circa 1919 across the street from his residence, he had marked success. After George's death his son Fred F. took over the junkyard and it became a well known landmark in Crown Point. It attracted countless customers, many of whom came not only to buy but to sit in the office to converse with the owner and who ever else was there.

When Fred Hall died his wife Mary sold the business out of the family. The junkyard continued on until a fire in the early 1960's it was rebuilt but never attained the previous status, and was torn down circa 1980 and duplexes were built for housing.

by Carol J. Hall

HALL, JOHN
F94

Little is known about John Hall before his arrival in Lake County, Indiana. He was born May 15, 1831 in England, area and town unknown. His parents names are unknown, but both were born in England. John's brother's name was Thomas and they had one sister. When John's mother died his father remarried and the 3 children left home.

John married a Miss North in England. John and Thomas came to America for a brief time, then both returned to England, where Thomas decided to stay. John and his then wife headed for America, while aboard ship his wife died and was buried at sea.

The earliest record of John in Lake County is his marriage to Catherine Melissa Loucks on July 4, 1869 in Crown Point. Catherine Melissa was the daughter of Peter Loucks and Dianna M. Kennedy. Catherine Melissa was born and raised in Ontario, Canada. The Loucks family is originally from the Palatinate, Germany, and is one of the oldest Palatine families in North America, having come here in the early 1700's.

The 1870 Federal Census shows John owning a small farm in Hobart Township assessed value of $800, which he later sold to buy a larger farm of 40 acres in Ross Twp. Here is where most of his children were born. John and Catherine lived on this farm until 1888, when John became ill; he mortgaged the farm to help pay expenses, but his illness lasted for some time and they lost the farm. They then packed possessions and children and moved to a house on Grant St. in Crown Point, where John died in June 1890. Catherine lived in the house until her death on Sept. 24, 1924. John and Catherine were the parents of 13 children. Many of their descendants still live in Crown Point area and in Lake County. Their children are:

1. Margaret (Maggie) b. 1870 m. Fred Stebbins in 1894. Margaret died a resident of Ohio in 1940.

2. Nellie Jane b. 1872 m. John Lewis Shaffer in 1892, she died in Crown Point in 1950.

3. Ada Adelsa b. 1873 m. Benjamin F. Zirkle in 1892. Ada died in 1950.

4. George Franklin b. 1875 m. Ida Mae Warchus in 1896. George died in 1939.

5. Daniel Barbour b. 1877 m. Bertha Shaffer, Daniel died in 1916.

6. John b. 1879 died 1880.

7. Charles b. and died in 1880.

8. Ida b. 1880 and died 1881.

9. John Abraham b. 1881 m. Alice Lillian McColley in 1901, died 1951.

10. Carrie Matilda b. 1883 m. John Henry Zirkle in 1903. Carrie died 1954.

11. Grace Valila b. 1886 m. PerryMorton, Grace died in 1938.

12. Raymond Harold b. 1888, died 1889.

13. Lauren Leroy b. the day his father died June 27, 1890 and lived only 6 months until Dec. 1890.

by Carol J. Hall

HALSTED, JAMES M.
F95

Ancestors Date Back to 1700's

James M. Halsted of Merrillville has three known ancestors who fought in the revolutionary war; Timothy Halsted for New York State, Lt. James Campbell Sr. of Penn. and Stephen Willcox of Penn.

Stephen Willcox is one of only three known revolutionary soldiers buried in our county of Lake; Willcox rests at the Pleasant View Cemetery in St. John Township.

This cemetery is very old, run down and mostly forgotten and Jim Halsted has been working with St. John Township Trustee Gary Scheub and the County Commissioners to get help to fix it up.

Authority is given county commissioners to appoint a five-member County Cemetery Commission and establish a tax base for the purpose of restoring and maintaining cemeteries established before 1850 which are without funds or sources of funds.

Revolutionary soldier Stephen Willcox was born in Dutchess County, New York in April of 1762 and grew to be a strong hardy boy, large for his age and served at a young age in the war with Capt. John Franklins Reg. which was commanded by Col. Zebulon Butler.

Willcox assisted in erecting the garrison at Wilkes Barre and doing guard duty in late 1778 and early 1779, serving a total of seven months.

The 1830 Census of Pen show Stephen Willcox still living in that state, however he shows up in Lake County on the 1840 Census.

Jim Halsted is a life long resident of Lake County, having been born January 2, 1912 in Hobart to Lula Maude Burge and Roy Woodhouse Halsted.

Jim has long been active in the Ross Township Historical Society and as a member acts as currator at the old John Wood Mill which was restored by the Lake County Park Dept. at the Deep River County Park.

He is also a member of the Lake courthouse Foundation and is the current Vice President of the Lake County Historical Society.

On Jim Halsted's mother's side family names of Burge, Demmon, Willcox, Morse, Bosworth and Campbell can be found. And on his father's side the names of Brown, Woodhouse, Fitch, Boone and Preston.

Family tradition has it that the Boone goes back to Daniel himself!

by Steven Yaros, Jr.

HAMMES, FR. JOSEPH
F96

Senior Salute

"Hello, friend," is the way Father Joseph Hammes answers his telephone. And, since 1926 when he came to Crown Point, that's the way he's greeted townspeople around the square even though he didn't know them by name. "My relationship with the public has been quite satisfying," he said.

"I like to think I've made some contribution to goodwill here in Crown Point; it's a city we can be proud of," he added.

When Fr. Hammes arrived at the Erie Depot after 12 years of schooling at St. Francis Seminary, Milwaukee, Wis., he was met by Fr. Phillip Guethoff and the gentlemen "exchanged priestly blessings," Fr. Hammes recalled.

"St. Mary's was my first parish and my only parish," he said. There were 250 families in the parish then; now there are 1200, he added.

Fr. Hammes was with Fr. Guethoff for 17 years before being named pastor. "During that time, he was turning pastoral responsibilities over to me," the 88-year-old pastor emeritus continued.

"Through the cordial support of the parishioners, the old school was remodeled, the church tuck-pointed, the interior twice painted, the vestibule built, a tile roof added, and a concrete sidewalk was poured." he said.

After the acquisition from Dan Steeb of five acres behind the church, playing fields were added with a ball diamond, parking space, and playground equipment.

"We had the first flood lights in Lake County. There were two softball games each night during the season," he recalled. NIPSCO gave me two poles for the lights, the telephone company gave me the same number. I remember driving my Pontiac to Chicago when the World's Fair closed for the wiring I needed," he said.

A part of Father's priestly duties which gave him much pleasure was providing private and group instruction, strengthening the Master's word: "Go and teach what I have commanded you." "I especially loved instructing the school children," he added.

Another source of happiness stemmed from being a charter member of the Rotary Club of Crown Point, and from being invited to serve as commencement speaker at the high school. "That was probably a first," he mentioned.

When Father retired as pastor of St. Mary's in 1972, his grateful parishioners gave him the home in which he's lived for the last 16 years. "I live in thanksgiving for my life. Doing God's work brings the greatest satisfaction and being a priest has solved many problems for me; love always does," he said softly.

In a treasured, framed wall hanging which belongs to Fr. Hammes are the words of an earlier priest and those words he has followed during his years as a diocesan priest: ". . . to be a member of each family, yet belonging to none; to teach, to pardon, to console. . . ."

by Jean Barrett

HANDLEY – HANLEY – HANDLY

F97

Origins and Migrations East to West 1620-1988

An old English name is found given to parishes and hamlets in Cheshire, Derbyshire, Staffordshire, and Worcestershire under the various spellings: Handley, Hanley, Handly; and where before the 15th century, the family bore arms in the County of Nottingham. In Ireland as bearer of arms between the 11th and 15th century, the name appears in Connaught and Roscommon, with the prefix of O, as O'Handley, O'Hanley or O'Handly.

As other groups left England for Scotland, Ireland, and later to America, so did the Handleys. The record books of Pennsylvania and Maryland, as early as 1620, show the name equally as popular under the old English spelling. A John Sigismund Hanley is found in early Augusta County, Virginia, records (but of German descent – Handel, Hanler, meaning peddler or tradesman).

The inconsistency of spelling is very evident in the census and other records of 1700 to 1900's, changing from one spelling to the other. About 1750-1780, many Handleys had settled in Pennsylvania and Virginia, and later West Virginia. After the War of 1812, many of them moved on to other states. During the War of 1812, many farms, homes, and estates were destroyed by the British raids on the Atlantic states. The Ohio Territory was opening up for settlement, with the completion of the National Cumberland Road, so the Handleys went. Later to move on to Indiana as that state opened up. In 1884, the Handleys moved on to Kansas and Nebraska, going by covered wagon. Kansas was a hard state to live in, with its severe blizzards, droughts, and grasshoppers, and in 1930, soil erosion created a dust bowl condition for a good part of the state. Discouraged farmers lost everything and left their farms and traveled to California and other states however they could, loaded down Model T trucks, hitchhiking, and by railroad.

The Handley family history follows parallel with the history of the United States. They took part in its wars: Revolutionary, Indian, Civil, and World Wars I and II. The Handleys took part in opening up of the West, starting farms as they went.

Handleys in Lake County and the state of Indiana came to this area in 1851 or 1858. James Handley was born November 4, 1794, in Loudon, Virginia, the sixth born of William. We do not know his mother, and only that William had a brother. James had five children by his first wife, Rachel (McDermit), in Richmond County, Ohio. She died in 1825 and James remarried Rebecca (Sanders) and had 10 children by her. Sometime between 1851 and 1858, they moved to Orchard Grove, Lake County, Indiana. James died in 1858 and was buried there.

John Douglas, first born of James, married Mary (Bishop) in Knox County, Ohio, November 16, 1848, and had 12 children, that also came to Orchard Grove, where the families farmed until 1883-1884, when they moved westward to Kansas to homestead, taking three months by covered wagon. George Washington, seventh born of John and Mary, and come back to Indiana to marry Anna Sarah (Perry) September 16, 1885, and settled here, having 10 children: Elmer, Alta, Ellis, Beula, Mary, Jennie, Eva, Alice, Raymond, and Vera.

Raymond Earl married Mary Alice (Rush) July 15, 1931, and had seven children, Raymond, John, Joan, Roland, George, Martha, and Thomas. Raymond and Mary were in business for 60 years in Crown Point, Indiana, in meat, meat and grocery, and drive-in restaurant. Raymond passed away December 6, 1982, and Mary is living at home with her son, Thomas, and daughter, Martha.

Raymond Arthur married Elizabeth (Valenti), had one child, who is now married and living in Ohio, and has three children. Richard and Theresa and children, Laura, Jeremy, and Rhonda. Raymond then married Betty (Held) and they have three children: Mark, Dawn, and Gregory. Mark and wife, Chirsty (Scott) have two children: Elliot and Myles. Dawn lives in Texas, Mark's family and Gregory live in Crown Point.

John Edward married Lovena (Williams) January 31, 1953, and had five children: Michael, Martin, Matthew, Mont, and Marcus. Michael married Janet (Paluch) August 8, 1980, and they have two children: Joshua and Sarah. Martin married Therese (Hanlon) November 10, 1984, and they have two children: James and Joel. Matthew married Dian (Oros) June 6, 1981. Mont graduates from Purdue May 15, 1988, and Marcus graduates Merrillville High School June 6, 1988.

Joan married Richard (Souther) and has three children, Catherine, David and Susan. Susan married Charles (Wagoner) and has one child, Monica.

Roland married Gerraldine (Randolph) and has two children, Tina and Douglas. Tina married Mitchell (Kormendy) and has two children: Derek and Zackry. Then Roland married Gayle (Gibbs) and has two children: Jeannie and Ryan.

George married Edna (Cunningham) and has two children: Theresa and Sherry.

Other Handleys stayed or came back to Indiana for Governor Handley was a cousin and has two brothers living in the LaPorte area. We were tied in for sure by another cousin in Las Gates, California, who put together the family tree.

It is very interesting to know one's roots, trees, and branches, and a challenge to keep up on the growth that goes on.

by John E. Handley

HANLEY, ROY AND LILLIE

F98

Mom and Dad Hanley (photo taken in 1968).

The Hanleys, like many other pioneers, contacted "western fever" at the conclusion of the Revolutionary War. They were a part of Kentucky's early history and served with the military from there during the War of 1812. Samuel Hanley married Miss Mary Ripple in 1804 and this union produced fifteen children. They farmed in several places including Muhlenberg County, Kentucky, until 1819. Their sixth child, David Hanley, was born on 5 July 1818. At the age of one year, David and his family moved to the northern part of Clark County, later called Edgar County, Illinois. David attended a local log school house and played with Cherokee Indian children. He worked on the family farm and made regular 30-day trips, by oxen, to the Chicago markets.

David was a successful farmer at the time of his marriage to Miss Hannah Peterson in 1842. David and Hannah had eight daughters and four sons. All of the children grew to adulthood, married, and had children of their own. Some of David's sons saw action during the Civil War. After this war, some of the children married and moved to other western states. Thomas Russell Hanley was the ninth born to David and Hannah and was too young for military service. He remained with the family until his marriage to Miss Maggie Dobson c. 1881. This married ended in divorce after ten years and two daughters. Thomas Russell

Hanley then married Miss Minerva Jane Cooper c. 1893 in Edgar County, Illinois. This married produced three children: Maude "Bobbe" in 1895, Mark Raymond in 1899, and Roy Paul Hanley in 1901. Maude married Dr. William Albert Zimmerman, on osteopath, in Mansfield, Missouri. Thomas and his two sons spent several years working on western cattle ranches until 1923. That year, the three men were drawn to the booming steel town of Gary, Indiana. Gary was just seventeen years old, and in many ways, just like boom towns of the "Old West." All three Hanleys got jobs with the Indiana Steel Company, later known as United States Steel, and purchased a building lot from the Gary Land Company.

They had L.I. Combs build a two story frame home at 833 Harrison Street in 1924. Mark Raymond Hanley was the first to marry and leave the Harrison Street home. He married a neighbor girl, Miss Mary Gloria Macedo, who had fled from the Azores during the great plague of 1924. They were married by Father Thomas Jensen on Saturday 30 January 1926. They had three children: Mark Anthony in 1928, Raymond in 1930, and Margeret M. in 1935. Mark Raymond Hanley was seriously injured in a wartime steelmill accident in the No. 3 blowing house on Thursday 6 January 1944. Thereafer, they sold their 520 Maryland Street home and moved the family to Mexico, Missouri, where he died on 2 January 1968.

Roy Paul Hanley married Miss Lillie Mae Hindsley of Medaryville, Indiana, on Monday 16 January 1928 in Valparaiso, Indiana. His father, Thomas Russell Hanley, moved to Chicago, Illinois, where he died c. 1936. Roy and Lillie Hanley became the parents of three children: Roy Donald, Richard Arlen, and Sharon Kay Hanley. Roy Paul Hanley remained with United States Steel until his 65th birthday and retirement in February of 1966. He was active in several Masonic organizations and served as the Master of Gary Lodge #677 F. & A.M. in 1944. During 1942 and 1943, he became active in organizing Masonic youth groups. He was the founder of the Steel City Chapter Order of DeMolay. A young man had to be 21 years of age to become a Masonic Lodge member. Because of the WW II draft and enlistments, the need of young men under 21, who had no Masonic contacts open to them, was apparent. The DeMolay membership was open to all boys between the ages of 14 and 21 without regard to their parents' affiliations or religious background.

WW II affected all areas of everyday life, including civic and social organizations. The Masonic groups had to make allowances for the new membership demands by performing initiation ceremonies after working hours and on Sundays to accommodate new members. 1944 saw the greatest increase in Masonic membership than in any other period of Gary's history. Changes were also made in DeMolay's structure because the young men were joining one week and enlisting the next week. DeMolay's term of office for officers was reduced from one year to four months to accommodate the fast pace of the war. The DeMolay Honor Roll included many of its members who served with distinction including three members who gave their life during WW II and the Korean Conflict. The Hanleys chaperoned all social activities and opened their home for many Jobs Daughters and DeMolay functions. These youngsters always referred to them as "Mom" and "Dad" Hanley. More than once, the Hanleys would be greeted by a group in public and they would draw inquisitive looks from other uninformed adults regarding the questions of parenting.

The Hanley's three children participated in Jobs Daughters or DeMolay as did their two daughters-in-law and two of their granddaughters. Mom Hanley passed away on Sunday 12 December 1971 and was laid to rest near her childhood home in the White Post Cemetery at Medaryville, Indiana. Dad Hanley followed her on Tuesday 25 October 1977 and is buried at the same place. They were survived by two sons, a daughter, eight grandchildren, and one great grandson.

by R.D. Hanley

HART, A.N.
F99

A.N. Hart

Martha Reed Dyer

Millionaire Ditch Digger

A.N. Hart (The founder of Dyer) was born at Akron, Ohio on April 16, 1816. He was the son of William J. Hart and Flora Norton, both of New England.

In 1850, Aaron Norton Hart went to Philadelphia where he became involved in the book publishing business under the name of Rice & Hart Book Publishers.

Mr. Hart came into the Chicago and Calumet area as a salesman for the publishers. He made some investments in land and soon settled in what is now known as Dyer. He engaged in the real estate business with Hart & Biggs Realty.

Hart soon became one of the largest land owners in Lake County, with most of his holdings in St. John Township. He started the Hartsdale farm which contained eight thousand acres of reclaimed swamp land. His keen eye observed that the immense Cady marsh could be drained and through an ingenious drainage system, which he developed, the water was drawn off into the Calumet River. This system was known as Harts ditch and flowed through Plum Creek in Dyer.

Eventually twenty thousand acres of fertile land was reclaimed for farming and settlement.

Mr. Hart married Martha Reed Dyer at Philadelphia in 1844. She was born in New Bedford, Massachusetts in 1824, and died January 4, 1897 at Crown Point. Hart took Mrs. Hart's maiden name of Dyer to name the town that he founded.

The Harts had four children, James W., Milton R., Malcolm T. and Flora Norton who married James H. Biggs of Cincinnati. Biggs was engaged in the real estate business, and was a dealer for the United States Cotton Press and Hay Press, manufactured in Michigan City by Haskell & Barker.

A.N. Hart met his death on January 12, 1883. While supervising the construction of a ditch cut through a bend in Plum Creek, the left hand bank caved in on him. A frozen edge fell and struck him in the region of the heart – killing him instantly. He was buried in the county seat of Crown Point.

His spirit of action and power live on today in the reclaimed land of North West Lake County.

by Steven Yaros, Jr.

HASEMAN FAMILY
F100

Henry Haseman Sr. came from Hagen, Germany and his wife Mary (Blume) came from Walringhausen, Germany. (Mary was the widow of Conrad Oltrogge who died in 1867. Their children were William and Mary.) Henry and Mary's children included: Henry F. Jr., Herman, Caroline (She was born December 29, 1872 and married Theodore Borges on April 20, 1902.); Sophia (She married William Tatge.); John (He was born on May 29, 1874 and died on August 16, 1894.); and Fred (He was born on June 4, 1889 and married Amanda Rosenbrock, who was born on January 19, 1892.).

Herman and Mary (Guritz) Haseman, lived in West Creek Township in Lake County and on the once known Ristenpart farm (his par-

Mrs. Henry Haseman, Jr. stands at right following the aftermath of the April 21, 1912 Tornado. Originally, the Frank Plummer Place, one mile south of the Lake Prairie Church near Lowell, Indiana.

ents lived southwest of them). In 1920 they moved northwest to Groton South Dakota. Their children were Marvin who married Marie Erickson; Ruby wife of Herbert Hinkelman; Ernest who married Marion Claus of Beecher, Illinois; Lucinda, single; Elsie the wife of Norbert Held of Dyer, Indiana; Erwin, who died at age 4 months; and Pearl, the wife of Fred Kuhlman of Beecher, Illinois.

Henry F. Jr. (born September 5, 1871) and Emma Guritz (born May 1, 1878, the daughter of William and Mary (Schaper) Guritz) married on March 3, 1898. (Mary and Emma were siters; and Herman and Henry were brothers.) They farmed the Arkenberg farm east of Crete Illinois before moving on in 1907 to a farm known as a Rotermund farm 1-1/4 mile west of Brunswick, Indiana on the southwest corner of 133rd and State Line Road (on the Illinois side of the road).

Henry and Emma's children included: William, the eldest who remained single; Helen who married Walter Dannenberg of Grant Park Illinois on May 1, 1927; Hildagarde who married Clarence J. Kurth of Grant Park on June 22, 1930; and Clarence who married Bernice Lohman of Beecher, Illinois on September 23, 1946.

Henry and his family moved to the Frank Plummer Farm west of Lowell, Indiana and south of the Lake Prairie Church in West Creek Township Lake County Indiana. (Living on nearby farms in Section 30, near Hadders Road, were: a brother of Emma (Guritz) Haseman; Louis and Emma (Wehrman) Guritz and their children Leona, Milford and Lucille; friends, August and Mina Hadders; new neighbors, the Eich family, and Henry Haseman's brother Herman and his wife Mary (Guritz), lived on the west side of the section.)

On April 21, 1912, around 6 p.m. a tornado touched down on certain areas throughout the Lowell area. The Plummer house was picked up with six of the Henry Haseman family in it and set down a few feet beside, and away, from the foundation. The children landed behind the two capsized stoves as the stove pipes fell apart. They were scorched by hot coals and a pot of hot coffee spilled over some of the family.

Every window was out of the house, the chimneys were off, straw and debris swirled around and all the contents "whirlwinded" out of the basement. Had the family been down in the cellar, they wouldn't have survived; it poured rain by the buckets full; they would have possibly drowned. Their belongings were hanging high up in the trees, most of which were uprooted.

The neighbors across the road luckily weren't home, their entire buildings were flattened to the ground. Only the hired man (who was home at the time) was saved. He was standing beside a horse, which served as protection from the storm.

Other neighbors took Henry's family in and in two weeks, the house was moved back onto the foundation and repaired. They were so lucky compared to the neighbor's great losses.

Henry's family moved west to the Illinois side of the State Line in the spring of 1913 and purchased the Charles Stadt farm. (The Stadt family bought the Brunswick Tavern before going on to Chicago, Illinois.)

Emma Haseman passed away on May 5, 1925. Henry remained on the farm, while the sons farmed. (Henry and the sons sold a 160 acre farm they owned in Minnesota near New Ulm, in the 1940's.) Henry who was born September 5, 1871 passed away in August 25, 1950.

Clarence and his wife Bernice (Lohman) remained on the farm, their daughter Mary Jane grew up there, she graduated from Beecher High School and married Terry Becker, son of Walter and Ione Becker on October 7, 1978, their children are Scott and Lisa Becker, reisde on county Line Road near Beecher Illinois.

by Mrs. Ralph Oldendorf

HAVENS, DANIEL AND LOLA
F101

Daniel F. Havens, known to everyone as "Doc", did not move to Lake County until he was in his fifties. He was born near Elwood, Indiana. His father's family had been in Indiana since log cabin days and his mother's family had come from Ohio. Early accounts of Doc in Elwood indicate that he was considered an enterprising young man with great promise. He was traveling in Union County with a church singing group, when he met Leora Bassett (always known as "Lola"), daughter of Charles and Mary Bassett. They were married in 1880 and left on their honeymoon in style with a pair of matched (but rented) white horses. They lived in Elwood where Doc was a tinsmith and plumber. They began to experience life's heartbreaks when their first child died of diphtheria just two days after the second was born. This second daughter also died of diphtheria when only three. Childless again, it was a couple of years before their son was born and six years later a daughter. Both of these children lived to establish families of their own.

With the economy in Elwood failing, the family moved to Indianapolis, where Daniel had a tin shop by his home. However, he became bedridden with a severe bout of "rheumatism" that lasted several years. Lola's sister, Mrs. Frank Hodson, was reporting the opportunities available in the new city of Gary and by 1920, full of hope, Doc and Lola decided to try for a fresh start there. Their son was married and remained in Indianapolis. Their daughter, Madeleine, was withdrawn from Shortridge High School in Indianapolis and entered Gary's Emerson High School as soon as the family made the move. She quickly discovered, however, that Shortridge had offered a college preparatory course not available in Gary and she was unable to continue some of her more advanced classes.

Doc never really got any momentum into a career in Gary. Lola became an art teacher in the Gary Schools but she died just two years after they moved to Gary. She has been described as a kind, sensitive person who was always there to help when there was a need and her sudden death at age 57 was a blow to all.

Three years after Lois died, Doc married her spinster cousin, Ella Kyger. They lived quietly at 548 Jefferson St. while Doc held a succession of jobs. Ella died in 1934 and soon after, Doc went to live with his daughter, Madeleine (Mrs. Joe Wildermuth). Doc's granddaughter, Dorothy Wildermuth, remembers the atmosphere in Doc and Ella's home as dark and quiet — not the place for a noisy youngster. When Doc moved in with the Wildermuths, however, he quickly adapted to the lively young family and was a "hit" in the neighborhood because he was available to remove warts and take the pain from burns. Later conjecture has pieced together the theory that Doc learned some healing techniques from his Uncle (Daniel Clymer of Elwood, Indiana — for whom he was no doubt named,) who practiced as a folk doctor. Although this uncle had no formal training, he was actually licensed as a Medical Doctor by the state of Indiana. When he was young, Doc may have spent a good deal of time with his uncle, which could also account for Doc's lifelong nickname.

In 1937, while visiting a sister in Kokomo, Indiana, Doc died suddenly with a heart attack. Life had often been difficult and Doc probably made little impact on his community, but he was greatly missed by his family.

by Dorothy Wildermuth Vekasi

HEIDBREDER, WILBUR H.
F102

Wilbur Henry Heidbreder of Crown Point, Ind. was born August 12, 1907 on the lower level of the Trinity Lutheran wooden school house which was also the residence of William H. Heidbreder and Ida (nee Bornmann) when they came from Quincy, Ill. in 1905, and William was the school teacher and principal, organist and choir director for 48 years of the Trinity Lutheran Church in Crown Point. Wilbur's parents spoke German in the home and he learned English when he started school where his father was his teacher for four years. His brother, Norbert, born May 5, 1912, is married to Neva (nee Burge) Biester and his sister Eleanor, born April 5, is married to Edwin Piepenbrink and lives in Western Springs, Ill.

At the age of nine during a family vacation in Quincy, Wilbur's mother became ill and he and his mother remained there for five years. During these eventful years, residing with his maternal grandfather, who was a Civil War veteran, Wilbur's interest in history was stimulated. Grandfather, Henry Bornmann, was a selfmade journalist and editor of a German daily paper in his post war years. He enlisted as a youth in the Union army because he believed in the freedom of slaves, and also became a friend of Booker T. Washington of Tuskegee Institute. Under this environment, Wilbur became interested in civics and political science.

He was confirmed in Quincy at St. James Lutheran Church and graduated from Crown Point High School in 1925. Wilbur participated in school in athletics and later he coached basketball and was an officer for Little League, Babe Ruth and American Legion Baseball programs. He played on the C.P. Baseball Team under the tutelage of Peter Henning, a pitching star of the Old Kansas City Federal League Team.

After graduation he was employed by the Lake County Title and Guaranty Co. He was encouraged by his boss, Edward J. Eder, for whom he had great respect and admiration to take a correspondence law course, which he did. March 16, 1934 he was married to Nina (nee Adank) who was also employed there by the title officer, Patrick Maloney.

To this marriage were born two sons. John William born January 7, 1939 attended Trinity Lutheran School in C.P. and was graduated from high school and from the University of Illinois with a Fine Arts Degree in Industrial Design. He is married to Joan (nee Breyfogle) and they have two children, Christa Berrell and William Christian.

Timothy Wilbur Heidbreder, the second son, born December 22, 1948 was married to Linda (nee Peters) of C.P. and three girls were born to this union, Juline Rachel, Angela Shea and Aimee Lynn. Timothy also attended Trinity Lutheran School, confirmed at Trinity Memorial Church and graduated from C.P. High School. He has his own business known as Crown Heating and Cooling.

After 19 years at the title company when Wilbur was offered a job at the First National Bank of C.P. by Paul Brown, he accepted and enjoyed an affiliation there for 30 years as officer and director. He retired on December 31, 1974.

Always having an avid interest in civic affairs, Wilbur worked behind the scenes many times with the Chamber of Commerce transportation commission in an attempt to retain railroad passenger service in the community of Crown Point and South Lake County, he was South Lake County Chairman of the American Red Cross, a staunch supporter of the Historic Board of Review of Crown Point, appointed by Mayor Richard Collins to maintain some of the city's historic architectural heritage.

He became involved in renovation and preservation of the old Lake County Courthouse for the purpose of establishing a county museum. The building was to be abandoned with the completion of a new complex for county offices north of town. In 1971 when Mrs. Joseph Brown of the Lake County Historical Society called a meeting of all the historical societies in the county for the purpose of acquiring the old courthouse, Wilbur was selected to chair the committee, and when the Lake Courthouse Foundation was formed in 1974 he served as President for 11 years on a voluntary basis and since retirement from this has remained as President Emeritus to date (1988). With the help of many volunteers the old courthouse was saved from the wrecking ball.

He has devoted much effort as Treasurer and board member of the Lutheran Home of Northwest Indiana in Crown Point, organized in 1978. He also has served on a number of committees in his own church, on the Calumet Mission Board and District and local areas of the Lutheran Church, Missouri Synod. He and Nina are members of Trinity Memorial Lutheran Church of Independence Hill, Merrillville, Indiana.

by Nina Heidbreder

HENNING, PETE
F103

"Pete" Henning of Crown Point, Major League Baseball Star

Ernest Herman ("Pete") Henning, regarded as one of the finest athletes in Lake County in the era before World War I, was born in Crown Point on December 28, 1887, to parents who had emigrated from Germany three years before. He started his career as a pitcher on the Crown Point baseball team, winning a Northwest Indiana league championship for them, and then moved into semi-professional ball with such teams as Hammond, South Bend, and Sturgis (Mich.). He reached the major leagues for two seasons, 1914 and 1915, with the Kansas City team of the old Federal League, which had teams also in Brooklyn, Newark, Baltimore, Buffalo, Pittsburgh, Indianapolis, Chicago, and St. Louis. The *Baseball Encyclopedia* gives him a record of 15 wins and 24 losses for the two years. He pitched in 63 games.

The prowess of the Crown Point team and its star pitcher was recalled late in life by Pete's nephew, Harvey Vandersee: "The ball park, with a grandstand seating about 1,500 people, was located on the east side of North Indiana Avenue at the Erie Railroad tracks. The high point of the week was Sunday afternoon, when a ball game was scheduled. Several hours before game time you could see people from all directions walking toward the ball park to see Pete Henning mow down the opposition. More times than not, he did just that. Crown Point had such a good team and park that they were able to schedule an exhibition game in Crown Point with the Chicago Cubs."

In 1939 a writer in the *Lake County Star* had similar recollections: "He must have been a pitcher from childhood, for one of our earliest recollections as a boy is that of slipping down to the oldtime ball games and squeezing under the fence to watch 'Pete' pitch. His reputation among the kids was solidly established: they believed him to be about the best in the world. the older folks thought so, too; for some of them arranged the game that brought the old Cub baseball machine out to play Pete's team, and we all had a chance to see the mighty Mordecai

Back row left to right: John Heidbreader, Christa Heidbreader, wife Joan Heidbreader, Julie Heidrreader and her father Timothy Heidbreader front row- Angela Heidbreader, Grandfather Wilbur Heidbreader, Aimee Heidbreader, Grandmother Nina Heidbreader and John William Heidbreader

97

Brown and his team-mates" (Nov. 10).

Perhaps because of Pete's losing seasons with Kansas City, the *Lake County Star* at his death pointed to an earlier season, 1910, as the "peak" of his career. In that year, in one game for Jimmy Callahan's Logan Squares in Chicago, he allowed only one hit, performing so brilliantly that the Chicago *Journal* commented: "Everything that a pitcher would want the big sod-buster had, and at the rate he was going he could have beaten any team in the world."

Among the highlights of his Kansas City career were two games early in the 1914 season against Chicago. The Chicago *Tribune* on April 18 reported his victory in a 13-inning game: "Big Pete Henning, a stalwart athlete of muscular proportions and calm mind, was voted the hero because he withstood the attack of the Chicagoans for the entire afternoon and at the finish looked as if he were just getting warmed up to the fight . . . Pete was also a Federal leaguer last year, and yet some folks think the Federal didn't have a thing a year ago." On April 27 the *Tribune* reported that a 12-4 victory for Kansas City over Chicago was won by long hits, "along with the fact that they had Pete Henning on the slab, the same tall, lanky hurler who beat the Chifeds down in Kansas City." He stood 5'11" and weighted 185 pounds.

Pete Henning's baseball career was interrupted by World War I. In summer of 1918 he reported to Camp Sherman, the enormous training camp in Chillicothe, Ohio, with Company B of the 336th Infantry. He was made corporal on August 17, and by the middle of October, a month before the Armistice, was in France. In February 1919 he was with the First Provisional Regiment at Camp D'Auvours, Sarthe, in northwest France. He sailed back to the States on the U.S.S. *Walter Luckenbach,* leaving St-Nazaire on June 4. He was soon playing ball again, for industrial and city teams; in 1920 he was on the Gary team of the American Bridge Company, credited with the team championship victory over Ambridge, Pa., repeating a 1911 performance. After retiring from baseball he played football with Crown Point area teams for several seasons, "with marked success," the *Star* reported.

Beginning about 1926 he worked for the Crown Point Telephone Company as a serviceman. He was active in the American Legion, the Fred Schmidt chapter in Crown Point, and six Legionnaires served as pallbears after he died in a freak accident on the "ideal stretch" of the Lincoln Highway (U.S. 30) east of Dyer, Indiana, early on the Saturday morning of November 4, 1939. He had stopped to push a stalled automobile and was struck by another car and crushed to death. Pete was the son of Friedrich Henning (1851-1928) and Wilhelmina Henning (1845-1932), and was survived by four sisters, Elizabeth (Mrs. John) Holst and Anna (Mrs. Karl) Vandersee of Crown Point, Clara (Mrs. Sherman) Barber of Lowell, and Ida (Mrs. Charles) Gumpper of Chicago.

by Charles Vandersee

HESS, JAY EMMITT FAMILY
F104

The history of the Jay Emmitt and Maxine Ellen (Steinard) Hess family in Lake County started in March, 1956 when Maxine, a brand new graduate of what was then Ball State Teacher's College, came to East Chicago to begin her teaching career. She completed that school year and returned to Franklin County, Indiana, the home of her parents, Wilkie and Beatrice Ellen (Dora) Steinard. Wilkie was a native of Franklin County, and Beatrice had moved there at the age of nine from neighboring Fayette County. She and Wilkie returned to Fayette County and lived on a rented farm after their marriage on February 17, 1926. On July 24, 1934, Maxine was born and in the following January the family moved to a newly purchased farm about one and a half miles distant, but back in Franklin County where the farm remains under the ownership of Maxine and her only brother, William.

Jay Emmitt Hess was born October 20, 1935 in Ross County, Ohio, the son of Jay and Verda Mae (Jenkins) Hess. He grew to manhood there attending local schools and graduating from Richmonddale High School in 1954. He then worked for the Norfolk and Western Railroad in Ohio, following the footsteps of his maternal grandfather, Charles Emmitt Jenkins. After meeting Maxine and deciding to relocate to Lake County, he took a position as block operator with the Pennsylvania Railroad where he worked until 1967, when he resigned to devote full time to his own business, Hess Detective Agency, which he had opened in 1961. This business flourished until the recession of the mid 80's, when he gave up the business to devote full time to safety escort, an interest from the security field.

Jay and Maxine were married on December 29, 1956 at the Blooming Grove Methodist Church in Franklin County, Indiana. They were blessed with children: Donald Eugene, Dale Edward, Charles Neal and an unnamed son who lived only seven hours.

Donald was born July 3, 1958, and is presently a licensed paramedic working for Town of Merrillville and Fagen-Miller Ambulance Service.

Dale was born June 14, 1959, married Kellee Ann Steele on November 12, 1983, and has one daughter, Ashlee Noelle born on October 4, 1985. Dale and Kellee were divorced in April, 1989. He is employed by Inland Steel.

An unnamed son was born and died on February 16, 1962. He is buried at Maplewood Cemetery, Crown Point.

Charles Neal was born September 26, 1963. He spent three years in the U.S. Army, and is completing requirements for a degree in recreational leadership from Taylor University, Upland, Indiana. Chuck, Don, and Dale are all graduates of Griffith High School.

Maxine pursued her elementary teaching career with time spent in East Chicago, Hammond, Lake County, and lastly, the Griffith system where she was honored for 25 years service in 1988.

Jay and Maxine also own Branches and Roots, a genealogy supply store and used book shop. The used book shop was formerly known as the Griffith Used Book Store.

by Maxine Hess

HESS, JOSEPH
F105

The history of the Joseph Hess family began in 1825 when Joseph Hess was born in the Alsace-Lorraine area of France. In 1846, at the age of 21, Joseph came to America, first settling in Chicago and then moving to Gibson, or West Point, on what is now Kennedy Avenue in Hessville, Indiana. At this point in time very little potential could be seen for the sandy and marshy area of northern Lake County with its scrub oak and cedars. The Michigan Central trains ended their tracks at West Point, where passengers disembarked to wait for a stage coach to Chicago, 20 miles away. Gibson Station was named for David Gibson who operated an inn at this site. He eventually sold the inn to Joseph Hess, who being a French baker, turned it into a restaurant for train passengers.

In 1849, Joseph Hess married Mary Sackley from Canada and moved about a mile south of Gibson, living across from the Concordia Lutheran Church on Marshall Avenue. Their only son, Frank, was the first male child born in North Township in 1853. Mary Sackley died in 1860 and Joseph Hess then married Elizabeth Natke and opened a general store in the 6900 block of Kennedy Avenue, the only other business being a blacksmith shop. This general store was the hub of the community. The main occupations of the settlers at that time were hunting, fishing and farming, with a few working on the railroad. Settlers would come into the store with corn or cords of wood to trade for supplies. Indians brought in their animal pelts for trading. These would have been Potowatomi Indians who did not release their lands in this area until 1832. They would come to visit their burial grounds along the Calumet River. The store served as post office with Joseph Hess being the postmaster for 40 years. It was also a place to vote, and Joseph was elected the first trustee in North Township, a post he held for 23 years. Joseph worked hard as Trustee to help build the two bridges over the Calumet River. The population of Hessville at this time was numbered about 50.

Joseph and Elizabeth had 11 children named as follows: George, William, Julius, Gustav, Albert, Joseph Jr., Edward, Emma, John, Lydia and Alice. Joseph died in August of 1895 and Elizabeth in 1917 and are laid to rest in Hessville Cemetery on 169th St. Located between Arizona and Parrish Avenues in Hammond, this cemetery is the resting place for many of the early settlers of the Hessville area.

Describing my branch of the Hess family, Joseph Hess's son George married Clara Tarnowski and they had six children, as follows: Erwin, Alfred, Robert, Lydia, Clara and Gertrude Emily born March 8, 1899. Gertrude was my mother and was 1½ years old when Clara Tarnowski Hess passed away in 1902. George could not keep the family together, so the children were raised by relatives. The three boys went to stay with Mary Tarnowski, Clara's sister and her husband Joseph Windish. Lydia was adopted by Frank and Martha Hess, Joseph Hess's first son. Gertrude was adopted by her mother's dear friend Jane Watts and her husband Ed Piper. Gertrude Hess Piper married Dewey Dishaw from Peshtigo, Wisconsin and I am their only child. I am married to Julius Housty and have two sons, Mark and Brian and a grandson Shane Housty. Erwin Hess married Viola Ingle and they had three children, Donald Hess of Portage, Erwin Hess of Hammond and Lorraine Hess Karr, now deceased. Donald Hess married Betty Brown and they had two children Donald Jr. and Candace and there are 3 grandsons, Daniel, Timothy and Andrew. Lorraine Hess married Martin Karr and they had two children, Dennis and Kathleen. Alfred and Clara did marry but there were no children from these unions. Lydia and Robert were never married. All of George's children are now deceased.

Lydia Hess was the last survivor of the original Hess family. She became the postmistress for 20 years after her father died in 1895. She lived in the residence at 6941 Kennedy for all of her life, never marrying. She was selected Queen of Hessville's Centennial celebration and was a legend in her own time. She was a staunch opposer in Hessville's becoming a part of Hammond in 1923. The 1920 census showed Hessville to have a population of 1,480 residents. Lydia passed away on February 18, 1949.

Joseph Hess and the other settlers of Lake County had to face a wilderness to provide their families with food, clothing and shelter. Self reliance, tolerance and a willingness to help each other helped them to survive. I am proud to be born into such a hard-working family who left me with such a wonderful heritage.

by Leana Housty

HESS, JOSEPH
F106

The Founder of Hessville

Joseph Hess was 21 when he came to the U.S. in 1846 from the Alsace-Lorraine region in France. He was born in 1825 and died in 1895. His father was also Joseph Hess and mother was Miss Dancro.

Joseph Hess was the first white settler in the area of Lake County, and also founded Hessville, Indiana. He became the first postmaster for almost 40 years. Joseph Hess married the daughter of William Sackley, a native of Canada. Her name was Mary Ann Sackley, but she died in 1860. She had one son named Frank Hess, who was born 1853. Joseph Hess' second wife was Elizabeth Natke, the daughter of Christian Natke and Marie (Warnock) Natke. Joseph and his second wife had eleven children. The names of the children are: George, William, Julius, Gustav, Albert, Joseph Jr., Edward, Emma, John, Lydia and Alice, who married Fred Scheuneman.

Frank Hess was elected City Treasurer in 1892, and he married Emma Haselback. After she died he married Martha Karsten. Frank and Martha had one daughter, Emma, plus an adopted daughter, Lydia. Lydia was the daughter of George and Clara Hess, and after Clara's death they adopted her. A more complete history of the whole Hess family from 1825 to today is at the Little Red School House.

by Kathleen Karr

HIGGINS, ERNEST
F107

Ernest Higgins was born 9 February 1914 in Smithfield, Grant District, Wetzel County, West Virginia to Enoch Higgins and Hulda Jane Hayhurst. Ernest grew up and attended school near his home. He also attended school in Monroe, Michigan. Enoch Higgins was born 5 November 1880 in Folsom, Wetzel County, West Virginia to Josephus Higgins and Mary Elizabeth Carson. Enoch Higgins married Hulda Jane Hayhurst 20 April 1902 in Wetzel County, West Virginia. Hulda Jane Hayhurst was born in Brink, Marion County, West Virginia 23 January 1886 to Andrew Coleman Hayhurst and Melinda Starkey. Enoch Higgins, a coal miner, died 27 August 1963 in Weston, Lewis County, West Virginia. His wife, Hulda Jane (Mayhurst) Higgins died 27 August 1957 in Folsom, West Virginia. Enoch and Hulda Jane Higgins are buried at Masonic Cemetery in Shinnston, Harrison County, West Virginia.

Ernest Higgins got his first job as a restaurant manager at a restaurant owned by Republic Steel in Monroe, Michigan. He met Katheleen Virginia Hyden while attending the Church of God in Monroe, Michigan. Ernest Higgins and Katheleen Virginia Hyden were married 17 August 1937 in Monroe, Monroe County, Michigan. Katheleen Virginia Hyden was born 26 March 1920 in Kentucky to Jesse Franklin Hyden and Laura Belle Garland.

While living in Monroe, Michigan, Ernest and Virginia Higgins first son, Jimmie Dean was born 27 April 1939. Then Ernest and Virginia Higgins moved to Cleveland, Ohio where a daughter, Sonja Modeane was born 27 April 1941. About 1941, Iva Pauline (Higgins) Ratliff (See John Ira Pegg Story), a sister to Ernest Higgins and her second husband, William Ratliff went to Cleveland and helped move Ernest and Virginia Higgins and their two children to Gary, Indiana because of the excellent job opportunities in the steel mills. Ernest Higgins soon got a job at Inland Steel Company in East Chicago, Indiana.

It was in Gary, Indiana that Kenneth Deon Higgins was born 1 March 1944 to Ernest and Virginia Higgins. The youngest son of Ernest and Virginia Higgins, Robert Charles Higgins was born in Gary, Indiana 28 July 1957. Their youngest daughter, Laura Jane Higgins, was born 29 October 1959 in Gary, Indiana. About 1965, Ernest and Virginia Higgins moved to Crown Point, Indiana.

Jimmie Dean Higgins married Janice Elaine Russell 18 August 1962 in Hammond, Indiana. Jimmie and Janice Higgins are living in Crown Point, Indiana with their three children. Sonja Modeane Higgins married Joseph Francis Hudgins 26 March 1961 in Highland, Indiana. Joseph and Sonja Hudgins are living in Remington, Jasper County, Indiana and they have two children. Kenneth Deon Higgins married Virginia Matthews 17 April 1966 in Gary, Indiana. Kenneth and Virginia Higgins are living in Crown Point, Indiana with four children. Robert Charles Higgins married Joanne Marie Reks 3 May 1979 in Crown Point, Indiana. Robert and Joanne Higgins are living in Crown Point, Indiana with one son. Laura Jane Higgins married Dan Neal and they have two children. They are now living in Cedar Lake, Indiana. Ernest Higgins is now retired from Inland Steel and he is living with his wife, Virginia in Crown Point, Indiana.

by John W. Pegg

HILBRICH FAMILY
F108

Hilbrichs To America

Nicholas Hilbrich was born April 29, 1806 in Nunkirchen, Germany, the son of Nicholas Hilbrich and Mary Bouwen and grandson of Jacob Hilbrich and Angela Willems of Neumagen, Germany. He was the fourth of five children. On February 10, 1829, Nick married Susana Kautenburger, daughter of John Kautenburger and Mary Palm in St. Mary Magdalena's Catholic Church in Brotdorf, Germany.

Early in March of 1847, Nick, age 40, his wife, Susana, age 38, and their seven children: Gertrude 17, Nicholas 15, Anna 12, John 10, Mathias 7, Frank 4, and Susan 1, left Brotdorf which is in the Saar region of Germany, a few kilometers northeast of Mersig. Traveling with Nick to America was his father, Nicholas, age 79. Their journey was to Antwerp, New York, and on to Lake County, Indiana, where some of their friends and neighbors settled a couple of years earlier.

It was in Antwerp where Nick bid good-bye to his only brother, John, who was sailing to South America. Legend has it that it was a nice, sunny afternoon when they set sail, but the captain of the vessel ordered all passengers to go below immediately. Within a few minutes the ship was tossing wildly in a violent storm. It was 38 hours before the storm spent itself and they were able to resume their course. Nick was the only passenger who did not get seasick. After they had proceeded for some distance, they passed vessels which had been caught in the storm and were without masts or sails, drifting aimlessly about. Nick never heard from his brother after that, and it was presumed that his ship had been lost in the storm. After the storm, there were other weather complications, so that unfavorable winds slowed the crossing time to three full months. During the last month of the voyage, the food on board ran low and the diet of passengers and crew dwindled to nothing but cornbread, sometimes called "Johnny Cake", and water. Nick go so tired of the stuff that he couldn't eat cornbread for a good ten years after he settled in America.

Upon his arrival in what is now Schererville late in the summer of 1847, Nick built a log home. As of this writing, the home still stands and is owned by and occupied by his descendants. A few doors away, 137 years later, on part of Nick's original 40 acres, a modern log home was built by and is the home of the Chris Hilbrich family who are 7th and 8th generation Hilbrichs on this property.

Nick began farming and making shoes for the early settlers as he was a cobbler by trade in Germany. Farming became his major trade. During July of 1848 a daughter, Catherine, was born. She died as an infant. In 1850, Peter, their 9th child, was born. Nick's mother, who remained in Germany, died in Brotdorf of 1848. Nick's father passed away in June of 1852 at the age of 83 years and 9 months. He is buried in St. John's cemetery. In April 1854, Susana passed away and Nick remained a widower until June of 1866 when he married Susana Aylen. She also was born in Germany. Earlier in 1866 Nick sold his farm which had grown to 520 acres to his sons Mathias and Nicholas Jr. Except for several 40 acre parcels, the farm was 40 acres wide and two miles in length, extending south from what is now 65th Avenue in Schererville to what would be 82nd St. paralleling the east side of the N.Y.C. RR. The home and barns are located on the extreme south end. The sons subsequently each separated the land into the individual farms. Nick Sr. continued to live with Nick Jr. and his family on the home site until his death on April 1, 1884. He had 64 grandchildren. His widow, Susana Aylen, passed away December 27, 1891.

The children of Nicholas Hilbrich all married as follows:

Gertrude married Nick Schutz of Dyer where they started one of Dyer's first saloons. It still operates as a tavern today. They had four children. Gertrude died October 15, 1911.

Nicholas Jr. married Margaret Bohney. They lived in the family home and operated the farm. They had 12 children. Nicholas died October 7, 1899.

Anna married Nicholas Koop and lived in Schererville. They had seven children. She died May 5, 1889. The descendants of this marriage changed their name to Cope.

John married Mary Peifer and lived on a farm in Cedar Lake. They had six children. Mary died and John married her sister, Ellen, with whom seven children were born. John and Ellen moved to Hammond where he died on March 5, 1899.

Mathias married Mary Bohr. They had ten children. After Mary's death, Mathias married Eva Wickman with whom one child was born. He lived on the farm in Schererville until his death on July 26, 1925.

Frank married Angeline Gehring. Seven children were born to this marriage. They lived in Crown Point and later in Hammond where he died on July 14, 1908.

Susan married Martin Young of Crown Point where they operated a saloon and raised seven children. Susan died in Crown Point June 27, 1919.

Peter married Barbara Rascher. They had four children and lived in Hammond where he was a policeman. He died October 20, 1928.

by James Hilbrich

HILBRICH FAMILY
F109

Hilbrichs Involved in Township's Growth

Roy C. Hilbrich was raised on the original Hilbrich farm, in Schererville, Indiana, where he was born on November 16, 1899, to Frank and Margaret (Schmal) Hilbrich. He attended St. Michael's grade school in Schererville and thereafter Dyer High School. His scholastic records show exceptional talent. It was in high school that Marie Fagen, the daughter of Michael and Anna (Lillig) Fagen of Dyer, caught his eye. Marie was born in Dyer, Indiana, on June 24, 1898. As classmates the graduated in 1917. With W.W. I in progress, Roy enlisted in the U.S. Navy. Marie began work at the Erie R.R. office in Hammond. Outside of her employ-

Patricia, Thomas, Marie, James and Roy Hilbrich 1945. Photo taken in Dyer.

ment, she was a trained vocalist and an accomplished pianist. Upon completion of his training at Great Lakes Naval Station, Roy was sent to Notre Dame University in South Bend, Indiana for college studies and Naval Officers Training. The war's end also concluded Roy's college studies as subsequently the Navy removed their students from active duty to a reserve status to complete their enlistment. He went to work at the Standard Car Wheel Plant in Hammond, and then on to the Hammond Dairy which became Bordens. He delivered milk for many years — first with horse and wagon, then by electric truck, and finally with trucks powered by gasoline engines. On June 5, 1923, Roy and Marie married in St. Joseph's Catholic Church in Dyer and they took up residence on Clinton Street in Hammond.

On February 13, 1926, their first child, James Michael, was born in their residence on Clinton Street. Following on April 7, 1927, a second son, Thomas Lee, was born on the farm in Schererville while Roy and Marie were visiting Roy's parents. On January 12, 1929, their last child, a daughter named Patricia Ann, was born in their new brick home which they had purchased on south Jackson Street in Hammond.

In May of 1929, Marie's father passed away and thereafter her mother, Anna, came to live with Roy and Marie. Anna longed for her friends, church, and the tranquility of Dyer. She offered Roy and Marie several acres she owned in Dyer on the west side of Nondorf Street if they would build there. The new home was built and in November of 1932, the family moved to Dyer. Anna lived with Roy and Marie in this house until her death in February, 1943. Roy and Marie also lived in this home the remainder of their lives.

During the 1940's and 1950's, Roy held a number of elected and appointed governmental positions. They were at the town, township and county levels. He was well recognized for his work in administering the St. John Township school system. Roy continued to work at Bordens until his retirement in 1962. Roy and Marie were both active, dedicated and devout members of St. Joseph's Catholic Church in Dyer. Marie passed away July 17, 1969 and Roy followed on January 14, 1972. They had a total of 14 grandchildren. Their children all married as follows:

1. James married Mary L. Scheidt. Children – Michael, Patrick, Sally, Chris, Peggy, Beth and Timothy

2. Thomas married Betty Burns. Children – Nancy

3. Patricia married John J. Rosinko. Children – Roy, Mark, Amy, Dan, Luke and John M.

by James M. Hilbrich

HILBRICH FAMILY
F110

Nicholas Hilbrich 1831-1899

A New Generation of Hilbrichs in a New Land

Nicholas Hilbrich was born on September 27, 1831, in Brotdorf, Germany, the son of Nicholas Hilbrich and Susanna Kautenburger. Leaving Brotdorf at age 15, he came to what is now Schererville with his parents, brothers and sisters. Nick helped his father build their log home and worked on the family farm. On May 5, 1860, he married Margaret Bohney in St. John Evangelist Catholic Church in St. John. She was the daughter of Nicholas Boh-

Margaret (Bohney) Hilbrich 1841-1927

ney and Catherine Muller. Margaret was born May 18, 1841 in St. John, Indiana. It is said that she was the first white child born in St. John Township. Margaret's and Nick's parents were both married in the same church (St. Mary Magdalene) in Brotdorf, Germany, although Margaret's parents lived in the neighboring village of Bachem. Nick and Margaret lived on the family farm and in 1866, just six years after their marriage, Nick's father sold his farm of 520 acres to Nick and Mathias (one of Nick's brothers) for $2,000 plus a contract to provide him with a home (one room), one acre of pasture for his cow and of all the grains, roots, and hay raised on the farm for as long as he lived. It is interesting to note that Nick Sr. completed this transaction just weeks prior to marrying his second wife. He had been a widower for twelve years.

Subsequently, Mathias and Nick split the farm, each having his own farm, with Nick Jr. and his family retaining the South part of the farm including the homestead and buildings. In 1877 Mathias sold 189 acres of his farm back to his brother, Nick. Nick engaged in dairy and grain farming and raised a family of twelve children. Nick and his father planted a large apple orchard. In addition to the apples supplying food for his large family, wagon loads were taken to the large cider press in St. John. The Hilbrich cellar was "known" for its endless supply of both sweet and hard cider. Many tales resulted from visits to this cellar.

In February of 1891, Nick deeded one-half acre of the extreme Southwest corner of his farm to St. John Township for a school. A frame schoolhouse was erected and school began that Fall. Officially it was St. John Township School #10, but in fact went by the name of Hilbrich School. This school was used through the 1904-1905 school year. In July of 1911, the one-half acre of property reverted to the Hilbrich Farm as called for in the original deed should its use for a school be discontinued.

Nick passed away on October 7, 1899. His widow remained on the farm with their son, Frank and his family, until her death on February 3, 1927. Nick and Margaret had 53 grandchildren. Their children all married and reared their families in the Calumet Region as follows:

1. Barbara (1862-1911) married John Hart — 2 children.
2. Mathias (1864-1928) married Amelia Ledoux — 1 child.
3. John (1865-1919) married Mary Austgen — 5 children.
4. Frank (1867-1946) married Margaret Schmal — 7 children.
5. Mary (1869-1956) married Henry Greiving — 3 children.
6. Susan (1871-1945) married Anthony DuBois — 4 children.
7. Nicholas (1873-1912) married Catherine Keilman — 5 children.
8. Margaret (1874-1925) married Ed Wachter — 1 child (died as an infant).
9. Bernard (1876-1952) married Margaret Keilman — 7 children.
10. Elizabeth (1878-1932) married Ed Hoffman — 2 children.
11. Othilla (1881-1963) married Anthony Kaiser — 2 children.
12. William (1885-1962) married Elizabeth Steuer — 14 children.

by James M. Hilbrich

HILBRICH, FRANK
F111

Hilbrich Homestead Remains "Home" To All

Frank Hilbrich, son of Nicholas Hilbrich and Margaret Bohney, was born and raised on the Hilbrich Farm in St. John Twp. Born September 1, 1867, he was the fourth of 12 children.

Upon reaching manhood, he worked tilling the prairies in the Brunswick, Klassville, and Eagle Lake areas. Two of the men he was working with at the time were John Mahoney and Herman Kleine. The latter related many of the activities of this three-some. While Frank was always known as a true gentleman, his strength was well recognized.

In 1898 he married Margaret Schmal, who was born in Klassville, Indiana on October 6, 1878 to Jacob Schmal and Catherine Schmidt. He soon returned to work the family farm, as his father died in 1899. It was there he and "Maggie" raised their family of seven children, as well as taking care of his mother who lived with him until her death in 1927. Frank's parents were very devout German Catholics whose religious example was carried forth by their offspring.

As the farm was still "home" to Frank's 11 brothers and sisters, as well as his many uncles, aunts and cousins, it was always a very active, fun-filled home. The development of the automobile and popularity of the railroad during this period made going home for a visit very popular.

In 1926, Frank retained 10 acres of the farm on which he retired (the remainder being sold). He built a new home on this 10 acres with a small barn, corn crib, hog house, etc. He also planted a new apple orchard. Interestingly, the new home was built where the "Hilbrich School" had previously stood.

Frank and Maggie each had a saying which was truly indicative of their characters. Frank would say "What we don't get done today, we'll do this afternoon." (His day always started at 4:00 a.m.). A typical comment from Maggie was, "You can put a lot of contented sheep in one barn." (She regularly did so, as her home was always home to many.) Frank passed away on November 8, 1946, his widow living until June 29, 1954. Their children all married as follows and raised their families in Dyer, Griffith, and Schererville.

1. Lawrence (1898-1981) married Genevieve Koshnick*. Children – Richard, John, Jean, Joan, and Mary Ann

Frank Hilbrich Family: Frank and Margaret (parents) seated with daughters: Margaret (Kushnick) on left and Katherine (Stark) on right. Standing left to right are Roy, Martin, Sylvia (Govert), Frank J., and Lawrence. Summer 1936

2. Roy (1899-1972) married Marie Fagen. Children – James, Thomas, and Patricia

3. Martin (1901-1984) married Edith Govert**. Children – Glen, Margaret, and Warren

4. Sylvia (1902-1977) married Leo Govert**. Children – Lawrence, Edward, Delores, Lois, Leo, and Janet

5. Margaret ("Pearl") (1904-1985) married Joseph Koshnick*. Children – Joseph, Rosalyn, and John

6. Katherine ("Katie") (1906-) married Edwin Stark. Children – Donald, Theodore, Judith, and Frank

7. Frank (1907-1984) married Esther Bieker. Children – Gerald, Mary Kay, Charles, and Karen

*Brother and Sister
**Brother and Sister

by James M. Hilbrich

HITZEMANN, EDWIN AND CLARA
F112

Edwin Hitzemann wife Clara (Keup) Hitzeman wedded 26 May 1920

Edwin Hitzemann was born 26 May 1896 Dyer, Lake County, Indiana, the son of Fredrich and Sophia (Seegers) Hitzemann. He was baptized 14 June 1896 at United Evangelical Zion Church (Deutsche ver. Evanglische Zions Kirche) and confirmed on 19 April 1910. He had a fourth grade education. He entered the U.S. Army 4 October 1917 and was sent to Camp Taylor, Kentucky. He was there about a month then transferred to Camp Shelby at Hattiesburg, Mississippi and remained there until he was sent to France. He sailed for France 6 October 1918 and was in Company D, 152nd Infantry, 30th Division. He was on his way to the Black Forest when peace was declared. He returned to the United States 13 April 1919 and was honorably discharged on 24 April 1919. After his discharge he returned home, spent a few days with his parents, then went to Andover, South Dakota to help his brother, Alvin, as a farm hand. There he met Clara Bertha Albertina Keup, the daughter of

(L to R): Lillian, Edwin and Raymond Hitzemann

Ernest and Mary (Mussack) Keup. They were married 26 May 1920 at Zion Lutheran Church, Andover, South Dakota. For their honeymoon they went to Hammond, Indiana to visit Edwin's parents. Edwin worked as a hired farm hand. The neighbors moved to Morristown, South Dakota (northwestern South Dakota on the North Dakota border — Corson County) and soon notified Edwin of a farm he could rent there. So Edwin and Clara moved to Morristown where their son, Raymond, was born. In less than two years Edwin and Clara decided to move back to Andover. They traveled by horse drawn wagon. Clara was expecting their second child at the time. Shortly after arriving in Andover, Clara gave birth to a daughter, Lillian. When Lillian was only 12 days old Clara died suddenly of a blood clot. Edwin then sold everything and with his two children moved back to Hammond, Indiana to live with his mother and father. They lived at 824 Carroll Street. He worked as a stevedore (laborer) in a freight yard for the Indiana Harbor Belt Railroad. He was a member of the Brotherhood of Railway and Steamship Clerk's Union. During the depression he got laid off so worked as a bartender at the VFW 802 Clubroom where he was a member. A friend let him continue to work one of his days at the Railroad and later the railroad hired him back full time. Edwin was a hard worker and loved to argue. He was a typical German — gruff, not much at showing his feelings but honest. He attended the Immanuel Evangelical and Reform Church (now Immanuel United Church of Christ). Edwin died 12 November 1943 at the Edward Hines, Jr. Veterans Hospital, Hines, Illinois. Children born to this union were: Raymond Ernest (1920) married Mae Evaline Brindley; and Lillian Clara (1922) married William Elsworth Shelvock.

by Ronna Lounsbery

HITZEMANN, FREDRICH AND SOPHIA
F113

Fredrich Hitzemann, wife Sophia (Seegers) Hitzeman wedded 8 Feb 1894.

Fredrich (Gotheb) "Fritz" Hitzemann was born 1 January 1871 Hanover Township, Lake County, Indiana; the son of Otto Charles and Maria (Mensing) Hitzemann (Sr.). He was baptized 22 January 1871 at the United Evangelical Zion Church (Deutsche ver. Evanglische Zions Kirche) now the Zion United Church of Christ. He was raised speaking German. On 8 February 1894 he married Sophia Seegers, daughter of Christopher and Dorothea (Kolling) Seegers at the United Evangelical Zion Church. Sophia also was baptized at the United Evangelical Zion Church on 26 February 1871. They farmed on the Illinois-Indiana border near Krietzburg with all the children being born there. The children attended Schellers School until they were 12 years old. They spoke German, not learning English until after they attended school. When they reached 12 years old they attended German School (a small school near the church) for two years for instruction for confirmation. Confirmation was done in high German so then the children needed to learn high German. At lunch time they would go to the cemetery to play. Grandma and Grandpa (Carl and Maria) Hitzemann's tombstone had a big ball on top of it which the children would take down and roll around. They would put the ball back before they went back to school. Grandma Seegers (Dorothea) lived with them. She refused to go

102

Fredrich Hitzemann Family. Front Row, L-R: Wilhelm, Sophia, Alice, Fredrich & Bernice. Back Row, L-R: Alvin, Edwin & Dorothea.

to any social functions so some one always had to stay home with her. The children didn't like her because of this. In 1920 Fred sold the farm and bought a home in Hammond — 824 Carroll St. Grandma Seegers continued to live with them until her death in 1921. Fred worked for the Indiana Harbor Belt Railroad but never received a pension. He also was custodian for the Immanuel Evangelical and Reform Church (now Immanuel United Church of Christ). In 1922 their son's wife died, leaving him with two small children to raise. Their son, Edwin, and his two children soon came to live with them. Sophia died 24 July 1928 from heart complications following surgery. Some time later Fred moved in with his daughter, Alice Beckwith on Drackert St. Fred had a way of telling jokes with a straight face so that you never knew whether to laugh or not. Fred died 14 November 1949. Children born to this union were: Alvin I(ndiana) (1894-1971) married Wilhelmina Barbara Thiemann; Edwin (1896-1943) married Clara Bertha Albertina Keup; Walter Harry (1898-1900); Dorothea Maria (1900-1962) married William McKinley Sauer; Bernice Emma (1905) married Edwin Helmer; Alice Sylvia (1909-1973) married Clifford Floyd Beckwith; and Wilhelm Fredrich (1910-1929).

by Ronna Lounsbery

HITZEMANN, OTTO CHARLES AND MARIA
F114

Otto Charles "Karl" Hitzemann (Sr.) was born 8 January 1819 in Hesse Cassel, Germany. It is believed he came to America around 1853 first settling in Illinois just south of

Otto Charles (Carl) Hitzemann, wife Maria (Mensing) Hitzemann. Probably taken 1890's.

Chicago, thought to be in Will County near the Indiana border. In 1853 he married Maria "Mary" Mensing (probably in Illinois). (Question on this — Maria states on 1900 census she came to America in 1855 but on the 1860 census her first child, Sophia, was born in Indiana. Sophia was born in 1853.) Maria was born 7 September 1833 in Hesse Cassel, Germany; and is believed to be the daughter of Christian and Dorothea Mensing (Mensching). The first two children were believed born in Illinois (some census say Illinois, some Indiana). Sometime around 1856/7 they moved to a farm only a few miles away crossing into Hanover Township, Lake County, Indiana near the town of Krietzburg. In the fall of 1858 twenty-three families on both sides of the Indiana and Illinois state line met to establish a church. It was called the German United Evangelical Zion Church (Deutsche ver. Evanglische Zions Kirche). Karl's signature is on the list of the founders of the church. Karl died 23 December 1886. After his death, Mary lived with her son, Otto, until her death 3 October 1907. Children born to this union were: Sophia (1853-1880) married Heinrich Thissius; Anna (1856-?) married ? Eierdem; Mary (1858-1872), Wilhelmina (1859 – by 1900) married ? Urbahns; Charles "Carl" (1863 – by 1900) married Emma ?; Otto Carl Jr. (1864-1940) married Louisa Claus; Heinrich (1867-1919); Fredrich "Fritz" (1871-1949) married Sophia Seegers; and Emma (1873-1890).

by Ronna Lounsbery

HLATKO, JOSEPH AND GERTRUDE
F115

George, born July 25, 1855, and Anna (Dianias) Hlatko, born July 25, 1863, migrated from St. Martins, Czechoslovakia where George was employed as a peddler, selling items such as pottery and china. They had 3 children: Mary born May 15, 1884, Anna born January 9, 1887, and John born in 1890. George served in Franz Joseph's army and was slightly wounded in the invasion of Bosnia. The family arrived in Halifax, Nova Scotia in 1892 and moved to Chicago, Illinois where George worked on the ship canal at Lemont, Illinois. They moved from there to Clinton, Indiana to work in the coal mines. Three sons were born in Clinton. George born December 13, 1900, Joseph born February 12, 1903, and Emil born April 25, 1906. George Sr. was struck and killed by an automobile in Whiting, Indiana on October 27, 1935. His son Joseph started work in the mines at the age of 12 for $1.40 per day. He completed 6 years of school. Joseph hopped a freight train and came to Chicago in 1927 and worked at various jobs until 1932 when he was hired by General Mills as a laborer at $.45 per hour. He was always civic minded, during World War II he was an air raid warden. After the war he was a leader in the urban renewal project at Turner Park in Hammond, Indiana. At General Mills, he was chairman of the safety committee and union official. He retired December 31, 1965.

Joseph married Gertrude Jeffery on June 4, 1932 in Crown Point, Indiana. They moved to Whiting, Indiana where their first daughter, Betty Louise was born on October 27, 1933. The family then moved to Hammond where Joseph Norman was born on November 11, 1938 and Karen Ruth was born on August 6, 1943. Karen died of leukemia July 7, 1949. Betty Louise married Dorris W. Campbell and lives in Dyer, Indiana. They have four children. Joseph Norman married Maureen Tonchef and lives in Munster, Indiana. They have two children, Katherine Lynn (Schafer) and Joseph Jeffrey; and one grandchild. Gertrude Hlatko passed away September 23, 1979. Joseph Hlatko lives at Lake Shafer near Monticello, Indiana.

Gertrude (Jeffery) Hlatko was born January 26, 1910 at Grisman (Lake Station), Indiana.

Her parents were Robert and Pearl (McPherson) Jeffery. She had 2 sisters, Bessie (Larson, Fusko) and Eliza Ann (McNutt) and five brothers, Edward, Richard, Lawrence, Marcene and Norman. When Gertrude was 11 years old her mother passed away and her father disappeared. The 3 oldest children went to live with their grandmother, Mary McPherson but the 5 younger ones were placed in the orphanage at Richmond, Indiana. This was very hard for them to bear. When the children were released at age 16, Richard and Eliza Ann were placed on farms. The 3 youngest came to live with Gertrude in Hammond until they went into the army in World War II.

Gertrude's grandparents, John Neal and Ann (Vidler) Jeffery migrated from Tumbridge Wells, Kent, England. John landed at Porte Live Providence, Quebec on May 3, 1871 and Ann landed at Baltimore on March 20, 1872. They lived in Chicago until August 14, 1873. At which time they purchased 10 acres of land in Hobart, Indiana. John and Ann had 6 children. John was struck and killed by a cattle train on the morning of November 1, 1877. Ann was never able to pay off the mortgage on the farm, but managed to pay the taxes and interest which meant driving to Crown Point every spring through hub deep mud in a horse and buggy. When the city of Gary was in its infancy, she sold the farm and bought a boarding house at the corner of 3rd and Broadway. With the help of her daughter Muriel, she sometimes fed 45 to 50 men 3 times a day. Ann lived to be 86 years old; she passed away May 26, 1929.

by Dorris W. Campbell

HOOTMAN, A. M.
F116

A.M. Hootman was born in Jeromeville, Ohio, Sept. 22, 1857. During his infancy his parents moved to Defiance County, Ohio, where young Hootman grew to manhood amid the forest, on the farm and in the blacksmith shop. At seventeen years of age, he taught his first school. He attended select schools, Hicksville High School, Bryan College and Valparaiso University, graduating in two courses.

He married Miss Carrie Elliott of Defiance, Ohio, in 1883, that year teaching at Aurora, Ill., in Jenning's Seminary. His first wife bore him one child, Claudia, and after four years of married life died. He was again married to Miss Delia Simpson, a teacher in Eureka, Ill., now the mother of his four children. Mr. Hootman was a teacher seven years in the Metropolitan Business College of Chicago. He served four years as police judge of Western Springs; two years as secretary of the Board of Education of that village in Cook Co., Ill. He was pastor and evangelist at Valparaiso two years; pastor at Lowell, Ind., four years; at Union City, Ind., four years; at Towanda, N.Y., Broad Street Church, two and one-half years; at Logansport, Ind., three years; he was president of the State Missionary Society in New York two years; president of the Second, Fourth and Sixth districts in Indiana. He is a graduate of Welmer's School of Suggestive Therapeutics, and is at present secretary and director in the South Bend Life Insurance Company at South Bend, Ind.

(Compiled from the Souvenir Album of Lake Co. Inc., Crown Point-Lowell, June 18-19, 1909.)

HORNER – CASTROGIOVANNI, BEATRICE
F117

Beatrice Horner (1980) at Cedar Lake, Indiana (born in 1910).

Looking Back Can Be An Adventure

There comes a time in one's life when looking backward can be an adventure in itself. Most everyone who has been blessed with reaching the "Golden Years" does this.

To put it in writing is this challenge so, please bear with me.

Born 27 January 1910, I am the third child, oldest daughter of Frederick E. Ervere born 1874 and Maude (Surprise) Wheeler born 1886. Both being of South Lake County pioneer families, they were married in Crown Point, Indiana in 1906, by the Rev. Timothy H. Ball who was a well known Lake County minister and historian.

The first Ervere home was at Sheridan, about 5 miles west of Lowell, Indiana on a farm owned by M. Fedler. By 1914 our family, now numbering six, moved to a farm 3 miles east of Lowell.

The first payment on that farm had come from England. My grandfather Frederick Ewer born 1843 had come from Liverpool where his father Harry Ewer was a barrister-land owner. Pioneer American Ewer became a South Lake County school teacher and taught until his death in 1894. He had married Adelia Van Slyke, widow of Jesse Wemple of Orchard Grove, and they are buried at Orchard Grove Cemetery, east of Lowell.

Inheritance money had secured the new farm home for our fast growing family. The hero of this story has to be our little 110 lb. mother. Her copper complexion and black hair showed the blood lines of her heritage as she claimed Wheeler, Surprise, and American Indian (Tischimongiano) heritage.

Going into the depression years of 1928 our family numbered seven boys and four girls. We as children worked, played and survived on a farm that consisted of dairy herds and all else that was common to family survival of those difficult years.

At age 17 I started working in other homes, usually using the only skill I knew – good old fashioned child care. I soon gained additional experience with children that took me from job to job.

Between 1928 and 1932 I also was having a lot of fun. The young people my age were riding in old jalopies and Model T Fords. We flocked from one county dance to another, most in South Lake County.

Those were the days of Name Bands seasonally booked at the big Lassen on The Water Dance Pavilion and Mid-Way Gardens at Cedar Lake. Smaller bands played in halls at Sheridan, Belshaw, St. Martin's, Brunswick, Dyer, and Spring Hill Grove.

By 1932 I married Peter Horner Jr. of Armour Town, Cedar Lake. He had worked for years in a general store in Cook, Indiana.

Every day that store sent out a grocery delivery truck that encircled the Lake and vicinity. I had fun riding with the driver now and then who happened to be my husband.

Those were the days of simplicity. We went in and out of most every kitchen door, greeted as friends. A bonus for me was when we also went into the back doors of many of those old hotels that flourished in Cedar Lakes' Hey Days.

Without realizing it, I was acquiring knowledge of Cedar Lake, its environs and its people. Also, I became acquainted with customers who patronized the big general store, at this time owned by John P. Schrieber.

Our honeymoon first home was rented from Horace and Clara Blizzard at North Cedar Lake. By 1936 we built a small home on the edge of Old Armour Town at N.W. region on what was the site of the Armour Schools.

By 1938 we adopted a tiny 3½ lb. baby girl. Now again I was using my childcare experience. In the course of the 28 years ahead we became a licensed foster home, working with 14 special care children and finally adopting and raising three girls.

In the course of working with children outside of my home over those same years I was doing what I called a hobby. That included asking questions, taking notes, and collecting memorabilia. The people I interviewed seemed to need someone who cared about their lives and memories as pioneers of this region.

From there on so much material, information, pictures, and artifacts accumulated in my home that by 1970 the town board of Cedar Lake suggested it be brought into the town hall – so continued a career that started from scratch.

We sold our home in 1977 and by that time we needed trucks to move our hoarded Cedar Lake artifacts to the Lassen Hotel for storage, as it was soon to be considered a town museum.

By this time we had a lot of ambitious history buffs who now were known as the new Cedar Lake Historical Association. Hopefully, their hard work will be recorded as we move on.

I now realize that my life education came from unusual sources. Having made a career of taking care of children, now we enjoy numerous, lovable grandchildren.

Also, I have used my autistic talent along the way teaching and entertaining with it.

Having a real privilege of living in Old Armour Town was a source of real memories to look back on now. I also credit Holy Name Parish and school for being very supportive when needed most as a family.

Meantime (not to be caught idle), I have traced my heritage back to on one of Champaign's men, Jacques Hertel who married the daughter of a Mohawk chief. Also, a Tischimonquian Canadian Indian and also back to the Puritan Lockwoods with several lines into England back to 1150's. In my "pipe" line Sir Richard De Pipe in 1578 was Lord Mayor of London. Also a Henry De Pipe who was a royal herald.

My closest Indian ancestor is La Rose Surprise whose grave site is marked by local girl scouts. It is in the Creston Cemetery; she is my great grandmother via my mother.

Much of this genealogy has been placed in local libraries.

I live today a stones throw from Old Armour Town. I became a widow in 1979 after nearly 48 years of marriage. In September of 1982 I married Sam Castrogiovanni and we continue to work toward the success of a museum that will visually display the history of a town that commands attention historically: "The Lake of the Red Cedars Museum."

by Beatrice Horner-Castrogiovanni

HUSSEY, JOHN EDWIN AND BERTHA MICHAELIS
F118

Bertha Michaelis (Berta Michyelis) was born on February 1, 1872 of Minnie Schmitke and John Michaelis. John Edwin Hussey was born on January 17, 1869, son of William Hussey. They met in Chicago, Illinois in the early 1890's. Bertha could only speak high German and worked as a waitress. John was a carpenter and boat builder and only spoke English. Yet they met and fell in love and married on January 30, 1892 in the German Evangelical Lutheran Church, St. Mathews in Chicago. Bertha was a tiny woman with dark hair and dark eyes. She was 19 years old. John was not much taller, with light thinning hair and blue eyes and of stocky build. He was 23 years old. They lived in Chicago at 2196 Fillmore where all five of their children were born, 4 girls and 1 boy: Elizabeth Emily Ann, February 21, 1893; Minnie Louisa Theresa, January 31, 1894; Ella Julia Marie, July 14, 1896; Hazel Margaret Martha, December 17, 1898; then Edwin Emil August, September 26, 1900, my father.

In the early 1900's they moved to Hammond, Indiana on the north side where John was a carpenter and a boat builder on the Calumet Harbor. Around 1911-1912 he opened a saloon at 530 Hoffman which he ran until about 1915-16. The family lived at the same address. Bertha died at age 40 on September 14, 1912 of pulmonary tuberculosis. She is buried in Oak Hill Cemetery in Hammond in section 15 or 16. There is no marker. John was left with the two younger children, Hazel and Edwin. The three older girls were either married or self supporting. John was a loud and happy story telling Irishman. He married a second time to a woman from Tennessee, Nettie, between 1912 and 1914. He sold his tavern and they moved to Tennessee, where a son was born, Leslie.

John's health began to fail while living in Tennessee. He came back to Hammond to live out his last days with Ella at 490 Chicago Ave., where he died on May 31, 1923. He was 54 years old. He is buried in Oak Hill Cemetery in section 16. There is no marker.

by Mrs. Joan Walker

INSCHO, DORIS
F119

Doris Inscho was born in Hobart, Indiana in 1894. She was the eldest of three children born to Nevin B. White and 'Bel Blackham White. Doris's parents were active in the life of the community and her father was the publisher of the Hobart Gazette.

Doris graduated from Hobart Township High School (which pioneered in busing, having a horse-drawn bus, with side curtains for bad weather). She spent a summer at Valparaiso University, then returned to her home area and taught school for five years.

Doris White married Leland S. Inscho and began her travels from Wyoming to West Virginia, finally settling in Wilmington, Delaware, where Leland worked for Hercules Co. They had four children, Mrs. E.I. Medon Edwards, Wilmington, Delaware; Mrs. D.C. MacFarland of Springfield, Virginia; Mrs. Bertus Thomae of Portage, Indiana; and Mr. Leland S. Inscho, Jr. of Evergreen, Colorado. They keep her young, she claims, with deep interest in their activities and those of their children and grandchildren.

While in Hobart, Doris contributed to the newspaper columns "Flue Dust" and "Keyhole Column". Since coming to Wilmington, Doris's poems have been published by First State Writers and the Delaware Federated Women's Clubs. A contest winning booklet 'Deeply High" was published in 1945. Currently her work is appearing in Women's Experience magazine.

Doris Inscho has been honored by the First State Writers with a lifetime membership because of her many contributions to writing in general and to First State Writers in particular.

Anita Mia

Reference –

In 1932, guns were dug up at Indian Ridge. These were Spanish guns of a very early make using wheelock mechanism which predated the flintlock. Considered to have been in the area pre 1670.

Legends tell of Spaniards coming up the Mississippi in their search for gold.

The raft that the men built would have been equipped with a sail and poles.

An ocean going ship could come up the Mississippi to about where St. Louis is today. The Illinois River comes in on an angle at this point. Up the Illinois two hundred miles the Kankakee River enters from the east – fifty miles up the Kankakee and Eagle Creek would come in from the north.

If they had been able to ask of the Indians, "Where is your treasure?" they would have been shown wampum with tiny seashells woven into it. Soft doeskin garments – clay pots – willow baskets – leather mocassins.

The strange malady that came upon the men after eating wild grapes and nuts was caused basically by the green hazel nuts – they are toxic if eaten before being roasted.

by Mrs. Bert Thomae

ISAKSON, GUSTAF ISAKSON LANS
F120

Born in Navestro, Sweden February 4, 1824, Gustaf Isakson Lans came to America in 1855 and became known as Gustaf Isakson. On May 17, 1860 he married Britta Marie Charleston in Porter County, Indiana. Marie was born November 23, 1833 in Krisdala, Sweden. She arrived in America in 1857. They lived on a farm located on the south east corner of Union Street and Highway #6. Gustaf and Marie were charter members of the Augustana Lutheran Church in Hobart. Church records show that they were the parents of seven children: Emma Sofia, Carl Oscar, Matilda Josephine, Charles Oscar, August Gilbert, Maria Sophia and Ellen Charlotte. Only three children lived to adulthood. Matilda married Victor Henricson, Ellen married Albert L. Johnson. August Gilbert born February 25, 1871, died November 15, 1939. Gilbert married Anna Sophia Lawson, the daughter of John and Louisa Sanstead Lawson, of Crocker, (Porter Co.) Indiana. Their four children are: Esther Sophia, Clarence Gilbert, Walter Raymond and Vivian Clara, who died at the age of six months. Esther married Ernest Theodore Nelson. Clarence married Lillian Swanson of Red Oak, Iowa. Walter was born July 16, 1903, and died January 3, 1981. On April 14, 1932, he married Oyjdal Marvel of Crittenden County, Kentucky, the daughter of John R. and Sarah Shewmaker Marvel. Their children are: Vivan

John Hussey and Bertha Michaels

Marie married Eugene Bokash, of Gary, Indiana, Raymond Gilbert married Linda Love of Flint, Michigan, Larry Edward married Victoria Marin of San Jose, Costa Rica. In 1872 Gustaf and Marie Isakson purchased the south east quarter of section 20, located north of Hobart. The history of this farm goes back to Wee-Saw a Pottawatomi Indian. This land was reserved for him by the treaty of Tippecanoe in 1832. The Indians had become indebted to George and William Ewing who headed a trading company in Fort Wayne, Indiana. August 28, 1838, Wee-Saw deeded this portion of his land to Hyacinth LaSalle, an Indian Agent. LaSalle deeded the land to William A. and George W. Ewing. For thirty three years the Ewings held title to this land. July 27, 1871, an administrator's deed was issued to George Stocker of Hobart. April 2, 1872, Gustaf Isakson and Mary, his wife, purchased the land. One hundred seventeen years have elapsed since that day and portions of the land are still owned by the descendants of Gustaf Isakson. Walter Isakson, the grandson of Gustaf, received a portion of this farm, in 1928, on which he set out apple and peach trees. Also in 1928 Walter and his brother Clarence started an automobile business at 55 North Center Street in Hobart. In 1945 this partnership was dissolved. Walter devoted the rest of his life to raising fruit and working at the carpentry trade. Walter was a life long member of Augustana Lutheran Church in Hobart. He was a charter member of the Hobart Historical Society and served as Vice President from 1965 to 1970.

by Oyjdal Isakson

ITTEL, JACOB AND KATHERINE
F121

Katherine Ittel was born on April 28, 1904, in New Orleans, to Carmello and Louise Canino. Katherine graduated from Crossman High School in New Orleans before moving to Lake County, Indiana. Katherine married Jacob Ittel (b. 5-19-1877) of Hobart on June 22, 1926, in Crown Point, Indiana.

Jacob Ittel was a resident of Hobart from 1900. He operated several businesses: a tavern, a hardware store, and Henderson's Ice Cream. He then organized Ittel Realty & Insurance in 1954. An original charter member of the Hobart Federal Savings & Loan Association, he was Chairman of the Board upon his death on July 5, 1964 in Gary, Indiana. He was also a charter member of the American Legion Post #54 and a member of the Hobart School Board for twelve years.

Katherine has been active and held various offices in the Legion Auxiliary Post #54 for 62 years. She was also Secretary/Treasurer of the First District Area. Katherine resides in Hobart, Indiana.

Jacob and Katherine had two children: Gilbert Walter Ittel, born December 3, 1929; and Donald J. Ittel, born August 9, 1934.

Gilbert received his B.A. from Indiana University. He was married to Marlys Miller (b. 7-13-30), who also holds a B.A. degree from Indiana University. They had five children: David Ittel, born June 16, 1956; Robert Ittel, born December 3, 1964; Thomas Ittel, born January 9, 1966; Jim Ittel, born August 4, 1971; and Richard who died as an infant. David Ittel married Nancy Johnson and had one son: Daniel John Ittel, born September 15, 1988, in Valparaiso, Indiana.

Donald attended Rose Poly Technical College. He married Ruth Anne Vician (b. 11-10-37) on October 3, 1959, in Gary. They have three children: Curt John Ittel, born February 10,1961; Kathy Anne Ittel, born November 16, 1963; and Mark Ittel, born November 20, 1967. Kathy married Jerry Oswald II and has one child, Jerry Devan Oswald III, born March 10, 1987, in South Bend, Indiana.

by Joanne C. Clark

JAMIESON FAMILY
F122

Robert Jamieson

Left to Right: Margaret Jamieson (Columbia U. 1906), Isabella Jamieson, Jim Jamieson and Edith Jamieson.

Sarah Catherine Jamieson, b. 3 March 1860, Kilbarkan, Scot., came to Boston 1881. Mathew Kuhn (Germany), b. 4 Dec. 1941, Griffith, In. Robt. Jamieson, b. 6-27-1834 Touch Corm, Scot., m. 4-18-59 Touch Corm, Sterling, d. 12-24-1907 Ross, In. (Caretaker). John, Ann Crow, b. 1775 m. 8-27-1800, Touch, Sterling (Scotch Royal Artillery) (Arthritis). Alex b. 4-18-1738, Mary Downie b. 8-30-1738, St. Ninian (Merchant). Robt. b. 5-22-1707, Jane Paterson b. 10-10-1713, St. Ninian. John b. July 1689, Isobel Conelan, St. Ninian. John, Janet Wingate.

Isabella Mark, b. 12-18-1841 Dunmore, Scot., d. 5-21-1924 Ross, In. James Mark b. 6-9-1799 Airth, d. Pleasant Ridge N.B., Canada (Gardener), m. 15 June 1832 Catherine Buchan b. 1-4-1811 Airth, d. 16-10-1847 Camden Foundry (Small Pox). John Mark, b. 1-22-178 Sterling, d. 5-12-1819 Airth, m. 10-6-1791 Helen Stewart (Gartnafuaran Line), b. 3-2-1771, d. unknown. James Mark, 9-22-1761 Sterling, m. 3-24-1778 Sterling 1799 Gardener Dunmore House. Margaret Miller b. 8-22-1759 Airth. William Mark, Airth, Scot., Margaret Wilson. James Mark, Mary Connchie.

by Marian Kuhn Gregory

JAMIESON, SARAH CATHERINE
F123

Sarah Catherine Jamieson was born to Robert Jamieson, a farmer, and Isabella Mark on 7th March 1860 at Kilbarchan, Scotland. She died in Griffith, 4th Dec. 1941, the year I graduated from Indiana University. Sarah married Mathias Kuhn at Crown Point in 1884.

The Jamiesons came to Chicago from Boston by train in 1881. Their plan was to farm in an area that promised a school. So they bought land on Elm and Colfax Streets in Griffith. The school was provided at Hartsdale, Indiana, which is located under the second viaduct south on Rt. 41. "Zippy" Davis was the teacher. Later at Jefferson School in Gary I accidentally met her. She remembered my father and the Kuhns of Schererville where she lived at one time. At that time my father was retired and lived in Florida.

Great grandmother lived 'till 1st of May 1924. I do not recall the lady, but she received recognition as a good scholar at Dunsmore School in Airth, Scotland. I have her award – a pen box in 1854 with a mother of pearl crest. Her mother died in 1847 when Isabella Jamieson was 6 years old. She was raised by Aunt Grant.

John Jamieson in 1775 had been in the Scotland Royal Artillery. He died a stooped old man with arthritis.

Alexander Jamieson in 1707 was a merchant in St. Ninian, where many of the family are still being buried.

Robert was born in 1834 at Touch Corm, Sterling, died 24th Dec. 1907 and was buried at the Ross Cemetery. He was a farmer but seemed to have the knack of taxidermy, braiding, glass blowing, and mending cup handles with metal. Robert was a fastidious gentleman farmer. One of his sons was trustee at the Glen Park School in Gary. The family at one time owned the land on which is now located the Beiriger School playground in Griffith, In. My father sold it to the Griffith School City during the 60's. Another son had a home in the Hoosier Prairie. I can remember the house because catnip grew in the vicinity, and orchids still line the ditch along Kennedy Ave. Botany was a fun subject for me because I had many knowledgeable teachers in the family and at school. I still have my grandmother's 70 year old cacti. One Christmas Cactus had 140 blooms and the other Easter Cactus 12. (These look like dahlias.)

The Isabella Mark Stewart line has been traced at the Mormon Library to Fleald in 1066. The line continued through James and William Stewart of Baldorran Sterling, Scotland – the Gartnofuaron line. After that followed the births of Andrew Stewart in 1719 and David Stewart in 1735 of St. Ninian. Finally William Stewart born 13th July 1760 of Sterling became the father of Helen born 3rd Feb. 1777 in Sterling. She married John Mark on 6th Oct. 1791. Helen died in Airth and John Mark, too, on 12th May 1819. Their son, James Mark, born 16th Sept. 1799 and Catherine Buchan born 1st April 1811 of Airth were married 15th June 1832. Catherine Buchan died young, 16th Oct. 1847 of small pox.

Sarah Catherine, my grandmother Kuhn, was skilled in gardening, cooking and knitting. She could quote poetry from the great masters primarily because she was belligerent and refused to eat oatmeal. (Either she was bright, belligerent or both.) I remember she could knit a pair of stockings in an evening, and found a mistake in a second. I remember seeing her lard down meat which when cooked was very tasty. She was 4 feet 9 inches but could move as swift as a deer. She never had much to say, but when she did, you moved. Her plants grew large and were very productive. She had her special treatment for plants.

Margaret Jamieson, her sister, graduated from Columbia University in New York 55 years before I did. She became an administrator of a hospital in San Jose, Cal. I checked the area when I studied at Stanford University in 1961.

by Marian Frances Kuhn Gregory

JORDAN, MARJORIE V.
F124

I was born in Ambridge on April 18, 1920. I came into the world a rather large baby. I won the fattest baby in Lake County that year and won two Teddy Bears to prove it. (I still have one of them.)

I remember the Ambridge (Riverside) Hotel that was a very large brick building complete with even a ballroom.

Lake County was a clean, safe, friendly and beautiful county. You could always find someone to help. Great neighbors to rely on were a way of life.

I remember buses and streetcars. Streetcars ran east and west only on 5th Avenue, and north and south on Broadway. Buses every 20 minutes on 5th and 8th Avenue.

I remember the best drinking water that has ever come out of a tap. I remember many relatives that would come in from Illinois, Iowa, Wisconsin and Michigan coming to the house and heading straight to the kitchen faucet for the world's best water.

I remembers Sundays after Sunday School, church and dinner. We would get in the old Model T Ford and drive thru the covered bridges in Crown Point. On those rides we would admire the beauty of the wild flowers, big trees and numerous varieties of birds.

Lake County, back then, had very few hills and curves and was basically flat. The exception was Miller Beach. It was the most scenic. The beach had huge sand dunes, crystal clear water, undertows (even as bad as they were) as well as all the grassy knolls. It was, at times, very difficult to find many people with a car back in the 20's and 30's. We always made sure we got a ride to Crown Point for the beautiful parades.

Getting back to Gary, there were neighborhood grocery stores every six to ten blocks. Schools were all in walking distance where you were able to come home for lunch. We were all healthy kids from all the exercise.

As a child I remember moving to the west side of Broadway that offered us Jefferson Park. There was no playground equipment but there were plenty of hills to roll down. As a child I used to think that the hills were so big, but as years went by and I grew older, I realized they weren't so big after all. My children also shared that same experience.

If the steel mills were working, there was always a smoky haze when you would go shopping on Broadway. Every dime store and several drug stores had a lunch counter. These seemed to be meeting places where you'd bump into a neighbor or classmate and chit chat. Each store had a special item that I liked and especially how cheap they were.

There were the YMCA and YWCA in town. I worked at the YWCA in the cafeteria at 6th and Massachusetts where some days the lines would stretch around the block. We all hustled to get people through the lines, whether you worked behind the steam table or out front clearing dishes. I worked six days, lunches and dinners. Lots of food, but that seemed natural as the Webbers were restaurant people then and I, a relative, followed in their footsteps.

I also remember a very large library that seemed to never end, my first elevator ride at the Gary National Bank that was Ten Stories High! Many good theaters, and the great rides into Chicago on the South Shore to see a live show and eat at a delicatessen. Then we'd ride back and walk home safely.

Oh, those were the best years of my life. I haven't been back in seven years now.

I hope this will help enlighten those that weren't there to see it and feel the security.

With the help of my oldest son, Scott G. Jordan, of New Port Richey, Florida.

by Marjorie V. Erickson (Mrs. Oliver Jordan)

JOURDAIN, JOHN
F125

Johann Nicolaus Jourdain, one of the pioneers of Lake County, Indiana, came to America in 1854 when he was 32 years old. He was born in Altvorweiler, Germany, June 30, 1822. John had one brother, Michael (Rachael DeWald), and one sister, Margaret (Bartelme), who also sailed to America. After arriving in the new country, John first lived in Crown Point, and then settled in St. John, where he met and later married Miss Johanna Klassen, a granddaughter of John Hack. She was born the 8th of March, 1840, to John Klassen and Elizabeth (Hack) Klassen, reportedly at sea while the Klassens were in voyage to America. John and Johanna's wedding took place May 14, 1857.

The Jourdains had seven children, all born in St. John Township: Elizabeth (Joseph Bohling); Anna (Nicholas Maginot Jr.); John (Emma); Susan (John Schaefer); Mary (John George Bohling); William (Anna Austgen); and Jacob. Their home was in town, located on the corner of Schmal Street and the Dyer-St. John Road.

John earned his living as a carpenter and cabinet maker. He was greatly in demand and turned out many articles of furniture for a number of homes in the township, as well as a number of pine boxes which were used as coffins. For a period of eighteen years he held the office of township assessor of St. John Township.

John Jourdain lived to the ripe old age of 85. He died November 18, 1907. Johanna died a couple of decades later on the 23rd of March, 1928. They are buried in the Catholic cemetery in St. John, Indiana.

by Jim Stephen

KAISER FAMILY
F126

John Jourdain

Jordan Michael Ham, age 2, at gravesite of his great, great, great grandmother, Eva Kaiser, buried in Maplewood Cemetery in Crown Point.

Kaiser Genealogy – Crown Point, Indiana

Eva and Peter Kaiser came to the United States from Germany in 1872. They were Catholic. He was born in 1840 and died in 1899. She was born in 1830 and died in 1901. They are buried in Maplewood Cemetery, which was established in 1871.

The Kaiser homeplace, property at 311 North Jackson Street once served as a candy store – the proprietor was Eva. It was part of a tract of 160 acres, the Railroad Addition, and

107

sold for $1.25 an acre, as recorded in LaPorte County Receiver's Office in 1839. Along with two other lots it came into possession of Eva and Peter Kaiser in 1892. In 1901, after the death of her husband, Eva bequeathed her property to her children. The property at 311 North Jackson Street, Crown Point, was bequeathed to Charles.

The children of Eva and Peter Kaiser were Angeline Hetzler Furnier, Nick, Peter, Marie, Margaret Thomen Wells and Charles.

Angeline H. Furnier had two daughters, Annabelle and Sylvia Kors. Sylvia's children were Howard Kors and Ethel. Howard was employed at Northern Indiana Public Service Company, and his children were Arlene Gumbiner and Ronald. Arlene's children are Heather and Laura. Ronald with his wife reside in Oakwood, Tenn. Their children are Kimberly, Keith and Kurt.

Nicholas Kaiser lived most of his life in Hammond, and was a realtor. His children were Frances Campbell, no descendants. Grace Masephol, whose son was Carlton. Mabel, who left no descendants, and Eva Witter, whose son was Verne. He had two sons, Lon and Dirk. Lon's children are Bret, Amy and Erin. They live in Texarkana, Arkansas. Dirk was a teacher in Crown Point, his last duties at Solon Robinson School. He lives in Chandler, Arizona, has one son, Dirk, Jr.

Peter Kaiser, Jr. was born in Rome, Italy, in 1872; he died in 1935. He was employed at the Letz Manufacturing Company, and invented the first heated incubator. His children were Nick, Margaret, Charles (Dutch) and Minnie Griffin. Nick was a local blacksmith for many years. His son is Clayton, and he is employed at the Northern Indiana Public Service Company. His children are Paula Rothermel, Joann Brady, Keith and Kenneth. Paula Rothermel has three children, Warren, Jr., Kenneth and Mimi, and lives in Tamarac, Florida. Joann Brady lives in Cuyahoga Falls, Ohio, and has two children, Jenifer and Shawn. Keith has one son, Keith, Jr.

Margaret Kaiser was married but has no children.

Charles (Dutch) Kaiser was a local grocer, a farmer, and a subdivider. He donated a tract of about four acres to the City of Crown Point. It is known as Kaiser Park and is located near the end of South Main Street. It is the location of the city's buried water reservoir. He had one daughter, Charlotte.

Minnie Griffin had three children, Edward Metz, Robert Griffin and Phyllis Stockwell. Edward resides in Bridgeport, Conn., has three children, Diana Giannini, Shirly and Gregory. Robert Griffin is a building contractor in Crown Point, has three children, Robert Jr., Kathleen and Kenneth. Phyllis Stockwell has one daughter, Debbie. Margaret Thomen Wells has one daughter, Ethel Beffa, who had one son, Charles of Rockford, Illinois. Eva and Peter's daughter Marie expired at the age of six.

Charles (Cuney) Kaiser was born in Crown Point in 1878, and died in 1955. He was a local blacksmith for many years, also served the city as street commissioner while Vincent Youkey was mayor. He later served as city night watchman. At the time, he and two others were the city police force. His children are Dorothy Hodges, Edna, Carl H., and Grace Malayter. Dorothy Hodges had one daughter, Judy Bellinger. Grace Malayter has no descendants. Carl H. (Cuney) Kaiser was employed as a mechanic, an expertise he acquired while he was employed in his father's blacksmith shop. Horse shoeing and buggy repairs were on the wane, automobile repairs then being required. He had one son, Carl J. (Cuney) Kaiser, who is an off set printer, operating a shop on East Goldsborough Street, a location within a block of where his earliest Crown Point ancestors settled. His wife is the former Frances Kucia. His children are Carl S. (Cuney), and Sherri. Sherri is married to Michael Ham, and has one son, Jordan Michael Ham as of July 1989. Carl S. married Sue Geis of Lowell.

This data was compiled by Virginia Kaiser by referring to a family owned abstract.

Other information and assistance were given by Margaret Kaiser and Alice Clay Watkins.

Charles Kaiser, his son, Carl H., and grandson Carl J. have all served as volunteers of the Crown Point Fire Department.

by Virginia Kaiser

KARR, MARTIN H.
F127

Long Time Resident

Martin H. Karr was born 3/30/1906 in Calumet City, Illinois and has lived 60 years in Hammond, Indiana, with his wife Lorraine (Hess) Karr and their children, Dennis and Kathleen. Martin's father was Martin Karr, Sr. born 1866 in Saarbrucken, Germany and died 1924 in Calumet City, Illinois. Martin's mother was Centi Hessler born 1879 in Germany and died 1965. Her father (John Hessler) was the first Village President of West Hammond in 1893, which is now called Calumet City, Illinois.

Martin had 6 brothers, Bernard, Walter, Arthur, Charles, John, and Joseph and 2 sisters, Emma, and Martha (Brom). Martin worked at Pullman Standard here in Hammond for over 40 years until his retirement in 1971. Martin's first wife was Opal Goodknight, no children and divorced. His second wife Lorraine Hess had two kids. Lorraine was born 4/28/1919; her parents were Erwin Hess and Viola (Ingle). Lorraine (Hess) Karr's great-grandfather was Joseph Hess, the founder of Hessville, Indiana. Lorraine was a long time member of the Hype Park Methodist Church. She died in 1986. She was a Girl Scout leader for 10 years at Edison Middle School during the 1960's.

Lorraine (Hess) Karr's father was Erwin Hess who was born 1891 and died 1965. Her mother was Viola (Ingle) Hess, born 1897 in Homewood, Illinois and died 1982. They were life long residents on Drackert Street in Hammond. Lorraine's grandparents were George Hess and Clara Tarnowski. Her great-grandfather was Joseph Hess who founded Hessville, Indiana. Lorraine has two brothers Erwin Jr. and Donald.

Here is a small portion of the family tree which can be researched at the Little Red School House in Hessville, Indiana:

Lorraine Hess, married Martin H. Karr, children Dennis and Kathleen, whose father and mother were Erwin Hess, married Viola Ingle, children Erwin and Donald, whose father and mother were George Hess, married Clara Tarnowski, had six children, whose father and mother were Joseph Hess, married Elizabeth Natke, who was his 2nd wife. Joseph Hess' first wife was Mary Ann Sackley who died in 1860. Joseph's father was also named Joseph and his mother was a Dancro.

by Kathleen Karr

KARSTENSEN, WALTER AND MARCELLA
F128

Walter and Marcella Karstensen

Marcella Piepho Karstensen was born to Elmer and Minnie (Triebold) Piepho on November 24, 1924 at St. Margaret's Hospital in Hammond, Indiana. She attended Schiller School in Hanover Township for all of her grade school. The first six (6) years of her schooling, Schiller was a one room school. When she was in seventh and eighth grades, it was a two room school. She attended Dyer High School which is located in the town of Dyer, Indiana, and graduated in 1942.

On September 20, 1947, Marcella married Walter Karstensen at Zion Evangelical and Reformed Church (United Church of Christ) south of Dyer, Indiana. Rev. H.J. Meier performed the ceremony. Walter and Marcella made their home south of Dyer, and in 1952 they built a new home on some of the land that Marcella's great-grandfather, Christopher Piepho, had homesteaded.

Walter was the son of Christ and Lula (Unruh) Karstensen. He was born at Grant Park Illinois and later attended Beecher, Illinois schools. For three years, Walter worked for the Buda Co. in Harvey, Illinois. In May, 1949, he started working for Northern Indiana Public Service Co. After working there for 34 years, he retired. Marcella worked at Buda until the arrival of their first son, Dennis.

Dennis was born on March 30, 1949 at Mercy Hospital in Gary, Indiana. Dennis attended Hanover Township grade schools through 9th grade, two years of High School at Dyer Central and his senior year at Lake Central High School in St. John from which he graduated in 1967. After high school graduation, Dennis attended DeVry Institute of Technology in

Chicago for two years. After receiving a AS degree from there, he went to California and worked for an aerospace company for five years.

While in California he met Alta Hood of Fremont, California, whose parents are John and Mae Del Hood. Alta attended Mission San Jose High School and graduated from there in 1969. After that she attended Biola College in La Mirada, California and received a BS degree in Nursing in 1974.

On April 14, 1973, Dennis and Alta were married at the Brethren in Christ Church in Upland, California.

In 1975, the young couple decided to move to Lafayette, Indiana so that Dennis could attend Purdue University. Alta worked as a nurse at Home Hospital while Dennis attended school. In 1977, he graduated with a BS degree in Electrical Engineering. They live in Chanhassen, Minnesota. Dennis is a Senior Engineer with Rosemount, Inc. in Eden Prairie, Minnesota. As of the year 1989, Dennis and Alta have four children: Cynthia, 12; Sharon 10, Janine 6, Kara 6.

Walter and Marcella's youngest son, Dean, was born April 17, 1951 at Mercy Hospital in Gary, Indiana. He attended Hanover Township grade schools and also Hanover Central High School from which he graduated in 1969. After graduation he worked in Chicago for six months for an engineering firm. He then decided to attend Purdue University, Calumet Campus, Hammond, Indiana. He received a BS degree in 1974 in Mechanical Engineering.

On September 21, 1974, Dean married Pam Barley, the daughter of Josephine and Pat Barley of Hammond, Indiana. The wedding took place in the Our Lady of Perpetual Help Church in Hammond, Indiana. After working for an engineering firm in Hammond, the couple moved to Channahon, Illinois, where Dean is employed at Quantum, in Morris, Illinois, as an assistant superintendent.

Pam attended grade school in Hammond, Indiana and graduated from Gavit High School in 1972. That same year, she took some classes at Purdue, Calumet Campus. In 1983, she attended a floral school, American Floral Arts, in Chicago, Illinois. In 1989, Pam graduated from the Joliet Junior College with an Associate Degree. As of the year 1989, Dean and Pam have two children: Dana, 12; and Randy, 10.

by Mrs. Walter Karstensen

KEILMAN, HENRY
F129

Four Generations on the Land

Henry Keilman born 9/12/1821 in Hesse Darmstadt Germany migrated with his family in 1840 to America. He located in Portage County Ohio and began a 3-year apprenticeship as a tailor. Henry operated a tailor shop in Randolph, Ohio for 1 year, then moved to Chicago, Ill. March 7, 1844 he married Susanna Palm, daughter of John and Catherine Palm of Prussia. In Chicago he operated a tailor-hat-cap store, also cut buffalo hides.

In spring of 1847 Henry and Susanna moved to the St. Johns area and began the first merchant tailor shop in the vicinity. He also began land and cattle buying, eventually owning 1,700 acres in what is now Lake County, Indiana.

Of his first marriage Henry and Susanna had 6 children: Philip, John, Lena (Neibling), Jacob, Margaret (Gerlach) and Catherine (Austgen).

After the death of Susanna, Henry married Anna Catherine Smith in 1873. Of this marriage no children were born. Anna Catherine died in 1878.

After the death of Anna Catherine, Henry married Mary Loehmer of Cook County, Ill. in 1879. Of this marriage were born Regina deceased in infancy, Nicholas, Joseph, Clara (Fritz) and Bernard deceased in infancy.

September of 1884 Henry ceded to Phillip, son of his first marriage, 82 acres of Section 9 and 10, Dyer area of Lake County. Phillip and wife Mary (Scheidt) had 10 children: H. Edward, Lillie (Weber), Estelle (Johnson), Mary (Barry), Carl, Herbert (killed in battle of Meuse Argonne France in WW I), Anthony, John, Alma (Gettler) and Philip W. Phillip and wife (Mary Scheidt) built the original farmhouse located on US 30. Here they were grain and cattle farmers. After the death of Phillip in 1910 wife Mary built a new residence just east of the farmhouse on US 30. She lived here until removing to the home of her daughter Alma (Gettler), meanwhile using her holdings as rental properties.

In 1942 after the death of Mary Scheidt Keilman, widow of Phillip, the estate was settled, the farmland and buildings were sold. The original farmhouse at 640 Joliet St. was purchased by Jeannette (Keilman) Schau, daughter of Anthony and Anna Keilman. Here Jeannette resides with her family. On this land in Lake County, Indiana originally purchased by Henry Keilman from the State of Indiana in 1854, five generations of his children have lived. Many of his great grandchildren and great-great grandchildren still live in this beautiful Lake County Indiana.

by Leona Mary Hilbrich

KENNEDY FAMILY
F130

The Bridge-Building Kennedys

Honest, painstaking workmanship lavished upon the exquisite covered timber bridges erected by the Kennedys has resulted in 6 bridges remaining in Rush County today for our enjoyment.

Paternal ancestors of the Kennedy family are believed to have come to America from Ireland about the middle of the 18th century. Family records date back to John Kennedy, who was born in Guilford County, North Carolina, July 26, 1782. He was married in 1805 or 1806 to Charity McMichael, likewise a native of above county, born May 9, 1790. To this union was born 10 children. Of these the 6th was Archibald McMichael, born August 25, 1818. The John Kennedy family emigrated to Indiana in 1826, settling on a farm 2½ miles south of Alquina in Fayette County. In 1834 the family moved to Rush County settling in a locality west of Arlington known as Beaver Meadow. John Kennedy moved to Platte County, Missouri in September 1845.

Archibald M., returned to Fayette County to farm, married Henrietta Langston of Union County, May 10, 1841. To this union were born Mary Josephine (Stoops), John Bennett, Emmett Loren, Emily Florence (Coleman), Charles Freeman and Franklin Perry.

Archibald began working at the carpenter trade in 1841, which he followed for 12 years. In 1853 he moved the family to Wabash County where he supplemented his carpenter work with small bridge construction. In 1857 he returned to Fayette County, then in 1864 settled in Rush County, acquiring 247 acres situated 4 miles northeast of Rushville where he erected a fine two-story home of brick made from clay taken from his premises and the dwelling was one of the showplaces of its neighborhood. It is still standing. He lived there until his death.

He was a self-educated man, at all times well informed. He was a colorful and able orator and invariably embellished his speeches with humorous stories. He was reared in the old Democrat school, but after the inception of the Republican party was one of its ardent supporters, being for many years a leader in local political affairs. In 1870 he was chosen to represent Rush County in the General Assembly and in 1876 was joint representative for Rush, Ripley and Decatur. In 1886 he was elected senator from Rush and Hancock. He was strongly advocated for Congress before the convention of the Republican party in North Vernon in 1874.

The bridge-building chapter began in 1870 when he was awarded the contract for a bridge over the East fork of Whitewater river one-half mile southeast of Dunlapsville in Union County. (After several years of endeavor to save this bridge and move it out of the Brookville dam area, it was destroyed by fire last year.)

Since he had erected a barn in 1849 on the Israel Freeman farm between Dunlapsville and Roseburg, it was natural that Archibald and son Emmett should go there in search of living quarters during the construction of the bridge. This period of residence provided an unexpected romantic interlude. On the day of arrival, May 8, 1870, Emmett met Martha Ann. Courtship blossomed and on September 14, 1870, they were married in the Freeman home. They immediately made their residence in Rushville and Emmett entered into active partnership with his father in bridge construction.

As was the custom in those days, the construction of piers and abutments, designated as substructure, was contained in a separate contract. The stone work was generally laid by someone else. The superstructure was made entirely of oak and pine. Most of them were constructed using the Burr truss construction which combines the arch and truss principles to permit long wooded spans with little or no midstream support. This insures great strength and rigidity without excessive bulk. A few shorter bridges did not have the arch.

Characteristic of the Kennedy bridges are the rounded archway above each entrance, the ornate brackets beneath the roof overhang of each gable and the scrollwork on the side trim of each portal. All the bridges had horizontal siding which added strength and all were painted white. Paint was prepared at the bridge site by mixing white lead and linseed oil in an old wooden tub. 4 were built with arcaded walkways on either side. The Raleigh bridge had a walkway on only one side.

During the era of greatest building activity, Emmett operated a large bridge timber yard in

Rushville, situated on the north side of the Cincinnati, Hamilton and Dayton Railroads, (Later B.&O.) east of the intersection with the Vernon, Greensburg and Rushville line (later Big 4). The yard was a block in width and 1½ blocks long. Although considerable native oak was used, the bulk used before 1900 was white pine shipped in from Michigan. It was easy to shape, cheap and plentiful. Emmett made periodic trips to Michigan by train to contract the white pine logs and expedite their shipment to the bridgeyard. The timbers were in most cases completely prepared for framing, even to boring the bolt holes, before being reshipped to the bridge site. It was said the Kennedy workmen became so adept at framing in the yard that the shaping of timbers was placed on a veritable "production line" basis. The time required to construct a bridge depended upon the length, the location and the difficulties encountered. For example the contract for the Vine Street bridge of December 23, 1891, specified to open the following March 1 was priced at $27.50 a lineal foot or a total cost of about $5,000.00. Tools most commonly used included a foot adze, in which the cutting blade is crosswise to the handle, the broadaxe, in which the blade is parallel to the handle, the tenon saw, a ship's auger and numerous types of planes for finishing and detail. An erection crew at the site normally consisted of 3 or 4 key men and 15 to 25 workmen customarily recruited from the ranks of local carpenters. Specifications and all erection details for the East Hill Bridge are on file in the Library of Congress in Washington, D.C.

Archibald withdrew from the business in 1883 and Emmett's brother Charles formed the partnership of Kennedy Brothers. Charles was severely injured in a fall from the framework to the stream below on the Circleville bridge and was incapacitated for several weeks. In 1886 Emmett took over the entire business.

Charles became a lawyer, became interested in horseracing and was Indiana State Board of Agriculture secretary. He later served in a similar capacity for west Michigan State Fair at Grand Rapids and was re-elected to the Indiana State Board until his death in 1921.

During the winter of 1872-73, Emmett was ill and, while convalescing, conceived the idea and built a model of the Kennedy bridges. This was something tangible to be seen and understood. He constructed a case into which the model fitted so he and his father could conveniently carry it to show and demonstrate to the Boards of Commissioners who let the contracts. The model is 42 inches long of burr arch construction, made in direct proportion to the large bridges, of scraps of bridge timbers and put together with bolts made by a local jeweler. It has the same number of posts, struts, lateral braces, bolts, clamps, keys and floor beams! It will hold weight of over 250 pounds and was made with a penknife. The records show the East Connersville bridge, considered by the family to be the masterpiece, was to carry 6000 pounds live load but was known to carry 20 tons many times daily. This is one of the many examples of the marvelous construction and strength of the bridges. The model has been loaned by the Kennedy family to the Rush County Museum where it may be seen.

In the 1890's steel and concrete bridges became popular and Emmett returned to general carpentry and the drilling of gas wells. His wife cooked the first meal with natural gas in Rushville September 14, 1899. He built barns, homes and school houses; also some furniture for family use.

The flood of 1913 destroyed the Long bridge at Metamora and Emmett and son Karl were called upon to reconstruct the two span structure.

Later the firm of E.L. Kennedy and Sons built the Norris Ford bridge in Rush County in 1916 and the last, the Mitchell bridge in Wayne County in 1918. The sons involved in the business were Karl (Dec. 15, 1893 – Jan. 26, 1967), Charles R. (March 29, 1882 – Nov. 12, 1962) and John W. (March 20, 1892 – Sept. 30, 1949). Another son, Leonidas L. (March 23, 1877 – Aug. 7, 1962) was not involved in the bridge business. Four children had died in infancy. One daughter, Mrs. Charles Herman (Nick) Tompkins, born April 28, 1879 died March 19, 1971 in California. One daughter, Mrs. Harry A. McMillin of Rushville, R.R. 7, survives.

E.L. Kennedy passed away at his home in Rushville December 13, 1938, having been manager of the bridge business all three generations, doing business as A.M. Kennedy, A.M. Kennedy and Sons, Kennedy Brothers, E.L. Kennedy, and E.L. Kennedy and Sons.

The 18 Rush County bridges are:

1873 Ferree, 2 mi. NE Milroy, A.M. Kennedy & Sons, (in use)

1877 Smith, 2 mi. NE Rushville, A.M. Kennedy & Sons, (in use)

*1878 Shelhorn, 2 mi. S. Milroy, A.M. Kennedy & Sons, purchased in 1933 by Lake County and re-built in Fairground Park, Crown Point (in use)

1879-80 Perkins, 2 mi. W. New Salem, A.M. Kennedy & Sons, replaced in 1964

1881 Mud Creek at Homer, A.M. Kennedy & Sons, washed out by flood in 1892; used as a sheep barn on farm nearby

1881 East Hill, east Rushville, A.M. Kennedy & Sons, replaced in 1940

1881 Swains Mill, 2½ mi. SW Arlington, A.M. Kennedy & Sons, replaced in 1959

1882 ½ mi. S. Arlington, A.M. Kennedy & Sons, replaced

1882 Raleigh, A.M. Kennedy & Sons, replaced 1953

1883 Circleville, A.M. Kennedy & Sons, taken out of use in 1942, after efforts to preserve were given up, it was torn down in 1949

1884 E. edge of Arlington, Kennedy Brothers, replaced in 1926

1884 Offutt's Ford, 2 mi. NE Arlington, Kennedy Brothers, (in use)

1884 Conn's Creek, 1.3 mi. S. Homer, Kennedy Bros., replaced in 1967

1884 1 mi. S. Orphan's home, no information, replaced

1885 Over Little Flatrock below Milroy, replaced (Facts are hazy on this)

1886 Moscow, E.L. Kennedy, Longest 2 span bridge in use in Indiana

1888 Forsythe, 2½ mi. NE Moscow, E.L. Kennedy, (in use)

1916 Norris Ford, 4 mi. NE Rushville, E.L. Kennedy & Sons, (in use)

by Mildred McMillin Benson

KLASSEN, JOHN
F131

John Klassen was born in Germany about the turn of the century, 1800. (The German spelling of the name Klassen is: Glassen.) Not much is known of his life there other than he married Elizabeth Hack, a daughter of John and Johanna Hack. The couple had three small children when they left their homeland for America: John, Mary and Ann.

The Klassens set sail for the new world in 1840, three years after John Hack and his family had immigrated. Their fourth child, a daughter Johanna (John Jourdain), was reportedly born in passage on the ship, March the 8th, 1840.

After the voyage, John and Elizabeth Klassen and their children traveled west across the country, and after many hardships they eventually landed in Lake County, Indiana, in the area which would later be known as St. John. They located on land close to Elizabeth's parents who helped them to get established in and accustomed to the country that was new and strange to them. John Klassen settled to the occupation of farming, and for many seasons worked the soil of his "Prairie West" claim.

Through the next twelve years six more children were born to the Klassens: Joseph (Margaret Schmal); Peter (Mary Herrman); Nicholas (Susanna Bohling); Susan; Francis Anthony (Magdalena); and Jacob (Mary Ann Stark).

John Klassen was a well known German-American farmer, and is counted among the early pioneers who helped aid in the development of the county. He and his wife Elizabeth are buried in the St. John Cemetery.

by Jim Stephen

KLEMME, JOHN
F132

Auctioneer

John Klemme, born May 17, 1864, the son of Henry and Caroline Klemme who lived at Endor, Illinois, just two miles west of the Illinois Indiana state line. Growing up in the area, educated, married Ella Corwin, a seamstress, of Lake County, Indiana on March 15, 1885.

In 1888, he began auctioneering in Illinois and Indiana, mainly the Crown Point, Indiana area, many of which were household and farm auctions.

Their children were: Edna (Janetske); Walter Klemme; Ruth (Hartman); and Ida (Adams). Mrs. Ella Klemme died in 1921. Later, in 1923, he married Carrie King.

The children always anticipated his return from an auction, as he would have lots of pennies, and small change from the sale. Tossed into the air, they would catch it and count the change, which was so much fun for children of that young age.

The Colonel, as he was called like most auctioneers have been over the years, auctioned many times at the Union Stock Yards in Chicago, Illinois; the Grand Champions, along with other prize stock.

After 40 years, he retired but still did some auctions from time to time; doing carpentry on

John Klemme, Auctioneer, 1904.

the side. He served as a Village Board Trustee for many years until his passing, April 25, 1952.

by Mrs. Ralph Oldendorf

KNOTTS, A. F.
F133

Hon. A.F. Knotts was born in Highland County, Ohio, Feb. 29, 1860. He was brought up on a farm near Medaryville, Ind., and received his early education in the country school. He afterwards taught country schools and the Medaryville town school. He entered the Valparaiso Normal, and in five years was graduated in the scientific, classical, engineering and law departments. He was president of the Central Indiana Normal School and Business College at Ladoga for two years, after which he was elected county surveyor of Porter County in 1886.

He had now laid the foundation for his larger life in his thorough school and business training. He began vigorously the practice of law in Hammond in 1887. He was elected Joint Representative of Lake and Jasper Counties in 1898. Through the Legislature, he succeeded in having a courthouse built in Hammond, and thus having practically a new county seat for his (the north) end of the county. On his return to Hammond he was elected mayor in 1902 at a time when strikes, riots, lockouts, graft and moral degeneracy, together with the sudden loss of the packing house, Hammond's main industry, made the sky look heavy for Hammond. There were now but three industries left. In a short time this city recognized that its mayor was awake, hopeful, practical, busy and tactful — a man that did things. Eleven new industries were planted in Hammond during the two years he was mayor, and the throngs of busily employed men learned that work at good wages was better than quarreling in idleness and want. Employees and employers shook hands and congratulated their mayor and his co-workers.

His reputation for doing things won for him the attention of Judge Gary of the U.S. Steel Corporation, and was the flag that stopped the train of opportunity at his station, which he promptly boarded, and on which he has been taking others with him, on a straight, broad-gauge track, on fast time, at his new and daring creation, the city of Gary. The pages of his numerous public acts constitute the book of his interesting biography. His name is written on the industries of Hammond, as it will be engraved on the very foundations at Gary.

(Compiled from the Souvenir Album of Lake Co. Ind., Crown Point-Lowell, June 18-19, 1909.)

KNUTSEN FAMILY
F134

In August, 1986 Ronald and Arlene Knutsen moved from the Logan Square area of Chicago, Illinois, where they were both raised, to Cedar Lake, Indiana.

Ronald (called Roy) was the second of two sons born to Ragna Leraas and Anton Knutsen on April 30, 1951 in Espeland, Norway, a small community fifteen miles from Bergen, Norway. The Knutsen family migrated to America in 1956 and settled on the northwest side of Chicago. Anton worked as a bricklayer and Ragna as an assembly line worker until their retirement. Roy's brother Jon became President of Bankers Tech/Colonial Bank in 1987. The Leraas-Knutsen ancestry dates back to the 1600's.

Roy has been employed with Illinois Bell Telephone Company since 1969 as a Service Technician. He is currently assigned to the Omnicom display for Illinois Bell at the Museum of Science and Industry in Chicago, Illinois.

Arlene Ann Walker (nicknamed Punky) was born to Beryl Elizabeth Pflugradt and Spencer Brennan Warner Walker at St. Joseph's Hospital in Chicago on December 18, 1950. She is a homemaker raising their two children. Her hobby is researching genealogy. The Pflugradt and Warner Walker family ancestry dates back to the early 1700's.

Arlene and Roy met while attending Kelvyn Park High School in Chicago. They were married on October 23, 1971 in the Norwegian Lutheran Minnekirren (little church) in Chicago. Their first child, Amy Renee' Knutsen, was born at West Suburban Hospital in Oak Park, Illinois on February 5, 1976. She is now a 7th grade student at Hanover Central High School in Cedar Lake. Their son, Richard Cory Knutsen (called Cory) was also born at West Suburban Hospital on July 21, 1983. In September, he will begin kindergarten at Jane Ball Elementary School in Cedar Lake.

by Arlene Knutsen

KOCUR
F135

Thomas and Maria Kocur came from Poland by Mr. and Mrs. Bocknowski in the late 1890's to East Chicago, Indiana. They lived in East Chicago, In. all their lives. Marie passed away and he raised their 5 children, Kathryn, Walter, Evelyn, Frank, and Joseph.

1. Kathryn was married Frank Bartz and had one daughter Georgene. Frank passed away and she married Louis Finn. He passed away and she married Victor Petertyl and he has passed away. No children from the last two. She lives in McHenry, Ill.

A. Georgene was married and had 2 daughters. All 3 live in Convent in Chgo, Ill.

2. Walter was married to Helen Sandor. Had a daughter Shirley. Helen passed away and he

From left to right: Amy Renee' Knutsen, Ronald (Roy) Knutsen, Arlene (Walker) Knutsen, Richard Cory Knutsen.

married Esther Sandor, sister of first wife. They had 3 children. Walter, Arlene and Sharon.

A. Walter Jr. passed away at birth.

B. Arlene is married and has 2 children. Marty and Karen Sue. She married Bernie Esboldt.

C. Sharon has one son Robert Jr. She married Robert Esboldt. Esboldt brothers from Dyer, In.

3. Evelyn was married to Loman Greene. Evelyn passed away. They had no children. Loman and his 2 brothers were on a fishing trip and they all drowned together in the year of 1974.

4. Frank was married to Sophie Piniak. They had 4 children Phyllis, Barbara, Robert and Thomas. After Frank passed away all 4 children were placed in foster homes. Don't know their whereabouts. Sophie has passed away also.

5. Joseph was married to Katherine Brown. They had 2 children. Ronald Raymond and Bonita Jean. Joseph worked at Inland Steel for 41 years. He also served in the Pacific Ocean part of it. Katherine worked at Carson Scott for 26½ years in Hammond. Joseph passed away May 18, 1977.

A. Ronald married Karen Sue Prugh and have 2 children Jennifer Sue and Ronald Joseph. Ronald works at Globe in Lowell, Indiana and lives in Hebron, Indiana.

B. Bonita not married. Works for Megadoon, which is with Burger King Inc. of Michigan. She lives in Hammond, Indiana.

Thomas Kocur (father) married Sophia Pawula and they had 4 children. Berniece, John, Edward and Genevieve.

1. Berniece married Joseph Buttinger from Chicago, Il. They have 3 children, Barbara, James and Paul.

A. Barbara married Del Arsenault and they have 3 children, Jeff, Brad and David. They all live in Chicago, Illinois.

B. James married Susan Hyry and they have 2 children. Emily and Amanda and they live in Washington, D.C. Lt. James is retired from the Navy.

C. Paul isn't married. Lives in Florida. He works for the Space Center.

2. John married Rose Szackar from East Chicago, Indiana. They had 6 children. Carol, John Jr., Robert, Thomas, Kathleen, and Janet. John passed away in May 1982.

2. Carol isn't married and is teaching in Hammond, In. at Our Lady of Perpetual Help School. The rest are all married have children, but don't know too much about them. They all live around the Calumet Region, except Janet and she lives in the state of Washington.

3. Edward W. isn't married. He is a retired Pipe Fitter which he worked in all the Mills in the Calumet Region. He does a lot of fishing and traveling.

4. Genevieve married Victor Wojtowicz from Chicago, Il. They have 2 sons, Victor Jr. and Edward. He worked at F.A.T.X. in East Chicago, In. He passed away in April 1977. She worked and retired from Illinois Bell with 44 years. Victor Jr. lives in Florida, neither son married.

Thomas and Sophia both have passed away. He in 1959 and she in 1975.

Five of the children are still living, 20 grandchildren, 25 great grandchildren.

by Katherine Kocur

KRINBILL, OSCAR A.
F136

Oscar A. Krinbill, of Hammond, county commissioner from the First District, is a man of wide business experience, made so by a long association with men of affairs in Lake County and by reason of being actively engaged in business himself. His entire life has been spent in Lake County, with the exception of two years in Kansas. Mr. Krinbill was born in Crown Point, August 3, 1863, his parents being George and Marie Krinbill, natives of Pennsylvania. They came to Indiana in 1851, locating at Cedar Lake, but later went to Crown Point, where they now reside. Oscar is one of eight children, six of whom are living. He received his education in the public schools, after which he studied pharmacy, and for a number of years was a drug-clerk in Hammond, and for ten years conducted a drug store of his own, retiring in September, 1903, to become manager of the Hammond Telephone Company, which position he still holds. On June 15, 1893, Mr. Krinbill was united in marriage to Miss Edith Weaver, daughter of Adam and Anna Weaver. By this union one daughter, Josephine Krinbill, was born. Mr. Krinbill is a staunch Republican. His knowledge of public affairs has well fitted him in the capacity of county commissioner, which position he has filled in a conservative manner and for the best interests of the county. He has been eminently fair toward all localities, and through him and his associates many improvements have been made in Lake County.

(Compiled from the Souvenir Album of Lake Co. Ind., Crown Point-Lowell, June 18-19, 1909.)

KUCIA FAMILY
F137

Peter Kucia, son of Madya and Frank Kucia of Poland married to: Mary, daughter of Frances and John Broer of Austria. Their children: Rosemarie, married to Greg Shafer. Their children, Jeffrey whose sons are Jason, Tim, Brian and daughter Julie.

Pat married Karl (Jerry) Gerlach. Their children Aimee, Jane, Jennie and Andrew.

Frances, married to Carl J. Kaiser. Their children, Carl Scott married to Sue Geis and Sherri L. married to Michal Ham. Their son is Jordon Michael Ham.

Peter Kucia Jr.

Marlene, married to Roger Van Slyke. Their children are Trisha, Debbie, Christopher and Steven.

Mary Anne married to David Wallace. Their children are Kevin, Michelle and Keith.

Michael married to Donna. Their children Angela, Kimberly, Vanessa and Jessica.

This family was a member of St. Mary's Catholic Church in Crown Point where the children attended grade school.

by Virginia Kaiser

KUHN FAMILY
F138

Clarence Kuhn, current Sec/Treas for the Town of Schererville.

Barbara (Minninger) Kuhn, Nick Kuhn and John Kuhn.

Marian (Kuhn) Gregory

Old News Photo: Seated left to right are William Gard, 13, Peter Kuhn 84 and his grandson, Clarence Kuhn, 14. Standing at rear, left to right: William J. Schiesser, president of St. Michaels Holy Name Society and Rev. Peter A. Biegel, pastor of St. Michaels Catholic Church in Schererville.

KUHN, AUGUST ROBERT
F139

August Robert Kuhn was born in the Dingam Jabay house across from Wicker Park in Highland, In., on 14th July 1886. August died 15th Nov. 1979 at Clearwater, Fla., where he lived with his wife, Agnes Mae Sturgess.

Shortly after his sister, Isabella Barbara Kuhn, a first grade teacher at Beveridge School in Gary, was born 27 Dec. 1888, the family moved to Hammond, In. Grandfather, Mathias Kuhn, built two houses on Indiana St. After Grandfather died, Nov. 1933, Dad collected rent once a month from those houses for Grandmother. It became a big event for me during high school days at Horace Mann in Gary between 1933-1937 to go to Hammond, collect the rent and eat at F.W. Woolworth's on the corner of State and Sibley. Before going home we would go across the street to Kaufman and Wolf to buy groceries.

Father was very impressed when he accompanied his father to Chicago where Grandfather helped build the Florida exhibit at the 1893 World's Fair. I'm sure seeing so many oranges from Florida made Dad decide to retire there.

In 1900 the family moved to Kennedy and Main St. in Highland, In. Dad commuted to Hammond to school by railroad. He would kill rabbits with a gun or stick and sell them at the station in Hammond. He and his dad drove a horse and wagon to Glen Park School via Ridge Road, which was dirt, to pick up Isabella every Friday, where she taught at age 18. In 1919 she attended Terre Haute College, and later helped start the Christian Church in Griffith. Matt Kuhn was a very giving and friendly person. He always sold his corn at a bakers dozen. And every Sunday night I would climb on his lap after dinner and listen to stories about Germany. Cousin Conleys lived behind Grandfather on True St. in Griffith. We spent every Sunday after church chasing wild flowers through what is now Hoosier Prairie and playing card games which helped me with my reading problem. There was always plenty of company in the Kuhn residence.

Grandfather refused to learn to read English even though my aunt was an excellent first grade teacher. I would always tease him about "Tirteen and Chica." He spoke broken English but was beyond reproach in arithmetic. In 1929 my father helped him build a sunparlor on our house at 564 Pennsylvania St. in Gary.

Mathias or Matt Kuhn was born January 1855 in Waldholzbach, Germany. He married Sarah Catherine Jamieson in 1884. They met at Hart's farm in Schererville, In.

The earliest record I have of the Kuhn family dates from Johann Kuhn born 21st Feb. 1759 in Waldholzbach, Germany. He married Susannah Maier, born 8th July 1798, from Nunkirchen, Germany. My how excited the officer at the Burgomaster was when he found this information in his records at Lasheim, Germany!

Their son, John, was born 21st May 1825 and died 1892 in Schererville, In. The family helped build Route 41 between Ridge Road and Schererville. He married Barbara Minninger who was born 9th May 1824 – 16 years after John's grandmother died in a flood near Waldholzbach, Germany.

The Minningers were bakers and farmers. They came to United States before the Kuhns and settled across from the Hoosier Prairie, now a government nature preserve on Main St. between Griffith and Kennedy Ave. My Kuhn cousins recount that the Minningers slept in a hay stack the first night in the area, and grandmother Minninger clutched her silver candlestick all night long.

John Kuhn and Barbara Minninger were married at Lasheim, Germany, 21st May 1849 and had six children. One, Uncle Peter, lived to age 95. He climbed to repair a roof two weeks before he died. He raised 12 children of which 9 are still living. Peter fed them on what he raised from their farm which is now Scherwood Forest south of Rt. 30 in Schererville. Kuhn males had railroad experience at the freight office in Hartsdale, which is located under the second viaduct south on Rt. 41 south from Rt. 6. The training helped my father excel as head of the shipping department at the Gary Screw and Bolt.

by Marian Frances Kuhn Gregory

KUKELKA, JOHN
F140

Brief History and Genealogy

John Kukelka was a member of an ethnic mix of Hungarians, Czechs, and Slovaks that entered the United States from the Austrian/Hungarian Empire in the late 1880's and early 1920's and became known as "Slavs." John Kukelka was a Slovak who came to the United States in 1893 to Whiting, Indiana to seek and find work in the new country. John sent for his wife Dorthia Antusak. John Kukelka was born in May 1860, and came to the United States in 1893 at the age of 40 years. Dorthia Antusak was born May 1862 and came to the United States at the age of 38 years. They had been married about 16 years. Dorthia was the mother of 12 children. She came to the United States with two children, one daughter, Gizella Kukelka, born April 1889, and one son, John Kukelka Jr. born January 1893. John and Dorthia Kukelka had a small farm at "Berry" Lake at the north end, sold milk, butter and eggs in Whiting, Indiana. Most of the Lake became the south tank field of Standard Oil Company. All the houses in "Berry" Lake were moved into Whiting on Schrage Avenue. John and Dorthia lived at 709 Schrage Avenue. In 1895 a son was born to John and Dorthia Kukelka. Anthony Stephan Kukelka, born December 14, 1895 (Anthony changed his name and birth date to Charles T. Kukelka to join the United States Army). Gizella Kukelka married Josep J. Tapajna. They had a grocery store at 711 Scharge Avenue (Dorthia Kukelka financed the building of this store building). Joseph Tapajna passed away in 1923. Joseph and his brother John founded the Tapajna Paper company in 1910. This first location at 5th and Washington Street in Gary, Indiana, was destroyed by fire and was moved to 8th and Washington. Gizella Kukelka (Tapajna) passed away at the age of 93 on September 9, 1982. Her home in Hammond, Indiana. Gizella had five children, William, Gertrude, Margaret, Irene, and Joseph Jr.

John Kukelka Jr. (birth and death unknown) was crippled at a young age, disabled as a result of injury in an accident. John never married. He lived all his life with his sister Gizella. Anthony Stephan Kukelka (Charles T. Kukelka) was born December 14, 1895. He passed away September 7, 1942 in Kansas City, Kansas. Charles enlisted in the United States Army on July 24, 1911, and had ten years consecutive service. Charles married Pauline Kathrine Dreiser, daughter of Paul Dreiser and Maria Bergweiler in Mayen, Germany, August 13, 1921 (World War I bride). Charles and Pauline had two children, one son, Harry C. Kukelka, one daughter, Mildred P. Kukelka. Charles departed this union in November, 1933. John Kukelka died in 1905 and Dorthia died in 1909. Both are interred at St. John Cemetery, Hammond, Indiana.

John and Dorthia (Antusak) Kukelka had three children in the U.S.A. as listed, along with their offspring.

1. Gizella Kukelka, b. ?, d. 9-9-1982, married Joseph Tapajna (birth and death unknown). They had five children: 1. William Tapajna, had two children Norman Tapajna and Kathy Tapajna. 2. Margaret Tapajna, married Joseph Leslie, had three sons, Joseph, Phillip, and Tim Leslie. 3. Irene Tapajna, married John McLeod, had three daughters, Shari, Marilyn, and Deborah McLeod. 4. Gertrude Tapajna, married Frank Martisovic, had two children, Frank Jr. and Marlene Martisovic. 5. Joseph Tapajna Jr., married Dorthy Runge, had one son, Joseph Tapajna.

2. John Kukelka, birth and death unknown, never married.

3. Anthony Stephan Kukelka (Charles T. Kukelka), b. 12-14-1895, d. 9-7-1942, married Pauline Kathrine Dreiser, had two children, 1. Harry C. Kukelka who married Margaret Fedorchak, had one son, Charles M. Kukelka, who married Lorrie Martin and had two sons, Christopher Kukelka and Bryan Kukelka. 2. One daughter, Mildred P, Kukelka, b. 3-27-1925, death unknown.

by Harry C. Kukelka

LAIL FAMILY
F141

When George Lail was a small boy he was captured by Indians at Ruddles Fort in Kentucky. The year was 1780, and George was seven years old, having been born in Micklenburg, North Carolina in 1773. The Indians adopted him, and moved to Cape Girorddeau, Missouri. George later married Louise Wolf. Their son, Robert, was born in 1824. His wife was named Lucy. Their son, Edward Leonius, married Ellen Allen whose father, Dempsey O. Allen, was the postmaster, and owned and operated a grocery store, and the local hotel in Carrier Mills, Illinois. Their oldest child, Robert Dempsey, was born on June 26, 1885, in Jackson County, MO. After a few years his mother died, and the family moved to Oklahoma. As a young man, R.D., as he was called, graduated from the School of Law at the University of Chicago by taking a correspondence course, and one year on campus at the university. He and a partner practiced law in Atoka, Oklahoma for several years. He was also the Indian agent, and represented them in court. At 32 years of age, he returned to the home state of his mother, and married Opal Ina Arnold, a great granddaughter of Captain Thomas Jefferson Cain, a Civil War veteran and land owner in Southern Illinois. Robert and Opal reared nine children. One daughter, Margaret Lenora, died in infancy. The old home place where the children were born and reared in Carrier Mills, Illinois, is empty since the family migrated to Indiana after World War II, but stands ready to welcome the family when they return for visits. Robert passed away in 1971 at the age of 85 years old. Opal still lives in her home in Hammond.

Left to Right, Front Row: Opal Lail, husband R.D. Lail, daughter Elaine Englebright. Second Row: sons Willard E., Norman Lee, Don W., John A., James C., Robert A., Thomas E., Charles Lamont. (Taken 1960 approx.)

Their children are Elaine Terry-Englebright of Crown Point; Robert Allen of Hammond; Thomas Edward of Dyer; Norman Lee of St. John; John Arnold and Don Wayne of Cedar Lake; Willard Emil of Galatia, Illinois; James Cleo of Dolton, Illinois; Charles Lamont of Merrillville. All are graduates of the Carrier Mills Community High School. Elaine (some years later) attended Hammond Business College; Thomas, Norman and John attended Murray State College, Murray, Kentucky; James attended Southern Illinois University and the University of Illinois; and Don attended Indiana University. Through the years the family has been active in church and political life. The sons were outstanding basketball players winning many honors.

Daughter Elaine married L.B. Terry of Chicago, and their children are Patricia Mae, Verna Leah, and Michael Erwin. After Mr. Terry's death she married Robert Amel Englebright. (See separate history of Terry, Englebright families.)

Robert Allen, oldest son of Robert and Opal, lives in Hammond. He recently retired from Ford Motor Company. He is a trustee for Hyles Anderson College, and a deacon at the First Baptist Church in Hammond. He married Bina Reynolds of Mitchellville, Illinois, a schoolteacher, and they reside in their home in Hammond. They have two children, Robert David, a store manager of Baskins in StratfordSquare in Bloomingdale, and resides in his home in Downers Grove, Illinois. He attended Gavit High School and Valdosta State College, Valdosta, Georgia.

Their daughter, Marianne, attended Hammond Baptist High School, Purdue University Calumet, and Sawyer College of Business in Hammond. After graduation from Sawyer's she stayed on as secretary to the academic dean. She is married to Raymond Reel, and they have one son, David Allen. Raymond, a graduate of Purdue University, is employed by a Chicago firm.

Second oldest son of Robert D. and Opal is Thomas Edward, who came to Hammond after attending college, and serving in the Armed Forces during World War II. He married Nurisha McBrierty originally from Greenville, Maine, and they lived in their home in Dyer until the death of Nurisha ("Tommy") in 1987. Thomas is a retired carpenter, and all attended Lake Central High School. Marie Carole, the older daughter, is a graduate of the University of Hawaii in Honolulu, where she resides with her husband, Richard Blackburn. She is owner/operator of a building supply firm. Richard is vice president of Hawaiian Flour Mills.

The oldest son of Thomas and Nurisha, Thomas Edward, Jr., attended Indiana University and the University of Hawaii. He lives in Honolulu. He served in the military there, and is currently a counselor for the U.S. Navy, and production manager of Theatrical Association in Honolulu.

Second daughter, Denise June, is married to Randall Purkey, and they reside in Lowell. Randall is a supervisor for a manufacturing firm in Gary, and Denise is a cashier. They have two children, a daughter, Danel, and a son, Jared.

Second son, Brent Allen, is a graduate of Tri State University in Angola, Indiana, and is employed by the R.H. Donnelly Company in Chicago as area manager. He married Barbara Jovanovich also of St. John, and they reside in Griffith. They have one daughter, Brooke.

The youngest son of Thomas and Nurisha, John Eric, is a senior at Purdue University Calumet where he is majoring in television engineering.

The third son of Robert and Opal is Norman Lee. After college, and serving in the Marines during World War II, he came to Hammond. He married Ellen Tucker, a schoolteacher from Logansport, and they have two children, Charles Anderson, a graduate of Lake Central

High School; and a daughter, Lora Ellen, who attends Calumet Baptist School in Griffith. Norman is co-owner of Lail Bros. Egg Farm, Inc., Satellite Sensations, and Uncle John's Flea Market in Cedar Lake. (See separate history of the farm.)

Fourth son, John Arnold, came to Hammond after college. He married Carole Wolber of Hammond, and they have one daughter, Cindy Kay, who is a practicing attorney in Indiana and Illinois. She is a graduate of Hammond Baptist High School, Bob Jones University in Greenville, South Carolina, and Valparaiso University. They reside in Cedar Lake where John is co-owner of Lail Bros. Egg Farm, Inc., Satellite Sensations, and Uncle John's Flea Market. In 1974 John ran for the office of State Representative. He served for two years in the Armed Forces.

Fifth son, Willard Emil, served in the Armed Forces for two years. He and his wife, the former Mary Walsh of Marietta, Ohio, lived in Hammond for some years, but the family now resides on their huge farm near Galatia, Illinois, where they raise black angus cattle, and he works on construction. Their only son, Willard Michael, is a graduate of Galatia High School, and a student at Southern Illinois University at Carbondale, Illinois.

James Cleo, sixth son of Robert and Opal, served in the Armed Forces for two years. He is an administrator of a hospital in the Chicago area. He and his wife, the former Donna Lee Lange of Dolton, Illinois, where they live, are the parents of a son, James Steven, and a daughter, Jodi Sue. James Steven is a graduate of Thornton High School where he excelled in sports as most of his uncles and his father had done before him. He is a graduate of Eastern University, and is employed in sales in Chicago. Jodi Sue is a graduate of Thornton High School, and is a senior at Eastern University in Charleston, Illinois, and majoring in elementary education.

Don Wayne, seventh son of Robert and Opal, served in the armed forces for two years. He is a former businessman in Hammond and East Chicago, and is married to the former Donna Lucille Remick of Lansing, Illinois. They have a son, Don Wayne, Jr., and reside in Cedar Lake. A son by a former marriage, Jason Cain, attends Hanover Central High School and resides with them. Don was a candidate for state representative in 1974. He is currently active in real estate.

Charles Lamont, youngest son of Robert and Opal, served in the Armed Forces for two years. He is married to the former Doris Anne Tallady of Milan, Michigan, and they reside in Merrillville. Charles is an engineer for the University of Chicago. They have two sons, Charles Lamont, Jr., and Kevin Rex. Charles Jr. is a graduate of Hammond Baptist High School, and a gifted pianist. He is attending Hyles Anderson College in Crown Point. Kevin attends Hammond Baptist High School where he excells in sports. Charles senior is a trustee for Hyles Anderson College, and a deacon at the First Baptist Church in Hammond.

by Elaine Lail-Englebright

LAIL – TERRY – ENGLEBRIGHT
F142

Robert and Opal Lail's only daughter, Elaine, was born and reared in Carrier Mills, Illinois, and attended Carrier Mills Community High School, and years later she attended Hammond Business College in Hammond.

She and her late husband, L.B. Terry of Chicago, are the parents of three children, Patricia Mae, Verna Leah, and Michael Erwin. The family lived in Chicago until L.B. joined the Armed Forces during World War II, at which time his wife and children returned to the home of her parents in Southern Illinois. After the war they migrated to Hammond, Indiana, because no housing could be found in Chicago.

Their daughter, Patricia, attended Hammond High School and Taylor University. She also studied at Anderson College, Ball State University, Detroit Bible College, University of Dijon in France, U.C.L.A., University of Southern California, and the Art Institute in Chicago. She taught school for seven years in Los Angeles. Married James Bernard Harder, an engineer from Glendale, California, and they have four children.

Their older daughter, Cherie Suzanne, is a student at Harvard University. During her high school days she was number one in the nation for extemporaneous speaking, and president of Girls' Nation in Washington D.C.

The other three children, Christopher Patrick, Nathanael Gregory, and Melinda Annelle are all at home. Christopher is an outstanding soccer player, and his younger brother is an excellent soccer and hockey player. Melinda is a pianist.

The family moved to Independence, Missouri, the fall of 1987 where James is utilities manager. Patricia is a registered interior decorator. The family is active in church work.

The younger daughter of L.B. and Elaine is Verna Leah, and she attended Hammond High School and Indiana University. She worked for the U.S. Treasury Department for ten years, and is currently attending North Hampton Community College in Bethlehem, Pennsylvania, to obtain a nursing degree. She and husband, Steven Aaron Moulton, have one son, Robert Arthur, who was a star football player at Southern Lehigh High School in Coopers-

Photo is of Elaine Lail-Terry and children, Patricia Mae, Verna Leah, and Michael Erwin. It was taken in Chicago at Christmastime 1963 when Patricia was home from Los Angeles where she was teaching English at a junior high school, Verna was home from Indiana University. Michael was a junior at Hammond High School. Elaine was employed as secretary of the plant manager of the plastics plant at General American Transportation Corporation in East Chicago, Indiana.

burg last year (87/88), and is a student at Penn State University. Steven was born and reared in Exeter, New Hampshire, and served in the navy. He is in management for an international company at their head office in Trexlertown, Pennsylvania, and the family resides in Coopersburg.

The Terry's only son, Michael Erwin, attended Hammond High School where he excelled in basketball. He attended Valdosta State College in Valdosta, Georgia, where he was All American for small colleges, and the University of Virginia. He has four degrees from the American Institute of Banking. He taught high school and coached football and basketball before going into banking. He served six years in the Indiana National Guard. He is senior vice president of a bank in Melbourne, Florida. He was Rotarian of the Year in 1986, and is currently president of the local Rotary Club. He is an honorary Kentucky Colonel, and last year he received the Paul Harris Fellowship award. He is currently serving on the Board of Directors for The Fellowship of Christian Athletes, Christian Businessmen's Association, Space Coast Writer's Conference, and the South Beaches Youth Basketball. He and wife, the former Wanda Kathryn of Miami, and a registered nurse, have two sons, Michael Scott and Mark Shannon. Michael Scott is an outstanding baseball player at Melbourne High School, and a budding poet. His brother Mark is an excellent basketball player, and plays in the junior high school band where he has received several honors. Both boys are soccer players, and in little league. The family is active in their church. Michael Scott is spending the summer months working at the Word of Life Resort in New York. The family resides in Indialantic by the Sea.

Always active in philanthropic groups, Elaine has served as president of the Hammond Intermediate Woman's Club, the Crown Point Woman's Club, the Crown Point Garden Club, the Big 10 Club of IFC, the Skyway Chapter of the National Secretaries Association in Hammond where she was Secretary of the Year in 1968, and has served on several mayoral committees in Crown Point. She writes for the Lake County Star, local newspapers. She was campaign manager for brothers John and Don Lail when they ran for state representative.

In 1968, Elaine and Robert Amel Englebright, a federal agent in Gary, were married. He passed away in 1973. Elaine continues to reside in Crown Point where she is still active in philanthropic endeavors, and is a free lance writer.

by Elaine Lail-Englebright

LAUERMANN, PETER
F143

Lake County history numbers the family of Peter Lauermann as one of the pioneer German clans of the area, arriving from Buschfeld, now in Kreis Merzig-Wadern of the Saarland, around 1839, as part of a group either accompanying or soon following John Hack, who founded St. John, the town that bears his name.

A cousin, Jacob Lauermann, was also one of the early immigrants. Lauermann descendants have made an important impact on the histories of the Calumet Region as well as of Stearns County, Minnesota, and areas of Nebraska, ultimately spreading through many parts of the United States and Canada, from Texas to Alberta and from Florida to California.

Locally, Lauerman Road in Cedar Lake memorializes the family and some of the descendants still live in that area. Many gravestones in local cemeteries testify to the presence of the family in Crown Point, Schererville, and Hammond as well. And hundreds of county residents can trace their Lauerman heritage through daughters who married into other pioneer families.

The early Lauermanns were farmers. One of the three sons of Peter gained tragic fame as the victim of a murder by a Swiss immigrant in Blue Island, Illinois, as he transported a load of oats to Chicago in 1857. Also bearing the name Peter, he left his widow, Elizabeth (also a Lauermann of Jacob's branch), with four sons: Peter, Nicholas, Jacob and John, who later pioneered in St. Cloud, Little Falls, and St. Joseph, Minnesota. The widow Elizabeth married Mathias Schneider and had three more children by him.

Mathias Lauermann, brother of the murdered Peter, farmed in the Cedar Lake area with his wife Maria Heiser, also a native of the Merzig area of Germany and part of another large pioneer family. Their numerous offspring remained for the most part in the vicinity for many years and included a son, Mathias, who founded a general store in what was then the town of Armour with help from Katherine Gard, his aunt, who had married into another of the pioneering German families of the St. John area. The younger Mathias Lauermann married a distant cousin, Mary Scholl, of the family who first settled in Schererville in 1857, also natives of Buschfeld. Her father, Peter Scholl, grandfather of the famous foot doctor, spent his declining years in the Lauermann home, and huge family gatherings celebrated his 90th birthday in 1908. In Crown Point was Nicholas Lauerman, brother of the older Mathias.

The younger Matt moved his store to Cook. Edward, Emil and Jerome, three of his sons, soon established a grocery business in Hammond, Lauerman Brothers (the family dropped the final "n" of the German name, although the Minnesota branch retains it). Mary Scholl Lauerman died in Hammond in 1924; Mathias in 1939. The oldest son, Joseph, moved to Seattle and later pioneered as a merchant in Edmonton, Alberta, where his children still live. Arthur, another son, lived in Hammond; his daughter, Marjorie Gaskell still resides there. Victor, the youngest son, became a merchant in Fowler, Indiana. Martha, the only daughter, wed Basil Davis, who was a telephone company lineman, and they moved to Gary. Basil died there in 1974 and Martha lived until 1981, a beloved grandmother of seven and a rich source of family lore.

Of the elder Mathias's offspring, John was a farmer in Cook; Michael was a postman in Calumet City; Angeline married Peter Wagner, a hotel owner in Morris, Illinois; and Katherine married Jacob Gard, son of Peter Gard and Angeline Hack, daughter of John Hack. Still other children included Peter, who moved to Morris; Mary and Conrad, who married brother and sister Bart and Eva Hepp; Susana married John Seberger; Elizabeth married a teacher, John Stommel. Each family had numerous offspring . . . to provide an adequate history of each would fill volumes.

by Paul A. Davis

LEDAK, ANDREW AND LOUISE
F144

Andrew and Louise Ledak

Louise Ledak was born on October 7, 1916, in Gary, Indiana, to Samuel and Josephine Centanni. She married Andrew Paul Ledak (b. 1-4-09) of Morris, Il., on October 7, 1944. They had one child, Sharon Ann Ledak, born August 17, 1946.

Andrew Ledak served as a Staff Sergeant with the Military Police in the United States Army during World War II. He was employed by U.S. Steel for 28 years until his retirement. The family then moved their home from Gary to Florida. Andrew Ledak died on May 3, 1987, in Brooksville, Florida.

Louise Ledak was a founder of the Lake County Association for Retarded Children. She has actively worked for the betterment of retarded persons both in Indiana and Florida for the past 37 years.

Sharon Ledak is currently employed in the East Center of the Lake County Association for the Retarded.

by Joanne C. Clark

LENBURG, JOHN HENRY
F145

Early Lake Station Resident

John Henry Lenburg was born on June 14, 1863 in Porter County. He was the fourth and youngest child of Claus and Christina Lenburg, and their only offspring to be born in the United States and to move to Lake County. John's parents immigrated to this country from Holstein, Germany in October, 1857. His brother, Jacob, was born onboard the ship that his parents, sister Anna and brother Claus traveled on to the U.S.

At age 11, John was an orphan. His father Claus died March 2, 1869 and his mother, Christina, five years later, on Sept. 24, 1874. Jacob was appointed as John's legal guardian. Following his parents' death, he worked as a hired hand on the William Lippart farm in Portage Township.

During his teen years, John escaped death, but not serious injury, in an accident that left him handicapped for the rest of his life. The accident happened when John tried to hop onto a moving train for a ride. He lost his footing on the ladder of a boxcar, fell under a car, and one of his legs was run over by the train. The leg had to be amputated below the knee. Ironically, John later became a railroad worker.

In the late 1880s, John moved to Lake Station. He was appointed Lake Station postmaster in May 1893. On Feb. 19, 1895 John a Lutheran, married Barbara Baumeister, a devout Catholic and a Lake Station native, at Saints Peter and Paul Church in Turkey Creek (now Merrillville). On their wedding day, John and Barbara rode in a sleigh over the snow to the church.

After serving as postmaster for 2½ years John took a job in the early 1900s with the Michigan Central Railroad. He operated the railroad's pumping station near Deep River in Lake Station.

John and Barbara built a home at 3131 Fairview St. There, they farmed, and reared three sons. Leo Nicholas was born on Nov. 8, 1895; Wilbur on May 1, 1897; and John George on Feb. 25, 1900. At age 14, Wilbur died on Nov. 13, 1911.

Although handicapped, John worked for the railroad until his death about 18 years later. He died Jan. 15, 1929 of heart failure at the age of 65. Barbara spent the last years of her life as a church volunteer. She washed, cleaned and ironed the altar linens and priest's vestments every Saturday for Sunday morning mass at St. Francis Xavier Church in Lake Station. She died Dec. 17, 1936 at the age of 74.

by John L. Lenburg

LENBURG, JOHN LEROY
F146

John Leroy Lenburg was born Feb. 18, 1924 at Methodist Hospital in Gary. He was the son of Leo N. and Mary (Ward) Lenburg who lived at 1034 Lincoln St. in Hobart. In 1935 the family moved to 3908 Jefferson St. in Glen Park a section of Gary. His parents also had a daughter, Joan, who was born July 8, 1928.

John attended school in Hobart and Gary. In December 1942, he enlisted in the U.S. Army Air Corps, and was assigned to the 760th Bomb Squadron, 460 Bomb Group. In 1943, he graduated from Lew Wallace High School. While in the service was promoted to technical sergeant and served as a flight engineer and gunner on "Miss Fortune" a B-24H bomber.

On June 30, 1944, at age 20, John was wounded when the bomber he was flying in was shot down over Hungary while he and the crew were on their 36th mission. John and the surviving crew were captured by the Hungarians and turned over to the German soldiers. He was sent to a P.O.W. camp in northern Germany, Stalug Luft IV. After a Russian advance to the area the Germans evacuated the camp and all were sent on a forced march that covered some 800 ki. John was liberated by the 104th division at Bitterfeld Germany in April 1945. He was discharged in October 1945 and had earned the purple heart and had received three citations of meritorious achievement plus other medals.

Two years later, on Thanksgiving Day, John met Catherine Galich, a Hobart High School graduate, at a roller skating rink in Hobart. He married her on Nov. 20, 1948 at St. Joseph the Worker Church in Gary. Catherine was born Sept. 15, 1929 in Gary to Mary and John Galich. She was reared on a farm in Hobart Township and attended school there. Before marrying John, she was a bookkeeper at Gary National Bank and Standard Steel & Spring.

John and Catherine have three sons. John Leo was born June 16, 1953 and twins Gregory and Jeffrey March 5, 1956. In 1958, John and his family moved to Anaheim, California. Catherine joined the Orange County Mother of Twins Club and served as the group's president from 1965-1966. John worked as an auto center manager with Sears Roebuck & Co. for 23 years, retiring in 1980. In 1987, John and Catherine moved to Hobart.

Their son Greg moved to Hobart in 1984 and married Edna Machnik, June 7, 1986. He is a graduate of Cal State Fullerton University. Greg has had 3 books published and works for the Portage Journal. His wife Edna works at the Lake County Public Library. Sons Jeff and John live in California. Jeff married Debby (Frangella) Bishop March 16, 1985. He is also a graduate of Cal State Fullerton and is the author of 8 books. John graduated from Cal State Long Beach University and married Karen Claussen Oct. 3, 1987.

John's sister Joan married Lake Station resident Andrew Garber May 12, 1956. She worked 28 years for First Federal Savings and Loan in Gary before retiring. Her husband owned and operated an insurance and tax business in Lake Station. They live in Hobart.

by John L. Lenburg

LENBURG, LEO NICOLAS
F147

Leo Nicolas Lenburg was born Nov. 8, 1895 in Lake Station. He was the oldest son of John H. and Barbara Lenburg, who lived at 3131 Fairview St. Leo had two brothers, Wilbur and John George. Wilbur was born May 1, 1897, and John, Feb. 25, 1900. Wilbur died Nov. 13, 1911 at the age of 14. John and Leo attended school in Lake Station and Hobart.

During World War I, Leo served in the U.S. Army Quartermaster Corps at Ft. Riley, Kansas. After the war ended in 1818, he found a job at the U.S. Steel Mill in Gary. He later was promoted to foreman and worked for the company for nearly 25 years. On Sept. 7, 1921, Leo married Mary Ward at the First Christian Church in Hobart. Mary was born in Williams County Ohio on June 25, 1903 and moved to Hobart after 1910.

Leo and Mary built their first home in Hobart on south Lincoln Street. While living there, they had two children. John was born Feb. 18, 1924, and Joan, July 8, 1928. Leo became a member of American Legion Post 54, and played the bugle in its Drum and Bugle Corps.

In 1935, Leo and his family moved to a house on Jefferson Street in Glen Park a section of Gary. In Glen Park, Leo was a member of the American Legion Post 214, and became commander of its Drum and Bugle Corps. He was also a member of the Masonic Lodge 718 Roosevelt Chapter, and during World War II, was a volunteer auxiliary fireman in the Civil Defense. At age 47, Leo died Jan. 8, 1943 at Hines Veterans Hospital in Hines, Illinois, and Mary died in Gary Apr. 6, 1969.

His brother, John, was a volunteer fireman in Lake Station during the early 1920s. During the Depression, he worked for the W.P.A. (Works Progress Administration). After the Depression eased, he found a job at the U.S. Steel Mill in Gary, working his way up supervisor in the Axle Mill. He was also a member of the Merchant Mill's baseball team.

In the 1930s, John married Bessie Targget of Chesterton. They built a home on U.S. 6, southeast of Deep River, in Hobart. On May 11, 1952, John died at age 52. Bessie married Anthony Grenis in 1953. Bessie and Anthony died in 1986.

by John L. Lenburg

LESZCZYNSKI, STANLEY FAMILY
F148

of Hobart, Indiana

Long time residents of Lake County include Stanislaw (Stanley) and Krystyna Leszczynski. Stanislaw was born to a poor peasant family in Sambori, Poland on Sept. 30, 1889. In 1913, Stanislaw and his younger brother Anthony immigrated to the United States, while their younger sister Mary remained in Poland with the parents. The two brothers settled in Wilkes Barre, Pa. and worked in the coal mines until 1916 when Stanislaw moved to Gary and enlisted in the U.S. Army on August 1, 1918. After his discharge on December 23, 1918, Stanislaw settled in Gary and started a textile factory in January 1919 at 1749 Virginia St. He became naturalized as an American citizen on May 12, 1919 and married Krystyna Ziolo from Chicago on June 2, 1920. Krystyna was born on July 23, 1892 to a well-to-do family in Tuchow, Poland. In 1916, the Ziolo family (consisting of the parents, Krystyna, 2 brothers and 3 sisters), immigrated to America and settled in Chicago in a nice home on Ashland Ave. Krystyna served as a nurse during World War I and in the early 1940's, she worked in the Hobart High School library mending textbooks and helped at St. Bridget church.

About 1923, the Leszczynskis lost their holdings in Gary and relocated to Hobart where they purchased the old Ensign farm southeast of town. The Leszczynskis engaged in farming, with other pioneer farmers in the area like Betz, Henry Bodamer, John Ensign, Henry Hoffman, George Lutz, and the Gruel Brothers, who operated an impressive dairy farm southeast of Hobart from about 1925 to 1936 when the farm was purchased by Mike Carozzo.

Top Row: William, Florence, Adolph, Marcella, Stanley. Bottom Row: Krystyna and Stanislaw.

The Leszczynski home in the 1920's. Used by Indians in the old days in their fur-trading business.

During the depression, Stanislaw worked on the WPA, helping to build the beautiful Hobart High School football field. However, his most notable vocation was farming, apparently as a result of his childhood days as a peasant in Poland. He could be seen driving his 1927 Model T truck delivering farm produce to places like Gary, Hobart, Valparaiso, and Whiting until his death on December 7, 1954.

The Leszczynskis had 6 children: Irenia (b. 1921 and died in infancy), Adolph (b. 2-9-23), Stanley Jr. (b. 8-19-24), Marcella (b. 9-27-26), Florence (b. 3-28-29), and William (b. 3-19-32). Adolph and Stanley were born in the old Ensign farmhouse (photo below). For many years this house was the oldest and last remaining homestead house in Hobart until its destruction by heavy snows in the winter of 1978. In the early days, the house was used by the Indians for their fur-trading business. Also nearby was a small one room, brick schoolhouse which ultimately got destroyed.

Adolph married Florence Dresbaugh from Gary on 12-29-50 and they had 7 children: George Dresbaugh, stepson (b. 8-25-48), Christina (b. 4-30-51), Adolph Jr. and Mary, twins (b. 5-18-52), Debra (b. 1-26-54), Stanley (b. 9-14-58), and Ruth (b. 3-7-60). Adolph continued to operate the family farm specializing in corn, oats, wheat, and beef cattle. At the same time he was employed as plant supervisor at the Bucciconi Machine Shop in Gary from 1951 until his retirement in 1990.

Stanley Jr. attended Purdue University, graduating in February 1947 after spending 2 years in the Army Signal Corps stationed in the Aleutian Islands. Stanley moved to Seattle, Wash. on January 19, 1949 where he worked as an Instrumentation Design & Test Engineer for a large Aerospace Company. He married Lois Erickson, a dietitian from Portland, Oregon on 11-3-56 and had 4 children: Stash (b. 8-18-59), Tina (b. 4-5-61), Linda (b. 12-4-62), and Patti (b. 2-3-67). Stanley became a recognized authority in his field of instrumentation and presented technical papers at several symposiums and supported the Air Force on many missile test programs in the field. He retired in 1990 after 41 years of dedicated service to the company and is currently engaged in gardening, Boy Scout support, and genealogy research on his family history. He is attempting to trace his ancestry back to the days of Leszczynski, King of Poland in 1704-1709. The family name comes from the word "leszczyna" which means hazel tree.

Marcella married Chester Kos from Chicago, Ill. on 6-18-49 and had 2 children: Janet (b. 5-25-50) and Sharon (b. 5-21-53). They reside in Hobart near the family farm and for many years, Marcella worked for Mitchell's Lumber Company. Chester worked as a bricklayer in the Lake County area and was a business agent in Bricklayer's Union #6 until his retirement in 1985.

Florence married Victor Nowasadski from Nanticoke, Pa. on 8-16-50 and had 2 children: Victor Jr. (b. 10-4-50) and Anthony (b. 11-17-53). They currently reside on California Street in Hobart, and both Victor and Florence worked many years in the Gary Steel Mills.

William married Loretta McNair (b. 1-28-36) a model, from Jackson, Miss. on 2-14-64 but she deceased on 6-2-70 with child. William then married America Norambuena-Casey, a school teacher, from Rock Island, Ill. (originally from Miraflores, Linares, Chile, South America) on 3-18-72. They had 2 children: James Casey, stepson (b. 11-28-69) and Kathleen (b. 8-30-75). America attended Black Hawk College in Moline, Illinois, Marycrest College in Davenport, Iowa, and Indiana University in Gary. William served in Korea and is currently employed at George Pacific in Gary, starting there in October 1964.

by William Leszczynski

LETZ FAMILY
F149

In 1879, Louis Holland Letz (1857-1908) and his wife Katherine Messerschmidt Holland Letz came to America. They brought their three little children — Eva (1875-1932), Ludwig (1879-1946) and Johannah (1878-1972). Their parents were sad to see the young family leave. Louis's father, Michael, had a shop in which he made farm tools and had hoped to have his son work with him.

The young Holland-Letz's went to Chicago but after a few years decided a small town was a better location for his little ones, so he boarded a train and headed for Indiana.

They came to Crown Point and soon Louis was setting up a machine shop — named Crown Point Manufacturing Company — located across from the Pennsylvania Railroad Station. By 1882, Louis had a simple feed mill on the market. He then experimented with a corn planter. When perfected, he sold his corn planter patent to International Harvester in Chicago.

As time passed, the company grew and so did the family. The Holland-Letz's had 10 children: Eva (1875-1932), Johannah (1878-1972) – Mrs. Louis Roffman, Ludwig (1879-1946), William (1881-1961), Marie (1883-1966) – Mrs. Ed Roffman, George (1885-1936), John (1886-1978), Carol (1888-1970) – Mrs. Harry Newton, Otto (1890-1942), and Ernest (1891-1909).

Though Louis and Katherine had 10 children, they only had 13 grandchildren. Ernest, their youngest, died of consumption at the age of 17. Two of the Letz children had no children. Of the grandchildren, only one grandson carried on the Letz name. Six of the grandchildren still live in Crown Point, — Arnold Roffman – son of Louis and Johanna, Dorothy Belanger and Florence Finck – Arnold's sisters, Edna Roffman – Marie and Ed Roffman's daughter, George Letz, Jr. – son of George Letz, and Adah Mueller (Mrs. Melvin W. Mueller) – daughter of John Letz. There are twenty-six great-grandchildren.

My best memory of the family is the family dinner on 2nd Christmas Day (December 26) — each descendant of the family taking turns at being host and hostess. This was a pot luck and always a wonderful time.

The Letz's have been active in the Trinity Lutheran Church all their lives.

by Adah Mueller

118

LEWANDOWSKI, ANN CENTANNI
F150

Ann Centanni Lewandowski

Ann Rose Centanni was born on June 7, 1929, to Samuel and Josephine Centanni. She was a life-time resident of Gary, marrying Peter Joseph Lewandowski (b. 4-9-23) of Iron, Michigan on October 2, 1948.

In his youth, Peter played Minor League Baseball in New Orleans. He was with the United States Army during World War II and operated a tank. He reportedly fought in the "Battle of the Bulge" in France. Peter was employed by the Gary Fire Department for approximately 25 years.

Ann Lewandowski was employed by J.C. Penney's in the Gary area for almost 20 years. She was a member of the Glen Park Democratic Club and the West Side Civic Club as well as Blessed Sacrament Church.

Peter and Ann had three children born and raised in Gary, Indiana: Karen Ann Lewandowski, born April 26, 1950; Patricia Ann, born April 19, 1953; and Peter Joseph, Jr., born October 22, 1961. Peter and Ann divorced in 1965.

Karen Ann Lewandowski graduated from Lew Wallace High School and was employed by the E.J.&E. Railroad for seven years. She married Rudy Dennis Mrak (b. 12-11-47) of Gary, on October 27, 1973, in Gary, Indiana. Rudy, a Vietnam Veteran, has been employed by both Western Electric and Indiana Bell. Four children were born to this marriage: Rudy Dennis Mrak, Jr., born February 19, 1976, in Crown Point, Indiana; Kimberly Ann Mrak, born October 3, 1977, in Hobart, Indiana; and twins, Jaclyn Ann Mrak and Joseph George Mrak, born January 8, 1979. The family currently resides in Portage, Indiana.

Patricia Ann married Steven Robert Pawlek (b. 1-12-50) of Gary, in 1970. One child was born to this union: Jennifer Ann Pawlak, born February 24, 1971, in Gary, Indiana. The couple divorced in 1972. Patricia then married Timothy Jeffrey Fields (b. 2-20-46) of Gary, on May 19, 1978 in Crown Point, Indiana. Mr. Fields is employed by the construction industry at U.S. Steel. Three children have been born in Merrillville, Indiana, to this union: Shane Ann Fields, born April 19, 1979; Sarah Louise Fields, born July 7, 1980; and William Haze Fields, born August 13, 1981.

Peter Joseph Lewandowski, Jr. received an athletic scholarship in baseball and attended Valparaiso University. He now resides in Valparaiso.

by Joanne C. Clark

LEWIS, ALBERT
F151

Albert Lewis was born in Bay View, Wisconsin in January, 1878 to John and Margaret Lewis who were both born in Wales.

Albert was one of nine children, Evan, David, George H., William, Bertha, Minnie, Ruth, Mae and Albert. His father was killed when the children were young and they were raised by their mother in East Chicago, Indiana. Albert was Police Chief in East Chicago and was then appointed Chief Probation Officer of Lake County, Indiana and served in that capacity for twenty-two years.

He married Lydia Maria Hutton, daughter of Levi and Gertrude (Fieler) Hutton, of Palmer, Indiana. They had three children, Gertrude Margaret, Irven, and Lydia.

Gertrude married Arthur Victor Berquist of Ludington, Michigan, Irven married Helen Jurgenson of Hammond, IN, and Lydia married Albert Brenneman of Pittsburgh, PA.

Albert died on September 21, 1933, his wife Lydia died October 26, 1956, Gertrude on September, 1984, Irven on December 7, 1989.

by Gerald Born

LITTLE, EARL B.
F152

(and Descendants)

Early history of the descendants of Captain Thomas and Myra Ames Little, early settlers of Lake Prairie community, West Creek Township, Lake County Indiana has been printed in prior history books of Lake County.

Earl Little (born 7-3-1901), son of Jesse and Martha Little, great-grandson of the above, has been a resident of West Creek Twp. his entire life. He attended school by riding or driving a horse. He graduated from Purdue University in 1924. He began farming by renting his father's farm.

On Oct. 1, 1925 he married Emarine Black, youngest daughter of Sarah and Thomas Black, also of West Creek Township. They celebrated their Golden Wedding anniversary in 1975. Emarine passed away in August 27, 1978 and was buried at Lake Prairie Cemetery.

They had two daughters Mary Virginia (born 9-20-1926) and Sarah Margaret (born 1-14-1928).

Earl married Winona Elliott Dennison on 7-2-1983. Winona (born 2-12-1930) daughter of Charles and Mildred Elliott, married Hardin Dennison on 2-5-1950 and divorced 6-1979. Winona had 2 daughters. Linda married Albert A. Peck (born 6-30-1960) on August 16, 1970. They have a daughter Tracy Lee (born 10-5-1971) and a son Scott Allen (born 1-2-1982). They live in Roselawn, Indiana. Kimberly (born 8-23-1962) married Richard Kevin Otey (born 8-6-1959) on 12-12-81. They have two children. Jeremy Kelton (born 4-10-1984) and Renee Michele (born 7-8-1986) in Fairfield, Il.

by Mary Mikels

LOVE, PETER KITWOOD FAMILY
F153

Peter Kitwood Love was born on May 28, 1867, at Washington Island, Wisconsin, one of eight children of Samuel A. and Ellen Jane (Mundell) Love who were married in 1850 in Ireland. He was named Peter Kitwood after a Methodist minister on Washington Island and preferred to be called by his initials P.K.

His father trained from childhood as a weaver, but after working at the trade for a few years, decided to go to sea. In the fall of 1852, in company with brother James, he left Ireland, due to religious turmoil, to settle at Detroit, Michigan. Samuel became a member of the crew on the steamer "Cleveland" and became the second mate. He and James moved to Washington Island, Door County, Wisconsin, in 1854 and for 17 years worked for the lumber industry during winter and sailed on the Great Lakes during the summer. Tragedy struck in 1870 when brother James drowned in a shipwreck. Saddened by his brother's passing, Samuel moved that same year to Lake County where he purchased 260 acres of good farm land north of the present site of Creston and farmed there for six years. He then moved to Leroy in Winfield Township where he operated a general store and was the postmaster. He also operated a hay business there, and along with sons John and William had a large hay barn at Creston. Sons Samuel, James, and Peter were all kept busy with these two business places in Leroy. In addition to John and William, Peter's brothers and sisters were Elizabeth, who is buried in Detroit, Samuel A., Mary A., James H., and Rosa.

Peter recalled that at age 4 in 1871 he watched the glow of the great Chicago fire at night from their yard at Cedar Lake and that he would cry because he was so frightened.

As a young man, Peter was a gifted left-handed baseball pitcher. He was offered a position with the I.I.I. League (Indiana-Illinois-Iowa) but refused the offer when he learned he would have to pitch on Sundays, which was against the religious beliefs of the family.

Peter Kitwood Love and Adda (Addie) May Gibbs, daughter of Harvey and Hannah (Carson) Gibbs, were married on April 25, 1889.

They owned and operated a farm one mile west of Leroy. They later moved to Leroy. Peter did dredging in Minnesota for several years. On occasion the family would accompany him.

Daughter Mabel Ellen was born on March 12, 1890; Edith Maude was born November 17, 1894; and Florence May was born July 16, 1901. Mabel Ellen attended Dublin School and graduated from Crown Point High School. On April 11, 1912, she married Joseph John Ross, a farmer, and son of John and Carrie (Kreis) Ross. To this union were born six children: Margaret Vivian, Marian Love, Harold Joseph, twins Donald John and Dorothy Jane, and Roland Eugene, who died at 10 years of age from encephalitis as a result of measles. Mabel E. died April 28, 1964, and is buried at Salem Cemetery.

Daughter Edith Maude attended Dublin School, graduated from Crown Point High School and received a degree from DePauw University, majoring in Latin. She was a teacher for many years. She married Carl Bars on August 31, 1926, at the Leroy Methodist Church. Their only child, Roberta, died at childbirth. Edith died June 7, 1969, and is buried at Salem Cemetery.

Daughter Florence May attended Dublin School, graduated from Crown Point High School, and attended Columbia College of Physical Education in Chicago. She taught for many years in Gary, Harvey, Illinois, and Hobart. On August 1, 1925, she married Lerton G. Muterspaugh in the Leroy home of her parents. They had no family. Florence M. died February 1, 1988, and is buried at Salem Cemetery.

Peter Kitwood Love died in Leroy on December 14, 1933, following a stroke. Addie May Love died in Leroy on May 3, 1949. They are buried at Salem Cemetery.

by Margaret V. Schlemmer

MAACK, ALBERT
F154

Albert Maack was born at Brunswick, Lake County, September 24, 1862, his parents being Mr. and Mrs. Peter Maack. Albert attended school in his native town until he was nineteen years old, applying himself diligently to his studies. He went to Crown Point to finish his education in the high schools. He followed up commercial pursuits, locating in Lowell, where he was actively engaged as a clerk, later going into business for himself. He was at all times a courteous and accommodating gentleman and was popular in both a business and social way. He was united in marriage September 10, 1889, to Miss Helen Kobelin, daughter of Mr. and Mrs. Wm. Kobelin, of Lowell. To this union two daughters were born. Mr. Maack was elected town clerk and treasurer of Lowell in 1886, which position he filled with satisfaction.

Mr. Maack and family moved to Hammond, where he was appointed assistant postmaster, which position he holds today, and virtually has full charge of the postal affairs of that city. Being an ardent Republican, he took an active part in politics, and for several years did valuable service as secretary of the Lake County Republican Central Committee. As a party worker he is active and clean. Four years ago he aspired to the candidacy for county treasurer, but failed to secure it. Nothing daunted and being of the "true-blue" type of Republicanism, he accepted defeat gracefully and "threw off his coat" for the cause. At the county convention held at Crown Point in March of the present year he was unanimously nominated for the office of county treasurer.

(Compiled from the Souvenir Album of Lake Co. Ind., Crown Point-Lowell, June 18-19, 1909.)

THOMAS MAUGER
F155

Thomas Lysle Mauger, taken in 1905.

Mineral Point(s) and Beyond

Thomas Lysle Mauger, who decided at a young age that he did not wish to following in his grandfather's footsteps and become a

Elsie Wilhelmina Mauger, taken in 1905.

Elsie W. and Thomas Lysle Mauger with their first child, Elmer Oliver. Picture taken at Indiana Harbor in June of 1910.

watchmaker and jeweler, left his home in Mineral Point, Wisconsin, to earn his living working on the railroads. "Water trains" took him across the Mississippi River into the western states as far north as Montana, where he sometimes worked as cook or ranchhand.

Lysle, which name he preferred to Thomas, was a "fireman" on the Elgin, Joliet, and Eastern Railroad when he met Elsie Wilhelmina Anderson in Waukegan, Illinois. They subsequently married there on May 15, 1905. Lysle was born in Mineral Point, WI, and was reared from age eight by his paternal grandparents, William and Mary Hannah (Davey) Mauger, of that city, when his parents, Thomas Davey and Anna Jane (Kelley) Mauger were divorced. His maternal grandparents were Timothy and Anna Mary (McCann) Kelley. His great-grandparents were from Wittenberg, Germany, Cornwall, England, and County Cork, Ireland, some of whom had emigrated to America and settled in Wisconsin.

Elsie Mauger was born in Fellingsbro, Sweden, and also reared by her grandparents until the age of eleven when she was brought to the United States by a sister of her mother. Her aunt had emigrated to this country in 1890, married, established a good home, and then returned to Sweden in 1898 to get Elsie. She and Thomas came to Indiana Harbor soon after their marriage upon the urging of his father who was in business there. Their first home was at 3610 Fir Street, and their second at 3825 Fir.

Early in 1908 Elsie contracted typhoid fever, and was not expected to recover. It was said to be the only case of typhoid in the entire area. It was so serious, in fact, that Lysle had started removing some of their furniture, which he was happy to start replacing when she showed signs of recovery. In 1910, Elmer Oliver was born, with Harold Kenneth, "Bud," and Clifford Damon soon following. Donald Leslie, Olvie Evelyn, "Sis," Leonard Everett, and Edna Irene were born at 4225 Carey Street which was in the Washington Park Addition, this home to be the permanent residence of Lysle and Elsie.

Lysle began working at Inland Steel Company on December 5, 1905. His first payday as a machine-helper and leverman was $21.24, which was for two 10-hour days and nine 12-hour days, a total of 128 hours. After quitting Inland in May of 1920, Lysle worked at Mark Manufacturing until September of 1921 when he then began working at the General American Transportation Corporation, and worked as a template maker until his retirement. He passed away on December 20, 1958.

Elsie's pleasure was tending her beautiful flowers and yard, and she still did what she could until she passed away at age 90 at the home of her daughter, Sis. She and Lysle celebrated their 50th Wedding Anniversary with all their children and fifteen grandchildren in attendance.

Elmer Oliver and Margaret (McGuire) Mauger were married on November 24, 1934 at Gary, IN, and made their home in the Hessville area of Hammond, IN. They were blessed with three daughters, Geraldine Ann, Margaret Mary, and Mary Jo, and one son, Elmer Bernard. Elmer's death occurred on April 10, 1969, and Margaret's on September 3, 1975.

Gary Arthur, Air Force Retired, and "Jeri" Ann Brown have four children, Gary Arthur, Jr., Julia Ann "Jill" Berg, Lisa Alane De Angelo, and Eric Arlen, and four grandchildren. James Anthony and Margaret "Peggy" Yonker have four children, James A., Jr., Eddie Joseph, Heidi Marie, and Gretta Ann. Elmer Bernard has two daughters, Nancy Lynn and Margaret Adlyn.

Harold Kenneth and Doris (Hill) Mauger were married on July 11, 1935, and have a son and a daughter. Harold Kenneth, Jr., "Ken" and Shirley Ann (Gates) Mauger have three sons, Michael Blaine, Patrick Allen, and Kevin Lyle, and two grandchildren. Ken served three years in the Army.

Willard Ezra and Virginia Ellen Frick have two daughters, Lisa Ellen Hughes and Sara Joan, and one granddaughter. Willard served four years in the Air Force.

Clifford Damon and Lovie (Borsits) Mauger were married on July 14, 1940, and have three children, Donald Borsits Mauger, Carolyn Diane, and Thomas Lyle. Donald Dennis and Arlene (Koedyker) Mauger have a daughter, Valerie Joan Wotkun, and two sons, Brian Dale and Gordon Keith, and three grandchildren. Donald served in the Army and Thomas in the Marines. Clifford passed away on October 18, 1968.

Donald Leslie and Ruth (Hudelson) Mauger, who were married on November 13, 1941, have a daughter, Jean Ann Colbert. Jean Ann has a daughter, Kirsten Dean, and a son, Paul Colbert. Donald served in the Army in World War II with time served in Japan.

Thomas and Olive (Mauger) Thomason were married on September 17, 1942. They have three children, Linda Evelyn, Laura Elsie, and Glenn Cooper. Linda E. Hug has a daughter, Heather Lyn. James Charles and Laura E. Claus have three sons, Jamie Thomas, Ryan Donald, and Joel Lucas. James served with the Army in Viet Nam. Glenn has a son, Glenn Damon. Thomas served in the Army in World War II earning five major battle stars in the European Theater of Operations.

Leonard Everett passed away on November 1, 1946, at the age of twenty-three, from injuries received in an automobile accident which occurred soon after he had completed serving four years in the U.S. Coast Guard in World War II. He was a Radioman 2nd Class aboard the U.S.S. Bath which was commissioned on November 14, 1943.

Myron Allen and Edna Irene (Mauger) Picard, who were married on April 13, 1947, have a son, Allen Everett, and a daughter, Karen Irene. Allen, who served in the Air Force, has a son, Wayne Allen, and two daughters, Tamara Lynn and Amy Marie. Emory Lavoy and Karen Manley have two daughters, Tina Marie and Venissa Wilhelmina. Myron passed away on June 24, 1971.

by Olive E. Mauger Thomason

THOMAS DAVEY
F156

Early "Indiana Harbor" Settlers

Thomas Davey and Anna Augusta (Kinney) Phalon Mauger were early settlers of the "Harbor" area of East Chicago, IN, having

Taken in Indiana Harbor in 1908. The three men to the extreme left are unidentified, but then from left to right they are at rear in doorway, Thomas Lysle Mauger, Thomas Davey Mauger, George Roop, Mr. Ford, the policeman, and Julius Cohen and his daughter.

moved from the Englewood district of Chicago, IL, around 1903. Thomas Davey was a salesman for the Irwin Packing Company. Their children at the time were William Joseph,

Grapevine Street from Michigan

Scene on Fir Street, Indiana Harbor, Indiana

121

Taken in Indiana Harbor about 1922 in front of 3812 Fir Street, the home of William Joseph Mauger, who is shown to the left with Andrew Chizmar.

twins, Addie Catherine (Brown) and Abbie Augusta (Blue), Robert Elsworth, Thomas Davey, Jr., and Maude Mae Phalon, who was Anna Augusta's daughter by her previous marriage, but was reared as the oldest child of the Mauger family. Two more sons, Frank Edison and Charles Benjamin, were born in East Chicago.

Thomas Davey, who was a coal and wood dealer and called "The Transfer Man," was born in Mineral Point, WI, on August 28, 1855. His parents were William and Mary Hannah (Davey) Mauger, William having been born in Wittenberg, Germany, on October 7, 1830, and Mary Hannah, born June 26, 1835 in Cornwall, England. Augusta was born on February 8, 1866 in St. John, New Brunswick, Canada, and came to the United States as a young bride of Edward Phalon. Edward passed away on November 10, 1893.

Thomas and Augusta lived on Grapevine Street, later to be named Grand Boulevard, while their new house at 3812 Fir Street was being built. Thomas had a barn and livery for his three teams of horses, meanwhile, and his son, Lysle, assisted him in their care. The Maugers were well known throughout the community and actively involved in its development. At the time of his death on February 21, 1927, Thomas was on the security force at Inland Steel. Augusta was actively involved as a member of the First Christian Church, the Harry C. Long Post, Women's Relief Corps, and the Woodmen's Circle, and passed away on July 6, 1928.

William Joseph and Grace (Olson) Mauger were married on June 10, 1924, and lived in the Harbor until their new home in Hessville was completed in May of 1927. They had two children, Robert Edmond and Lois Jean. Robert and Carolyn (Wascher) Mauger have three children, Cheryl Lynn Barbosa, Karen Ann Moody, and Robert Edmond, Jr., and two grandchildren. Robert served in the Quartermaster Corps in Korea after graduating college. Thomas and Lois Jean Luchene have a daughter, Therese Marie (Bevacqua) Rigsby.

William Joseph served his country in the Field Artillery in World War I with much of that time being served in France. The money that "Bill" sent home to his mother was saved by her and used to purchase a player piano when he returned home. He retired from Inland Steel Co. with forty-six years devoted to his job. He passed away on August 12, 1964, and Grace passed away on October 11, 1980.

Howard Littleton and Abbie Augusta "Blue" Clark were married in East Chicago on August 20, 1917. Howard was a 2nd Lieutenant in the 59th Regiment of the 5th Infantry stationed at Gettysburg, PA at the time. The Army was his career and he attained the rank of a full Colonel. After his death on September 18, 1945 at Fort Oglethorpe, GA, he was interred at Arlington Cemetery, as was Abbie Augusta, who passed away in Sarasota, FL on March 8, 1953. They had two sons, Howard Warren and William Arthur, who also were career Army men. Howard W. and Elizabeth Whiting (North) Clark were married on March 13, 1943, and have two daughters, Leslie Littleton and Anne Critcher Schaefer, Jr., and one grandson. Howard also attained the rank of Colonel and just recently passed away. William Arthur died while serving his country on April 18, 1945 at Luzon. He is interred in the U.S. Cemetery, Batangas, Philippines.

Oliver C. and Addie Catherine "Brown" Hall were married on June 30, 1920. Addie suffered a heart attack on March 19, 1922, with death following two days later.

Robert Elsworth and Mary (Palkovich) Mauger were married on May 16, 1941, and their family includes four sons, Raymond Arthur, Gary Frank, Robert, Jr., and Richard Dean, and one daughter, Roberta Ann. Raymond and Sharon have a son and a daughter, and one grandchild. Richard and Roberta Ann Knight have two sons, and one grandchild. Robert Elsworth, who was retired from Youngstown Sheet and Tube Co., passed away on April 16, 1977.

Thomas Davey, Jr. and Emma (Kane) Mauger were married on September 25, 1922, and had a daughter, Adeline Mary, and a son, Thomas William. Peritonitis developed after an appendectomy, and Adeline passed away on November 20, 1939, at the age of fifteen years. Thomas William and Mary Magdaline (Sertich) Mauger were wed on March 2, 1946, and have a son, Thomas Dale, and a daughter, Mary Adeline. Thomas Dale has two sons, Thomas, Jr. and Jeremy Ryan. Ronald Brack and Mary Adeline Hatfield have two daughters, Christina Marie and Cindy Marie. Thomas William served in the European Theater of Operations in World War II, and in the Pacific during the Korean Conflict. He is a Major in the National Guard. Thomas Davey, who was a machinist at Inland Steel Company, and at one time ran for East Chicago Councilman, passed away after surgery at age 47, on June 5,

Indiana State Bank and Post Office, Indiana Harbor, Indiana

Auditorium Building, Indiana Harbor, Indiana

1949. Emma passed away on July 6, 1981.

Frank Edison "Packy" Mauger was very well known in the Harbor section of East Chicago, where he was associated with Warren "Sonny" Sheetz who operated the Auditorium Bar and Grill. His latter years were spent in Hot Springs, Arkansas with his wife, "Press." Frank died on April 4, 1985, and his wife about ten years previously.

Charles Benjamin and Alice Maple (Oakley) Mauger were married on February 4, 1926 and had three sons and two daughters. Warren Davey and Margaret (Gyerko) Mauger have two sons, Glen and David, and two grandchildren. Warren served in the Army in World War II. Prospers and Joanne Oakley Franchimont have two sons, Richard and Michael, and a daughter, Susan. Desmond and Deborah Ann Quinn have six children, Daniel, Patricia, Maurine, Sean, Erin, and Patrick, and three grandchildren. Charles Franklin and Sharon Mauger have two daughters, Keri and Kelly. William Clark and Karla Mauger have four children, Kimberly, Kirsten, William, and Katrina. Charles Benjamin, who was a retired employee of Youngstown Sheet and Tube Company, passed away on April 17, 1982. Alice passed away on January 5, 1979.

by Olive E. Mauger Thomason

JAMES WARD
F157

A Bit of "Flying" History

Some of the headlines in the Hammond Times newspapers in April of 1911 were: Romance Revealed When Girl Marries Aviator, East Chicago Girl Elopes with Airman, We Fly at Nashville, Wife Will Soar with Husband, Scolds Hubby for Short Trip, Aviator's Wife Brings Home Prizes, Hero of 1800 Flights Quits the Air Forever. Some of the comments of Thomas Davey Mauger of Indiana Harbor were: "I don't like his occupation, give me terra firma, if that don't beat the Dutch, I've nothing against my son-in-law I've never seen him, I'm afraid he flies pretty high for me."

Miss Maude Mae Phalon Mauger and James J. Ward had a "whirlwind courtship" having met at a Thanksgiving dinner the previous year. Maude packed the necessities for a weekend stay in Chicago at the home of Ward's chief mechanic, Fred Ratsch. But she and Mrs. Ratsch "slipped quietly away" to Nashville on Friday night to attend the Aviation Meet that was in progress for the week. Whether it had all been arranged beforehand or whether the young couple settled it after they met in Nashville was unknown, but they were married on Saturday.

Maude planned on accompanying her aviator husband on one of his ascents in Nashville, but was unable to do so because of the strong winds. In anticipation of a flight by her, Mr. Ratsch had built a seat on Ward's machine to accommodate her. For his flights there, James received a prize of a silver cup and $250 for making the highest ascent, a distance of 5000 feet. Other aviators participating were Lincoln Beachy and John McCurdy. Ward's first flights were made in Chicago where he had attracted the attention of Glenn Curtiss who speedily added him to his staff of aviators. His wife first flew in Wichita, KS, where Ward stayed in the air about three minutes, but was scolded for "not making the flight longer, and not going higher." By 1914, though, Jimmy Ward had "quit flying forever" to engage in a "legitimate business." "I have made 1800 flights without a serious mishap," He said. "My nerve is as good as ever, but I'm through. The reason is – Mrs. Ward."

by Olive E. Mauger Thomason

James Ward about to take his wife, Maude Mae (Phalon) Ward, for her first flight in Wichita, KS on May 4, 1911.

MAXWELL, GEORGE
F158

George Maxwell was born February 17, 1840, the eldest son of James and Permelia (Banks) Maxwell, who were married in New York state November 1, 1834. As a child George lived along the shore of Lake Erie in Madison Township, Lake County, Ohio, until 1853, when he moved with his family to Lake County, Indiana. George worked as a farm laborer, for James Holstead, in Ross Township, as a young man 20 years of age. George was married to Maria Adline Strong in Porter County, Indiana on November 19, 1862. Maria was born May 12, 1842 in Porter County, Indiana, a daughter of Orson Webster and Lucy Emeline (Cadwell) Strong. George owned 40 acres of land in section 16, Ross township, Lake County, Indiana, the same land formerly owned by his parents. George and Maria had two sons, John Wesley, born April 19, 1864, and Lenzo Eugene, born October 1, 1865, both in Ross Township, Lake County, Indiana.

At the age of 24, George was enrolled as a private of Company B, 151st Regiment Indiana Volunteers, at Valparaiso, Indiana, on February 6, 1865, and mustered into service at LaPorte, Indiana on February 8. He was six feet tall, with hazel eyes and black hair. About June 1, in the line of duty in service at Tullahoma, Tennessee, George suffered an illness which continued until his discharge to his home in Deep River September 19, 1865, shortly before the birth of his second son. The chronic illness continued until his death on December 25, 1865, leaving his widow with two very young children to raise alone. Maria later applied for a pension for her husband's service during the Civil War, which she received until her death, in Ross Township, on March 16, 1885.

John Wesley Maxwell was married to Vernissa Jane Crisman, in Lake County, Indiana, on September 24, 1885. Jane was born September 21, 1866, daughter of George W. and Catharine (Mareness) Crisman. They had three children: (1) Earl, born December 1887 in Lake County, Indiana, was married to Grace Brovine October 23, 1909. Their daughter Helen, born August 24, 1916, died as a teenager, in California; (2) Ruth, born December 30, 1888, married Joe Wollenhaupt July 20, 1910, and they had two children; (3) Verna G., born March 21, 1891, married Dr. Eugene F. Carey July 21, 1916. They lived in Chicago on South Halsted Street. They had no children. John W. Maxwell died in April 1939 and Jane in 1945, both in Chicago, Illinois.

Lenzo Eugene Maxwell was married February 6, 1890 to Saloma Hardesty, born in Indiana May 2, 1860, a daughter of Harmon and Isabell (Milner) Hardesty. Their children were Harry W. born June 15, 1891 in Union Township, Porter Co., Indiana, married June 15, 1914 at Valparaiso, Indiana to Elsie May Ditlow, born November 16, 1893 in Union Township, daughter of Abraham and Anna (Cremer) Ditlow. Children: Clyde Orville, born March 21, 1915 Porter Twp., Porter Co., Indiana; Bernice Alvera, born May 18, 1917 in Union Twp., Porter Co., Indiana; Lois Barbara born 1919 in Center Twp., Porter Co., Indiana; Annadel May born Sept. 15, 1921 in Valparaiso; Burl Harry, born July 1923 in Valparaiso; Mary Jane born March 1935 in Valparaiso. Harry died April 21, 1963 and Elsie died January 26, 1974, both in Valparaiso.

Isabelle, born May 25, 1894 Union Twp., married Rinehart H. Eikelberg Jan. 6, 1917 at Valparaiso. He was born Jan. 20, 1892, son of Henry and Lena (Moss) Eikelberg. They lived in Michigan City, Indiana and had 10 children: Infant daughter born and died Sept. 3, 1917; infant son born and died June 14, 1918; Everett Norman born July 20, 1919, died October 26, 1989; Lucille Ruby born Nov. 26, 1920, died April 15, 1989; May Isabell born May 6, 1922; Robert Walter born Nov. 27, 1923, died Feb. 28, 1987; Allene Rose born Aug. 23, 1925; Wayne and Ward, twins, born May 8, 1927; Alice L. born Oct. 27, 1928. Saloma died Nov. 4, 1895, of typhoid fever, as a result of drinking water from an open well.

Lenzo married a second time to Louisa Jane Weiler, on November 3, 1897, in Porter Township, Porter Co., Indiana. She was born May 18, 1864 in Porter Township, daughter of John Leonard and Christina (Riecker) Weiler. They had two daughters: (1) Ruby C. born Sept. 4, 1898 in Porter Township, married Marion Grant Daniels May 25, 1926 in Porter Township. He was born Aug. 24, 1901 in Morgan Twp., son of Milan and Susan (Stanley) Daniels. They had one child, Doris Jean, born April 21, 1927 at Leroy, Lake County, Indiana. Ruby and Grant continued to live in her parents house after their death. Darrell Sanders, son of Doris, and his wife, Virginia, presently occupy the house on the Maxwell farm in Porter Township formerly owned by Lenzo and Louisa Maxwell, then by his grandparents, Grant and Ruby Daniels. (2) Ruth Pauline, born Aug. 21, 1900 at home in Porter Township, was married to Robert S. McGinley on May 16, 1923 at the Maxwell home in Porter Township. Robert was born April 28, 1901 in Union Twp., Porter Co., Indiana, son of Robert L. and Inda Leona (Judd) McGinley. They had three daughters: Geraldine Ruth and Betty Lou born in Michigan City, Indiana, and Carol June born at home in Hebron, Indiana. Geraldine (Mrs. Theodore Weiss) presently lives in Valparaiso. Betty (Mrs. Leslie Williams) is a resident of Center Township, Porter County, Indiana, and Carol (Mrs. Arthur Lageveen) resides in DeMotte, Indiana.

by Betty L. Williams

MAXWELL, JAMES
F159

James Maxwell was born June 20, 1814 in Armagh County, Ireland, to parents of Scottish ancestry who died in Ireland. When James was sixteen years of age, he left Ireland and came to New York state, where he was married November 1, 1834 to Permelia Banks. Permelia was born June 16, 1816 in Schoharie County, New York, a daughter of Mr. and Cathrine (Rhodman, or Rodman) Banks.

James and Permelia Maxwell remained in New York for a few years and then went to Madison Township, Lake County, Ohio, arriving there by 1840, where they lived until 1853. That year they left Ohio, and then settled on Section 8 of Ross Township, Lake County, Indiana. James and Permelia were the parents of five children: (1) Hanna A., born April 13, 1837, was married to Joseph Green April 13, 1853 in Lake County, Ohio; (2) Sarah P. born January 11, 1839 was married to Luther Smith February 12, 1854 in Lake County, Indiana; (3) George, born February 17, 1840, married Maria Adline Strong November 19, 1862 in Porter County, Indiana; (4) John, born March 13, 1846 in Lake County, Ohio, died November 9, 1862 at Scottsville, Kentucky, of illness contracted while on a march in the line of duty, while serving in Company A 73rd Regiment Indiana Infantry; (5) Jane M. born March 3, 1848 in Lake County, Ohio was married to Asa P. Brown December 5, 1865 in Porter County, Indiana. James Maxwell died September 27, 1862 and was interred in the Woodvale-Deep River cemetery.

Permelia married, for her second husband, Thomas P. Wilcox, a widower, on October 11, 1865 in Lake County, Indiana. Thomas had five children by his first wife, Sarah, who died April 8, 1863 in Lake County. They were Catherine born ca 1845, in Pennsylvania; George born 1850 in Pennsylvania; Rhodi or Ruey born ca 1854; Mary E. born ca 1858; and Cora born ca 1862, the latter three in Indiana.

Thomas and Permelia left Lake County and moved to Boone Township, Porter County, Indiana by 1870. There Thomas P. and his son, George, worked at the trade of wagon makers. Permelia (Banks) (Maxwell) Wilcox died January 21, 1877, in Kansas.

by Betty L. Williams

MEEKER, HENRIETTA AND CHARLES
F160

Henrietta Meeker was the second child of Sherman Meeker and Elizabeth (Cress), born 10 May, 1854. She married Elliott Bibler 22 February, 1872. They had one son Alphius, born 12 December 1872. She died 1 February, 1876.

Charles Meeker, born in Calhoun County, Michigan on 2 November, 1857 was the son of Sherman and Elizabeth (Cress). He was schooled in the school district of Center Twp. and assisted his father and brothers on the farm until his marriage to Rose Sweeney on 22 September, 1880. She was the daughter of James and Elizabeth (Johnson) Sweeney, born 17 July, 1859 in Center Twp. and educated in the same school as her husband. They farmed for about 10 years but in 1891 they moved to Crown Point where Charles established an agricultural implement business, which he later expanded to include buggies and wagons. On 17 September, 1914, his wife Rose died and he was alone until 4 October, 1926, when he married Marie Gunschivich. He was a prominent business man, a Trustee of Center Township, active in civic affairs. (see T.H. Ball's Hist. of Lake Co. published 1904) Charles died 22 June, 1935.

by Ruth Demmon

MEEKER, HIRAM
F161

Hiram Meeker, born 10 March, 1835, in Wyoming County, Penn., was the son of Joseph L. Meeker and Hannah (Bronson). He enlisted Oct. 1861 in Co. A, 57th Regiment of the Penn. Volunteers. He was injured during the war but served as a steward in an army hospital in Smoketown, Md. until his discharge in the spring of 1863. After the War he lived for a time in the Lafayette, Ind. area where he married Mary Bryan 7 Jan. 1864. She was the daughter of John and Susan (Graves) Bryan. In 1869 they came to Crown Point, Ind. where he established a Nursery southeast of town, and an orchard across from the Fairgrounds. They had three daughters, Adeline who married Julius Rockwell, Alta who married William Thompson, and Josephine (not married) who assisted her Father in the business in his later years and who carried on after his death. Mr. Meeker was said to have been a remarkable man, active in civil affairs, and was well known for his integrity and his knowledge of small fruit, shrubbery, shade trees and nursery stock which he sold throughout the area.

He died 6 May 1922 at the age of 87. His obituary said he "retained the ambition, activity and virility of youth", and "that he was indeed Crown Point's youngest old citizen".

by Ruth Demmon

Top: William Heinze, Richard Dyer, Roe Rockwell Dyer – granddaughter, Irl Rockwell – grandson, Will Thompson, Middle: Alta Meeker Thompson, Addie Meeker Rockwell, Josephine Meeker. Bottom: Hiram Meeker, Robert Dyer (great-grandson), Hortense Rockwell Heinze (granddaughter), Irene Mulhern Rockwell.

MEEKER, J. FRANK
F162

J. Frank Meeker, was the youngest son of Sherman and Elizabeth (Cress) Meeker, and was born in Center Twp. 11 December 1868. He had the distinction of being one of the youngest of the log-cabin children of northern Indians, having been born in the "primitive and pioneer log cabin" that his father had made his home when they first came to the county. He attended the Center Twp. school, but at the age of 13 he came to Crown Point to continue his education, graduating from High School. He entered the school of Law at the University of Michigan where he graduated with the class of 1892. He returned to Crown Point and began his practice. His obituary said of him, "He was recognized from the first as a lawyer of brilliant attainment. He came to be recognized as an authority on questions developing on county law and his victories contested by opponents in higher courts to their loss achieved fame for him." He served as deputy prosecuting attorney for 2 terms and in 1901 was appointed County Attorney. He was running on the Republican ticket for the Circuit Court Judgeship, but a week before the primary on the 15th of May 1914, he died of a heart attack.

He married Stella Colby the daughter of Mrs. Catherine Colby, 24 March 1894. She was a native of Lake County and "had the distinction of being the only woman at the time qualified and had obtained admission to the bar of Lake County." She was said to have been a lady of unusual literary talent and possessed legal knowledge many attorneys might envy. They had one daughter, Stella, born 22 August 1898.

by Ruth Demmon

MEEKER, JOSEPHINE
F163

Josephine Meeker was born in Crown Point, Ind. 7 September, 1871, the daughter of Hiram and Mary (Bryan) Meeker. She grew up there and graduated from Crown Point High School in 1889. She was a born teacher, who spent the next 25 years teaching in the local school system until her mother's final illness forced her to retire. After her mother's death in 1914, she assisted her father in the nursery business which she continued after his death issuing a catalogue with many new and unusual varieties of trees, shrubs, and flowers. It was said that the business showed an unusual growth because of her efforts.

She was very active in the First United Methodist Church where she taught Sunday School for over 50 years, and served on the Church Board until she was in her 70's, and was most interested in mission. She was active in the Women's Club, County Historical Society, Daughters of the Union Veterans, but her first love was the Garden Club where one of her last projects was to help organize the May Basket Project for the sick and shutins. Her home at 215 S. Court Street was surrounded by beautiful flower gardens which she tended, sharing her flowers with her friends and neighbors until her last days.

She never married. She was loved by everyone but most of all by her nieces, nephews, and their children. She died surrounded by her family on 2 April, 1958, at the age of 87.

by Ruth Demmon

MEEKER, SHERMAN
F164

Sherman Meeker, oldest son of Joseph L. Meeker and Hannah (Bronson), was born 28 April, 1829, in Wyoming County, Penn. He married Elizabeth Cress 4 Nov., 1849, in Carbondale, Penn. where their first son Nathan was born 4 November, 1850. The land being hilly and rocky, they started West and by 1854 were as far as Illinois. In 1855 they were in Calhoun County, Michigan where children Henrietta was born 10 March, 1854, and son Charles was born 2 November, 1857. About 1859 they headed south to White County, Indiana, and then into adjoining Carroll County, finally settling in 1867 on farm east of Crown Point, Indiana. Here on 11 December, 1868, another son, James Frank, was born. In later life Sherman and his wife left the farm to Nathan and spent their retired years in Crown Point. Mrs. Meeker died 18 May, 1906, and Sherman died 14 February, 1910.

Nathan Meeker, was the oldest son of Sherman and Elizabeth (Cress) Meeker, born in Wyoming County, Penn. 4 November, 1850. He was a well-known and prosperous farmer of Center Township on the old Meeker homestead. He was educated in the public schools, reared to the farm life and remained at home assisting his parents until his marriage. He married Isadora Craft, daughter of Thomas and Lucinda (Forsha) Craft 29 April, 1874, and they began their married life as renters in Kankakee County, Illinois. In 1878 they returned to Center Twp. on the homestead farm of one hundred and sixty acres.

They had two children, Goodman and Maud, both of whom died during their first year. A third son Thomas, born 8 October, 1884, married Edna Smith 29 January, 1907. They had Lola (Charles Aylesworth) and Harold b. 29 Aug., 1914.

by Ruth Demmon

MEYER, JOHN
F165

It seems that in about 1840 there were five Meyer families in the Cedar Lake area: John Henry Meyer Family, Dietrich H. Meyer, Fred Meyer, Henrich (Heinrich) H. Meyer, and John H. Meyer. There is no record of their parents having lived here. They were all cousins and some of them were born in Germany.

I will follow the John Henry Meyer family. John Henry (1805-1893) married Anna Margaret Beckman (1808-1876) and they purchased 341 acres of land on the northwest side of Cedar Lake. They are buried in the cemetery in Meyer Manor. They had four children: Anne Meta (1832-1888), John Henry Jr. (1833-1877), John (1838-1919), and Anna Marie Meyer (1841-1877). They all had big families.

Anne Meta married John Borger and they had 9 children.

John Henry Jr. married Anna Christine Daescher. They had 12 children. He was known as the prairie Meyer as he farmed the flat land just south of Brunswick.

John Meyer married Elizabeth Sophia Plietner. They had 8 children. They stayed on the family land where the Eller-Brady Funeral Home now stands. He was known as the Lake Meyer or Hog Meyer as he lived on the lake and raised a lot of hogs.

Anna Marie Meyer married Antone Carston and they had 4 children.

A man by the name of Nordyke was the first squatter on this land. He sold to a Mr. Schultze who lived there in a log cabin until 1852. John Henry Meyer lived there until his death and his son John Meyer then became owner of the property. His son, Otto Meyer, became the next owner.

In 1922, Otto Meyer sold 30 acres of land on the northwest shore of Cedar Lake to Mr. Samuel Bartlett for the purpose of subdivision for summer homes. This wooded area is known as Meyer Manor. He also sold Mr. Bartlett the wooded area west of the farm house in 1927.

On July 4, 1974, the Cedar Lake Auxiliary of Veterans of Foreign Wars in Cedar Lake dedicated a memorial in the Meyer Manor Cemetery to William Van Gorden, a Revolutionary War soldier, who is thought to be buried there. He came here in 1837. The Lake county land did not come up for sale by the U.S. government until 1839, when the government purchased it from the Pottowattomi Indians.

John Meyer, son of John Henry Meyer, had 8 children that lived to be adults: John Jr. (1866-1942), William (1868-1934), and Lewis (1870-1959) — (these sons, when young, moved

Meeker Reunion 1939. Top: Helen Rosenbaum, Elmer Rosenbaum, Thomas Meeker, Roe Dyer, Addie Meeker, Mr. Bibler, Alta Thompson, Harold Thompson, Stena Thompson, William Heinze. Middle: Herman Rosenbaum, Irl Rockwell, Julius Rockwell, Irene Rockwell, Arlene Thompson. Bottom: Harold Meeker, Ruth Rosenbaum, Ms. Thomas Meeker, Josephine Meeker, Hortense Heinze. Bottom Row: Richard Dyer, —, —, —, —, Sue Heinze. (some family names unavailable).

to Missouri to farm on land their father purchased for them as their inheritance). Otto A. Meyer (1874-1937) married Alma Kuhn of Chicago, they had 2 sons, Herbert and Harold; Elizabeth (1877-1944) married John H. Letz, they had 3 children; Edward (1876-1965) moved to Chicago and worked there, married and had one son; Margaret (1879-1965) married William Steeb and lived in Crown Point, they had 4 children; and Albert (1881-1948).

At the turn of the century (1900) the Meyer children walked a mile and a half to school. They went to a one-room 8-grade school. The mail came by boat. The mail man blew his whistle and one of the family would run down the hill, get in a boat and row out. Visitors that came by train got off at the station on the west side of Cedar Lake and then came by boat to the Meyer home. There was a mud road, but the boat travel was better. My grandfather built a stairs from the top of the hill, where the house was, to the lake. This was a good way to get down to the shore.

by Adah Mueller

MIKELS, MARY VIRGINIA LITTLE
F166

(Descendants)

Mary Virginia (born 9-20-1926) daughter of Earl and Emarine, born in Lake Prairie community and resided in Lake County attended schools and graduated from Lowell High School in 1944. Mary is a registered nurse receiving her degree in 1969.

On 9-28-1945 she married Fletcher Wayne Lain (born 11-19-1922) son of Henry and Elizebeth Lain of North Judson, In. They divorced in Jan. 1955. They had 4 children who attended area schools and graduated from Lowell High School.

William Earl (born 9-11-1847) married Lynda Price (born 11-26-1948) daughter of Roy and Delores Price of Griffith, In. on 2-27-1971. Lynda is a registered nurse receiving her degree from Purdue University. They purchased the farm from his grandfather Earl Little.

Henry Leland (born 7-10-1949) married Nancy Esther Forkner (born 9-5-1952) on 5-25-1974. She is the daughter of Glen and Mary Forkner of Veetersburg, In. Henry served 4 years with the U.S. Navy and is a Vietnam veteran, then attended Ball State University. He is an over the road truck hauler. Nancy holds a Master Degree from Ball State University and teaches in the Tri-Creek School system. They reside in Lowell. They have 2 children Mary Frances (born 4-13-1981) and Jesse Earl (born 4-16-1982).

Martha Alice (born 12-22-1950) resides in Charleston, Il. where she has worked for the Trailmobile Company since 1973. First starting with the Pullman Company in Hammond, In., she was transferred to Chicago and then to Charleston.

Rebecca Joyce (born 8-14-1952) holds a Master Degree from Purdue. She is employed by the Carrol Consolidated school system since 1974 where she is the Library Media Specialist at the high school.

On November 22, 1962 Mary married Harold R. Mikels (born 7-6-1915). He is the oldest of 12 children born to Robert and Avah Mikels of Battle Ground, In. He owned and operated the Hill Top Restaurant and Service Station on US 41 from 1948 to the late 1961. He was one of 6 brothers who served in W.W. II. He retired from Globe Industries Inc. in 1981 and they now reside in New Port Richey, Fl. Harold has 3 sons also graduated from Lowell High School.

Richard Leon (born 10-21-1944) married Janet Marsh (born 9-15-1951) daughter of Forrest and Helen Marsh of Markelville, In. on 8-10-1974. Richard served in the U.S. Navy 4 years and is a 3 year veteran of Vietnam. They both graduated from Ball State University. Rich manages a printing company and they reside in Muncie, In. They have 2 children Eric Richard (born 10-8-1975) and Amanda Christina (born 5-17-1977).

John Robert (born 7-29-1949) married Judy Kay Dile (born 7-29-1949) daughter of Maude File of Shelbyville, In. on 1-6-1968. John served 4 years in the U.S. Air Force, stationed in Minot, N.D. He holds a barber license and is employed with the Lanny Parris Barber Shop in Lowell, In., where they reside. They have one son Ryan Robert (born 8-18-1976).

Pat (born 1-22-1951) served 4 years in the U.S. Navy aboard the USS Long Beach. He was married to Judy Hoover in 1973 and divorced in 1984. On June 29, 1986 he married Rebecca Sue Pierce Bower (born 1-4-1954) of Lafayette, In. He has 3 step-children John (born 3-2-1975), Patricia (born 10-4-1976) and Michael (born 2-6-1981) and 1 son Andrew Stephen (born 12-6-1987). They reside in West Lafayette. Pat is a car painter for Shaver Pontiac in Lafayette, In.

by Mary Mikels

MILLER, MAUREEN FAGEN
F167

Robert and Maureen Miller

On December 5, 1930, Maureen was born. She attended St. John Township School as did her sister Donna and brother Mike. She graduated from Stephen's College in Columbia, Missouri in 1951 and an hour after graduation married Bob Miller, son of Ralph and Mary (Rutledge) Miller of Schererville. They moved into an apartment above the Highland funeral home and lived there ever since, moving three times to larger apartments. Bob worked full time for the EJ&E Railroad and part time for Nick. Bob had death psychosis which he overcame within a year. In 1955, he took a leave from the railroad and attended mortuary school. After being licensed, he went to work full time for Nick. In 1970, Bob and Maureen purchased the Dyer and Highland funeral homes. They bought the Royce Funeral Home in Griffith in 1974 when their son Larry married. He moved in and managed the home until he and his family moved to Highland.

Larry is a funeral director and embalmer. He and his wife Hillary Jane have four children: Kristi, Robert, Richard and Ryan.

Jerry is a paramedic, lives in Highland, and has three children: Marcia, Angela and Thomas. He was coordinator and president of the Fagen-Miller Ambulance Service until 1989 when he became operations manager for Community Ambulance in South Bend.

Terri married Bill Webb from Schererville. Terri is the office manager at Fagen Miller, Inc. Her husband is licensed as a funeral director and a paramedic. Terri was citizen of the year 1987 in Dyer for her volunteer work. They have two children: Jennifer and William Robert and reside in Dyer.

Gary, unmarried, resides in Griffith above the funeral home. He is an EMT and CEO of Fagen-Miller, Inc. Gary was awarded the Indiana Jaycees Ten Outstanding Men of the Year award in 1988 as was his father 24 years before.

Bob died suddenly in 1981. His family continues the family business.

by Maureen Miller

MILLS, ARCHIE
F168

Archie Lou Mills was born 5 November 1895 in Crown Point. He was a descendant of two early Lake County families. His maternal grandfather, Nathan Wilder, was the son of Rueben Wilder who brought his family from Ashtabula County, Ohio to Indiana in 1836. They settled in the present town of Dyer. Archie's fraternal grandfather, John Mills, came to Crown Point in 1862 after serving in the Civil War. John was buried in Maplewood Cemetery in Crown Point.

Archie was the first of four children of George W. Mills and Estelle Mae Wilder Mills. He was followed by one sister, Estelle (Hart) and two brothers, George Jr. and Arnold. The family lived in Crown Point, Hammond and Burnham, Illinois. Their father at one time was a cement contractor in the Burnham area. Archie remembered driving the horse and wagon used to haul material to the construction sites. He attended Hammond High School but left school in 1913 when his father died as a result of injuries suffered in a fall during a fire in a local plant. He later completed his education by correspondence and graduated as an electrician and specialist in electrical maintenance.

His children remember many stories he told of his boyhood in the Calumet Region. He learned to swim in the Grand Calumet River and told of fishing and boating on the river from Burnham to Calumet Avenue in Hammond. He and his sister also had fond memories of riding on a raft on the Kankankee River when they visited their paternal grandmother's family, the Grangers, who lived on the river near Shelby, Indiana.

April 12, 1916 Archie L. Mills married Naomi Anderson at the First Christian Church in Hammond. Three children were born to them, Edna Ruth (Huntington), Richard Clyde and Kenneth A. The family lived in Hammond and the children attended Irving School and Hammond High School.

In 1936, after working for a number of years for the Hammond Electric Company, Archie founded Mills Electric Company. When World War II ended, his son Richard, following his discharge from the U.S. Navy, returned to the company as a partner.

In later years, after the death of his first wife in 1967, Archie married Alfrieda Augustyn, June 28, 1969. They bought a home in Highland. He continued to operate his business and lived an active life until his death, September 9, 1976.

Mills Electric is now owned by Richard C. Mills and his son Richard Jr. They are training a new generation to take over the business as Richard C. Mills III has also joined them.

by Edna R. (Mills) Huntington and
Kenneth A. Mills

MILLS, JOHN
F169

John Mills was born February 6, 1832. He was the youngest of the ten children of John Mills and Elizabeth St. John of Hamburg, N.Y.

He left his family in New York at the age of thirteen and came to Indiana to live with his brother Alfred in Porter County. In the 1850's John moved to Michigan where he met Miss Olive Granger of Mt. Clemens. They were married in Detroit May 17, 1855. They stayed in the area several years.

In 1860 John moved his growing family back to the Calumet Region, and by 1862 they were living in Chicago. September 17, 1864 he enlisted in the Union Army and was assigned to Co. E, 1st Regiment U.S. Vet. Volunteer Engineers as a Private. The company was sent to Chattanooga, Tennessee to work on the fort and strengthen the fortifications. A premature blast injured John Mills causing partial blindness and resulted in his being completely blind in his later years. He was mustered out September 26, 1865 at Nashville, Tennessee.

The family moved to Crown Point, Indiana where the parents were to remain the rest of their lives. Olive Granger Mills died December 28, 1887; she had outlived several of her ten children.

John was married to Mrs. Eveline Sprague Bryant on May 13, 1890. They lived in Crown Point until his death March 21, 1901.

He was buried in Maplewood Cemetery in Crown Point after burial services at the Methodist Church conducted by Rev. T.H. Hall. The John Wheeler Post of the G.A.R. conducted a grave side service.

Three sons survived John Mills. They were Charles of Sandwich, Illinois, Earl of Poinette, Wisconsin, and George of Hammond. There are many descendants still living in Lake County.

by Edna Huntington

MINER, HAROLD E. "DOC"
F170

Harold E. "Doc" Miner was born at Nelson, Nebraska, October 25th, 1889, the son of Daniel and Eva Ackerman Miner. The family moved to Peoria, Illinois, during the late nineties, where father Daniel Miner died in 1898, leaving his young family, consisting of wife Eva, son Harold and daughter Maude, practically penniless. Following her husband's death, Eva Miner moved with her two children to a cottage in her girlhood hometown of Kirkwood, Illinois, where she was able to secure employment to support her family. However, before Harold could finish the common school, his mother's health declined to where she was compelled to cease working; thus causing Harold to leave school before reaching the age of fourteen years. It was at this time that he was able to secure employment as a helper to the local CB&Q Railway station agent and found an opportunity to begin the study of telegraphy.

Deprived of further formal schooling, Miner devoted all possible time to research and study; soon becoming well-versed in electricity, chemistry, and kindred subjects. It was also noteworthy that like Abe Lincoln in his diligent research after knowledge, he acquired a versatile vocabulary, together with an expertness in spelling that would have been highly creditable to a college-trained person. He also became so authoritative in his study of chemistry, that while yet in his early thirties, he was employed for two years as an instructor in Chemistry at the Palmer College of Davenport. While teaching Chemistry at Palmer College, Miner availed himself of the opportunity to take up the study of Chiropractic. Upon completing the course in Chiropractic, he was united in marriage, June 28, 1921, to Miss Stella Elizabeth Breyfogle of Crown Point, Indiana, who had also just graduated from Palmer School. Whereupon the newly wed Doctors of Chiropractic decided to make their home in Hammond, Indiana where they opened offices in the Rugg Building. Stella soon found it necessary to devote her time and attention to her home, while husband "Doc" continued practice. They had two children during this time; (John (Jack) and daughter Lois May.

Later in life, Miner joined his son John Holton (Jack) Miner in the establishment of an electronics firm in Hammond, the Miner Electronics, Inc. with offices, laboratory and warehouse situated at 7331 Calumet Avenue; and secured from the Motorola Corporation a franchise for the installation, maintenance and servicing of their public address and communication systems, now in operation in the major industrial plants, refineries, businesses, police, fire and numerous other business has grown and developed into a sizeable and highly important as well as lucrative business. The business is now under the direction and control of son Jack, who is a graduate of Purdue University in electrical engineering; and resides with his wife Helen Kuhn Miner, at 238 Belmont Avenue, Munster; together with their four children, Janice, Jeffrey, Joel, and John.

Mrs. Stella Breyfogle Miner continues to reside in the family home at 8254 Northcote Avenue, Munster; while daughter, Mrs. Lois Mary Scroggs, a graduate of Indiana University in business administration; resides with her husband Leroy Russell Scroggs, at Lake Mohawk, Sparta, New Jersey; together with their three children, Carol, Kenton, and Claudia. Mr. Scroggs is an airline captain with United Airlines.

by Ralph Miller Dunn

MINNINGER, CECIL AND MARY
F171

Cecil (Dolly) Minninger and Mary (Born) Minninger. Gerald Born in background.

Cecil Earl Minninger, or "Dolly" as he was commonly called, was born in 1898 near Lowell, Indiana, the son of Michael and Annie S. (Templeton) Minninger. He was educated in the schools of Lowell. He met his future wife on a double date, with Gay Nichols, who would later become his sister-in-law, when she married John Born. Mary Born was dating Ernest Bahr, whose brother would much later become her second husband, and she would become "Dolly's" wife.

Dolly and Mary Martha Born, the daughter of Roscoe Conklin and Ella Almeda (Stowell) Born, were married in Lake County, May 15, 1926, and started their married life at Schneider, Indiana. Here "Dolly" built a house on the northwest edge of town where there was plenty of room for him to have his "coon" dogs, as hunting was his passion in life. Mary soon was installed in the Schneider Post Office as postmistress, a position she would hold for the next 30 years.

127

In the late 30s Dolly and Mary purchased the then IGA store, which had formerly been owned by a man and wife named Bruckman. Here they would run a general store that would be a landmark in the community for many years, with the post office occupying a corner of the store. Previously, it had been located about a block north of the general store.

Tragedy struck in 1947 when "Dolly," who was a member of the volunteer fire department, was called to a fire. The car in which they were driving was hit by a fast moving locomotive and he was killed, thus ending his carefree days hunting and fishing along the Kankakee River.

Her brother, John Born, answered her call to manage the store soon after Dolly's death and for the next ten years he managed and eventually owned a portion of the store. She continued working in the post office. When John sold his part of the business, she continued to own the building, but only work in the post office. When the business came back to her, she had married by then married Neil Bahr, who had been recently widowed. He had two daughters, Norma and Carol. They continued to operate the store, changing it to a Royal Blue Store until health caused them to retire. Neil died in 1975 and she died in 1976.

Mary Minninger's grandparents were Emanual and Phoebe (Gordon) Born and Myron and Lestina (Sutzer) Stowell. Emanuel Born has been treated elsewhere in this work. Phoebe Gordon was born May 23, 1849 in Ohio, the daughter of Oliver P. Gordon and Catherine Beam. Catherine Beam or Boehme was born about 1815 in Maryland, the daughter of John and Nancy (Zimmerman) Beam. John Beam was born December 28, 1783 in Germany and settled for a time in Maryland. He was a miller by trade, the profession of his forefathers in Germany. His death occurred at Flowerfield, Michigan on June 14, 1853 and he is buried in the Flowerfield Cemetery, St. Joseph County, Michigan.

Family tradition states that the Boehme family descended from Jacob Boehme through his son, Tobias. Jacob Boehme was a simple shoemaker before he underwent an enlightening experience which caused him to ponder the creation of the universe. He was born at Altseidenberg, in Upper Lusatia, a hamlet among the hills, some 10 miles southeast of Gorlitz. His father was a well-to-do peasant, and his first employment was that of herd boy on the Landskrone, the only education he received was at the town-school of Seidenberg, a mile from his home. In his 14th year he was apprenticed to a shoemaker, being judged not robust enough for husbandry (1589). By 1599 we find him settled at Gorlitz and married to Katharina, daughter of Hans Kuntzschmann, a thriving butcher in the town. Boehme's authorship began in his 37th year (1612) with a treatise, *Aurora, oder die Morgenrote im Aufgang*.

This work was widely circulated and he became well known as a German mystic in England under the name Behmen. George Fox and the Quakers absorbed much of his philosophy into their religion. In Sweden, a man by the name of Swedenborg incorporated Boehme's ideas into his new religion. He was widely quoted. Boehme claimed a direct illumination and for that reason had difficulty with the church. His writings have traces of Paracelsus (1493-1541) and Kaspar Schwenkfeld (1490-1561) the first Protestant mystic. He died in 1624 after writing some seventeen volumes which were published under the title, *Der Weg zu Christo*, on New Year's Day 1624.

On the maternal side of her family the Stowell family is traced elsewhere in this work. Her mother's mother was Lestina Melvira Sutzer, who was born November 22, 1850 at Patch's Grove, Grant County, Wisconsin to Philip and Catherine (Cox) Sutzer. Philip was the son of Henry and Susan Sutzer, natives of Virginia, who settled in Ohio before coming to Wisconsin. Lestina Sutzer married Myron H. Stowell on February 28, 1866 at Defiance County, Ohio and they had seven children, Emma, who married Wm. Frederick Kimball, Anna C., who died in 1869 at Rolling Prairie, LaPorte County, Indiana, Loren Lorenzo, who married Martha and moved to Washington state, Ella Almeda who married Roscoe Conklin Born on January 1, 1901 in Lake County, Indiana, Etta, who married Edwin L. Sanders and Warren DeWain, who married Celena LeBlanch Cabana and moved to Washington. Delila died in 1878.

by Gerald M. Born

MOORE, ANDREW
F172

Andrew A. Moore who came to West Creek Township with his family in 1837. Photo taken about 1862.

The Rest of the Story

My grandmother Daisy (Moore) Thomas, who was born in Lowell, Indiana, September 23, 1872, was proud of her family heritage. Therefore, as a child, the names of her parents and grandparents became familiar to me. I remember she said that her grandfather Andrew Moore had seventeen children and outlived four wives. In recent years I became interested in genealogy, especially as it pertained to family history and personal stories, and I learned "the rest of the story".

Her grandfather Andrew A. Moore was one of the early day pioneers in southern Lake County, arriving in West Creek Township in 1837. It is likely that he came with his family by horse-drawn wagon and that his sister Anna and her husband Derastus Torrey traveled with them. They helped organize the M.E. church there in the summer of 1838. Andrew was the first Justice of the Peace in West Creek Township, and his brother-in-law was one of the first county commissioners, Torrey Bridge (over West Creek?) was no doubt named for the Torrey family.

Andrew was the son of Andrew and Hannah (Cole) Moore. He was born in the autumn of 1806 in Windsor, Broome County, New York. His maternal grandfather was Nathaniel Cole, a Revolutionary War patriot for whom a large, present day park in Broome County, N.Y. was named. Andrew married Aurena Hine, daughter of Ambrose and Sally (Judson) Hine, in Broome County about 1825 and the following children were born there: Andrew Franklin Moore, who was born about 1826; Ambrose H. Moore, born 11 Mar 1829; Daisy's father, James Nathaniel Moore, born 23 May 1831; and Derastus Torrey Moore, born about 1834. On the way west, their fifth son, William R. Moore, was born in Adrian, Michigan, 13 May 1836. Their only daughter, Mariah, was born in Lake County about 1838. She married John P. Meader in Kankakee County, Illinois in 1856 and moved to St. George, Kansas. Her brother Ambrose and the Torrey family moved to Kansas at about the same time.

Although Andrew owned 160 acres in West Creek Township, for a number of years he and his family lived a few miles west in Sherburnville, Illinois. Their sixth and last son, Isaac W. Moore, was born there about 1843. Aurena died sometime between Isaac's birth and Andrew's marriage in Lake County in 1845 to Mrs. Jane Brown, a widow. Martha Jane Brown was Jane's daughter by her previous marriage. Andrew and Jane's first-born was Lewis Albert Moore. They also had three daughters: Melissa, who died at age 36, having never married; Ellen, who married Isaac Rhodes; and Clara, who married Elsworth Fry.

The Civil War years were tragic times for the Moore family. All of Andrew's seven sons volunteered for service for the Union. Subsequently, three died, and the four who survived suffered

Andrew's son, James N. Moore. Photo taken about 1890.

life-long disabilities. First, Isaac died in battle at Gallatin, Tennessee, at age twenty, in December 1862. Then Derastus, known as "Torrey", died in a hospital in Nashville, December 1863, two months after having his right elbow and left ankle broken by enemy fire at the battle of Chicamauga. Later, his leg was amputated. Torrey left a widow named Ruby (Strickland) and three children in Stegar, Will County, Illinois; Alfred, born in 1856; Ida Ellen, who died young; and Irena Jane (known as 'Jennie'), born in 1858. Jennie married Avery Rumsey in Lowell in 1875 at the Church of the Red Cedars. Torrey's widow Ruby married George Lokie in Kankakee County, Illinois in 1869. And lastly, Andrew and Jane's son Albert was only eighteen when he died in a hospital at Kendalville in April 1864. Isaac and Albert, as well as James, have their names engraved on the Three Creeks Monument in Lowell. Torrey and William served with Co. H 100th Illinois Volunteers.

Andrew, the oldest son, was known as Frank. He married Emily Hine in Will County, Illinois in 1848. During his term of service in Co. F 64th Illinois Volunteers, he was sick in a hospital at Paducah, Kentucky for about six months in 1862, then for about four months in Decatur, Alabama in the summer of 1864. When he was mustered out after the war, his pay was docked for "losing two shelter tents and one haversack on the march from Atlanta to Savannah, Georgia." His health was "frail" as a result of bowel disease which he became heir to during the war. His son Orlando F. Moore also served.

William married Sarah R. Hamilton in Kankakee County, Illinois in 1859. In the battle at Stone River, Tennessee, he was wounded directly over his heart by a musketball, causing permanent damage to his heart and lungs. In his pension papers he stated, "It is impossible for me to do any kind of work that jars me, such as riding horseback, chopping wood, and plowing is very hard on me . . . also pitching hay or handling sacks of grain."

After the war, William and Frank became partners in a sawmill at Argos, Marshall County, Indiana, but the work was too strenuous for them. William returned to farming. He lived in Argos until his death in 1893. Frank went west to Coos Bay, Oregon, a few year after the war and he died there in 1881. His brother Ambrose was living there with his family. Ambrose had married Sarah Ann Pattee in Kansas in 1861, and he and Sarah operated the Arago Hotel in Empire City for many years. Ambrose was listed as a school teacher and suffered from paralysis in the 1880 Coos County, Oregon census. He was also a Justice of the Peace. His Civil War record is unknown. He died in Oakland, California in 1892, and he was buried beside Frank in Coos Bay. Frank's headstone says, "Rest, Comrade."

James married Mary Ault in Crown Point in April 1856. He enlisted in the 12th Indiana Cavalry, Co. G. In the thick of battle in the South, he was disemboweled by a mini-ball. He cleaned his wound in a nearby stream and bound it, and therefore survived. Nearby lay a young Southern boy who was wounded in much the same way. Even though the boy was an "enemy", James saved the life of Jesse Vick. They became friends and corresponded for a great many years. James got "state's malaria" in the south and was affected by it for the balance of his life. He out-lived all his brothers, dying in Lowell of pneumonia in 1913.

According to an 1883 historical sketch, Andrew Moore sold his property in Sherburnville in 1865 and moved to Lowell where he "engaged in mercantile life until 1872 when he retired". His second wife, Jane, died in 1870, and is buried in the Lowell cemetery. Then he married his third wife, Mary Tilton, in Lowell. Nothing is known about her but it is assumed she died prior to 1875 when he married Eliza Cleaver. Eliza was the widow of Worcester "Wooster" Cleaver, a pioneer of Sherburnville, and when she died in 1897 in Lowell at age 71, she was buried in the Sherburnville cemetery beside her first husband. She and Wooster had five children: Sarah Ann, Caroline, Rebecca, Jasper, and Morris Cleaver. Although all were grown when Eliza and Andrew were married, Eliza's children, as well as Martha Jane Brown, were apparently counted as part of Andrew's "seventeen children", which accounts for all seventeen. And, contrary to family tradition, Eliza, his fourth wife, out-lived him.

Andrew lived in Lowell until his death September 22, 1888. According to his obituary from the Argos Reflector where his son William and daughter Ellen were living, "he had sickened suddenly, sank rapidly, and died full of years, having almost reached his 82nd birthday". He was buried in West Creek cemetery but the headstone is no longer there.

by Dorothy Schroeder

MOORE, JAMES N.
F173

The Moores of Lowell were Pioneers

James N. Moore was born in Binghamton, New York, May 23, 1831, the third son of Andrew and Aurena (Hine) Moore. He came west to West Creek Township, Lake County, Indiana with his parents and brothers in 1837 when he was six years old. He grew up to be one of Lowell's leading contractors and builders, and he laid out an addition to Lowell. It is very probable that some of the buildings he built in Lowell and southern Lake County are still standing. Beginning in the late 1860's he had a contract with the Union Pacific railroad to build depots along the first transcontinental railroad line. Upon his return from the Western frontier, he related that he and his crew had one memorable skirmish with unfriendly Indians, and also he was bitten once by a rattle snake.

James married Mary Ault, an auburn haired beauty, in Crown Point on April 20, 1856. The writer of this family history has the old daguerreotype which was taken on their wedding day. The photo is enclosed in a framed folder which has mother-of-pearl insets on the cover and red velvet on the inside. Mary, who was born November 11, 1833 in Brookston, White

Daisy Moore at the organ. Taken about 1888

Herbert Thomas and Daisy Moore. Photo taken 1893

Mary (Ault) and James N. Moore's wedding picture, April 20, 1856

129

Lorus Thomas as she looked when she graduated from Everett High School in 1915

County, Indiana, was the daughter of Andrew Ault and Keziah Jane Moore (no relation to Mary's husband James). Keziah was the daughter of Mary Campbell and James H. Moore who were married in Lexington, Kentucky in 1810. Andrew Ault was the son of Michael and Hannah (—?) Ault. Michael, his son Andrew, and their families were pioneers in Porter County, Indiana about 1835 where Andrew opened the first general store in Washington Township in 1836.

In 1843 tragedy struck the Ault family in the form of cholera. Mary lost her mother, newborn twin sisters, her sister Elizabeth, and Amizi Moore (Keziah's sister?) within a three month period. She had previously lost her only other sister, Hannah. After the tragedy, the family moved to Lowell. In 1846 Mary's father, Andrew Ault married Mary Jane Bradshaw. Keziah Jane Ault, who was born September 29, 1847, was undoubtedly their daughter. It is not known what became of Andrew's second wife or their daughter, but Andrew died in 1848, leaving Mary and her brothers, John and Isaac, orphans. The children rented an apartment above Halsted's store "after which the duties and responsibility of a housekeeper and mother was assumed by the little sister", according to family notes. Although Mary was only fourteen, she was an expert seamstress, and she maintained that she supported herself and her brothers with her sewing.

Mary's brother John Ault married Loretta Thorn in 1855. As soon as her brother Isaac returned from serving in the Civil War, he married his cousin Nancy Ann Moore, daughter of William C. and Elizabeth (Cleavinger) Moore. Both brothers lived in other areas while their families were growing up, but they returned to the Lowell area, as did most of their children. Some of their descendants are probably still living in southern Lake County.

After James and Mary were married, they lived on their farm about four miles west of Lowell where their first-born daughter was born. She lived less than a year, and their second daughter Amy was born in 1858. Amy went up to Crown Point with her parents when James enlisted to serve the Union in 1863. (See related story: "Andrew Moore — the rest of the story") Then he moved his family into the town of Lowell. At that time there were only eleven (according to Amy's obituary) houses and a grist mill there. After the war, their son Bertie was born in 1867, and he died of pneumonia a few months later. The twins, Edwin and Edson, were born in 1869. And lastly, their daughter Daisy was born in 1872.

Amy married Marcellus Smith in 1879, and she died in 1955 at age 96½ years, after living on Fuller's Island for a great many years. Edwin married Emma Mudge about 1888; and Edson married Grace Ebert about 1893. Edson and Grace were the parents of Carl Moore who, with his wife Metha, were long time residents of Cedar Lake. Carl died in 1966. Much of this Moore family history would have been lost forever except for his interest in his heritage and his willingness to share the information.

James and Mary's daughter Daisy was a photographer's model when she was in her teens. She met Herbert Thomas of Battleground, Indiana, while they were both attending college in Whitewater, Wisconsin; she was studying music, and he was studying to be a telegrapher. He was the son of Rachel Barcus and John Marion Thomas. Daisy and Bert were married in Lowell in 1893. Their first two daughters were born in a log cabin near Battleground in Tippecanoe County — Vernal and Lorus — and Mildred was born in Lafayette.

In 1898, James N. Moore accompanied his daughter Daisy and her three children on the train west to a small town named Machias in Snohomish County, Washington State, where Bert was already employed as the depot agent. First, James added several rooms on to their very small house, then he returned to Indiana. After that, James and Mary traveled to Machias by train almost every summer for a few years; they said the Indiana summers were too hot for them. James built a house each summer to help pay for the trip and their "vacation" while Mary helped Daisy with the children. Some of the houses he built around the turn of the century are still being used as residences.

After a few years went by, James' health became frail and they no longer made the trip west. James died in Shelby of pneumonia in 1913. At the time of his death, he was the only charter member of the Masonic Lodge of Lowell, and he had been the Master Mason for a longer time than anyone else. Mary died at the home of her son Edson in Hammond in 1921.

When their daughter Daisy first came to Machias in 1898 with her three daughters, she soon learned that she was a pioneer to a new frontier. Machias was a tough little town that had seven saloons and a dance hall — and no church. Consequently, she became the leader in bringing respectability to the community. She started a temperance union, and she was instrumental in the building of the first church. She was not only one of its charter members but she played the organ there for a great many years.

Daisy and Bert's family grew until they had twelve children — ten daughters and two sons. She often left her oldest daughters in charge of the younger children while she became a widely known and much respected mid-wife. She always claimed that she had brought the late Senator Henry "Scoop" Jackson (of Everett) into the world. Bert was killed in an accident in 1922 when he fell from a roof of the Big Four Inn while removing the snow.

One of the biggest events in the community's history took place one day in the summer of 1927. Just as family, friends and neighbors did in the pioneer days of Indiana, they all assembled on a wooded hill which overlooked the valley to build a log house for Daisy. The men cut trees and dragged them into place, put up the roof and framed in the windows — all in one day — while the women prepared a feast for the crowd. Daisy loved her new home and lived in it until she was about seventy years old, until she could no longer walk back up the hill after walking to the store at Machias.

The log house in the woods not only became a landmark in the valley but some of Daisy's grandchildren's happiest memories go back to their Hoosier grandmother's home, including the writer of this family history who can still picture her there as she played the organ while she sang "Whispering Hope". She was dearly loved and very much respected by all who knew her. She died in Snohomish in 1957. (Author's note: The writer of this story is the daughter of Daisy's daughter Lorus who married Edward M. Gemmer in 1920. Lorus is now 94 years old and lives near her daughter Dorothy in Quincy, Washington. Dorothy is a member of the Northwest Indiana Genealogical Society.)

by Dorothy Schroeder

MORSE, ROBERT
F174

Born October 5, 1874 in Blythe, England

At the age of seven, his mother Sarah Jane Perry Morse brought Robert, his brother, Harry, and sister Sarah Jane to America, after her minister husband died. By age 14, Robert was at work in the coal mines in Carbon Hill, Illinois. In his later years, he met a school teacher, Estella Emily, who taught all grades in a one room school house. They married May 1, 1901. In 1908, Robert came to Gary, Indiana to work at the American Bridge Company and find a home for his family. In 1909, Estella and Robert brought their four children to their new home at 15th and Grant Street. Their four children were Mildred, Robert, Beatrice, and Winifred. The area was sparsely populated and sandy, but soon grew in population. Robert Morse worked over 40 years at the American Bridge Company and they lived in the same house until their deaths in 1958. Five more children had been born to them from 1910 to 1923: Dorothy, Kenneth, Marjorie, Florence and Jeanne.

All the families stayed in Gary and watched its growth, and were downtown for the 50th celebrations. Summer days were spent at Lake Michigan. First by the lake near the Bridge Company and later at Marquette Beach. The fishing shacks were still there until a few years ago.

Six of the children attended and graduated from Froebel school. The last three attended and graduated from Tolleston school and Marjorie and Florence were charter graduates in 1937. The young people went to dances at Miller's "Gay Mill", the "Miramar" across from Froebel school, the McHallon on 5th Avenue, the Polis Hall in Tolleston, or the many church halls in the city.

Gary had ethnic neighborhoods – distinct ones. Serbians at the Southeast, Irish the East, Slovakian nationalities the West and the elite had the North. The Greeks were around 13th Avenue East and West of Broadway, There were many family run food stores, candy stores, drug stores, hardware stores, etc., no major chains, not until later years. Old street cars took you to town, which was Broadway. You walked anywhere else. So few could afford cars until later years. So many landmarks of the early 1900's are gone, any that are left are in disrepair! But memories are not tarnished.

Mildred's husband Kenneth Kniesley worked for the City of Gary. Robert L. Morse worked at U.S. Steel. Beatrice's husband Hurshel Sullivan worked on the E.J.&E. Rail Road. Winifred's husband Nick Jankovich established Gary's Airport (61st & Broadway). Dorothy's husband Fred Millard worked for Railway Exp. in Gary. Kenneth Morse worked at Inland Steel in Indiana Harbor. Marjorie's husband Russell Clements worked in many Gary markets as a butcher. Florence's husband Joseph Schuman worked at U.S. Steel. Jeanne's husband Basil Vargas was a truck driver.

by Florence Schuman

MOSNY, GEORGE
F175

George and Viola Mosny at their 50th wedding anniversary celebration, Oct. 27, 1973.

The name Mosny appeared in Indiana Harbor, IN in 1902 when the family moved from Illinois where they lived in Lemont and the Irondale section of Chicago on Torrence Ave. They moved into the area of the 3400 block of Guthrie St. and occupied several buildings in that neighborhood. George Mosny, Sr. had come from Czechoslovakia in 1890 – at that time it was considered Hungary – followed by his wife, Mary, in 1892. There were five boys in the family. In chronological order they were George, John, Joseph, Michael and Paul. Before coming to Indiana, George, Sr. sold religious books and after coming to Indiana Harbor, he opened a saloon.

All the boys attended the East Chicago public schools. Joseph was the only one who went to college and became a well-known lawyer in East Chicago. Three of the Mosny boys served their country in W.W. I and were fortunate to return home well and healthy. George served with the U.S. Air Force Signal Corps, 28th Aero Squadron. John served with the 168th Aero Squadron. Joseph was in the R.O.T.C. at Indiana University, then served in the regular army for only about three months before the war was over.

After the service years, George ran a bicycle shop in partnership with his brother John and a man by the name of William Moore. George kept his interest in airplanes strong by having one of his own which he delighted in flying around the lake front area and over into Illinois. He often gave airplane rides to anyone brave enough to fly at that time.

In 1923 George married Viola R. Ehrhardt of Forest Park, IL. He met her when he roomed in Forest Park for a time with a friend of Viola's family. Viola wanted to learn to drive a car, and her parents asked the young man to teacher her. Not only did Viola learn to drive, but this turned into a courtship and led to marriage. They moved into an apartment over the insurance office of the Riley-Westberg building on Main Street where George managed the insurance department for Riley-Westberg. In 1926, George, Viola and year old Margaret moved into a home on Hemlock St. near Washington High School where, at this writing, Viola still lives.

During the depression in 1931, George left the Riley organization and began his own insurance and real estate business, Insurance On A Higher Plane. About this time a second daughter, Shirley, was born. For a while the business was operated from the Hemlock St. office in his home with Viola doing the office work. Eventually, there was an office on Main St. and finally, for most of the years of the business, George operated from 3476 and 3478 Guthrie St. Both these buildings had belonged to the Mosny family. George retired in 1965 and sold the business to Manta and Hurst.

George was proud of his country, belonged to the American Legion, VFW, and was secretary of Draft Board #6 during W.W. II. He belonged to several civic organizations, the Masonic Lodge and the First Methodist Church. He passed away in March of 1984 at the age of 89.

Joseph Mosny married a young school teacher by the name of Geraldine Coonrod from Forest, IN. Joseph, as mentioned above, was a lawyer and had an office on Main St. in the First National Bank of East Chicago building. The Joseph Mosnys were active in the American Legion also. This branch of the family had two daughters, who, early in their adult lives moved out of the state. Joline, the oldest, moved to Florida. Betty, a violinist, lived in several different states, playing with several symphony orchestras. She now lives in Texas where she has been associated with the Houston Symphony. Joseph died in 1949.

John Mosny went to work at Inland Steel after the bicycle shop years with his brother. He married Lillian Marciniak, a local Indiana Harbor girl, and they lived for a time on Deodar St. and a much longer time on Columbus Dr. There was one son, John Dennis, known as Dennis to avoid confusion of two Johns in the family. Dennis lives in Highland, and he and his wife, Irene Hlad, had four children, two boys and two girls. All of the children are married, and as this history is partly to trace a family name, it should be mentioned that there is only one male Mosny so far in the younger generation. So far this youngster lives in Lake County. John passed away in 1968.

Paul Mosny was a man of variety – at least in his working life. He held jobs as a mailman, milkman, did decorating and remodeling – at which he was very good – and eventually worked at Standard Forge. He married a Whiting girl, Genevieve Prus. They had two daughters, Eleanor and Lorraine. Paul passed away in 1964 and Genevieve passed away in 1974. Eleanor lives out of state, and Lorraine passed away in 1974, the same year as her mother.

Michael Jay Mosney (note change of spelling – his choice) worked around the Indiana Harbor area at a variety of jobs, married a local girl, had one son, William. After the marriage dissolved, Michael left for the west coast where he worked from California to Alaska. He finally settled in Seattle where he now resides with his wife, Josephine. He is the only living senior Mosny of the Indiana Harbor Mosnys. His son, Bill, lives in the east and has only been a resident of Lake County for a short time as a youngster and during his high school years.

There was one daughter born to the first George Mosny during a second marriage after his first wife passed away in 1906. The daughter, Anne, has lived most of her life in Lake County with the exception of about 20 years in Chicago.

Margaret and Shirley, daughters of George, Jr. both married. Margaret to Milford Christenson of Griffith where they live now. Shirley married William Ashby of Hammond, deceased as of January, 1988. Shirley lives in Ohio where she and Bill spent most of their married life.

This is the story of the Mosny family of Lake County, IN. There are other Mosnys scattered around the country, but it has been difficult to find a close relationship with any of them.

by Margaret M. Christenson

MUELLER, MELVIN W.
F176

The Melvin W. Mueller family was formed when Adah H. Letz and Melvin W. Mueller were married on August 25, 1940 at Trinity Lutheran Church in Crown Point.

Adah, a daughter of John H. Letz and Elizabeth nee Meyer, was born and raised in Crown Point. Melvin was born and raised in LaPorte, son of John Mueller and Laura, nee Tanger, in LaPorte. Melvin's father worked for Allis Chalmers for many years. Adah's father was president of Letz Manufacturing Company for a long time.

Mel met Adah at a church youth meeting. He moved to Crown Point shortly before they were married and worked at Letz until it closed in 1965. They have a big family.

The oldest Ann is married to Jim Semsar and they have 3 children. They live in Baraboo, Wisconsin where she teaches school and Jim is a photographer.

Beth is married to Kirk Horn. They have one daughter and live in Missoula, Montana. Beth is director, Information Office of U.S.D.A. – Forest Service, Northern Region. Kirk also works for the U.S.D.A. as director of Game and Wild Life for North West region of U.S.

131

Melvin J. works for the E.J.&E. Railroad and has ever since he returned from serving in the army stationed in Korea. He has 2 children.

Elaine, wife of John Green, lives in Colorado Springs. She is cook book editor of the Cook Books Current, Inc. Publishers. Her husband, John, works for Hewitt Packard. She has one daughter.

Annette and her husband Greg Hales live in Burke, Virginia. Both of them work for the government. Annette in the State Department and Greg in the Communication Department. They have 2 children.

Marilou and her husband, Mitre Jovanoski, live in Crown Point. She is manager of the mini branch of First Bank in Crown Point. He works in the mills. They have 2 children.

Ruth and her husband, Dan Aubuchon live in Demotte. Ruth works in the Demotte State Bank and Dan works in the mills.

Our eighth child, Richard lives in Crown Point with his wife Kathy. He works at Inland Steel. They have 2 children.

Adah is active in several church groups at Trinity Lutheran Church.

Mel is also active in church and has become very interested in the Lake County Antique Agricultural Society. He has obtained a Letz feed mill built in 1917. It is in running order and he goes to the farm and steam shows and grinds corn for the people attending the shows.

Life has been interesting. Each child has his own personality.

Holidays are wonderful. We always have at least eighteen for dinner. The hostess makes the meat, potatoes and rolls and the rest of the meal is brought in by the rest of the family. We have many beautiful memories of these gatherings.

by Mrs. Adah Mueller

MUNDELL, ELMORE HARTE
F177

He was born 12/20/1830 in Harrison Co., VA, the son of Joseph and Amanda Melvina Sigler Mundell. At the age of 4, he came to Hobart with his parents and grandparent Samuel Sigler in a covered wagon. They settled on the west side of present Hobart where they lived until his death. During the Civil War, he and two brothers, Alonzo and William, enlisted in the Union Army of the Cumberland with General Grant. A fourth brother, James, had a foot deformity and was left home to take care of his parents. Will was killed at Murfreesboro, TE, and Alonzo was shell shocked at Missionary Ridge, while Elmore was invalided out with malaria which left him in poor health the rest of his life. He was a literate man and read a newspaper every day of his life. While fishing with his daughter Alice beside a bridge one day, an old dilapidated buggy and broken down horse appeared. "Oh, look at the poor old man!"' his daughter said. "Poor old man, hell" he said, "that's old Jules Demmon and he could buy and sell me a dozen times!". Naturally, she later married Julius's grandson. Married twice, he had children Charles and Sarah Ann by his first wife and Jane, Alice, Mae, and Elmore Harte by his second wife. On 5/11/1907 he passed away and is buried with his wife in Old Hobart Cemetery. His obituary concluded, "Thus one more reveille has sounded, the lights are out, and one more noble soldier has answered the bugle call and awaits the coming of his remaining comrades, where they will enjoy the reunion around one great campfire in the presence of the 'Great Commander'."

by Ruth Demmon

NASOLOSKI, ANTHONY AND THERESA
F178

1st Row: Josephine Centanni, Theresa Centanni Nasoloski, Lillian Schulties and baby Charlotte. 2nd Row: Anne Centanni and Louise Ledak.

Theresa Marietta Centanni was the seventh child of Samuel and Josephine Centanni. She was born on August 2, 1924, in Gary, Indiana, and graduated from Froebel High School. She married Anthony Walter Nasoloski (b. 4-27-21) of Gary, on October 1, 1949, in Gary, Indiana. Theresa has been a dedicated supporter of St. Joseph the Worker Church in Gary for 25 years. She also has been active and held various offices in the American Legion Auxiliary Post #214 for the past 19 years.

Anthony Nasoloski was a 1939 graduate of Lew Wallace High School. He spent four years in the U.S. Navy Seabees as a Second Class Petty Officer serving in the Aleutian Islands and South Pacific. He is an active member of both the American Legion and the Holy Name Mens' Organization at St. Joseph's Church.

The Nasoloskis had three children, all born in Gary: Gloria Ann, born February 27, 1952; Toni Marie, born January 13, 1954; and Anthony Walter Nasoloski Jr., born February 20, 1958. All these children graduated from Lew Wallace High School.

Gloria Ann married John Smederovac (b. 11-23-47 in Gary) on May 11, 1974, in Gary, Indiana. John was a Hospital Corpsman in the U.S. Navy. They have one daughter, Kathleen Marie, born May 11, 1979. Gloria attended Indiana University in Glen Park for two years.

Toni Marie has been employed at the Lake County Mental Health Center. Anthony received an A.A. degree from Rangely College and is now employed by U.S. Steel.

by Joanne C. Clark

NEUDORF FAMILY
F179

Nicholas and Catherine (Contz/Kunz) Neudorf sailed to America from their German home in the early 1840's, when they were both in their thirties. (The meaning of the German name "Neudorf" in English is new town or burg.) The Neudorfs traveled westward, and eventually came to Lake County, Indiana, settling on land located on the Jackson Highway (Cline Avenue) in St. John Township, August 4, 1845. (A stone marker indicates the location of the home and the adjoining land.)

Nicholas and Catherine had one child when they immigrated to America, a son, Nicholas (Jr?) (1836-1912) (Mary Ann Backes). Their second child, a daughter, Catherine (1842-1916) (William Wirtz Jr.), was born in Illinois, before they located in Indiana. Two more children were born after they arrived in Lake County: Peter in 1846; and Margaret in 1850.

The Neudorfs cleared their unimproved land and made it suitable for farming. (The field south of the homestead marks one of the highest points of elevation in Lake County.) They raised general crops annually, and had a sizable herd of dairy cattle, the milk of which was shipped off daily by truck or rail to Chicago, Illinois. There was also a fine orchard south of the house consisting of various fruit trees, and a grape arbor on the north side where the garden and peonies were.

The two Neudorf sons learned farming at an early age while working the fields with their father. In later years Nichcolas (Jr?) reared his large family on the Neudorf homestead. He married Mary Ann Backes on January 31, 1861. She was born the first of January, 1841, a daughter of Mathias Backes and Catherine (Seberger) Backes, also homesteading farmers of Lake County.

Nicholas (Jr?) and Mary Ann were to have twelve children, seven of which lived to adulthood: Nicholas (III?) (1861-1933) (Anna Lasser); Katherine (1863-1917) (Joseph Sutter); Mathias (1864-1956) (Coelistia Keilman) (Mary Loyce); Peter (1866-1945) (Anna Marie Doffin); William (1869-1945); Mary (1871-1929); and Andrew (1873-1963).

Three of Nicholas (Jr?)'s sons, Peter, William and Andrew, became farmers and spent their entire lives working the soil of the family farm. Mathias was a cement mason and also operated a coal yard in Merrillville, Indiana, while Nicholas (III?) located in Illinois. Katherine and her husband settled on a nearby farm, and Mary stayed at home and helped with the domestic chores for her brothers there.

Through the years as the family grew, the Neudorf farm became the site of an annual "Neudorf-Backes" reunion. It was held in August, and was a much anticipated event of both young and old, from the 1930's until the middle 1960's, when the last patriarch, Andrew, died at the age of 90. Soon afterwards, the homestead was sold. The home and barns were abandoned and destroyed in the following decades, and all that now remains of the Nicholas and Catherine Neudorf farm, and their family's lengthy existence on the land they so proudly claimed nearly a century and a half ago, is the stone marker, covered with weeds — ending another chapter in Lake County, Indiana's history!

The Neudorf name still continues on in the Chicago, Illinois, area, through the descendants of Nicholas (III?), who married in the early 1890's, and settled in the "Windy City" when he was a young man.

by Jim Stephen

NICHOLS FAMILY
F180

One of the early Nichols families in Lake county came from Maryland to Fairfield county, Ohio about 1804 and then to Lake county, Indiana about 1864.

Eli Nichols and his brothers Jacob, Samuel, and John settled in Lake county. Eli was born Nov. 16, 1817 in Fairfield county, Ohio, the son of John and Mary Louise (Polly) Lantz Nichols. Eli married Catherine Johnson Dec. 6, 1838 in Fairfield county where she died in 1863. Eli and Catherine were the parents of Zura, Henriett (or Harriet Minerva), Rebecca A., Albina, James, Mary M., John, Benjamin, Charles, and Walter Scott Nichols. Eli died in 1907 in Lowell.

Walter Scott Nichols was born May 6, 1860 in Fairfield county. He married Mary E. Dinwiddie (1861-1888) in Lake county on Sept. 1, 1880. They had two boys: John Bernard, born June 24, 1881 and Harry, born Aug. 7, 1883. After Mary's death, Walter married Caroline Baker (Carrie Becker) (1871-1944) on Dec. 11, 1892. Walter and Carrie had two children: Lolita, born Jan. 6, 1905 and Leonard, born Oct. 11, 1910. Walter died May 21, 1929 in Lowell and is buried in the Lowell Memorial Cemetery.

Walter Scott was a prominent landowner and successful farmer of the area. His family told many anecdotes of his love of horses, and swift horses in particular. Walter was most capable and could do whatever was needed, from carpentry to bricklaying, building his own homes. He was an inventor of varied items and a designer of farm equipment, an amateur watchmaker and an engraver.

Harry and John Bernard Nichols, sons of Walter and Mary, were farmers in Lake county. John B. married Margaret J. Turner in 1903 and their children were: Mary, Florence, Mabel, Bernard Jr. and John Milford. John B. died Sept. 1956. Harry married Carrie Topping (1883-1937) and their children were: Walter, Harold, and Leota. Harry married second Ida Schilling. Harry died in 1957.

Lolita Nichols, the daughter of Walter and Carrie, married Karl Wendel (1903-1936), son of Henry and Louise D. Wendel of Crown Point. Lolita was recognized for her musicianship, having attended De Pauw University. She was a legal secretary and for many years was employed in that capacity in the Appellate and Supreme Courts of Indiana. Lolita and Karl had three children: Carolynne, Robert, and Margaret. Lolita died in 1956 and is buried beside her husband in the Lowell Cemetery.

Leonard Nichols of Lowell, son of Walter and Carrie, married Patricia Connelly and their children were: Gerald, Keith, and Andrea.

Eli Nichols' brother, Samuel (1842-1918) married Flora Fowler. Samuel and Flora are both buried in Lowell. Eli's brother Jacob (1824-1906) may have married three times. His first wife was Elizabeth L. Hight of Marion county, Ohio. Their children were: Ella?, Herschel J., Marshall A., Mary, Cecelia, Jane, Bertha A., and Milford E. By his second wife, Julia A. Henderson, whom he married in 1872?, he had Libby, Ralph, Salina (Celina), and Henry. There may have been a daughter Emma by Julia or by his third wife. Another brother, or perhaps a half brother, to Eli was John Nichols (1805?-1896). John married Elizabeth Bibler in 1826 and later to a Diana (1818-1882). The latter was a native of New York.

Eli's father was John Nichols, born Aug. 8, 1783/4 in Cumberland, Maryland. John was married twice, first to Catherine Markee (or Keys), a native of Germany. Second he married Mary Louise (Polly) Lantz in 1814 in Fairfield county, Ohio. Mary was born in 1799 in Lancaster county, Pennsylvania, the daughter of Martin and Caty Barr Lantz. Mary died Nov. 1, 1860 and is buried in Lancaster, Fairfield county. John's children were: Jacob, John, Samuel, Joseph, Abraham, George, Catherine, Perry, Mary, Henry, Jesse, and Martin. John died Dec. 19, 1867 and is also buried in Fairfield county, Ohio.

Eli's father John was apparently the son of Joseph (born Dec. 24, 1753) and Frances Nichols, grandson of John and Martha, and gr-grandson of John Nichols. The latter was born about 1709 in Frederick county, Maryland and deeded his plantation "Butter and Cheese" to his sons John and Asa in 1791.

The Nichols family is numerous in Maryland and there is need for more research.

by Carolynne (Wendel) Miller

OLDENDORF, CONRAD JR. FAMILY
F181

Conrad and Christina (Ohlendorf) Oldendorf in 1892

Conrad Oldendorf Jr. (Conrad Sr. and Engel Maria's son) married Christine Ohlendorf on July 4, 1861. Christine born August 15, 1844 in Idensermore, HessenSchaumburg, Hannover, Germany to Henry and Christine Sophia (Senne) Ohlendorf. Their ten children included the following.

Sophia (born November 17, 1862) married Hans Henry Wehmhoefer on December 13, 1883. He was born December 19, 1860 (his father was Conrad). They farmed his father's farm located 1 3/4 mile west of her parents' farm. In 1912 they moved to Minot, North Dakota to farm. Sophia passed away in October 11, 1940 and Henry on August 16, 1944. Their son, Louis had an Implement Dealership in Bismarck, North Dakota.

Louise (born July 18, 1865) married Fred Meier, Jr. Fred was born April 3, 1869 in Crete, Illinois. They moved to a farm, purchased by the Oldendorf family, in Iowa with three of their children. Later, they returned to Crete to farm.

Christine (born October 13, 1867) married August Hartman on April 6, 1890. He was born April 14, 1859. (William Hartman was August's brother) August was originally from Woodworth Illinois, which is where they returned to farm. On April 17, 1892, during delivery both Christine and their baby son, Waldemar, died. August returned to Crete and several years later married Emma Ruhe. They raised five children.

Caroline (born March 17, 1870) married Herman Borchers on February 16, 1896. He was born on December 13, 1870 near Kreitzburg, Indiana to Henry and Maria (Jordening). They farmed his fathers farm until they retired in Crete, Illinois. Their children were Ella, Emilie, and Alvina, who died an infant on June 3, 1898.

Conrad III (born July 20, 1872) died May 7, 1873 at age 22 months.

William (born February 22, 1874) married Louise Schrage of Crete. They moved to Iowa to farm. Their daughter Florence was born in Iowa on December 20, 1899. They returned to the area in 1903 and acquired land, west of the Oldendorf farm on Bemis Road in Crete, Illinois, for farming. They built an addition around the home that they purchased and farmed there until their retirement. Florence married Clarence Hahn in September of 1922. They took over Florence's parents farm until she and her husband retired. Then they moved to a home in Crete once known as the William Sallers home, located at the edge of town, it soon became surrounded with additional homes.

Henry (born June 6, 1877) married Wilhlemina Becker of Hanover Township in Lake County Indiana. After their marriage they farmed the "Wakely" farm just off Klemme Road and Exchange. They had three children: Melvin, Donald, and Raymond; who died in infancy. Melvin married Therese (Dorman) of Chicago and farmed near Dyer, Indiana and later near Beecher, Illinois, where they resided. Donald married Ruby Bixeman and continued farming the family farm.

Dick (born December 24, 1879) married Wilhelmina Moeller on June 15, 1904. She was born July 7, 1879 in Crete, Illinois. They moved to a farm, across the road from the Fred and Louise Meier in Iowa, they farmed it along with their children Martin, Ray, Ed, and Helen. The family returned to farm near Beecher, Illinois and later near the Crete-Monee area.

Edward (born June 23, 1882) married Emma (Piepho) on February 5, 1908. She was born on October 2, 1889 to August and Dorothea (Wille) who farmed the corner of 113th and Calumet Avenue. Ed and Emma farmed the Oldendorf family farm (the Homestead farm). They had three children: Dora, Harriet and Ralph.

Emilie (born October 24, 1885) married Gus-

133

tave Schroeder November 16, 1905. He was born July 29, 1883 in the Beecher, IL area (his father was John Schroeder). They farmed two miles south in Hanover Township in Lake County Indiana. Later they farmed west of Indiana/Illinois State Line Road until they retired in the town of Crete, Illinois. Their children were Harry, Helmuth, Florence, Wilmer, Else, LeRoy, Herbert, and Ruby. (Helmuth died an infant.)

Building improvements were made on the Oldendorf farm in 1876. A large corn crib was built just south of the barn. It held grain in the upper story and ear-corn below. The lower area was designed with storage on both sides of a center driveway, which was used for wagon storage.

There were quite a few parties, with lots of music and dancing, held in the Oldendorf house, especially with all the childrens weddings receptions. One of Conrad Jr.'s buddies recalls one particular evening when the fiddlers were playing. Conrad, who was enthusiastically dancing, fell through the floor into the basement. The music stopped and there was total silence; until they heard Conrad Jr. yell, "Hey! Don't stop the music, I'll be right up!"

Plans for a new house soon followed that incident. In 1903, a large house (for that time period) was built. The neighbors teasingly called it the "Mansion on the Hill." Emma (Piepho) Oldendorf used to tell of how before her marriage to Edward, she and her mother would drive by the house, as it was being built, never dreaming that she'd be one of the first to live in it. (Her mother and Edwards mother often got together to "spin" wool on their spinning wheels.)

Florence, Conrad and Christine's granddaughter, recalled that as a little girl she remembers coming out from Iowa and visiting Grandma Christine who contracted tuberculosis. Christine died on December 27, 1904 after living in the new house only one year; having raised the children in the smaller house.

Conrad Jr. died on December 8, 1906, two years after his wife Christine. It was said that he was a well known and likeable person and with a certain pride in his horses. The boys used his team at the burial, at St. John's original church site, and the horses "neighed" throughout the service at the cemetery on the hill.

by Mrs. Ralph Oldendorf

OLDENDORF, CONRAD, SR. FAMILY
F182

Conrad Oldendorf Sr. arrived in New York Harbor on May 12, 1851, and came to America on a 457 1/4 ton ship called the *Bark Emma* that left from Bremen, Germany; D. Edzarde was the captain of the ship. Conrad Sr. was accompanied by his wife Engel Maria, and their children (those born in Germany); his mother-in-law Catharine Wassman (born November 11, 1790); and his widowed mother, Katharine Oldendorf (born July 22, 1778 in Helse Germany).

Conrad Sr. and his family came to Hanover Township in Lake County, Indiana less than a month after their arrival in America. He established an interstate farm, that stretched across both sides of the Indiana/Illinois State Line

The farm that Conrad Oldendorf, Sr. walked to on Rte. 55 from his Homestead on the State Line, to help his families farm. 1869 – 1894.

Road at west 117th; immediately south of Bemis Road. The farm included 13 acres in Illinois and an adjacent 135 acres in Section 13 (Hanover Township) in Indiana; 28 acres of woodland was purchased later. (Conrad Sr. filed his first land grant claim on June 9, 1851. These grants were signed, deeded documents of Presidents Tyler, Fillmore and Pierce. Claims for the Illinois property were filed in Chicago, Illinois.)

A log cabin was built for the family, on the Indiana side of the State Line Road, where they lived until their house was built. A barn was built on the Illinois property for the horses, cows, and hogs; with a loft for storing the long prairie grass used for feed. A small storage crib was built for ear corn and grain.

Conrad Sr. and Engel Maria's children include the following:

Conrad Jr. (born September 25, 1838) married Christine Ohlendorf on July 4, 1861. Together with Conrad Sr., they farmed the homestead farm.

Sophia (born May 3, 1847) died on September 20, 1862 at age 15.

Henry (born March 3, 1853) married Maria Borchers on April 8, 1875. Conrad Oldendorf Sr. acquired a 160 acre farm that Henry and his wife farmed on the "Nine Mile Stretch" on Rte. 55 between Lowell and Crown Point in Section 4.

Caroline (born December 10, 1856) married August Fischer, Sr. (son of John) on March 22, 1876. Conrad Oldendorf Sr. established a 160 acre farm in the northwest 1/4 of Section 4, on July 8, 1869. Later, Caroline and her husband August acquired the farm. The farm was located to the east of the Henry Oldendorf (Caroline's brother) farm. A provision was made in the deeds for a strip of land to be used as an access drive between farms. Caroline and August's had two children, Sophia and August Jr. Sophia was born on July 7, 1884. She married Christ Moeller of Crete and they lived in Steger, Illinois. She died of tuberculosis 10 years after the marriage. August Jr. was born on September 25, 1879 at Woodworth, Illinois. He married Mayme Fiegle of Crown Point on April 20, 1913. She was born on April 11, 1891. They farmed southwest of his dad and north of his Uncle Henry and Aunt Maria. August, Jr. and Mayme's children were Leona Marie, born March 29, 1917 and died on July 17, 1946, Leonella who married Robert Roffman on June 6, 1942 (Robert died on June 20, 1965). Leonella and Robert's daughters are Jerilyn and Leonette. (Mayme died in 1945 and August in 1962.)

Wilhelmina (born September 14, 1834) and Otto Behre were married while living in Germany. Otto was born in Riepen, Rodenburg, Churhessen Germany. They came to America on the same ship as her parents and settled on the north side of 113th Avenue upon their arrival. Later they moved to rural Wells, Minnesota.

Catharine (born March 27, 1836) married Hans Henry Tatge on September 16, 1857. He was born July 8, 1821 in Ogelsdorf, Guttenberg, Germany and resided on a farm located on Bemis Road (Crete Township, in Illinois) just 3/4 mile from the State Line Road.

Dorothea (born April 27, 1850) married Henry Rehborg on January 1, 1870. Henry was born March 3, 1884 in Bakedorf, Churhessen, Germany. They resided and farmed in Woodworth, Illinois, in Iroquois County. Their son Ernest farmed a farm next to them and prospered in that part of the state. Descendants of Dorothea and Henry still own and farm the original full section of Oldendorf farm and land in Osceola County, IA.

Engel Maria, born on September 9, 1812, died on November 14, 1860. Katharine, Conrad Sr.'s mother, died January 2, 1870. After Engel Maria's death, Conrad Sr. continued farming and providing for his family. He often walked from his farm on State Line Road to the "Nine Mile Stretch" to help his son and son-in-law with their farming. He took the short cut through the fields and startled the farmers. He'd stop to chat before continuing on his way home again. After Dorothea's wedding he walked a cow and a calf to Woodworth, Illinois as part of her dowry. (Descendants now say 55 it's to far to drive" at reunion time.) Conrad helped establish the Interstate Creamery, which was built in 1891 on his property. He later remarried. His second wife was Dorothea Matthias, born February 11, 1801 in Riepen, Rodenburg, Grafshafi, Hannover, Germany. Dorothea died on January 3, 1886. Conrad Sr. was born on September 14, 1810 and died on September 14, 1894.

by Mrs. Ralph Oldendorf

OLDENDORF, EDWARD FAMILY
F183

Edward Oldendorf (Ludwig Edward Oldendorf) married Emma Maria Catharina Piepho on February 5, 1908. Edward, the son of Conrad and Christine Oldendorf Jr. was born on June 23, 1882. Edward's brothers and sisters include: Sophia, Louise, Christine, Caroline, Conrad III, William, Henry, Dick and Emilie. Emma was born on October 1, 1889 to August and Dorothea (Wille) who farmed on the corner of 113th and Calumet Avenue in Hanover Township. Emma's sisters and brothers include: Herman, Elmer, Ora, Ida and Dora.

Edward and his family continued to farm the family farm. He made several farm building improvements, such as building a tool shed, cowshed, brooder house and chicken house.

Edward and Emma's children include the following:

Dorothea ("Dora") married Otto Paul on October 9, 1934. They farmed the Paul farm 1-1/2 miles north of Brunswick, Indiana. They had one child, a son named David.

Harriet married Gordon Kennett of Chicago on May 6, 1940. They resided in Thorton, Illinois. Their children are John, Donald, and

Edward and Emma (Piepho) Oldendorf in 1938.

Brenda, Melody, Ralph, Cherie, Mark, Oldendorf family in 1973.

Cynthia. (Harriet presently lives in Chicago, Illinois.)

Ralph married Melody Kurth of Monee, Illinois on August 21, 1949. Their children are Cherie, Mark and Brenda.

Edward loved music, he often played the violin, harmonica, organ and accordion. He was a quiet, kindly, likeable person who was the second youngest of a big family. He didn't say much and he didn't waste any words when he did talk; which was not often. Emma was a warm, honest, cheerful person who had a sincere interest in people. She was very active in Church activities and was a home nurse, caring for elderly or ill people in their homes while their families were away.

Edward died on August 30, 1942. Ralph continued the farming tradition, as well as cared for Emma who was ill until she died on April 20, 1961. (When Ralph married, part of the family home was converted into an apartment for Emma. This allowed her to entertain and have some privacy.)

by Mrs. Ralph Oldendorf

OLDENDORF, RALPH EDWARD FAMILY
F184

Ralph Edward Oldendorf, son of Edward and Emma, was born October 1, 1921. Ralph had two sisters, Dora and Harriet.

Ralph married Melody Mae Kurth on August 21, 1949. Melody, the daughter of Clarence and Hildagarde ("Hilda") Kurth, was born January 4, 1931. Ralph and Melody met at a dance in Monee, Illinois. At the time they met, Melody was living in Green Garden, Illinois 7 miles west of Monee. She graduated from Peotone High School. They were married at the United Church of Christ in North Peotone. After the ceremony they had family and friends over for a dinner reception at the Kurth's family home and later a dance at the Monee Ballroom.

Ralph and Melody's three children include: Cherie, Mark and Brenda.

Cherie Lynn was born March 22, 1951. She graduated from Hanover Central High School in 1969. She met Kenneth Francis Zahora in school and they married on August 21, 1971. They reside in Indianapolis with their children Aimee Laraine and Nathaniel Edward. Ken is a teacher and Cherie a teachers assistant in Indianapolis.

Mark Edward was born on September 8, 1954. He graduated from Hanover Central in 1972 and married Lana Jean Freix of Markham, Illinois on April 12, 1975. He was employed at Garrett Industries in California when he died on July 4, 1982 leaving one son Ralph Edward II, the 7th generation in America.

Brenda Sue was born on September 14, 1960 and graduated from Hanover Central High School in 1978. She married Pat Alan Thunherst from Crete, Illinois on April 16, 1988. Pat graduated from Crete Monee High School in 1976. Brenda is employed at the Institute of Financial Education in Chicago, her husband at Portion Packaging of South Chicago Heights, Illinois.

Together Ralph and Melody operate the family farm, which was designated with a Hoosier Homestead Award in 1976. This award is given to those whose farms remained in the same family for at least 100 years.

Ralph and Melody are known for their love of music and dancing. Ralph has sung for various functions in the area and as a young man was involved in various talent shows. Melody an accomplished pianist and organist, was the organist at the Zion United Church of Christ for 20 years. Ralph enjoys his wife's music so much that he had speakers installed on the house so he could hear her playing the organ just about anywhere on the farm. At the end of a long exhausting day when the lights are ready to be turned out, if someone notices an announcement for a public dance, energy is suddenly revitalized and away Ralph and Melody go!

by Cherie Zahora and Brenda Thunherst

OLTROGGE, CONRAD FAMILY
F185

Mary Oltrogge and her husband, William Bauermeister, Jr. in 1903.

Conrad Oltrogge was born in Harste, a province of Hannover, Germany. Mary Blume, Conrad's wife, was born in 1840 in Waldringhausen, a province of Hannover, Germany. When she was 20, Mary arrived in New York Harbor, from Germany, on May 16, 1859 aboard the *Wesser*. Her family was known to have settled near Watseka, IL. Conrad owned land in Section 18. It was located directly north of the Otto Paul farm, east of 121st, along Calumet Avenue.

Conrad and Mary had four children. One son died an infant, on February 20, 1865. Henry Conrad was born on September 9, 1867 and died on March 22, 1868. William was born on September 15, 1862. He married Minnie Ohlenkamp on May 2, 1893. (Minnie was born October 3, 1865. They farmed twenty miles south in the "marsh area" and then moved to a farm near Lowell. The home was the enlarged "first brick school house" in the Lowell, Indiana area. The barn was new and large; many recall some of the barn dances held there in the loft, and the good times they had there. William and Minnie had two children: Tillie, who married Archie Doty and Alice, who married Cecil Doty. Maria was born on February 6, 1864. She married William Bauermeister, Jr. (William was born on April 22, 1853. He owned his father's farm.)

Conrad died on October 6, 1867 and subsequently the property east of 121st and Calumet Avenue was sold. Mary then married Henry Haseman Sr. (He was born October 22, 1841 in Hagen, Germany. At the age of 16, Henry came to America on a ship called *H. Von Gagern* on July 3, 1857.) Mary and Henry Sr. resided on the west side of State Line Road (the Illinois side). They had several children, which they raised along with the children from Mary's first marriage.

by Mrs. Ralph Oldendorf

ORR, ROBERT
F186

Governor of Indiana

Samuel Orr, the progenitor of Gov. Robert Orr, was born in Newton Ardres, County Down, 87 miles from Dublin, Ireland, Oct. 11, 1810. He married Martha Lowry there and they sailed for America the following year. The couple landed at Baltimore and traveled on to Pittsburgh by wagon and stagecoach.

For two years he remained in Pittsburgh as an employee in a grocery. There he met James Laughlin. In partnership with Laughlin, he opened a pork and general merchandise business in Evansville, Ind., which he carried on for a number of years. This enterprise was reorganized into the wholesale grocery and iron trade, with new associates. In 1862 Orr dropped the grocery line and began the iron business exclusively. The company prospered and continues today as Orr Steel Co., Division of Shelby Steel Inc.

Orr had substantial investments in the railroad and banking business. At the time of his death he was president of Evansville National Bank.

His obituary stated, "In deeds of charity he was foremost among the men of his day." As a benefactor of Wabash College, his death brought the president of the college, the Rev. Joseph Tuttle, to Evansville for three days to conduct the obsequies.

Samuel Orr was a life-long Presbyterian and to the Walnut Street Church was liberality itself. He was the father of three children, among whom was:

James Laughlin Orr, who was born in Evansville. His birth occurred soon after the family moved into a new, two-story brick residence that stood on the southeast corner of Second and Vine Street.

In 1852 James Orr accompanied his father on a trip to Ireland to visit relatives. They traveled by rail to Milwaukee, by lake steamer from there to Buffalo and from Buffalo by the Eric Canal and railroad to New York City where they took a ship to Belfast. The boy of 14 years was left with relatives to go to school in Northern Ireland. Later he returned and entered his father's iron business. With the outbreak of the Civil War he enlisted in the Union Army and by 1864 was a captain in the Quartermaster Service assigned to the trains of the Second Division.

Soon after his discharge from the Army he married Kate Ann Howes, an Evansville girl then living in Memphis, Tenn. About 1881 they bought a home at 716 W. First St. in Evansville which now bears the number 412 S.E. First St. At the death of his father in 1882, a new partnership was formed under the name of Orr, Griffith & Co. In 1900 the firm name was changed to Orr Iron Co.

James and Kate Orr had six children; three died in infancy. Among the three who lived to be adults was:

Samuel Lowry Orr, who attended Yale and began his industrial career soon after graduation with the class of 1894. He became president of the company when his father died in 1918. Like his grandfather, he was president of Old National Bank, which succeeded Evansville National Bank. He joined with nine other men in the purchase of Shroeder Headlight Co., which became Sunbeam Electric Manufacturing Co. Orr was engaged in many other business ventures.

He was also active in community affairs. It was through his efforts and those of his brother-in-law, George Clifford, that Evansville College was brought to the city. He was a Rotarian for 33 years.

Orr was survived by his wife, Louise Dunkerson Orr, and three children, among whom is Gov. Robert Orr.

The Dunkerson Family

Thomas Dunkerson (also Dunkenson) was born May 20, 1763, in Spotsylvania County, Virginia. He married Lucretia, daughter of Thomas and Phoebe Moore, Dec. 3, 1785. The tax rolls for 1788 lists for him one slave and four horses. In the following year he acquired 228 acres. In 1810 the family moved to Christian County, Kentucky, where Thomas died in 1835.

Thomas and Lucretia Dunkerson had 10 children, among whom was:

Washington Dunkerson, their ninth child, who was born in Virginia just prior to their removal to Kentucky. He married Marcissa Jane Blackwell in Henderson County, Ky.

Washington died in 1847 leaving an estate which was sold at auction for $322.90. A detailed list of the property survived. It included a wagon, $25; a roan mare, $25; a roan colt, $37.50; 38 barrels of corn, $51.29; books and pamphlets, $6.25. He was a minister of the Christian Church and had four children among whom was:

Robert K. Dunkerson, who lived in Evansville after 1861 when he came from Henderson, Ky. In Evansville he was engaged in the tobacco business being in the firm of Brown, Dunkerson & Co. This was succeeded by White, Dunkerson & Co. with a large warehouse at Water and Locust streets.

Dunkerson's banking connections date from 1865 when he became a director of Evansville National Bank, which was followed by Old National Bank in 1892. He became president of the bank in 1901 and held that office until his death. His business ventures were legion. He bore a heavy interest in the Evansville, Paducah & Cairo Packet Line. His interest in the river and its traffic led to the naming of a boat in his honor which ran for many years in the Green River Line. "Mr. Dunkerson's prudence and business sagacity amassed a fortune."

He married July 25, 1871, to Laura Shaw Casselberry, "daughter of one of the city's first and most prominent families." They had two children, of which Louise (Dunkerson) Orr was one.

Thomas Evans Casselberry was born in 1790 on the Fourth of July, in Providence, Pa. In 1806 he moved with his parents to what is now Posey County, Indiana. He had some education and even more native intelligence. He was a man of affairs and active in public life. He left a substantial estate to his wife, Rachel Jane Carson, whom he married in 1816. He secured his marriage license in Vincennes. They had eight children, among whom was:

Isaac Stroud Casselberry, who was born up on a farm in Posey County Nov. 26, 1821. He graduated from the Medical College of Ohio in 1845 and formed a partnership with Dr. M.J. Bray of Evansville. In a very short time he "became known as one of the leading physicians in this section of the state."

At the outset of the Civil War he received the appointment of surgeon of the First Indiana Cavalry. Following the war, he resumed practice and "was one of the most zealous, energetic and self-sacrificing physicians in the county."

He served on the Board of Health and was one of the founders of the Evansville Medical College.

He contributed many papers to medical journals and was a charter member of the Indiana State Medical Society and a permanent member of the American Medical Association.

Dr. Casselberry married April 20, 1847, Louisa Garven of Gettysburg, Pa. They had two children, one of which was Laura (Dunkerson) Casselberry.

Much credit for this article is due P. Grady Morein, university librarian, University of Evansville, and James Churchyard, 3124 Bermuda Drive, Costa Mesa, Calif. Churchyard has recently compiled "Our Family Museum, A Collection of Family History Notes," which deals at length with the Orr family.

Willard Heiss, a certified genealogist, is a fellow of the National Genealogical Society and the American Society of Genealogists and chairman of the genealogy section of the Indiana Historical Society. He writes Ancestoritis, a column which appears in the Free Time section of The News each Saturday.

by Willard Heiss

OWENS, SETH
F187

Seth was born in New York state 3/29/88, but moved to Lake Co. in 1836 with his mother Elizabeth, sisters Sarah and Elizabeth, and brother Elizur. They had come from New York after the death of Elizabeth's husband. His mother purchased eighty acres from the U.S. Government Land Office in St. John township on 4/10/1843, where Seth commenced farming. On 6/18/1854 he married Nabby Glazier Baker, by whom he had children Warren Clark, Phebe Elizabeth, Sarah Ann, Ransome Andrew, Malinda Lucretia, Allice A., Clara Augusta, David Eleezer, and Martha Louise. The latter married William Demmon, youngest son of Julius Alonzo Demmon, and thus tied another pair of pioneer families together. Seth was the first township supervisor of St. John township. Elizabeth, Seth's mother, donated one acre of her land ". . . to be used as a burying ground . . . ". It was known for years as the Dutton Cemetery, but today is called Pleasant View, and is the burial place of many of the earliest settlers including the Wilcox, Demmon, Owens, and other families. Seth died 3/25/1880 and lies in the Pleasant View Cemetery.

Nabby Glazier Owens was the daughter of Benjamin and Phoebe Chapman Glazier who came here from Ohio in 1836, and granddaughter of Revolutionary soldier Benjamin Glazier of Massachusetts. Born 1/12/1830, she passed away on 4/2/1899 and also lies at Pleasant View.

Both Seth's sisters remained single all their lives. Brother Elizur went west during the gold rush, was never heard from again, and presumably perished as did so many on the perilous trip.

by Ruth Demmon

PAUL BROTHERS
F188

Otto J. Paul I taken in 1920

On August 27, 1856 the three Paul brothers, Heinrich Christoph ("Henry"), Johan Heinrich ("John") and Otto Johan were granted permission via barons to leave Minseln; from Krietzruhe, a province of Hannover, Germany. Armed with a royal signed and sealed document of government officials they left for America.

The three brothers took the first ship available. It took the usual six weeks to arrive at New York Harbor. After a few days, they received directions and proceeded on the route to Hanover Township, Lake County, Indiana.

John chose to settle one and a half miles east of the town of Crete, Illinois on the north side of Exchange Road on the first curve. A descendant, Helen Paul (Ehrhardt), wife of the 1930's famed Baseball player, W. Ehrhardt, lived there until recently.

Christoph chose to settle in Washington Township in Will County, Illinois near Eagle Lake/Beecher Illinois. (Several descendants, one of which is, Norbert Paul and wife, Annabelle (Cassill) have always kept in touch with visits to relatives over most of the states.)

Otto preferred the site south of 121st on the east side of Calumet Avenue, which he purchased on October 1, 1865. He built a sod house on the east side of the barn, on a little knoll, until there was time and money to build a small house and barn later.

Otto was born on August 19, 1847 in Kreitzruhe, Hannover, Germany. His wife, Engle Maria ("Mary" Russel) was born January 29, 1852 and they were married on October 17, 1869. She was a sister to William and Herman, who farmed the two farms adjacent and to the southeast on 125th, of Otto and Mary.

Otto then purchased an additional tract of land known as the 100 acre Henry Eggers farm in February 8, 1875. Henry Eggers was later a sponsor to one of Otto's children. Later, an addition was built onto the house making it a comfortable home. The children that came to visit then; and in later years were fascinated by the two staircases.

Otto and Engel Maria's children included: Wilhelm Paul, born February 24, 1870; Henry, born on June 24, 1873; Christoph who was born January 9, 1881 and died on August 17, 1886; and Louise, (known as "Lizzeta" or "Lizzie"), born June 15, 1887, who later married John Teske on December 22, 1907 and resided in Washington Township in Will County, Illinois.

Engel Maria passed away on December 28, 1903, her husband Otto continued farming with his son Henry and Henry's family until his passing on October 31, 1927.

by Mrs. Ralph Oldendorf

PAUL, HENRY FAMILY
F189

Henry Paul, son of Otto I and Engle Maria (Russel), was born on June 21, 1873. He married Regina Ohlendorf on December 20, 1900. Regina, whose parents were Henry Ohlendorf and Wilhelmina (Arkenburg) was born on January 20, 1875 in Crete, Illinois. She had been a seamstress and also an avid bicycle rider, which was unusual for those years.

Their only son, Otto Henry was born on February 24, 1906. Regina died on March 23, 1906 due to complications stemming from the delivery.

Carrie Becker, a neighbor came to help care for the newborn baby as well as take care of the housekeeping. On September 2, 1906, Henry and Carrie married. Carrie raised Otto as her own son. Henry and Carrie had one baby of their own; however, the baby died an infant.

Henry often spoke of Otto I, his father, farming with horses and using the thatched roof barn that Otto I built. In 1900, he built the shingle roofed barn as the tall prairie grass known as "slough hay" only lasted ten years and were a lot of work to install and maintain. (It was upon Regina's, his first wife, insistence that a new barn be built.) Henry enjoyed farming with horses, he hated to think of a barn with no horses. His son Otto and grandson David always used the tractors to do their share of the farm work.

Henry would recall when Otto, his father, kept his buggy mainly for driving out to his favorite fishing spots at Cedar Lake. As a boy, Henry would go along with his father to the

Three Paul Generations. To the left is David, Henry, and Otto II, on the right; posing during work in the year 1947.

Meyer farm, at the north end of the lake. Otto would fish in the lake from a fence and pull the fish in one after another, drop them into a two bushel grain sack. Henry would chuckle and say, "that was about the time when blue gills jumped into your boat at Cedar Lake." (Old-timers would tell of walking across Cedar Lake, stepping first on one fish and then another. Another one would spin the yarn further and quip, "Yah, you would walk on 'em in those days, now the fish supply is getting so sparse there is a lot of water in between.") Henry always enjoyed fishing when his work was done, but he thinks his Dad enjoyed it even more.

Henry lived and farmed on the Paul homeplace, except for four years after confirmation. He attended school at Zion United Church of Christ (known then as the Zion Evangelical and Reformed Church) schoolhouse. During those years, he was taught by Pastor Wahl and Schmidt. After that, he went to work for his uncle, in a brick yard in Chicago, Illinois. He was one of a four-man crew, a clay handler and moulder. He worked with two truckers. The first man placed the clay in the moulds; the moulder shaped them and Henry, a trucker, with a mould of six bricks ran them outside, placing the bricks on racks to dry. It was very hot from four in the morning to nine at night. The heat of the brick oven was so great during the day, as 7,000 bricks made the quota in five hours.

Henry and Carrie enjoyed having customers come to the farm for cream and butter, he would always entertain visitors with historical or humorous stories. Both were missed after they died, within one year of each other; Henry on February 9, 1967 and Carrie on January 31, 1968.

by Mrs. Ralph Oldendorf

PAUL, OTTO FAMILY
F190

Otto and Dora (Oldendorf) Paul. October 9, 1934

Otto Paul, the only son of Henry and Regina (Ohlendorf), was born February 24, 1906, in Hanover Township, Lake County, Indiana near Brunswick. He was named after his grandfather. Otto received his schooling at Schiller School, two miles north of Brunswick.

Otto and his father, Henry, farmed on the homestead, one and one half miles north of Brunswick. During World War II, Otto worked at the Elwood Arsenal in Elwood, Illinois and did carpenter work on the side. In his later years, he drove a milk truck for Adolph Niemeyer of Brunswick. (Milk was first picked up from farmers in eight gallon cans and later with a bulk tank truck into which the milk was pumped and delivered to the Dixie Dairy at Gary, Indiana for processing.)

Otto married Dorothea Christine ("Dora") Oldendorf. She was born October 9, 1910 to Edward and Emma (Piepho) Oldendorf on State Line Road in Hanover Township (rural Dyer). She attended Schiller School and the Zion United Church of Christ, known then as the Zion Evangelical and Reformed Church. Dora worked in Blue Island for a number of years before she married. She was an accomplished soloist and pianist for socials; a life of the party wherever she appeared. She and Otto enjoyed ballroom dancing besides movies and joined many couples in these get togethers for entertainment.

Otto and Dora lived in Crete Illinois for a time; Eagle Lake, Illinois and the first farm south, on the Illinois side of State Line Road, of Dora's homeplace.

Their only son David Otto Paul was born on August 30, 1935 and was christened at his parents church. He attended Crete Elementary School and graduated from Dyer High School 1953. He began working at the Steel Mills. He married Charlene Terry of Chesterton, Indiana on June 15, 1957; and shortly thereafter he entered the army. Their daughter Sandra was born on January 21, 1958 at Fort Hood, Texas. Later, he was transferred to Fort Carson, Colorado. When he completed his service, David and his family returned to Brunswick. His wife, Charlene decided to live with relatives in Oklahoma and raise Sandra there. Sandra attended Oklahoma University; resided at Clairmore, Oklahoma.

David's second wife, Sue Alsman, was born on January 6, 1945 and lived in, or near, Calumet City. Their son Edward was born in their home in Kreitzburg on May 20, 1966; their daughter Lisa was born October 2, 1967.

Both Henry and Carrie Paul passed away within a year of each other (Henry died on February 9, 1967 and Carrie died on January 31, 1968. Their son, Otto, died soon after on February 25, 1968, leaving David to farm the Paul Farm near Brunswick, Indiana.

David, at that time, was working at Burson's Steel Corporation in Illinois. In 1972, longing for Colorado, which he liked so well when stationed in the army, he decided to sell the farm. He and his family headed for the west and invested in a business in Montrose, Colorado.

David later moved back to the Cedar Lake area, and worked at Sauk Steel Corporation in Illinois. Sue stayed in Montrose, Colorado with the children. Edward and Lisa attended the Pamona Elementary School in Montrose. Moving to Craig, Colorado, they then attended the Moffat County High School there, in 1980.

Edward first entered the Little Britches Rodeo Circuit and then the Quarter Horse Shows, on the western slopes of Colorado; riding from Montrose to Durango; Denver, on to the Colorado/Utah border. His horse was named Bueno Star, which he rode from the age of twelve until he was eighteen years old. Lisa, joined him at age eleven until she was twenty years old. Her horse was named Star Rocket.

Later, Edward returned to the Cedar Lake, Indiana area and graduated from Hanover Central High School. Employed at various jobs, he remained with an area Lumber and Hardware Company. Within a few years, he met and married Juanita Fitch on September 5, 1987 and resided in rural Cedar Lake, Indiana. Juanita is the daughter of Sherman and Alice (Zyp) Fitch of Cedar Lake. Edward and Juanita's son, Benjamin Edward Paul, was born on October 11, 1988, the sixth generation in the Paul family.

Lisa Paul graduated from Moffat County High School in Craig, Colorado and is currently residing there with her mother.

by Mrs. Ralph Oldendorf

PAVELL, MIKE
F191

Mike and Anna Pavell came to America like so many immigrants from Eastern and Central Europe with anxious expectation. Theirs was the expectation that America could fulfill dreams of economic opportunity and prosperity. Anxious, in that, as with all immigrants from all places in all times, they would be able to accept the dangers and the risks and the high adventure of setting out to a strange place with different customs and language. Mike was not totally without knowledge of America when he left his Slovak village of Samudovce in the eastern part of Czechoslovakia in 1937. Others from that village had gone before, some had even returned. Stories of opportunities and success in America abounded in the village of Samudovce as it did in villages throughout Eastern and Central Europe. Success in America was well known in the house of young Mike Pavlo. His uncle, for whom he was named, Michael Pavlo had gone to America in 1907 at 14 years old along with his uncle on his mother's side, Jan Estovk and his cousin Paul. Now the children of Samudovce heard of Michael Pavlo's success, how he had changed his name in America to "Pavell" and how he owned a "big" ranch in Montana. Such dreams sent young Mike Pavlo to America to join his uncle on that ranch in Montana.

In the Berta household, where daughter Anna was growing up, information about America consisted not only of the messages received from relatives and friends, but a result of a much more direct knowledge. The father of that house, Michael Berta, had been to America, had worked in the coal mines of Pennsylvania, and had returned with enough money to purchase a fine farm for his family. America was indeed the land of rich opportunity.

Anna Bertova was much younger than her future husband, but the families were closely linked. Mike's father had remarried after his first wife and young Mike's mother, Zuzanna Estovk, was killed by an artillery barrage of the village in 1918. Young Mike (born 14 August 1914) and his infant brother Juraj were left motherless. Their father Jan Pavlo married a young widow named Anna Hresko whose maiden name was Durovcikova. The Durovcik family was well known in Samudovce and Michael Berta, Anna Pavell's father, was married to Zuzanna Durovcikova another daughter from the same Durovcik household. So the connection between the two families was set, and even though there was a twelve year age difference, Mike and Anna were a likely match for marriage as the old villagers saw it.

War and the tragic aftermath of global conflict had occurred before Anna reached the age of marriage. Mike, who arrived in America before the war began, adopted the anglicized spelling of "Pavell" as his uncle had done, had served in the American Army winning not only his citizenship, but the right to bring a "war-bride" to America. Arrangements were made and Anna Bertova of the village of Samuldovce set forth alone for the new world and marriage to a man she had not seen since she was ten years old. After difficulties at Ellis Island, the usual mix up of bureaucratically arranged papers, the young twenty year old Anna Bertova (born 17 March 1927) arrived in Montana early in the year 1948. Anna Bertova and Mike (Pavlo) Pavell were married on the 26th of January 1948 at Havre, Montana.

Their first child, Anna Ruth, was conceived on the high plaines of Montana, but, because of complications during the pregnancy which forced her parents to move to Whiting, Indiana, was born 21 May 1949 at St. Catherine's Hospital in East Chicago, Indiana.

In the fall of 1948, Mike and Anna Pavell had taken up residency in Whiting, surrounded and insulated by the large community of Slovaks in those neighborhoods. Many of them were relatives from Samudovce or nearby villages. Mike went to work for Youngstown Sheet and Tube and Anna began to study for her citizenship. Hard work and sacrifices enabled the Pavell family to prosper. On 6 September 1950 Mike and Anna Pavell began to build their American dream as they moved from the Slovak community of Whiting to a farm which they had purchased on Burr Street just south of U.S. 30 in Crown Point. Mike continued to work at Youngstown Steel from which he ultimately retired after 31 years of service as a machinist in 1980. The Pavells started raising chickens on their new farm, adding though this labor to the hope for prosperity in their new life.

The new family in Crown Point also began to grow in size. Son Milan David was born 24 February 1953 at St. Catherine's Hospital in East Chicago, Indiana, and son Michael Daniel was born at the same hospital on 16 September 1954. The last of the Pavell's four children, Joseph John, was born on 1 July 1956 at Mercy Hospital in Gary, Indiana.

Mike and Anna Pavell from the little village of Samudovce in Eastern Czechoslovakia worked hard to earn their American dream: a good life for their family. Their children grew to maturity, completing education and starting careers. Mike and Anna sold the old farm house and built a new home on the original Burr Street acreage in 1966 where they still live enjoying their retirement, their family, and their grandchildren.

Their son, Milan, married 4 October 1975 to Markita Marie Wakefield, daughter of Mark and Mabel Wakefield of Crown Point. They have two sons, Brent David Pavell, born 11 March 1980 and Paul Joseph Pavell, born 23 August 1983. Their daughter Anna Ruth married on 19 June 1976 to Daniel Lee Padberg, son of Edwin and Lyda Fay (Ruffin) Padberg of St. Louis, Missouri. Daniel and Anna have three children: Kathryn Anna Padberg, born 3 January 1980, John Michael Edwin Padberg, born 1 February 1983, and Daniel Lee Padberg, Jr., born 16 September 1984. Mike and Anna Pavell's son, Michael Daniel, married on 9 July 1983 to Lori Lynn Pollock, daughter of Ronald Pollock and Phyllis (Kahn) Nicholson. Michael and Lori Pavell have a daughter, Lindsey Danielle, born 10 Nov. 1986. The fourth Pavell child, Joseph John, is not married.

The lives and accomplishments of Mike and Anna Pavell represent the richest rewards America can offer. To work hard to build a good life, free from terror or tyranny. And so that promise of America continues to attract immigrants and continues to bless the lives of all Americans with the rich diversity that comes from our country's unique blend of ethnic peoples from all over the world.

by Daniel L. Padberg

PEGG, JOHN IRA
F192

In Memoriam of Robert Eugene Pegg, October 16, 1955-April 30, 1982.

John Ira Pegg was born in Smithfield, Grant District, Wetzel County, West Virginia, 24 June 1922 to John Ira Pegg Sr. and Iva Pauline Higgins. John Ira Pegg Sr. and Iva Pauline Higgins were married at her house at Maxburg, Wetzel County, West Virginia, 29 January 1922. John Ira Pegg Sr. was working as a coal miner when he died 19 January 1926 at Wyatt coal mining camp, Harrison County, West Virginia. He is buried at the Higgins Cemetery on the farm of Josephus Higgins, grandfather of Iva (Higgins) Pegg at Deadfall, Grant District, Wetzel County, West Virginia. John Ira Pegg Sr. was born about 25 July 1897 in Bebee, Wetzel County, West Virginia to Joseph Bernard Pegg and Lucinda C. Kiger. Iva Pauline (Higgins) Pegg, a daughter of Enoch Higgins and Hulda Jane Hayhurst, was born 13 December 1903 at Folsom, Wetzel County, West Virginia. John Ira and Iva Pauline Pegg had another son, Bernard Eugene who was born 29 September 1924 in Smithfield, West Virginia.

With hard times affecting everyone, Iva (Higgins) Pegg took odd jobs to help support her two sons at home. Then on 3 May 1927, Iva Pauline (Higgins) Pegg married William Arch Ratliff in Oakland, Garrett County, Maryland.

Young John Ira Pegg grew up and attended school in several communities. He attended school in Clarksburg, Harrison County, West Virginia, Jordan, Marion County, West Virginia, Newton Falls, Ohio, and Monroe, Michigan. About 1938 when John Ira Pegg was in the 9th or 10th grade of school, he joined the Civilian Conservation Corps. He was with the 1664th Company CCC Camp Paradise in Eckerman, Michigan. He was with the Civilian Conservation Corps until he enlisted in the United States Army on 5 June 1940. He served with Company D 35th Tank Battalion in the 4th Armored Division of the Third Army in Europe during World War II.

About 1940, John Pegg's mother Iva (Higgins) Ratliff and his step-father William Ratliff moved to Gary, Indiana from Monroe, Michigan because there were excellent job opportunities in the steel mills in northwest Indiana. John Pegg's mother and step-father both got a job at Inland Steel in East Chicago, Indiana. They moved from Gary to the Indiana Harbor section of East Chicago too. John Ira Pegg was honorably discharged from the United States Army 20 October 1945 at Camp Atterbury, Indiana. After arriving in northwest Indiana, John Pegg got his first job at Inland Steel. Later he started driving truck from coast to coast. He also worked at United States Steel in Gary, Indiana and Union Carbide Corporation in Whiting, Indiana. About 1955 he joined the Carpenters Union local 599 in Hammond, Indiana.

After dating Arlene Willis of Gary for several months, John Ira Pegg and Arlene Willis were married on Thursday evening, 17 August 1950 at 8:00 p.m. in a church ceremony in Gary, Indiana. Arlene Willis is the daughter of John

The Pegg Family, left to right: Robert Eugene, Arlene, John William, John Ira and Joyce Arlene. Photo taken about 1960.

Vernon Willis and Hazel Beatrice Mulvany.

John Ira and Arlene Pegg had the following children: John William, Joyce Arlene, and Robert Eugene. They lived in Gary, Indiana sixteen years where they raised their children before moving to Griffith, Indiana in 1968.

John William Pegg was born 30 June 1951 in Gary, Indiana. He grew up and attended school in Gary and graduated in May, 1969. He attended Indiana University, northwest campus in Gary, Indiana and Training Systems Institute in Hammond, Indiana where he obtained his computer education. He is now employed with the Veterans Administration Data Processing Center in Chicago, Illinois.

Joyce Arlene Pegg was born 28 January 1954 in Gary, Indiana. She grew up and attended school in Gary and Griffith and graduated in 1972. She married Lester Dale Vermilyer on 6 September 1981 in Three Oaks, Berrien County, Michigan. Dale Vermilyer had two children from a previous marriage. They are Dale C. Vermilyer (born 25 September 1965 in Hammond, Indiana) and Constance P. Vermilyer (born 30 October 1968 in Hammond, Indiana). Dale and Joyce Vermilyer are now living in Palm Harbor, Pinellas County, Florida. Lester Dale Vermilyer was born 20 September 1940 in Laporte, Laporte County, Indiana to Lester A. Vermilyer and Ethel L. Newland.

Robert Eugene Pegg was born 16 October 1955 in Gary, Indiana. He grew up and attended school in Gary and Griffith and graduated in 1975. Robert attended Automotive Mechanic School after high school graduation. He married Carolyn Kay Comer on 5 August 1977 in Crown Point, Lake County, Indiana. She is the daughter of William Edgar Comer and Beverly May Kallas. She was born 28 April 1961 in East Chicago, Indiana. Robert and Carolyn Pegg have two daughters, Lia Marie and Amy Lyn. Lia Marie Pegg was born 10 June 1977 in Crown Point, Indiana and Amy Lyn Pegg was born 28 July 1981 in Munster, Indiana.

Robert Eugene Pegg died 30 April 1982 in East Chicago, Indiana from fatal injuries obtained from the 15 April 1982 collapse of a portion of the Cline Avenue Bridge which was under construction in East Chicago, Indiana. He is buried at Chapel Lawn Memorial Gardens in Schererville, Indiana. He was living in Schererville, Indiana with his wife, Carolyn, and his two daughters, Lia Marie and Amy Lyn, when the bridge accident happened.

John Ira Pegg retired from the Millwright Union local 1043 of the United Brotherhood of Carpenters and Joiners of America in Portage, Indiana in 1986. He became a member of the Masonic Order, lodge 716, in Gary, Indiana in 1960. John Ira Pegg and his wife Arlene are still living in Griffith, Indiana. William Arch Ratliff, step-father of John Ira Pegg died 30 June 1959 in Gary, Indiana. He is buried at Ridgelawn Cemetery in Gary, Indiana. William Ratliff was born in Burnsville, West Virginia 26 October 1907 to William Ratliff and Lillie Cutlip. About 1974, Iva Pauline (Higgins) Ratliff, mother of John Ira Pegg, moved back to Wetzel County, West Virginia near New Martinsville. About 1980, she moved to Pine Grove, Wetzel County, West Virginia. Iva Pauline Ratliff died 14 December 1981 in New Martinsville, Wetzel County, West Virginia. She is buried with her second husband, William Arch Ratliff at Ridgelawn Cemetery in Gary, Indiana. Realizing how important education is to everyone, John Ira Pegg returned to high school and graduated in 1976 in Griffith, Indiana.

by John W. Pegg

PENDLEY, MICKEY E. FAMILY

F193

Colonial American Family in Crown Point

This Crown Point couple have family ties to Indiana long before their respective families moved here and before the sixteenth state came into being in 1816: A Virginia ancestor of Mrs. Pendley's in 1779 accompanied George Rogers Clark to Ft. Vincinnes, and a Virginia ancestor of Mr. Pendley's in 1812 accompanied General William Henry Harrison to the Battle of Tippecanoe.

Mr. Mickey E. Pendley, an only child, was

Marie Lewry on left visits with daughter Buckett Pendley in her Sun City, AZ cacti garden, 1984.

The Mickey E. Pendley Family 1964. Front left to right: Trent and Brett, back Mickey and Buckett.

Rebe Pendley on left found Chicago a second home when a child in Marion, IL as her father owned real estate throughout the city. Here shown at a 1955 family wedding in the Silver Forest room of the Drake Hotel with her aunt Mrs. Leon Sanders, husband Elgan, and cousin Carmen Sanders.

Mickey Pendley on right c: 1944 playing cards in Michiana Shores with cousins Jackie Lurie, Chicago and Donald Rosko, Gary.

born March 30, 1935 to Reba [nee Romans] and Elgan Pendley in Marion, Illinois. When a young child in 1939, Mr. Pendley moved to Lake County, Indiana after his Grandfather's Pendley-Wilkinson Coal Mining company in Marion closed during the Great Depression, and his father, Elgan Pendley, transferred to the Inland Steel company where he remained employed for thirty-nine years through his retirement in 1978. In the Calumet Region Mickey's mother, Reba Pendley, joined her two sisters, one Lorraine Rosko who lived nearby on Gary's West side and Goldie Lurie who lived in Chicago's South Shores Pill Hill neighborhood, and he grew up amongst his many cousins joining them each weekend at one of their homes or occasionally spending weekends at the family's beach resort in Michiana Shores.

During the War years Mickey's mother managed Pendley's Grocery Store in East Chicago's Indiana Harbor area, and he waited on the stores patrons at their ice cream bar. The store was sold soon after WWII and Mrs. Pendley later opened a beauty salon in South Hammond which she operated with a sister for thirty years. Mickey thereafter found employment working at Chicago's Merchandise Mart and for his Uncle who opened Royal Bedding in Chicago, est. 1920 and manufacture of Restonic Mattresses which at one time supplied over thirty furniture stores in Northwest Indiana.

Mickey and his parents were continental travelers and often spent weekends exploring the midwests many resorts and toured the other American states during their summers. In 1964, Reba and Elgan were honored by the Four Winds Yacht Club for having taken the longest cruise around Lake Michigan, and in 1981 Elgan served as President of North West Indiana's Wally Byam Caravan Club Chapter. From the end of WWII through the 1970's Mickey's parents vacationed for several weeks each winter in Miami Beach, until 1978 when they established a winter home in Melbourne, Florida; a quieter community on the Atlantic shore where several other family members and friends have also made their winter homes, and where on a clear day they can watch the NASA space shuttles lift off from Cape Canaveral.

Not having lost her passion for travel in retirement, Mrs. Reba Pendley has joined her daughter-in-law and her sisters for overseas adventures nearly every summer since 1977, and the foursome from the Calumet Region leave their husbands behind to tour and shop at their lengthy leisure. Mrs. Pendley's first voyage abroad at sixty took her half way round the globe to visit a grandson in Israel, and since then has toured Great Britain, Ireland and the majority of central Europe.

In 1984 Elgan and Reba Pendley observed their fiftieth Wedding Anniversary with over sixty friends at a Melbourne Hotel.

Mrs. Mickey E. Pendley [Bertha Ellen Lewry] was the youngest of four children born to the late Marie and George S.W. Lewry, in East Chicago's St. Catherine's hospital, and was named in honor of her great auntie, Lady Bertha Sanderson-Perkins of Rushden, Northamptonshire, England who had visited her parents Hammond home in 1935 or shortly before her birth. Though her father's family was English, her mothers family were all old colonials some having arrived in Charleston as early as 1680 from Martinique and subsequently married into the Stevenson family thereby linking them to two U.S. Presidents and several members of Congress. In 1914 her mother, Marie Lisle, moved from Lima, Ohio to Valparaiso, Indiana where she attended college and later taught school in the Indiana Dunes area and in 1920 met and married George S.W. Lewry, grandson of Furnessville's merchant and Postmaster Lewry family. The elder Lewry's had settled in Chicago shortly after their arrival in the States during the 1850's from Brighton, Sussex, England, their ancestral home since 1592, and moved into the Indiana Dunes in 1858. The Lewry family's 1863 home, typical of mid-Victorian and Sussex architecture still stands on U.S. route 20 in Furnessville, and the family and their store are portrayed in Edwin Way Teales autobiographical "Dune Boy."

Mr. and Mrs. George S.W. Lewry after their marriage in 1920 settled in Hammond's Saxony area where they raised a family of four children: Robert Lisle; Margaret Ann; Deloras Jeanne; and Bertha Ellen nicknamed Buckett, and while Mrs. Lewry became a homemaker and community leader, he became a labor organizer for the local 210, columnist for the Hammond Times and a radio talk show host for the Voice of Labor in Chicago. In 1938, Mr. Lewry died from the results of an industrial explosion at Sinclair, and Mrs. Lewry resumed employment first with the City's [Hammond] Assessors Office, then for awhile with the Edward C. Minas Department store and eventually with the Sinclair Oil Co. from where she retired in 1962 and moved to Sun City, Arizona.

Mrs. Lewry had been a frequent visitor to Phoenix since 1940 when having to remove her

Marie Lisle Lewry and George S.W. Lewry, Nov. 1926. A one time Hammond Councilman candidate their Chestnut Street home saw Presidential candidates to dinner as well as his aunt Lady Bertha Sanderson-Perkins of England, and her aunt and author Me Agnes Rouget deLisle of Manhatten and Paris.

Rebe Pendley on left with the Lewry sisters: Daughter-in-law Bucket Pendley, Crown Point; Jeanne Nestor and Marge Smolinski, Highland, and visiting Trent D. Pendley at the Western Wall in 1977.

141

PENDLEY, TRENT D.
F194

Walnut Hill, established 1967, the country home of Buckett Pendley in Crown Point.

Trent in 1984 stands in front of his G.G. Grandparents home in Furnessville. Const. commenced in 1863 prior to Mr. Lewry's being drafted into the GAR Indiana 9th Co. E. The house and long gone general store were featured in the 1876 Historical Atlas of Porter County.

eldest son from Purdue University and send him to Arizona because of his asthma. Thereafter Marie Lewry and her three daughters became regulars on the Santa Fe Super Chief making routine visits to see her son, and by the time she retired to Sun City in 1962 he had already established a new branch of the Lewry family in the American Southwest.

Mrs. Lewry's affinity to gardening took on a new repertoire in Arizona and instead of lilac, irises and grass lawns, her garden in Sun City grew a collage of cacti, olive, palm and grapefruit trees, amongst pebble lawns and a collection of rocks from her walks in the surrounding desert. Mrs. Lewry returned to the Dunes country each spring to visit her three daughters and their families, and each July visited her native Ohio to inspect the graves and landmarks of several generations of her Stevenson and Lisles ancestors. Marie L. Lewry died in June 1987 at the age of 87 in Sun City, Arizona, and was interned in the Lewry family's century old garden in the Furnessville Cemetery, which is now surrounded by the Indiana Dunes National Lakeshore. A Plaque in Furnessville commemorates a garden of one hundred trees which were planted in her memory in the American Independence Park in the Judean Hills near Jerusalem, Israel.

During the 1940's both Mickey Pendley and Buckett Lewry as she is widely known, grew up on the 170th block of Chestnut Street in south Hammond, but didn't meet one another until they were students at Hammond Tech. High School. They were married August 14, 1954, and shortly afterwards Mickey joined his father with the Inland Steel Co. where he has been employed for as many years. During the 1950's this couple also purchased a home in Hammond's Saxony area and only a block away from Mickey's parents home on Oakdale Ave., which was next door to the setting for Lee Zacharias' 1981 novel "Lessons," and had been a 1959 feature in the Hammond Times. Not only was Mrs. Mickey Pendley at home on Hammond's southside just blocks away from her childhood home on Chestnut Street, but she was also just a few minutes from her two sisters and their families in Highlands Brantwood neighborhood.

In Saxony Mickey and Buckett raised a family of two sons: Trent D. Pendley and Brett T. Pendley who were both born at the University of Illinois Lying Inn Hospital in Chicago. The children were within walking distance to the Woodrow Wilson Elementary School built in 1948 which Buckett's mother and father had been so instrumental in having had built, and the former was asked to lay the cornerstone on the new school.

Mickey and Buckett's Howard Avenue home was portrayed in a fall 1967 issue of the Hammond Times shortly before the family moved to Crown Point. The new family home, a custom build colonial cape cod rests on eight acres in the Valparaiso moraine and was named Walnut Hill for the estates abundance of black walnut trees. This family home became the setting for many family and holiday gatherings with the children's cousins arriving from Flossmoor, Munster, Highland, Michigan City and Chicago's gold coast. Here the family hosted piano recitals in their music room and saw international guests arrive from England, Colombia, Israel, Iran, the Philippines, Turkey and Venezuela.

During the 1970's Mrs. Pendley a respected oil artist turned her energies and home studio towards interior design and eventually into real estate and construction. In 1978, Mrs. Pendley founded Buckett, Inc., a residential construction company, and she is responsible for a bicentennial block of grand homes along Shorewood Drive in Valparaiso, each depicting an era of American architecture. In 1987, Mrs. Pendley opened another branch of her business with American Dream Realty with offices in a turn of the century home at 150 North Main Street with Crown Point's Courthouse square.

by Trent D. Pendley

He Who Plants a Tree Plants Peace, its a Tree of Life.

Trent D. Pendley, Crown Point, a fifth generation Dunes country resident, spent his early years in Hammond, and when age ten in 1967 moved to Crown Point to his father's country estate, Walnut Hill, located in a forested area of the Valparaiso Moraine. In Crown Point he became a charter member of the Hub Swim Team and was subsequently active with various organizations at Crown Point High School such as the student council. During his collegiate years Trent was a summer employee at the Inland Steel Co. and secured a TOPS award in 1976. He was a member of the Crown Point Young Democrats and in 1980 campaigned for Senator Birch Bayh in Lake and Monroe Counties.

Following his studies at Indiana University, Bloomington and the Hebrew University of Jerusalem, Israel he joined the nations current migration to the sunbelt, and in 1983 moved to Scottsdale, Arizona to be near his maternal grandmother, Marie L. Lewry, and her winter home in Sun City and also other friends from the Calumet Region who had moved to the Valley of the Sun.

Though Trent is a member of the board of his mother's Buckett, Inc. real estate and construction company in Crown Point and remains a contributing correspondent for the local Illiana News on which he has served as a staff member and also as an editor since the papers inception in 1975, he has also maintained residences in Scottsdale, Arizona and Midland-Odessa, Texas where he works managing stores for Barry's Jewelers of Los Angeles.

Trent is Vice President of B'nai B'rith Perm-

Trent D. Pendley stands along the lakefront of his native city, Chicago, where his family first settled in the 1850's making him a fifth generation Dunes Country resident. From this vantage point a century later in 1979, he can point out landmark skyscrapers to which his family has connections.

Trent D. Pendley with his cousin Marion Perkins Bryon in Feb. 1988 inspecting a family garden outside the castle walls in Amberly, Sussex, England. Marion's mother and Grandmother visited the Indiana Dunes in 1935 and 1910 respectively.

ian Basin Lodge 2409, and is active with the UJA locally, in Phoenix and Dallas, and has visited Northwest Indiana's adopted Israeli neighborhoods of Ramat Eshkol in Lod, and Petah Tikvah in Amishav both near Tel Aviv. Through Keren Kayemeth LeIsrael Trent is responsible for the planting of hundreds of trees in the Judean Hills throughout Israel many in honor of citizens of Northwest Indiana and some planted with his hands. In 1988 he dedicated a grove of trees in Israel's American Independence Park named in memory of his late maternal grandmother Marie L. Lewry.

Trent D. Pendley is keenly aware of his deep American roots and his ancestors roles in struggling for religious and civil liberties in colonial Charleston during the 1690s; Their parts in the American Revolution and early connection to the Old Northwest; Heavy losses and migrations during the Civil War; Mercantile experiences in frontier Chicago and the Indiana Dunes. Trent is an avid correspondent, a bookman, and collects family memorabilia and works of art. A hobby is to visit family landmarks from generations past on both the American and European continents. He has written several articles of history on Northwest Indiana and has been asked to give talks on his world travels and on his late family uncle, Justin Robert DeLisles, M.D. a colleague of Louis Pasteur and one of the world's original bacteriologist who at the turn of the century searched for a cure for syphillus with Wasserman, Metchnikoff and others.

When in the Dunes Country visiting his parents Walnut Hill and their Irish Wolfhound pet, Trent often drives to the Indiana Dunes National Lakeshore for which he has a special affection, and to the 1863 home and dune forest neighborhood of his great great grandparents, Sarah and William Lewry in Furnessville. He also visits his Temple Israel in Miller Beach where he retains membership and has served on the congregations Social Action Committee.

Mr. Pendley in the spirit of his early American ancestors keeps abreast of political current events, has lobbied his Hoosier solons on Capitol Hill and holds membership in the Democratic Party, the ACLU and several other Liberal, progressive and environmental organizations.

by Trent D. Pendley

PIEPHO, AUGUST AND DOROTHEA
F195

August Piepho was born on November 17, 1858, in Hanover township north of Brunswick. He worked for his father and also for a farmer near Lowell, In. By working away from home, he learned the English language.

On July 12, 1885 August married Dorothea Wille. She was born in 1866 in Illinois to Friedrich and Maria (Kneif) Wille. The Wille's home was on the Indiana-Illinois state line.

At the time of August and Dorothea's marriage, they received from their parents, 80 acres, a wagon filled with oats and a team of horses. All of the buildings were built by the young couple. A barn was built before their marriage. After their marriage, they lived in the barn until their house was done. It was the custom of the day to board the people that were working for you.

These early years, people did a lot of walking to get places. They had spring wagons and later on a buggy. Once a month they went to the store for supplies. Stone for foundations was hauled from the quarry and it was an all day trip.

August and Dorothea were parents of seven children: Herman, married to Bertha Blume; Clara, who died at the age of 1 year; Emma, wife of Edward Oldendorf; Ora, wife of Otto Russell; Elmer, married to Minnie Triebold; Ida, wife of Carl Pfau; and Dorothea who was single. Sometimes Dorothea was called Dora and later Dorothy. Ora and Ida were teachers in the Lake Co. schools until their marriages and then they taught in Illinois. Dora taught in Lake Co., Indiana.

In 1884 August purchased 40 acres from his father, which were part of the original homestead acres.

They lived on this farm for their entire married life and on July 12, 1935, they celebrated their golden wedding anniversary.

by Mrs. Walter Karstensen

August and Dorothea Piepho in July, 1935. This picture was taken around their golden wedding day.

PIEPHO, CHRISTOPHER AND CATHERINE
F196

Early Day Residents

Christopher Piepho was born on June 20, 1826, in Kohlenfeld, in the Province of Hanover, Germany, to Johann and Engle (Bergmann) Piepho. He was a shoemaker by trade. In 1852 he immigrated to the United States, having sailed to New York. On December 1, 1852, he acquired a land grant from the government for 80 acres located in what is now

143

Christopher Piepho, Sr. (Father), Christopher, Jr., August, Heinrich, Engel Marie, Wilhemine, Catherine Piepho (Mother) Circa 1870.

Hanover Township about 8 miles west of Crown Point. This was known as Hanover Prairie and is still referred to by this name on occasion. He homesteaded this land and in order for him to take possession, he had to live on it for a certain number of days. He built a shack to stay in and furnished it with the barest necessities.

In 1853, he purchased approximately 72 acres from the United States government.

On December 28, 1855, Christopher married Catherine Seegers at the St. John's Lutheran Church at Eagle Lake, Illinois. Catherine was born on September 10, 1834, in Mesmarode, Germany.

They were parents of ten children. Christopher Jr., August, Karoline, who died at the age of 2 years, 7 months; Katharina, who died at the age of 3 months; Heinrich, Engel Marie, Wilhemine, Sophia, Luisa, and a stillborn infant.

In 1857, several of the area residents living in a school district north of Brunswick, petitioned for a schoolhouse on Section 12, Range 10. Christopher Piepho was one of the petitioners. A small frame school was built, but not immediately.

Christopher was a charter member in 1859 of a church then known as German United Evangelical Zion Church (now Zion United Church of Christ).

In 1867, Christopher bought 80 acres from a neighbor and in 1882, he purchased approximately 106 acres.

Catherine died on October 23, 1890, and Christopher on December 6, 1891. They were both laid to rest in the church cemetery.

by Mrs. Walter Karstensen

PIEPHO, DOROTHEA NUELLA
F197

Dorothea ("Dora") Nuella Piepho was born on December 10, 1901. Her parents, August and Dorothea (Wille) Piepho, lived in rural Dyer Indiana, in Hanover Township, on a farm located at 113th and Calumet Avenue. Dora taught for a number of years at Dyer, Schiller and various other schools in the area.

Dorothea Nuella Piepho, 1939.

Dora's sisters and brothers include: Herman, Emma, Elmer, Ida, Ora, and Clara. Herman was a Justice of the Peace in this area until he became a Postal carrier on the main "run" between Chicago and Cincinnati. He married Bertha Blum (the Reverend Blum's, of Zion United Church of Christ, daughter) and they moved to Cincinnati, Ohio. Emma married Edward Oldendorf who farmed nearby on a farm located on the State Line Road. Elmer married Minnie Triebold and farmed the homeplace at 113th and Calumet Avenue. Ida married Carl Pfau who farmed a farm located at 117th and Calumet Avenue. Ida was a teacher at New Elliott, Schiller, and other various schools before her marriage. Ora married Otto Russel and resided in Beecher Illinois. Ora also taught school at Brunswick, Dyer and St. John, Indiana schools. Clara died when she was one year old.

The following story was written by Dora toward the end of her convalescence with tuberculosis. She died in her parents home on May 18, 1944.

Sunset and Sunrise

I am tired today. Physically I feel very comfortable — and very weak. Mentally, too I am not strong today — sometimes discouraged and tired from wondering how it will all turn out. What can I do to get back to a more pleasant and wholesome condition and state of mind? Some folks would recommend a few jokes or a jolly story. The doctor would probably say I need a good meal. My pastor would tell me to read the twenty third psalm. No doubt all of these things would help, but I believe that what I really need is to see a beautiful sunset.

I learned to appreciate the value of sunsets when I was working. After a hard days work in the schoolroom, a lovely sunset never failed to make me feel rested, content, and at peace with the world. You see, I had to drive ten miles every evening. Fortunately, my home was west of the schoolhouse, so I missed nothing of the beauty and the splendor of the western sky. It did something to me. Somehow, mere things did not matter so much. I forgot about the petty troubles I had had that day — that disobedient child; the unexpected visitor who came just when we had decided to leave off that final geography lesson and have instead a general housecleaning of untidy desks. That third grade reading test that had bothered even the brightest of my pupils — how could I remember those in the light of such beauty. I could forget for a while the responsibilities which I know must be faced next day. Three sets of questions must be ready before morning. Those pictures of the Little Red Hen must be ready before morning. Those pictures of the Little Red Hen must be traced for the little folks. That arithmetic problem — but why go on?

As I say, I forgot these things and felt absolutely at peace with the world. The miraculously blended colors soothed me. It was a time for solitude and meditation, deep and holy thought. I could almost hear a stillness and peace saying "Peace, be still."

A sunrise is nice too — but different. Whereas the evening horizon gorgeous, a sunrise is glorious. Watching it gives me new hope — new courage. Many people think a sunrise even more beautiful than a sunset. For myself I have not "lived" it as I have the evening phenomenon, so I am partial to the latter. There seems to me to be this difference; a sunrise inspires one to go and do things while the sunset invites one to come and rest.

I cannot see the sunsets now — only reflections of parts of them in the glass of the windows. I miss them more than I can say. Yet, I know they are there. A beautiful sunset gives me again the feeling that all is well.

Some how I hope that when my time comes to leave this world it may be at eventide and that there may be a sunset in the west. I think I could not be afraid then. That peace that so often has permeated my being will surely not fail me then. I will be satisfied to go with the sunset — and for those left behind there will be a sunrise next morning.

by Mrs. Ralph Oldendorf

PIEPHO, ELMER AND MINNIE
F198

Elmer and Minnie Piepho on their wedding day December 30, 1923.

Elmer Piepho was born in Hanover Township on January 4, 1895 to August and Dorothea (Wille) Piepho. He attended a small one room school in the neighborhood. When a young man, he took six week course in agriculture at Purdue University. He worked for his father on the farm. In 1919, he purchased his first car.

A friend introduced Elmer to a young lady whom he later married. Minnie Triebold was born in Winzlar, Germany, on July 24, 1899, to Wilhelm and Wilhemine (Ackemann) Triebold. At the age of 14, Minnie left Germany on Oct. 3, 1913, and arrived in Baltimore, Maryland, on Oct. 17, 1913. The boat she came on was the Seidlitz. It made a stop in Philadelphia, Pennsylvania first.

This boat was a one (1) chimney boat. The more chimneys a boat had, the faster it would go. The trip to America was delayed because the Sedlitz got an urgent call from another boat that needed help and it turned around and picked up thirty (30) passengers from the boat in trouble.

When Minnie arrived in the United States, she went to Crete, Illinois where she lived with an uncle and aunt. It was required that she attend school until she was 16. She went to a Crete, Illinois public school where she learned the English language. She then worked for farmers near Beecher and Crete, until Elmer and Minnie's marriage.

They were married on Dec. 30, 1923, in the home of the groom by Rev. E.H. Stommel, pastor of St. John's Evangelical Church (United Church of Christ) of Crown Point, Indiana.

One daughter, Marcella, was born to Elmer and Minnie on November 24, 1924 at St. Margaret's Hospital in Hammond, Indiana.

In 1945, they purchased the home place after Elmer's parents' deaths. Elmer spent his entire life on this one farm. He died on December 24, 1964, and a year later Minnie moved from their farm to a new home which had been built on their land. In 1989, she is still residing in this home.

by Mrs. Walter Karstensen

PILLER, SARAH
F199

(and Descendants)

Sarah Margaret Little (born 1-14-1928) daughter of Earl and Emarine Little graduated from Lowell High School in 1946 and attended Purdue University. Sally married Eugene Piller (born 3-2-1922) of Willard, Ohio who holds a civil engineering degree from Purdue University on 6-14-1948.

After 5 years of traveling while being employed by B.F. Goodrich he accepted a job with Bower and Bower Construction Company of Princeton, N.J. They reside in near-by Blawenburg, N.J. Gene retired in 1985. They have 3 daughters.

Jane Marie (born 2-3-1959) married Bruce Wilson on 1-17-1987 and lives in Palo Alto, Ca. They are expecting their first child in August 1988.

Patricia Ellen (born 6-30-1961) married Jack McArdle. They have 1 daughter Kailen (born 4-25-1987). Jack teaches and coaches at a private school. They live in Long Island, N.Y. Patty is a Real Estate Appraiser.

Julie Diane (born 2-19-1963) lives, works and goes to school in Nashville, Tn.

by Mary Mikels

REDAR, MATHIAS
F200

Mathias Redar, with his wife, Maria, and their children comprised one of four families who traveled together from Germany to America in May of 1838. They landed in Lake County, Indiana, and settled in "Prairie West" — later to be known as St. John. The other families were those of Joseph Schmal, Peter Orte, and Michael Adler. They were friends of John Hack in Germany, and were originally to sail at the same time as the Hack family, but for some reason the plans were changed and they didn't make the journey until the following year.

The Redars departed the old country on the ship, Erie, from the port of Le Harve, France, and after a rough journey of 30 days, disembarked at New York City, New York. From there they continued on their travels westward across the states, enduring many hardships along the way.

The route the Schmal family took to Lake County is known, and being the people at that time always traveled together in groups for safety reasons, it is assumed that these families all traveled together. They left New York City by canal boat and journeyed to Buffalo, New York. From Buffalo, they continued on by wagon train to La Porte, Indiana, where a team of oxen and a covered wagon were purchased to complete their trek.

Mathias Redar was about 40 years old, and Maria, about 35. They were not to live a long life in America. Reportedly, Mathias became ill with pneumonia and died in the winter of 1838-1839, the first death of a white settler in St. John Township. Maria soon followed her husband in death. She died in the spring of 1839.

The Redars had six children when they immigrated: Peter, John, Mathias (Jr?), Michael, Anna and Jacob. After the deaths of Mathias and Maria, it is not known where the children lived, or who reared them. There are no Redars listed in the U.S. Census of 1840 for Lake County, Indiana.

But unlike their parents, the Redar children were to live long and prosperous lives in the land they sailed to in their youth. The sons became farmers, and John also had quite a large holding of land in Schererville. Five of the children are known to be buried in St. Michael's Cemetery in Schererville: Peter (1820-1878); John (1821-1884); Mathias (1822-1892); Anna (1826-1887); and Jacob (1838-1916).

by Jim Stephen

REDAR, MATHIAS, JR.
F201

Mathias Redar (Jr?) came to America with his parents when he was a lad in his teens. He was born in Prussia, June 4, 1822, a child of Mathias and Maria Redar. The young Redar settled with his family in Lake County, Indiana, shortly after they immigrated in the summer of 1838. He later went on to marry Margaretha Spanier in October of 1848.

Margaretha too came from Prussia, and immigrated with her parents. She was born the 25th of July, 1831, and was one of eleven children of Jacob and Catherine (Herrmann) Spanier, early pioneers of the county.

Mathias Redar was a farmer, and he and his young wife made their home in St. John Township. They were to have eight children, some of which married members of prominent families in the Schererville area: Margaret (1851), (Mathias Peifer); Adam (1853), (Susan Raascher); Mary (1855), (Peter Stephen); Mathias (1856), (Susan Schumacher); John (1867), (Mary Schmidt); and Jacob (1872). Catherine (1850), and Peter (1859), died in childhood.

Mathias Redar lived to be elderly, and saw many changes in the development of Lake County. He died at the age of 69, on the 25th of February, 1892. Margaretha only lived to be 48 years old. Her death occurred March 3, 1880.

The Redars are buried in St. Michael's Cemetery, Schererville.

by Jim Stephen

REEDSTROM, ERNEST LISLE
F202

E.L. Reedstrom's reference library is a collection of over 30 years. Most books are autographed by his cohorts.

Local Historical Illustrator

Nationally known for his authentic paintings, book and story illustrations dealing with the Civil War period, the early Western Frontier movement and Indian and military tactics, Ernest Lisle Reedstrom is considered an expert in his field.

Born December 8, 1928, in Chicago, Illinois, he was the son of Ernest Earl (a farmer and mail clerk) and Helen (Kruslak) Reedstrom. His family soon moved to Lisle, Illinois, then back to Chicago's northwest side where he enrolled in the Art Institute of Chicago and studied until 1945. Later that year he decided to head West and landed in Apache Junction, Arizona, near the Superstition Mountains.

During the next five years, Lisle and two partners, using half wild burros, packed and guided many groups into the Superstitions. He encountered numerous old-time cowhands, prospectors, Indians and soldiers from whom he heard many wild hair raising tales.

These were his traveling years, when he worked at fencing ranches, cooked for ranch crews, painted scenery on adobe walls for ranchers and for business buildings in town, and prospected for gold, working both placer and lode claims. It was during these times that he found and accumulated an assortment of historical relics which now comprise a part of his reference "museum."

After the war in Korea started Lisle entered the U.S. Army in 1951 and served a 13½ month tour of duty with a Mobile Army Surgical Unit in Korea. He was honorably discharged in 1952 and returned home to Apache Junction and married Shirley Ellen Plucinski.

Lisle and his wife Shirley presently reside on a 5½ acre farm in Cedar Lake, Indiana with their son Wesley Lisle and daughter Karen Lee. He and his wife are owners of The One Stop Ad Agency – Advance Advertising.

Lisle is an active member of The Western Writers of America, the Little Big Horn Association, the Company of Military Historians and the Westerners (Chicago Corral).

He has authored and illustrated four books: Bugles, Banners and Warbonnets (for which he won the Spur Award in 1978 from the Western Writers of America), Historic Dress of the West, Scrapbook of the American West, and U.S. Military Uniform and Accouterments in the Apache Campaign.

Besides illustrating children's western coloring books and illustrating and drawing maps for historical books, as well as illustrating chapter heads and book jacket designs, Lisle has written over 100 articles for national magazines.

Two of these were on the infamous John Dillinger, one entitled John Dillinger Public Hero and Public Enemy, appeared in Guns & Ammo Annual 1975 and the other John Dillinger, Bad Shooter, Bad Driver, Bad Guy appeared in the September 1979 issue of Guns Magazine.

The author has a vast wall to wall personal collection of western reference books of over 30 years and most of them are autographed personally by the authors.

Lisle gives talks for groups on many subjects (for a minimum fee to cover his time) some of these talks are accompanied by color slide shows.

Reedstrom's subjects are the U.S. Military, especially the cavalry, American Indians and Westerns. His paintings have appeared in books and on book covers.

His art hangs in many places throughout the country, in doctors, lawyers and publishers offices, and in schools, libraries and private homes.

His books are descriptive and extensively researched. They are a must for the collector's bookshelf and for students of that period of time that is now gone forever – except for that captured between the pages of Lisle Reedstrom's books by his careful research and embellished with his unique style of art!

by Steven Yaros, Jr.

RIECKER FAMILY
F203

George Riecker was born May 21, 1823 in Wurttemberg, Germany, a descendant of a family who were organ makers in Wittenberge, Germany. George emigrated, embarked at Liverpool, and arrived in New York on September 20, 1851. George had three sisters who also emigrated to the United States, Barbara, who came to U.S. in 1851, married Charles Willman July 3, 1864; Anna Catharine born January 1, 1825, in Germany, married at Lancaster, New York, in 1856, to Christian Weiler, and settled in Lake County, Indiana; Christina born Oct. 9, 1836 Wurttemberg, Germany, married John Leonard Weiler July 6, 1857 in Porter County, Indiana, and settled in Porter Township.

George was married to Catharine Weiler October 13, 1854 in New York. Catharine was also born in Wurttemberg, Germany, on July 6, 1833, daughter of Johannes Weiler and Eva Katharina Echnter. Soon after their marriage, George and Catharine moved to Indiana. George applied to the Porter Circuit Court for naturalization on October 6, 1855. They settled in Lake County near Deep River, where he followed the occupation of farmer, and had a family of seven children: (1) John Levi born Sept. 11, 1855, married Fredericka (Ricky) Wahl Sept. 18, 1884 in Lake County. They lived at Beatrice, Nebraska and had three children, Bertha; Glen; and a child that died very young; (2) William Gottlieb born Nov. 10, 1857, married Alice Catherine Jones Feb. 24, 1881 in Lake Co., In, and they were the parents of six children: (1) Lottie E. was born in Lake Co., Indiana Oct. 13, 1881 and married Warren Luther Jeffers Oct. 11, 1905 in Hamilton County, Nebraska; (2) Emery Charles born May 2, 1884 at Hebron, Indiana, married Gretta Dart April 17, 1907; (3) Elnora Alice born Sept. 12, 1886 at Crown Point, Indiana, married Harvey Peterson; (4) Mabel Eliza born June 1, 1890 in Hamilton Co., Nebraska, died Nov. 10, 1946, married Claude Wright Dec. 8, 1909; (5) Linne Rose born Dec. 28, 1891 in Hamilton County, Nebraska, married Claude Wright July 17, 1947; (6) Zelma Olive born March 28, 1902 at Hamilton Co., Nebraska, married Gerald Miller July 12, 1927. William died at Aurora, Nebraska on Nov. 25, 1940. Alice died June 4, 1911 in Hamilton Co., Nebraska. (3) Caroline C. born March 26, 1860, died August 23, 1870 and is buried in Deer Creek Cemetery, Winfield Township, Lake County, Indiana; (4) George E. born Aug. 1, 1862, died July 2, 1884, buried Deer Creek cemetery; (5) Mary Catharine (Cassie) born November 27, 1864, married Michael Wahl March 12, 1884 in Lake County, IN. Their first 3 children born in Lake County were Grace Elnora, born March 10, 1886; Clarence born 1889, died 1898, Hebron, Indiana; and Esther Mae born 1892, a school teacher in Hebron, died May 1962 in Valparaiso, Indiana. The family moved to Hebron, Indiana where their fourth child, Floyd Milfred, was born Sept. 2, 1894. Floyd married Anna Pearl DeCook in Valparaiso on January 20, 1926. They had 4 children, Barbara Ann (Mrs. John Bastin); Jeanne Marie (Mrs. Willis R. Ziese); Michael; and Janet Ruth (Mrs. John Edward Lauer)./ (6) Henry D. born July 17, 1867, moved to Beatrice, Nebraska in November 1891, and married Alice A. Willey. They had a son living in Beatrice, and a daughter Cynthia; (7) Anna born January 18, 1870, died August 27, 1870, buried Deer Creek cemetery, Lake Co., IN.

George Riecker was drafted for service during the Civil War, on November 11, 1864, at the age of 41, and mustered in at Michigan City, Indiana, to serve with Co. H, 42 Reg't Indiana Infantry for a period of one year. He was 5' 7½" tall, with gray eyes and black hair. He was mustered out at Louisville, Kentucky on July 21, 1865. George contracted an illness while serving at or near Savannah, Georgia in December 1864, which later caused his death, on September 4, 1870, at Deep River, Indiana. At the time of his death, George was the owner of 40 acres in Ross Township, the southwest Quarter of the northeast quarter of Section 33, Town 35, Range 7 in Lake County, Indiana.

After the death of George, his widow married Gottlieb Stegmeier, a native of Wurttemberg,

Germany, in Lake Co., Indiana, June 24, 1871. Gottlieb had been working as a laborer on the Riecker farm. Gottlieb purchased this farm from the estate in 1873. Three children were born to Catharine and Gottlieb: (1) Christina, born April 22, 1872, died November 13, 1873; (2) Rosa born July 20, 1874, married Sept. 20, 1898 to James Arthur Frame, and died April 19, 1954; (3) Emma F. born Nov. 27, 1881, married William Graham November 24, 1903 in Lake County, Indiana.

Gottlieb Stegmeier died April 15, 1913, in Ross Township, from tuberculosis. Catharine died November 22, 1915, both in Lake County, Indiana.

by Betty L. Williams

ROACH, PARIS A. AND EDNA L.
F204

Paris A. Roach Family. (front) Joan, Lois, Erma (rear) Edna, Paris, Jean. Taken in 1944.

Early Gary Residents

Paris Arbuth Roach came to Gary at the age of 21, about 1923, to find himself a steady job. He worked in the steel mills for about 5 years and saved his money. On 28 April 1928 he returned to Dana, Ill. and married Edna Laura Tucker. Paris was born 16 Oct 1902 in rural Corryton, Knox Co., Tenn. He was the 4th of 11 children of Marshall and Martha/Mattie Tuma (Bright) Roach. Marshall was the son of James Franklin/Frank and Dianna (Dunsmore) Roach. Mattie was the daughter of Andrew Jackson and Anna Eliza (Carnes) Bright. About 1909 Marsh and Mattie Roach moved to Fairbury, Livingston Co., Ill., near some old friends from Knox Co., Tenn., to try to better themselves. When he was old enough, Paris worked as a farmhand with his father for several local farmers. By 1920 his parents had saved enough money to purchase 80 acres from Marshall's sister near Mayland, Cumberland Co., Tenn. They loaded their furniture and animals in a boxcar and moved back to Tenn. but Paris returned to Ill. and continued working as a farmhand.

Edna Laura Tucker, born 26 Dec 1906 near Minonk, in Clayton Twp., Woodford Co., Ill., was the 3rd of 10 children of Oliver Ashmer and Emma Geneva (Martin) Tucker. Oliver was the son of Edward A. and Eliza Ellen (Nelson) Tucker and Geneva was the daughter of Presley A. and Eleanor Virginia (Bane) Martin. Ollie and Geneva lived on a farm near Dana, in Minonk Twp., Woodford Co., Ill. (just West of Livingston Co.) that had previously belong to her grandparents, Jotham and Rebecca (Clegg) Martin, which had been purchased by their son, Presley A. Martin, from his father's estate. Oliver never owned the farm but raised his 6 children that survived on it. In the summer of 1921 and 1922 Paris worked on Oliver Tucker's farm and lived with them. By 1923 he had moved to Gary, Ind. and was working in the steel mills. He continued his friendship with the Tuckers and in 1928 he married their daughter, Edna.

Soon after their marriage Paris and Edna had a 5 room red brick bungalow built at 336 Hayes Street in Gary. It was one of the first 3 houses built on the block and is still there today, 61 years later. In 1966 they moved into their summer cottage on Lake Dale Carlia, near Lowell, Ind., that he and his sons-in-law had built in 1955. In June of 1967 the sold the house on Hayes Street.

Shortly after their marriage Paris started working for Wade Williams at his Sinclair Service Station on 19th and Madison St. By the next year he had his own Sinclair Station on 15th and Pierce St., next to the Dixie Dairy Co. This proved to be a blessing in disguise as the Eskilson's of Dixie Dairy kept his growing family of 4 little girls in milk all during the Depression and Paris continued to buy Dixie Dairy products for the rest of his life. In late 1934 he moved his business to 1033 Broadway where it remained until his retirement in 1959. (See related story – Roach's Service.)

Paris and Edna had 4 daughters born in Gary Methodist Hospital. Lois June Roach was born 11 June 1929. She married Jerome Edward Sattler, son of Fred and Barbara (Voeller) Sattler from the Tolleston area, on 2 Dec 1950. They live in Forest Hills Subdivision of Merrillville and Jerome is employed at Handy Andy's on Broadway. They have 4 children. Cheryl Jean (Mrs. Mark) Lamarre, of Niles, Mich., has 2 daughters: Alissa Rochelle and Kristin Renee. Russell Jerome Sattler married Rachelle Reinhold of Lafayette, Ind. and they live in Two Harbors, Minn. with their son, Ryan Scott, and are expecting again in Sept. Dale Howard Sattler is still single and travels the West in his work with an oil research company. Randall Robert Sattler married Susan (Morrison) Dupree and lives in Houston, Tex., with their 1 year old daughter, Kodi Kristin.

Jean Louise Roach, second child of Paris and Edna, was born 1 Sept 1930. On 11 July 1954 she married Robert Dean Bryner, son of Harold and Gladys (Camp) Bryner of Hammond. They have 2 sons: Jeffrey Robert and David Russell. Jeff married Linda (Cowser) Brown and they live in Dyer with Linda's young daughter, Julie Brown. They are the owners of Lake Cycle of Merrillville. Dave is single and works for the Welsh Oil Co. in Merrillville as a computer programmer. Bob is retired from Indiana Bell Telephone and they live in Crown Point.

The third child of Paris and Edna is Erma Jane Roach, born 27 Sept 1931. She was married 16 Feb 1952 to William Covault, son of Benjamin A. and Ida O. (Vorhees) Covault of Hammond. (See related stories – Ben and William Covault.) They had 3 children: Thomas William Covault, D.V.M. who married Jacquelyn Marie Ream of Michigan City, Ind.; Jerry Jay Covault, who died in 1957 at age 15 months; and Cathleen Louise (Mrs. Kenneth E.) Seramur. Both children live near their parents in rural Hebron. Bill and Erma own their own business, Meta-Braze, Inc., in Valparaiso where they manufacture brazing paste. They have 3 grandchildren: Lindsay Ream and Eric Thomas Covault; and Kate Elizabeth Seramur.

Paris and Edna's youngest, Joan Marie, was born 13 Oct 1935. On 15 Jan 1955 she married Glen A. Smith, son of Vernon and Bertha (Nellinger) Smith of Flanagan, Ill. Their children were: Phyllis Marie, of Milwaukee, Wisc.; Scott Allen, who died at 14 months in 1960; Vern Curtis of Peoria, Ill.; and Steve Allen who married Jaynet Cwick and lives in rural Dana, Ill. with their sons: Eric All and Brent Thomas. Glen and Joan live in rural Flanagan where they operate a large farm.

In 1960 Edna suffered a stroke which left her an invalid. After retiring from the station Paris went back to work for the Buy Low Food Stores in Tolleston and on Grant St. where he managed the Dairy Dept. until the end of 1967. In late 1973, when Paris became too ill to take care of her, Edna moved into the Lake Co. Convalescent Home. He died on 2 March 1974 but she lived 11 more years. On 27 June 1985 she died and was buried beside him at Calumet Park Cemetery near Merrillville in the family plot of their daughter, Erma Covault. May they rest in peace.

by Mrs. Erma J. Covault

ROACH, S.F. FAMILY
F205

Bud and Jessie Roach.

Sylvestor (Bud) Roach and Jessie Luttrell were born at the turn of the century near Knoxville, Tenn. A few years later both of their families moved to Illinois where both Bud and Jessie attended the same one-room country school near Fairbury, Illinois. They started dating in high school – "in a horse and buggy."

After graduation, in the spring of 1918, Bud served in the army (World War I) until shortly after the Armistice. The couple was married on Dec. 4, 1919, in Pontiac, Ill., and migrated to Manitoba, Canada, the following April to engage in pioneer farming. Wayne Eugene had been born in Ill. in 1921, and Juanita and Madelle were born in 1922 and 1925 in Manitoba.

In 1926 the family returned to the U.S. and Bud hired in at the Carnegie, Ill. Steel Co. (now U.S. Steel) shortly afterward. Gary, In., was home until his retirement in 1964. Three sons, John, James, and Gerald were born in 1927, 1931 and 1936. The children graduated from Tolleston High School.

In April, 1965, Bud and Jessie went to work at Beechwood Lake Baptist Youth Camp, Bloomfield, IN., where they stayed for about seventeen and a half years. They returned to this area in Jan. 1983, Bud's second retirement.

Wayne Eugene, a Purdue graduate, served in the U.S. Air Force, experiencing the Battle of the Bulge. After World War II's end, he married Reva Hulse and to that marriage three children were born: Wayne Jr., Elaine and Brent. Wayne E. Sr. is a retired supervisor from Amoco Oil Co., Whiting, since Jan., 1981. The couple resides in Crown Point.

Juanita, an Indiana Univ. graduate, married Robert F. Tucker, and they adopted two daughters Denise and Darleen. Juanita retired from teaching in the Gary Community School system in June, 1985. The Tuckers reside in Hobart.

Mardelle the daughter who was born in a log cabin near Minitonis, Manitoba, married Fred G. Spiker. Two sons, Fred W. and Gary D. were added to the family. Mardelle retired from Wisconsin Bell Telephone Co. in 1983, due to illness. She died on Dec. 28, 1984, after a long battle with cancer.

John served in the U.S. Navy, 1945, and married Margaret Pryle, 1948, after his tour of duty in Japan. Margaret died in 1970, leaving a son, John Jr., and a daughter, Nancy. John Sr. married Miriam Moore, 1971, and the couple now live in Phoenix, Az. John is step father to Miriam's children: James, Jeff, Elizabeth and Jeanne. He is a retired Supervisor from Merchant Mill, U.S. Steel Co.

James married Lorraine Nelson and their children are Pamela, Janis, and James Jr. "Jim" is a supervisor of retail sales for Mid-Central Food Sales, Inc. He and Lorraine reside in Hammond. Jim served in the U.S. Army.

Gerald served in the U.S. Marine Corps and later married Rosemary Popa. Their 2 sons are Gerald Jr. and Jody. "Gerry", a graduate of the FBI Academy, retired from the Portage Police Dept. after 20 years of service. He and Rosemary are presently living in Buckeye, Az.

Bud and Jessie celebrated their 69th wedding anniversary on Dec. 4, 1988. They are living in Camelot Estates, Portage, In. They have experienced tremendous changes in their lifetimes: from horse and buggy days to space exploration, from a Model T to an air-conditioned automatic shift automobile, from a log cabin with Bud and a neighbor acting as a mid-wife for the birth of a daughter, to open heart surgery for Jessie in 1966.

by Juanita Roach Tucker

ROACH, WAYNE EUGENE FAMILY
F206

Wayne Eugene Roach was born in Strawn, Illinois, November 3, 1920. A few weeks later he was taken to Manitoba, Canada near Minitonas by his parents Jessie T. (Luttrell) Roach and Sylvester F. Roach, where they staked out a homestead farm. Two sisters were born there: Juanita Roach (Tucker) and Mardell Roach (Spiker). After over six years of farming and trapping they were lured to Gary, Indiana to make "big" wages at U.S. Steel.

Eugene, his family called him, started school at Glen Park grade school in Gary. After three years the family moved and he then attended Merrillville grade school, later moving to Cedar Lake School and for a year at a one room country school near Danforth, Illinois where he was the only 6th grader. The family moved back to the Tolletson area where he graduated in 1938. After one year at Indiana University he went into the Air Force as an electrical specialist on P-38 planes serving in England, France, Belgium and Germany.

He returned to his job at Standard Oil Company Refinery in Whiting, Indiana where he became a Supervisor. He continued his education at Purdue night classes and in 1964 received an Associate Degree in Industrial Engineering. He worked at the Refinery until he retired on January 1, 1981. He and his wife Reva (Hulse) Roach now live in Crown Point. Reva (Hulse) Roach was born on December 27, 1924 in Gary, Indiana. She lived on Bridge St. with her parents Jesse H. Hulse and Bernice M. Hulse until 1946 when she married Wayne Eugene Roach. She has an older sister Audrey M. Hulse (Mathias). She attended Ambridge grade school and Horace Mann High School. She worked awhile at Gorden's Department Store and during the war worked as crane operator at the American Bridge Company.

In February 1946 she married Wayne E. Roach (Eugene) (Gene). From that union three children were born: Wayne Eugene Roach Jr., Elaine Lavonne Roach (Thomas), and Brent Lee Roach. They lived on Taney St. in Ambridge until 1967 when they moved to Crown Point. The children followed their Mother's footsteps attending Ambridge grade school and even some of the same teachers. Wayne, Jr. and Elaine went on to graduate from Horace Mann High School and Brent from Crown Point High. Both Wayne Jr. and Brent graduated from Purdue University. Wayne Jr. received a Masters Degree from Ohio State, and is living in Tucson, Arizona with his wife Donna and daughters Kelly and Allyson. Elaine is now divorced from Richard Thomas and lives in Crown Point with two daughters, Janet Lee and Amy Rae. Brent lives at Lakes of the Four Seasons with his wife Cynthia, daughter Jennifer Lynn and son Kyle Wayne.

by Wayne Eugene Roach

ROCKWELL, JULIUS
F207

Julius Rockwell, son of Timothy and Malinda (Brown) Rockwell, was born 21 November, 1861. He married Adaline (Addie) Meeker about 1884. She was born in Cass County, Indiana, 1 August 1865, the daughter of Hiram and Mary (Bryan) Meeker. They had four children, all born and raised in Crown Point. Rae Inez, born 1885 married Richard Dyer of Hammond. Julius Irl, born 1887, married Irene Mulhern and in retirement moved to Florida. Harry Meeker, born 1890, became a mining engineer, married Dell Gowans, and spent his life in Toole, Utah. The youngest daughter was Hortense, born 1895, who married William Heinze. Addie died 24 April, 1943, and he joined her 4 October, 1944.

William Thompson, son of Alexander and Mary Jane Watson, was born on a farm about a mile south of U.S. 30 in Ross Twp., 5 August, 1870. He married Alta Meeker, daughter of Hiram and Mary (Bryan) Meeker, in Crown Point 18 April, 1894. In the early 1900's he and his family moved to Chicago where he was a salesman for the Armour Co. Some years later he came back to Crown Point and opened a grocery and filling station next to his home across the Lake County Fair Grounds. In later years, he and his wife spent their winters in Florida. He died in Crown Point 13 March, 1935.

Alta, his wife was born 1 April, 1868, in Carroll Co., Indiana. She, like her sister, graduated from Crown Point High School and became a teacher in the local school system until her marriage. They had 4 children; Harold Hiram, born 1897, married Ernestine Rosenbaum and lived in Hobart, Ind.; Helen Mary, born 18 May, 1901, married Elmer Rosenbaum and they also lived in Hobart where Elmer was a building contractor. Two sons Keith, born 1904, and Walter, born 1906, both died as children. Alta died 7 April, 1949.

by Ruth Demmon

ROGERS, JOSEPH S.
F208

Joseph Samuel Rogers was the first son born to Calvin Mahlon Rogers and Martha Elizabeth Beattie who were married January 11, 1867. His father Calvin Mahlon was born July 17, 1848 in Portage County, Ohio to Joseph C. Rogers and Charlotte Cox Gilbert who were married January 6, 1835. His mother Martha Elizabeth was born August 5, 1847 to Samuel R. Beattie and Sarah J —. Samuel R. Beattie, born in 1820, is the son of Robert Q. Beattie who was born in Cumberland County, Pennsylvania March 11, 1791 and on January 30, 1815 he married Mary Kelso, born 1798. In 1838 the family moved from Cumberland County Pa. to Richland County, Ohio and located on a farm near Mansfield.

It is thought that when Samuel's brother James Q. Beattie emigrated to William County, Ohio in October of 1849 that he also went, as the 1850 Federal Census of Ohio shows Samuel R. (age 30) a cabinet maker (born in Pa.) with his wife Sarah J. (age 27) born in Ohio and a son Joseph (age 4), Elizabeth M. (age 3) and Samuel W. (age 1) all in Williams County, Ohio along with brother

James and his family.

Joseph Samuel Rogers was born July 31, 1872 and he married Ida Mae Marks who was born January 29, 1877 and died July 3, 1938. She was the daughter of William H. Marks and Sarah Matilda Shimp. Joe and Ida lived most of their life in Waterloo, Indiana and had three children: Violet Mae born May 4, 1902 who married Carl O. Borrner, Mahlon Joseph born January 25, 1904 and Wanda Sarah (Doris) born July 1, 1907 who married Steven James Yaros of Tolleston (Gary), Indiana.

From around 1912 thru 1930 Joe and Ida Rogers lived in Gary, Indiana.

On April 6, 1947 Joseph S. Rogers passed away and he is buried in the Waterloo Cemetery beside his wife.

by Steven Yaros, Jr.

ROSENBAUM, ELMER
F209

Elmer Rosenbaum was born near Salt Creek in Porter County, Indiana, 28 February, 1890, the second child of Herman and Johanna (Granzow) Rosenbaum. He was raised on the family farm north of Wheeler and was educated in the Trinity Lutheran School in Hobart, and when his parents retired from the farm, he too moved to Hobart. He married Helen Thompson 27 September, 1923. She was the daughter of William and Alta (Meeker) Thompson of Crown Point. His life was spent building quality homes all over the area including in later life his own small subdivision known as "Cleveland Terrace" on the east side of Hobart.

Elmer and Helen had three children. Ruth born 28 April, 1926, married Floyd Demmon in 1947, who is the family genealogist and lives in Hobart. Herman, born 19 September, 1935, married Nancy Jenkins in 1956, and is a builder like his father, living in Hobart. Peggy Ann, born 1 June, 1940, married Robert Nevin in 1963 and became a nurse, living in Orland Park, Illinois.

Elmer died 19 February, 1968, and Helen 2 July, 1981. Both are buried near his parents in Hobart's Crown Hill Cemetery.

by Ruth Demmon

ROSENBAUM, HERMAN JULIUS
F210

Herman Julius Rosenbaum was born in Rattai Province, Prussia, January 1859, the son of Johann and Ernestine (Kallies) Rosenbaum. The family had for several generations owned and operated the local mill. At the age of 22 in September, 1881, he left his home for America, traveling to Wanatah, Indiana, where he stayed with relatives for awhile. He worked as a laborer on the "Wolf Farm" where he met and married Johanna Granzow 26 October, 1886. She was the daughter of Theodore and Kristina (Netzow) Granzow who had emigrated from Pomerania.

Within 10 years they had their own farm north of Wheeler, Indiana, where they raised their 11 children. Paul (Edith Cary) remained on the farm; Elmer (Helen Thompson) of Hobart; Hedwig (Carl Briney) of Hobart; Martha (Vincent Boyd) owned Boyd Construction Co.; Clara (Dan Haxton) of Wheeler; Ernestina (Harold Thompson) of Hobart; Ewald (Viola Kegebein, Lillian Baumer) of Hobart; Emma (Leslie Storey) of Hobart; Herbert (Ruth Ritter) of Hobart; Albert (Harriet Casper) of Hobart; and Myrtle (Frederick Rampke, Eldo Bell) also of Hobart.

In the early 1900's Herman and Johanna built a home on Lake Street in Hobart and left the farm to their son Paul's care. They were members of Trinity Lutheran Church in Hobart from its beginning and their children were educated in its Church's Day School.

Herman died 2 October, 1928 and Johanna 21 August, 1954. Both are buried in Hobart's Crown Hill Cemetery.

by Ruth Demmon

ROSS, DONALD J. FAMILY
F211

Donald J. Ross was born on February 26, 1923, to Joseph and Mabel Love Ross in their farm home in Center Township west of Leroy. He had two brothers, Harold and Roland, and three sisters, Margaret, Marian and his twin, Dorothy. He attended Washington Elementary School in Center Township and graduated from Crown Point High School in the class of 1941. He was active in sports in high school. He also played on the local softball team and on the Goldbrick football team for several years. His 38½ years service in the United States Steel Mill in Gary was interrupted by the three years he spent in the U.S. Army during World War II and the three years he worked with the Dillabaugh Moving Engineers.

On September 28, 1946 he married Phyllis Dillabaugh, daughter of Ellis and Lora Shay Dillabaugh, in Leroy Methodist Church. She was also a product of the local school system, having moved to Center Township in 1947 from the town of Crown Point. She had a half brother and half sister, Grant and Shirley Dillabaugh and three brothers, Donald, Ellison and Howard Lynn Dillabaugh.

Donald built a home on the Northwest corner of the family farm and it remains their home. The marriage was blessed with one son, Jerry, born January 20, 1948 and two daughters, Judith, born April 8, 1950 and Janet born April 20, 1953. All three attended Washington School in Center Township and graduated from Crown Point High School and Purdue University, West Lafayette, Ind. Jerry married Karen Pearson of Sheridan on January 25, 1970 and became an astronaut in 1980. He flew on the shuttle, Atlantis in November, 1985 and again in December 1988. On the 1985 mission he enjoyed two six hour space walks while experimenting on "Ease" and "Access" – forerunners to building the space station. He is presently scheduled for another flight aboard Atlantis in June, 1990. Judith married Michael Futa, a pharmacist of South Bend, In. on August 22, 1970, and taught elementary school in LaPorte, Ind. Janet married William Rattazzi, an electronic technician of Vine Grove, Kentucky, July 11, 1987 and taught in the Junior High School in Crown Point. They have one son, Joseph Ross, born November 3, 1988. Jerry and Karen are parents of Amy, born March 30, 1971, who is attending Purdue University, West Lafayette and Scott, born April 23, 1972 who is a senior at Friendswood, Texas High School. Judi and Mike are parents of five sons, Adam, born November 14, 1975; Matthew, born October 24, 1978 and Michael, born March 30, 1982 – all students in the Granger, Ind. school system. Also Scott, born July 22, 1986 and John born February 13, 1989.

The family, though not geographically close, stay in close touch and enjoy as many family reunions as possible, at least once a year or more.

by Donald J. Ross

ROSS, HAROLD JOSEPH FAMILY
F212

Harold Joseph Ross was born to Joseph John and Mabel Ellen Love Ross, on August 29, 1919, at home on their farm in Winfield Twp., Leroy, Indiana. The oldest son of six children, he attended Leroy and Washington grade schools (both two room schools) and graduated from Crown Point High School in 1937. Helping his father farm, he also worked at Letz Manufacturing Co. until drafted to serve in World War II from April 1941 to September 1945. He served in the Quartermaster Corp. as a mechanic, three years being spent in England. Upon honorable discharge, he returned to Letz Mfg., later joining Crown Point Telephone Co. in 1946, as a lineman.

On May 29, 1948, he married Mary Ann Diesslin, of LaPorte, Indiana. Born at home on the farm, on October 27, 1923, she was the third of five children of Gustaf Adolph and Clara Helen Hummel Diesslin. She attended Center Twp. Grade School, graduated from LaPorte High School, and received a B.S. in Home Economics and Science from Purdue University in 1945. First teaching Home Economics, she then became the first County Home Demonstration Agent, White County Indiana ever had.

Their family increased with the birth of four sons. Keith Harold was born May 18, 1949 in Gary, Indiana. He attended Leroy and Winfield grade schools (both two rooms), graduated from Crown Point High School, and received a B.S. in electronics engineering technology from Purdue University. He is a supervisor of systems engineering for Allen-Bradley Division of Rockwell International. He married Mary Eileen McCarthy, a special education teacher from Gary, Indiana on September 2, 1978. Mary was born on March 23, 1947. A son Andrew Keith was born December 30, 1980. They live in Mentor-on-the-Lake, Ohio.

Harold's second son, Lanny Alan was born March 19, 1951 in Gary also. He attended Leroy, Palmer and Winfield Twp. Elementary schools, also graduating from Crown Point High School, and received a B.A. in Business Administration from Indiana University. Living in Arlington Heights, Illinois, he is a salesman for Frito-Lay.

Dean Eric, third son, was born September 3, 1952, in Gary. He attended Leroy, Palmer, and Winfield elementary schools, Taft Junior High School, and graduated from Crown Point High School. He received a B.S. in Horticulture from Purdue University. Dean is a Horticulture specialist for the Arlington Heights Parks

Department, both living and working in Arlington Heights, Illinois.

Fourth son, Kent Lee was born June 26, 1958 in Gary. He attended Winfield Grade School and Winfield Twp. Elementary school, graduated from Crown Point High School, and received a B.S. in Psychology and another B.S. in Electronics Engineering Technology, both from Purdue University. He is an Automatic Test Equipment Engineer for Allen-Bradley Division of Rockwell International. On August 6, 1983, he married Mary Catherine Horban, a registered nurse, from Rochester, Indiana. Mary was born in Rochester on May 28, 1960. Son, Jacob Robert, born March 8, 1986 and daughter, Kristin Marie, born May 18, 1988, complete the family, now living in Huntsburg, Ohio.

Mary Ann returned to teaching three years when three of the boys were all in college at the same time. Crown Point Telephone Co. was bought out by Illinois Bell Telephone in 1954 and Harold became Construction supervisor of an area covering from the Kankakee River to Lake Michigan, in Lake Co. Indiana. In 1976, the Commerce Commission forced the sale of Illinois Bell Telephone in Indiana, to Indiana Bell Telephone Co. within the state boundaries. Thus Harold retired in 1982 with thirty-six years service to Indiana Bell Telephone Co.

Harold and Mary Ann had a house built by Cooper Bros. in Gary; brought out to a corner of Harold's father's farm, in Winfield Twp., on wheels, and set on the constructed foundation. So in April 1953, this three acres became the home for our young family. We later purchased four and a quarter additional acres immediately behind the original piece.

The boys raised chickens, and rabbits, and we all gardened, and Mom canned and froze hundreds of quarts of fruits and vegetables each year. All the boys clothes were made at home, as were Mary Anns and some of Harolds. School activities and activities at Leroy Methodist Church were very important in our daily lives. All repair work, be it mechanical, electrical, car repairs, carpentering and etc. were proficiently done by Harold. The hard working, frugal training from our parents German heritage worked well for us and in training our offspring. All four sons earned most of the money for their education. We all loved nature and spent vacation each summer traveling all over the United States with our four sons. We had great fun together!

by Mrs. Harold J. Ross

ROSS, JOHN, JR. FAMILY

F213

(1860-1900)

John Ross Jr. was born December 4, 1860 on the farm that his father owned one mile west of what was to become Cassville, later named Leroy. He worked on the farm and attended Dublin School which was located one mile west of Leroy at the southwest corner of 139th Ave. and Arizona St. Hannah Carson was a teacher there the winters of 1864-1866. She married a local farmer, Harvey Gibbs in 1868.

John Jr. married Carrie E. Kries (1865-1936) of North Judson, Indiana on March 22, 1888. Carrie was born in Bavaria and came to the United States in 1867 when she was two years old. Carrie's father, Jacob Kries, was a well known farmer and lumber merchant in North Judson. John continued to farm his father's farm. He raised hay and oats which were shipped to Chicago by rail, to feed horses there.

John and Carrie's children were Joseph John (1889-1976), twins Charles E. (1892-1985) and Cornelius (1892-1892), Edna A. (1898-1983), and Mary J. (1900 – living today). Cornelius died at the age of three days. Joseph, Charles, Cornelius and Edna were all born on the farm. In 1899, John Jr. built a new house for his family in Leroy. Being ill at the time, this made him closer to his doctor. Thus Mary J. was born in Leroy and this house was her home most of her life.

John Jr. died at age thirty-nine. This left Carrier to raise the four children. To provide for them, she rented the farm out, sold poultry and eggs and boarded men who worked on the Pennsylvania Railroad. What an admirable lady! Once a year, she took the train into Chicago to buy fabric for clothing and household use, also other yearly supplies. She took her family to the Presbyterian Church in Leroy. Later it became the Leroy Methodist Church.

Joseph John married Mabel Love and they had a farm just across the field from where he grew up. Charles E. continued to farm his father's farm. Edna A. married Richard Wright and they lived on the Wright farm near Salem, later moving to Lansing, Illinois. Mary J. worked in the Calumet region from 1918-1955, living in Hammond then. She retired in 1955 from Combustion Engineering, and returned to Leroy. Mary J. is still a resident of Leroy, living in the house she was born in.

John, Carrie, Joseph J. and Charles E. are buried at Salem Cemetery. Cornelius E. is buried at Southeast Grove Cemetery and Edna A. is buried at Maplewood Cemetery in Crown Point, Indiana.

by Mrs. Harold J. Ross

ROSS, JOHN, SR. FAMILY

F214

(1826-1898)

John Ross, Sr. was born in Ireland on January 2, 1826. The potato famine of 1845 through 1847 was probably the reason he departed for the United States. He departed Londonderry on the Steamship Basque Affghan and arrived at Philadelphia, Pennsylvania on May 31, 1849. In 1856, he purchased eighty acres of land approximately five miles east of Crown Point for one dollar and twenty-five cents an acre. This land had been homesteaded only four years before his purchase. He appeared in Circuit Court and was naturalized at Lake County on June 5, 1860. In 1864, he deeded a right of way through his property for construction of the Chicago and Great Eastern Railroad, later called the Panhandle, and then the Pennsylvania Railroad. The railroad was a blessing for local farmers for they could ship their milk and grain to many markets. The railroad also made traveling much easier. Mrs. Hannah Gibbs states in her book, "we heard of a wonderful thing that was going to happen, a town was going to be built close to the John Ross farm, and during the summer of 1869, we could see the store building going up." Amos Edgerton was the man that built the store and a dwelling house for his family. The town, established in 1869 was called Cassville after Dr. Cass who had a practice there. It was later re-named Leroy.

John Sr.'s wife Jane Wilson was born in Ireland and died in 1889. Their children were Isabelle J., Robert, Anneliza, John Jr., and Joseph Andrew. John was a farmer his whole life near Leroy. He raised hay and oats which were shipped by rail to Chicago to be sold as feed for horses. The children attended Dublin school which was located one mile west of Leroy at the south west corner of 139th Ave. and Arizona St. Hannah Carson was a teacher there the winters of 1864 through 1866.

Joseph Andrew died at age twenty-two months and Annaliza died at twenty-eight. Robert married Maggie J. McKinney on January 1, 1880 and they had three sons; Marshall, Walter, and Harry. Robert, with his sons farmed and operated a sawmill near Southeast Grove for many years. Isabelle lived most of her life with Nettie Gordon at Palmer. Nettie was a sister to Robert's wife Maggie. John Jr. married Carrie Kries of North Judson and continued to farm the land that his father had farmed for many years.

John, his wife, Jane, Isabelle, Robert, Anneliza and Joseph Andrew are buried at Southeast Grove Cemetery. John Jr. is buried at Salem Cemetery a few miles east of Palmer.

John Ross Jr. was basically a farmer and had a lot of acreage in Center, Eagle Creek and Winfield townships. Some of his original acreage, purchased in 1856, remains in the family in 1989. Great grandson Harold J. Ross owns one parcel in Winfield Township. Another parcel, also in Winfield Township, which grandson Earl Charles Ross owned until his death in 1985, is now owned by great, great, grandson, Dean E. Ross.

by Mrs. Harold J. Ross

ROSS, JOSEPH JOHN FAMILY

F215

Joseph John Ross, oldest child of John and Carrie (Kreis) Ross was born on October 9, 1889, in the family farm house one mile west of Leroy. His grandfather, John Ross, Sr., came from Scotland, and his mother, who was born in Germany, came to America when two years of age with her parents Jacob and Wilhelmina Kreis. Joseph's father passed away at age 39, which left his mother with four children to raise — Joseph John, Earl Charles, Edna Anna (Richard) Wright, and Mary Jane. Charles' twin brother, Cornelius, died shortly after birth. Joseph was almost 11 at the time of his father's death.

Joseph attended Dublin School, which was located on the southwest corner of what is now 139th and Arizona Streets. It was a one-room school and students had to walk to school and also help start the fire in the stove to heat the room on cold days. He attended Crown Point High School, rode the train from Leroy, and walked from the train to high school at North

Ward School, located on North Street in Crown Point. He graduated from high school in 1907, then went to Purdue University and took a one-year course in agriculture.

Joseph was planning to marry Mabel Ellen Love in 1911, but developed a serious illness and went to Colorado and stayed with his mother's sister and her husband, Mr. and Mrs. Allen Reichard, for a year to regain his health.

On April 11, 1912, he and Mabel were married at the home of her parents, Peter K. and Addie M. Love in Leroy. He took up farming that spring on an 80-acre farm his mother purchased from Henry Battermann and she got him started at farming by purchasing equipment and cows at farm sales. Later he bought 27 acres, for a total of 107 acres. Charles helped his brother farm the first summer. Some of the crops raised on the farm through the years were corn, which had to be husked by hand during some mighty cold weather; wheat and oats, which had to be husked by hand; clover and alfalfa hay, which had to be put in the mow or stacked in the field after the mow was filled. This work was done with using horses and manual labor. Buckwheat, soybeans, and potatoes were also raised.

All farm jobs were done by horse power until the middle 1930's. Joseph usually milked 8 to 10 Holstein cows by hand and took the milk to the creamery in Leroy. When the creamery burned down, milk was then shipped on the train. Later on, milk was picked up by truck.

Threshing bees were common. Several farmers banded together, using a neighbor's threshing machine to thresh the grain. The housewife would prepare a huge meal for 10-12 men.

In 1935 a new barn was built with lumber from his mother's woods. His cousins, the Ross brothers, from Southeast Grove, sawed the wood for the barn.

During the depression Joseph raised navy beans, which were cleaned by hand, to sell along with eggs to get extra money to buy some groceries to feed the family.

Poland China pigs, Rhode Island red chickens, and white ducks were also raised on the farm.

At one time Joseph baled hay for different parties around the country, and jacked up an old Buick to use the wheel power to operate the baler.

Joseph and Mabel were married 52 years when she passed away on April 28, 1964. To this union were born six children — three daughters: Margaret Vivian (George) Schlemmer, Marian Love (Robert) Kazda, both of Crown Point, and Dorothy Jane (William) Tholke of Cincinnati, Ohio; and three sons: Harold Joseph (Mary Ann nee Diesslin) and Donald John (Phyllis nee Dillabaugh) of Crown Point, and Roland Eugene, who passed away at the age of 10, due to encephalitis as a result of measles. Donald and Dorothy are twins. There are 15 grandchildren and the great-grandchildren now total 22.

In July 1967 Joseph married Lottie (last name not known) of Alton, Illinois. After her death in June 1968, he married Nannie Gray of Carbondale, Illinois, on September 28, 1968. In May 1969 Joseph sold his farm and moved to Florida, living in two different homes. From Florida, he and Nannie drove all the way from Florida to Pasco, Washington, with all their possessions (both were in their 80's). From Pasco they moved to Cedar Lake, Indiana. After a short time they moved again to Florida; from Florida to Mt. Vernon, Indiana, living in two different homes. Nannie died in Mt. Vernon July 6, 1975, after almost 7 years of marriage and seven moves for Joseph and eight for Nannie while in their 80's. On October 11, 1975, Joseph married Rosa Simmons in New Haven, Illinois, and Joseph moved from Mt. Vernon, Indiana to New Haven, Illinois, where he died September 18, 1976, 3 weeks short of 87 years of age. Rosa died March 2, 1977, in New Haven. Joseph and Mabel are buried at Salem Cemetery.

by Margaret V. Schlemmer

RUSSEL, OTTO
F216

On a whim, a friend of Otto Russel, talked Otto into taking the Watkins wagon and route as a very young man. He'd go as far as Peotone, Illinois and other surrounding areas; staying overnight at friends or customers homes.

After several years, Otto went into the insurance business. He began dating Miss Ora Piepho, a teacher, in a courtship that lasted ten years. She was the daughter of Dorothea (Wille) and August Piepho, whose farm and residence was at the corner of Calumet Avenue and 113th; approximately three miles north of Brunswick, Indiana.

Otto's parents were Wilhelmine (Claus), also known as Mina, who was born on April 16, 1863 and Herman Russel, born June 30, 1861. They were married August 21, 1881, in Hanover Township in Lake County, Indiana. Their farm was on the north side of 125th, just east of Calumet Avenue. Their children were: Clara, who married Ben Reichert; Alma, who remained single; Ben, who married Bernice Seegers; Harry, who married Wilhelmina Kohlscheen; Lydia, who married Harry Fick; and Herman, Jr., who married Mary Rust. At age 82 years, Otto's mother, Wilhelmina, died on December 25, 1945. His father, Herman Sr., died on April 27, 1931 at age 70 years. (Otto's brother Ben was the last of the family to run the farm.)

Otto was born on January 7, 1888. His wife Ora Piepho was born July 26, 1893. She was a very kindly person who had taught at Schiller, Dyer, and Brunswick schools. They married June 10, 1925 and resided in Beecher, Illinois. Their son, Richard Otto, was born on June 14, 1930 and their daughter, Jeanette D., was born on December 8, 1937. Ora died on December 24, 1937.

After Ora's death, Otto went into the tree-trimming business until he died in 1962. Jeanette went to live with her aunt and uncle in rural Dyer, Indiana. She grew up, attended Dyer High School and married Arthur Klemme. Their children include Cory, Becky, April, Kurt, Dianna and Kevin. They resided in Munster and later moved to DeMotte, Indiana.

Richard remained living with his father in Crown Point, Indiana, after his mother's death. He obtained his education and served several years in the army. Upon his return, he worked for the Remington-Rand Corporation and was sent to various parts of the country. He married Peggy (Nyles) Russel and resided in New York for quite some time. He then returned to Chicago with his wife to be near where their only son, Thomas born in 1966, was attending college. Richard underwent treatment for multiple sclerosis at Hines Hospital. He died in his home on February 13, 1986.

by Mrs. Ralph Oldendorf

SCHAEFER, JACOB
F217

Jacob Schaefer, a native of Germany, is counted among the early settlers of Lake County, Indiana. He was born February 1, 1806, in Nudlingen, Germany, and was reared and educated in the old country. (The meaning of the German name, Schaefer, in English is: shepherd.) As a young man of 26, Jacob married to Miss Margaret Willem, also a na-

On a whim, Otto Russel took over his friends Watkins Route for about three years. This photo was taken the year of 1912.

Jacob Schaefer (1806-1887)

John (1854-1934) and Susan (1864-1955) (Jourdain) Schaefer.

tive of Germany, a daughter of Linus willem and Katherina (Schafer) Willem. They were united in marriage the 11th of February 1832. The couple were to have nine children, five of which were born in Germany: Jacob (Magdalena); Bartholomew (Magdalen Bohling); Margaret (Francis P. Keilman); Johanna (Frank Rettig); and Cecelia (George Ludwig).

In the mid 1840's the Jacob Schaefer family sailed to America and eventually landed in Lake County, Indiana, where the other four children were born: Michael; Elizabeth (Nicholas Thielen); Barbara (Peter Barman); and John (Susan Jourdain).

The Schaefers first lived in Center Township and then around 1863, they settled in St. John Township. Jacob purchased from the government a 560 acre farm near the Beaver Dam (three miles east of Crown Point), land which he tilled and cultivated for twenty some years. The immigrant became fully Americanized when he was made a citizen by naturalization on the 14th of December, 1854.

Jacob Schaefer died at the age of 81, on December 19, 1887. Margaret preceded him in death by three years. She died the 4th of February, 1884. They are buried n the St. John the Evangelist Church Cemetery, St. John, Indiana.

From the 1904 History of Lake County, Indiana, by T.H. Ball.

by Jim Stephen

SCHAEFER, JOHN
F218

John P. Schaefer of St. John Township was a life-long resident of Lake County, Indiana, and for many years had been one of its prominent farmers and representative citizens. He was frugal, industrious and a good manager all through his career, and at the prime of his years had acquired a competence in a fine landed estate. He also identified himself with various community interests, and was an all-round successful man, a fine example of sterling American citizenship.

Mr. Schaefer was born in a log cabin in Center Township of Lake County, on the 9th of February, 1854, a son of Jacob Schaefer (1806-1887) and Margaret (Willem) Schaefer (1813-1884). He was nine years old when the family moved over into St. John Township, where he was educated in the county school until the age of twelve. John then remained at home and assisted his father in the cultivation of the farm. Later the two went into partnership and for many years worked their farm together.

On October 9, 1883, John married Miss Susan Jourdain, who was born in St. John Township, October 5, 1864, a daughter of John Jourdain (1822-1907) and Johanna (Klassen) Jourdain (1840-1928), old settlers of Lake County. John and Susan lived with his father and mother on the Schaefer farm, and had seven children, six of which lived to adulthood. The first child, a daughter Margaret, died as an infant. The other six children were: a second daughter named Margaret (1887-1951) (Joseph Wachter) (Adam Wirtz); Edward (1888-1961) (Rosalia Echterling); Carrie (1890-1977) (Norbert Bohling); Cecelia (1893-1927) (Edward Schutz); Mayme (1897-1987); and John (1904-1963) (Anna Fisher).

At the time of his father's death in 1887, John bought the homestead and continued grain farming, gradually adding to his estate interests as he prospered. He owned over five hundred acres in the Beaver Dam area, east of where the homestead was situated, and a seventy-three acre farm in St. John on Joliet Street, east of the Monon Railroad tracks. John and Susan located on this farm in 1901, having lived on the Schaefer homestead previous thereto. John gave most of his own labors and attention to the seventy-three acre farm, where he did general farming and stock-raising, and rented nearly all the rest of his land.

John Schaefer tilled his fields with teams of horses – he never owned or used a tractor. Working two plow teams of five horses each, John would alternate plow teams after each round trip of cutting the land, giving the horses an opportunity to rest. Mr. Schaefer kept between 20 to 25 head of horses, and raised 4 or 5 colts a year. Many a field of timothy hay was planted to feed these animals, and at the end of harvest, when the barns were full, any extra hay was shipped to Chicago, Illinois, via the Monon Railroad.

Mr. Schaefer was a Democrat as far as concerns national politics, but in local affairs he tried to vote for the best man, regardless of what party tag he bore. He and Susan had church membership with the St. John Catholic Church.

In their later years in 1919, the Schaefers moved to the town of Crown Point, where they lived out the remainder of their lives at their home on East Joliet Street. They then joined St. Mary's Church. At this time their son Edward farmed the Schaefer homestead, and John would walk from town to the Beaver Dam area and back almost every day to assist his son in the labors of the farm. In October of 1933, John and Susan Schaefer celebrated their Golden Wedding Anniversary with a host of relatives and friends.

John Schaefer died at the age of 79, on January 20, 1934, with his wife and children at his bedside. He was the last of nine brothers and sisters to answer the call to leave his loving family. Susan lived to be 90 years old. She died on the 30th of June 1955. John and Susan are buried in St. Mary's Cemetery, Crown Point.

The Schaefer homestead was sold in 1936, after being in the hands of the same family for nearly 75 years.

From the 1905 History of Lake County, Indiana, by T.H. Ball; additional information: Jim Stephen.

by Jim Stephen

SCHAFER, CLARENCE J.
F219

Former Schererville Town Official Dies

Clarence J. Schafer, often called the oldest politician in Schererville died after a short illness at the Lake County Convalescent Home. He was 91.

Schafer was the grandson of Nicholas Scherer, the founder of Schererville. Schafer joined the fire department in Schererville in 1914 and was a member for 48 years and its chief for 32 years. He was also retired from the New York Central Railroad, where he worked for 56 years. He was a veteran of World War I.

Schafer was elected to the Town Board in the late 1920s and served on the board for more than a dozen years, including an eight-year stint as board president. He also served on the town Plan Commission, and was building commissioner, and a member of the contractor licensing board.

Schafer was awarded the first community service award from the Schererville Town Board in 1981.

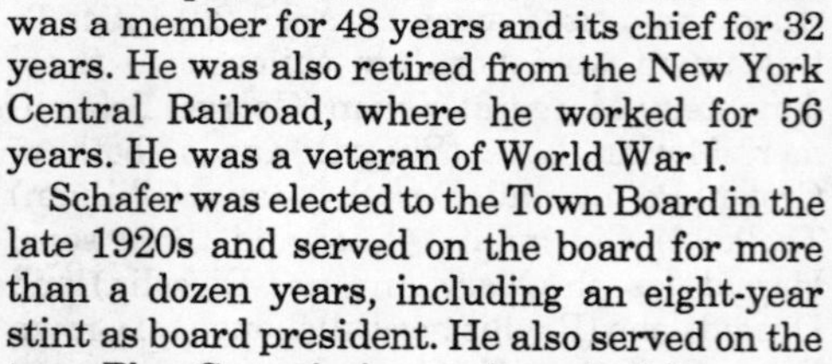

SCHEERINGA, JAKOB
F220

The Jakob Scheeringa homestead in 1906, Leek, Groningen Province, Netherlands.

Jakob Scheeringa (1856-1941), Grietje Heuker (1863-1917).

The Scheeringas Arrive in America

Jakob Scheeringa was born on February 16, 1856, in Sebaldeburen, in Groningen province, the Netherlands. He was the ninth of twelve children of Hemke Scheeringa and Maartje Snip. Jakob had four brothers and six sisters. One brother died only one week old.

Grietje Heuker was born May 28, 1863, in Niebert, in the same province. Grietje's parents were Egbert Heuker and Margareta Datema. Grietje had one older sister, Saapke.

In May 1885, Jakob married Grietje. They had 10 children, 8 boys and 2 girls.

Jakob and Grietje were very poor and never owned any land in Holland. There was a class system at the time, so if you were born poor, you stayed poor. My great-uncle Tony, now age 85, recalls his father weeding the garden with tears falling to the ground, not knowing how to feed his large family. Jakob's daughter Margaret got rickets because of poor nutrition. The family had a few piglets, milk from cows, and chickens for food.

The Scheeringa family lived in a typical Dutch house with attached barn. The homestead is shown in the 1906 photo. The older boys slept in the barn, the younger children in a closet-bed recessed into the wall. The children walked 2 miles each way to a 4-room school in Eenamatil.

The Scheeringas watched as more families left for America. The two oldest boys, Hemke and Egbert, decided to go, and boarded a ship on May 8, 1911. Soon after, their brother Hotse left too. When Harm, the next son, talked of going across, Grietje finally said, "If Harm goes, we all go, even the babies."

On April 27, 1912, just 12 days after the Titanic sank, the family boarded the ship *Noordam* at Rotterdam for America. They had $200 to their name, so Jakob's son Hemke, already in Hammond, paid their passage. The ship arrived at Ellis Island on May 7, 11 days later. There they boarded a train for Hammond to meet their sponsor, Ed Van Til. When they arrived in Hammond, the Van Tils provided some food and a house in Munster.

The family pooled their earnings the first two years. The third year they rented a 40-acre farm on 45th Avenue in Griffith. They bought some tools at an auction and started farming.

The family prospered. Jakob bought a 2-horse buggy with frills. When he came down the road, people would say, "Here kompt Scheeringa!" My grandfather Harm would relate this story with great pride in later years.

On August 1, 1917, Jakob's wife Grietje died of pneumonia at age 54.

Jakob lived with his son and daughter-in-law, Harm and Tena, until 1935 when their twins were born. Tena became too busy to care for Jakob, so unhappily, he went to live with another son, Ralph, and his wife Julia.

Jakob died on January 12, 1941, also of pneumonia caused by flu. He is buried with his wife in Hope Cemetery on Kleinman Road in Highland.

by Ken Scheeringa

SCHEERINGA, HARM
F221

Harm Scheeringa in Groningen, Netherlands.

The Second Generation

Harm Scheeringa was born November 17, 1893, in Pasop, in Groningen province, the Netherlands. He was the fourth of ten children of Jakob Scheeringa and Grietje Heuker.

Harm lived in a typical Dutch house with an attached barn. The six oldest brothers, Hemke, Egbert, Hotse, Harm, Martinus, and Roelf slept in the barn. The younger children, Margaret, Tonnis, and Renatje slept in a closet-bed recessed into the wall.

The children walked two miles each way to a four-room school house in Eenamatil. Harm

Harm and Tena Scheeringa family in 1950's. Back Row: Julia, Herman, Anthony, Ronald, Grace. Front Row: Jeanette, Harm, Tena, Thelma.

153

Tena Schoon Scheeringa

went through the sixth grade. Then he hired himself out to a farmer.

In 1911, Harm's older brothers left Holland for America. The next year, on April 27, 1912, just 12 days after the Titanic sank, the rest of the family boarded the ship *Noordam* at Rotterdam for America. The family only had $200, so Harm's brother, Hemke, already in Hammond, paid their passage. The ship arrived at Ellis Island on May 7. There they boarded a train to Hammond to meet their sponsor, Ed Van Til. The Van Tils provided some food and a house in Munster.

The very next day, Harm went to work for Peter Kikkert, a farmer, for $1 per day. The family pooled their earnings the first two years. The third year they rented a 40-acre farm on 45th Avenue in Griffith.

During World War I on August 1, 1917, Grietje, Harm's mother, died of pneumonia. Harm's brother Hotze was drafted and sent to France. In 1918, Harm and his brother Martin were drafted and sent for training to Fort Custer, Michigan. They were not yet American citizens, so they applied for, and received, a discharge from service six months later.

Harm married Tetje (Tena) Schoon on April 9, 1919. Tena was born on May 5, 1897, in Roseland, Illinois, the only child of Jacob Schoon and Jeltje Piersma. In 1907, the Schoons moved to Munster. Tena attended Munster Christian School through seventh grade.

Harm bought a 9-acre farm at 3915 Ridge Road in Highland. He peddled his vegetables in Gary.

In the next 15 years, Harm and Tena had seven children, Julia, Grace, Jeanette, Herman, Anthony, and the twins, Thelma and Ronald. All seven children were born in the tiny bedroom at the house, delivered by Dr. Malmstone. When the twins were born, Sadie Schoon Bosch lived with the family for a few months. Julia quit high school to help, too.

In the early 1940s, Harm bought a 240-acre farm at the corner of US41 and 45th Avenue. Harm's son and son-in-law, Herman and Harry Vander Noord, farmed the land for a while. In 1953, Harm moved his family from the farm on Ridge Road to a new house at 2331 45th Avenue.

Through the years the residential neighborhood was swallowed up by businesses. Harm gradually sold parcels of his land. Most of the farm became a sprawling complex known as Hampton Apartments.

Harma retired about age 65. He loved gardening. His favorite flowers were mums and he kept his children supplied with his favorite vegetable, green beans.

On September 1, 1963, Tena died of congestive heart failure. Harm lived alone for five years.

On March 14, 1969, at age 75, Harm remarried to Tena's first cousin, Bessie Schoon. Bessie was born in 1894, the daughter of Klaas Schoon and Sijtje Kloosterboer. Bessie was the widow of Jacob DeGroot who had died in 1947.

Harm and Bessie were married for 13 years and spent 9 winters together in Florida.

Harm and Bessie sold their 45th Avenue home to his son Anthony. They then moved into Hampton Apartments. After one year, Harm had a series of small strokes. Bessie could no longer care for him, so Harm was placed into Rest Haven South nursing home in South Holland, Illinois, on November 19, 1979. Bessie moved into the adjacent Holland Home so she could visit Harm easily. Much later, Bessie herself moved into Rest Haven South where she still lives today.

Harm lived in Rest Haven for three years. He died at age 89 on December 18, 1982, of heart failure.

At his funeral, one grandson from each of his children's families served as pall bearers. He was buried alongside his wife Tena in Hope Cemetery in Highland.

by Ken Scheeringa

SCHOON, JACOB
F222

Jacob Schoon was born on November 21, 1862, in Broep op Langedyk, in the province Noord Holland, the Netherlands. He was the seventh and youngest child of Abram Schoon and Guurtje Kaas. Of the seven children, only Jacob and his brother Klaas survived childhood.

Jacob Abrams Schoon

Back Row: Harm holding baby Herman, Dena Tysen, Tena and Jeltje (Piersma) Schoon. Front Row: children Julia and Grace.

In 1883, Jacob's father, Abram died. That same year Jacob and his mother left Holland for America. They settled into a house located at 341 105th Court in Roseland, Illinois. There Jacob was a carpenter by trade.

Guurtje, Jacob's mother, died on May 12, 1895 at this house. She was buried in the Old Holland section of Homewood Memorial Gardens, Homewood, Illinois. Her grave is unmarked and its exact location unknown. Her death certificate lists her name as Widow Schoon.

A month after his mother's death, Jacob married Jeltje Piersma, a local bar maid. Guurtje had strongly opposed this marriage while she was alive.

Jeltje was born on January 7, 1866, in Oldeboorn, in Friesland province, the Netherlands. She was the third of five children of Pier Piersma and Tetje de Jong. Jeltje had four brothers, Eit, Jacob, Gutse, and Harmen. Her brother Eit died as an infant.

Jeltje emigrated to America in 1891 and settled in Roseland, Illinois. Here she met Jacob Schoon, whom she married on June 24, 1895.

Two years after they were married, Jacob and Jeltje had their first and only child, a daughter, named Tetje.

In 1907, Jacob moved his family to Munster, Indiana. Tetje attended the Munster Christian School through the seventh grade.

The Schoon family moved again to a home near Ridge Road in Highland. While they lived there, Tetje met and married to Harm Scheeringa on April 9, 1919.

In 1920, Jacob became very ill with stomach cancer. In March, he was admitted as a patient to West Suburban Hospital in Oak Park, Illinois. His condition did not improve, so he underwent stomach surgery on March 24. At first Jacob seemed to recover, but then he died at the hospital on April 15 at age 57.

Jacob was buried in Hope Cemetery in Highland.

Jeltje, Jacob's widow, had suffered most of her life with a disfiguring face cancer. Jeltje rarely appeared in public without wearing a hat and veil, and almost never allowed herself to be photographed. The photo shown here may be the only existing photo of her.

Jeltje's face cancer advanced and her health failed gradually. By 1930, she had become chronically ill. On Christmas Eve, the Hammond Times town reporter notes she is severely ill.

Early Christmas morning in 1930, at age 64, Jeltje died in her home at 544 Ridge Road in Highland.

Jeltje is buried in Hope Cemetery, located on Kleinman Road, in Highland. She is buried in a single grave, one row apart from her husband Jacob who had preceded her in death ten years earlier.

by Ken Scheeringa

SCHEERINGA, ANTHONY

F223

The Third Generation

Anthony Scheeringa was born on January 23, 1931, in Highland. He is the fifth of seven children of Harm Scheeringa and Tena Schoon. Anthony has four sisters, Julia, Grace, Jeanette, and Thelma, and two brothers, Herman and Ronald. All the children were born in a tiny bedroom of a house located at 3915 Ridge Road in Highland.

Anthony attended Highland Christian School, located on Highway Avenue at the time, adjacent to the First Christian Reformed Church.

Anthony and his brothers and sisters worked hard on the family farm from a very young age, learning how to plant onions, pull mustard and turnip greens, and do the other farm chores. Modern conveniences were added later, including an electric vegetable washer in the barn and a toilet under a stairway in the house to replace the outhouse.

Anthony preferred working outdoors over school work, so he quit high school in his freshman year.

On January 12, 1951, Anthony married Ruth Sikma. Ruth was born on March 16, 1931, the eighth of nine children of Harry Sikma and Cora Jonkman. Ruth had five brothers, William, Henry, Donald, Harry, and Cornelius. A brother, another Henry, had died at age one. Donald was retarded and he died in 1951 at age 24.

Ruth also was raised on a farm, located on Torrence Avenue, the third house north of US30. Ruth's father decided he needed his children home to help work on the farm so she was not given the choice to attend high school.

After they were married, Anthony and Ruth moved into a house owned by his father Harm at 3906 Highway Avenue in Highland. Ruth became a housewife and the mother of two sons, Kenneth, born in 1952, and Wayne, born three years later.

At first, Anthony worked for Martin Rispens' seed store, delivering seed and loading boxcars. In the summer of 1951, he farmed with his brother Herman.

The next year, Anthony opened a fruit and vegetable stand at 9625 Indianapolis Boulevard. The Bounty restaurant is located there today. He operated the stand for six years until 1958.

During these same years Anthony also worked as a laborer for Bill De Young, a mason contractor, and then as a carpenter for Vander Noord Brothers.

Anthony became less interested in farming and more interested in carpentry. While he worked for Bill De Young, he began building houses at night after work with his neighbor, Harold Zeilenga, who worked for a brickyard. They built homes for three summers from about 1955 to 1957. In 1955 Anthony built a new home for his own family on Waymond Avenue, adjacent to his father's farm on 45th Avenue.

A few years later, in 1958, Anthony and Ruth's oldest daughter Janet was born. That same year, Anthony and Harold formed a new partnership, Scheeringa and Zeilenga General Contractors, and went into the homebuilding business full time for themselves. Many homes in the region were built by this partnership throughout the 1960s.

In 1960, another daughter, Joyce, was born. The family outgrew the small house on Waymond Avenue, so Anthony built a new larger home at 3646 44th Street in Highland. The youngest daughter, Jill, was born in 1963 while they lived there.

All the children attended Highland Christian School in Highland and Illiana Christian High School in Lansing, Illinois.

Anthony's second son, Wayne, decided he too would become a carpenter. The Scheeringa and Zeilenga partnership had dissolved about 1970 and a new partnership, Scheeringa and Son, was formed in 1973. This partnership continued for the next ten years.

In 1983, Wayne joined Timothy DeVries to begin their own homebuilding business known as Scheeringa and DeVries.

The home building boom of the 1960s and 1970s went bust in the early 1980s. Work in the area was scarce. The Scheeringas accepted work as far away as Indianapolis to bring them through the hard times.

By the mid 1980s, business improved, and the Scheeringa and DeVries company prospered. Soon they had to hire help to meet the greater demand.

Anthony turned to remodeling work by himself, but he often worked with Wayne and Tim when they were short of experienced help.

Today, all the Scheeringa children are married. Ken lives in Lafayette, Indiana, and Jill lives in Williamsport, Pennsylvania. The three other children live in the Calumet region, near the hometown.

Anthony and Ruth have eight grandchildren, with two more expected this year. Ken and Martha have twins, Wayne and Patricia have three children, Gary and Janet Roeda have two, while Paul Musielak and Joyce have one. Mark and Jill Burchfield are expecting later this year.

The family photo was taken at Christmas in 1986 in Anthony and Ruth's home. They purchased the house on 45th Avenue in 1978 from his father, Harm, before he was placed in a nursing home.

by Ken Scheeringa

Anthony and Ruth Scheeringa Family (Christmas Day 1986). Standing: Anthony, Joyce, Paul, Gary, Jill, Mark, Ken, Martha. Seated: Ruth, Derek, Janet, Jackie, Joshua, Pat, Koryn, Austin, Wayne.

SCHEERINGA, KENNETH

F224

The Fourth Generation

Kenneth Scheeringa was born on February 22, 1952, in Hammond. He is the oldest of five children of Anthony Scheeringa and Ruth Sikma. Ken has one brother and three sisters, Wayne, Janet, Joyce, and Jill. All the children were born at St. Margarets Hospital in Hammond.

Ken attended Highland Christian School in

Ken and Martha Scheeringa with twins, Jamie and Keith, June 19, 1988.

Highland and Illiana Christian High School in Lansing, Illinois. He decided to become a meteorologist. He attended Purdue University-Calumet campus for two years, then transferred to the West Lafayette campus where he completed his degree in 1974.

Meteorology jobs were scarce in 1974 due to hiring freezes in the government, so Ken accepted a research position at Purdue University. After three years working in weather and crop yield research, he was promoted to computer specialist. The new position involved working closely with the National Weather Service office on the Purdue campus, which he enjoyed very much.

Ken was a long time bachelor, and surprised his parents when he announced his engagement to Martha Floyd of South Holland in 1986.

Ken had met Martha in February, 1986, at a Singles Retreat at Cedar Lake Bible Conference Center in Cedar Lake, Indiana. They began a letter exchange. To the surprise of them both, Martha had cared for Ken's grandfather, Harm, when he lived in Rest Haven South nursing home in South Holland, Illinois. It would be five years later, however, before Ken and Martha would meet for the first time.

Ken had become quite interested in genealogy in the months before he met Martha. On their first date, they made a stop at a local cemetery to seek out Ken's ancestors. Martha must have begun wondering just what she was getting herself into!

During the next Singles Conference at Cedar Lake in July 1986, Ken and Martha became engaged. They were married the following Easter weekend on April 18, 1987.

Martha Floyd was born on November 15, 1959, in Elmhurst, Illinois. She is the sixth of nine children of Glenn Floyd and Margaret Goring. She has five sisters, Peggy, Edith, Clara, Nancy, and Sandra, and three brothers, Carl, Charles, and Brad.

Martha attended Madison Elementary School in South Holland, Coolidge Junior High School in Phoenix, and Thornridge High School in Dolton, Illinois.

Martha was interested in medicine, and attended several medical trade schools. She obtained her certification for Nursing Assistant and Emergency Medical Technician. Beginning in 1977, she worked as a nurses aid at Rest Haven South nursing home in South Holland. She left this position in 1982 due to poor health.

After they were married, Ken and Martha rented a house at 1326 North 28th Street in Lafayette, Indiana. In December, 1987, they bought their first home at 3605 Navarre Drive in Lafayette.

A few days later, on January 8, 1988, Ken and Martha became the proud parents of twins, Jamie Lynne and Keith Philip. They were born at Home Hospital in Lafayette.

In January, 1988, Ken assumed duties as the Indiana State Climatologist, a position at Purdue University. Ken is responsible for archiving weather data taken within the state of Indiana.

Martha is a full time mother and homemaker, caring for the newborn twins at home.

by Ken Scheeringa

SCHEIDT, ANTHONY
F225

Red Brick House on Joliet St.

Anthony Scheidt was born 4/27/1831 in Lorraine, France to John and Agatha (Blattner) Scheidt. In 1844 he migrated to the south edge of Cook County, Illinois. He married in 1852 Marianne Schaller born 1832 daughter of Joseph and Mary (Hummel) Schaller. Anthony and wife Marianne operated a 124 acre farm in the Strassburg area just west of the Illinois-Indiana line. Here 5 children were born to them; only the oldest, daughter Mary, survived the typhoid epidemic which carried off 4 of the children. In 1860 the family removed to Chicago where they kept a grocery, saloon and boarding house on the west side of Chicago.

In 1861 Anthony moved his family to Dyer, Indiana where he became landlord of the State Line Hotel at the southeast corner of Hart and Joliet Streets. The State Line House is an interesting part of the area history. Farmers and drovers from as far south as the Kankakee River made the hotel their overnight stopping place while taking their cattle and grain and produce to the markets in Chicago. It was a one-day drive from Dyer to the Chicago markets, and after transacting their business they would stop over at the hotel on their return trip. The hotel remains as the Sports Grill today, after many changes of ownership.

Four more children were born to Anthony and Marianne after their return to Dyer. Mary born in 1850 married Phillip Keilman and lived at the Keilman farm on Joliet St. east Dyer. Anthony married Susan Hilbrich and lived in Chicago. Edmund married Mary Schutz and lived in Hobart where he operated a general store in partnership with H. Edward Keilman, son of his sister Mary. Barbara and Matilda were unmarried and lived out their lives in the red brick home on Joliet Street in Dyer.

Anthony maintained the State Line Hotel until he sold it in 1875. He bought half-interest in the Dyer Mills, continued overseeing his farm in Illinois, and entered a swine-breeding venture with George F. Davis of Dyer. By 1882 Anthony owned the red brick house on Joliet Street, 24 acres in the Town of Dyer area, the Illinois farm, and property in Chicago aggregating $25,000. He died March 5, 1895, survived by his wife Marianne who died 1/7/1914. Two unmarried daughters, Barbara and Matilda, lived on in the red brick house, the family home. They augmented their income by keeping a board and room house for single men employed by the local railroads. When travel by car became a vogue the two sisters posted a "Tourists" sign and accommodated many travelers on US 30. After the death of Barbara in May of 1934, Matilda sold the red brick house to Joseph Hoffman, keeping a small two-room suite for herself until her death.

In 1985 the 408 Joliet Street was zoned commercial. It was taken over by Exhaust Masters. The residence was retained and adapted to the needs of the business for which it was purchased. Family members of Anthony Scheidt who still live in the Dyer area are pleased to note the care taken to preserve this lovely old home which is one of the very few remaining of the original homes built in the Town of Dyer.

by Leona Mary Hilbrich

SCHLEMMER, GEORGE EDWARD FAMILY
F226

George Edward Schlemmer was born on July 4, 1912, to George J. (Johann Georg) and Anna (Becher) Schlemmer in Crown Point at 124 North Ridge Street. He was their only child.

George's elementary school years were spent in Trinity Lutheran School, where all eight grades, taught by William Heidbreder, were housed in the old frame building at the corner of Grant and North Streets, which was also where church services were held. George was graduated from Crown Point High School in 1929 and then attended Gary Business College, taking a 2-year general business course. Here he met Margaret Ross, who was to be his future wife, who was taking a secretarial course.

George and Margaret Vivian Ross, daughter of Joseph John and Mabel Ellen (Love) Ross were married on April 11, 1937, at the Leroy Methodist Church. This date was also her parents' silver anniversary. They lived in Gary for six months while their brick home at 116 North Ridge Street was being built. Nick and Fred Hoffman were the builders.

George worked for Standard Brands, Inc., a wholesale grocer company, in Gary for 27 years. They were distributors for Fleischmann Yeast, Chase and Sanborn coffee, and baking supplies for bakeries. He also worked for a short time for Housewares, Inc., Gary and for Calumet Park Cemetery.

In 1963 George began working for the Crown Point Post Office and worked there for 17½ years until he retired in 1981. He was serving as a window clerk at the time of his retirement.

The Schlemmers were active in Trinity Lutheran Church. George served as chairman of the congregation for three terms and was serving in this capacity at the time of the dedication of the new Christian Life Center in 1976. He was a financial secretary for 29 years, and served for two terms as secretary of the Christian Board of Education; also chairman. He served 28 years as secretary and president of the Calumet Lutheran Dart Ball League.

George was interested in sports and helped organize St. Mary's softball league, officiated as officer and manager of city girls' softball league, and Babe Ruth League. Another community effort was helping with the Hub Pool drive. He also held an office in Girl Scouting.

Margaret has been a member of Trinity Lutheran Church for almost 40 years and during those years belonged to Lutheran Women's Missionary League, and Trinity League, serving in various offices, and was a member of the choir for 17 years. Margaret was a 50-year member of the Leroy Fidelis Federated Woman's Club, a 50-year member of the Crown Point Garden Club, and a 45-year member of the American Legion Auxiliary, Post 20, and served in numerous offices. Margaret also was a Brownie leader and a Junior Garden Club leader.

Four daughters were born to this union. Twin daughters Karen June and Sharon Jane, both graduates of Concordia Teacher's College, River Forest, Illinois; Maurine Margaret and Ruth Ann, both graduates of Ball State University, Muncie, Indiana.

Karen is married to Jonathon Baker, a farmer and dairyman. They have two children, son Jeffrey, a Bonduel High School graduate, and daughter Diane, Bonduel High School sophomore. Karen teaches elementary students in Shawano, Wisconsin, her 25th year of teaching.

Sharon and husband John Schulenberg with children Christopher, a Manchester College graduate and employed as an accountant in Fort Wayne, Indiana; Gretchen, a freshman at Ball State University, Muncie, Indiana; and Andrew, a fourth grader, live in Rensselaer, Indiana. John is an elementary school teacher with 25 years of teaching and Sharon is employed by the city library with 21 years of service. They celebrated their silver anniversary in June, 1989.

Maurine was stricken with a disabling disease while in her final quarter at Ball State University and makes her home in Crown Point with her mother. She received a B.S. degree in general arts, with a major in elementary education in 1973, completing her education by correspondence courses.

Ruth Ann is married to Michael Whiley, who attended Ohio State and Ohio University and is advertising manager for a shopping news service. She has a B.S. degree in elementary education from Ball State University and taught for 17 years in Lancaster public schools in Lancaster, Ohio, where they live. Their son Jonathan is a high school junior. He is interested in the band.

George died on May 19, 1981, at age 68, and is buried in Maplewood Cemetery, Crown Point. George had the distinction of living his entire lifetime on North Ridge Street, Crown Point.

by Margaret V. Schlemmer

SCHLEMMER, JOHANN GEORG FAMILY
F227

Johann Georg Schlemmer was born December 10, 1875, to John and Margaretha (Schramm) Schlemmer in Crown Point, Indiana, at 118 North Ridge Street. He was the last of seven children born to this union and the only one born in Crown Point. His parents came to the United States from Bavaria, Germany, and chose Chicago as their first home. It was under the laws of Cook County, Illinois, that they took out naturalization papers March 3, 1857. His father opened his first dry goods store in Chicago and moved his family and business to Crown Point around 1872.

Johann Georg chose to be called George J. and received his education in the Crown Point schools. Upon graduation he began working for his father until his father's death on January 30, 1899. He then went into business with his brothers William and Frank and formed the Schlemmer Brothers Dry Goods Store. George's sisters were Sophie and Emma, who never married. Brother William also never married and brother Frank married Paulina Fraas on February 7, 1887, and lived at the corner of East Joliet Street and Jackson Street, Crown Point. They had no children. Frank was a longtime member of the Crown Point volunteer fire department. Sophie, Emma, and Will remained at 118 North Ridge Street until their deaths. A brother John G. died in 1872 at 5 years of age of scarlet fever and a sister Eliza died in 1873 at one year of age. The mother Margaretha died on July 15, 1904.

On October 19, 1904, George J. married Anna Marie Magdaline Becher, daughter of Jacob and Henrietta (Marthinich) Becher of Chicago, and began housekeeping in their newly constructed frame home at 124 North Ridge Street on a section of the parents' original property. Anna's two brothers were John Becher of Berwyn, Illinois, and William Becher of Oak Park, Illinois. A son, their only child, George Edward, was born on July 4, 1912.

They were members of Trinity Evangelical Lutheran Church. George J. was a financial secretary for many years. He was also on the Board of Director for the Commercial Bank at one time.

A favorite pastime on Sunday afternoons was playing croquet. In the mid-30's the men became interested in playing dart ball in the Calumet area. Anna enjoyed playing pinochle and bridge. It was a common practice to exchange Sunday evenings with friends or neighbors for a social get-together of visiting or playing cards. Anna was well-known for the delicious 3-layered tri-colored cake she would bake, iced with mocha icing. She also loved animals, although they had none of their own, and befriended the neighbors' dogs. The neighborhood children loved to gather in their yard for various games. They still talk about "Schlemmer Stadium."

Anna died on March 7, 1941, at the age of 62 after several years of poor health due to high blood pressure. She didn't live to see any of her grandchildren. George J. died on December 13, 1943, at the age of 68. His twin granddaughters, Karen and Sharon Schlemmer, were one year old on November 26 of that year.

George J. and Anna are buried in Maplewood Cemetery, Crown Point.

by Margaret V. Schlemmer

SCHMAL, ADAM
F228

Adam Schmal, the youngest son of Joseph and Anna Catherine (Spidler) Schmal, was a child of ten when he sailed with his family to America in the spring of 1838. He was born in the Rhine Province of Germany, June the 24th, 1828. Reared in Lake County, Indiana, on the Schmal homestead in St. John, Adam received an English and German education. Like his father, he grew to be a farmer; and later became prominent in political life.

On April 29th, 1851, Adam Schmal married Margaret Rassier-Rasher, a native of Germany, born on the 11th of June, 1827. Margaret and her parents came to Lake County in 1842, and lived near Cedar Lake. Adam and Margaret Schmal were the parents of ten children: Barbara (John Wachter); Joseph; Frank; Lillosa (John George Bohling); Peter (Elizabeth Reeder); George (Margaret Sweeney); Margaret; Catherine (Henry Schmidt); Albert; and Frederick (Theresa Berg) (Elizabeth Barfeldt). Joseph died at the age of six years; Frank, at the age of three months; and Albert live until fourteen years of age. George was the founder of Schmal's dairy of Crown Point, Indiana; and Frederick, hotel owner and merchant at Lowell, Indiana.

Adam Schmal and his family first lived on a farm in St. John Township. Soon after his marriage he became interested in civic welfare, and was the first Republican ever elected as Township Trustee of his township. In 1859, Mr. Schmal was elected County Commissioner of Lake County, and in 1862, he was re-elected, during which term he served the board as president. Adam, resigned this position in 1867, and was elected County Treasurer, an office he held until 1971 — being a most satisfactory official.

It was also in 1867, when the Adam Schmals moved to a home at the County Seat, on north East Street, across from Adam's good friend, John Krost. In February of 1873, he purchased 160 acres of land in Center Township, about five miles south of Crown Point. After building a house here in 1875, Adam moved with his family to this location, where he continued to buy more land from time to time, until he owned 380 acres of good farm soil. Mr. Schmal retired from farming in 1886, and bought a home on Court Street in Crown Point.

On March 15th, 1889, Mrs. Schmal passed away after a lingering illness. Some time later, in May of 1890, Adam, together with an old friend, Peter Simon, of Chicago, Illinois, made a trip back across the Atlantic to see his former homeland. Mr. Schmal found many old landmarks he remembered from his early childhood. The old stone house the family left in 1838, had not changed.

In his later years, Adam was cared for by his children. After and illness of nearly two years, he died in his home on Court Street, February 1, 1897, and was laid to rest along side his wife, Margaret, at St. Mary's Cemetery in Crown Point.

Adam Schmal (1828-1897)

Adam Schmal had been a very successful farmer in Lake County, Indiana, and lived a full and helpful life in social and community affairs. He was very interested from his early boyhood in the political welfare of the county, and was always an ardent Republican.

by Jim Stephen

SCHMAL, JOSEPH
F229

Joseph Schmal, pioneer of "Prairie West," was born in the Rhine Province of Germany, February the 6th, 1784. He spent most of his life in the Fatherland and was a carpenter by trade. As a young man in the early 1800's, Joseph was united in marriage to Anna Catherine Spidler of the same locality. She was born on the 11th of November, 1785. The Schmals were to have quite a large family of sons and daughters: Margaret, John, Joseph, Catherine, Angelina, Regina and Adam.

One day early in the year 1838, a letter addressed to Joseph was received by him in his carpenter shop. He hurried to the house to read the letter to his wife, Anna, because it contained important news from their old friend, John Hack, who, with his wife and family, had immigrated to America the year before. Mr. Hack wrote in flowing language about the fertility of the soil in Lake County, Indiana, where he had established a home for his family in what is now known as St. John.

Although Joseph Schmal was at that time a man of 54 years, and had successfully followed the carpenter trade for 36 years, he discussed with Anna, and their children, the advantages of joining their friend, John Hack, in the new world. One deciding factor in favor of the Schmal's sailing to the United States was that their eldest sons would have soon been drafted into military service.

For many weeks preparations were made to leave the Fatherland for a new world. One can imagine the tearful farewells on leaving their relatives and good friends for the uncertainties of a long and dangerous voyage across the Atlantic Ocean in a sailing vessel.

The Schmals set sail in the spring of 1838, from the port of Le Harve, France, aboard the ship, Erie. After 30 days of rough passage the family arrived in New York City on the 25th of May. From there to Buffalo, New York, by canal boat was another long, tedious trip. They continued on from Buffalo by wagon train to La Porte, Indiana, and finally to Lake County by team. (A team of oxen had been purchased along with a covered wagon to complete their travels.)

On their journey to their destination, the Schmals met hostile Indians, who frightened them many times while they were camping along the way. After numerous days of hardship they arrived safely in Lake County, and were joyously received by their friends, the Hack Family.

But there was little time for visiting, as they had to establish a claim, clear the land to secure logs with which to build a cabin. Joseph Schmal selected a homesite in St. John Township, in the general vicinity of the Hack property, east of present day Route 41, and settled to the occupation of farming. (A stone marker located at the bend of Schmal Street (93rd Street), at the southwest corner of the Lake Hills golf course, marks the site of the Schmal homestead.)

Joseph was not a young man when he immigrated, and he did not become very fully Americanized. But he lived a reputable life in his new homeland, where he reared his family and made a good home.

The Joseph Schmals were the second German family to settle in "Prairie West." Over twenty years later, on the 8th of May, 19, Anna Catherine Schmal died and was laid to rest in the St. John Cemetery. Her devoted husband, Joseph, then 75 years old, was so grief stricken that he followed her to the grave in ten days, thus ending a well spent life.

by Jim Stephen

SCHMAL, JOSEPH AND CATHERINE
F230

Children of

The first marriage to take place was that of Margaret to John Rhein, in 1839, and it is said that their oldest child, Mary, was the first baby born in St. John Township. There were six children born of this union: Mary, Barney, Joseph, John, Regina and Angeline.

John married Miss Barbara Rassier-Rasher, and settled on a farm in St. John Township. To them were born John Jr., Margaret, Mary, Regina, Barbara, Nicholas and Catherine.

Another son, bearing his father's name, Joseph, became a prominent farmer in Hanover Township. He was married to Miss Barbara Keiffer of Illinois. There were twelve children in this family: Catherine, Mary, Joseph, Barbara, Adam, Johanna, Jacob, Frank, Louis, Aurelia, Alfred and Amelia.

Catherine married Peter Ludwig and settled on a homestead located between Crown Point, and St. John. Thirteen children were born to this union: Catherine, Barbara, Mary, Rachel, Joseph, Peter, Margaret, John, Elizabeth, Jacob, Regina, Adam and George.

One daughter, Angelina, marrying a son of the Hack family, Mathias, was for many years an active, energetic, well known, and much respected woman in the life of Crown Point. The Hacks had three sons: John, Joseph, and William.

Regina first married John Berg, and to this union three children were born, namely: Nicholas, John and Adam. Soon after the death of Mr. Berg, Regina married John Leinen. They were blessed with two girls, Barbara and Regina.

Adam became prominent in political life, and held for two terms the office of County Treasurer. He was united in marriage to Miss Margaret Rassier-Rasher and they were to have ten children: Barbara, Joseph, Frank, Lillosa, Peter, George; Margaret, Catherine, Albert and Frederick.

Submitted by Jim Stephen

by Rose Schmal (1884-1979)

SCHMAL, JOSEPH, JR.
F231

Joseph Schmal, Jr. was one of seven children of Joseph and Anna Catherine Schmal. He was born in Rhenish Prussia, Germany, November the 8th, 1817, and was a young man of 21 when he came with his parents to America in 1838. Joseph became one of the early settlers of Lake County, Indiana, when Indians still formed a part of the population.

He had received a fair German education, and soon after his arrival in St. John Township, Joseph engaged in work on the Illinois and Michigan Canal for over two years, receiving $24 a month. In the wintertime he chopped wood and did carpentry, a trade he had learned from his father while still in the old country. Joseph's work on the canal took him into Illinois, where he met Miss Barbara Keiffer. She was born in Germany, June 10, 1819, a daughter of John and Eve Keiffer, both natives of Germany.

Joseph and Barbara were married on May the 8th, 1841, at Joliet, Illinois, and of this union there were twelve children: Catherine (Ahles) (Maack); Mary (Frederick Gerbing); Joseph G. (Johanna Thielen); Barbara (Henry Ebert); Adam, Johanna, Jacob (Mary Schmidt) (Catherine Schmidt); Frank (Adelia Buckley) (Hattie Griesel); Louis (Magdalena); Aurelia (Frederick Ebert); Alfred (Caroline Hermann); and Amelia.

A short while after his marriage, Joseph Jr. purchased forty acres of land in St. John Township, and engaged in farming. By 1853, Mr. Schmal had increased his acreage to one hundred and twenty, at which time he sold the land and moved to a farm at Brunswick, in Hanover Township. At this location Joseph had erected a large frame house and some outbuildings, and over the years he had accumulated a landed estate of some one hundred and thirty-two acres. He hauled his products to Chicago, Illinois, by ox team. His fields of hay were cut with a scythe, and his wheat and oats were cradled.

Joseph Schmal Jr. attained more than ordinary success in life, and was noted for his industry and economy and good sense. He was an active politician of the Republican school, and supported the Party's doctrines and principles from the time of its organization. For some twenty or twenty-five years during the early history of Lake County, he was the United States mail carrier between Crown Point and Brunswick.

On the 29th of December, 1893, Joseph Schmal Jr. died at the age of 76. Mother Schmal reached the advanced age of 85 years, and resided with her son Alfred and his wife, who took care of her during her declining years. She died February 1, 1908. Joseph and Barbara Schmal are buried at Brunswick, Indiana.

Compiled from writings and local history books

by Jim Stephen, 1988

SCHOENBECK FAMILY
F232

Approx. 1948 Herman & Rose (Neipiepho) Schoenbeck, at their farm home on State Line Road in Hanover Twp.

Schoenbeck's On The State Line

Henry Schoenbeck came to the United States in 1856 from Hesson, Germany. In 1857, following his marriage to Engel Solke, they purchased land in Hanover Township on the state line northwest of Brunswick. This became the family farm.

In 1871, he purchased 38 acres increasing the family farm to 83 acres. Henry and Engel worked and lived on this farm until it was passed down to their son, Henry II in the early 1900's.

Henry II and his wife, Anna Steiber, worked the farm with the help of their five children until Henry's death in 1924. At this time his son, Herman, continued working the farm.

Although Herman was a farmer at heart, his ability as a blacksmith was known throughout the county. On rainy days, when the field work was impossible, area farmers would travel to the Schoenbeck Farm for the needed repairs on wagons and other machinery.

Herman's general contracting talent was put to use in building many area houses and barns. Frequently exciting the neighborhood when he would dynamite out rocks and stumps prior to building.

Herman and his wife, Rose Piepho, were married in 1922 making them the third generation to raise their children on the family owned farm. They were also the third generation to be active members of Zion (Hanover Prairie) United Church of Christ.

Their son, Virgil, still resides in Lake County, while the only daughter, Virginia Heldt lives in Grant Park, IL. Another son, Herman, lives in Steger, IL. Sons Leland and Raymond are deceased.

The family farm was sold following the death of both parents in 1956.

by Herman Schoenbeck

SCHOLL, PETER
F233

Arriving in Chicago in 1852, Peter Scholl, Sr., and his wife Susanna Lehnen Scholl, were met by his cousin Peter Lauermann and brought to Lake County, where the family settled on a farm on the ridge south of the old U.S. 30, not far east of the present site of St. Michael's Catholic Church in Schererville.

Johann Becker and Margaret Kleser were maternal ancestors of both the Scholl and Lauermann families, as their daughters Barbara and Elizabeth had married, respectively, Peter Scholl and Peter Lauermann, parents of the immigrants, and lived in Buschfeld, a town in what is now Kreis Merzig-Wadern in the Saarland of Germany.

The Scholl immigrants came to America with four or five children, including twins born in March of 1852. Peter, the oldest child, was 8 years old when the family left for America, taking a three-masted sailing boat from Rotterdam, spending 37 days at sea. After three days in New York, they spent seven days on a train to Chicago.

Susanna died in 1869 and is buried in the St. John churchyard; Peter, Sr., died in 1910 and is buried at St. Michael's, Schererville.

Jacob, another son, eventually took over the farm. He and his wife Mary Fotre had nine children, and many of them made their mark in Lake County annals. The oldest son, Charles, was ordained a Catholic priest. Having served as pastor of a number of parishes in the dioceses of Fort Wayne and Gary, he retired from his last pastorate in Lake Village. The Calvary in St. Michael's churchyard marks his final resting place. His sister Rose became a nun, Sister Salome, who was a noted hospital administrator in the Franciscan order.

Katherine, the eldest daughter, married Nicholas Austgen, of another pioneering German family of Lake County.

Joseph Scholl, survivor of the twin brother mentioned above, married Harriet Grieser and farmed near Ames, Iowa. Suzanne, his sister, married Peter Fotre, brother of Mary Fotre, Jacob's wife, and lived in Chicago. Nicholas Scholl wed Emily Box and lived in San Bernardino, California; their daughter, Suzanne Goodge, lives in Seattle.

Matthias married Elizabeth Schulte and moved to Juniata, Nebraska, where he operated a general store in an area populated by offspring of many Lake County German families, including such names as Lauerman, Frohnen, Bohr, and Beiriger. Having no children, they came back to Lake County to retire.

Another daughter, Mary Scholl, married Mathias Lauermann and lived in Cedar Lake, caring for her father, Peter Scholl, Sr., in his declining years. That family has a separate account in this book.

Peter Scholl, Jr., the oldest son, had a distinguished career, being a man of many talents. He substituted for his father during the Civil War, serving with Company D in the 83d Indiana Regiment during the siege of Vicksburg. He later bought a farm in La Porte County and eventually established a well-known dairy in La Porte, with a branch in Michigan City. He raised a family of 13 children, struggling through the loss of his first two wives, leaving him with five small children. He was blessed with a third wife, Ella Lusso, who gave him eight more children and outlived him.

Son of Clara Hanna, Peter's second wife, was William M. Scholl, who inherited a tradition in the shoe business from his grandfather, who had been a shoemaker upon his arrival in Lake County, the practice then being to go from house to house to make the shoes. The actual tools are now in Cedar Lake's historical museum. William studied in Chicago to become a doctor, and his revolutionary foot-care products made history and are sold throughout the world. Although William did not marry, descendants of his brothers and sisters are found throughout the U.S.A. and in Europe as well, keeping the Scholl name alive.

by Paul A. Davis

SCHREIBER, PHILIP
F234

Philip Schreiber born in Indiana on June 28, 1868, was the seventh and youngest child born to Michael and Anne (Sauer) Schreiber both born in Germany.

In 1889 Philip Schreiber married Elizabeth Miller in the St. John Catholic Church, in St. John, Indiana. Elizabeth, Philip's bride was Elizabeth Miller who was born in Indiana on December 17, 1870, and was the fourth and youngest daughter born to Peter and Elizabeth (Getschinger) Miller.

Philip and Elizabeth purchased a farm in Cedar Lake. The address now is 9005 W. 117th Avenue, Cedar Lake, in Hanover Township. The Schreibers were farmers and had a threshing machine that traveled throughout the area doing threshing for other local farmers.

Philip and Elizabeth had ten children. Eight boys, William, Edward, Philip, Michael, Gilbert, Walter, Theodore, and Clarence and two daughters Sylvia (Schutz) and Laura (Thomas). The living children are Walter, Clarence and Sylvia, all of Cedar Lake, Theodore of Michigan, Laura of California.

After Philip and Elizabeth passed away, son Clarence carried on the duties of the family dairy farm. He married Loretta Higgins of Chicago on September 15, 1945 and had one daughter Loretta. After Clarence retired and daughter Loretta married Larry Nelson of Crown Point in 1977 the Nelsons are continuing the operation of the grain farm.

Larry and Loretta have two sons, Phillip born October 7, 1980 and Dean born January 3, 1983.

Clarence and the Nelsons all reside on the family farm.

In December 1976 the Schreiber farm was presented the Hoosier Homestead Award for having the farm in the family for 100 years.

by Loretta Nelson

Top Row: Gilbert, Michael, William, Walter, Clarence, Edward. Front Row: Philip, Laura, Elizabeth, Phillip, Sylvia, Theodore. Picture taken at Golden Wedding Anniversary at the Schreiber Farm (July 1939).

SCHULTIES, LLOYD AND LILLIAN
F235

Lloyd and Lillian Schulties – 1956

Lillian Antoinette Centanni was born on November 15, 1909, in New Orleans, and came to the Gary area with her parents, Samuel and Josephine Centanni, as a child. She married Lloyd Nicholas Schulties (b. 12-15-09) of Maple, Wisconsin, on May 31, 1930, in Gary, Indiana.

Lloyd Schulties was employed by U.S. Steel until his retirement. He was involved in part time enterprises with the O'Day Construction Company and with tugboat operations at the Calumet Harbor Port.

Lillian was the owner-operator of Lillian's Beauty Shop in Gary and the Sunshine Dress Shop in Glen Park. Lillian and her husband built their home in the Glen Park area; they currently reside in Mankato, Minnesota.

Lloyd and Lillian had two children who were born and raised in Gary: Charlotte Louise Schulties, born June 4, 1940, and Sylvia Ann Schulties, born September 10, 1942. Both children graduated from Lew Wallace High School.

Charlotte Louise Schulties received a degree in Practical Nursing from the University of Minnesota in 1961, and a B.S. from Mankato State College in 1972. She married John David Pugh (b. 7-25-34) of Mankato, Minn., in June, 1976, in Mankato. They have one son, David Lloyd Pugh, born July 1, 1978, in New Ulm, Minnesota. Charlotte's husband, John, is a successful farmer, and the Pughs have made their home in Mankato.

Sylvia Ann Schulties received a B.A. from Midland College and M.A. from Miami University. She married Paul Krebs (b. 2-4-44) on August 18, 1962, in Gary, Indiana. Paul also received a B.A. from Midland College and then received a M.A. from the Lutheran School of Theology. Two children were born to this marriage: Mark Paul Krebs, born February 4, 1964, in Freemont, Nebraska, and Philip John Krebs, born November 19, 1968 in Beach Grove, Indiana. Mark recently received his B.A. from Wittenberg University. Sylvia and Paul have made their family home in Connersville, Indiana.

by Joanne C. Clark

SEEGERS FAMILY
F236

Christoph and Karoline and Christoph and Dorothea Seegers

Johann Heinrich Christoph Seegers was born 2 October 1821 in Mesmerode, Germany in the Province of Hanover (located northwest of the city of Hanover near the town of Wunstorf). It was a small village surrounded by farmland. Everyone lived in the village and went out daily to work on the farmland they owned or worked on. The nearest church was two to three miles away in Idensen. They walked to church. Christoph was the son of Johann and Sophie (Behrens) Seegers. He was a farmer and linen weaver by trade and attended the Lutheran Church at Idensen. On 19 October 1851 he married Karoline Engel Marie Schreek in Idensen. She was born 29 May 1826 in Gross-Munrel, Germany; the daughter of Heinrich and Engel (Flebbe) Schreek. In 1853 a son, Christopher, was born to them. In 1854 Christoph and Karoline came to America following his brother, Conrad, who had come the year before. They settled in Hanover Township, Lake County, Indiana. In the fall of 1858 twenty-three families on both sides of the Indiana and Illinois state line met to establish a church. It was called the German United Evangelical Zion Church (Deutsche ver. Evanglische Zions Kirche). Christoph's signature is on the list of the founders of the church. On 20 June 1865 Karoline died leaving him with several small children to raise. Children born to this union were: Christopher (1853-1924) married Maria Claus; Sophia Caroline (1855-?) married Fred Batterman Jr.; Mary Sophie (1857-1865); Heinrich (1859-1865); Heinrich W.C. (1861-1863); and Conrad W. (1862-1862). Christoph's brother, Conrad, had also died in January that same year leaving a wife, Dorothea, and several children. So for survival purposes Christoph and his sister-in-law, Dorothea, married on 7 September 1865. Dorothea had a total of thirteen children between her two marriages with Conrad and Christoph. Known children born to Christoph and Dorothea were: Anna (1866-1949) married #1 Heinrich Seehausen #2 –? Sego; Mary (1868-?); Sophia (1871-1928) married Fredrich Hitzemann; Frederick (1873-1873); Emma (1875-1875); Maria (1877-1877); August (1878-1880); and one more child that died at birth or in infancy. Christoph died 19 March 1880. After his death, Dorothea married a third time to a widower neighbor, Fred Batterman Sr. on 4 September 1884. He was born 2 February 1819 in Hanover, Germany. On 8 September 1885 Fred passed away and by 1900 Dorothea was living with her son, Fredrich. Dorothea died 8 November 1924 in Lake County, Indiana.

by Ronna Lounsbery

SEEGERS, CONRAD AND DOROTHEA
F237

Heinrich Christoph Conrad Seegers was born 17 August 1824; the son of Johann and Sophie (Behrens) Seegers. He was born and raised in Mesmerode, Germany in the Province of Hanover near the town of Wunstorf. He attended the Lutheran Church at Idensen. He was a farmer and shoemaker by trade. In 1853 Conrad Seegers and his friend, Catherine Dorothea Sophia Kolling sailed for America aboard the ship "Ella" arriving in New York 3 June 1853. Dorothea Kolling was born 28 May 1834 in Mesmerode, Germany; the daughter of Heinrich and Anne Engel (Doepke) Kolling. It is believed Conrad and Dorothea may have first settled in Will County, Illinois near the Indiana Border possibly marrying there. A short time later they moved into Hanover Township,

Lake County, Indiana. In 1854 his brother, Christoph, and his family followed Conrad to America also settling in Hanover Township. On 6 January 1865 Conrad died. In June that same year, Christoph's wife, Karoline, also died. This left Christoph and Dorothea both with young families to raise so brother and sister-in-law, Christoph Seegers and Dorothea Seegers, married on 7 September 1865. Their story is continued under the Christoph and Dorothea Seegers history. Known children born to Conrad and Dorothea were: Sophia Karoline (1859-1868); Conrad (1862-1876); Dorothea (1863-1905) married Heinrich Claus; and Maria D. (1864-1865).

by Ronna Lounsbery

SEEGERS, HEINRICH AND CHRISTIANA
F238

A third Seeger brother, Heinrich Friedrich Wilhelm, was born 3 May 1837 at Mesmerode, Germany; Province of Hanover. He was the son of Johann and Sophie (Behrens) Seegers and attended church at Idensen. He immigrated to America following his two brothers, Conrad and Christoph in 1863. It is not known where he first settled but it is thought to be in Will County, Illinois. A short time later he married Christiana ? Christiana was born in January 1846 in Wuerttemberg, Germany. She had immigrated with her family in 1847. By 1880 Henry and Christiana are located in Hanover Township, Lake County, Indiana where Henry was a farmer and ran a saloon. Known children born to them were: Henry (1865-?); Frederick (1867-?); Conrad (1871-?); August (1879-?); and Ila (1892-?); and seven more children died at birth or in infancy.

by Ronna Lounsbery

SCHERER, NICHOLAS
F239

Nicholas Scherer and his wife Frances

Schererville Pioneer

Schererville was founded in 1865, when Nicholas Scherer located in the area while he was working for the Great Eastern Railroad (now the Pennsylvania Railroad). He was born in the Saar Valley of Germany on June 29, 1830, and came to America with his parents, John and Mary Scherer. The family arrived in St. John in 1846 and later moved to Dyer where, in 1865, John Scherer died at the advanced age of 103. Mary Scherer died five years later in Schererville at the age of 99 years.

Nicholas had worked grubbing stumps for farmers to repay them for his passage to America. He then sent for his brother Matthias, and in 1849 they opened a saloon in St. John, which was the first in Lake County. Later they opened a distillery in Dyer.

Nicholas Scherer married Frances Uhlenbrock in 1862 when he lived in St. John. They were the parents of seven children: Anna, who became Mrs. Nicholas Schafer; Margaret, who married Adam Gerlach; Nicholas Jr., killed by lightning in 1893; Theresa, who became Mrs. Jacob Austgen; John G., who died in 1892; Joseph, who died in 1891; Mary, who died in her teens.

In 1873, the residents of Schererville presented to the Bishop of Fort Wayne a petition written by Frances Scherer asking to establish a Catholic parish. Nicholas Scherer donated 4½ acres for the church and parish cemetery.

Soon a white frame church, dedicated to Saint Michael the Archangel, stood at the site. The Bishop blessed St. Michael's on September 28, 1874.

Nicholas Scherer was a man involved in his community. As a pioneer of Lake County he used his many talents and interests to help and form this northwest corner of Indiana.

After a very active, useful life, he retired in 1895 and in 1907, at the age of 74, he passed away at his home at 33 Wilhelm Street, Schererville. Funeral services were held at St. Michael's church and he was laid to rest in the shadow of the Archangels steeple!

by Steven Yaros, Jr.

SHERMAN, JOHN AND HELEN
F240

Helen Czapko was born on January 19, 1919, in Gary, Indiana. She is the youngest child of George and Anna Czapko. She married John Michael Sherman, Jr. on January 26, 1936, in Gary, Indiana. They made their home in the Gary area.

John Sherman is a graduate of Froebel High School. He was employed by various divisions of U.S. Steel for about 11 years. In 1955, he obtained employment in Plant Protection at U.S. Steel and worked in this capacity until his retirement in 1980. John has been a member of the Masonic Lodge and has been a Shriner for almost 20 years.

Helen Sherman, a Froebel High School graduate, worked at Indiana Wholesale Suppliers for almost 12 years. She and her husband have been members of St. Mary's Eastern Orthodox Church.

The Shermans had four children born and raised in Gary: Joelle Dee Sherman, born November 16, 1936; Sandra Kay Sherman, born July 27, 1940; Lois Faith Sherman, born September 3, 1943; and Jon George Sherman, born November 19, 1946. Joelle and Sandra graduated from Lew Wallace High School; Lois and Jon graduated from Horace Mann High School.

John and Helen Sherman – 1967

Joelle Sherman married Joseph Szyllagi on March 8, 1956, in Gary, Indiana. Three children were born to his marriage: Beth Szyllagi, born December 15, 1956; and Deana Szyllagi, born November 1, 1959; and Joseph Michael Szyllagi, born April 13, 1964. Joseph was employed by Illinois Bell. They divorced in 1976. Joelle later married William Pippin and currently resides in Tellulah, Illinois.

Sandra Kay married Douglas A. Vincent (b. 6-26-40) of New York, N.Y., on June 19, 1964, in Tulsa, Oklahoma. One child was born, Gay Lynn Vincent, on July 28, 1966, in Houston, Texas. A second child, Judi Ann Vincent, born March 26, 1970 was adopted by Douglas and Sandra when she was eight months old, in New Orleans, Louisiana. Douglas Vincent is a college graduate. Sandra completed a medical technology course after high school. She died in 1974, in Edmond, Oklahoma.

Lois Faith Sherman has two children: Kimberly Sue Cain, born March 31, 1977, in Tulsa, Oklahoma; and Holly Michelle Cain, born August 4, 1978, in Oklahoma City, Oklahoma. Lois was married to Milton Popa on February 14, 1989, Valentine's Day, in Schererville, Indiana. Milton is employed by American Chemical, and Lois is a Farmer's Life Insurance Agent. They have made their home in Schererville, Indiana.

Jon George Sherman received a B.A. from Franklin College and served in the Air Force for four years. He married Alice Elizabeth Brenning (b. 7-1-50) of Columbus, Ohio, on January 10, 1970, in Columbus, Ohio. They have two children: Stacie Renee Sherman, born July 7, 1977, in Columbus, Ohio and Michael Paul Sherman, born January, 1981, in Columbus, Ohio.

by Joanne C. Clark

SHORTRIDGE, ERNEST L.
F241

Ernest L. Shortridge is another Lowell boy, who, by energy, perseverance and intelligence, has to his credit the honor of being one of the best court reporters in the State of Indiana. He was born on a farm near Lowell, June 11, 1873, and received his education in the public schools of that place, after which he went to Valparaiso College and took a thorough course of stenography and business training. He took up his residence in Hammond, where he has taken an active part in commercial and political affairs and come prominently before the public eye. In 1901 he was appointed court stenographer of the Superior Court of Lake, Porter and Laporte counties, which position he holds at the present time.

Mr. Shortridge was bred a Republican and has taken an active part in the campaigns for his party's cause since 1892 in such a strenuous manner that he was made chairman of the Republican Central Committee in 1902, which position he held until 1904, his conduct of the campaign during that period giving satisfaction to the party. So highly was he held in the esteem of his party friends that when, in the campaign now on, he announced himself as a candidate for the office of county clerk, he had no opposition and received his nomination by acclamation. Mr. Shortridge was married to Miss Misha Mathis, of Hammond. They have one daughter, five years of age, living, and one bright little daughter whom death reaped a short time ago.

(Compiled from the Souvenir Album of Lake Co., Ind., Crown Point-Lowell, June 18-19, 1909.)

SIMON, EDWARD
F242

Edward Simon, of Hobart, Democratic candidate for representative of Lake County, was born in Buffalo, N.Y., thirty-three years ago. He was educated in the public schools and St. Joseph College of that city. It was there he learned the cigar-making trade. In 1892 he went to Chicago, where he engaged in the restaurant business for a year, when he came to Lake County, and opened a cigar factory at Liverpool. His business increased so rapidly that he sought a larger place, and located at Hobart, where today he employs fourteen people in his factory. It is his individual and manly efforts, hustle and business tact and square dealing that have brought his establishment creditably before the public. Mr. Simon, who, since his residence in Hobart, has been an energetic member of the volunteer fire department, advocated and worked for the organization of a society of the volunteer departments of the county, and was instrumental in forming the Lake County Volunteer Firemen's Association, two years ago, and was selected as its first president, and the first annual tournament was held at Hobart. At the last meeting of the association, which now embraces the volunteer departments of the Tenth Congressional district, Mr. Simon was reelected president. He is an ardent Democrat and a faithful worker for his party, and soon after going to Hobart he was made township chairman, and two years ago was selected as county chairman of the Democratic Central Committee, because of his faithful, energetic work, and he was thus brought in close touch with the Democratic leaders of the county. While the nomination for representative came without any solicitation, he nevertheless appreciates the honor.

(Compiled from the Souvenir Album of Lake Co. Ind., Crown Point-Lowell, June 18-19, 1909.)

SIMS, REX
F243

Rex Sims – The Soldier

The Army Years

Rex Sims was drafted into the Army in November of 1950, soon after the outbreak of the Korean Conflict. He received sixteen weeks of basic training at Fort Riley, Kansas, where he was taught the obligations and requirements of a fighting soldier — to kill and be merciless! During this training period the young recruit was also tested for suitability as a candidate for Officers Training School; Airborn Training; and, N.C.O. School (Noncommissioned Officer). At the end of his basic training, the test results all came down on the same day. Rex had passed all three and had to make a decision.

The weather in Kansas for the winter of 1950-1951, was quite severe, with temperatures down to 15 degrees below zero. For two of the choices of Rex's continued Army training he would have stayed on at Kansas, in the freezing cold weather. The third choise was to be in Georgia, where the temperature was 85 degrees. Rex chose the third!

At Fort Benning, Georgia, Private Sims began his Paratrooper Training. Here he was taught and learned to jump from a 35 foot mock tower; a 250 foot tower; and later, to jump from aircraft. After this training, the soldier's Regiment, the 507th, was sent to join the 187th Regiment in Sasebo, Japan, but they never got there. Because of the big "Push" in Korea at that time, the unit went directly to Inchon.

Here in Korea, all of Rex's time was spent under combat conditions — on the line, or in outpost duty patrols. He slept on the cold, hard ground at 40 degrees below zero; lived in trenches where the mud was knee-deep, and in holes where the rats were larger than cats. Rex's Company — Company F, 7th Infantry Regiment, 3rd Division — lost on the average of 75 soldiers a week. Unable to secure enough replacements from the States, Company F was comprised of American, Puerto Rican, and Korean "ROK" Soldiers.

During the one skirmish in the Chowon Valley, the enemy had a Big Push on Company F's outpost located three miles ahead of the main line, and before the three day battle was over, there was an estimate of 10,000 dead Chinese and North Korean Soldiers in the trenches and all around the outpost. This battle was in the heat of August, and there was quite an odor in the area for days.

Escaping death a number of times in combat, Sims once took three burp-gun slugs above the brim of his helmet, and wasn't aware of it at the time as they didn't knock his helmet off. And from another incident in action, to this day he carries around shrapnel in both legs.

In six months from the time of basic training, Rex went up the ranks from Private E2 to Master Sergeant. Possessing the qualities of a leader, Sims was offered a Battlefield Commission, but he turned it down, the reason being he would have been transferred to another Company — he preferred to remain with the dwindling number of men he had been with from the time of basic training.

The Master Sergeant saw his share of the dead during the Korean Conflict, and put a lot of miles under his feet. He had been in Korea; Tokyo, Japan; and China; and also swam in the Yellow River in a heavy current. At the time of his discharge, Rex had made a total of 50 jumps.

His combat over, the paratrooper came back to the States and was discharged from the Service at Fort Benjamin Harrison, Indianapolis, Indiana, in May of 1953. At this time the Army had offered Rex a position as an R.O.T.C. instructor at Purdue University, but the battle fatigued soldier just wanted to get out of the Service. Some time later, however, Rex did join the Army Reserves.

by Jim Stephen

SIMS, REX
F244

Rex Eugene Sims came to Lake County, Indiana, as a young man in September of 1949, a few days before his nineteenth birthday. He came seeking employment, with all his worldly goods packed in the back of a '36 Ford, and all his monetary possessions packed in his back pocket.

The second of six children, Rex was born September the 5th, 1930, to Noel Cline Sims (1903-1981) and Maria Elizabeth (Burkhart) Sims (1905) of Odon, Indiana — where he spent his youth and received his education. A curious child interested in the mechanics of things and how they worked, Rex spent many an afternoon tinkering in the workshop of his father's large garage. He could also be found

Rex and Betty (Stephen) Sims

with the neighborhood boys, swimming and fishing in the surrounding creeks, coal strip pits, and gravel pits. And with these comrades Rex also pulled the ordinary childhood pranks! Another sport he enjoyed was hunting — especially for rabbit and quail.

As a youngster, Rex worked on his grandfather's farm, and on some of the Amish farms in the area. For a time he performed domestic chores for his parents when they lived on a farm before moving into town. Rex had a couple jobs at filling stations in Odon, where he pumped gas, and did mechanical work on cars, first at the Ford Garage and later at a Shell Gas Station. This was during a period of time from the eighth grade through high school.

Rex went to Odon Elementary School, and Odon High School, where he graduated with the class of 1949. In these years for fun and amusement, Rex and friends followed the midget racing circuit, and enjoyed the time trials and races at the Indianapolis Speedway. They would also travel to Jasonville State Park for the Indiana State swimming meets, and, where they too often swam.

After graduation Rex sought employment, some kind of a profession where he could better himself and work at for the rest of his life. He managed a truck stop on the midnight shift for a while, and also looked into other positions at different places. Undecided what to do, and unable to find suitable work in the local area, Rex joined with another job hunter and headed up north to "The Region." After some time he found employment with the Inland Steel Company in East Chicago, Indiana, where he was hired into the electric shop as a learner.

A friendly person with an outgoing personality, Rex made many new friends and soon started dating the sister of one of them, Betty Lou Stephen. Rex and Betty had met on a blind date arranged by her brother, Roy. Over a period of time they got to know each other rather well, and enjoyed each others company, but their relationship was soon interrupted.

When the Korean conflict broke out in 1950, Rex was drafted into the Service, and entered the Army in November of that year. After his war experience, fulfilling his military obligations, Rex returned to Lake County, Indiana, in the spring of 1953, and soon married his sweetheart, Betty Lou Stephen.

Betty was born in Schererville, Indiana, February the 23rd, 1934, the tenth child of Michael Stephen (1883-1960) and Catherine (Sutter) Stephen (1889-1950). She spent her youth in Schererville, and attended St. Michael's Grade School; and later went to Dyer High School in Dyer, Indiana. Soon after the death of her mother, Betty went to live with her sister and brother-in-law, Margaret (Stephen) and Walter Baumgartner, in Chicago Heights, Illinois, where she remained until the time of her marriage. During this period Miss Stephen worked in the maternity ward nursery at St. James' Hospital in Chicago Heights; and later as a cashier at a large grocery store there in Illinois.

Rex and Betty's wedding took place at St. Agnes' Church in Chicago Heights, on the 11th of July, 1953, and it being the "Coronation Year," Betty wore a tiara. The young couple then honeymooned for a week at the Wisconsin Dells.

The Sims first lived in a trailer at East Chicago, Indiana, and soon after the birth of their first child, they moved to an apartment, which was also in East Chicago. After renting a number of years, they bought their first home in 1957, located on Cline Avenue, south of Main Street in Griffith, Indiana. On Rex's birthday in 1960, they moved across town to North Jay Street where they currently reside.

Rex and Betty Sims have four children, three sons and one daughter: Eugene Alan (6-4-1954) (Pat Yankauskas); David Lee (1-22-1957) (Sue Buikema); Daniel Michael (3-10-1960) (Andrea Ruhs); and Cheryl Lynn (2-7-1966) (Kevin Frisk).

After his Korean years, Rex returned to the electrical department at Inland Steel, where he has continued to advance himself, working up through the ranks to foreman, general foreman, and section manager. He is still training to date, once or twice a year on different courses. Chairman of a committee on large motor and generator maintenance for the A.I.S.E. (Association of Iron and Steel Engineers), which is world wide for Inland Steel, and of which he is a member, Rex travels around the world much of the time for the steel company.

For relaxation and enjoyment Rex golfs, and also likes to get away now and then on little trips and spend a few days hunting and/or fishing — continuing the interest he attained for these sports in his youth. His sons, being sports minded too, often accompany him on these little excursions, and at times their wives will go along fishing, as they also enjoy the recreation. Betty's interests and favorite pastimes are sewing, quilting, crocheting, and cooking, the latter of which the family enjoys the most! And through the years, she too has become quite a fisherman.

The Sims are a very "family-oriented" family, and host numerous get-togethers, on holidays and other occasions, for their children and their growing families; and they all work together and help each other out on projects around their homes.

by Jim Stephen

SMITH, CLARENCE
F245

Clarence Smith

Into Thy Hands O Lord

Clarence Smith was born in Crown Point in 1905 and came to Schererville at the age of four. He attended St. Michael School and served as an altar boy at St. Michaels until after his marriage.

From 1923 to 1925 he attended Electrician's school in Chicago. At age 16 he joined the Catholic Order of Foresters and was a 50 year member at the time of his death.

Started working for the Pennsylvania Railroad at the age of 18 in Hartsdale yards and in 1931 he went to Colehour yards in South Chicago where he worked until his retirement. Worked a total of 38½ years on the railroad. Worked for 3 years for the Town of Schererville reading and repairing water meters.

Married Cecilia Grimmer Schererville in 1927, and they would have been married 50 years on June 1st. of this year.

Five children, Thomas, who preceded him in death in 1952, Patricia Michael and Dorothy Doctor of this parish, Major John Smith, United States Marines of Woodbridge, Virginia and Cel Reickhoff of Munster. 16 grandchildren.

"Smitty" was a volunteer fireman when he was young, served as a charter member and past-president of the Schererville Lions Club, served on Board of Directors of Schererville Civic Fund, Member of St. Michael Holy Name Society, worked for many years on St. Michael Thanksgiving Clothing Drive, Vice-President of Schererville Centennial Celebration in 1966. Chosen as Lion of the Year in 1974, and Schererville's Distinguished Citizen in 1969. Also reigned as Grand Marshall of Crossroads Parade, 1969.

In the early 1940's' he served as Scoutmaster, Assistant Scoutmaster, in Schererville. Also served as Committeeman, Merit Badge Counselor. Recently made honorary member of Schererville Girl Scouts. Recipient of Scouting's highest honor, The Silver Beaver Award, in 1967.

"Smitty" was a familiar face at the Church Festivals, and every Sunday he could be found in the Church basement helping the men who sorted and counted collection envelopes.

Into thy Hands O Lord do we commit the fighting soul of Clarence P. Smith (better known as Smitty) who passed away February 4, 1977.

Smitty will be missed by this town and this parish as this spunkie little guy was involved in many activities and projects of both. A life time of credits were listed in his obituary yet they took only a minute to read and they will soon be forgotten – only his fighting spirit will be remembered as it was as American as his last name.

At Communion standing next to his coffin with the song of Let there be Peace on Earth ringing through the church ones thoughts ran that Smitty had fought his last great battle in life and had won the lasting Peace of God.

His Funeral Mass ended with the singing of the Battle Hymn of the Republic sung and it seemed very fitting as every life (as was Smitty's) is full of battles and the spirit that he brought to his battles, his life were truly examples of individual courage and faith in his fellow man.

by Steven Yaros, Jr.

SMITH, LUTHER
F246

Luther Smith was born in Ohio December 7, 1833, a son of Jacob, born 1800 in Connecticut, and Hannah, born 1859 New York, Smith. Jacob was a farmer in Ross Township, Lake County, Indiana. Luther married Sarah P. Maxwell February 12, 1854 in Lake County, Indiana. Sarah was born January 11, 1839 in New York state, a daughter of James and Permelia (Banks) Maxwell. Later in 1854 Luther acquired land in Section 17 of Ross Township which he began farming.

Luther and Sarah were the parents of six children, all born in Indiana. (1) Emma Permelia on October 31, 1855; (2) Elbert Eugene on April 5, 1857; (3) Sarah Jane born August 10, 1859, died October 10, 1867; (4) Adner Adair born November 17, 1862; (5) Jacob born April 1864, died June 21, 1864; and (6) Ambrose Luther born May 29, 1865.

Luther was enrolled in Co."B" 151st Regiment of Indiana Volunteers in Valparaiso on January 27, 1865 and mustered into service February 8 at LaPorte, Indiana. While in the service and in line of duty, at Tullahoma, Tennessee, Luther contracted a physical ailment requiring hospitalization, was transferred to Indianapolis and furloughed to his Deep River home where he died August 10, 1865. Sarah applied for, and was granted, a pension to help with the support of her children. Sarah died August 9, 1871 at Crockery, Ottawa County, Michigan. Sidney Lawrence, of Nunica, Ottawa County, Michigan, was subsequently named legal guardian of the Smith children.

by Betty L. Williams

SPENCER, MAX JACOB
F247

Max Jacob Spencer was born April 30, 1914 in White Heath, Illinois to Matthew Jacob Spencer and Dixieanne (Jordan) Spencer. His family moved to Hammond, Indiana in 1926 where his father was employed as an electrician at Pullman Standard. Max attended Hammond grade schools and graduated from Hammond High School in the Class of 1933. He worked briefly at a gas station, Youngstown Sheet & Tube and Grasselli Division of DuPont Chemical Company, and then was a salesman for Hostess Cake Division of Wonder Bread Company in Hammond for 11 years. He was a distributor for Maurice Lenell Cookie Company from 1947 until his death in October, 1975. Known as the "Cookie Man."

Max married Vivian Berquist of East Chicago on November 25, 1939. They had two children, Brian Arthur Spencer born 2/22/42 and Susan Christine Spencer born 7/2/45. They lived in East Chicago until 1945 when they moved to Crown Point, Indiana.

Max was a member of the United Methodist Church, served as Sunday School Superintendent for seven years, member of Lake Lodge #157 Free and Accepted Masons, Orak Shrine, South Bend Consistory, past president of Crown Point Lion's Club, City Cancer Chairman in 1958, Crown Point Community Chairman for three years, City Councilman for three terms, served five years on the Crown Point Planning Commission, served on the Annexation Committee, Streets and Sidewalks Committee and Industrial elopment Committee, Precinct Committeeman for fifteen years. He died while he was running for a fourth term as City Councilman.

by Gerald Born

SPOHN – (RANDHAN) MEDLIN
F248

Former Residents

I was born into the family of Sylvan and Minnie Spohn, July 11, 1908. My family had come to the Kouts, Indiana, from Adams County, Ohio in 1899. At the time I was born the family lived about three miles north east of Kouts, Indiana. When I was about one the family moved to the Barney Williamson farm two and one half miles east of Malden, Indiana. We lived there until I was about twelve years of age. The family then moved to a small farm north of Valparaiso, Indiana, still in Porter County.

At the age of six I started to school. My sister Edith and I walked the two and one half miles to school and home again each day. In the winter when it would snow Dad would take us in the bob-sled with the horses. I remember many things we enjoyed while living east of Malden. One special time was a visit from my oldest brother who lived in Ohio. He came in a Model T Ford with a shiney brass radiator. That was probably the first car I had ever seen. But two years later we had a greater surprise; in 1916 Dad came home with a new Model T Ford. This one didn't have a brass radiator but it was even more special, "It was ours." We would go to Valparaiso once a week to buy groceries. We hardly had a trip without a flat tire and when it rained we stopped and buttoned the side curtains to keep from getting wet. I remember after the "Big Tornado" that went through the Kouts area, mom took us to see the devastation it had caused. We went by the place where I was born, all that was left of the house was the floor. Sitting there was a rocking chair rocking away. I remember the first airplane I saw and a Zeppelin Dirigible.

In 1920 we moved to the farm north of Valparaiso. We went to school at Cooks Corners. When I graduated from eighth grade I attended Valparaiso High School. Later I worked at McGills Mfg. in Valparaiso. In the Spring of 1926 we moved to Hammond, Indiana.

I married Robert R. Randhan, in Valparaiso, May 8, 1926. We lived in Gary, Indiana. Robert R. Randhan II was born February 21, 1935 and for years later Judith Ann Randhan was born February 18, 1939. Robert R. Randhan I died May 13, 1941.

In July 1942 we moved to Miller, Indiana. While living there we went to church, and became members of Central Baptist Church, Gary, Indiana. In 1944 I became active in the Lake County Chapter of Child Evangelism Fellowship.

I married Benjamin F. Medlin in June 1948. We moved to Michigan City, Indiana in the fall. In 1957 both Ben and I felt the Lord had called us to work full time in Child Evangelism Fellowship. We were asked to come to Port Huron, Mi. where we moved Jan. 1, 1958. We worked together as a team to reach the children with the Gospel. I attended the Leadership Training Institute for C.E.F. and graduated in August 1958. Benjamin died in 1974 and I continued to work until I retired Jan. 1, 1979.

Judith and I took a trip in Sept. 1986 to visit her son who is in the U.S.A.F. in Germany. We traveled all up and down the Moselle River, to Innsbruck, Austria, to Garmish and through Bavaria. We took the train, the cable car up to the top of the highest peak of the Alps in Germany, Mt. Zugspitze. Also went to Trier, where we saw Porta Nigra and the Roman Bridge, parts of which were built there in the second century. We went to the Memorial site Concentration camp at Dachau, where the Jews were persecuted in World War II. We went through a number of castles, some were ruins, others were maintained the way the Kings lived in them. Two were built at the orders of King Ludwig II. One had 200 rooms. He lived in the older one most of the time. He later went insane and died mysteriously.

Robert R. Randhan II has two children, Brian, born June 26, 1958, Rita born April 1, 1961 and a foster son Robert Charles, born July 21, 1975. He is currently married to Jackie.

Judith Ann married James Murphy Jan., 1956. They have a son David Alan. B. May 11, 1959. She married David Thompson. They had three children, Susan Thompson Fleury, B. Oct. 31, 1961 Patricia Ann Thompson, B. Feb. 21, 1964, and Michael David, B. Nov. 8, 1965. David Thompson died March 28, 1968. Judith is currently married to Robert Forstner.

I have six Greatgrand children:
David Alan Murphy II, B. July 9, 1982 and Amanda Renee Murphy, B. Feb. 22, 1986. Shane Reily Fleury, B. June 12, 1983 and Taylor Ryan Fleury, B. July 23, 1985. Bryan Richard Thompson, B. Jan. 30, 1985 and Kayla

Michelle Thompson, B. Dec. 3, 1987.

Robert Randhan II lives near Hebron, Indiana and Judith Ann Randhan Forstner, Susan Thompson Fleury, Patricia Ann Thompson and Michael D. Thompson live in Port Huron, Michigan as I do.

by Mary E. Medlin

SPOHN – BAILEY
F249

Earl Kenneth Spohn born April 11, 1914 Indiana to Sylvan Sinclair and Minnie Warren (Miller) Spohn of Adams County, Ohio and Valparaiso, Indiana. Lived on a farm until his health caused him to move to Caption, New Mexico. Married Pearl Mae Cheever September 3, 1938 in the Valparaiso Christian Church. One daughter, Carol Mae born January 7, 1953 in LaPorte, Indiana. Carol Mae married November 16, 1972 in Roswell, New Mexico Robert Lee Bailey born March 30, 1949 Hot Springs, New Mexico. They have two children: David Thomas Bailey born June 3, 1979 Roswell, New Mexico and Karen Mae Bailey born November 30, 1984 Roswell, New Mexico.

Earl Kenneth Spohn died June 3, 1985 age 71 in Capitan, New Mexico.

by Lois Brown

SPOHN – BROWN
F250

The Spohns have been traced back to Maryland. David Spohn born about 1789 and his wife Hannah, born about 1790. She died between 1860-1870. They lived in West Union, Adams County, Ohio, Tifflin township. David was a blacksmith, farmer and minister of the Gospel. He was 80 in the 1870 Census.

Their son, Laymon was born about 1832 in Adams County, Ohio. He was a farmer. He married Sara Jane Thompson born about 1831 in Ohio. Sara's parents came from Pa. Children: Fleashia (23), Carlton G. (21), Chester L. (19), Laura Belle (14), Sylvan Sinclair (12), born 21 February 1868, and Viola May (7). (1880 Census).

Sylvan lived in a house with three sides and lots of sugar maple trees. He married Minnie Warren Miller 26 February 1890. Her parents William J. and Louise Miller. In 1899 Sylvan and his family came from Ohio to Porter County, Indiana to live. They lived in and near Kouts, Indiana until about 1909 when they moved to the Barney Williamson farm, 160 acres, 2½ miles east of Malden, Indiana. They also lived north of Valparaiso, Indiana and in Hammond, Indiana. They had eight children:

1. William Laymon B. 26 June 1891 in Ohio; married Maude Sininger in Ohio. Died in Ohio January 1922. They had no children.

2. Nellie May B. 16 June 1893 in Ohio; married 1. Ralph Wood. 2. Albert McGrath. Died November 1971 in Roswell, New Mexico. Buried in St. Whitley, IN. No children.

3. Elizabeth Jane B. 28 December 1895 in Ohio. Married Claude Fryar in Indiana 26 February 1917. They farmed the Arnie Small farm north of Haskell, IN., and the Bunnel farm northwest of Wanatah, In., until they bought their home in Wanatah, In, in 1944. Claude died in December 1971. They had three children: Louise, Lois (there was a son born between Louise and Lois who died three days after birth).

A. Louise married Arthur Ailes and have five children: Sharon, Roger, Linda, Lila and Donna.

B. Lois married Nick Polite. They have a daughter Joanne and live in Wanatah, IN.

Elizabeth (Aunt Bett) came to the family reunion this year (1988) age 92.

4. Harry Curtis B. 19 December 1897 in Ohio. Married 1. Rose Barber, 2. Helen Dinse, 3. Mary Walker. Harry and Rose had a daughter Mary, she married Randall Yager 29 June 1962. Harry died in a car accident December 4, 1985. He was on his way to spend the winter in Florida. He was just 15 days from being 88 and was still farming his 350 acre farm near Kouts, In. Randall and Mary now own the farm and moved back from Florida to live there and farm it. They have four children: Rosemary Helen, Michelle Marie, Randall Jr. and Mark.

5. Ruth Clara B. 27 June 1900 in Porter County, Indiana. Married Frank William Brown 28 September 1921. Loudean a girl friend had introduced them. They were married in the parsonage of the First Christian Church, Valparaiso, In., accompanied by Mr. and Mrs. Claude Fryar. Frank William was born in South Boston, Washington County, In. 28 May 1897 and died 28 January 1968 in Jeffersonville, In., buried in Walnut Hill Cemetery in Jeffersonville. William Haymon brought Frank William up north to work on farms possibly the Ostermeyer farm. Ruth had scarlet fever in December of 1935 and died on January 9, 1936, buried in Ridge Lawn Cemetery in Gary. Frank William had served in the U.S. Army in World War I. They had seven children:

A. Katherine Minnie B. 13 Oct. 1922, married Joseph Kocur and lives in Hammond, In., Joseph worked for Inland Steel and Katherine worked for Carson, Pirie, & Scott. Joseph died 18 May 1977 buried in St. Johns Cemetery Hammond, In. They had two children: Ronald Raymond and Bonita Jean.

B. Frank William Brown Jr. B. 15 December 1923 married Blanch Burke, had four children: Linda, Frank, Steve and Phyliss. 2nd marriage Atha Hosch, three children: Floral, Cindy, Frank. Frank served in the Army Air Force in World War II. He works for the Post Office and lives in Hobart, In.

C. Alvin Earl B. 28 February 1925 married Sylvia Newbolds, he worked for J&L Steel of East Chicago, In. Alvin died April 24, 1981 buried in Elmwood Cemetery in Hammond, In. Fourteen children: David, Jerry, Kenneth, Sharon, Larry, Paul, Billy, Jeff, Patricia, Anthony, Danny, Carla, Elizabeth, and Ruth. David died in 1971. The 1,236th Vietnam War Indiana serviceman killed in war since 1961. Kenneth died in 1953.

D. Harry Kenneth born 9 November 1927 married Daisy Goodman. Have four children: Glenn, Sandra, Diane, and Brian. Harry served in the Air Force. Lives in Dyer, Indiana. Members of the Dyer Baptist Church. Daisy worked for Lake County Schools retiring in 1988. Harry works for J&L Steel, East Chicago, IN.

E. Doris Lynn (twin of Donna Lee) born 4 September 1931. Worked for G.A.T.N. in East Chicago, In. Lived in Hammond, In. Died 1970 in Colville, Washington.

F. Donna Lee born 4 September 1931 died Dec. 1931. Buried in Ridge Lawn Cemetery, Gary, In. (twin of Doris).

G. Carroll Gene born 19 November 1934. Married Lois Jean Helms. He was raised by his father's sister Anna and her husband Horace Burger of Indianapolis after his mother died when he was one. Worked for Youngstown Sheet and Tube (now J&L Steel) in 1957. Now works for Indianapolis Power and Light Co. Two children: Natalie Sue and Lance William.

6. Edith Edna born 3 September 1905. Married Chauncey Herrick 2nd marriage to Robert Gillies. She had two daughters: Evelyn, Virginia. Edith died 26 February 1944. Buried in Hollywood Cemetery, Hollywood, Ca. Evelyn married Delvin Hall and had twelve children. Virginia married Kenneth Campbell and had two sons.

Sylvan Spohn family: Sylvan, Minnie, Elizabeth Fryar, daughter Louise, Frank Brown, Edith Spohn, Earl Spohn, Ruth Spohn Brown, Claude Fryar, Mary Spohn, (Picture taken about 1917)

7. Mary Eva born 11 July 1908. Married Robert R. Randhan, 8 May 1926 in the parsonage of the First Christian Church, Valparaiso, In. Harry Spohn and Mamie Randhan were witnesses. They had two children: Robert R. and Judith Ann. Robert R. Sr. died May 13, 1941, buried in Calumet Park Cemetery Merrillville In. Mary married Benjamin F. Medlin June 11, 1948. They moved from Michigan City, In. to Port Huron, Mi. Jan. 1, 1958 to be Missionary Directors to the Children of St. Clair, Co. Mi. under Child Evangelism Fellowship Inc. Ben died Sept. 17, 1974 and is buried in Lakeside Cemetery, Port Huron, Mi. Mary celebrated her 80th birthday this year (1988) at the Spohn-Brown Reunion.

A. Robert married Jane Pavlov and they had two children, Brian and Rita. Robert is now married to Jackie and they live near Hebron, In.

B. Judith married James E. Murphy and they had a son David. 2nd, David L. Thompson and they had three children: Susan, Patricia and Michael. (David Thompson died March 1968). Judith married Robert Forstner December 1971 and they live in Port Huron, Mi.

8. Earl Kenneth born 11 April 1914 married Pearl Cheever in August 1938. They have a daughter Carol Mae. Earl worked on farms in Porter and LaPorte counties. He bought a home in Wanatah, In., and worked for a Farm Implement Business. They moved to New Mexico in 1960 because of poor health. He died June 3, 1985. Buried in Capitan Cemetery, NM.

The Spohn children grew up on a farm 2½ miles east of Malden, In. their dad did a lot of carpenter work so the children had to help on the farm. Sylvan bought a two row corn cultivator and taught Ruth to use it. This was the first two row cultivator in the community pulled by horses so it wasn't easy and many hills of corn were covered with dirt. Edith and Mary had to walk behind and uncover any corn that got covered. When Earl started to school he was not strong so Ruth would drive the children 2½ miles to Rising Sun school in the horse and buggy. In 1916 Sylvan bought a Model T Ford and taught Ruth how to drive.

On week-ends everyone would go to Gramma and Grandpa Spohns, the men worked on the farms and the women would cook the meals. Playing the piano and singing made for a lot of good memories. Sunday they would go to church.

Sylvan and Minnie celebrated their 60th wedding anniversary February 1950, in Wanatah, In. at Earl's home. All the living children were there.

There have been three Spohn-Brown Reunions: 1986, 1987, 1988 held in June and it has been so nice to talk, see, share stories, and pictures, and fellowship with family.

Thanks to Elizabeth and Mary for information of this wonderful family and all of the families who have made possible this information for our family history.

by Lois Brown

STEPHAN, JACOB
F251

Jacob Stephan, an early settler aiding in the development of Lake County, Indiana, was born March 4, 1823, in Neumuhle, Bavaria, Germany, and lived in Brecken, Bavaria, Germany. He came to the United States as a young man in his twenties, via Canada, and into Michigan by stage coach, landing in Detroit. After some time Jacob settled in Lake County, homesteading on unimproved land east of what is now Schererville. (Route 30 goes through 13 acres of this land.)

On April 17, 1850, Jacob married Miss Anna Koerner, born in Germany, April 20, 1832. They were the parents of twelve children: John Leo (Barbara Dubs/DuBois); Peter (Mary Redar); Katherine (Adam Schubert); Barbara; Louis; Frank; Anna; Michael; Elizabeth; Maria (Fred Lukmann); Joseph; and Barbara Margaret (Arthur Hunt). All were baptized in the log chapel which now rests on the Catholic Church property in St. John, Indiana. Many of the children, however, died in their youth.

When the pioneers arrived they lived in tents. They cut down trees and built log cabins. Jacob and his contemporaries also had to dig wells and clear the land for planting crops. Those that were already settled helped the new comers to get started. In later years Jacob built a colonial type two story home.

Several times a year the pioneers would get together and drive with their horses and wagons to Chicago, Illinois, to trade their products, such as corn, wheat, etc., for supplies they needed. It was not safe for one farmer to go alone. On some of these trips Jacob would trade for a bolt of calico, a material much used at the time for making house dresses. Anna would sew a dress for herself and the girls in the family from the same bolt. Jacob also traded his products for boots. Not everyone in the family had a pair. In the winter, those who did the chores or went somewhere wore the boots.

The children had a long way to go to school, and in winter time when the weather was very bad, Anna used to teach them at home. In the summer months the farmers let the cows graze on the prairies, and tied a bell around their neck so as to tell where the cows were. Jacob was a little hard of hearing so he would hold up one of the children to listen for the sound of the bells.

The German immigrant became fully Americanized in September, 1860, when he was naturalized. Jacob died January 7, 1890. Anna died the same year on the 2nd of November. They are buried in St. Michael's Cemetery, Schererville.

In 1894, the Stephan homestead was sold to Killian Schubert. The house is still standing, and is located on Burr Street, between Route 30 and County Road 330.

by Florence Stephan and Jim Stephen

STEPHEN, ALFRED
F252

Alfred Edward Stephen, Michael and Catherine (Sutter) Stephen's second son, was born in Schererville, Indiana, March 15, 1916. He spent his early years in the local community where he attended St. Michael's Grade School, and later, Dyer High School, in Dyer, Indiana. Al liked to hunt and spent many a day as a young man pursuing his interest, returning home more than a few times with a number of fowl or hare. And being one of ten children, Al's bounty was a much appreciated depression day supper.

An ambitious person with a sense of business, Al entered that field in 1933, opening a Standard Oil gasoline station on the corner of

Dan and Al Stephen, July 27, 1963

Routes U.S. 30 and U.S. 41, by Teibel's Restaurant. He had many a meal there at the restaurant's coffee shop, and over a period of time got to know one of the waitresses, Olive Halton, rather well. Al dated her and she later became his bride.

Miss Halton was born April 3, 1918, a daughter of the Halton's of Spencer, Indiana. She came to Lake County, Indiana, in the late 1930's seeking employment. Al and Olive were united in marriage on the 22nd of September, 1938, at St. Michael's Church in Schererville. Over the years the couple adopted two children: a daughter, Sharon Kaye, in 1942 (James Bauske); and a son, Daniel Raymond, in 1945.

Alfred Stephen went into partnership with Orville Gilliam, forming "Stephen and Gilliam Standard Service," around 1939. Orville was a truck driver who patronized Al's station. They became friends and when Orville tired of driving they went into business together. Stretching out in their business pursuits, Al and Orville expanded with a fleet of trucks. Among other things, "Stephen and Gilliam Trucking" hauled: steel, from the mills in Gary, Indiana, across the states; grain, to the large Cargill elevators in Chicago, Illinois; and Indiana Limestone, from the quarries in Vincennes and Terre Haute. (The limestone facing on the Prudential Building in Chicago, was hauled by Stephen and Gilliam Trucking.)

An outdoorsman, Al loved the sports of hunting and golfing. Continuing his lifetime interest, he went on many hunting trips: South Dakota, for pheasant; Cairo, Illinois, for goose; and out west for deer and elk. Through the years he had a number of fine hunting dogs including, Irish Setters, English Shorthair Pointers and German Shorthair Pointers.

In his younger day Al was a caddie at the Lake Hills Country Club. He enjoyed the venture and went on to become an excellent golfer, winning many trophies which he proudly displayed. At his peak, Al had a handicap of seven. Olive also enjoyed golfing and they spent many a sunny afternoon on the course. During the winter months Al and Olive would bowl together on leagues. For several years he owned the bowling alley in St. John, Indiana, which is now the V.F.W. Post 717.

A generous person, Al made many charitable donations to organizations in the community.

In the mid 1960's, the successful businessman became seriously ill and sold his interest in the business to his partner of over 25 years. Months later, Alfred Stephen died of cancer at the age of 50, October 19, 1966. He is at rest in St. Michael's Cemetery, Schererville, Indiana.

by Jim Stephen

STEPHEN, DOROTHY
F253

Leonard and Dorothy (Stephen) Vander Lugt.

Dorothy A. (Stephen) Vander Lugt, daughter of George J. Stephen (1887-1975) and Anna L. (Soelker) Stephen (1890-1988), was born February the 28th, 1913. She recalls her early years in Schererville, Indiana, ice skating on Schubert's pond with her cousins and friends, and coasting down Schulte's hill. A memory of summer is playing baseball where the Scherwood Club is today. After graduating from St. Michael's School, Miss Stephen became a hairdresser in a beauty shop in Hammond, Indiana.

Her husband, Leonard Vander Lugt, was born in Iowa, August 26, 1906, the son of Lewis Vander Lugt (1880-1952), born in Delft, Holland, and Magdalena (Sluiter) Vander Lugt (1887-1960), from Rotterdam. The Vander Lugts had first settled in Iowa, and moved to Indiana in 1926. Dorothy and Leonard were married on May 25, 1935. They had met at a dance at Deep River, Indiana. The couple first rented a house in Glenn Park, a suburb of Gary, Indiana, before buying a house in Lansing, Illinois, in 1937. They later moved to a home with five acres in Lake County, Indiana, on Route 41, near Route 8, in 1945.

To Dorothy and Leonard two children were born: Ronald L., April 4, 1940 (Cheryl Teasdall, July 20, 1944); and Diane G., December 15, 1947 (Bernie Weston, May 15, 1942).

In 1955, the Vander Lugts vacationed in Colorado, visiting Leonard's brother and family. Liking that part of the country, they moved to Boulder, Colorado, in 1957, where Leonard worked for the Dow Chemical Company. He retired in 1971.

Dorothy and Leonard have three grandchildren: Mark Vander Lugt, 1963; Brian Weston, 1970; and Wendy Weston, 1974.

Son Ron and family moved to Escondido, California, in 1975, and works for Hewlitt Packard. After visiting Ron twice, once in January, and seeing oranges and flowers, etc., in the middle of winter, the Vander Lugts were much impressed with the city. (Escondido is located 25 miles north of San Diego.) Diane and her family also vacationed there and liked the area. In 1981, they all made the move to California, and enjoy being together once again. Diane and Bernie own California Gold Gymnastics of Escondido, where they train girls in the sport of gymnastics.

Dorothy and Leonard Vander Lugt are content and happy in their California home, where they can be with their children and grandchildren.

by Dorothy (Stephen) Vander Lugt and Jim Stephen

STEPHEN, EDWARD ADAM
F254

Edward (1877-1945) and Carrie (1881-1968) (Scholl) Stephen.

Edward Adam Stephen was born in the Schererville, Indiana, area and, except for some brief periods of time, lived there most of his life. He was born June 16, 1877, and was the second son of Peter and Mary (Redar) Stephen.

At approximately age 13, he worked on the Hart farm near Schererville. In those days if young children of farmers did not have enough work at home they would be employed by another farmer. This was true for most of the youth of that period. Later Edward gained employment as a section hand for the Pennsylvania Railway. He was eventually promoted to section gang foreman for the railroad.

John Stephen (1893-1974) on left with bow tie; Edward Stephen (1877-1945).

Edward met Caroline "Carrie" Scholl who was born on May 10, 1881, to Jacob and Mary (Fortre) Scholl. They were married October 10, 1899, in St. Michael's Roman Catholic Church, Schererville. Edward and Carrie lived in Dyer, Indiana, and Lansing, Illinois, while he continued his work with the railroad. In addition, he started an evening business of barbering men's hair to gain extra income for the family. However, Edward eventually lost his hearing and had to resign from his railroad employment. It was at this time that Edward and Carrie decided to start a new way of life and return to farming.

They lived on the Schiessle farm in Schererville; the Bieker farm in Lake Hills; and finally bought an 80 acre farm which was owned by the Liesenfeldts. The location of this property was near Schererville's Lake Hills Country Club.

Edward and Carrie Stephen had five children: Marie (1902-1985), (Jacob Schweitzer); Rose (1903-1985), (Aloysius Schreiber); Irene (1906-1975), (Eugene Schreiber); Helen (1916-1970), (Lawrence Huseman); and Howard (1923), (Lucy Mae Yates).

Edward had many interests. One was driving a horse-drawn school bus (circa 1916) for Schererville. His route to pick up children was in Hartsdale (just north of Schererville, and now incorporated into the town) and along the old Route 30 (County Road 330).

Edward also enjoyed concertina playing for pleasure and pastime. He and his brother John played together. During the 1920's, he and some friends played their music numerous times for dances at the old Halfway House, which has since been destroyed by fire. They also entertained on the farm for reunions and neighborhood gatherings. This provided a communal source of entertainment and fun.

Harvest time and grain thrashing was a laborious task for the area farmers of that period because of the available field equipment and machinery. In fact, it oftentimes involved cooperative assistance among the farmers to help each other before winter. The women of the community would prepare and cook food for all the helpers. When harvesting was finished, the farmers would have a celebration on one of the farms. Edward would entertain with his concertina while others played cards and enjoyed the festive occasion.

Edward continued farming his 80 acres of land until the time of his death, August the 28th, 1945. By this time all the children were married. Carrie remained on the farm a number of years and later moved to a home in town on Joliet Street. She died March 6, 1968, at the age of 86. Edward and Carrie Stephen are buried in St. Michael's Cemetery in Schererville.

by Mrs. Howard (Lucy) Stephen

STEPHEN, GEORGE
F255

Wedding photo, George (1887-1975) and Anna (1890-1988) (Soelker) Stephen.

George Jacob Stephen formerly of Schererville, Indiana, was born June 5, 1887, the fourth son of Peter Stephen (1854-1928) and Mary (Redar) Stephen (1855-1931). As a young man, he first worked on the "Section" for the Pennsylvania Railroad in town, and later as a car inspector for the E.J. & E. Railroad.

George married Anna Lena Soelker from St. John, Indiana, on the 3rd of November, 1909. She was a daughter of Henry Soelker (1859-1915) and Anna (Osweiler) Soelker (1863-1951). George and Anna had met at a dance in St. John. For a short while they lived with his parents, and later rented a small house in back of the public school in Schererville. The Stephens had one child during this time span, a daughter, Dorothy, born February 28, 1913. By 1916, George had built a house on the west end of his father Peter's property on East Joliet Street. A large barn that was on his father's land was torn down, and with part of the lumber a two car garage was built.

In his early married years George raised chickens and pigs in the back yard. He had a hunting dog and house pets: a cat, "Tabby"; a Boston bulldog, "Bozo"; and later, another Boston bulldog, "Bobo." At different times George had two race horses. In the summer during Fair week, and a while before, the horses would be in Crown Point, Indiana, training for, and running in the races held at the Lake County Fairgrounds. When George bought his first car, a Model "T" Ford, he sold the horses. George enjoyed hunting, fishing, and gardening. Quite often he and friends would go to South Dakota, pheasant hunting.

The years passed, and George retired from the railroad at age 65. When he was 71, in 1958, he and Anna moved from Indiana to Boulder, Colorado, with the help of their daughter Dorothy and her family, who had moved there in 1957. It was good for all to be together again – their homes were only one mile apart. George and Anna both enjoyed working in the yard; he his garden, and she, her flowers. Soon they had the new yard looking as nice as the one in Schererville. In a short time George had many good friends in Boulder, and fished east of town and in the mountains west of Boulder, in Netherland, Colorado.

In Anna's earlier years she loved to crochet, making tablecloths, bedspreads, rugs, etc., many of which are still being used by the family.

George suffered a stroke in May of 1975, and passed away at age 88, on September 14th the same year. Anna lived by herself until her 90th birthday and then went to live with her daughter, Dorothy, and son-in-law, Leonard Vander Lugt. In 1981, when e family moved to Escondido, California, Anna had her first airplane flight. She was 91 at the time. Anna died February 22, 1988, at the age of 97. George and Anna Stephen are buried in Mountain View Cemetery, Boulder, Colorado.

by Dorothy (Stephen) Vander Lugt

STEPHEN, HOWARD
F256

Howard and Lucy (Yates) Stephen

Howard Edward Stephen was the fifth and last child born to Edward Adam Stephen (1877-1945) and Caroline (Scholl) Stephen (1881-1968). He was born on 4 June 1923, in St. John Township, Lake County, Indiana. The Stephens owned an eighty acre farm in Schererville, where they raised dairy cows and field corn crops.

As a child, Howard rarely had time to spend with school mates because of his chores on the farm. The work there was considered more important than education and Howard did not have the opportunity to attend high school. Social contacts during Howard's later teen years were also very limited, as there was only a minimal amount of time to venture beyond the farm land and establish his own social circle. When he did interact with his friends the time was mostly spent at ice cream parlors or roller rinks. In 1943, however, Edward met someone special, and new hopes and dreams were formed.

Lucy May Yates was the third child of David Clarence Yates (1890-1973) and Anna Nevada (Hardesty) Yates (1898-1985). She was born on 9 November 1922, in Guston, Kentucky, and in 1924, migrated with her family to Hammond, Indiana. Lucy does not remember the train ride to Indiana, but does recall the depressed period of the late 1920's and early 1930's, when food was not plentiful, and new clothing was not affordable.

Miss Yates attended Catholic grade school and went on to Hammond High School. In June 1941, she graduated, and furthered her education at the Hammond Business Institute learning clerical skills. After finishing her training, Lucy was hired as a secretary for Northern Indiana Public Service Company. Her dream, though, was to become a wife and mother rather than a business career woman. This dream was soon realized during a double date. Lucy began the evening with one fellow, and ended up with her girlfriend's date. That exchange of partners eventually led to her marriage.

Howard Edward Stephen and Lucy May Yates were joined in matrimony on 9 June 1945, at St. Ann's Catholic Church in Lansing, Illinois. The couple began their married life on the Edward Stephen homestead, where they assisted in running the farm. Here Howard and Lucy shared many experiences and established a stronger love, respect, and appreciation for each other. Their farming future was, unfortunately, shortlived.

The small Stephen farm was draining the family's financial resources, and in addition, Howard's father, Edward, was seriously ill. Shortly after Edward's death, the family had to decide whether or not to continue the operation. Considering all the economic and social factors of this period, the decision was made to sell the farm, and Howard and Lucy had to make new choices for their future.

Relocating in Hammond, so Howard could seek employment in the industrial region, the couple had to establish a different social setting, lifestyle, and financial base. Howard was also faced with the task of being retrained in a totally new occupation. Fortunately, he had the innate sense of creativity and was quick to learn a new skill. He was hired by Combustion Engineering as an assembler and craft welder; and later by Pullman Standard as a welder and fitter. Lucy was busy maintaining the household, and in time, raising three children: Edward Howard (3-19-1949) (Patricia Ann McCullough); Kathleen Marie (7-6-1951) (David Stanek); and Charles Anthony (5-13-1958) (Michelle Warneke).

Even though Howard lives in the city, the blood of a farmer flows through his veins, and every year he and Lucy plant a garden. At the end of summer they both "can' and "put up" the fruit of their labors, as much for the enjoyment of it as for it's practical value. Lucy is interested in genealogy and has done a lot of research on her family, the Yates and the Hardestys, as well as Howard's family.

In 1987, after being in the same home for twenty some years, Howard and Lucy moved to a home a number of blocks south. They were somewhat forced to make the change because of the deterioration of their old neighborhood. Howard is retired from the Pullman Standard

Company, and enjoys carpentry and working with wood. He is currently involved in "personalizing" their new home, rearranging the kitchen and building new cabinets, as well as other projects throughout the house.

From a research paper by: Kathleen (Stephen) Stanek, 1987 and Edited and additional information: Jim Stephen, 1989

by Kathleen (Stephen) Stanek and Jim Stephen

STEPHEN, JOHN
F257

John (1893-1974) and Mathilda (1898-1983) (Schumacher) Stephen.

John Stephen, a well known farmer of Schererville, Indiana, was reared to the occupation of farming. He acquired his agricultural pursuits, which later were to be his chief occupation and livelihood, while working his father's land. The fifth son of Peter and Mary Stephen, John was born January 8th, a wintry day in 1893. He lived in Schererville all his life, and continued to work at home and assisted his parents until the time he received employment on the Pennsylvania Railroad. John was about 19 then, and for two or three years he worked the "Section" from Schererville to Crown Point, Indiana, walking there and back, inspecting the rails. He received 10 cents an hour, and later when he was given a 1 cent raise, John thought he had the world! For three years he worked for Jacob Seberger in Schererville, and helped build his new barn after the first one had burned down.

John courted Mathilda Schumacher, a young girl of the local community. Born September 9, 1898, Tillie grew up in her parents home in Schererville. She was a daughter of Henry and Mary Schumacher. John and Tillie were married on October 24, 1916, in Schererville, at St. Michael's Church, where they celebrated their golden wedding anniversary in 1966. They had four children: John George (7-23-1917), (Virginia Bol); Florence Mathilda (9-21-1919), (Francis Berens); Leona Marie (1921-1934); and Ella Mary (1-18-1932), (James Ball).

The Stephens first rented a farm on Cline Avenue in Schererville, and then about 1920, they moved to the other side of town to their farm on Lincolnwood Road. John and Tillie rented there too for many years, and then later bought the 140 acre farm. During the more than 40 years the Stephens farmed the area, they kept 50 to 60 head of cattle. They performed the daily chores side by side, getting up at 5 o'clock every morning to milk the cows and feed the animals. Then at 4 o'clock in the afternoon they had to do the milking and feeding all over again. The couple raised corn, oats, soybeans, and hay. John worked his fields with a team of horses up to the time he purchased a second-hand tractor, a McCormick Deering 1020. In 1944, he bought an International Farmall H, his first new tractor.

Tillie took care of chickens and turkeys. They were her hobby, and her way of raising spending money. She raised some 500 chickens and 100 turkeys each year, and at holiday times had to call on her sisters to help prepare the fowl for customers. With eight sisters (and two brothers) she had plenty of help.

John was well-known in the county for his concertina playing. He was in demand for weddings, square dances and house parties. He performed regularly on Saturdays at Finklestein's Halfway House between Crown Point and St. John, Indiana, with his band: John Shelfo played the saxophone and Ray Moss was on drums. They played from 9 p.m. to 1 a.m., and even later when an enthusiastic crowd would pass the hat. Many times John and Tillie would stay out so late, him playing and both dancing, that when they got home it was almost time to milk the cows. The concertina was an enjoyment to John, but it was also a necessity during the dark days of the depression, for without the income earned on the occasions of his performing, there would not have been enough money to pay the bills.

The hard working Mr. Stephen also looked for extra work with his team of horses at the time of the depression. He found it in plowing gardens for private individuals and in digging basements. The latter was accomplished by hitching the team to a "slip" – a huge shovel. Sometimes the team was used with a "wheeler" – a scoop mounted on two wheels. Three times as much earth could be moved by this method as with the slip.

Tillie's talent was displayed in the rugs she knitted and crocheted to decorate her home, and won prizes with at the Lake County Fair. She also had a way with flowers, filling her garden every year with roses, peonies, dahlias, and cannas. Feeding the threshing crew was a highlight of a farm wife's year. All the farmers in the area would work together threshing, filling silos, shredding corn, and storing fodder, while the women would cook a feast. The big meal was served at noon with an entire table covered with food. Usually the men ate so much they had to take a nap before heading back into the fields. By suppertime the farmer's appetites had returned for the lighter community meal shared then.

John and Tillie retired in 1960, and their son, John, took over the farm, raising grain for a decade after the cattle were sold. Meanwhile the Stephens began selling off parcels of their land, with the first 10 acres going to the developer of Sherwood Forest. Stephen park in Schererville is named after John and Mathilda, who donated 10 acres and made another 10 acres of land available to the town to form a 20 acre park. It is only one of several developments on their former family farm. Grimmer and Watson Schools are located in fields where John used to plant corn and beans. The now long-ago farm also includes Spring Hill and Shady Oaks subdivisions.

On September 20, 1974, John Stephen died peacefully in his sleep at the age of 81. Mathilda lived to be 85. She died November 22, 1983. They are buried together in St. Michael's Cemetery, Schererville.

John and Mathilda Stephen contributed substantially to the development of Northwest Indiana and the expanding Schererville Community, where they raised their family, shared their friends and made their living.

From the Post Tribune interview by Eleanor Meyer, 1978. Additional information: John Stephen, Jim Stephen.

by Jim Stephen

STEPHEN, JOSEPH
F258

Joseph Stephen (1912-1972)

Joseph Michael Stephen, a man of diverse interests, was the second child born to Michael Stephen (1883-1960) and Catherine (Sutter) Stephen (1889-1950) of Schererville, Indiana. He arrived at midnight, the 30th of November, 1912. When asked whether she wanted her son's birthdate to be the last of November or the first of December, Catherine chose December 1st. Joe grew up in the Schererville area, spending many days at the John Stephen farm, an uncle, and also at the Neudorf Brother's farm in St. John Township, uncles on his mother's side.

As a young man attending one of the local dances he met his future wife, Teresa Cecelia Bohling, a daughter of Norbert Bohling (1888-1954) and Carrie (Schaefer) Bohling (1890-1977). Teresa was born on the Bohling farm in St. John Township, March 10, 1916. They were married October 2, 1937. Joe and Teresa lived all but the first two years of their married life in Schererville, at 125 West Joliet Street, a wooded area on a natural sand ridge located on the former Sauk Trail. The home belonged to his aunt, Mary (Sutter) Leinen. At first they rented the house (circa 1912), and later bought it. Many improvements were made to the Stephen home through the years. To Joe and Teresa were born three children: Patricia Ann, October 5, 1938 (James Klein); James Lawrence, May 26, 1941; and Stephen Robert, April 24, 1944 (Janet Golcher).

A one time member of the Lake County Saddle Club, Joe had a number of fine horses, and handsome western saddlery as well. Sometimes on snowy, winter evenings the sounds of sleigh bells could be heard in the Schererville area when Joe would hitch "Duke" to the sleigh and take the family out for a ride. There was a lot of livestock up on the hill a "125 West" over the years, ranging from cows and horses, to pigs and chickens, to cats and dogs.

Joe also liked to golf. Throughout his life he enjoyed the sport and became accomplished at it. He and some of his brothers caddied at the golf course in Lake Hills when they were boys, working most of the day carrying bags of golf clubs up and down the hills. Teresa's main interest, apart from being a wife and mother, has always been her plants and flowers. She has spent many happy hours working in the yard. Some of her plants are original to the place, being those of Mary Leinen. A number of other flowers were received as starts from a neighbor, Miss Lizzie Helfen.

For some time in the 40's and early 50's, Joe operated a gas station in Schererville for the Standard Oil Company, located on the northwest corner of the intersection of U.S. 30 and U.S. 41 – "Crossroads of the Nation." During World War II the filling station was shut down for a period of time when Joe was needed to work at the steel mills in Gary, Indiana, for war production. But he is best remembered for another occupation.

Like his father before him, Joe was a school bus driver, driving for the St. John Townships Schools. He was a much loved and respected school bus driver for over twenty years, and took a lot of pride in his buses, frequently having his family help to keep them clean and polished.

After a lengthy bout with cancer, Joseph Stephen died at midnight July 3, 1972. He is buried in St. Michael's Cemetery in Schererville, along with his father, grandfather and great-grandfather.

by Jim Stephen

STEPHEN, MICHAEL
F259

Michael Stephen, a life-long resident of Schererville, Indiana, was born September 20, 1883, the third son of Peter Stephen (1854-1928) and Mary (Redar) Stephen (1855-1931). He spent the days of his boyhood and youth in Lake County, and acquired his education in the district school. He later went on to be the first bus driver for the School Town of Schererville, driving a team of horses and a wagon.

Michael married Catherine Sutter, a daughter of Joseph Sutter (1858-1917) and Katherine (Neudorf) Sutter (1863-1917). Kate was born November 2, 1889, and was reared on the Sutter farm located south and east of Scherer-

Michael Stephen

ville, on the Jackson Highway (Cline Avenue). She passed the time of her adolescence in the local area and went to school in Schererville, where she received a common education.

Mike and Kate lived with his parents in the town of Schererville their early married years. Six children were born during this period: Lucille (1911), (Anthony Grau); Joseph (1912-1972), (Teresa Bohling); Alfred (1916-1966), (Olive Haltom); Lawrence (1917), (Anne Evans); Margaret (1920-1983), (Walter Baumgartner); and Walter (1922), (Dorothy Stroyeck). Then in 1924, Mike and Kate had a home of their own built on the west side of his father's land at 330 East Joliet Street. Over the next ten years four more children were born: Robert (1925), (Jean Ott); Rita (1927), (Dale Myers); Roy (1929), (Dorothy Hill), and Betty Lou (1934), (Rex Sims). Three of the Stephen boys served in the Armed Forces in World War II. Lawrence was in the Navy, and Walter and Robert were in the Army.

In the early 1900's, as a young married man working on construction for the Pennsylvania Railroad, Mike suffered a very serious back injury resulting in a permanent spinal disorder. After the accident he was unable to take care of the bus wagon and his horses by himself, so his brother John assisted him, and Mike continued to drive the bus a number of years; sometimes going as far as the southwest corner of the township to pick up children attending school in Schererville. He also drove children to the high school in Dyer, Indiana.

Mike enjoyed gardening, but the pride and joy of his yard was the hedge, as many of the neighborhood children of the time will remember! He also took great pleasure and satisfaction in his annual harvest of concord grapes. A favorite pastime of Kate's was relaxing in her rocker after the many chores of the day, oftentimes whistling.

Although in pain throughout his adult life as a result of his spinal injury, Mike earned his livelihood working for the Pennsylvania Railroad, and retired in the middle 1950's. He died February 19, 1960, and was preceded in death ten years by Kate, who died February 28, 1950.

by Jim Stephen

STEPHEN, PETER
F260

Peter Stephen, a native of Lake County, Indiana, was the second of twelve children born to Jacob Stephan (1823-1890) and Anna (Koerner) Stephan (1832-1890). (The surname was changed from "Stephan" to "Stephen" sometime this century.) Peter was born on the Stephan homestead in Schererville, August 12, 1854. His early years were spent on his education in the local school and in working on his father's farm, along with his many brothers and sisters, doing such chores as his age and strength permitted. He grew to be a tall, lean young man with a pleasant disposition.

He courted and later married Miss Mary Redar, a young lady of Schererville. The marriage took place June 23, 1874. Mary, born March 24, 1855, was the daughter of Mathias Redar (1822-1892) and Margaret (Spanier) Redar (1831-1880); and a granddaughter of Mathias and Maria Redar who came to America in 1838, and were one of the first German families to immigrate and settle in the county.

Peter and Mary Stephen had six children, four of which lived to adulthood: Edward (1877-1945), (Carrie Scholl); Michael (1883-1960), (Catherine Sutter); George (1887-1975), (Anna Soelker); and John (1893-1974), (Mathilda Schumacher). A son Mathias (1875), and a daughter Margaret (1879), died at an early age.

Peter was a farmer for many years, tilling and cultivating the soil of his Jackson Highway farm in Schererville, and later worked for the railroad. For seven years in the 1920's he was employed as janitor of the two-story public school in town.

The majority of their years together, the Peter Stephen family resided in the home he had built in Schererville, located at 346 East Joliet Street. It was constructed in 1886, the date being noted by a grandson, Walter. While doing some remodeling in the 1960's, Walter found an 1886 "Indian Head" penny under a window sill, placed there in custom by one of the carpenters of the time. When the house was built, Joliet Street was one of the main roads in the Lake County area, known as the "Main Road" or road to Joliet. Years before it was called the Sauk Indian Trail, going as far as Detroit, Michigan, and Joliet, Illinois, the main path in the land at the southern tip of Lake Michigan. Two of Peter's sons, Michael and George, later built homes on their father's land.

Peter, a gentle man, beloved by his family and those around him, lived to be 74 years of age. He died February 9, 1928. Mary died June 27, 1931, at the age of 75. They are at rest in St. Michael's Cemetery, Schererville.

by Jim Stephen

STEPHEN, RITA
F261

Rita K. Stephen, formerly of Lake County, Indiana, the daughter of Michael Stephen and Catherine (Sutter) Stephen, was born April 27, 1927. Her early years were spent in the Schererville area where she received her education attending St. Michael's Grade School and later, Dyer High School. Rita spent a lot of time sledding on the Keilman hill with the neighbor

Rita Stephen – 1940's

kids, and also enjoyed many a Saturday evening in the mid to late 40's, baby sitting for the children of her brother Joe and his wife, Teresa.

Miss Stephen held a number of jobs in the local area. She worked at Mary's Restaurant in town; as janitoress at St. Michael's Grade School; and as maid at "Meyers Castle" in Dyer, Indiana. Rita also washed the walls of private individual's homes for spending money.

In 1946, Rita went to work at Sauzer's Restaurant in Schererville, and continued working there for three years. It was there where she met Dale F. Myers. He was in the Air Force and planned to make a career of the Service. They got to know each other, and in December of 1949, Rita and Dale were married. Dale was born August 8, 1926, the only child of Samuel Walter Myers and Jennie Dell (Fieres) Myers of East Chicago, Indiana. Mr. Myers was a carpenter; and Mrs. Myers, a school teacher.

The newly married couple's first home together was at Chanute Air Force Base in Illinois. From Chanute Field the Myers traveled to Carswell Air Force Base in Fort Worth, Texas, in 1951. The following year they were transferred to Barksdale Air Force Base at Shreveport, Louisiana. After staying there for eight months, Rita and Dale moved in 1951, to Lockbourne Air Force Base in Columbus, Ohio, the city where they currently reside.

The Myers have five children:

Samuel Walter (11-18-1952), who in 1974, married Loretta Iacaboni. They were blessed with a beautiful girl in 1982, Angela Marie. Sam is a graduate of Ohio State University, and is presently a lineman with Ohio Bell;

Cynthia Louise (7-31-1957) married Michael Kennedy in 1977, and has four red-headed children: Patrick Michael, 1982; Christopher Michael, 1983; Kellie Kathleen, 1985; and Katie Pauline, 1987;

Vernon Alan (4-16-1959) has three children and two stepchildren. He married Linda Parsley in 1984. Their children are: Terri Parsley,1979; Michael Parsley, 1983; Vernon Alan Jr., 1985; Christina Marie, 1986; and Brian Anthony, 1988. Vernon is janitor of the family's parish church in Columbus;

Michael Stephen (10-7-1962) is an accountant, a graduate of Ohio State University; and

Catherine Mary (6-28-1964), who wed in 1985 to Russel Hall. The Halls have one daughter, Ashley Marie. She was born in 1986. Cathy is a waitress at Bob Evans Restaurant; and Russ works for Lincoln Village Foods.

Dale Myers is retired from the Service and until recently did odd jobs, from which he has also retired. Rita's pastime is going shopping with her daughters. She belongs to the "Senior Stars," and is on the telephone and bingo committee at church — to organize the bingo crew twice a week. Rita manages the kitchen in the bingo hall on these occasions. She also enjoys entertaining the grandchildren.

Rita and Dale Myers have lived in Columbus, Ohio, many years now. They started to establish roots there after their decision in 1960, to make the city their permanent home.

by Jim Stephen

STEPHEN, ROBERT
F262

Robert Stephen 1987

Robert William Stephen, son of Michael and Katherine (Sutter) Stephen, was born on the 15th of October, 1925, Indiana, where he received his education. As the years advanced Bob grew to be a likable person, a lot of fun and always ready for a good time — a cheerful individual with a disposition much like that of his paternal grandfather.

Bob entered the U.S. Army in 1943, at Camp Shelby, Mississippi, and in 1944, he entered the European Theatre of Operation — France, Germany, Belgium and Austria. Seeing much action during World War II, he earned numerous medals: Rhineland Campaign; Central, with three major battle stars; European-African; Middle Eastern Theatre; Combat Infantrymen Badge; Good Conduct; Occupation Ribbon; and Presidential Citation (Unit).

Back home in Indiana after the War, being a conscientious and civic minded young man, Bob devoted much time to the Schereville Boy Scouts, taking them camping, on paper drives, and on various other activities.

When the Korean Conflict broke out in 1950, Bob again saw action. Entering at Inchon, Korea, joining the First Cavalry Division, he served 13 months on the front lines as a machine gunner (BAR), and as squad leader. Medals earned: National Defense Service Medal; Korean Service Medal with Silver Service Star; Republic of Korea Presidential Unit Citation; D.A.G.O. #35, 4 June 1951; Combat Infantrymen's Badge; Bronze Star for galantry in action; and the Purple Heart.

Robert Stephen was united in marriage to Jean Marie Ott, daughter of Homer and Mae (Reichert) Ott, October 4, 1952, at Holy Name Church, Cedar Lake, Indiana. Bob met Jean on a double date with his sister Margaret, when the girls were cashiers at a grocery store in Chicago Heights, Illinois. The couple had three children: Robert William Jr., 1953; Mary Catherine, 1955; and Martin Thomas, 1958.

Honorably discharged from the Army for disability in 1956, Bob and the family lived in Dyer, Indiana, a good many years and later left Lake County, and moved to Chicago Heights, Illinois, Jean's hometown. During this period Bob was employed by Keyes Fibre Company in Hammond, Indiana.

On the 25th of January, 1974, Jean Marie Stephen died as the result of an accident at home that caused a massive brain hemorrhage.

The Descendants of Robert William Stephen Sr. and Jean Marie (Ott) Stephen

Robert William Stephen Jr. married Deborah Ann Foley in 1975. They reside in Chicago Heights, Illinois, and have three children: Christine Ann, 1977; Robert William III, 1979; and Lawton Aaron, 1982.

In 1976, Mary Catherine Stephen married Kenneth Foster Blanchard. The Blanchards have two children: Kenneth Foster Jr., 1977; and William Charles, 1978. They reside in Portland, Oregon.

Martin Stephen is single at this date and also lives in Portland.

Robert William Stephen Sr. married Grace L. Lewis in 1976, and moved to Gresham, Oregon, the following year. In 1987, Grace died after a lingering illness.

Bob currently lives in Oregon, and on September 1st, 1988, married Nickie Espinosa. The Stephens have made Portland their home.

by Jim Stephen

STEPHEN, STEPHEN
F263

Stephen Robert Stephen was born in Lake County, Indiana, in 1944, to Joseph Stephen (1912-1972) and Teresa (Bohling) Stephen (1916) of Schererville. He grew up in the local community and received his education attending St. Michael's Grade School in Schererville, from 1950 to 1958, and Dyer Central High School in Dyer, Indiana, from 1958 to 1962.

Among Steve's many hobbies and interests were sports, cars, drawing and aircraft. He enjoyed the natural beauties of the outdoors and the terrain of the area, and spent many a day hunting in the surrounding fields and fishing in the neighboring lakes and ponds. Steve played baseball in little league; basketball in grade school; and in high school he wrestled and was on the varsity football team, and became a letterman. Also in his high school years Steve customized his red '53 Chevy Bel-

171

Stephen R. Stephen

Air convertible, and worked at Sauzer's Waffle Shop in Schererville.

In the fall of 1962, Steve went to College where he cultivated a couple more interests — those of drawing and flying. At Ball State University in Muncie, Indiana, he enrolled in R.O.T.C., and majored in Art, a subject in which Steve became proficient and adept in many different media, and for which he received a B.S. Degree. But of all his interests, there was one which was the strongest.

At an early age Steve became interested in aircraft and had the dream of flying. As a child and teenager he read many books on the subject, and constructed numerous model airplanes, some of which were motorized and flew. With his R.O.T.C. background and his desire for flying, Steve entered the United States Air Force in 1966, was commissioned a Second Lieutenant and received his pilot training in the F-4 Phantom Fighter at Reese Air Force Base (AFB), Texas.

Lt. Stephen then served in the Vietnam War from 1968 to 1969, being assigned to the 469th Tactical Fighter Squadron (TFS), Korat Royal Thai Air Force Base, Thailand. Flying 202 combat missions (506 flight hours) into North and South Vietnam and Loas, he received 3 Distinguished Flying Crosses, 20 Air Medals, the Vietnam Campaign Medal and the Republic of Vietnam Defense Medal. At this time Lt. Stephen was promoted to the rank of Captain. He also designed and painted the famous P-40 War Hawk shark teeth on the F-4E Phantom Aircraft for the squadrons 24 aircraft deployment to Vietnam in 1968. (The F-4 Aircraft currently located in the Pacific Area of Operations still retain this proud symbol of America's aviation history.)

Captain Stephen's next tour of duty was with the 401st Tactical Fighter Wing (TFW) at Torrejon Air Base, Madrid, Spain, from 1969 to 1973, as a member of NATO Alliance, deployed with the 307th TFS to Air Bases throughout Europe. In 1972, he attended Squadron Officers School.

Back in the United States, assigned to the 50th TFW, 71st TFS and the 63rd FS, Captain Stephen was at Mac Dill AFB, Tampa, Florida. At this base from 1973 to 1977, he served as instructor pilot, preparing new pilots for world-wide combat operations in the F-4 Phantom. From 1977 to 1979, he was stationed at Nellis AFB, Las Vegas, Nevada, attached to the 474th TFW, 429th TFS, where he received his next promotion.

As a Major, Stephen served one year with the 314th Air Division, Osan Air Base, Korea, where he attended Air Command and Staff College, and was Chief of Fighter Training Exercises. Next came "Red Flagg," back again at Nellis AFB, Las Vegas, this time with the 4440th Tactical Fighter Training Group, from 1980 to 1983. Here Major Stephen was Director of Flying Operations, responsible for conducting realistic Air Combat Training Exercises for over 5000 United States Air Force, Navy, Marine and Army Aircrew members per year, over the world's best training ranges. At this command Stephen was promoted to Lieutenant Colonel and attended Air War College.

He then traveled to Florida, where he was with the 31st TFW, 307th TFS, at Homestead AFB. Here from 1983 to 1987, Lt. Colonel Stephen served as F-4 instructor pilot, Director of Wing Weapons, 307th TFS Operations Officer, and Assistant Director of Wing Flying Operations. His most enjoyable assignment was as Operations Officer of the 307th TFS, where he received the "Top Gun" Award, and the Top Instructor Pilot Award. Also at this assignment he earned a Masters Degree in Aviation Technology from Embry Riddle University of Aviation, was nicknamed "Snoopy" by his men, and was promoted to the rank of Colonel.

Snoopy next was assigned to Headquarters, USAF, Pentagon, Washington D.C., in 1987, where he is directly involved in policy and decisions regarding present and future Air Force, force structure requirements. Colonel Stephen currently resides in Centreville, Virginia, with his wife and family, and remains active in his hobbies and interests as time permits.

In 1967, the then Lieutenant was united in marriage to Janet E. Golcher at Laughlin AFB, Del Rio, Texas. Janet was born in 1940, to Harry F. Golcher(t) (1897-1955) and Marguerite E. (Wiseman) Golcher(t) (1911-1968), of Glenwood, Illinois. Steve and Jan had met through mutual friends while still back in the Midwest. A daughter, Marguerite ("Margo"), was born in 1968, while the couple was stationed at Tampa, Florida, and a son, Sean, was born at Madrid, Spain, in 1970.

Colonel Stephen R. Stephen has flown over 3500 flight hours in the F-4C/D/E Phantom II Fighter and has received many decorations and awards: two Meritorious Service Medals; three Air Force Commendation Medals; three Distinguished Flying Crosses; twenty Air Medals; the National Defense Medal; Achievement Medal; Marksmanship Awards; the Air Force Outstanding Unit Award; Training Unit Award; three Overseas Tour Awards; Longevity Ribbons; and the Republic of Vietnam Defense Medal, and the Vietnam Campaign Medal.

by Jim Stephen

STEPHEN, WALTER
F264

Walter Stephen

Walter Andrew Stephen, "Nick," was born in Schererville, Indiana, February 12, 1922, at the home of his paternal grandparents, the sixth child of Michael and Catherine (Sutter) Stephen. He attended St. Michael's School from 1928 to 1935, and received his high school education at Dyer, Indiana, the following years. His first year of employment was in 1939, at the Keilman Company Block Works by Dyer, receiving $50 per month, working six days a week. In 1940, Walter started working at the Inland Steel Company in Gary, Indiana, upgrading himself to $40 per week.

He was drafted into the Army in January of 1943, and fought in World War II. Decorations earned: Cloister of Five Bronze Stars – all battle stars; European Theatre Medal; and Honorable Discharge in December of 1945.

An energetic young man, Wally worked as an apprentice carpenter for three years and was given a Journeyman Carpenter Card. He remodeled several older homes in the area and built himself two new ones. The first in 1955 on 68th Place, and the other in 1959 at 66 Redar Drive, both located in his home town.

Walter met his wife, the former Dorothy Stroyeck of Decater, Illinois, in 1940, when she was working as a waitress at Teibel's Restaurant in Schererville. She was born December 13, 1921. The ceremony which united Dorothy and Pfc. Walter in marriage at St. Michael's Church, Schererville, took place March 18, 1944, and was planned with war-time simplicity, but nevertheless retained the splendor of traditional nuptial rites. The Rev. Peter A. Biegel officiated. Wally and Dorothy have three daughters: Esther Marie, September 10, 1948 (Ronald McCauley); Carol Ann, February 15, 1951 (Arthur Hamilton); and Shirley Rae, April 30, 1954 (Paul Nelson).

Returning to Inland Steel in 1948, Wally worked as roll finisher. In 1963, he moved into the supervision ranks, was sent by Inland to Purdue University on two different occasions, and was given an Industrial Degree. He served as a Schererville Volunteer Fireman from 1960 thru 1968, moving up in the ranks to Captain in eight years.

In November 1967, Walter went into the political game in Schererville, and won the seat of 1st Ward Trustee, holding that position for seven years. He also held a four year seat on the Town Planning Commission, and was Town Board President for three years.

For fun and relaxation, Walter enjoys a good game of golf, a sport he became interested in and learned while working as a caddie at the Lake Hills Golf Club in St. John, Indiana, during the depression in 1932. He is still playing today and is pretty good at age 66! Also, several times through the years, Wally has enjoying hunting and fishing in Minnesota, South Dakota, and Canada, and he goes fishing every chance he gets.

Retired from Inland Steel Company, March 1, 1981, Walter is currently involved with the Veterans of Foreign Wars. A long-time member, joining sometime after World War II, he has held a number of high offices at Post 717 in St. John: Quartermaster, Trustee, Hall and Bar Manager, and twice, Commander. Moving into the 1st District, he has served as guard, Junior Vice Commander, Senior Vice Commander, and Commander (1987-1988), with 4,700 veterans under his command. Walter has traveled throughout the States working for the Vets, including: Washington D.C., New Orleans, and Evansville, Indianapolis, and Clarksville, Indiana.

Walter and Dorothy reside in the home he built on Redar Drive, and have seven grandchildren: Kevin, Richard, Thomas and Lisa Marie McCauley; Joshua Hamilton; and Amy and Eric Nelson.

by Jim Stephen

STEWART FAMILY
F265

Andrew Allison Stewart (1836-1908) was born in the Parish of Coylton, County of Ayr, Scotland, the son of James Stewart and Jean Allison. Andrew emigrated to the United States in 1849 and married Mildred Amelia Lindsley (1858-?) in 1876. She was a descendant of David Lindley (1759-1845), a soldier of the Revolutionary War. Andrew and Mildred lived in Alberta, Canada, for several years, and their three oldest children were born there. They were the parents of four children: Jeanet (Jessie) Gibson (1879-1965) who married Alexander Dow in 1899 and lived most of her life in Gary, Indiana; Andrew A., born 1881 in Canada and died in Pennsylvania; Mary Mildred, born in 1885, who was a Christian Scientist healer in Portland, Oregon, and married to Harry Clay; and John Alan (1893-1950), the subject of this history.

Dr. John Alan Stewart (1893-1950) was born September 15, 1893, in Chicago, Illinois, the youngest child of Andrew Allison Stewart and Mildred Amelia Lindsley. He earned his doctorate in dentistry at Indiana University and began his practice in Gary, Indiana, in 1920. He lived briefly in California but returned to Gary in 1925 and continued his dental practice at 848 Broadway until his death on April 7, 1950. He was a 32nd degree Mason and became a Noble of the Mystic Shrine on December 2, 1944.

Mary Ann Vukin (1910-1957), born June 29, 1910, in Escanaba City, Michigan, served as Dr. Stewart's receptionist in his dental practice until she married her boss on June 17, 1932, at Blue Island, Illinois. She was the oldest child of Marko D. Vukin and Barbara Glivar who emigrated from Karlovac, Jugoslavia to the United States in 1905 on the S.S. Kaiser Wilheim II. Mary Ann lived most of her life in Gary, Indiana, and died there on August 24, 1957.

Dr. and Mrs. Stewart had one child, Mary Janet Stewart, born September 4, 1941, who currently resides in Hammond, Indiana. After her mother's death, she lived with her father's sister, Jessie Stewart Dow, in Gary while she finished high school. She graduated from Lew Wallace High School in 1960. She earned her Bachelor of Science degree in Physical Education in 1964 from Indiana University and taught school in Chicago, South Suburban Illinois, New London, Connecticut, and Lake County, Indiana, for several years. In 1982 she earned her Master of Science degree in counseling from Purdue University and is currently a Deputy Chief Probation Office and Head of the Intake Division for Superior Court of Lake County, Juvenile Division, in Gary, Indiana.

by Mary Janet Stewart

STOWELL FAMILY
F266

The founder of the family was the Norman knight, Adam, who came over with William the Conqueror in 1066. His services were rewarded by giving him the manor called de Cothelstone, one of the oldest homes in England, situated six miles from the Bristol Channel, in Quantock, County Somerset. It was built long before 1066 by a Saxon king and queen, with many buildings immediately surrounding it including a church, eleven farm houses and fifty-four cottages. It was retained by them in an unbroken line from the time of the Norman Conquest until 1820.

The name Stowell comes from another manor, de Stawelle, also in Somerset County, which also came to the family at that time. The titled branch continues to spell the name Stawell, while the U.S. branch has adopted Stowell.

The family was very influential in the 12th, 13th, 14th, and 15th centuries and in the time of the Civil Wars was the most prominent family in southwestern England, as they had acquired by marriage or purchase some 26 additional estates with churches and lands attached to them. They were royalists and staunch supporters of the Stuarts. When the Parliamentary Party and Cromwell came into power their estates were confiscated and their mansion house and the church badly damaged and Sir John Stawell was imprisoned for several years in the Tower of London.

On this side of the Atlantic an important event for the family occurred in 1635 when a large colony from Hingham, England landed in the New World to settle in Hingham, Massachusetts. Among the colonizers was a ten-year old boy named Samuel Stowell. Since his name does not appear in the ship's log, it is probable that he came in the company of a relative on his mother's side, or a friend whose name was not Stowell. His name does not appear in the Hingham records until his marriage in 1649.

Samuel Stowell became a blacksmith. He not only shod the horses and repaired all the wagons, farming tools and implements, but what was more important kept the fire arms with which they defended their homes and property in working order. His descendants all married into the best families of Hingham and Newton. He died at Hingham November 9, 1683.

His wife was Mary Farrow, daughter of John and Frances Farrow, born in Hingham, County Norfolk, England September 22, 1633. After her husband's death, she married Joshua Beal, who lived on an adjoining lot.

Their son, David Stowell, was baptized at Hingham April 8, 1660 and married a second time to Mary Stedman, daughter of Nathaniel and Temperance Stedman. David was undoubtedly a man of great strength of character and of good social standing, for all his children married well. This was especially true of his daughter, Mary, who married John King, and their children occupied prominent positions in the early days of our country.

Nathaniel Stowell, their son, was born about 1703 and died at Pomfret Connecticut on March 11, 1757. He married at Newton on October 22, 1731, Margaret Trowbridge, daughter of James and Hannah (Bacon) Trowbridge. Her ancestor, Thomas Trowbridge, was from an influential family in Exeter, England, where they had come into prominence when Henry VIII granted them a title for establishing wool routes from the highlands of Scotland to the port at Exeter. Theirs is one of the few titles brought to this country from England and retained here.

Their son, Oliver Stowell, was born at Pomfret December 7, 1744 and died at Abington, July 20, 1836 aged 91 years. He married Abigail Strickland, daughter of Jonathan and Joanna Strickland. He was a physician, who studied at Harvard and opened his practice at Stafford, Tolland County. Prior to his marriage he served with the forces of the American Revolution. He was also an active force in forming the Abington Public Library.

In passing it might be noted that Augustus Oliver Artemus Stowell, one of their sons, was a noted lawyer in his time and one of the early members of the Mormon church. He later became disillusioned with the church and returned to Westfield, New York where he was admitted to practice in the Supreme Court of New York in 1808. His son, William Rufus Rogers Stowell, however, continued with the Mormon church and was a Captain of a military company in the pilgrimage over the desert to Salt Lake City.

However, it is their son, Loren Lorenzo Stowell, who was the progenitor of the Stowells in northwest Indiana. He was born at Stafford, Connecticut March 3, 1795 and died at Lowell, Indiana between 1872 and 1879. He married Mary Matilda Reed, whose mother's maiden name was Ruth Daskum. She was born March 12, 1799 and died October 6, 1842 in Kalamazoo County, Michigan. We know little of his early life. He first appears in the records of Sherman Township, Huron County in the 1820 census. Huron County is located at the extreme western end of the Ohio Western Reserve, that portion of land in Ohio that had been part of Connecticut, when the state's claim stretched to the Mississippi River. It is known as the "Firelands" for land was given to those Connecticut residents who had property burned by the British during the Revolutionary War. Six of their children were born here.

An account of his life will be found in this volume.

by Gerald M. Born

STOWELL, JOHN E.
F267

John Stowell was born in Sherman township, Huron county, Ohio June 13, 1824 to Loren Lorenzo Stowell of Connecticut and Mary Matilda Reed of New York. His mother died when he was eighteen years old and he went to live with Hale Bates, a native of Vermont, who taught him the blacksmith's trade and with whom he came to Porter township, Porter County, Indiana in 1843. He made his home with them until he was married to Rhuey Ann Powers (his obituary says Shumway) January 1, 1851, who was living with the Warner F. Sampson family in Boon Township, Porter County. This union was blessed with six children — three boys and three girls, five of which survived their father, one son Loren dying in infancy.

In 1859 he moved from Porter County to West Creek Township, Lake County, Indiana where he lived much of the time in or near Lowell, with the exception of time spent in and around Kankakee, Illinois about 1880.

When his country became involved in the Civil War he heard the call for assistance and enlisted in Company A, 73rd Indiana Infantry on August 6, 1862 from which organization he was honorably discharged July 1, 1865; having served faithfully for nearly three years.

He was wounded in the left leg by a gun shot that shattered the tibia. This skirmish occurred at the Battle of Stone River in Tennessee in January, 1863. The wound never did heal properly and he was unable to devote full time to his occupation as teamster and farmer.

Later in life he was employed at the pumping station, Lowell, where he never missed a day when the weather would permit, going there to see that things were in order, until within ten days of his death on December 10, 1902 at Shelby, Lake County, Indiana.

John E. Stowell united with the Christian Church, Shelby under the pastorship of Rev. Appleton. His funeral occurred from the Christian Church, Lowell. The members of Burnham Post G.A.R., of which he was a member, turned out forty-four strong to pay this last tribute of respect to their dead comrade. Five members of his regiment acted as pallbearers, George S. Clark, Oliver Surprise, D.C. Pulver, Orin DeWitt, N.J. Phillip and in addition H.H. Purdy.

The children of John E. and Rhuey Ann (Powers) Stowell were: Homer J. Stowell (1852-1932) who married Emily D. Hayhurst (1856-1940) on February 17, 1875 and they had six children, Charles Stowell, Nora May, who married Charles D. Cleaver, Clifford Thornton Stowell, who married May Whitaker, Royal Franklin Stowell who married Gertrude Thomas, Floyd Stowell and Ethel Ruby who married Robert E. Pemble.

Alice Stowell (1857-1919) a twin daughter married Wm. B. Howie (1842-1884) of England. They had Grace Howie and Elsie E. Howie, who married first Grant W. Lawbaugh and second Enoch D. Jones.

Alice (Stowell) Howie then married William W. Sanders, Jr. and they had Burnie M. Sanders, Estella M. Sanders, who married Grant W. Lawbaugh, Mary M. Sanders, who married Fred Reed and Gilbert W. Sanders, who died in infancy.

Alice's twin, Adelia Stowell (1857-) or "Addie" married "Matt" or Manford Cross (1859-1942) who worked at the Brown Ranch. Their children were Mary Augusta or "Rhoda" Cross who married Leonard Harmon, Samuel Cross, who married Ada B. Camblin of Morocco and second, Beatrice Chamberlain, Cass Manford Cross, who married Nora E. Herckle first and later Edna M. Jones, Amos George Cross or "Toad", who married Helen Myrtle Baster, John Cross, who married Mae Warner, and Rhuey Ann Cross, who married Frank Press first and Albert Hiatt second.

Harriet Stowell, the third daughter of John E. and Rhuey Ann (Powers) Stowell married Samuel McDonald and moved to Hardman, Oregon.

Frank Stowell (1859-1932) married Helen Dollish and lived at Chicago Heights, Illinois. They had three sons, Bert, Frank and Peter.

John E. Stowell's first wife died on August 14, 1882 and he married Mrs. Ruth Gragg, who in turn died in 1885. He was again married to Mrs. Eliza A. Doolan, who preceded him by only a few weeks, dying September 16, 1902.

John E. Stowell and his wife are buried at the Lowell Cemetery.

by Gerald M. Born

STOWELL, LEWIS M.
F268

Lewis M. Stowell was born July 19, 1828 at Sherman Township, Huron County, Ohio to Loren Lorenzo and Mary Matilda (Reed) Stowell. He married Mary Ann Treece, the daughter of Benjamin and Eva (Eaton) Treece on December 3, 1854 in Porter County, Indiana. Some of

their six children were born at Clay Township, LaGrange County, Indiana, while some of the older children were born in Cedar Creek Township, Lake County, Indiana. By 1880 the family lived in Monroe Township, Pulaski County.

Their children were Eva Alvaietta Stowell born September 11, 1855, George W. Stowell b. 1857, Laura A. Stowell born November 6, 1868 at Lowell, Charles D. Stowell born October 29, 1866, Jes (Josiah Eaton) Stowell born December 10, 1869 and Lettie May Stowell born 1872.

Eva married John Franklin Latta and had Marvin, Silas E. "Ted," Mary Blanche, Jesse Elmer, John Dick, Edith M., and Virgie. Marvin married Cora P. Surprise, Ted married Della M. Regnier, Blanche married Howard Doty, Jesse married Harried Belle Strader, Dick married A. Belle Williams, Edith married Harry Nave and Virgie married Lyle Ruley.

George Stowell married twice. By his first wife Mary he had Floyd Stowell, who married Sarah J. Harding. He was also married to Maude Day.

Laura Stowell married Daniel C. Foley, who was born in New York. They had John, who married Ida, George Francis, who married Myrtle, Charles Carlton, who married first Blanche Sharp and then Nellie Bales, Lewis Patrick, who married first Rae Rose Morris and second Jesse Stowell, Mary Margaret, who married first a Balser and then Fred A. Marsh and Lola Mae. The latter two children were born at Lowell.

Charles D. Stowell married Hattie Jane Cotrill, the daughter of Penisla and Mary Jane Cotrill and had 11 children, Marvin, who first married Cecil Lamphire, Helen, who married John Haskell, John, who married Helen Troy, Jessie, who married Lewis Patrick Foley, Elizabeth Ruth, who married Earl Burkholder, Monson, who married Ruth Nelson, George, who married Mildred Pollock, Charles Eugene, who did not marry, Lewis, who married Virginia Maxine Garvey, Margaret, who married John Burski and Faye, who did not marry.

Jes Stowell was twice married. His first wife was Margaret Loretta Smith, daughter of John and Jane (Britton) Smith. They had James Elmer, who married Eleanor Phillips, Delbert, who was unmarried, Iva Grace, who married first Harold Hurst and had Robert, and William Heelan, who were the parents of Wm. Heelan, Cecil Stowell married Wm. Earl Gast, Mildren Stowell married Elsworth Clem and Ada Maude married Lowell M. Dionne. By his second wife, Pearl Head, daughter of Lewis and Mary Ann Head, Jes Stowell had Mary L., who married Edward A. Stuhlmacher, Jessie Ruth, who married Delbert Fischer, Ethel Irene, who married Carl Allen, Etta Mae, who married Daren Spitler, Laura Ann, who married Delbert Mathew and Dora June, who married Robert Gene Brunton.

Lettie May Stowell married Edwin Haskell, the son of Giles and Elizabeth (Albright) Haskell. They had Faye, who married Ruth Whelon, Bethel, Nina, Wilbur, Leon Earl, and Grayce, who married Elmer Witt.

It is interesting to note that Elizabeth (Albright) Haskell became the second wife of Myron H. Stowell after the death of the mother of his children. Giles and Elizabeth Haskell had Perry Haskell, who married Mary Elizabeth, Frank Haskell, who married Emma J. Umstead, Ed Haskell, who married Lettie Mae Stowell, and Charles Haskell, who married Mary A. Latta.

Space does not permit the listing of the many descendants of Lewis M. and Mary Ann

(Treece) Stowell, but they are scattered over a wide area of northwest Indiana and different points throughout the nation.

by Gerald Born

STOWELL, LOREN LORENZO
F269

Was born at Stafford, Connecticut March 3, 1795, the son of Oliver and Abigail (Strickland) Stowell and died Lowell, January, 1872. He married Mary Matilda Reed, daughter of Mr. Reed and Ruth Daskum. She was born in Connecticut March 12, 1799 and died October 6, 1842, Kalamazoo, Michigan. Very little is known of Loren Stowell's early life.

He grew up in a very stable New England family in the communities of Pomfret and Abington, Connecticut, where his father was a doctor. As a very young man, he fought in the War of 1812 to protect his country. He may have enlisted in New York state where many of the Reeds lived and it may have been there that he married his wife, but this is not recorded in family records.

He joined the tide of immigration to "the Firelands", which were located in Huron County, Ohio and were reserved for Connecticut residents who had lost property during the Revolutionary War. Huron County is located at the extreme western end of the Ohio Western Reserve, that portion of land in Ohio that had been part of Connecticut, when that state's claim stretched to the Mississippi River. Loren Stowell and his family are found here in 1820 and 1830.

The first six children were born in Sherman township: Laura (b. 1820) m. Homer Field, Oliver H. (b. 1822) died in Michigan in 1843, John E. (b. 1824) m. Rhuey Ann Powers, George Washington (b. 1826) m. Margaret Rice, Lewis M. (b. 1828) m. Mary Ann Treece, Marcus Lafayette (b. 1830) m. Mary Elizabeth Fuller. The last two children were born at Brady, Kalamazoo County, Michigan: Myron H. (b. 1832) m. Lestina Melvira Sutzer and Loren (b. 1835) died in 1845 or 46. The Stowells of Northern Indiana descend from these children.

From the *History of Kalamazoo County, Michigan* printed in 1880 we find that Lorenzo Stowell in the company of Bradley S. Williams, a native of Genessee County, New York and later a resident of Huron County, Ohio came to Michigan in the month of August, 1835, and made his home in Schoolcraft township on Prairie Ronde and pre-empted the farm he owned in Sections 5 and 6. The reason he and Mr. Stowell chose this locality was because it abounded in better timbers than any other. Lorenzo Stowell settled in 1838, which was a very sickly year.

The early land records of Kalamazoo County, Michigan show that Lorenzo Stowell owned 160 acres of land in Section 5. Shortly after the census of 1840 was taken his wife and oldest son died. After the death of his wife, he was left with six children all under the age of eighteen. His only daughter, Laura had married two years prior to the death of her mother and was then living in Wisconsin with a child of her own, so she could not assume the responsibility for rearing her brothers. It is not known exactly how Loren dealt with the situation, but from later records it appears that the children were placed in the homes of friends and relatives for care.

All trace of Loren Stowell is lost during the next 12 years, but during that time he moved to Indiana. It is not until his second marriage in Porter County, Indiana on August 2, 1854 to Emily A. Hyde that he reappears. He had a son, Loren Stewart Stowell, born about 1856 by this marriage.

Loren S. Stowell, age four, appears in the household of John and Rachel Reed of Eagle Creek township, Lake County, in the 1860 census, indicating that his mother had died and that he had been placed with them. It appears that John Reed died in the next decade, for Loren Stewart Stowell appears in the 1870 census as Stewart Reed, age 14, living with his foster mother Rachel Reed, who in turn was living with James and Emily Fuller in Cedar Creek township. Stewart Stowell lived with his half-brother, John E. Stowell, at Momence, Illinois in 1880 and later settled at Shelby, Indiana with his wife, Mrs. Elsa (Burroughs) Fuller. By 1900, he is shown in the West Creek census and my grandfather, Roscoe C. Born, is boarding with him and his wife.

Loren Lorenzo Stowell married a third time to Elizabeth Gibbs on March 25, 1857, and by 1860 he and his wife are living in the town of Lowell, and his occupation is listed as gardener. By 1870 he has no occupation listed so it is assumed that he had retired. Elizabeth Stowell, his wife, is found in the 1880 census of Shelby, but he is not, indicating that he died in the 1870s. It is not known where he or any of his wives are buried.

He left a rich heritage to his children. Although the family was separated, there is every indication that when they reached adulthood they reestablished contact with one another. John E. Stowell died in Lake County and is buried in the Lowell Cemetery. George Washington Stowell died in Salem, Oregon. Lewis M. Stowell is buried in the Sanders Cemetery, West Creek township, as is Myron H. Stowell. Marcus Lafayette Stowell went to Kansas and died at Saxman in 1893. Four of the sons of Loren Lorenzo Stowell fought in the Civil War — Lafayette with Co. D, 42nd Illinois Infantry; Lewis M. Stowell with Co. A, 99th Indiana Infantry; John E. Stowell with Co. 2, 73rd Indiana Infantry; and Myron H. Stowell with Co. H., 42nd Illinois Infantry.

by Gerald M. Born

STOWELL, MYRON H.
F270

Myron H. Stowell was born June 10, 1838 at Brady, Kalamazoo County, Michigan to Loren Lorenzo and Mary Matilda (Reed) Stowell. At his mother's death in 1842 he was placed with relatives to be reared. He appears in the 1860 census of Cedar Creek township in the household of Charles and Juliet Martin. Nearby lived his father with his second wife. Myron was then 21 and engaged in farming.

Myron H. Stowell enlisted in Company H, 42nd Illinois Regiment Volunteer Infantry at Kankakee, Illinois on August 17, 1861 and was discharged three years later on September 17, 1864 at Lexington, Kentucky. He returned to Lowell until September of 1865 when he moved to Defiance County, Ohio, where he married Lestina Melvira Sutzer, the daughter of Phillip and Catherine (Cox) Sutzer, natives of Ohio and Indiana, respectively, who was born November 22, 1850 at Patch's Grove, Wisconsin. They probably met through the Stringham family, who lived near Lowell, for L.P. Stringham helped survey the town of Patch's Grove. Lestina's half-sister, Mary Stier, married Henry Stringham some years later in Lake County.

The Sutzer family came from Virginia where the grandparents, Henry and Susan Sutzer were born in 1781 and 1784, respectively and were probably of Swiss or German stock. They appear to have spent some time in Pennsylvania before settling for awhile in Ohio in the 1820s where their children were born. They were living with their daughter, Margaret (Sutzer) Burton, the wife of George W. Burton at Grant County, Wisconsin in 1850. Their sons Phillip (b. 1829) and Henry (b. 1826) were in the same county.

Later generations report that Phillip Sutzer died about 1856 and was "buried in the woods." Catherine Sutzer, who was 27 at the time came to Defiance County where she married George Stier, a widowed farmer with three children, and they had two daughters, Mary Ann (b. 1860) and Lucia A. "Lucy" (b. 1862). After George Stier's death in 1868 Catherine had a hard time caring for her family, which included John and Sarah Sutzer and the two Stier girls. Catherine made a living for her family from farm produce, blowing eggs from their shells and filling these shells with her maple syrup, walking to Defiance to sell these along with vegetables, eggs, sauerkraut and wood to stores there.

Catherine (Cox) Sutzer Stier married again to Loren G. Waters and they had three children, Eunice May, Charles L., and Amos Girden. Mr. Waters died about 1874 and Catherine loaded her family, with the exception of Lucy, who was left with the John Shock family to help his wife care for her children and Lestina Stowell and left for the west in a covered wagon, finally settling at a point near the LaSalle, Putnam County, Illinois line below the Illinois River, where she lived with her fourth husband, Joseph Morreaux, a Canadian fisherman. Catherine died about 1894.

(L. to R.) Etta, Emma and Ella Stowell. Handley-Lowell Indiana

After their marriage Myron H. and Lestina Stowell left for LaPorte County, Indiana where they received a Bible from the LaPort County Bible Society on July 28, 1866 and their first child Emma Leorah was born at Rolling Prairie on February 21, 1867. She was followed shortly by their second child Anna C. who was born February 2, 1867. In March 1869 they again returned to Defiance County where their third child Loren Lorenzo was born on April 13, 1871 in Farmer township. Ella Almeda followed in Noble township November 6, 1873 and their fifth child Etta May was born October 22, 1875, Tiffin township. Their sixth child Delila was born in Adams township August 19, 1877 and the last child, Warren Dewain Stowell was born August 14, 1879 at Defiance.

Then disaster struck, for Lestina died on April 6, 1880 at the age of thirty, leaving a family of five living children. After finding homes for his children with friends and relatives, Myron returned to Shelby soon after 1880. Etta was living with her aunt, Mary (Stier) Stringham in Lake County, Indiana, Emma was in Genoa Junction, Walworth County, Wisconsin with her uncle, Homer Field, and Lorenzo Stowell was in the same county. Ella may have been staying with her uncle, Stewart Stowell, who was a half-brother of Myron. Warren Dewain was given to Otis C. Myers and his wife Nancy, natives of Vermont, to raise and he later took the Myers name as his own.

On May 12, 1881 Myron married his second wife, Mrs. Elizabeth (Albright) Haskell, the widow of Giles Haskell of Shelby. She had four sons, Franklin, Perry, Edwin and Charles Haskell. After her death he chose for his third wife Mrs. Martha Jane Cole, who survived him. No children were born to the last marriages. Mr. Stowell was a quiet and unassuming man, honest and honorable in all his dealings and was highly respected by all his acquaintances.

His funeral occurred from the Pine Grove church, West Creek on July 13, 1911. Nathan Worley preached the funeral. Music was supplied by Mrs. Raymond McCarthy, Miss Nellie Hale and William Sheets. Mrs. Harry Sanger presided at the organ. Six of his comrades, T.W. Bacon, Oliver Surprise, Sam Nichols, H.H. Purdy, George S. Clark and H.H. Ragon bore him to the last side of the Sanders graveyard, where the burial services were rendered by the Grand Army of the Republic. His death occurred at the Old Soldiers Home, Lafayette, where he had gone when his wife was no longer able to care for him.

by Gerald M. Born

STRINGHAM, HENRY J.
F271

Henry J. Stringham was born in March, 1852 at Ceder Creek Township, Lake County, Indiana and is probably the grandson of Stephen Stringham (b. 1789, NY) and Catherine (b. 1794, PA) who are found in the 1850 census of Ceder Creek Township along with their children Davis S. (b. 1824, IN), James H. (b. 1826, IN), William G. (b. 1829, IN), Nancy Ann (b. 1832, IL), and Eliza Ann (b. 1834, IL). Tradition has it that two other children were also from this family, L.P. Stringham (b. 1819, IN) who married Lavinia Smith on December 6, 1841 in Lake County, and Peter Stringham (b. 1823, IN) who married Susanna Lofler on July 21, 1842, Lake County.

Stephen Stringham was a farmer, who was elected to the first Board of Commissioners in 1837 along with A.L. Ball and Thomas Wils. From an early history we learn that Leonard Stringham had charge of a post office near Lowell, "Outlet Post Office was established and located at a point about one mile east of the site of Lowell, with James H. Sanger, Sr. as Postmaster. He kept it for some years, when it was moved to a point half a mile west, and was kept by Leonard Stringham."

From a history of Grant County, Wisconsin we find that L.P. Stringham laid out the town of Patch's Grove about 1850 and it was here that the Stringhams became acquainted with the Sutzer family, who would ultimately supply Henry J. with his mother-in-law. Catherine (Cox) Sutzer was a pioneer along with her husband, Philip Sutzer, and his brother, Henry Sutzer, and his wife, Phebe, and their sister, Margaret (Sutzer) Burton, wife of George W. Burton with whom their parents, Henry Sutzer (b. 1781, VA) and Susan (b. 1784, VA) lived.

When Philip Sutzer died in 1855, Catherine "buried him in the woods" and went to Defiance County, Ohio with her three small children, Lestina, John and Sarah Sutzer and married George Stier, a farmer from Baden, Germany, who had four children, Caroline and Henry Stier, who had been born at Hanover, Germany to his first wife, and Louisa and Frederick by his second wife, Frederica Holborn, also a native of Germany. Another daughter, Frances, had already left home by the time of George Stier's second marriage.

George Stier and Mrs. Catherine (Cox) Sutzer had two daughters, Mary Ann Stier (b. May, 1860, OH) and Lucia A. "Lucy" Stier (b. Sept. 1862, OH). After George Stier's untimely death on April 30, 1862 at the age of 48, Catherine was left with five children of her own and four of his to care for and the responsibility was great. Catherine made a living for her family from farm produce, blowing eggs from their shells and filling them with maple syrup, and walked to Defiance to sell these along with vegetables, eggs, sauerkraut and wood to stores there.

For her third husband Catherine Stier chose Loren G. Waters, who had two children by his former wife, Betsey and Lon Waters. By this marriage she had three children, all born at Tiffin Township, Defiance County, Ohio, Eunice May (b. 1866), Charles L. (b. 1870), and Amos Girden (b. 1872).

After the death of Loren Waters, Catherine loaded her children, with the exceptions of Lestina, who had married Myron H. Stowell, and Lucy, who was left to care for the children of Mrs. John Shock, into a covered wagon and started west. Unfortunately her route has not been documented, nor how long she stayed at different places.

Catherine (Cox) Sutzer Stier Waters reached Lake County, Indiana about 1873 for it was here that her daughter, Mary Ann Stier, married Henry J. Stringham on Christmas day, 1879. Catherine Waters did not stay long, for in the 1880 census of Putnam and LaSalle Counties, Illinois, she is found with her fourth husband, Joe Morreau, living south of the Illinois River in the "marshes of Illinois."

In 1880 Henry J. and Mary Ann (Stier) Stringham were living in West Creek Township, along with their niece, Etta Stowell, who was just four years old and had been sent to live with them after the death of her mother, Lestina Stowell, at the tender age of thirty. Etta lived with them and other relatives until her marriage on February 14, 1894 to Edwin Lowell Sanders in Lake County, Indiana.

By 1900 Henry Stringham and his wife had moved to Napolean Township, Defiance County, Ohio. By then they had five children, Arville (b. 1882), Alviras (b. & d. 1883), Van Wesley (b. 1889), and Willard V. (b. 1892). The record of the fifth child is not available. His brother, Clifford Stringham (b. 1841, IN) was also living with them. By 1910 they had moved with their family to First and Dawes Street, Toledo, Lucas County, Ohio. Arvilla married a Lacey and had two sons, Dale and Mervin, and Willard had six children. Van married but did not have children.

While living at Toledo, Henry J. Stringham became a foreman at an automobile garage, and his two sons, Van and Willard were chauffeurs there. Mary Ann (Stier) Stringham died August 16, 1936 at Toledo and is buried in the Willow Cemetery. Many of the family still live in the Toledo area.

by Gerald M. Born

STRONG – DOCKWEILER
F272

Lois Strong was born April 30, 1930 to Howard Strong and Rena (Steinhilber) Strong in Hammond. Howard and Rena moved to Palmer shortly after Lois was born. Lois attended Palmer School and Crown Point High School.

After graduation in 1948 she worked a short time at Letz Manufacturing Co., Millers Grocery and Hubers Grocery until she met and married Kenneth Dale Dockweiler July 15, 1950.

Kenneth was the second son of Clarence Dockweiler and Minnie (Peters) Dockweiler. They were originally from Lansing, Illinois. When Kenneth was a small boy, they moved to

Henry J. Stringham and his wife, Mary Ann (Stier) Stringham, and their daughter, Arville, 1890.

Lois and Kenneth Dockweiler in front of their camper, 1985.

a farm south of Dyer where he attended Katz Corner School for 5 years. They moved again in 1940 where Kenneth finished grade school at Center and attended and graduated from Lowell High School in 1948.

After graduation he worked on a farm and for Henderlong Lumber Co. In January of 1949 he was employed by Northern Indiana Public Service Co. in Crown Point; first as a groundman, then a lineman, crew supervisor, assistant general line supervisor, general line supervisor. He was with NIPSCO for 36 years until he had a fatal heart attack August 1985.

Lois and Kenneth attended Trinity Lutheran Church in Crown Point. They were both 10 year 4-H leaders. They have 2 boys, Duane and Bruce and 3 girls, Peggy Ann (Bruce) Torbeson, Brenda Sue (John) Mitchell, and Shirley Jean (Fredric, Jr.) Collins. There are also 7 grandchildren. Anastacia Lee, Adam Jennings and Chad Everett Torbeson; Charity Hope, Joshua Cain and Sara Krystal Mitchell; and Olivia Michele Dockweiler.

Their 5 children were in almost every project offered in 4-H with Mom and Dad helping as their leaders bringing home several champions.

In 1960 we moved from Crown Point to a 40-acre farm in Winfield Township. Here Kenneth was able to farm part time, which was his first love, as well as work at NIPSCO. Kenneth always had a very large garden from which Lois canned and froze items. We also had some of the 4-H animals slaughtered for the table.

Just recently Lois was able to get into DAR on her great, great grandmother's line.

Kenneth and Lois and their family enjoyed camping most of their married life, traveling all over the United States whenever time would allow.

by Lois Dockweiler

STRONG – STEINHILBER
F273

50th Wedding Anniversary photo (1979) of Howard C. Strong and Rena B. Strong.

Lifetime residents of Lake County, Indiana, Howard C. Strong, born November 19, 1907 son of George W. and Matilda Busselberg Strong and Rena B. Steinhilber, born October 2, 1908, daughter of Jacob and Amanda Blakeman Steinhilber were married in Valparaiso June 26, 1929 and settled in the Crown Point area.

Ancestors of Busselberg and Steinhilber migrated to farms in the Winfield Township in the 1850's and 1880's respectively, from Germany. Grandfather Blakeman came from Oxhill, Warwickshire, England about 1840. Rena's maternal grandmother came from New York state, Hannah Jane (Mrs. John) Blakeman was the daughter of William and Louisa Wood Miller; also, George Strong's grandparents, Orson and Emaline Cadwell Strong. Howard traced his lineage through his great-grandmother, Emaline Cadwell Strong to his Revolutionary ancestor, John Cadwell whose ancestors came to America about 1640.

Howard and Rena had two children, Lois Strong Dockweiler, wife of Kenneth Dale Dockweiler, who were parents of 2 sons, Duane Dale and Bruce William and three daughters, Peggy Ann Dockweiler Torbeson, Brenda Sue Dockweiler Mitchell, and Shirley Jean Dockweiler Fredric Collins; and son Wayne (Donna Pluto) Strong, parents of two sons, Marc George and Eric Paul and two daughters, Dian Jean and Lori Ann. Strongs also raised Raymond Strong, son of Howard's brother Arthur and was openhouse for several other nieces and nephews.

In the early 1930's, Howard bought a milk route, transporting 8 gallon cans of milk, picking them up at the farms and taking them into Crown Point. He enlarged his routes until he reached a total of 400 cans daily which he transported to Chicago, 150 miles daily roundtrip. This required a fleet of 4 trucks and a semi-trailer and 5 men with Howard driving a schoolbus from Winfield Township to the Crown Point High School and managing his business, which he did for sixteen years.

After selling his routes in 1948, he became a fieldman for the Borden Dairy, having obtained his training on the job. His duties included procuring milk through a contract negotiated with the farmers and check back periodically to see that they produced it in a sanitary manner, thus maintaining the Grade A requirements for the cities of Chicago, Gary and Hammond. This required up to 300 miles of driving daily as his territory varied from time to time from Wisconsin, Joliet Illinois and as far as Peru, Indiana and Holland, Michigan. This earned him the title of Licensed Sanitarian, work which he continued until retirement in 1972.

Both Howard and Rena were active in civic and church-related activities, serving for 25 years as Republican Precinct people in Winfield Township and in various offices in the Salem United Methodist Church, located just across the line in Porter County, where they held their membership, later transferring to Crown Point United Methodist Church.

Besides raising their family, Rena found time to raise a large garden, preserving the vegetables and fruits and cure the meats which Howard and his brother, Elmer butchered. Rena served as County President of the Lake County Home Demonstration Clubs in 1951 and 1952 (which numbered 55 clubs at that time). Later she served as Worthy Matron of Lake Chapter #408, Order of Eastern Star. Rena was employed in the advertising department of *The Lake County Star*, leading newspaper in Crown Point for ten years.

Howard belonged to Crown Point Lodge #157, F. & A.M. and was active as a member of the Ancient Nobles of the Mystic Shrine of Hammond. He helped organize and was a charter member of its Temple Guard, also, Porter County Shrine Club both of which he served as president. Howard passed away in 1982; Rena still resides in Crown Point at this writing.

by Rena B. Strong

STRONG, ASA
F274

Asa Strong was one of the early pioneers of Lake County, having brought his family to Indiana in June 1837. Asa, a native of Connecticut, migrated to the town of Sheridan, Chautauqua County, New York, in the year 1811, and remained there until he moved to Lake County. The Strong family settled on Section 28 in Ross Township, where they had a farm of 80 acres.

Asa had a family of six children: (1) William O., the eldest, was born November 3, 1809 in Spencertown, Columbia County, New York, married Jane A. Howe, and remained in Sheridan, where he died January 26, 1892; (2) Marilla Strong was married to Horace Cross February 20, 1839 in Lake County, Indiana; (3) Amanda M. married Francis Barney January 17, 1843 in Lake County; (4) Orson Webster, born October 11, 1818, married Lucy Emeline Cadwell June 11, 1840 at Wheeler, Porter County, Indiana; (5) Asa J. was born August 1, 1820, married Frances (Fanny) Watts November 22, 1842 in Lake County; (6) Daniel Herbert, born March 14, 1826, married first Alma Cross, October 28, 1844, in Lake County. Alma died October 31, 1896 and Daniel married his second wife, Adelia L. Ewer, December 22, 1897.

Orson Webster Strong was born in New York October 11, 1818. As a young man of 19, he worked on his grandfather's ship, the John Strong Steamship Lines. Orson left New York and went to Michigan prior to his arrival in Indiana, by December 1, 1836, being one of the early settlers of Union Township, Porter County. Orson was married at Wheeler, Indiana on June 11, 1840, to Lucy Emeline

Cadwell. She was born July 6, 1823 at Fabius, New York, daughter of Chester and Phila (Daniels) Cadwell. Orson and Emeline owned a farm in section 27 of Union Township, directly across the Lake-Porter County line road from his father, Asa Strong. Orson and Emeline had a family of 13 children: (1) John D. born November 22, 1840, married Margaret Jane (Jennie) Morris, who died April 1, 1888 near Des Moines, Iowa. John married 2nd Isabel (Zanna) Clark July 27, 1890 at Merrick County, Nebraska; (2) Maria Adline was born May 12, 1842, married George Maxwell November 19, 1862, in Porter County, Indiana. George died December 25, 1865 and Maria March 16, 1885, both in Ross Township, Lake County, Indiana; (3) Charles Wesley born March 13, 1844, married Ida M. Niles in Porter County, Indiana on March 10, 1873; (4) Orson W., Jr. born June 6, 1846, died September 21, 1846; (5) Philo Amelia born September 19, 1847, died June 30, 1848; (6) Chester Oron born May 14, 1849, died December 31, 1874; (7) Margaret Ruth born April 14, 1851, married Sylvester P. Chandler March 23, 1877, in Lake County, Indiana; (8) Louis Henry born August 2, 1853, died March 30, 1854; (9) Henry Lewis born May 10, 1856, married 1st Lanetta Adella Niles March 14, 1877, in Porter Co., Indiana, and 2nd Amy Viola Bloodgood in Central City, Nebraska on October 6, 1894; (1) Laura Rosetta born July 17, 1858, married John Albert Whalen May 23, 1882 at Hobart, Indiana; (11) Hiram born May 17, 1861; (12) Celestia born February 18, 1866, died March 22, 1866; (13) Anna A. born September 28, 1869.

Orson Webster Strong died November 3, 1875, in Union Township, of typhoid fever. In 1888 Emeline moved to Kansas with the family of her daughter, Mrs. John A. Whalen, remaining there for several years. In 1897 they moved to Livingston, Montana, where Emeline died April 1, 1901. She was a sufferer of asthma and it was this disease which finally caused her death.

Asa J. Strong remained on the home farm, which he acquired from his father, Asa, in 1841. Frances, wife of Asa J., died February 9, 1880, and he spent most of his remaining years with his son, Thomas. Asa J. suffered from rheumatism for many years, and died at the home of his son, Thomas, in Ross Township, on February 17, 1899. Thomas remained on the home farm, which he had acquired when his father died, until 1902, when he moved to Hobart with his family.

by Betty L. Williams

STURGESS – POLHAMUS – BULL
F275

Agnes Mae Sturgess was born 17th Feb. 1892 in Joliet, Il. She is the daughter of George Mynell Sturgess born 23rd April 1860 in Surrey, England, and Clara Elizabeth Polhamus born 15th Nov. 1863 in Wilmington, Il. Clara Elizabeth was a charter member of the Gary Methodist Church. George died 27th Sept. 1927 and Clara died 17th May 1915 in Gary, In.

George Mynell's father, Charles Sturgess, was born 13th Nov. 1833 at Courteen Hall Northumberland, England. John, Charles' father, moved out of London because of the terrible strikes of the times.

George Mynell's mother, Eliza Blake, was born Oct. 1834 at Nissington, Northumberland, Eng. She died in childbirth 1872 in Guelph, Canada. Most of this Blake family moved to Australia.

Charles, while blind, went by covered wagon to California. Three of his children went with him. Charles was buried at Forest Lawn Cemetery in Cal. in 1918. George Mynell stayed behind in Chicago, Il., to study electricity. Sometime later he helped put electricity into the second Palmer House in Chicago.

Later he worked as an electrician with P. Gleason in Joliet, Il. In 1903 George and family moved to Buffalo, N.Y., where he worked with electricity at the Lackawanna Steel Co. P. Gleason started up U.S. Steel in Gary, In. George Mynell was called to come back to the midwest in 1910 as night superintendent of the Electrical Dept. of U.S. Steel. George Mynell died in the company hospital in 1927.

Clara Elizabeth Polhamus has a well-known family history in N.Y. Theodorus Johannes Polhamus was born 1598 at Backerchen, Bavaria, which no longer exists. His parents and family were teachers and ministers. Johannes attended Heidleberg University in Germany. He became a protestant minister. He was called as a Dutch missionary to Brazil. On his trip back to Netherlands his ship was captured by Spanish. He ended up in N.Y., and finally died 9th Sept. 1676 in Flatbush, Long Island. He was considered an excellent linguist but a poor speaker. However, he seemed to be loved by the church members. Princeton University has the original copy of the land grant given by Peter Stuyvesant to Johannes. Johannes also had a church in Lewes, Delaware.

Grandchild, Daniel Polhamus, was born about 1758 in Dutchess Co., N.Y., (DAR #0714527) and married Annatje Meyer. Issac was born 1797 in Kingston, Ulster Co., N.Y., and married Anna Mower about 1815.

Daniel moved up the Hudson River and across the Mohawk Valley in N.Y. to Ontario Co., where my great grandfather, William, was born 1st Jan. 1826 to Issac and Ann. When Issac's wife died before 1845 their land was divided into 9 parts. So William, Levi and Augustus moved to Bureau Co., Ill. In 1853 William married Nan Ann Bull born 1836 in Knox Co., Ohio. Her father was Eli Bull, born 1814 in Md. His father, William Bull, married Deliah Cole 28th May 1800 in Baltimore, Md., by a Baptist minister, Absolum Butler. In 1806 twins, Ephraim and Honour Lewis, were born at Berlin, Worchester Co., Md. Between 1810-1817 William taught school in Adams Co., Pa. William, a farmer in Knox Co., Ohio, died in 1832.

Many of the Sturgess family were goal oriented but were fun loving off the job. Fred and George C.W. were educated at Armour Institute (now I.I.T.). Glen graduated from Purdue University. Two of them had an artistic bent, including Agnes Mae who also made a fine Sunday School teacher. Agnes Mae worked for Gary Post and Doyne plumbing and heating. She married August Robert Kuhn 24th Dec. 1914 and died in Clearwater, Fla., 10th July 1971.

by Marian Frances Kuhn Gregory

SURPISE FAMILY
F276

Surprises of Lake County

In 1833 when that first settler Pierre Surprenant brought his wife LaRose and his six month old son Henry to the region of present day Lake DaleCarlia, they called a small log cabin home.

By 1835 the area was being called Pleasant Grove, and there with the Potawattomie Indians as neighbors, the (Suprenant) Surprise family took root to eventually number eight living children.

As adults, sons Oliver and Harvey Surprise served in the Civil War. Then Harvey, Elizabeth and Lovina went to live in the Osage territory of Kansas and Oklahoma.

William, Henry, Oliver, Armenia and Alvina stayed in south Lake County.

To make a point let us follow the life of Alvina Surprise. Alvina, born 1842 at Pleasant Grove, in 1857 married William Wheeler of Liverpool, England, a veterinarian.

They built a log home at today's 9305 W. 173 Avenue (southwest of Creaton), homesteading the land.

By 1886 the family numbered nine living children, all born in that log cabin home. In 1890 William Wheeler died, right at the time plans were being made to build a new two-story house.

After his death a new home was built. The house was completed but rough and lonely were the years ahead for the tiny widow and her brood, but with the loyal aid of the older children the family persevered.

When those three boys and six girls became of marriageable age, one at a time they chose life partners who were members of other regional pioneer families.

Charles, the eldest son, married Elizabeth Jacqua, a Cedar Lake schoolteacher. He was a well-known carpenter who helped build many historical buildings around Cedar Lake. Among those were the Armour Bros. Hotel and the big Lassen Dance Pavillion, and the Surprise (William) and Bernard homesteads.

Their 10 children were born here, but by 1900 the family moved to Michigan.

Son Jessie stayed on to help farm the Wheeler homeplace and cared for the mother until her death in 1926.

Now note the old family names as we follow the other Wheeler marriages:

John married Maude Taylor who was a descendant of pioneer Obadiah Taylor. Ella married Hamlet Taylor, descendant of Obadiah. Jennie married John Taylor, descendant of Obadiah. Eunice married William McCarty of the pioneer McCartys. Bertha married Oscar Edgerton of another Cedar Lake early pioneer family. Maude, the youngest, married Fred E. Ewer of Robinson Prairie and Orchard Grove pioneers. Those united old families of this Wheeler relationship go a long way as we try to explain why everybody is someone else's cousin.

A reunion of the Surprise Clan in 1907 at Cedar Lake shows faces that tell what a couple of generations did to mix up all of the old-time families of that region.

Those were the years when all of the grandchildren came and went, in horse and buggy, visiting the little old grandmother living still on the Wheeler homestead. They ran in and out of the remains of the old log home as it stood alone now, being used as a storage shed. To the west was the old open well, still equipped with a crank and rope that raised and lowered a bucket into its depths.

These children and their children's children are now part of the proliferation of those pioneer generations. Relating people of this explosion is enough to give the most enthusiastic genealogist a real headache trying to disentangle the branches of his family tree.

by Beatrice Horner

SURPRISE, CHARLES L.
F277

Charles L. Surprise, deputy clerk of the United States District and Circuit Courts at Hammond, Ind., was born near Lowell on Nov. 11, 1884. During his infancy his parents, Oliver and Carlinda Surprise, moved to town, where they still reside. In 1903 he was graduated from the Lowell High School; the same year he won the county oratorical contest at Hammond, gaining honors for himself and his school. The following fall he attended Northwestern University. Then he clerked and studied law in Atty. S.C. Dwyer's office until his appointment in August, 1906, to the deputyship at Hammond. Mr. Surprise is also an employee of Knotts & Bomberger, corporation lawyers of Hammond. He is an active member of the M.E. Church, a Republican, and in good favor with his wide acquaintance in the county.

(Compiled from the Souvenir Album of Lake Co. Ind., Crown Point-Lowell, June 18-19, 1909.)

TAYLOR, OBADIAH
F278

Obadiah Taylor

1762-1839
A Revolutionary Soldier Who Lived and Died in Lake County, Indiana

Paper ready by Arthur B. Taylor, at Gary meeting 1926

Mr. President, Ladies and Gentlemen:

This year marks the 150th anniversary of sesqui-centennial of the Declaration of Independence. It may seem strange but there is only one known veteran of the Revolutionary army buried in Lake County. Obadiah Taylor, my great-great-grandfather, the subject of this sketch, was born in Deerfield, Mass., in 1762 and died in the pioneer settlement known as West Point at Cedar Lake, Indiana in the year 1839, and is buried in the old pioneer West Point cemetery at Cedar Lake.

On his father's side of the family line he was descended from the Taylors of Deerfield, and on his mother's side of the family from the Sawtells of Deerfield. Both families were of Puritan Stock.

Adonijah Taylor, the father of Obadiah Taylor, owned a farm of some two hundred acres in Deerfield. He operated a saw mill and grist mill upon his place and named it Indian Hill. He built a house on the farm in 1770. It was there that Obadiah Taylor was born. The old house is still standing. The farm is now owned by Geo. E. Sanderson and is known as the Whately Glen Farm.

At the age of 18, Obadiah Taylor enlisted in the Continental army. His war record is given as follows. "Taylor, Obed (also given Obadiah). Descriptive list of men raised to reinforce the Continental Army for the term of six months, agreeable to resolve of June 5, 1780, returned as received of Justin Ely. Commissioned by Brigadier General John Glover, at Springfield, July 10, 1780; age 18 years; stature 5 feet 8 inches; complexion dark; engaged for the town of Montague; arrived at Springfield, July 10, 1780 under command of Capt. Daniel Shays; also a list of men raised for 6 months service and returned by Brigadier General Paterson, as having passed muster in a return dated Camp Totoway, Oct. 25, 1780; also pay roll for six months men belonging to the town of Montague raised for service in the Continental Army during 1780; marched July 9, 1780; discharged Jan. 9, 1781; service 6 months, seven days including travel (140 miles home,) (mass. Soldiers and Sailors in the Revolution – Volume XV Page 415).

It is worthy of note that his father and five older brothers served in the Revolutionary Army. His Father was one of the minute men who marched on the alarm of April 19, 1775. His father later was a first lieutenant at Fort Ticonderoga. Late in the year 1777 he is mentioned as a commander of the block house at Lake George Landing, south of Lake Champlain.

Obadiah Taylor married Abigail Williams of Deerfield. She was doubly descended from Robert Williams, the first Williams to arrive in America. Her father was Dr. Thomas Williams who studied medicine with a cousin Dr. Thomas Williams, whose brother founded Williams College. On the maternal side of the family tree, she was a granddaughter of Major Elijah Williams who was a son of Rev. John Williams, Puritan pastor of Deerfield, the Rev. John Williams who was carried away in captivity by the Indians.

After the close of the war, Obadiah and several of his brothers moved to Rensselaer County, New York, where they lived for many years.

Here were born five sons, Obadiah Taylor, Adonijah Taylor, Feb. 11, 1792, Horace Taylor, 1801, Leandor Taylor, Seymour Taylor and six daughters, who became Mrs. Dorothy Lilley, Mrs. Betsey Edgerton, Mrs. Almire Palmer, Mrs. Miranda Stillson, Mrs. Thoda Gifford, Mrs. Rachel Hurlburt. Most of this large family later moved to Erie County, Pennsylvania, where the aged mother died in 1837.

Dr. Calvin Lilley, son-in-law of Obadiah Taylor had emigrated westward to the St. Joseph country, as northern Indiana was then called, and had become one of the pioneer settlers of South Bend, Indiana, in the year 1830. He sent back word to the East of the possibilities of this new territory. In the year 1832 Obadiah Taylor and several members of the family made a trip to what is now Lake County to look the country over, but did not stay here. In the spring of 1836, the families of Dr. Calvin Lilley, Horace Edgerton, sons-in-law, and Adonijah and Horace Taylor, sons together with the aged father, Obadiah Taylor, emigrated to Lake County and settled upon the east side of Cedar Lake. The Adonijah Taylor house and mill was located where Binyon's hotel property now is. The Horace Taylor house stood where the Stanley or Enoch Peterson house now stands. The Dr. Lilly tavern and store stood upon the northeast bank of the Lake. Other members of the family and their relatives followed. A large community which soon took the name of West Point, began making preparations to locate the county seat of Lake County at West Point.

by Steven Yaros, Jr.

THOMAS, GEORGE
F279

The Story of George Thomas (Tamas)

George Tamas – was born in Iladia Romania – April 20, 1886. He started to learn his trade at the age of twelve. He was in a school for four years learning the trade of furniture making – graduated at the age of sixteen then went out on his own to make a living making furniture by hand. He made his mother a seven room house of furniture and at the age of twenty years old he came to America. He then went to work for some furniture factory in St. Louis, Missouri; he also worked in car barns making street cars, etc. His original name was George Tamas, but when he came to America he used the English pronunciation and spelling – Thomas. He received his citizenship papers five years after coming to America. He started to collect wood from all parts of the world spending his money on this collection. He wanted to make something to show his appreciation of being able to become an American citizen of this free country called America, so he made the Flag and the table of North America. He died in a nursing home at the age of seventy four on November 2, 1959. He suffered with multiple sclerosis of the bone.

179

THOMPSON, ALEXANDER
F280

Alexander Thompson was born 10 July, 1838, in the town of Streetsboro, Portage County, Ohio, the third son of John and Elizabeth (Cockburn) Thompson who came to this country from Scotland in the early 1830's.

He was raised and educated in Portage County, and spent a year at Hiram College in Ohio. In 1861 he enlisted in Co. E of the 1st Ohio Volunteers and served a short time. He married Mary Jane Watson in November of 1862, in Chicago, Illinois. After their marriage they spent a short time farming at Paxton in Ford County, Illinois, moving in 1865 to Lake County, Indiana, where he bought a farm in Ross Twp. He was the Lake County Assessor for 2 years and served 18 years as Ross Township's Assessor. In 1897 he retired from the farm and moved to Hobart.

Mary Jane (Watson) Thompson was born at Ridgeville, Lorain County, Ohio, 30 June, 1833. She was the oldest of eight children born to John and Elizabeth (Colley) Watson, both natives of England.

Alex and Mary Jane had three sons. Fredrick was born in 1863 and married first Estella White, and when she died Amelia Treibus. Hugh was born in 1878 and died in a train accident at the Ainsworth Crossing of the Grand Trunk RR in 1909.

William married Alta Meeker and had four children. Keith and Walter died at a young age. Harold (1897-1971) married Ernestine Rosenbaum and daughter Helen (1901-1981) married Elmer Rosenbaum.

Mary Jane died 26 August, 1914, and Alexander in January, 1917. Both are buried in Crown Hill Cemetery in Hobart, Twp.

by Ruth Demmon

THORNBURG FAMILY
F281

The Thornburg Origin

Eldred, second Baron of Kendall married Edgitha. Eldred was the son of Ivo de Taillebois. Edgitha was a granddaughter of King Ethelred II (978-1016)

Ketel, son of Eldred and Edgitha, married Christiana.

Orm, son of Ketel and Christiana, married Gunilda, daughter of Gospatrick and Christiana. Gospatrick was born 1026 – Earl of Cumberland, 1067. Gospatrick traces back to Malcolm II, King of Scotland, 1005 to 1034.

Orm and Gunilda had two sons whose family line traces to the Thornburg's:

1. Robert Ormson: married Christiana, daughter of Anketin de Meynwarin.
2. Gospatrick Ormson: married Egilina Engaine

I trace Robert and Christiana first:

3. Peter, son of Robert and Christiana
4. Roland, son of Peter – died before 1259
5. Amice, daughter of Roland; married William de Lascelles
6. Alice, daughter of William and Amice; married Rowland de Thornburgh
7. William de Thornburgh, son of Rowland and Alice
8. William de Thornburgh (died before 1351); married Elena de Culwen. This marriage united with the Gospatrick line.

Gospatrick and Egilina traced to Elena de Culwen:

3. Thomas, son of Gospatrick and Egilina, married Grecia De Culwen. Thomas died 1200.
4. Patrick de Culwen, son of Thomas and Grecia
5. Gilbert de Wirkington (also de Corwen; De Curruwenne), son of Patrick
6. Patrick of Dregg; married Alina
7. Thomas, son of Patrick and Alina, married Juliana de Pickering.
8. Elen (Elena de Culwen), daughter of Thomas and Juliana, married William de Thornburg who died before 1351. Elen's sister, Alice married John de Pekering (Pickering). A lawsuit in Assize roll 1440 authenticates this as it shows involved – Rowland de Thornburgh and his mother, Elena, widow of William; also John de Pekering and his wife, Alice.

Another interesting pedigree shows Walter (who married Emma), another son of Robert and Christiana, and a brother of Peter, having a son named Nicholas whose son was Rowland de Thornburgh who married Alice, daughter of William and Amice.

The combined line carries on thusly:

9. Rowland de Thornburgh, son of William and Elena, married — Lengleys (?). Note reference to lawsuit above.
10. William – claimant to Asby, 1364 (?)
11. Roland
12. Roland – under age in 1375
13. Roland
14. William Thornburg of Hamsfeld, esquire, living in the reign of King Henry VI, 1422-1461; married Eleanor, daughter of Sir Richard Musgrave.

by Charles C. Thornburg

THORNBURG – MUSGRAVE FAMILY
F282

Through the marriage of William Thornburgh (Thornborough) to Eleanor Musgrave, daughter of Sir William and Margaret Betham Musgrave, a connection is made all the way back to Charlemagne, King of the Franks. I thought it worthwhile to record it here as other genealogies are confused about the proper Eleanor Musgrave.

Charlemagne, King of the Franks, Emperor of the Holy Roman Empire, and founder of the Carolingian dynasty was born about 742 and died January 28, 814. Among many, he married the Swabian princess, Hildegarde about 771.

Louis I, the Pious, born 778, died June 20, 840. He married Judith, daughter of Guelph I in 819.

Charles II was born June 23, 823 and died October 6, 877; married Ermintrude, daughter of Odo, Count of Oleans.

Louis II was born November 1, 846 and died April 10, 879. He was called "The Stammerer". He became King of France on his father's death and reigned only two years. He married Adelheide, the second wife.

Charles III, The Simple, was born September 17, 879, the posthumous son of King Louis II and Adelaide or Adelheide. He died October 7, 929. He married Edgiva, daughter of King Edward of England and granddaughter of Alfred the Great.

Louis IV (From beyond the Sea) was born about 921 and died September 10, 954. He lived in England in exile until he was recalled in 936 to become King of the Franks. He married Princess Gerberga, daughter of Henry I, Emperor of Germany.

Princess Gerberga, the daughter, married Albert I, Count of Vermandous.

Herbert III, Count of Vermandois. He was born about 956 and died about 1000. He married Ermengarde, daughter of Reinald, Count of Bar.

Otho, Count of Vermandois, was born about 999 and died May 25, 1045. Married Bavic.

Herbert, Count of Vermandois and of Valois, was born about 1032. He married Adele de Vexin.

Adelaide, Countess of Vermandois, married Hugh the Great, Duke of France.

Isabel de Vermandois married Robert de Beaumont in 1096, son of Roger and Adeline de Beaumont.

Robert de Beaumont II was born about 1104 and died April 5, 1168. He married Amice, daughter of Ralph Seigneuer about 1120.

Robert de Beaumont III died in 1190 during his return from the Crusades. He was the third earl of Leicester. He married Petronilla, great granddaughter of Hugh de Grandmesnil, the Domesday tenant.

Margaret de Beaumont who died January 12, 1235 married Sir Saier de Quincy, 1st Earl of Winchester, who died as a Crusader November 3, 1219 in the Holy Land.

Roger de Quincy, 2nd Earl of Winchester, Constable of Scotland died in April, 1264. He married, 2nd, Margaret, daughter of Prince David of Scotland.

Margaret de Quincy died about 1280. She married in 1238 William de Ferrers, Earl of Derby.

Joan de Ferrers married Thomas de Berkeley, Lord of Berkeley in 1267. He was the son of Maurice and Isabel FitzRoy de Berkeley.

Maurice de Berkeley, Lord of Berkeley was born about 1281 and died May 31, 1326 Eva La Zouche.

Isabel De Berkeley died July 25, 1362. She married Lord Robert de Clifford first. She married second, Sir Thomas de Musgrave of the Musgraves of Westmorland.

Sir Thomas de Musgrave of Musgrave died at the beginning of the reign of Edward II (1307). He married Sara, sister of Sir Andrew of Harcla.

Sir Thomas de Musgrave, a minor in 1310. Sheriff of Westmorland, 1340 to 1344; of Yorkshire from 1360 to 1365. Died in 1376. He married Isabella, daughter of Maurice, Lord Berkley. She died in 1362.

Sir Thomas de Musgrave owned Crosby Garret in 1382. Died in 1384. He married Margaret, daughter of Sir William Roos of Yolton in County York. Margaret was his first wife.

Sir Thomas de Musgrave, Lord of Hartley, was born in 1337 and died in 1409. He married Elizabeth, daughter of Sir William Fitzwilliam.

Sir Richard Musgrave of Musgrave, living in 1422. Believed to be buried in Kirkby Stephen Church. He married Elizabeth.

Thomas Musgrave of Musgrave, Esquire. Died January 3, 1447. Married Joanne, daughter of William, Lord Dacre, living in 1456.

Sir Richard Musgrave of Musgrave, died

November 9, 1464. Buried at Kirkby Stephen, Westmorland. Married Margaret, daughter of Sir Thomas Betham of Betham, Westmorland.

Eleanor Musgrave, daughter of Sir Richard and Margaret Betham Musgrave, married William Thornborough (Thornburgh) of Hamsfield and Selside. (Number 7 in my Thornburg line.) Note Eleanor's brother Thomas Musgrave of Musgrave and Edenhall, who inherited, married Joan, daughter of Sir William Stapleton. Thomas died before October 20, 1458 as Joan is shown as a widow on that date.

by Charles Thornburg

THORNBURG, CHARLES COLLIER, III
F283

The Thornburg Pedigree to Charles Collier Thornburg III – 1976

The following pages depict and analyze the Thornburg origin tracing back to Ivo do Taillobioso and King Ethelred II. I start my genealogical line here however using at the start the Solside Hall pedigree accepted by *Nicholson and Burn*.

1. William de Thornburghe of Thornburghe in York County; married a daughter of Sir John Croker of London. There is no doubt but what the family originated in the North Ridings of Yorkshire. The town of Thornborough together with the Thornborough Moors and Circle exists today north of Ripon.
2. Sir William Thornburgh of Thornburgh, knight; married Anne, daughter of Richard Maleverer, esquire.
3. John Thornburgh of Hamsfeld, esquire; married Elizabeth, daughter of Sir Henry Pierpoint, knight.
4. William Thornburg, esquire; married Catherine, daughter of William Hilton, esquire.
5. Thomas Thornburgh, esquire; married Jane, daughter of Sir John Dalton.
6. Henry Thornburgh, esquire; married Elizabeth, daughter of Matthew Booth.
7. William Thornburgh of Hamsfeld, esquire; married Elianor, daughter of Sir Richard Musgrave of Musgrave, knight.
8. William Thornburgh of Hamsfeld, esquire; married Elizabeth, daughter and heiress of Thomas Broughton of Broughton in Lancashire, esquire.
9. Rowland Thornburgh of Hamsfeld, esquire; married Margaret, daughter of Sir Geoffrey Middleton of Middleton Hall, knight.
10. Sir William Thornburg of Hamsfeld Hall, knight; married Thomasine, daughter and co-heir of Sir Robert Bellingham of Burneshead, knight. Sir William died in 1552. Dame Thomasine died in 1582. In the Kendal Parish Church in Westmorland in the north east corner in the Bellingham chapel can be found a small marble tablet in her memory. Above it is the arms of the Thornburg family with a total of six quarterings. The inscription is marred by cracks but is still plainly discernible. It shows her to be the daughter of Sir Robert Bellingham and the wife of Sir William Thornburgh and that she died on August 11, 1582 – "This world, she left there of not loth, Almightie God hir soule receave, To hevenly blis she humblye craved." All pedigrees relating to the American Thornburg's (except that of Delmar Thornbury) include and continue on from Sir William and Thomasine of Hampsfield Hall.

Sir William participated in the invasion of Scotland in 1547 and was knighted by the Duke of Somerset at Roxburgh.

In 11, my lineage carries on to a son, William, but another son of William and Thomasine should be briefly mentioned here — Nicholas Thornburgh of Whitwell, esquire married Isabel, daughter of Robert Sakeld of Thornesmonby. It is believed that the first Thornburg to arrive in America, Thomas, in 1616, was a descendant of Nicholas. Delmar Thorbury differs, tracing the American immigrant, Thomas back to a Nicholas, son of William Thornburgh and Elizabeth Broughton.

11. William Thornburgh of Hamsfeld, esquire; married Ethelred, daughter of Sir Thomas Carus, Justice of the King's Bench. In the Cartmel church exists a small marble slab showing Ethelred to have died on March 3, 1596, that her father was "Justice Carus", her mother Katherine, and her husband, William Thornburgh, who was the second son of William and Thomasine.
12. Rowland Thornburgh of Hansfeld, esquire; married Jane, daughter of Sir Thomas Dalton of Thurnham in Lancashire, esquire.
13. William Thornburgh, esquire; married Catherine, daughter of Edward Langtree in the County of Lancaster, esquire. This William in 1637 sold Hampsfield and in 1641 sold part of the manors of Whitwell and Selside. In addition to Rowland, the heir, they had two other sons, Richard and Charles. It is said they became followers of George Fox.
14. Charles Thornburgh of Methop (east of Cartmel); married Elizabeth (born 1645), daughter of Thomas Leyburne and Dorothy Lascelles of Cunswick and Witherslack. (Thomas Leyburne was the 3rd son of John Leyburne (died 1663) and Catherine Carus of Halton.
15. Robert Thornborough, emigrant to Ireland where he resumed the name of Thornborough; married Sarah Jackson in Cootehill, 1686. Irish Quaker record accepted in America.
16. Edward Thornborough; married Jean. Edward and two brothers, Thomas and Walter, emigrated from Ireland between 1714 and 1726.
17. John Thornbury (Thornesburgh) married — Davis, da. of John and Mary Davis.
18. Thomas Thornburg; married Diana Peat (Piat). Thomas in Allegheny County census of 1800 as Thornebrough. Census of 1810 as Thornsburgh. Thomas and Diana established the Thornburg farm of over a thousand acres in Robinson Township, Allegheny County, Pennsylvania on area now named Borough of Thornburg. Thomas died in 1833. Shown in census of 1830 as between 80 and 90. Diana is indicated in census of 1800 as between 35 and 45. In census of 1830 as between 70 and 80. In the Pennsylvania Archives the transcript for taxables in 1781 shows Thomas Thornbrough listed for 400 acres in Robinson Township. The list published by Washington County D.A.R. (1955) shows Thomas Thornbrough in the 1784 tax lists. (Washington County in these years included all of Pennsylvania south of the Ohio River and west of the Allegheny and Monongahela. Allegheny County was cut out of the north portion, including Robinson Township.

On January 13, 1806, James and Lydia Brisson by deed conveyed 402 acres "situate on Chartier's Creek" to Thomas Thornburg. Thomas left a will dated September 15, 1831. His son, Jacob, received 200 acres. The rest was divided up among the other children.

19. Jacob Thornburg married Jane Lorain. Jacob born 1784, died 1880. In census of 1860, 1870, 1880. Shown as 97 in June census of 1880. Died in August. Jane Lorain was born in 1788. Shown in census of 1860 as blind. A brother of Jacob, John, is shown in census of 1810 as Thornsburgh and over 26.
20. John Thornburg married Eliza ?. John born 1824. In census of 1860, 1870, Dead before 1880. Eliza born 1828. In census of 1870 as 40. In census of 1880 as 50 and a widow.
21. Charles Collier Thornburg married Nina Boice. Charles born 1857. In census of 1860, 1870, 1880. Nina Boice born 4/11/1859. Died 1938 at Hobart, Indiana. Charles died 3/22/1884. Tombstone, Chartiers Cemetery.
22. Charles Collier Thornburg II married Bernadine Erskine. Charles born, Crafton, 6/16/1884. Died 1950, St. John, Indiana. Bernadine Erskine born 12/30/1890. New Cumberland, West Virginia. Died 1951, Cedar Lake, Indiana.
23. Charles Colliere Thornburg III married Lillian Coleman. Charles born 10/22/1906 in Ingram, Pennsylvania. Lillian Coleman born 9/21/1913 in Hinckley, Minnesota.
24. Charles Jason Thornburg married Helga Klepsch. Charles born 11/6/1938 in East Chicago, Indiana. Helga Klepsch born 8/23/1941 in Austria.
25. John Norman Thornburg married Jane Elizabeth Harvey. John born 10/30/1946 in East Chicago, Indiana. Jane born 1/22/1952 in Battle Creek, Michigan.
26. Children of Charles and Helga: Charles Jason II born 4/10/1965, Lackland Air Force Base, Texas; Carla Renate born July 2, 1968, Davis Monthan Air Force Base, Arizona; Erie Tyson Thornburg born July 21, 1972, Homestead Air Force Base, Fla.; Lee Robin Thornburg born September 1, 1977, Altus AFB, Oklahoma.

by Charles Thornburg

TRUAX, LULA
F284

Lula Myrtle (Haynes) Truax came to Gary about 1920, with her second husband Claud Jerald Truax. With them were her 2 daughters by her first marriage to Harry E. Mooney, Margaret Louise Mooney and Lola May Mooney, and Lula and Claud's son Claud Edward who was born in Des Moines, Iowa.

Claud J. served in the U.S. Army during W.W. I and was a railroad man for E.J.E. RR. Claud was also known for his photographic memory. Claud died April 30, 1930. Claud and Lula had 3 children: Claud Edward b. Jan. 1919 m. Rose Rendina June 1945. Claud served in the U.S. Navy during W.W. II in the South Pacific. He died Dec. 1986. Roy Forbis b. Sept. 30, 1921, m. Alice Doolin Nov. 1944, died 1951. Edna Glenn b. Oct. 1927 m. Ernest Floyd Maatheus Sept. 1947.

Lula's two older daughters: Margaret Louise b. Jan. 1914 New Boston, Ill., m. Allen O. Shaffer Aug. 1929; she died April 22, 1980. Lola May b. Mar. 1916 New Boston, Ill. m. Archie E. Hall Nov. 1938 died April 6, 1980.

Lula worked as a housekeeper and maid until the beginning of W.W. II, then she went to work at the cafeteria in U.S. Steel. After the war she owned and managed a local grocery located at 25th and Clark Rd. Gary until 1950.

Lula was also very involved with the Church of the Nazarene in Tolleston, even after the church moved to Aetna she was still a board member and attended church regularly until 1965 when a car accident crushed her hip and she could no longer drive a car. Lula did not like to be dependent so she would seldom ask for rides to church, so started her many hours of religious sermons via the radio and television evangelists. She still gave financial and spiritual support to her church.

Lula lived in Gary from 1920 to 1971, when she moved to Merrillville. She was 89 years 1 month and 27 days old when she passed out of this life.

by Carol Jean Hall

TULEY, WILLIAM T.
F285

William T. Tuley of St. John.

William T. Tuley was born in Hammond, Indiana on July 20, 1916. His parents, Eureka and William Thomas Tuley had six children, Maysie, Vera, Gladys, Lilah and the twins Winifred and Bill.

The parents moved to Hammond from LaPorte County, Indiana in 1902 when the elder Tuley became a railroad fireman and eventually an engineer with the Indiana Harbor Belt Railroad.

The family dates back to France in 1572, when the family fled to England when the French Government started to round up and kill the French Huguenots (Protestants).

Almost one hundred years later, in the mid 1600's, three Tuley brothers came to America, landing in South Carolina. There the brothers split up, one going to New York, one to Virginia and the other going to Louisiana.

The Virginia branch of the family came to Kentucky in the very early frontier days, and helped to settle what is now Louisville, Kentucky.

Bill Tuley's great, great grandfather, born in 1768, brought his family from Grant County, Kentucky to LaPorte County, Indiana in 1834. He passed away in Clinton Township, LaPorte County in 1837.

Bill attended Wallace and Washington grade schools in Hammond, and graduated from Hammond High School in 1937. In 1942 he entered the armed forces and became an Infantry Staff Sergeant with the 87th Infantry Division. The 87th Division distinguished itself in combat through France, Belgium, Luxembourg and Germany. During combat Tuley received a bronze star for heroism.

After the war Tuley was made First Sergeant of a Military Government Detachment in Zwickau in East Germany. When the Russians took control of the city Tuley and his men were assigned to the same duties at Obernzell, Germany, located on the Danube River, not too far from the Czechoslovak border. He remained there until December of 1945 when he was sent home to become a civilian again.

During his working life Tuley spent 20 years as a printer with the W.B. Conkey Co. This company later became a part of the Rand McNally Publishing Co. From there he went to the Times Newspaper where he worked for another 20 years. When he left the Times he was employed by the Hoosier Bank in Hammond to run their in-house print shop. When he retired from the bank in 1981 he purchased the print shop from the bank and went into business for himself, locating first in Dyer and then in Schererville where he finally sold the business to Minuteman Press, but remained as a partner with the new owners.

In 1947 Bill married Helen Bruhn of Hammond, and after living in Hammond and Griffith for several years they moved to St. John in 1956. In 1959 Bill entered politics and was elected to the St. John Town Board. He served on the Town Board for 20 years, the last 17 of which he was the Town Board President. During that time he also served as President of the Northwest Indiana Council of Small Cities and Towns. He was also President of the Northern Indiana Town Trustees Roundtable Association. This organization was made up of Town Board members from towns in the 10 county area of Northern Indiana.

When he retired from politics in 1980 he wrote a book covering the 150 years history of St. John, Indiana.

Bill was a very devout baseball fan, and in 1938 he organized his own semi pro baseball team called the Hammond Braves. By the time the team disbanded after the 1947 season they had compiled an envious record of victories, winning five different league championships, and runner up in the State Semi Pro Tournament. Twice they placed seven men on the Indiana All State Semi Pro Team.

In 1979, 32 years after the team disbanded, the Hammond Historical Society asked Tuley to write a book on the story of the Hammond Braves. Using old box scores, newspaper clippings, photographs and memories, the book was printed and turned over to the Historical Society for their archives and distribution to the various libraries.

by William T. Tuley

VAGNER, VACLAV AND ANNA PODANOVA
F286

Steve Buras "Early Hammond Residents"

Vaclav Vagner

"Early Hammond Residents"

Edna Anna Podanova and Vaclav Vagner met in Prague, Czechoslovakia in 1909. They fell in love and planned a new and better life in America. Vaclav was a salesman of machinery and Anna was a pastry cook in a wealthy home. They worked and saved and Vaclav was the first to travel to America, arriving in the Calumet region in April 1910. He first found

Anna Buras "Early Hammond Residents"

work at the Betz Surgical Instrument Company in Hammond. Edna Anna followed her sweetheart and arrived in April 1911 in Hammond. Anna, as she preferred to be called, was 27 years old and Vaclav was 29. Anna was a small woman with thick brown hair and grey green eyes. Vaclav was of medium built with light brown hair and brown eyes. What an exciting future they had before them! They were very much in love and worked hard to save for their own home. Anna and Vaclav first rented a large house and soon it was full of boarders: co-workers of Vaclav and men of the area who had heard of Anna's delicious meals and pastries. How hard Anna worked cooking, cleaning, and washing all the laundry by hand on a washboard. A daughter was born to them on November 30, 1912, Helen Marie. Soon they had saved enough money to purchase a brick home at 5623 Howard Ave. in the city. Vaclav changed jobs and went to work at the Standard Freight Car Plant nearby. He rode his bicycle to work everyday. Life was good and they were very happy. In the spring of 1919 Vaclav became ill with pneumonia but was anxious to return to work. It was too soon and he suffered a fatal heart attack at work and died on April 4, 1919. He was just 37 years old. Anna was now a young widow with no family to help her and her small daughter. She went back to what she did best: cooking. She went to work in a restaurant in downtown Hammond while kind neighbors looked after little Helen. It was there that Steve Buras, a young man from Greece, first saw Anna. He became a regular customer for his meals as his barbershop was nearby. Anna and Steve courted and were married. Steve moved to the Howard Avenue home and there a daughter was born in 1922, Ruth. Tragedy struck when Ruth died at 2 years 6 months of age from complications from measles. Soon a second daughter was born to Anna and Steve, Sophie. The family was again happy and complete. The daughters grew up and moved away to being their own lives. Anna and Steve lived out their lives at the Howard Avenue home. Steve died at age 67 in 1955 and Anna lived on until 1966 to age 83. Helen moved back to live in the home until her death in 1985 at age 73. The home was sold but still stands strong and sturdy as the strong and sturdy people who once lived there. I am proud of my ancestors and all they stood for. How brave they were to come to a strange land and leave all that was familiar behind. They never looked back but always looked to the future. Anna and Vaclav were my grandparents and Steve was my step-grandfather. The oldest daughter Helen, was my mother. The youngest daughter Sophie married and lives in the west.

by Mrs. Joan Walker

VANDERSEE, HARVEY FREDERICK
F287

Harvey F. Vandersee

Vandersee Family of Crown Point

Harvey Frederick Vandersee, production manager for Letz Manufacturing Company and Helix Corporation, Crown Point, and Lutheran lay leader, was born in Crown Point on October 23, 1907, youngest of four children of Karl Louis Vandersee (1871-1932) and Anna Emma Bertha Henning Vandersee (1881-1960). Both parents were born in Germany, his father leaving Bremen alone at age sixteen. Karl worked in Crown Point delivering beer with a wagon and team of horses for Crown Brewing Company, and later at the Letz factory on an unloading crew and as night watchman. Harvey's mother came at age three with her parents, Wilhelmina Henning (1845-1932), and Friedrich Henning (1851-1928), a laborer, who on arriving in the Crown Point area took up railroad work. Besides Anna, there were four Henning girls and one boy, Ernest H. ("Pete"), who became famous in the area as a baseball pitcher, eventually playing professional ball (see separate story).

Harvey Vandersee was born with the help of a midwife in the family house on North Grant Street in Crown Point, in "Bridgeport," near the Pennsylvania Railroad station. In his youth this area consisted of a grocery store, a butcher shop, several saloons, Rusty's bowling alley, a building for the two-wheel fire cart, Cordia Cadwell's barber shop, and a vacant lot or two. Harvey graduated from Trinity Lutheran School, three blocks away, which his mother also had attended; in his day it was a one-room school, with about 55 pupils in eight grades, under William Heidbreder. German was still taught, which he hated, and never learned. He attended Crown Point High School for two years, working six nights a week setting pins at the two-lane bowling alley. Wages, 30 to 50 cents a night, depended on the number of bowlers. Saturday meant getting up at 5:30 a.m. to clean and polish the alleys and to sweep up the establishment, which also had a pool table, lunch counter, and soda fountain. In summers there was fresh ice cream from Logansport, in steel containers packed with ice in wooden kegs, to be picked up by hand truck from the evening train at the Pennsylvania depot.

Disliking school at all levels, also feeling the need to work "to help the family survive," as he later recalled, Harvey left high school to work at Zurbriggen's grocery store on the corner of Grant Street and Goldsborough. He recalled no influence from any of his high school teachers — "a very poor lot," except for Charlotte Wheeler in Latin, "who respected her pupils, and they responded in kind."

After one year at the grocery store, he was offered a job at the Letz firm, at $17.50 a week, the work schedule then being ten hours a day, six days a week (five and a half days in summer). He started as assistant to Howard Towle, who was in charge of production and cost control. When Towle left after two years, Harvey was asked to take over his duties; he was to hold the post of production manager some 25 years. These included the busy years of World War II, during which time the Letz firm, producing feed grinders and roughage mills, was instrumental in sustaining agricultural production critical to the national war effort. The well-known American writer Flannery O'Connor mentions a "Letz mill" on a Georgia farm in her postwar story "The Displaced Person." In the early 1950s, foreseeing the probable close of the once-prosperous firm, Harvey Vandersee joined Helix Corporation, a new concern which at that time was also engaged in manufacturing farm equipment. He was production manager with the growing firm the same length of time as at Letz, and was in charge of inventory when he died at age 76.

Nephew of Crown Point's famous baseball player, "Pete" Henning, Harvey Vandersee was himself a baseball enthusiast. He managed a Crown Point baseball team before his marriage; thereafter he concerned himself with family and with Trinity Lutheran Church in Crown Point and its daughter congregation, Trinity Memorial in Independence Hill, which he helped found. He was for several years a school board member at Trinity, the parochial school then consisting of three rooms, and helped found Boy Scout Troop 72. At Trinity Memorial he was congregation president and active in calling on prospective new members. In both parishes he taught Sunday school for many years; a highlight of his life was a trip to Israel in 1969, seeing places he had encountered in his teaching. He served on the mission board of the Calumet District of the Missouri Synod, at the time Good Shepherd Lutheran

Church, a black parish in Glen Park, Gary, was founded, and he served the District on various other boards and committees. Though not active in politics, he considered himself a Republican of the Robert Taft philosophy.

In 1935 he met Louise Amelia Bauer (born October 25, 1907), a teacher at Ford School in Lafayette, Indiana. She was seventh of twelve children of Andreas J. Bauer (1870-1949), a farm worker and apprentice cobbler in Bavaria, Germany, who had emigrated in 1886, and Barbara Babette Leitner Bauer 1872-1950), who came with her parents in 1888 from Middle Franconia in Bavaria. Louise's parents operated a farm south of Lafayette, near Shadeland, cooperating with Purdue University in various agricultural experiments. A short account of the Bauer family and farm appears in a five-volume Indiana biographical history published in 1931, with Andy Bauer symbolizing the American "self-made" man, having arrived in Tippecanoe County "with only a dollar." Two of Louise's sisters, Minnie and Lillian, had already married Crown Point men, Carl Pfeil and Vernon Heintz; the marriage of Harvey and Louise took place on the front lawn of the farm June 20, 1937, their honeymoon in Colorado Springs. Louise Vandersee, who had attended Indiana State Teachers College in Terre Haute, and Purdue University, then devoted herself to her family, except for some substitute teaching. Among her talents was sewing; for many years she made virtually all her own clothing. Not a gardener in the strict sense, she gained great satisfaction from daily attention to her lawn and flowers. Especially in later years she enjoyed rendering Bible passages from rhyme, and was notable in the neighborhood around 153 North Ridge Street for hospitality to children and unobtrusive instruction of them.

Both Vandersee children were born in Mercy Hospital, Gary, and graduated from Trinity Lutheran School in Crown Point and from Crown Point High School. Their son, Charles Andrew Vandersee (born March 25, 1938), graduated from Valparaiso University and received his Ph.D. in English from UCLA, on Woodrow Wilson and Danforth national fellowships. Since 1964 he has taught at the University of Virginia, Charlottesville, where he has also been associate editor of *The Letters of Henry Adams* (Harvard University Press) and director of the undergraduate Echols Scholars Program. Their daughter, Barbara Anne Vandersee (born October 4, 1941), graduated from Valparaiso and received her M.S.W. from the University of Denver. She is a licensed social worker in Portland, Oregon, working for Lutheran Family Services, and with her husband, Larry W. Foster, owns and trains award-winning Old English sheepdogs. She is author and publisher of a book about the breed, *Companions, Competitors, and Clowns*.

Harvey Vandersee died at home of a heart attack on June 27, 1984, preceded by brother Leslie (1902-1920) and sisters Irene (1905-1936), who worked for the Indiana Leather Specialty Company, and Lucille (1903-1984), a stenographer for Letz. Louise Vandersee died at St. Anthony's Medical Center on November 21, 1983, survived by a brother and six sisters.

by Charles Vandersee

VEKASI, MICHAEL AND ELIZABETH
F288

Although born in Nagy-Szelmenc, Ung Megye, Hungary, Mike Vekasi came to America when young and almost all of his childhood memories were of Donora, Pennsylvania. There he had a meager education but a wide assortment of life experiences. He was about twenty-one when he came to Gary, Indiana, with his parents, Peter and Julianna (Pataki) Vekasi, to whom he was devoted. Most of his life he worked as a crane operator in the open hearth but he also liked to tell of delivering sewer pipe to Glen park and especially of his experiences when, for a couple of years, he drove an ice wagon in what must have been one of the seamier sections of town.

As a young man, Mike enjoyed sports. In Donora he had played on a football team called the Donora Independents. There was a Catholic baseball league in northern Lake County and Mike was the catcher on the St. Emeric's team for a while. If they were short players, the priest would play outfield for them. Mike described it as fun with a good crowd to watch.

In August, 1924, at the First Hungarian Reformed Church, Mike married Elizabeth Bazin, daughter of John and Barbara Bazin. Shortly thereafter Mike was injured at the mill when he was crushed between the crane and a wall. He was fitted with a brace but the mill doctors as well as the doctors at Mayo's Clinic offered little hope that he would return to normal activities. Although time and perseverance proved them wrong, he did suffer pain from the injury all of his life. Even as his memory was failing in old age, he would speak of the horrors of that accident. However, it did not prevent him from completing over 40 years of service at U.S. Steel's Gary Works before he retired in 1958.

In 1925 Mike and Elizabeth had a son, Michael Eugene, who attended Jefferson School then on to Horace Mann. There were no more children until 1943 when their daughter, Linda Sue, was born. By that time their son was a student at Purdue University and soon joined the Army Air Corps where he became a navigator. Both Mike and Elizabeth completed their naturalization process to become American citizens in 1946. The following year their son married Dorothy Wildermuth. He then went on to graduate from Purdue, move to Michigan, and rear three sons. Linda graduated from Horace Mann High School, married Ted Drygas, and moved to Hobart. In 1974 Ted was killed in an accident. After Linda reared their two sons, Anthony and Andrew, she married Joseph Garcia.

Mike and Elizabeth lived at 840 Van Buren St. all of their married life until about 1968 when they moved to 5140 Delaware. Elizabeth's health began to fail and she died in 1970. Mike lived alone for about five years then took up residence with his daughter. He died in 1987. He was a man whose devotion to parents and his family, loyalty to his employer, and integrity of person earned respect from all who knew him.

by Dorothy Wildermuth Vekasi

VEKASI, PETER AND JULIANNA
F289

Near the turn of the century in a small Hungarian village in the foothills of the Carpathian Mountains Peter and Julianna (Pataki) Vekasi grieved over the loss of yet another child. Their first-born , Michael, was now a strapping young lad, but all the children that followed had died at birth. The doctor said Julianna must not have any more children for awhile. Both Peter and Julianna were orphaned young and were anxious to establish a family of their own. They were very poor, and, like so many others at that time, America appeared to be the solution of their problems.

Peter journeyed to Pennsylvania and was soon able to send for his wife and son. They moved to Donora, Pennsylvania, and soon rejoiced over the birth of a healthy daughter, whom they named Gazella. The children that followed, however, all died. By about 1913 word of the opportunities available in the young city of Gary, Indiana, reached them and they moved on.

In Gary Peter found work in the wire mill and in time his son became a crane operator in the open hearth. They settled into the life in Gary, joined St. Emeric's Catholic church, and resided at 1833 Washington St. then 941 Adams St. Finally, in 1923, they built a three story residence with a flat on each floor at 840 Van Buren St. It was a multilingual neighborhood of immigrants from many different nations. Although Peter preferred speaking Hungarian, he was conversant in English. Julia, however, never became comfortable with the English language.

Both of their children were married in 1924. Mike married Elizabeth Bazin, daughter of John and Barbara (Papp) Bazin. Gazella married Edward Boer, who had a grocery store on Massachusetts St. between 5th and 6th Ave. called "The First Store." For a while, each family occupied a flat in the house on Van Buren St.

In 1928 at 57 years of age Peter had a stroke and soon after he died. Mike bought the house on Van Buren from his mother. The Boer family moved to Tolleston and Julia resided with them most of the time. Julia was nearly 76 when she died in 1945. She is buried next to Peter in Calvary Cemetery in Garyton. The family they had longed to establish has come to pass. From their two children they had four grandchildren, eight great-grandchildren, and the next generation continues to expand. Many of these descendants are still residents of Lake County.

by Dorothy Wildermuth Vekasi

VIDLER, ANN
F290

(January 9, 1843 to May 26, 1929)

Ann Vidler was the oldest daughter of Benjamin and Emma Vidler of Tumbridge Wells, Kent, England. She was one of 14 children; 11 boys and 3 girls. When quite young, she was married to Benjamin John Packham. To this couple was born one son, Benjamin. Ben's

Ann Vidler Jeffery

father was quite a musician and played the violin for party's and clubs a great deal. He was very much in demand, which kept him away from home. Many times he would be kept all night, he got less interested in his home and stayed away more and more. Finally, he went away and nothing more was ever heard from him. Mrs. Packham was forced to break up her home and return to her parents with her small son. She then went out to service, or as we would say in this country "to work". She worked in very wealthy gentlemen's houses where there were about 14 servants kept at one time. She continued working until she met and married John Neal Jeffery on October 2, 1870, witnessed by Charles Beuer and Mary Ann Beuer and Albert N. Young.

The following year they decided to come to America. Mr. Jeffery came first, he landed at Port Live Providence, Quebec on May 3, 1871, Chicago May 8th and Hobart, IN August 14, 1873. There he purchased 10 acres of land at what is now the intersection of Old Ridge Road and Liverpool Road, from John G. Earl. His wife joined him shortly afterward, landing in Baltimore, MD March 20, 1872, Chicago March 23rd and Hobart, IN August 14, 1873.

To this union were born 6 children; James Richard, Robert William, Biveon Charles, Adelaid, Walter and Muriel. Mr. Jeffery met death very suddenly on November 1, 1887 when on his way to work he was struck by a cattle train. He lived for a few hours, he was 38 years and 7 months.

Mrs. Jeffery labored on alone and managed to raise her children until the boys were old enough to work for the local farmers to help their mother along. There was a mortgage on the home that she was never able to pay off, but she managed to keep the interest and taxes paid and provide for her children. It was very hard driving to Crown Point every spring and fall in a buggy through hub deep mud. It was very slow traveling.

When Gary, IN was born, all the Jeffery children, except Muriel were married. Mrs. Jeffery and Muriel thought they would try their hand at the boarding house business. So she sold the home place in Hobart and bought a boarding house at what is now 3rd and Broadway in Gary. Her place was only a tarpaper shack as were the rest of the houses at that time. They did very well, feeding 45 to 50 men three times a day. Later, when Gary started to grow they were forced to give up the place to make room for more permanent buildings.

From that time on Mrs. Jeffery made her home among her children, going from one to the other. Whenever a new baby came along she was usually there to lend a hand, but she was getting on in years. When she was 80 years old she traveled to Duluth, MN, to spend her 80th birthday with her daughter, Muriel, traveling both ways alone. In 1926 she had a sick spell and the doctors gave her up and said she would only live for a few hours. She lingered on and then one day she announced that she would not take any more medicine and she didn't. She began to get well and did a lot of sewing and needle work for about three years.

She was very fond of riding and on the 4th of February, 1919, her grandson Walter Edward took her for a ride through Hobart and all the familiar places. She was very pleased but quite tired and complained that here eyes were hurting when she returned home. From that time on she failed rapidly. She passed away May 26, 1929 at age 86 years 4 months and 17 days. Leaving 4 sons, 2 daughters, 36 grandchildren and 6 great-grandchildren. Ann Vidler Jeffery is buried near the East entrance in the Hobart, Indiana Cemetery.

by Dorris Campbell

VILMER, W. E.
F291

W.E. Vilmer, photographer of high rank, began his business career in 1886, at Crown Point, where he is still located. He is a member of both the National and State Associations of Photographers, and also of the Indiana Art League. He has just been elected president of the State Association, in which he previously served three years as its secretary.

In 1904 he was commissioned by a Pennsylvania art concern, to go to Indianapolis and make a series of photographs of Vice-President Fairbanks. He is owner and publisher of several copyrighted pictures sold extensively in the art stores of the country, and is possessor of numerous medals given by both the State and National Associations.

Compiled from the Souvenir Album of Lake Co. Ind., Crown Point-Lowell, June 18-19, 1909.)

VUKIN FAMILY
F292

Markel (Marko) D. Vukin (1886-1943) was born April 25, 1886, in Karlovac, Jugoslavia. He emigrated to the United States aboard the S.S. Kaisar Wilheim II and landed in New York on September 5, 1905. In 1910 he lived in Escanaba City, Michigan, and worked as a spare man in a hardwood flooring company. Most of his adulthood was spent in Gary, Indiana, although he did return to the Michigan area and lived in Benton Harbor and Read City from 1921 to 1925. He worked as a laborer for the CIS Corporation in Gary. He lived in this country 37 years before he became a naturalized citizen of the United States on November 10, 1942. He died in 1943 in Gary, Indiana.

Marko married Barbara Glivar (1889-1959) in February, 1905, in Karlova, Jugoslavia. She was born January 4, 1889, the daughter of Stephen (1865-1939) and Katherine (1870-1938) Glivar, and she emigrated to the United States in September, 1909. She was a short, stocky, Croatian woman noted for her excellent cooking skills, her famous sauerkraut, and her staunch Catholicism. Her granddaughter, Mary Janet Stewart, remembers that she made the best home made nut bread in the world. She also remembers Barbara making kielbasa, blood sausage, and her own special cheese. After Marko's death, Barbara continued to live in Gary with her brother, John Glivar, until her death on March 2, 1959.

Barbara and Marko had nine children: Mary Ann (John Alan) Stewart (1910-1957); John (1912-1939); Josephine (Chauncey) Smith (b. 1914); Katherine (Robert) Murray (b. 1916); Joseph (1919-1974); Caroline (William) Bonner (b. 1921); Stephen (b. 1938) and married to Judith; Donna Esther (Matthew) Bleicher (b. 1926); and Barbara Jean (Gordon) Powers (b. 1931). Most of the children stayed in the Lake County and Porter County, Indiana, area and raised their families here.

As the oldest child in the family, Mary Ann Vukin quit high school in her sophomore year to help her family financially. She was 15 years old when she went to work as a receptionist in the dental office of Dr. J. Alan Stewart in Gary, Indiana. Seven years later (June 17, 1932) she married her boss. They had one child, Mary Janet Stewart, born September 4, 1941, who currently resides in Hammond, Indiana. Jan graduated from Lew Wallace High School in 1960. She earned her Bachelor of Science degree in Physical Education in 1964 from Indiana University and taught school for several years. In 1982 she earned her Master of Science degree in counseling from Purdue University and is currently a Deputy Chief Probation Officer and Head of the Intake Division for Superior Court of Lake County, Juvenile Division, in Gary, Indiana.

by Mary Janet Stewart

WALKER, RICHARD A. AND JOAN F.
F293

"Present Day Residents"

Joan Edwina Frances Hussey was born and raised in the Calumet region, first living in North Hammond with her father and mother, Edwin and Helen Wagner Hussey, then at age 7 returning from Boston, Massachusetts with her mother after her parents divorced. Joan and her mother lived in the upstairs apartment in her Grandparents Buras' home at 5623 Howard Avenue in the central part of Hammond. The apartment was cozy and she was looked after by her grandmother while her mother worked through the WW II years and after. Joan attended Lafayette Grade School and then graduated from Hammond High School. While still in high school she met a young man newly arrived from the south,

The Richard and Joan Walker Family

Richard Arlen Walker. He had come to the Calumet region from Huntingdon, Tennessee to work at Inland Steel. He was 18 years old and she 16 when they met and fell in love. They dated then married on October 27, 1954. Their first home together was an apartment on Becker Street in Hammond. They lived there a little over a year until Rich was drafted into the Army for 2 years (to serve 16 months in Italy). When he returned home in December 1957, they finally could start to build a life together. Joan and Rich worked and saved to buy their home in Highland where they still live, and April 1961 they moved in. None too soon for their first child Jeffrey Michael was born on August 6, 1961, soon followed by James Patrick on August 15, 1963 and finally Jill Ann and Janet Marie on July 24, 1965. "Twins"... Their family was complete and the house full to bursting now! Thru the years the family grew and prospered. The children attended and graduated from Purdue Calumet, Indiana University N.W. and I.V. Tech. Rich continues to work at Inland Steel as a Supervisor in the Power and Fuels Dept. and Joan is employed in a law office.

by Joan F. Walker

WASSMANN FAMILY
F294

Mrs. Catharine Wassmann, widow of Henry I, was born on November 11, 1790 in Idensen, a province of Hannover, Germany. She immigrated on the ship, *Bark Emma* with the Conrad Oldendorf's; the Otto Buehre family, along with her son, Henry, and family who arrived in New York Harbor on May 12, 1851.

Her daughter, Engel Maria Wassmann, was married to Conrad Oldendorf, Sr., of the same area. Her son, Christoph, born August 20, 1822, later married Sophia Rohe, born 1825; Henry Wassmann, born December 27, 1825, married Dorothy Rohrsen, born 1835; Second wife, Anna Kapperman, born November 29, 1845; Sophia Wassmann, born October 3, 1835 was married on November 9, 1851 to Conrad Tatge, who was born on May 26, 1827.

Henry and Anna (Kapperman) Wassmann. Circa 1897.

From New York, they settled near the Metropolis of Chicago, Illinois. A few years later, they moved to a farm one half mile north of 121st Av. (SE corner of Sec. 12 and NE Corner of Sec. 13 platt map). Henry continued the farm labors to which he was reared, in that locality until 1870. The son, Henry, Jr. was born on March 17, 1850; had been educated in the German schools of this country, and assisted his father farming. On December 10, 1874, he married Sophia Meier, born February 20, 1854, the eldest daughter of John O. Meier, of rural Crete, Illinois. Their children were: Millie, John, Herman, Edward, Henry, Fred, Louis, Elsie, Walter, and Paul; Sophia, died at age three years; Engel, at age sixteen years.

Christoph Wassmann, born 1823, married to Sophia Rohe, born 1825, had four children who were: Henry, Sophia, Mary, and one daughter who was born in 1858 and died in 1861.

Sophia Wassmann, born October 3, 1835, on November 9, 1851 married Conrad Tatge, born May 26, 1827, entered politics as a Republican elected to offices of: Highway Commissioner, Township Collector, Justice of the Peace, Clerk of Circuit Court, of Will County for eight years, and resided in Joliet, Illinois, for a time.

Their children were: Caroline, Sophia, William H., Emilia, Gustavus, Emma, Amanda, and Juliana. H. William, died at one month old, Henry C., infant, Christine, age two years, and Conrad W., an infant.

Dietrich Wassmann, known as Dick, born November 22, 1860 near Brunswick, Indiana, the son of Henry Wassmann, owner of the farm near Brunswick, with brothers, H.H. Wassmann of rural Crete, Illinois; Herman, and Christoph of Lake County, Indiana, and a sister Mrs. William Zemke. On August 26, 1883, Dick married Louise Engelking, also of Lake County. Their children were Mrs. A.H. Radi, Clifton, Texas; Mrs. August Griese, Lockwood, Missouri; William H., of Sibley, Iowa; Clara; Rose; Fred, and Walter Wassmann.

In September, of 1883, Henry Wassmann, son Dick, and Charles Griep, and several neighbors, left Indiana and headed west from Chicago, Illinois to Glendive, Montana, and on to Bismarck, North Dakota. Unable to find anything suitable, the group split up. So, by way of St. Paul, Minnesota, to Sheldon, and Bigelow, Minnesota; Dick decided to try Sibley, Iowa. In Osceola County, he bought several pieces of land, among which was the I.G. Ireland farm in Sec. 34, (platt map) where he settled on a very productive farm. William H. and wife were living at Sibley at the time. Later, Dick sold the farm to William Zembke. It was then that Dick acquired the Osborn property in the town of Sibley, Iowa and entered politics in 1896, under the Democratic ticket. Having been Treasurer for six years, he moved on to accepting the position of Assistant Cashier with the Bank of Ocheydan, Iowa for seven years; deceased on January 20, 1911.

The children of Henry Wassmann and Dorothy Rohrsen were: Sophia, Christine, Henry, Diedrich, William, Gustave, Christopher, and Herman. Henry Wassmann's first wife died at age thirty-seven on May 1, 1872, in rural Brunswick, Indiana. On June 20, 1872, he was united in marriage to Anna Kapperman, of Hannover, Germany, born November 29, 1845, who had immigrated two years earlier. Their children were: Henry, Lena, Fred, Emma, Mary, Anna, Rose, Louise, Anna, died at age six years, and Louise, died at age one year, both of diphtheria.

Christine Wassmann, wife of George Redeker, of Osborn, Kansas, later, moved to North Dakota; William married Sophia, of Quincy, Illinois; Gustave, single, of Brunswick, Indiana; Herman married Minnie Dohrman, of Sibley, Iowa; Herman's second wife, Katharine Behrens; and Christoph of Sibley, Iowa.

by Mrs. Ralph Oldendorf

WASSMANN, FRED FAMILY
F295

Fred Wassmann, was born February 3, 1875 near Brunswick, Indiana. On June 4, 1899, he married Emma Behrens. After their marriage, they farmed with his parents on the homestead at first; but for twenty-four years, farmed the one south of the homeplace. Then they moved to a farm south of the Oldendorf Homestead for twenty years. Their children were: Lillian, wife of Arthur Bernhard who farmed near Brunswick, Indiana, east on the state line; Helen, wife of Albert Seehausen, of Chicago Heights, at first; Linda, wife of Paul Wukasch, second

Fred and Bertha (Behrens) Wassmann

husband, Oscar Junge, of Chicago, Valparaiso, and presently, Lafayette, In.; Margaret wife of William Seehausen, of Beecher, Illinois and Texas; Clara, wife of Leonard Teske, Eagle Lake, Illinois; Marie, wife of Henry Grieving, Jr., of Dyer, Indiana; Lucille, Freeport, Illinois, at first; Rose, wife of Henry Haake.

A sister of Fred, Lena, married Herman Paul, of Minnesota. One brother lived at Crystal City, Texas. Emma wife of Alfred Wehling of Beecher, Illinois; Mary, wife of William Hinze of Beecher, Illinois.

The Henry Wassmann farm in the mid-section, 12 SE (platt map) was later known as the Harvey Dust farm and the Fred Wassmann farm was later known as the Herman Brands farm.

by Mrs. R. Oldendorf

WEAVER, H. V.
F296

H.V. Weaver was born on a farm near Reading, Hillsdale Co., Mich., Aug. 16, 1856, his parents being H.H. and Hattie Weaver. Young Weaver attended the public schools of Reading until he was eighteen years old, when he left the parental roof and went forth to see some of the world. Later, having satisfied his desire for travel, he took up the study of undertaking and embalming as a profession. He also studied medicine and his being associated with medical men aided materially in his proficiency in his chosen work. Mr. Weaver graduated from Clark's College of Embalming at Cincinnati, Ohio, and has his diploma from that institution. He also has a license issued by the State Board of Health of Indiana, and one from the State Board of Health of Illinois. He is acknowledged to be one of the best funeral directors in this or any other locality, performing his duties with a quiet ease and courtesy that have won for him many warm friends and supporters, who readily recognize and appreciate his valuable services. At present he is connected with the mercantile firm of Hoevet & Ruge, of Lowell.

Mr. Weaver was united in marriage Nov. 11, 1891, to Miss Hattie Flynn, of Rensselaer, and to them have been born three children, two boys and one girl. He and his family are held in high esteem by all for their many rare qualities.

(Compiled from the Souvenir Album of Lake Co., Ind., Crown Point-Lowell, June 18-19, 1909.)

WEBER FAMILY
F297

Ronald William Weber was born in Chicago, June 12, 1933, and lived on the south side with his parents, Donald Carl Weber and Evelyn Alma Larson Weber. Theresa Dolores Carlascio was born in Chicago, November 5, 1935. She lived on the south side also. In fact, three blocks from Ron. She lived with her parents, Rocco Carlascio and Theresa Musto Carlascio and an older brother Richard Rocco. It was believed that Ronald and Richard played together at one time or another, because they had a friend in common, John Christianson.

The Weber's moved several times in Northwest Indiana, Hamlet and Kingsford Heights and then settled in Gary, with two more children, Richard Thomas and Nancy Jean.

Ron came from Gary to Chicago to meet Theresa, they were both dating friends of each others. Then one night each got stood up by their dates, so Ron and Theresa decided to go on a date. In preparation for their marriage they discovered many things they had in common, such as both being baptized at St. Leo's Church, Chicago. On August 28, 1954, they were married at St. Helena's Catholic Church on 101st Street and Normal, Chicago. At their reception they found that they had much more in common. For example, many of their relatives and friends knew each other. It was like a reunion of neighbors, relatives and friends. These friendships continued and grew throughout their married life.

Ron and Theresa lived with the Carlascio's for a year and a half, at which time their first child Loretta Anne, was born, on July 14, 1955.

During February 1956 they moved to 1435 East End Ave., Dyer, Ind. They lived there for seven years through the birth of their second daughter, Katherine Anne on May 2, 1957 and their third daughter, Judith Anne, on June 25, 1960 and their son, Paul Allen on June 17, 1961.

On June 29, 1962 they moved to their present location, 9393 Old Lincoln Hwy. in the old town of Deep River. They lived in an old home, built in 1849, by Nathan Wood, son of John Wood, who settled the area. This ten room house was a big challenge to them, coming from a five room ranch. Also, they had to do a lot of remodeling to update the house.

They had a large garden in the backyard and they canned 1,000 jars of food the first year. Each year it dwindled to just freezing a few items now and then.

On September 20, 1971 another daughter, Margaret Anne was born.

Ron worked for Republic Steel Company when they were married, then he went on to several other companies trying to find his nitch in life; such as Peter Wheat Bread Company, Martin Oil Service Stations, Borden Milk Company. Then in September 1958 he became a heavy equipment mechanic. He enjoyed this job a lot. Ron was also a member of the 113th Engineers of the National Guard of Indiana.

Theresa was a homemaker. She raised the kids, gardened, canned, and eventually got involved in Dyer Junior Women's Club and Girl Scouts as an assistant leader. After moving to Deep River, she became more involved in Girl Scouts, Eastern Star, Jobs Daughters, Cub Scouts, DeMolay, and church activities.

After the formation of the park the family became involved in the Deep River Park as volunteers.

On July 10, 1976 Loretta Anne married Stephen Dwayne Bannwart from Wanatha and had three children, Tanya Elizabeth born January 25, 1981 in Fort Wayne, Ind. Michael Adam was born December 5, 1984 in Hammond, Ind. Mathew Aaron was born November 28, 1987 in Michigan City, Ind. On August 19, 1983 Judith Anne married David Michael Case from Hobart, Ind. On March 26, 1983 Katherine Anne married Brian Everett Trager from Porter County and had two children, Kyra Brianne born July 3, 1984 in Valparaiso, Ind. and Kyle Morgan born on August 15, 1986 in Virginia Beach, VA.

by Theresa Weber

WEILER, CHRISTIAN
F298

Christian Weiler was born in Eislingen, Wurttemberg, Germany December 9, 1826, one of nine children born to John George and Joanna (Kuemmel) Weiler, and grandson of John George and Barbara (Bihr) Weiler. His father and grandfather were cartwrights in Eislingen. John was a member of the Richter (judges) who were members of the village council. Joanna was from Kitzen, a little place with only a few houses, about 4 miles from Eislingen. In Germany the Weilers followed the protestant religion. Up to the 19th century there were either Protestants or Catholics. The denomination depended on the ruler's faith. The Duke of Wurttemberg adopted the Protestant denomination shortly after Luther's Reformation, and thus his people (to which the Weilers belonged) had to adopt it too. In this country the Weilers were Mennonites.

Christian Weiler emigrated to the United States from Harve in France and arrived at New York on the 15th day of May 1853. He was married in 1856 to Anna Catharine Riecker, at Lancaster, New York. Anna was born January 1, 1825 in Germany. Soon after their marriage Christian and Anna left for Indiana. Christian applied to the Circuit Court of Porter County, Indiana for naturalization on August 15, 1856, at the age of 29 years. Christian and Anna settled in section 33 of Ross Township, Lake County, Indiana. His land was on the Lake County side of the Lake-Porter County division road. Their first house was a log cabin. Later on a new house was built in front of the log cabin. They were the parents of four children: (1) Mary Ann, born August 28, 1857, married Willet B. Sykes March 25, 1878; (2) George born August 10, 1859, died October 24, 1902, was married to Ida Lucetta Burge February 21, 1884; (3) Christian, Jr. born November 20, 1861, died May 15, 1879; (4) John E. born August 4, 1864, died May 21, 1940, married Ida L. (Burge) Weiler, his brother's widow, on June 28, 1905.

Christian Weiler was drafted for service during the Civil War, was mustered into the 17th Indiana Infantry, and assigned to Company I, at Michigan City, Indiana, on November 11, 1864. He was 37 years of age, a farmer, with blue eyes, brown hair, and was 5 feet 6 inches tall. In October or November of 1864 he was enrolled in Company E of the 15th Regiment of Indiana Mounted Infantry commanded by Captain Garvey, and received his honorable discharge in June 1865 at Indianapolis.

While Christian was away at war, his brother John, who lived in Porter Township, would walk the six miles from his house to Christian's to check on the family once, and sometimes twice, a week. This was about a two hour walk each way.

In June of 1865, while in the line of duty at Macon, Georgia, Christian contracted a disease due to hardships and improper diet and also suffered severe sunstroke, caused from very great exposure. The injuries caused him to partially loose his hearing in later life, and he also suffered from brain damage.

Christian's daughter, Mary Ann Weiler, was born August 28, 1857, and married Willet Bound Sykes March 25, 1878. Willet was born Dec. 21, 1850 in Tioga County, Pennsylvania, son of Charles N. and Susannah (Waldron) Sykes. Willet and Mary Ann left Lake County, Indiana and settled in Claytonia, Nebraska, where their five children were born, Susie Ann; Jennie Emily; Irvin; Ward; and Ora. Willet died December 24, 1924 and Mary Ann died June 9, 1936.

George Weiler, son of Christian, was born Aug. 10, 1859, and married Ida Lucetta Burge Feb. 21, 1884 at Valparaiso, Indiana. Ida was born Aug. 11, 1865 in Ross Twp., Lake Co., Indiana, daughter of Cyrus and Koziah (Blake) Burge. George and Ida had two children: (1)Arthur George born March 23, 1885 at Crown Point, married Olive Myrtle Thompson Dec. 21, 1910 at Hebron, Indiana. They had an adopted son, Albert, who married Viola Verna Phillips on Jan. 1, 1929. Olive died Sept. 6, 1938 at Gary, Indiana. Arthur married 2nd to Mary Jane Boone. (2) Pearl Jessie, born July 16, 1890, married Richard August Doepping Jan. 24, 1912, son of Rinehart and Sophia Doepping. They had one son, Earl George, born July 7, 1915, who married Mildred Antrim of Hebron, Indiana. Earl presently occupies the Christian Weiler homestead farm. Richard died Dec. 21, 1928, and Pearl married his brother, William Karl Doepping October 31, 1936. Pearl died August 2, 1983, at the age of 93.

John E., youngest child of Christian and Anna Weiler, was born Aug. 4, 1864, and married Ida L. Weiler June 28, 1905 in Lake County, Indiana. Ida died April 5, 1937 at her home near Deep River. John died May 21, 1940 at his home, following a stroke of paralysis.

Christian Weiler died October 8, 1895 at Logansport, Indiana. Anna died at the home of her daughter, Mrs. William Sykes, in Wilbur, Nebraska, December 13, 1900. Her remains were shipped to Ainsworth, Lake County, Indiana, for interment beside her husband in Deer Creek cemetery.

by Betty L. Williams

WELLS, RODMAN H.
F299

Wells Founding Father

Rodman H. Wells was born in Crown Point, June 6, 1838, the son of Henry and Adaline Wells natives of Massachusetts. Both of his grandfathers were also from Massachusetts and both served in the war of 1812.

Rodman's father Henry came into Lake County, in 1836 from Michigan and started farming in the vicinity of Crown Point. Henry and his wife attended the Presbyterian Church and were the parents of five children. Henry was appointed as the first sheriff of Lake county and later was elected Sheriff and County Treasurer.

Rodman H. Wells was reared on the family homestead at Crown Point and attended the public schools there. He worked on the family farm until the Civil War where in August of 1862 he helped raise a company of infantry and enlisted as a private, although he was offered a second lieutenancy.

He served for nearly three years and participated in the Vicksburg campaign but was sent home because of ill health.

After the war he worked again on the family farm and entered the livery business at Crown Point which he carried on for 25 years. In the year 1899, he sold out his establishment at the county seat and in partnership with his son opened large stables at Hammond.

Both before and after the Civil War, Rodman worked as a deputy sheriff and in 1882 he was elected sheriff, as his father before him. He served as sheriff of Lake County for two, two-year-terms or four years.

Rodman H. Wells was a member of the Baptist Church and in 1860 he married Nancy J. VanHouten, a daughter of James and Sallie Ann VanHouten. But after only eleven years Nancy died and left no children.

In 1872, Rodman married Emily W. VanHouten, a sister of his first wife and they had two children.

On Thursday, October 11, 1906 Rodman H. Wells died unexpectedly of paralysis at the age of 68 years.

by Steven Yaros, Jr.

WENDEL FAMILY
F300

Robert Earl Wendel of Lowell, Margaret (Wendel) Budney of Binghamton, New York and Carolynne (Wendel) Miller of Indianapolis are three Crown Pointers born to Lolita (Nichols) and Carl (Karl) Louis Roy Wendel. Although Carl and his brother Harold Arnold Wendel were natives of Illinois, the Wendel family settled in Crown Point about the year 1908. Carl was born July 19, 1903 in Lansing, Illinois and died in an automobile accident in December 1936.

Harold Wendel who was born January 2, 1908 married Edith Taylor in 1935 and died October 20, 1983 was a prominent member of the Crown Point community. He built the first radio station WLBT in Crown Point and for many years owned the Wendel(l)'s Radio and Electric Service on North Main Street. He was with the Crown Point Fire Department for 33 years. His wife Edith was a direct descendant of the Revolutionary soldier Obadiah Taylor. Harold and Edith had no children.

Henry Wendel and Louise Dorothea Marie Brey were the parents of Carl and Harold (Bud). Henry and his siblings Amanda, Ida, Selma, Arnold, Laura, Elsa, Charles, and Fritz were the children of Charles and Sophia Lem(c)ke Wendel. Henry who was born November 28, 1877 in Illinois married in 1901 to Louise owned a greenhouse and operated the Crown Point Floral Company from the corner of Grant and North streets. Henry died in Arizona in November 1933 and is buried in the St. Lucas Cemetery in Chicago. His wife Louise Brey was born in Manitowoc, Wisconsin on August 23, 1878, the daughter of Henry and Augusta Schroeder Brey(e). Louise died June 4, 1965 and is buried in the Lowell Memorial Cemetery.

Charles (or Karl Charlie) Wendel, the father of Henry was born January 15, 1845 in Germany and made a nine week journey from Alsace Lorraine to America at the age of about 17. He settled in Chicago where he worked for his future father-in-law Frederick Lem(c)ke. Charles, the son of Ernest and Elsey Peters Wendel died December 17, 1918 and is buried in the St. Lucas Cemetery in Chicago. Charles' brothers and sisters were Henry, Robert, Walter C., Arnold, Elmer, and Earl. Charles married Sophis Lem(c)ke who was born October 24, 1851 in Germany and died January 20, 1922 in Chicago. Her sister Frederike (1858-1940) married Henry Wendel, a brother of Charles. The parents of Sophia, Frederick and Carolina (Schmidt) Lemcke were natives of Mecklenburg, Germany who settled in Illinois about 1854. Frederick died November 26, – at the age of 76 years.

Henry Brey(e), the father of Louise Brey Wendel was born December 25, 1854 in Mecklenburg, Germany, the son of August Brey. Henry married February 2, 1877 to Augusta Schroeder, the daughter of Johann (or August?) and Wilhelmine Schroeder. Augusta was born June 9, 1857 in Hamburg, Germany and died March 13, 1884 in Manitowoc, Wisconsin. Henry Brey married for his second wife Annie Andrews. Henry died December 4, 1886 in Manitowoc.

August Brey was born January 9, 1833 in Mecklenburg, Germany the son of Fritz (or Fred) Brey (1812-1879) and Helena Luckoff Brey, also natives of Mecklenburg. August died November 3, 1895 in Manitowoc, Wisconsin. His wife Frederica Lueth, the daughter of Hans and Louisa Lueth, natives of Germany, was born in 1829 and died in 1915.

Although some of the vital statistics and cemetery inscriptions noted in this sketch are documented, the remainder of the family information was primarily that given to the author by her grandmother Louise D. Brey Wendel.

by Carolynne L. (Wendel) Miller

WHEELER, HAROLD L.
F301

Region Native Stays Because 'it's home'

Crown Point — There must be something in Northwest Indiana that makes it an attractive place to live. After all, descendants of families who arrived in the 1800s still live here.

Real estate appraiser and Crown Point resident Harold L. Wheeler is a descendant of Solon Robinson, one of the earliest settlers of Crown Point. Connecticut-born Robinson came to the Region in 1834, and many of his family members have remained here.

Aside from service in World War II, attending college and working for a couple of years after college, Harold L. Wheeler has spent his life in Northwest Indiana.

Wheeler's also has been involved in banking and agriculture. His wife, Marty, is the Center Township assessor. They have children and grandchildren who've chosen to stay in the area.

Wheeler said he's stayed here because "it's

home."

"I was so damned glad to come back here after World War II," he said.

"Along with that, it's really a unique area in the whole world. We're close to the Great Lakes. We have excellent soil conditions. Being mid-continent, the routes of transportation and communication really cross here. So we are uniquely positioned. We have a tremendous cross section of people here," he said.

Wheeler said he has a very optimistic view of Northwest Indiana "in particular because of our transportation and our distribution of power, both gas and electric. Our supply of people adds up to being a hell of a place to carry on commerce and industry."

Wheeler said the area has suffered some from its singleness of purpose in relying on the steel mills to provide continued employment. "We have a great potential to diversify and to recover," he said.

His recommendations on how to do that? "Quit crying and get back to work. If you don't know what to do, find something."

One down side to the area is its image of corrupt politics. "Until the general public is willing to clean house in their own particular political persuasion, this will continue to have a stifling effect," Wheeler said.

The federal investigations into corruption at the county government level "should serve as a frightful example to the newcomers and to the oldtimers that they better mind their P's and Q's or they'll do big time — and they should — for violating the public trust," Wheeler said.

"I think the federal government has shown us the way, but we need to take over. Until we do that, we've got a long way to go," he said.

Wheeler said his ancestors stayed here because many were born here, and they liked it. Robinson chose this area because the Indians liked it, Wheeler said.

Robinson was the first postmaster of Crown Point. He became the first county clerk in 1837, and he also helped build and pay for the first county courthouse.

A long line of Robinson's descendants have continued in distinguished service to their country, their county and their city. They also had their hands in running two weekly newspapers that are still published in Crown Point.

Harold L. Wheeler's great-great-grandfather, Col. John, became the county surveyor in 1853. Col. John Wheeler was also the editor and publisher of The Crown Point Register, starting in 1857.

Col. Wheeler sold the newspaper when he went off to fight in the Civil War with the Twentieth Indiana Regiment. He was killed at Gettysburg in 1863.

Col. Wheeler's son, John J., married Belle Holton, a granddaughter of Solon Robinson, in 1870. John J. Wheeler bought The Lake County Star, another weekly newspaper in Crown Point, in 1880. John J. Wheeler also served as Crown Point postmaster, starting in 1892. He was assisted by his son, Fred Y. Wheeler, who later also became postmaster.

When John J. Wheeler died in 1917, son Fred took over editing The Star. Fred's daughter, Charlotte Wheeler Verplank, took over the editing chores in 1947 when she and husband Bert purchased the paper. The Star remained in the family until the Verplanks sold it in 1973.

Harold L. Wheeler's grandfather, Harold H., was the first mayor of Crown Point. Harold H. was the son of John J. Wheeler and the brother of Fred Wheeler. He was also a lawyer and county clerk.

Harold L. Wheeler's father, John Ward, was an engineer well-known for his work in World Wars I and II and the Korean War. He helped build the Alcan Highway in Alaska.

by Petra Luke

WILCOX, STEPHEN
F302

He was the son of Elisha Wilcox and was born 4/29/1766 in New York, but seven years later he and his family moved to Wyoming Co., PA. During the Indian invasions he helped erect the Wyoming Garrison and served during the Revolution with the Connecticut Line. A contemporary said he was ". . . large for his age and an uncommonly strong and handy boy". After the Revolution, he lived in Bradford Co., PA until nearly seventy, but moved with his wife Rachel Campbell Wilcox and their son, James Campbell Wilcox to Lake Co., IN, where they settled along Sauk Trail in Ross Twp. He died 12/19/1847 and is buried in Pleasant View (the old Dutton) Cemetery west of Merrillville. He is one of three Revolutionary soldiers believed to be buried in Lake Co.

Rachel Campbell Wilcox, the daughter of James Campbell and Jane Knox, was born 10/9/1769 in Blandford, MA, and died 6/30/1847, being buried with her husband in Pleasant View Cemetery. Her daughter, Nancy Harriet Wilcox would later marry Julius Alonzo Demmon and tie these pioneer families together.

James Campbell Wilcox married Susan Bosworth and had children Gowin, Hiram, Harriet, Jeffrey, Hamden, Sally, Stephen, Mary, Norman, Rachel, and Inez. He was born 7/11/1809 near Harrisburg, PA, and died 1/19/1864. He too is buried at Pleasant View Cemetery.

by Ruth Demmon

WILDER, REUBEN
F303

Reuben Wilder was the first child of Reuben Wheeler Wilder and Eunice Bailey, who were married at Sterling MA on 6 Feb 1783. Reuben Wheeler Wilder, farmer and schoolteacher, eventually a resident of Geneva OH, was a *Mayflower* descendant through his mother Phoebe (Wheeler) Wilder, descended from William and Susannah White and son Resolved. His father, Jotham Wilder, fought at Bunker Hill at the age of 65.

The family is found at Saltash (Plymouth) VT in the 1790 census, but sometime prior to the 1800 census they moved on, probably to the Norwich NY area, where Reuben's youngest sister Polly was born on Christmas Day, 1802. By about 1805, Reuben met and married Polly Eunice Herring, also originally from Massachusetts, and settled on a farm in Onondaga County NY, where their three oldest children were born: Almon on 21 May 1806, Mary Relief on 25 Oct 1809, and another who died in infancy.

By the time of the birth of their fourth child, Hiram Ordell, on 22 Oct 1811, the family had joined the elder Wilder generation at Batavia NY. There Reuben enlisted in Capt. Richard Godfrey's company at the NY militia in the War of 1812 and served as 1st sergeant from 14 Nov to 4 Dec 1812.

After the War of 1812, after the birth of Louisa in 1813, but prior to the birth of Betsey on 25 Feb 1815, both Wilder generations moved farther west, to the Kingsville OH area, where the younger children were born: Reuben B. on 20 Aug 1817, Cephas on 10 Sep 1819, Nathan W. on 8 Aug 1821, Sarah on 10 Sep 1823, and Riley on 17 Sep 1826.

The family attempted a move west to lower Michigan and were driven out by Indians, but later were successful travelling across the states of Ohio and Indiana, driving their stock along with them, Riley riding the lead horse of the spike team, until they reached the Illinois state line. In about 1837 they settled southeast of a small but rapidly growing town called Chicago, in the area now known as Dyer, and were among the earliest pioneers there. On one trip to Chicago for supplies, the oxen they had driven got loose at night, and the next day they hunted for them in swampy, boggy land, where now stand some of Chicago's tallest buildings whose foundations reach some forty feet underground to bedrock.

By this time several of Reuben and Polly's children had married and established families of their own, some remaining back in northeast Ohio-northwest Pennsylvania; Betsey (Wilder) in Richmond OH, and Hiram and Louisa (Potter) in Pennsylvania. The others joined their parents in the Chicago vicinity; Almon at Crete IL, where he was a prominent citizen; Mary Relief (Hitchcock, Barber) lived at Dyer until her parents' deaths, later at Hobart IN; Reuben B. and Cephas both owned property at Dyer, although Cephas' residence was Chicago. Nathan settled in Crown Point IN after residence near his sister at Hobart.

After Polly's death at Dyer on 4 Aug 1846, Reuben remarried, to Mrs. Jane Holmes, who then became known and loved as "Mother," and whose name was passed on down through the generations. On 30 Aug 1858 Reuben died at Dyer. It is likely Reuben and Polly are buried in unmarked graves in the old Dyer pioneer cemetery, near where their oldest son Almon's first wife Anna (died 5 Mar 1840) is buried.

by Ramona E. Pekarek

WILDER, REUBEN, JR.
F304

Reuben Wilder Jr. was an early settler of Lake County. He came from a family proud of its early American roots and carried on the tradition of its pioneer spirit when he brought his family to the Calumet Region.

Reuben Jr. was born in 1783, the oldest child of Reuben Wheeler Wilder and Eunice Bailey. His father, Reuben Wheeler Wilder, farmer and schoolmaster, was a Mayflower descendant through his mother Phoebe Wheeler. Her great great grandparents, William and Susannah White, came to America in 1620 with the first arrivals. His grandfather, Jotham Wilder, was an early veteran of the Revolutionary War who fought at Bunker Hill. Reuben Wheeler Wilder was also a Revolutionary War veteran, he served with a Massachusetts Regiment in 1779.

The Wilder family moved from Massachusetts to Vermont and on to Norwich, New York by 1802. There Reuben Jr. met and married Polly Eunice Herrin in 1804. They settled on a farm in Onondaga County, NY. Three children were born there and a fourth was born shortly after they moved to Batavia, NY to join the elder Wilders in 1811. The War of 1812 had begun and Reuben Jr. enlisted in Captain Richard Godfrey's Company of Militia as a 1st Sergeant.

The war ended and the two Wilder families moved west to find new land. They settled near Kingsville, Astubula Co., Ohio, and bought farmland. Five more children were born to Reuben Jr. and Polly as the years passed.

In 1834, the older children had married and left home. Almon, the eldest son, Mary Relief and Betsey lived in Ohio, Louisa and Hiram had moved to Pennsylvania with their families. The younger children were growing up and looking to the future. Tales of the rich land farther west challenged them to follow the family tradition and move on seeking a new life, becoming pioneers again.

Reuben Jr. and Polly, although in their late middle years, agreed to join the family in the venture. Michigan was their destination as the preparations were made and farewells were said to the remaining family.

It was with high hopes they started, driving their stock before them, the heavy wagons following, each member had their assigned task each day as they made their slow progress west along the trail. They met a set-back early in the journey when they found they could not go to Michigan. The Indians were hostile and they were driven off the trail. It was too late to go back and the decision was made to continue westward to Indiana or Illinois.

They crossed the prairie land and found that many others had made the journey before them. There were small villages, larger towns and scattered farms along the way as they continued on with the promise of government land ahead. They found the land they sought on the border, just as the Sauk Trail entered Illinois. It would someday be called Dyer.

The land was cleared and planted, a cabin and outbuildings were built. Shelter was important for safety as well as comfort for the family. Wild game for food was plentiful, there were many small animals and birds, but there were predators as well. Wolves and wildcats prowled at night and snakes abounded in the tall grass.

Through the years on the Sauk Trail, they saw much of the life of the area. There were often Indians on the trail in the early days, soon they were followed by the new settlers who poured in from the eastern states and Europe. Farmers of the area took their produce to sell in the growing town of Chicago and farmers from Illinois passed on their way to take their grain to Woods Mill near Hobart.

The hard years passed, and in 1846 Polly Eunice Wilder died. It is believed that she and other family members were buried in an old pioneer cemetery in Dyer. Reuben married Mrs. Jane Holmes on August 12, 1847. She became a beloved second mother to his family. Reuben lived until 1858, after his death, Jane Holmes Wilder moved to Crown Point to spend her remaining years.

It is known that in 1840 and 1850 several of Reubin's sons owned property in Dyer. The oldest son, Almon, who with his family followed to Indiana, owned land on both sides of the state line but sold after the death of his first wife. He moved to Crete and married Mrs. Louisa Raymond. He farmed there for many years and became a prominent resident of the community. Reuben's sons Cephas and Reuben Jr. also sold their Dyer land and moved on, Cephas to Crete, IL and later to Grand Junction, Michigan. Reuben B. married Nancy Ann Parks and lived near Crown Point. Another son, Nathan W. owned land in Dyer until 1851 when he and his wife, Bloomey Jane McLaughlin moved to a farm in Cook Co., IL. He returned to Lake Co., IN after the death of his first wife and his second marriage to Sarah Loucks in 1866. They lived near Hobart until 1880 and spent their remaining years in Crown Point. Riley, Reuben's youngest son, married Minerva Coldwell. They lived in Dyer until 1852 when they moved to Baraboo, Wisconsin to join her parents. Two daughters of Reuben and Polly Wilder, Sarah (Parks) and Mary Relief (Hitchcock-Barber) married and remained in Lake Co., IN.

There are many descendants of Reuben Wilder living in Lake Co., IN today. They remember their American roots with pride. They are also proud that there have been members of the Wilder family in Lake Co. for over 150 years!

by Kenneth A. Mills, Edna (Mills) Huntington, Ramona E. Pekarek

WILDER, RILEY
F305

Riley Wilder, son of Reuben and Polly Wilder of Kingsville and Conneaut OH, accompanied his family to Dyer IN, where he became enamoured by a neighbor, Harriet Minerva Caldwel ("Colwell"), whom he married on 30 May 1847. Harriett was the second child of John and Minerva (Hill) Caldwell, who were married 23 Mar 1828 at Colchester VT, but residing at Westford VT at the time of Harriet's birth on 4 July 1830. In 1837 the Caldwells moved to Lake County, IN, but in 1847 they migrated farther west, to Baraboo WI, leaving Riley and Harriet behind, where Minerva Jane was born on 15 Mar 1848 and Reuben Jasper on 22 Dec 1849. But by 1852 Riley and Harriet moved to Baraboo to be near the Caldwells and attracted by the fertile farmland of central Wisconsin.

In Wisconsin the young family expanded, adding Eunice Augusta ("Gusty") on 1 Jul 1853, Mary Louisa on 20 Jan 1856, John Riley on 11 Jun 1858, Martha Ann on 18 Sep 1863, Harriet A. on 31 Aug 1861, Frank Edwin on 31 Mar 1865, Charles Fredrick ("Fred") on 14 Nov 1868, Lilly on 24 Mar 1871, and Almon Cephas on 19 Feb 1874. Harriet and Lilly died young, but the others grew to adulthood at Baraboo.

Harriett Minerva, B. 4 July 1830, Westford, VT; m. 30 May 1847, St. John Twp, IN; D. 26 June 1905, Baraboo, WI

Martha Ann Richardson, Almon Cephas, Reuben Jasper, John Riley, Frank Edwin, Eunice Aldrich, Augusta, Mary Louisa Richardson, Charles Fredrick, Harriett Minerva (Caldwell) Wilder, Riley Wilder, Minerva (Jane) Martiny.

Riley Wilder, youngest son of Reuben and Polly (Herring) Wilder B. 17 Sept. 1836 Kingsville, Ohio; D. 31 Aug 1908, Baraboo, WI.

The oldest, Jane, married August Martiny, a French-speaking Belgian immigrant and Civil War veteran, and together they raised their family on a farm adjoining that of Riley, west of Baraboo at Freedom. In their later years Riley and Harriet lived with Jane and August, and it is through Jane's granddaughter, Evelyn Stewart of Baraboo, we have some clear memories of these ancestors.

According to Evelyn, Riley always had a VanDyke beard, was a small man, and bent, his final affliction, passed on to each generation from then on known as the "Wilder back." His ailment did not hinder him as he sat, but he bent forward very deeply when he walked. Harriet was little and frail, but with very large, bright brown eyes. Her hair was parted in the middle and kept black by dipping her comb into a clear colored mixture in a jar on her bureau. She combed her hair very smoothly down over her ears to a bun in the back, and she deliberately avoided "plaited hair, etc." In her little dress with a little white collar she looked like Old Mother Hubbard. Evelyn recalled a visit when August drove his fringeless surrey, carrying Riley and Harriet, to their home along the Wisconsin River. Riley gently led Harriet into the house for an all-day visit. They brought along a bag of brown sugar with a sizeable bag of walnut meats tucked in the top, and during the visit they made fudge for everyone, a treat to delight especially the children.

On 26 June 1905 Harriet died of heart failure, but Riley survived until 31 Aug 1908. From the previous October until July he had visited his children and their families in South Dakota. But after a fishing trip at Delton with his friend John Iber he succumbed to a lung and throat ailment. To their own children Riley and Harriet devoted their lives, worthily preparing them for adulthood in many ways, but especially remembered are the daily worship services in their home.

The children who settled near Hartford SD were Reuben, Gusty (Aldrich), John and Fred. Reuben never married, but his farming efforts there are memorialized by his 1882 historic homestead designation. Fred's descendants organize family reunions each July at Storm Lake, IA. Mary Louisa married George Richardson and settled in a farming community at Bryant, SD. Their son William Riley Richardson, farmer, Baptist minister, and schoolteacher, left writings including our account of Riley's move from Ohio to the pioneer settlement near Chicago. Martha married George Richardson's brother Walter, a Civil War veteran, and they spent most of their lives at Cadott, WI. Frank sunk family roots at Baraboo, but he ended his life in an oil rig accident at Coalinga, CA. Almon became a railroad engineer residing at Waukegan, IL, and relatives recall him to be a friendly man with the habit of frequently checking the time on his pocket watch.

by Ramona E. Pekarek

WILDERMUTH, ELIAS AND OLIVE
F306

The oldest of Henry and Barbara (Burns) Wildermuth's nine children, Elias Wildermuth was born March 2, 1850, in Pulaski County, Indiana. Included in the household were Henry's two children of his first marriage. Pioneering was part of Elias' heritage. His ancestors had come to Pennsylvania from Germany in the mid-eighteenth century. They moved on to Ohio just as it was achieving statehood and then on to Indiana in time to be original purchasers of land in Pulaski County, Indiana. Elias' mother, born in Germany, came to this country when she was eleven and married Henry on her eighteenth birthday. Although her grandchildren remember her singing German lullabies, she was not allowed to speak German in the home while Henry was around.

In 1875, Elias married Olive Herrick, the daughter of Joseph and Sarah Elizabeth (Hickman) Herrick. Joseph had come to America from England when he was eighteen, served in the Union Army during the Civil War, and, eventually, became a farmer in Pulaski County. Elias and Olive had four sons: Harry, Ora, George and Joe. Their only daughter died at birth.

As a young man, Elias taught school in a walnut log schoolhouse near his farm in Van Buren Township, Pulaski County. Farming, however, was his chief occupation until 1904 when he retired to Star City.

Perhaps partially motivated by the pioneer spirit of his ancestors, Elias, at age 56, chose to participate in the founding of a new city on the shore of Lake Michigan. This decision to move to Gary was encouraged by his two older sons. Harry, who was a locomotive engineer for the Pennsylvania Railroad, passed through Lake County on his regular run from his hometown of Longasport to Chicago and caught the excitement generated by all the activity in northern Lake County. Even before Elias moved to Gary, both he and Harry had purchased land there. Elias' son, Ora, a new graduate of Indiana University, had moved to Gary in 1906. In the spring of 1907 Elias packed the family's possessions in a wagon, hitched up the team and, with his ten-year old son, Joe, made the three day trip from Star City to Gary — a distance of 75 miles. Olive followed on the train.

Shortly after arriving, Elias opened Gary's first feed store. With a whole city to carve out of the sand dunes, hundreds of horses were needed to pull the grading equipment. The business of selling hay, oats, corn and straw flourished. There was a spur of the railroad in front of the shack store and, although he always kept some feed on hand in the store, most of it was sold from the railroad car. At first the family lived above the store, but soon built a home at 425 Jefferson St.

Elias became an active citizen of Gary. When the first iron ore shipment was to arrive in Gary, the US Steel Corporation invited the leading citizens of the town to ride the boat from the South Chicago Harbor to the new Gary Harbor. Elias was among those invited. For the next several years Elias ran the store, invested in the construction of couple of buildings, and found time, in 1910, to be an enumerator for the US Census.

After a short illness, Elias died on January 2, 1915, and was buried at Oak Hill Cemetery. Two of his sons preceded him in death. In December 1907, George was found decapitated along side a railroad track. The murderer was never found. Harry died in a railroad accident in 1910. Joe continued to live at home with his mother who opened her home to boarders — some of whom became Joe's life-long friends. After Joe was married, Olive lived with them at 660 West 8th St. Joe's wife always spoke of her Mother-in-law with great affection. Olive's granddaughter, Maxine (Ora's daughter), was a frequent visitor and the two were very close. Olive Wildermuth died in 1925 and was buried along side her husband.

Representing a generation older than many who were part of the formative years of Gary, Elias and Olive Wildermuth lent their spirit and experience to this burgeoning new city full of 20th century pioneers and became forever a part of its history.

by Dorothy Wildermuth Vekasi

WILDERMUTH, JOE AND MADELEINE
F307

In the upstairs back bedroom of the family's farm house in Pulaski County, Indiana, Joe Henry Wildermuth was born on July 6, 1897. Named for his two grandfathers, Henry Wildermuth and Joseph Herrick. He was the fourth — and last — son of Elias and Olive Wildermuth. In 1907 he moved with his parents to the fledgling town of Gary, Indiana.

Ten-year-old Joe became Gary's first newsboy, selling Chicago papers like hot cakes to the construction workers returning home from work on the steel mill. He also had the only agency in Gary for the *Saturday Evening Post* and sold the first *Gary Tribune*. When his father hired an architect to design a commercial building he planned to have built, Joe was intrigued. It was the beginning of Joe's commitment to a career as an architect. When only thirteen, he worked for a summer in an architect's office and, while a student at Emerson High School, he prepared plans for a schoolhouse addition for the Board of Education. In 1920 he graduated from the School of Architects at the University of Illinois and returned to Gary to become its first hometown graduate architect. During these years, he enjoyed sum-

191

mer sports. He became the tennis champion of Gary at one time and had a golf trophy for his efforts on the links.

About this time Madeleine Havens moved to Gary with her parents, Lola and Daniel (known as "Doc") Havens. After graduating from Emerson High School, Madeleine entered Northwestern University. Her mother died in the spring of 1922 and the following fall, Madeleine did not return to college. On January 18, 1923, she married Joe Wildermuth at the home of her aunt and uncle, Gertrude and Frank O. Hodson.

While Joe's mother was living, the young couple shared a home with her. Later they moved to 755 Arthur St. It was a friendly neighborhood with Fourth of July block parties, and with baseball games in the middle of the street. Their two children, Richard and Dorothy attended nearby Horace Mann School.

Madeleine became active in the social life of Gary and was a member of the Beta Gamma sorority. Their home was frequently the scene of social gatherings as well as always serving as a focal place for their children and the neighborhood. The children were allowed to use the living room for their self-produced plays which included rigging up sheets for the stage curtains, arranging chairs for the audience and selling homemade candy at the door. By the time Joe arrived home in the evening, however, everything was back in place.

Joe became Gary's school architect. In addition to schools, he designed for Gary many libraries, several churches, the Court House and Jail and, when only thirty years old, he was the architect for Gary's Memorial Auditorium. The Auditorium's cornerstone was laid at an exciting time in Gary's history. The headlines of the *Gary Post-Tribune* screamed "Visitors Marvel as Steel City Marks Advance with Ceremonies." The brand new Gary Hotel housed the out-of-town dignitaries who had come to witness Gary's "Discovery Days." It was a tight schedule with an inspection of the new Post-Tribune building at 2:30, the laying of the cornerstone for the City Hall at 3, the ceremony for the Memorial Auditorium at 4 and the formal opening of the Commercial Club at 5. Because the auditorium was designed to be used for many school activities, the ceremony at that site featured students with Joe the only adult speaker. Wanting to make the proper impression, 30-year-old Joe had rehearsed his speech at home. When the city fathers saw the series of events falling behind schedule, they asked Joe to shorten his speech, which, of course, he did. Family members were all present, but their memories of the events were overshadowed by a small boy. As Joe delivered the abridged version of the speech his three-year-old son, sitting on his uncle's shoulders to witness the ceremonies, shouted, "Daddy, you forgot something!"

Joe and Madeleine's world was shaken, when Dick, barely six, was hit by a car and suffered a fractured skull. The following year, while coming home from school, he was seriously injured when struck by a speeding truck. He seemed to be recovering from these injuries when a serious infection left him with an illness that required bedside teachers for a good part of each school year. This was reversed after 1937 when Madeleine took the children to Florida for an entire winter.

During the depression, Joe's architectural office stood empty while Joe worked as Assistant Manager and Chief Appraiser for the United States Home Owners Loan Corporation for Northern Indiana. Because the architectural work had required frequent evening meetings with school boards, etc., Joe's evenings had been frequently interrupted. Madeleine commented that the depression was the only period when the household was on a predictable schedule.

Joe authored a treatise, "Real Estate Valuation" in 1934 and the following year one on schoolhouse design. For a brief period, Joe took an interest in politics, and at one time was elected as a representative to the Democratic state convention.

When the economy improved and Joe returned to his architectural career, he resumed his work with Gary schools and libraries. He also designed buildings throughout Indiana including the Indiana State Board of Health Building, a hospital at the Soldiers and Sailor's Children's Home in Knightstown, and many buildings at Indiana University. Joe was on the Indiana State Architectural Board for thirteen years serving as Chairman for several of those years.

In 1935 Joe helped organize the Gary Federal Savings and Loan Association and he served on its board from the beginning. For a time, after retiring from his architectural work, he served the bank as Vice President, then President, retiring in 1962.

In 1939 the family moved to 8805 Lake Shore Dr., which immediately became the summer gathering spot for the Horace Mann High School friends of their children. Even in the winter, when the tennis court in front of the house was flooded for ice skating or there was snow for tobogganing at Marquette Park, their home would fill with young people. During World War II Dick served in the Army Air Corps; but summertime continued to find the girls — and any boys home on furlough — at the Wildermuth's beach home. Madeleine helped out at the Gary Service Men's Center, and regularly invited sailors from the Great Lakes Station to join the young people in the fun at her home.

Back when the children were young, a regular Sunday afternoon activity for the Wildermuths was to drive out into the countryside and look at farm land. Although Joe's family moved off the farm when he was quite young, he always insisted that he was a farmboy at heart. Eventually, he purchased some land southeast of Crown Point near Leroy. With little architectural work available during the war, Joe determined to learn everything about modern farming. He was in contact with the Agricultural School at Purdue and all but haunted the Lake County Farm Agent. Under Joe's direction, the farm transformed from a place of questionable buildings and land production, to a thriving, profitable farm with showplace barns and home. Joe personally went to Texas to purchase cattle and was perhaps his happiest when checking the conditions on his farm astride his Texas cow pony. Shortly after the war, they sold the lake house and moved to the farm. They also maintained an apartment in Gary at the Vesta Court apartment building (1619 W. 5th Avenue), which Joe had designed early in his career and later owned.

Joe tended to become totally engrossed in what he was doing and cared little for conforming to convention. This combination often caused his actions to appear bizarre to others and the family had a whole repertoire of what they called "Joe Stories." One such time, Joe happened by a farm auction and stopped in. He soon began to participate and ended up the high bidder on a large sow. To transport his purchase, he just put down the top of his convertible, placed the hog in the passenger's seat and drove down the highway — unconcerned about the astonished stares.

Throughout the years the Wildermuths held membership in City Methodist Church where Madeleine participated in the West Side Division, where their teenage children were active in the Epworth League, and where their daughter was married. In 1947 — within two weeks of each other — each of their children was married. Richard married Helen Cole, daughter of Amos N. and Lillian (MacAdoo) Cole. A graduate of the University of Michigan Architectural School, Dick practiced architecture in northern Indiana for most of his career and is responsible for many of its public buildings. After rearing their two children, Helen began a movement to clean up Gary's appearance garnering help from industry yet keeping a grass roots appeal. She served as Gary's commissioner for beautification under Mayor Richard Hatcher. In 1972, they moved to New England. After graduating from the University of Wisconsin, Dorothy married Michael E. Vekasi, son of Michael and Elizabeth (Bazin) Vekasi. They moved to Michigan where they reared their three sons.

By 1953 Joe had retired from his architectural business in Indiana and built a home in the Florida Keys, where he practiced architecture on a limited basis. Each summer, however, they returned to their Indiana farm residence. Their children and five grandchildren were frequent visitors to their home on the farm and in Florida. In later years they summered with their daughter in Kent County, Michigan and, when Joe died at the close of 1972, he was buried there. Madeleine survived him by six years.

by Dorothy Wildermuth Vekasi

WILDERMUTH, ORA L.
F308

"It was dark outside, but the lights were bright on the Christmas tree. Everything was waiting. Then we heard the sleigh bells. Dick and I ran to the door to let in Uncle O and Aunt Cordie. Now the magic of Christmas Eve could begin." That is the way Dorothy (Wildermuth) Vekasi remembers her uncle, Ora L. Wildermuth. He was a good deal older than her father and not a daily part of her life, but holidays always brought the families together. Uncle O, with his sense of history, was wont to save things of the past — like the sleigh bells — so they could be a part of the future.

Ora Wildermuth's past harkened back to an era that was hard for his niece to imagine. Born in 1882 he attended a district school in Van Buren Township, Pulaski County, Indiana. It was a one room school and the teachers often had no more than an eighth grade education. In class the students were drilled in the fundamentals, and, as they hiked through the forest from their farm homes to school, running their traps on the way, they learned firsthand about woodmanship and the ways of nature. Continuing an education past eighth grade proved a challenge, but Ora seemed to thrive on challenge. He had to travel to Star City for high school, where, by his fourth year, he was the only student and the trustee refused to hire a teacher for one student. Undaunted, Ora boarded in Winamac, and completed high school there. He credited his farm upbringing and the education he received in Pulaski County, both in and out of the classroom, with giving him the breadth of background upon which he drew the rest of his life.

After high school Ora taught school for a season, then enrolled in Indiana University. For the next four years he divided his time between studying and earning money to continue. In 1906 he received a LL.B. from Indiana University Law School, was admitted to the bar, and moved to northern Lake County where a new town was being carved out of the sand dunes.

For someone who liked challenges, the embryo town of Gary was the place to be. He arrived in August 1906, when there was little besides a mill under construction and few people other than the construction workers. He worked for a couple of months laying concrete for the first blast furnace. With families beginning to arrive it became evident that there was a need for a school. A three-man school board was chosen with A.F. Knotts president and Ora was named teacher. Recalling those days when he and Knotts were rooming together at the old Fitz Hotel, Ora jokingly commented, ". . . the teacher had no difficulty in reaching his board, and the board was in comparatively frequent touch with the teacher, at least physically, for we slept in the same bed and he who slept in the back had to get in first for there was not room to walk around the bed." The schoolhouse was located just north of what was to become 4th Ave. and the west side of Broadway. Its space for 36 students was not adequate for the number of youngsters and the story goes that, when the seats were filled, the door was closed. If you wanted an education, you couldn't tarry on the way to school. The need for books was quickly apparent and a committee of women suggested holding an oyster supper in the schoolhouse. They wondered about attendance, but word was sent to the construction camps and on the appointed night the schoolhouse was jammed. Enough money was raised for 75 books. Thirty years later Ora was quoted, "I took charge of the collection [of books], though I didn't know a thing on earth about handling a library. The youngsters found some cardboard somewhere and cut up cards. I'm sure our system wouldn't pass muster now."

Before winter — across Broadway from the schoolhouse — Ora constructed a tar-paper covered shack in which he lived and had his first law office. Because on cold nights tramps were wont to break into the schoolhouse and use the books to fuel a fire, the books were moved to Ora's office. Thus, within a few months, Ora Wildermuth had become Gary's first resident lawyer, first schoolteacher, and first librarian.

All of his life Ora maintained a law practice in Gary with offices at 690 Broadway. He was the first president of the Gary Bar Association and chairman of the committee on admissions to the bar from 1916 to 1925. He belonged to Bar Associations in the District and State as well as the American Bar Association. He was Gary's first city judge serving from 1910-1914. He is credited in a 1943 American Library Association Bulletin with rewriting Indiana's library laws and by Charles Roll in "Indiana 150 Years of American Development" with being identified with much of the important litigation that came before the courts during his years of practice. At a gathering of Gary pioneers in the mid 1905's, Judge Wildermuth was asked about the stories that circulated about his ridiculously low fees. He responded that those stories were greatly exaggerated and added, "First they said I defended a fellow charged with petty larceny and charged him $10. The next time around the charge was grand larceny and my fee was $5. Finally the said the charge was first degree murder and my fee was $2."

Interest in education became a lifetime commitment for Judge Wildermuth. In 1929 he was elected to Indiana University's Board of Trustees and continued on the board until he retired in 1951, serving as president for nearly thirteen years. At retirement he was named President Emeritus for life. He was one of the incorporators of the Indiana University Foundation and a member and officer of its board. He also served as a trustee of the Waterman Institute for Scientific Research. Ora's interest in educational institutions expanded and, in 1939, he was elected president of the Association of Governing Boards of State Universities and Allied Institutions. In a tribute from this organization, Ora was described as a "gentle, wise, scholarly man" with a "youthful spirit" who had a "lasting influence on the future of public education and of higher education." Indiana University awarded him an honorary LL.D. in 1952, and in 1971, named its Intramural Center in his honor.

Ora also had a lifelong dedication to library development. In 1908 in Gary he and William Wirt, the founder of the Gary public school system, felt Gary needed a full-fledged library. Ora researched the legalities of setting up a library board and found that the law required five years of residency for board members. Because Gary had not existed that long, it was a requirement that needed circumventing. Believing in the autonomy of a library board, the two men devised a method of establishing a library under the school board but run by a library board which merely reported its actions to the school board. Although awkward in the beginning, this system allowed the library board to be in existence from the start and, once the law allowed, totally independent. On March 30, 1908, the library was officially begun with the first board consisting of Msgr. Thomas Jansen as president and William A. Wirt, Mrs. John E. Sears, and Ora L. Wildermuth as members. Even though they had yet to get a stick of furniture or a book, the board hired a librarian, Louis J. Bailey. Later Ora commented with a chuckle, "Smartest thing we ever did." In the fall, when the library opened, it had 936 books, a traveling library of 250 books and 75 magazines. Ora remained a member of the library board for 50 years serving as president for 35 of those years. The Branch Library in Miller is named for him.

As with education, Ora Wildermuth's interest in libraries expanded and he served as president of the combined Gary-Lake County Library Board from 1940-1948. He became president of the Indiana Library Trustees Association and held various offices in the Trustees Section of the American Library Association which, in 1943, awarded him its Citation of Merit for his work as a trustee. In an address to that organization honoring Judge Wildermuth and recounting his role in establishing the Gary Library, Laurance J. Harwood said, "There was not [even] the oft-mentioned blade of grass from which to make two grow. He planted the first blade."

In a 1946 letter to I.U. Alumni Secretary, George G. Heighway, Wildermuth commented on his joy in working with the University and the Gary Library, but noted that it left little time for his law practice. He concluded, "Paradoxical as it may seem, one many enjoy living so much that he starves himself to death." Despite these tugs on this time, his interests were not limited to law, education, and libraries. In the early days of Gary, he was part of a group that gathered in the only place they could find — above a saloon — to organize an interdenominational church. Later he assisted in the organization of Gary's First Congregational Church and was a member of its board of trustees from its inception. During World War I he was a "Four-Minute Man" receiving a certificate of honor signed by Woodrow Wilson, and during the depression he was Chairman of the Governor's Committee of Unemployment Relief. Judge Wildermuth was a democrat, and, when young, he was active in politics. He was a member of the old Commercial Club in Gary and was the sixth President of the Chamber of Commerce for a year. He was an active advocate and patron of the YMCA, where his favorite sport was volleyball. For a time he was a director of the Indiana State YMCA. He was one of the original organizers and officers of Turkey Creek Country Club.

Judge Wildermuth showed leadership in commercial ventures serving as President of Gary and Southern Railroad Co. from 1918 until it was sold in 1928 and President of Gary and Hobart Traction Co. from 1916 to 1924. For a time he was Vice President and Director of Barnes Ice and Coal Co. in Gary, Secretary and Director of Lake City Ice and Coal Co. of Michigan City, and a Director of Glen Park State Bank.

Cordelia Wilds, daughter of John and Sophia (Kelley) Wilds, and Ora Wildermuth were married in Peru, Indiana, on September 3, 1907. Their daughter, Maxine, graduated from Emerson High School in 1927. She married John Tula who died in 1962. She is still a resident of Lake County. After a long illness, Cordelia died April 23, 1941. The following year Ora married Mae R. (Arnold) London, who had been Porter County Clerk for a number of years. Ora was widowed again in 1951 and four years later he married Mildred (Polak) Frolik, a long time teacher at Horace Mann High School.

For many years Ora resided at 626 Pierce Street in Gary in a large formal house surrounded by ample grounds enclosed in a wrought iron fence. A tunnel connected the garage to the basement where Ora had set up a small woodworking shop. Ora loved wood and would seek out some special piece that had meaning for a retiring president or governing board and would then fashion it into a gavel as a gift. Ora also built an informal home at 7432 Lake Shore Dr. Later in life, after a serious illness, he wintered in Naples, Florida, where he maintained a residence as well as one at 5251 E. 6th Place in Gary. While in Naples, he served on the Collier County Library Board of Trustees and was a member of the Florida Library Trustees Association.

Ora Wildermuth died in Gary on November 16, 1964. Funeral services were held at the City Methodist Church with Herman Wells, President of Indiana University, giving the principal eulogy. He is buried at Oak Hill Cemetery. He will, of course, be remembered for his many accomplishments. He will also be remembered as a man in touch with his roots, yet ever interested in the present and how he might best serve it. He was the consummate storyteller — always including a sprinkling of humor.

by Dorothy Wildermuth Vekasi

WILLE, FRIEDRICH FAMILY
F309

Friedrich and Maria (Knief) Wille. Circa. 1885

Friedrich Wille was born July 23, 1823 in Ohndorf, HessenSchaumburg, a province of Hannover Germany. He married Maria Knief who was born April 11, 1825 in Riepen, Hessen-Schaumburg, Hannover, Germany. Her parents were J.H. Christoph Knief of Riepen and Ilse Maria (Piepho) of Beckedorf, Churhessen, Germany. Friedrich and Maria left their homeland for America in 1849.

After arriving in America, they found their way to Chicago, Illinois where Friedrich learned of a place to farm in the area of Elk Grove, Illinois. They farmed in Elk Grove; then decided to move to Indiana. On January 10, 1852, he purchased a land grant that was issued by President Pierce for land located in Section 12. This land was located on the side of 113th Avenue. On April 15, 1853, he purchased another piece of property in the N.E. section of Section 12. The 1860 census shows their residence in Hanover Township, Lake County Indiana. In August 1859, the Zion United Church of Christ, known then as the Hanover Prairie Church and also as the Zion Evangelical and Reformed Church, was built directly across from Friedrich's property.

The Wille's neighbors to the west were George and Margaretta Bottner. George, born in 1837, and his wife Margaretta (Theobald), born in 1835, were from Germany. He was a tailor there. Old records show that George, had worked as a tailor in Dyer. They had two sons: Charles born in 1860 and George Jr. The Bottner property was in the vicinity of where George Charles later built his home.

Friedrich and Maria, having been members of the Elk Grove Lutheran Church, then became members of St. John's (Eagle Lake) Lutheran Church in Washington Township in Will County Illinois. Some of the children were baptized, confirmed and married there. Later, they transferred to the new church directly across the road from their property on 113th Avenue.

On a knoll just across the road from the church, Friedrich built a house, a barn and some outbuildings. Livestock, especially the chickens, occasionally would break out and get onto the church property. So to solve the problem without any "Fuss," Friedrich moved all the buildings to a parcel of land owned by the Wille family (relatives) that lived on the Illinois side of State Line Road, north of 113th, in Crete Township, Will County. Of course, buildings were not so large to move at that time. (Over the years this land in Illinois had been owned by Philip, August, John and William Wille. The buildings, under new ownership, remain on that same site on well maintained property.)

Friedrich and Maria's children included: Henry and Engelein, both of whom died in infancy; Maria, born in Elk Grove Illinois, who married Conrad Bock of Hannover Germany and resided in rural Beecher, Illinois; J. Fred, born in Elk Grove, who married Wilhelmina Ostermeier and resided in Wells, Minnesota, he later married his second wife, Maria Wente (both wives were from Beecher, Illinois); Sophia, who married Henry F. Batterman II and resided near Dyer; John F., who married Sophia Katz of Kansas and moved to Morris Minnesota; Henry Carl, who married Louise Hueper, of Lake County, and then resided in Wells, Minnesota; William, who married Louise Seehausen and in 1906 moved to Enid, Oklahoma; Dorothea, who married August Piepho and resided in rural Dyer, Indiana; and Wilhelmina, who married Fred Fiene of Beecher, Illinois and resided in Freeborn, Minnesota.

by Mrs. Ralph Oldendorf

WILLIS, ARLENE
F310

Arlene Willis, the second daughter of John Vernon Willis and Hazel Beatrice Mulvany, was born 9 August 1932 in Omega Township, Marion County, Illinois. John Vernon Willis, the son of John Littleton Willis and Cynthia Ann Hall, was born 2 April 1909 in Marion, Williamson County, Illinois. Hazel Beatrice Mulvany was born in Omega Township, Marion County, Illinois, 23 March 1908 to Samuel Jesse Mulvany and Lulu Etna Gordon. John Vernon Willis married Hazel Beatrice Mulvany 25 March 1928 in Salem, Marion County, Illinois.

The other two daughters of John Vernon and Hazel Beatrice Willis were Norma Marceline and Shirley Joyce. Norma Marceline Willis was born 15 March 1930 in Salem, Marion County, Illinois. She married John Henry Rabatine 29 October 1949 in Hammond, Indiana. John Henry Rabatine was born 18 December 1924 in Hammond, Indiana to John H. Rabatine and Laura Griese. John and Marceline Rabatine have four daughters, Jessica Ann (born 11 August 1951), Jennifer Lee (born 11 August 1951), Karen Lynn (born 6 August 1952), and Susan Kay (born 21 October 1954). John and Marceline Rabatine are now living in Hobart, Indiana.

Shirley Joyce Willis was born 15 August 1939 in Hammond, Indiana. She married William John Cook III 26 November 1957 in Gary, Indiana. William John Cook III was born 17 December 1937 in Hammond, Indiana to William John Cook Jr. and May Mitchell. William and Shirley Cook have three sons and one daughter, William John IV (born 6 July 1958), Jeffrey Willis (born 10 May 1960), Steven Dane (born 3 August 1962), and Nancy Michelle (born 14 December 1966). William and Shirley Cook are now living in Manassas, Prince William County, Virginia.

John Vernon and Hazel Beatrice Willis came to northwest Indiana from southern Illinois about 1933 because of the wide variety of jobs available in northwest Indiana. Since the World's Fair was in Chicago, John and Hazel Willis took their two daughters, Marceline and Arlene to see the World's Fair for the first time.

About 1935, John Vernon Willis joined the Carpenter's Union Local 599 in Hammond, Indiana. About 1954, he started his own business which was Vern's Cabinet Shop and the shop was located at Mount Street and 25th in Gary, Indiana. He specialized in custom made kitchen cabinets using all wood parts. He operated the business for about two years. John Vernon Willis became a member of the Masonic Order, Lodge 716 in Gary, Indiana about 1954 too. He was the first male secretary for the Order of the Eastern Star for two years. Hazel Beatrice Willis was a member of the Order of the Eastern Star and a past matron too. John Vernon Willis was a past high priest of the Masonic Order and he was a past president of the Carpenter's Union local 599. He was the first president of the Carpenter's Credit Union in Hammond, Indiana.

Arlene Willis grew up and attended school in Gary and Hammond, Indiana. Arlene also attended school in Indianapolis, Indiana when her father, John Vernon Willis, went to work on the construction of the Veterans Administration Hospital. Arlene got sick often during her childhood and it prevented her from completing high school. Arlene Willis worked at the Austin Drug Store on 11th Avenue in Gary, Indiana in 1949. She worked at the Pig Restaurant on State Street in Hammond, Indiana in 1945. She also worked at Goldblatts Department Store in Gary, Indiana and Vogel's Restaurant in Hammond, Indiana. While working at Austin Drug Store, Arlene Willis met a young man who offered to take her to work because she was walking to work sometimes. Sometimes, she did take a bus to work. This young man that Arlene Willis met was John Ira Pegg. Everyday, John Pegg would come and see if Arlene Willis was walking to work and he offered to give her a ride to work. After several times, she relented and accepted a ride to work.

After dating for several months, John Ira Pegg and Arlene Willis decided to get married. They were married 17 August 1950 in Gary, Indiana (See John Ira Pegg Story).

About 1960, Arlene (Willis) Pegg and her two sons, John William and Robert Eugene, lost their hearing. No medical explanation can be given and proven what caused their loss of hearing. They continued to carry on their normal daily lives even though they wear a hearing aid.

As Arlene's mother, Hazel Beatrice Willis got older, she too lost her hearing. Realizing the value of education, Arlene (Willis) Pegg returned to high school and graduated in 1976 in Griffith, Indiana.

On 6 November 1980, Arlene's father, John Vernon Willis died after a long illness at Saint Margaret Hospital in Hammond, Indiana. He is buried at Elmwood Cemetery in Hammond, Indiana. John Vernon Willis and his wife Hazel Beatrice were living in Hammond, Indiana when he died. Hazel Beatrice Willis is now eighty years old and continues to live in the Calumet Region.

by John W. Pegg

WOOD, GEORGE F.
F311

This prince of good fellows is a product of Crown Point. He was born April 29, 1870, his parents being Martin and Susan Wood. Martin Wood was one of the pioneer lawyers of Lake County, having practiced in Crown Point for over forty years. He served one term in the State Legislature. He died in 1892, but his wife survives, aged seventy-eight years, and makes her home with her children, of whom she has eight, three daughters living in Hammond and one in Kansas; one son in Topeka, Kansas; one in New York City; one in Kansas City, and Geo. F., who resides in Crown Point.

George attended the public schools of his town, and later entered his father's office and read law, and later studied in the office of J. Frank Meeker, and was admitted to the bar of the Lake County Circuit Court. Twelve years ago Mr. Wood was made county constable of Lake County, which position he has filled conscientiously and fearlessly. In his uniform of blue that he wears at all times, he looks the officer that he is. He is familiar with every nook and crook in Lake County and has rendered valuable services to sheriffs and their deputies in apprehending lawbreakers. He is highly respected by all, even crooks, because, while he is firm, he is very congenial. George always carries his trademark with him — the best disposition of any man in Lake County.

(Compiled from the Souvenir Album of Lake Co. Ind., Crown Point-Lowell, June 18-19, 1909.)

WOODS, BARTLETT
F312

The Grand Old Man of Lake County

Bartlett Woods was born July 15, 1818 at Winchelsea, England but spent most of his childhood in Hastings. His father, a postmaster, had two more sons, William and Charles, and a daughter, Charlotte. At eighteen years of age, Bartlett and his brother Charles sailed for the United States in May, 1836. After fifty-seven days at sea, they arrived in New York in August and traveled by boat through the Erie Canal, arriving in Michigan City. After living in Michigan City for a year, Bartlett came to Lake County by stagecoach in 1837. On March 6, the same day he arrived in Lake County, he filed a claim for land which was signed by Solon Robinson, Registrar; the price, $1.25 per acre.

Four years later, he married Sarah Ann Griffin. This union gave them a son, Edmund Bartlett, who later died in Tennessee during the Civil War. Shortly after Sarah's death, Bartlett moved to Chicago for a short time to work with his brother, William, who had come later from London. Tiring of city life, however, Bartlett returned to the farm in Lake County to begin his career as an important early pioneer of the area.

Feeling the need for a housekeeper, in 1847 Bartlett hitched oxen to a wagon and travelled seven miles to Liverpool. Here he persuaded one of Samuel Sigler's daughters, Ann Eliza, to become his wife. That same evening he brought her back to the farm, bag and baggage. Ann Eliza Sigler Woods was characteristic of the pioneer woman. She made all the clothes with just a needle, spinning her own yarn. She would gather rye straw to make straw hats. She cooked over an open fireplace and was known for baking a barrel of flour a month. Being raised in Virginia, she loved her corn bread, a delicacy which Bartlett would eat only as a last resort.

This union produced some notable offspring. The most prominent was Samuel B. Woods, active in public affairs, author, philosopher, farm and civic leader whose life spanned a century of Lake County history. There was Will G. Woods, a well-known area farmer and president of the Peoples' State Bank of Crown Point. And, Walter L. Woods who was a prominent Chicago businessman. There was a daughter, Charlotte Woods Merrill, married to the Hammond resident. Their daughter, Ethel, graduated from the University of Chicago with honors at age fifty-two. And, Lottaville, the general vicinity of the Blockhouse on Cleveland, was named after Charlotte. Another daughter of Bartlett, Alice Woods Cormack, produced a son, Bartlett Cormack, who became a prominent author and playwright. His most famous Broadway hit was "The Racket". Other plays included "Tampico", "The Painted Veil", and "Hey Diddle Diddle". Some of his works were made into Hollywood films such as "This Day and Age", "The Beachcomber", and "The Unholy Partners", the latter adaptation starring Edward G. Robinson.

When Bartlett came here he was not an experienced farmer and depended much on his wife, Ann who was more skilled in her knowledge of farming.

The Grand Old Man of Lake County was eulogized as an honest, honorable, and upright man; dealing fairly and honestly with all whom he had business, always ready and willing to take up the cause of the people, and so fair and straight-forward was he in his discussion of all public questions that he held the respect of friend and foe alike. At thirty years of age he began his active role in Lake County public affairs. He served as State Representative in 1861 and again in 1865, serving the best interests of his constituents. He also served two terms as Commissioner of Lake County and was president of the Lake County Fair, Old Settlers Association, and the Farmer's Institute. He is credited with organizing the Free Soil Movement in Lake County, and, thus, the founder of the Republican Party in Lake County. As a delegate to the Wigwam Convention in Chicago, he helped nominate Abraham Lincoln to run for President. Bartlett Woods believed deeply that as a citizen one must take an active role in the affairs of the county as well as the country.

The Grand Old Man of Lake County was not so unique as he was typical of our early pioneer ancestors to which most of us can attest. They were hard-working and active both in their own affairs as well as those of public concern. They were individuals, strongly opinionated and extremely persuasive; persuasive not for any power or clout they could wheel, but rather for the prestige and respect gained because of their words and their actions.

Presented on May 17, 1975, to the Lake County Historical Society by Bruce L. Woods, great-great grandson of Bartlett Woods.

by Bruce Woods

WRIGHT, EVERETT AND MARY
F313

Everett and Mary (Nichols) Wright

Everett Marshall Wright was born June 27, 1899 at Armstrong, Vermillion County, Indiana, to Reece and Leona (Davis) Wright. The parents later moved to Hammond, where they constructed a brick apartment building on Sibley Street. Two of his sisters also located here, Tressie, who married a Steffy and Odie, who married a Hammond policeman and lived on Elizabeth Street. By his first marriage Everett Wright had Gwen, who married Glenn Hawkins of Crawfordsville and had two children. His second marriage produced no children.

He was a fireman on the New York Central when he met Mary I. Nichols who was visiting friends at Schneider, Indiana, not far from where her parents, John Livingstone and Clara Maude (Graves) Nichols were managing the Linderholm farm, Fernwood. They were married at Danville, Indiana on January 26, 1928 and held a dance in celebration at Lake Village, Indiana on the second floor of Hogan's General Store, which was attended by friends from far and near.

They set up housekeeping in Hammond on Drackert Street and lived there a number of years until Everett became an engineer on the New York Central, the occupation he followed for the rest of his life. In the fall of 1936 they purchased the house at 27 Elizabeth Street, now owned by their nephew, Gerald Born. Mary opened an antique shop in the carriage house, which had been used to liver a horse and buggy when the house was first built by Mr. Norris, one of Hammond's early pharmacists in 1919.

While the country was in the depths of the depression Mary opened the house to roomers, women teachers in the Hammond school system and continued this until World War II, when she took in men boarders, who were employed in the steel mills and were contributing to the war effort. She also was active in local politics, being a Democratic Precinct Committeeman. She also helped Mr. Argus prepare for auction sales and assisted during the sale. After this phase of her life she raised and sold German Short Hair Pointers.

Enjoying travel, she made several trips to the west coast and to New England, Mexico, and Canada. When Everett died in 1957 she continued to live in her home at 8 Ruth Street, Calumet City until 1961, when she moved to Morocco to live in a 14 room mansion built by her uncle, William Nichols for Phillip Smith. She lived here until 1984, when a firebug on the local fire department torched her house and she lost everything. She died four years later. Before moving back to Newton County she studied with noted art instructors at the Chicago Art Institute and continued her studies with Ora Jones, an artist of note. She exhibited many of her oil paintings at the county fair where she won many ribbons.

Mary Wright had roots deep in the history of northern Indiana and Illinois. Her grandfather, Jacob Nichols, left from Hill's Tavern in Momence, Illinois in 1849 for the California Gold Rush and returned ten years later via South America on the ship, Olive Branch, to marry and farm. He raised a family of eight children, with his wife Mary Jane Johnson, the daughter of Leland and Phoebe (Vail) Johnson. They were: William (1861-1917) married Luella Potts, Mary Ann (1865-1964) married Nelson Teeter, John (1868-1935) married Maude Graves, the daughter of Harvey Newton and Louisa Gay (Archibald) Graves, Mary's parents, Clarence, unmarried, Arthur (1875-1934) married Flora Ohms, Sarah Jane (1880-1972) married Henry Slusser, Lavina (1883-1963) married George Corbin, Samuel (1877-1959) married Etta Lahr of Lafayette.

Her great-grandfather, William Nichols, was born on the Manor of Leeds in Fauquier County, Virginia, the son of Samuel Nichols. He married Mariah Van Gundy and was an early settler in Ross County, Ohio, when the capitol was located at Chillicothe. Later the family moved to Columbus and opened the first tavern in that city, and he thereby lost his good Quaker standing for being too worldly. William Nichols then moved to Terre Haute and later to Momence (then Will County) where he constructed a handsome two-story brick home with materials he had shipped by ox cart from Vincennes. The Nichols homestead is located at Six-Mile Grove and the Nichols cemetery is nearby. The family owned some 1200 acres near Momence.

Her grandmother, Mary Jane Johnson, was from an old Quaker, Long Island family. The progenitor, Thomas Vail came to New York from England in 1630, married Sarah Wentworth, sister of the Governor, and started a family that was destined to play an important role in American history. His son, Joseph Vail died in 1698 and his son, Moses Vail married Phebe Platt, who was killed by being thrown from a horse carriage when her children were small. Micah Vail, their seventh child was born September 29, 1730 at Huntington, NY and married Mary Briggs. He moved first to Dutchess County, NY and later to Danby, Vermont, where he and four other families helped lay out the town in 1760. He was moderator of the town meetings, which were first held in his home. Capt. Micah Vail, a member of the Committee of Safety, associated with Ethan Allen and others in defending the town against the land-grab-struggle between New York and New Hampshire. He became one of the six original captains elected by the Green Mountain Boys, who would serve only under officers chosen by themselves. His son, Moses Vail (1755-1809), married Lucy Seeley and his son, Ephraim Vail (1787-1852), married Sarah Averill and were the parents of the above Phoebe Vail. He died at Momence October 12, 1852.

by Gerald Born

YAROS, JOHN FAMILY
F314

From 1880 to 1920, almost four million immigrants arrived in the United States from the old Austria-Hungary Empire. These were an ethical mix of Hungarians, Czechs, Slovaks, Slavs, Croats and Serbs. In this country, they became collectively known as Slavs.

Concentrating in Pennsylvania and in the cities of Chicago, Akron, Toledo, Milwaukee and Detroit, Slavic laborers provided much of the muscle needed for America's iron, steel, and coal industries.

Our Slovak ancestor John Yaros fit this pattern having come to the U.S. in 1885 at the age of 19 from Hungary and his future wife Anna Marcinak came here in 1890 from Hungary also at the age of 20.

It is said they were married in Philadelphia in 1889 when John was 24 and Anna 21 years old. The 1900 Federal Census finds them in McKean County, Keating Township, Pennsylvania with five children and John as a laborer in the chemical works. Our families last name was misspelled in the census the way it sounds Yerrish and long time friends John and Anna Platko and their five children are listed right alongside of them in that census.

Land records show the 50 acres in Semethport, Pennsylvania were purchased on August 23, 1899 from John Platko for $150.00 and sold October 8, 1908 for $94.47.

The family then moved to Batesville, Oklahoma and stayed for approximately three years moving back east in 1911 to Gary, Indiana.

John and Anna Yaros lived at 1236 Cleveland St. in Tolleston, right behind Beverage School and John worked in the Wheel Mill at Gary Steel Works.

John Yaros died on March 19, 1927, at the Cleveland St. address in Gary at the age of 59 years and was buried on March 21, 1927 at Calvary Cemetery in Portage, Indiana. Anna Yaros died seven years later in 1934 and was also buried at Calvary.

John Yaros and Anna Marcinak had eight children as listed below:

John J. Yaros (born 12-28-1891) married Veronica Kurdelak.

George G. Yaros (born May 1893) married Maybelle Stacker.

Anna Mabel Yaros (born 10-14-1894) married Glenn Edward Smith Sr.

Mary (Marie) Yaros (born 7-9-1896) married George G. Yaros.

Susanna (Thelma) Yaros (born 7-6-1898) married John Elmer Pettit.

Rose Yaros (born 3-12-1901) married Elij Gile and on his death George Thomas.

Michael Yaros (born 4-3-1903) married Helen Echols and then June Fitzgerald.

Steven James Yaros (born 3-21-1906) married Wanda Sarah (Doris) Rogers.

by Steven Yaros, Jr.

YAROS, MIKE
F315

Mike Yaros as a leading semi-pro hurler with Rock Island of the Mississippi Valley League. Photo taken 1931.

Semi-Pro Baseball Pitcher

Mike Yaros, one of the best sandlot pitchers ever to come out of Gary, passed away May 8, 1988 at St. Margaret Hospital in Hammond at the age of eighty-five. Mike was born April 3, 1903 one of four boys (John, George, and Steven) and four daughters (Anna Smith, Marie Yaros, Thelma Pettit and Rose Gile Thomas) to John Yaros and Anna Marcinak.

At an early age Mike left school and went to work in the steel mills and started pitching ball for mill teams such as the Locomotive Shop.

YAROS, MIKE H. FAMILY

F316

Mike Yaros player-manager for Spencer Coals of Chicago. Mike is in the center, front row, with hands on bat boy.

The Yaros Family. Front Row: Left to Right: Mike, Jr., Margaret, Laura, Edward. Back Row: Left to Right: Harry, Bertha, Donald, Pauline, Elizabeth

Mike and Mary Yarns

Mike Yaros was just a youngster when he made his debut in semi-pro baseball under the wing of former Gary Fire Chief Wilfred Grant. After a couple of successful seasons with the Firemen, Mike transferred his activities to South Bend with the disbandment of the Firemens Ball Club.

Then for the next few seasons (around 1934 and 35) Mike was South Bend's leading semi-pro hurler, working with the Studebakers and the South Bend Indians. Mike also played ball in the early years for the Moline Plowboys, the Burlington Bees, and Rock Island, all of the Mississippi Valley League.

From 1936 thru 1938 Mike played for Duffy Florals and at Shewbridge field in a 1 to 0 pitching duel beat the great Satchel Paige and his Negro National League All-Stars before a crowd of 6,000.

Also, while pitching for the Duffy Florals, Mike entered the semi-pro hall of fame when he shut out the Connor Empires of Spring Field, Illinois without a hit in the second game of a double header at Shewbridge Field. The Florals won the game 4 to 0.

During 1939 and 41 Mike was a player-manager for Spencer Coals of Chicago. After that he retired from active ball but continued to coach. In 1949 and 1950 he was manager of the Music Maids of Chicago in the National Girls Baseball League.

Mike Yaros married first Helen Echols and then June Fitzgerald and has three sons: Robert, Timothy, Brian, and a daughter Mary.

Mike was a member of the Pitch & Hit Club of Chicago (a professional baseball organization) and he attended many of the Gary Old Timers Banquets.

Some of the headlines in the papers of the 30s describing Mike's ball playing are as follows: "Yaros Pitches Superb Ball; Lines Out Long Three-Bager." "Yaros Stars in Moline's Double Win Over Buns." "Too Much Yaros — Mike Tosses Great Game — Wins by 5 to 0." "Yaros Is Hero as Mates Bunch Hits Off Verdi." "Mike Yaros Twirls Shut Out Ball Against Bears." With Mike Yaros twirling a phenomenal brand of ball the Hobart Cubs turned back the Merrillville Bears." "Yaros Superb as Studebakers Win from Elkhart 4-1." "Mike Yaros Hurls Peerless Ball for Studebaker Nine." "Yaros Turning in Sensational Work for Studebaker Club."

But one of the best compliments given to Mike was related in a Friday July 9, 1937 column Speculating in Sports by John Whitaker as follows:

Caleb White's son, Ralph, who once had a trial with the Cardinals, will tell you that the world's greatest pitcher is not Dizzy Dean, Carl Hubbell, Van Mungo — "The king of them all," says Ralph, "is none other than Satchell Paige, the superman of the colored league, who is now on tour outside the U.S." Paige was beaten only twice all last season, pitching something like 50 games, six of them on successive days when his collection of stars won the Denver semi-pro tourney — a Whiting citizen, the veteran, Mike Yaros, pitched for Duffy Florals last September, when Paige was beaten 1-0 in Chicago. White still talks about Mike's wonderful control that afternoon. Ralph had played against all the colored lads at Denver and knew their weaknesses. "I never caught an easier game in my life," says Ralph. "Mike could have hit a dime all afternoon, whether he was throwing speed or curves."

Mike H. Yaros came from Austria-Hungary at the age of 22, arriving on Ellis Island, New York on July 6, 1907. He first lived with his brother John in Gary, Indiana. Mike met his wife Mary Kochmar in East Mauch Chunck, Pennsylvania while visiting relatives there. The two were married on February 23, 1914 in Carbon County, Pennsylvania and moved to Tolleston.

The family lived in Tolleston until 1926 when Mike heard about land available in Independence Hill, just outside Merrillville. One of the first three families to settled in the area, Mike and Mary built a home on two acres of land located one block west of what is now Highway 55 on U.S. 30.

Mike began working at U.S. Steel and would be an employee for 40 years, serving as crane operator and a crane inspector. While in Tolleston, they also began a family. Six of the eventual nine Yaros children were to be born before they moved to Independence Hillo: (from oldest to youngest) Pauline (husband Darrold Brackett), Margaret (husband Paul Mackanos), Mike F. (Wife Leona Linton), Elizabeth (Husband Joseph Canale), Edward (wife Ruth Murray) and Harry (Wife Betty Lisius).

A large vegetable garden was planted on 1½ acres and many fruit trees were planted. The garden helped provide the large family with necessary foods for canning, etc. One of the first tasks the family accomplished upon moving to their new property was to construct a 92-foot well which was operated by hand. This well is still in service but now operates electrically.

Although there was little else built in Independence Hill when Mike settled there, the family was able to travel to Gary and the county seat of Crown Point by way of street car because the new community was located between the two cities. The cost was ten cents.

The family witnessed the tremendous explosion of construction and population over the years, which was aided by better roads built in the area. The construction of the larger, modern Lincoln Highway (U.S. 30) caused many residents of the area, including the Yaros; to lose part of their property to the government. Along with I-65, U.S. 30 was a major factor in Merrillville's shift from a rural to a more urban environment.

Mike travelled the stone roads from Gary to Crown Point in a 1920 Model T truck, enduring many rough rides and flat tires. Later, the family would own a Model T family car. The more modern transportation method of driving met the older method of taking the street car head-on one day while Mike Sr. was driving with sons Ed and Harry. Mike asked the boys to look for street cars, but somehow they missed seeing one street car, which hit the back of the car. The only damage was to the sturdy old car's bumper, which fell off.

The Yaros family grew even larger in the Independence Hill house. The last three children were born here: Laura (Husband Fred Schilling), Bertha (Husband Russell Bearby) and Donald. All nine children attended Merrillville schools. The children recollect the winter of 1936 when a snow storm hit, stranding all of the children at school. A sled owned by the Kaiser family was used to transport the kids back home. During another major blizzard, a sled was used to take food from Moniger's Grocery Store on Highway 55 back to the Yaros household.

While in school, the younger Mike played varsity basketball and also was a star of the track team. Marge and Mike were varsity cheerleaders, as was Bertha. Laura was named by eldest sister Pauline after school teacher Laura Lennertz. Laura later would have Miss Lennertz as a 6th grade teacher. Bertha Agnes was named after Agnes Fieler, who helped deliver her as a baby. The children enjoyed swimming and other summer-time activities at Fancher Lake in the Lake County Fairgrounds. At that time, the children in the community were told that the lake was "bottomless," that an underground passageway existed between Fancher and Cedar Lakes.

Businesses were few and far between in Independence Hill during its founding; quite a change from the modern day strip malls. The nearest establishment was Kitchel's Corner — a gas station, motel, restaurant and grocery store. Several of the Yaros children were employed there. This was the business which had the first television set in the area. Telephones in the community were part of "party lines" for many years. A nearby farm on the northeast corner of U.S. 30 and 55 was owned by the Keuhl's and served as a source for the Yaros' fresh milk.

Mike, Ed and Harry served in the United States Army in World War II. In an unfortunate turn of events, their mother Mary died at the young age of 45 on September 14, 1943 while the boys were at war. Younger brother Donald also served in the Korean War.

In 1944 the Independence Hill Fire Department was organized as a volunteer station. Harry and Donald served in the position of fire chief for many years, when the station was responsible for much of Ross Township. The volunteer fire department was formed after the DeFoor home on the northwest corner of U.S. 30 and 55 was destroyed by fire.

Mike, Sr. passed away at the age of 88 on October 24, 1975, but the old Yaros home still is occupied by brother Donald. The house has been the principal gathering spot for countless family reunions and holiday celebrations over the years.

Sons Ed, Harry and Don followed in their father's footsteps and worked at U.S. Steel for many years. Mike, Jr. served as management for A&P Food Stores for 20 years and now works for the Merrillville Public School System. Ed Yaros retired and moved to Naples, Florida and has a daughter Kathy Mudrich (Husband Donald) and two grandchildren, who reside in Valparaiso. Harry and wife Betty Yaros remained in Merrillville and have a daughter Michelle Wildes (Husband Tim) and two grandchildren, from Hobart. Mike and Leona Yaros, Merrillville, have a son Michael (Wife Judy) and three grandchildren in Blairstown, New Jersey.

Pauline and Darrold Brackett retired to Marco Island, Florida and have two daughters: Cheryl Seamples (Husband Marcel) and Gale Cannon (Husband Tom), each with one child and each residing in nearby Naples, Florida. Marge and Paul Mackanos also retired to Naples. Their daughter Marsha Carlson (Husband Dr. Milton) resides in Champaign, Illinois and has four children. Son Tarry (Wife Carolyn), of Marion, Ohio, has three children (one deceased).

Elizabeth and Joseph Canale are parttime residents of Marco Island and Schererville. Their daughter Jeri Marabel (Husband Steve), of Naples, has one daughter of her own. Laura and Fred Schilling of Merrillville, have three children. Lori Schilling-Joyce, their daughter, resides in Lake of the Four Seasons with husband Robert. Sons John (Wife Lorena) and Randy (Wife Cindy) both reside in Phoenix, Arizona. Randy and Cindy have one daughter. Bertha and Russell, of Munster and Marco Island, have two sons. Mark (Wife Lori) resides in Long Grove, Illinois and Scott is a law student in Bloomington, Indiana.

YAROS, STEVE
F317

of Independence Hill

Steven James Yaros was born March 26, 1906, one of eight born to John Yaros and Anna Marcinak who were married in Philadelphia in 1889. The family owned 50 acres in McKean County, Keating Township in Pennsylvania and sold it in October of 1908 and moved to Bartlesville, Oklahoma and stayed approximately three years, moving back west in 1911 to Gary, Indiana.

John and Anna lived at 1236 Cleveland St. in Tolleston, right behind Beverage School and John worked in the Wheel Mill at Gary Steel Works.

When Steven was old enough he too went to work in the steel wheel plant of U.S. Steel Gary Works and was to work there for 47 continuous years, retiring in 19–. It was in these early years he met and married Wanda Sarah Rogers (better known as Doris) who had come to Gary with her parents and brother Mahlon around 1912. Doris' father was Joseph S. Rogers, son of Calvin Mahlon Rogers and Martha Elizabeth Beattie. Her grandparents on her father's side were Joseph C. Rogers and Charlotte Cox Gilbert married January 6, 1835 in Portage County, Ohio. Doris' mother was Ida Mae Marks who was born January 29, 1877 to William H. Marks and Sarah Matilda Shimp. Ida died July 3, 1938.

Steven and Doris rented an apartment at 11th and Garfield and then rented a home at 1209 Garfield, both in Tolleston (part of Gary, Indiana). Here were born their oldest daughter Faye Ellen on August 30, 1926, then another daughter JoAnn, then their oldest son Steven Jr. (Sonny) was born on his mother's birthday July 1 (1935), then son Larry Eugene was born December 16, 1938. In the early part of the 1940's they bought a lot and built a home from Henderlong in Independence Hill at 8209 Kathryn Drive, Crown Point, Indiana (now part of Merrillville).

Here son Duane Jon was born November 25, 1940 and later daughter Sandra Lee was born September 27, 1948. And finally, Terry David was born November 17, 1953.

The family were charter members of Immaculate Heart of Mary Catholic Church in Independence Hill and three sons and a daughter were married at its altar.

All children graduated from Merrillville High School except daughter Sandra Lee who graduated from Andrean Catholic High School on Broadway in Merrillville.

Mother Doris Rogers was born July 1, 1907 and died on July 26, 1962 after suffering many years with cancer.

Steven Yaros Sr. lived many years in retirement at the old homestead and died June 20, 1985 near the age of 80.

Daughter Faye Ellen married Charles E. Milner of Philadelphia and they had three children: Michael, Curtis, and Stephanie Faye.

Daughter JoAnn married James H. Whalls of Canada and they had Darlene, Cherrie and Marsha. In January of 1961 she was divorced and in October she married Ralph McHone and they had Cynthia, Jeannie, Melody, Anita, Angela, Tabathia and Lynnette.

Steven Jr. married Polly Ann Casagranda of Crystal Falls, Michigan and they had Karen Lynn and James Steven.

Larry Eugene married Nancy Lee Franklin of East Gary and they had Duane Edward, David Alan, Shawn Joseph and Jason Andrew.

Duane Jon married Janet Carol Helbling of Independence Hill and they had Kelly Dee, Windy Lynn and Robin Jean.

Sandra Lee married Merlon A. Clayton and they had Kristen Kaye, Kortney Casandra and Kyle Christopher.

Terry David never married; he became instead our all American Special Olympic star.

by Steven Yaros, Jr.

YAROS, STEVEN
F318

Of Shererville

Steven James Yaros, Jr. was born July 1, 1935 on his mother's birthday. He was the first born son of Wanda Sarah (Doris) Rogers and Steven James Yaros of Tolletston.

Sonny (Steven Jr.) had three brothers and

three sisters, namely: Larry, Duane and Terry; and Faye, JoAnn and Sandy.

Steven Sr. and wife, Doris, rented an apartment at 11th and Garfield where Steven Jr. was born and then his parents rented a home at 1209 Garfield in Tolletson (part of Gary, Indiana).

Paternal grandparents John and Anna (Marcinak) Yaros came to this country from Hungary in 1885 and 1889 respectively, and were married in Philadelphia in 1890 when John was twenty-four and Anna twenty-one years old.

In 1908 they sold their fifty acres in Semethport, Pennsylvania and moved back to Bartlesville, Oklahoma and stayed for approximately three years, moving back east in 1911 to Gary, Indiana.

John and Anna Yaros lived at 1236 Cleveland Street in Tolletson, right behind Beverage School and John worked for Gary Steel Works (U.S. Steel) in the wheel mill. Their eight children in order of birth were: John J., George C., Anna M., Mary (Marie), Susanna (Thelma), Rose, Michael and Steven James (the father of our subject, Steven James Yaros, Jr.)

On the maternal side, Steven's grandparents were Joseph Samuel Rogers and Ida Mae Marks. Joe and Ida lived most of their life in Waterloo, Indiana, and had three children: Violet Mae, Mahlon Joseph and Wanda Sarah (Doris, the mother of our subject). From around 1912 through 1930, Joe and Ida Rogers lived in Gary, Indiana; however, both of them are buried in Waterloo, Indiana.

In the early part of the 1940's Steve and Doris built a home in Independence Hill (now part of Merrillville, Indiana). Steve Sr. worked for U.S. Steel (Gary Works) for forty-seven years in their steel wheel plant.

The family were charter members of Immaculate Heart of Mary Catholic Church in Independence Hill and three sons and a daughter were married at its altar. All their children graduated from Merrillville High School, except their youngest daughter who graduated from Andrean Catholic High.

Our subject, Steven Jr., graduated from high school in 1953 where he was a four-letter man and co-captain of his football team and was named to the Calumet Conference first team at right end.

In 1955, he was drafted into the United States Navy and spent six months in Okinawa and six months in Japan as a Navy Hospital Corpsman attached to the Third Marine Division.

Upon his release from the service in November 1957, Steve Jr. went to work for Strom Machinery Corp. of Hammond as an export manager/shipping-receiving clerk. Around this time, he also became a member of the Catholic Young Adult Noll Club, and became its president and editor of its monthly newsletter and was awarded the Gary Diocesan Eagle of the Cross Award for his outstanding work.

In 1961, he met Polly Ann Casagranda of Crystal Falls, Michigan, through the CYA Noll Club and they were married June 9, 1962 and rented an apartment above the home of Bob and Mary Jean Fischer on Monroe Street in Hammond. On April 27, 1963, their daughter, Karen Lynn, was born at St. Margaret's Hospital.

Soon after that, Steve, Polly and daughter rented a home at 1916 St. John Road, Schererville from Jule Bell, owner and founder of Bell Appliance. On April 13, 1965, their son, James Steven, was born at St. Margaret's in Hammond.

In February of 1966, Steve joined the Lake County Sheriff's Department (now called the Lake County Police Department) as a patrolman working both in the jail and on road patrol. In 1971, he was promoted to the rank of Detective and in late 1972, he made the rank of Sergeant — a swing supervisor between jail and patrol. Twice while Sergeant, Steve led his men into the riot-torn sections of the county jail to retake it from rioting inmates. From 1975 to 1979, he was a jail turn supervisor with the rank of Lieutenant and then he was appointed Division Commander of patrol with the rank of Captain. From 1979 through 1983, he held the responsible job of Department Training and Planning Coordinator. (In May of 1982, he had been appointed Major and Assistant Chief).

In 1983 and 1984, Captain Yaros held the position of Deputy Warden of Operations and as his last assignment (from 1984 through 1986) he was the Corrections Division Personnel Director and Training Coordinator.

Steve retired from the Lake County Police Department on May 4, 1986, as a Captain with twenty years of service. While on the Department he was one of seven who formed the Lake County Police Association, Local 71 of AFL/CIO and served as Second Vice President in 1984 and 1985.

Steve was also responsible for starting a police cadet program and award program and a suggestion plan for the police department; and along with Sergeant Van Scoyk, started a chaplain's program for inmates and staff. He also did PR work for the department at parades, mall shows and the Lake County Fair.

Steven was editor of his parish (St. Michael's) monthly newspaper for four years, during which time he wrote forty-five editorials and articles which he later published in a small collection booklet, "From the Editor's Desk — For God, Country, and Man."

Steve was active in the Lake County Historical Society for about a dozen years, being a past president and historical secretary. During this time, he was editor of the society's newsletter. For a while, had a weekly historical column entitled, "Heritage Trail" appearing in the *Schererville Villager* in 1978. Steve later published eleven of these articles into a small pamphlet.

Steve served on the Lake Court House Foundation for about six years, as its vice president in 1984-1985, under President Wilber Heibreader. Steve was also one of the featured stars on the video tape, "Back to the Future," produced by the old Sheriff's House Foundation and the Crown Point Chamber of Commerce.

Since his retiremrent in 1986, Steve has spent sixteen months as a history book project director in Lake County, Indiana, for Curtis Media of Sioux City, Iowa, and worked part time for Sea World of San Diego, California, as a park operations host.

In December of 1988, Polly and Steve sold their home at 1624 Terrace Drive in Schererville and at this writing have relocated to Lake Havasu City, Arizona. Steve has taken a job with American Dream Homes as sales counselor having passed his Arizona State real estate examinatin in December of 1989.

by Jim Stephen

BUSINESS STORIES

ORCHARD GROVE CHEESE FACTORY
B1

The settlement of Orchard Grove had a cheese factory in the early days as well as a store and a post office. Though it had great financial difficulties under management of strangers, it ended a successful enterprise in the hands of home folks. But this difficult birth of the cheese factory made Orchard Grove known by the big court trial.

"In 1875, Warren, Carter, and Company of Chicago built a cheese factory in Orchard Grove, having a capacity of 8000 pounds of milk per day. It was operated from June until October. During that time it piled up a $2000 deficit. The milk farmers were alarmed and attached the property of the company. A few hours after the writ of attachment was issued, steps were taken by the company to get rid of the property or beyond the reach of their creditors. Soon after the property was attached the Ames Iron Works of New York replevined the engine. When the case came to trial in the circuit court, it was decided against the Ames Iron Works, who appealed to the Supreme Court to compromise with the Iron Works but that company demanded dollar for dollar. They perhaps got a dollar of expense for every dollar of their claim. While this action was pending, the property was sold under an order of the court. George Handly and Jerry Kenney bought the factory and ran it for seven or eight months a year for several years."

Then Mr. Kenney made a settlement whereby Mr. Handley was sole possessor. In 1890 Frank Tilton, an experienced cheese maker, acquired the factory from Handley. At first he paid $.70 per hundred weight but later in the summer to $.60. At the same time Mr. Tilton ran a grist mill in the other end of the same building where he ground both feed and flour. He had a far reaching business as people came from miles in all directions to buy his products. Also, hogs, meat, lard, fruit, vegetables, honey, butter, milk, and cream. His family lived upstairs. The building was later converted to a barn when farming became Mr. Tilton's chief interest. Fern Vandercar still has the cash book from that venture which makes interesting reading.

by Bessie Kenney

LETZ MANUFACTURING COMPANY
B2

The Letz Manufacturing Co. filled a valuable place in Crown Point history and for many families that lived in Crown Point and also in the life of the farmers in this country. The Letz feed mill ground grain to feed the livestock of our farmers and made it possible for many a farmer to survive during the depression and the drought in the 1930's as well as during normal times.

Louis Holland-Letz (1852-1908) came from Steinbach in Thuringer, East Germany in 1879. His father, Michael Holland-Letz made farm tools in Germany. Young Louis went to the university and then came to the United States as he felt his future was greater here. He brought his wife, Katherine Messerschmidt and 3 young children to Chicago, but came to Crown Point a year later.

Louis established a modest machine shop and foundry in 1881 across from the Pennsylvania Railroad Depot, called it Crown Point Manufacturing Company. Here he soon had made a grinder mill that would enable farmers to process their own grains to feed their livestock.

He got a patent on his mill in 1882. In 1895, he secured broad patent rights on a type of burr or grinding plate that improved the performance of his mill.

The original series of machines, primitive by today's standards, was so far advanced for its time, won the coveted gold medal against all competition at the 1893 Columbian Exposition in Chicago and repeated the victory in 1904 at the St. Louis World's Fair.

Louis, with the help of his sons, made a corn husker and shredder in 1896, a corn crusher in 1909, an all-purpose roughage mill in 1912, and separating mill in 1916.

A new factory with warehouse and office building was completed in 1891 on a different location on East North Street and Indiana Avenue and named Letz Manufacturing Co.

After the death of Louis Letz in December 1908, his sons, George, John, Otto, and daughters Eva and Carol (Mrs. Harry Newton) continued the business.

In 1909, a new line of feed mills was especially designed for crushing corn in addition to grinding small grains.

In 1916, the old structure was raised and replaced by a modern factory, foundry, and warehouse.

The first mill was run by "horse power". Visualize a wooden merry-go-round revolving on a central axle which turns on a series of gears and shafts. Picture two horses hitched to a merry-go-round so they walk in a endless circle. Imagine a gear train, driven by the horses motion, and driving a feed mill through a flat belt from a speed-jack. Such was the power of the first mill.

Before long, the horse power device was replaced by the puffing portable steam engines. The steam engine was replaced with the "oil pull" engine. With the beginning of the 20th century, the modern internal combustion engine, stationary and tractor-type, was used to power the mills.

By 1920, the business had grown and an addition was needed to adequately fill the demands for their products.

During the depression in the 1930's the factory continued to prosper and gave employment to many Crown Point men. The mill saved many a farmer, as it made it possible for them to prepare their own feed for their livestock. Letz Manufacturing Co. made roughage mills, fodder and hay choppers, corn and grain grinders, silo fillers, and grinder mixers.

For a long time during the early years of this century, Letz was the biggest company in south Lake County. 180 men were employed.

Due to changing conditions on the farm after World War II, the business declined and the Letz Manufacturing Co. closed in 1965.

by Adah Mueller

INTERNATIONAL HARVESTER FARM EQUIPMENT AGENCY
B3

The old Livery Stable on Washington St. in Lowell was operated by Emory Hathaway in the early 1900's. Later Frank Plummer was the proprietor of an Implement Shop, there.

In 1919, Flynn V. Russell came from Williamsport to purchase the Plummer Implement business, with a Mr. Hunter, as a partner. The Co. sold products of the McCormick-Deering International Harvester Co. In a short time Flynn Russell was able to buy out his partner.

Harold Sorensen began working for Flynn Russell in 1922, and after Flynn's death in the early 1940's, Sorensen purchased the business with a partner Vincent Junglas, whom he later bought out in 1947. Dorothy Homfold began working there as a Secretary-Parts lady in 1943. On Feb. 6, 1944, she and Harold Sorensen were married.

In 1949, Harold Sorensen moved the business into new, larger brick buildings on Rt. 41 near the junction of Rd. #2. In 1950, he won an award for selling the most "C" model tractors in N.W. Indiana.

Harold Sorensen's I.H.C. Agency on Rt. 41, West of Lowell.

In 1951, he sold the business to Robert L. Davis, who eventually built a smaller building on Rd. #2 east of North Hayden. The International Harvester Agency is now owned and operated by Don Bales Inc., at that location.

The Sorensen brick buildings on Rt. #41 were sold to the Lake Co. Highway Dept., who presently conduct their south county operations from that location.

by Dorothy Sorensen

HISTORY OF LAIL BROS. EGG FARM, INC.
B4

Sign on Lail Bros. Egg Farm, Inc.

Lail Bros. Egg Farm, Inc. is owned and operated by two brothers, John A. and Norman L. Lail. They opened their doors to the public in 1970.

They are not the first owners of an egg farm at this location. In 1926 a commercial enterprise called The Taylor Poultry Farm was started up at this location by Harvey Taylor and his wife, the former Joyce Frame. He was a commercial chicken breeder who specialized in crossbreeding the leghorn strain with the white rock strain. The Farm was known nationwide as a prominent and successful business until Harvey's death in 1955.

The Farm was purchased in 1955 by Orval Bishoff. He developed the operation under the name of Cedar Lake Poultry Farm as a commercial shell egg unit, and operated with an inventory of 80,000 laying hens until 1969.

About this time John Lail was looking for a new business. He had been operating a credit corporation in Blue Island with 29 employees. After looking over the farm, he decided to buy it. His brother, Norman, superintendent of a large construction company became a partner in the firm. He was an invaluable asset with his vast knowledge of building.

48,000 chickens were purchased, and the Lail Brothers were in business. You can still find the freshest eggs ever at the farm.

Both brothers are graduates of Murray State College, Murray, Kentucky. Both have served their country in the armed forces.

John is married to the former Carole Wolber of Hammond. They live on the farm with daughter, Cindy Kay, a practicing attorney in Illinois and Indiana.

Norman is married to the former Ellen Tucker, a school teacher from Logansport, and they have two children, Charles Andrew and Lora Ellen.

In 1977, due to economics, a variation in buying and selling was started at the farm. Other merchandisers were invited to participate in the commercial aspect of the farm. This was under the auspices of Uncle John's Flea Market.

In 1983, Norman, because of his expertise in the field of electronics, opened a new venture of selling and installing satellite television receiving equipment, calling it Satellite Sensations. He is an expert in the electronics field.

Lail Bros. Egg Farm's commercial operation has a 62 year history, and enjoys an excellent reputation with its neighbors. It is known throughout the community for its charitable and cooperative nature.

by Elaine Lail-Englebright

RADIO WLBT IN 1926
B5

"Welcome to Uncle John's Flea Market Saturday and Sunday" pointing to the sign on the left is co-owner John A. Lail and on the right is co-owner Norman L. Lail.

At age 18 Bud Wendel operated Crown Point's First Radio Station.

Bud Wendel was Crown Point's First Disc Jockey, Station Owner

Long before today's radio waves began to criss-cross Crown Point, an enterprising young Hub resident began the city's first radio station. The year was 1926. Few persons remember WLBT. The call letters stood for "Where Lovers Become Tied", reminiscent of the era when Crown Point was known as the "marriage mill."

During the time, Crown Point Judge "Spot" Kemp married thousands of people including actors who traveled long distances to come to this city.

The station was owned and operated by Harold "Bud" Wendel who along with his wife Edith still resides in Crown Point.

At the age of 18 Bud or "Buster" Wendel as some folks called him, was an electronics mastermind. He and several others constructed the station mainly out of spare parts.

Electronic devices and equipment were very costly for young Wendel in 1926, and often he improvised or created "homebrew" equipment to suit his needs.

His 100 watt transmitter reached across the city of 1310 kc. (now KHZ) on the AM dial.

The antennae were 20 foot spreaders, with five horizontal radiators. They were attached to two old windmill towers that stood near his father's greenhouses near the corner of Grant and North Streets.

The station had no fixed schedule and no advertisers. It operated first out of Wendel's home. Later studios were constructed where attorneys Edward Reardon and David Wilson have their law offices today on North Court Street.

The station also operated from the top floor of the Crown Point Community Building, when the structure was known as the old American Legion Hall.

Wendel's programming consisted of news, public service programs and music.

For a small station with no budget, new records were expensive. Frequently ASCAP and other publishing houses pressed for royalty uses from broadcasters, thus limiting the playing of records on WLBT.

The little station however continued to grow in popularity. Write-ups in the Star and Register Newspapers in the late 20's alerted listeners to this new form of entertainment that featured people that everybody knew around town. Residents huddled around large round cabinet radios, or used "catwhisker radios" to hear their local station.

Many times a week a local band called "Bakers Harmony Boys" played informal concerts over the station. The band was composed of Crown Pointers Harry Baker, Luther Randolph, Dr. Archibald Farley, Fred Young and Vernon Heintz.

Heintz recalls the time that a local truck driver Dick Bielefeld put up a Western Union operator to send a fake telegram to the station. The telegram was allegedly from a listener in Tennessee who had enjoyed hearing Heintz sing the favorite "Mary Lou", on the show. The staff was first amazed that the station could be heard from such a distance, and were later dishearten when they learned that the telegram was a hoax.

Wendel says that the station was a challenge to build and operate. His nonprofit hobby attracted the likes of Crown Points Fred Hall and Grant Fredericks, to work at the station. Grant Fredericks owned a plumbing supply store on South Main Street, where Kentucky Fried Chicken is today.

He presently resides in Gary, and for sometime was the station's main announcer. Fred Hall was the station's engineer.

Together the trio ran the operation for about two years, until interest, and finances, failed.

In his later years, Wendel managed TV repair shops on North Main Street. One shop occupied the building where Crown Point Cleaners is today, the other the site of Phil and Son Shoe Repair. He often toyed with going back on the air, but this never materialized. Ironically, he lives just around the corner from the studios of Crown Point's present radio station, WFLM.

At age 71, Bud is still interested in electronics and spends much time tinkering with appliances, old TV's and homemade projects. Once in awhile he'll talk on his CB radio.

Even though WLBT has been silent for nearly 50 years one often reads about the unusual characteristics of radio waves. After leaving the transmitting tower some waves travel further than others, especially at night. Others leave earth and go out into outerspace. And perhaps, just perhaps, somewhere in our galazy the former signals of WLBT are out there still traveling through space to let aliens know that some 50 years ago, Bud Wendel was our pioneer broadcaster from Crown Point.

by John R. Ghrist

THE BROWN'S POINT THRESHER COMPANY
B6

In 1917 as America entered World War I there was a need for greater grain production and farmers were urged to plant a larger acreage than usual. It happened to be a very good growing season especially wheat and oats.

Wheat was needed for human food not only in America but to supply our Allies. In those days the farm the city and the Army moved by horsepower so oats were needed to feed the horses. Even Standard Oil delivered their products to the farm by horsepower until 1920.

The large acreage and high yield led to a shortage of threshing outfits. A group of farmers living north of Crown Point in Ross Township faced with a long wait for a custom thresher decided to go on their own. They purchased an outfit that was offered for sale in Illinois. They organized "The Brown's Point Thresher Company named after the Brown's Point School which was located on the William Wirtz Farm. The twelve original owners were Henry Kuehl, William Wirtz, A. G. Mosier, John Wirtz, Fred Streubig, Chris Baldner, Oscar Streubig, Henry Luebke, Frank DeLau, Peter Wirtz, Harry Woods and Chris Fieler.

Within two years A.G. Mosier's share was purchased by Chas. Swanson and he is the only one still of this group. In fact not very many of the second generation are still living.

The farms in this group started at 73rd avenue on the north to 93rd avenue on the south and from Grant Street on the east to the St. John Township line on the west. 73rd avenue was the only hard surfaced road in the area. The rest were just mud in wet seasons and dust in dry seasons. It took about three quarters of an hour to drive a team from the Baldner farm on 93rd avenue to the Fieler farm on 73rd avenue.

Threshing usually started the last week in July and with good weather could be completed in three weeks. It took much longer in 1917 as they started later in the season.

The thrashing machine was a 30-60 Red River Special next to the largest machine manufactured by the Nicholas-Shepard Co. There were usually eight men with teams and rack wagons to haul the bundles to the machine. There were four men in the field to pitch the bundles on to the wagon. It took four good men with two box wagons holding 55 to 60 bushels to keep the threshed grain hauled away from the machine and shoveled into the bin.

There was a crew of three to operate the outfit, a separator man, engineer and water boy. The separator man or thresher kept his machine oiled, the belts tightened and made the adjustments necessary to get the grain all threshed out of the straw and cleaning it without blowing it out with the straw. The engineer needed skill to keep enough water in the boiler and a hot enough fire to generate enough steam for power. The water had a team and tank wagon and it was up to him to have water on hand as needed. Sometimes he would have to go a mile for water.

The housewife job was to have a big dinner ready at noon and the men usually would be hungry and they would do justice to her skill.

The Brown's Point Thresher Company existed for about 23 years with no serious differences between the stockholders and it finally disbanded with the coming of the combine and a new era in farming.

by Henry P. Fieler

ADVANCE ADVERTISING
B7

Shirley and Lisle Readstrom, owners of Advance Advertising, have resided at the same address for over 30 years and have done advertising for the Lake County area as well as for out-of-state companies. Their experience has involved every aspect of product development, such as creative design, art work and printing.

Advance Advertising specializes in creating a complete package of ad promotion and is "The one stop ad Agency."

Founder of Advance Advertising is historical illustrator and author Ernest Lisle Reedstrom of Cedar Lake who has written and illustrated four books: Bugles, Banners and Warbonnets, Historic Dress of the Old West, Scrapbook of the American West and U.S. Military Uniform and Accouterments in the Apache Campaign.

Lisle has also written over 100 articles in national magazines, two of which were on the infamous John Dillinger. John Dillinger Public Hero and Public Enemy appeared in Guns and Ammo Annual 1975 and John Dillinger, Bad Shooter, Bad Driver, Bad Guy appeared in Guns Magazine in September of 1979.

Lisle Reedstrom is an active member of: Western Writers of America. Little Big Horn Association, Company of Military Historians and The Westerners (Chicago Corral).

by Steve Yaros

C AND C IRON, INC.
B8

C and C Iron, Inc.

C and C Iron was founded twenty-five years ago in 1963 by the Chandler and Crist families as an ornamental railing and stairs fabrication firm. Both John Chandler and Bud Crist were employed elsewhere full time. John was an ironworker with local number 395, and Bud worked in business with Platak Meats.

After putting in eight hours plus days, they worked evenings in a garage making the railings. Bud did most of the sales and installation, and together they made the rails and stairs. John's wife, Gerry, kept the books.

In 1965 the company built a small building in the former vegetable garden and field area next to the Crist's home which later became 6409 Hendricks. In the summers during the busiest season, Bud's wife Sharon, answered the phone and assisted customers with selections.

In 1966 Bud began full time employment in C and C Iron. Sharon continued to teach school to help support a new business venture. For the next few years, Bud worked many hours a week in the business and John continued as an ironworker and part-time entrepreneur. Many residences were constructed in the area at this time. A small 6-ton truck crane was purchased, and house beams and columns soon became another phase of the business.

As the natural growth of the business occurred, John began working full time also. During the 1970's, small scale fabrication and field erection jobs were done. Soon intermediate size fabrication and larger steel erection jobs were completed. A full scale Whitney Automated Beam Line, including a full conveyor system with overhead crane capability, was installed.

Additional building space was added periodically. At present the business consists of 7500 square feet under roof with an outside yard over 42,000 square feet, serviced by two gantry cranes. A full office staff, detailing department, and shop management staff are part of daily operations. The book work, still overseen by Gerry, is totally computerized for payroll, inventory, job estimating, job costing and jobs in progress.

Along with owning and operating the business, the Crist's and Chandlers have been busy in many activities. Each family raised a son and a daughter. Both sons are now employed in the business. Both John and Bud were officers in the Indiana Subcontractor's Association. John is on the Board of Directors of the Construction Advancement Foundation and chairman of its Legislative and Governmental Affairs Committee. Bud has been elected for two four-year terms to the Merrillville School Board and has served as Board president for four years. Gerry is an officer in the Merrillville Chapter of Business and Professional Women. She is also an officer in District #311 of the National Association of Women in Construction. Gerry is liaison for Indiana Department of Highways for the State of Indiana. Sharon continues to teach and is active in the Teachers' Association and in the teaching of Gifted and Talented Students. Both families have been active during the last thirty years in the Trinity Free Methodist Church now located on Grand Boulevard in Merrillville.

Many homes in the area are resting on a basement beam and columns which were fabricated and set by C and C Iron. Many businesses in the area contain steel fabricated and erected by a 25 ton mobile crane operated by Bud.

One of their challenging jobs in 1980 was the fabrication of the steel for the Holiday Star Theater, the Convention Center, and the Holidome in Merrillville. The major 14 by 81 feet girder over the stage of the theater is the longest clear span girder, outside of the steel mills, in Northwest Indiana.

Other jobs include 1100 tons of structural steel for the Unarco Leavitt Tube Mill in Blue Island, Illinois, 1050 tons for the Interstate Plaza in Highland, 1500 tons for the Oak Lawn Illinois Sports Complex, 1200 tons fabricated and trucked to the Keystone at the Crossing area for a 17 story highrise in Indianapolis. Presently, the Performing Arts Center in Munster is being fabricated and erected.

The success of C and C Iron is the result of God's guidance, family encouragement and an extremely dedicated work force, many of whom are talented in several areas of expertise.

by Sharon Crist

REGION REALTY CO., INC.
B9

Region Realty Co., Inc. was founded in March, 1983, by James M. Gasvoda, a Schererville resident. It is located on the main floor of the Scherer-Villa office building at 2301 Cline Avenue, Schererville, Indiana. The business is a corporation, with family members as Officers.

James Gasvoda is a life-long Hoosier, graduating at Purdue University in 19??, with his major in business and economics. He is an active participant and sponsor to the community, Church, Schools, governmental projects, charitable organizations and non-profit organizations. He is a member/associate member of the Schererville Chamber of Commerce, Merrillville Chamber, Northwest Indiana Better Business Bureau, Hammond Optimist Club, Pirates, Schererville F.O.P. and more.

In 1984, Region Realty expanded their Real Estate operations to Munster, Indiana, at 8230 Calumet Avenue, under the direction of Nancy Echterling. Ms. Echterling is the recipient of many coveted real estate sales awards, selling over 20 million!

In 1985, Region Realty was asked to join a national referral Service "Network 50." with Patricia M. Kelley, as Relocation Director. Mrs. Kelley's personal portfolio includes recognition and awards from the Board of Realtors, and successful transferring of buyers to and from our "Region"!

Region Realty has a fine professional and competent record. The thrust of the two facilities is to provide the highest level of real estate expertise, professionalism and service to the residential real estate market in the northwestern region of Lake, Porter counties, Indiana, and adjacent Illinois communities.

by Pam Jessup

WAYNE'S FRAME AND BODY SHOP
B10

Steel was in its heyday in 1969 in Gary, Indiana, when Wayne's Frame and Body Shop came into existence. The way it started and evolved can almost be told like a fascinating "story-book" tale.

At that time Leo Harris, was the owner of Indiana Body Shop, Inc., at 4010 West 4th Avenue, an established heavy-duty truck repair facility. He had decided to change his career objective, and had put his establishment up for sale.

Wayne Tice, an ex-truck mechanic and ex-truck driver, owned the truck stop next door to Indiana Body Shop. When he heard of the sale, Wayne eyed the large facility with a deep down feeling of "opportunity knocking." Quietly, he began to look into how he could come up with the money necessary to purchase what he began to call "his dream."

After talking with his wife, he added up his assets and liabilities, then decided he could take out a mortgage on his home. After studying this information and pulling the midnight shift at the truck stop, he walked over one morning to talk to Harris.

"These are my assets, Leo," Wayne said. "I want to buy your company, Can we talk a deal?"

"Let's talk," Harris said.

Within a few short weeks Wayne and Harris had agreed upon a deal satisfactory to both parties. But, by this time, Harris had laid off most of his employees. His crew had gone from somewhere around ten employees to only four; the shop foreman, Frank Itczak; the front-end alignment specialist, Roland Sikorski; the all-round truck repairman, Charles Cochran; and the office clerk, Amy Garza.

Shortly before the day the keys changed hands, Wayne confronted the men in the shop and told them that if they would stay he would do his best for them. They agreed to stay. Then, Wayne approached the office clerk.

"Amy," he said, "I'm beginning this job with a lot of trucking experience, but I know nothing about the way this office is run. I really need you; however, I can't pay you any more than what you're making now, and I don't know about raises. But I promise you that if you work for me I'll make it worth your while someday."

Throughout the next sixteen years Wayne lived up to his promises. The years were full of ups and downs, but "Wayne's" came through better than ever. New equipment was added, and an addition to the main building and a new paint booth were built. The parts department graduated into over-the-counter sales, with Wayne's son, Ron, serving as Parts Manager. The crew rapidly grew to twenty employees. All these improvements began to bring in annual sales of over a million dollars.

Work on the floor escalated from body work, frame and front-end work to heavy-duty fabricating and chassis alterations on all types of trucks and trailers. Wayne's had become a one-stop repair and parts procurement facility.

But eventually it came time for Wayne to think about retiring. He announced to his crew that he'd consider selling to any or all of them. After a year's time, Wayne and his wife accepted an agreement and signed papers with the new owners—their son, Ron Tice, and the office manager, Amy Garza.

Co-owners Ron and Amy re-named the organization A.R.E., Inc., dba Wayne's Frame and Body. They asked Wayne (on semi-retirement) to be General Manager. Later, northwest Indiana's poor economy led the new owners to ask Wayne to assume the position of shop foreman full time.

On June 30, 1989, Wayne's Frame and Body will be twenty years old. Still among its twenty employees are Frank Itczak (now the Service Manager), Roland Sikorski (head Front-end Alignment Specialist), and Amy Garza (Co-owner). One of the four original employees, three are still working for the firm. That fact, in itself, tells the story of Wayne's!

"Wayne's" is not merely a firm or company—it's a way of life.

by Amy Garza

GAINER BANK 1907–1988
B11

A group of employees and officials of the United States Steel Corporation formed Gary State Bank in 1907 to meet the needs of the incoming steelworkers.

However, due to poor economic conditions and the panic of 1907, construction of the 5th and Broadway Office was not completed until March of 1908. On the first day, deposits totaled $379. After Gary State Bank was in business a few short months, deposits had reached $90,000. Over the next five years, deposits reached $1 million.

Through the years, the 5th and Broadway Office was continually remodeled. Then it was razed and a new $1 million structure was constructed and operating in 1928.

Enter W.W. Gasser as vice president, Gary State Bank. After a brief apprenticeship, Mr. Gasser replaced retiring President Lawrence W. McNamee. Mr. Gasser was the first professional banker to lead the institution. His cre-

ROACH'S SERVICE IN DOWNTOWN GARY

B12

The site of which the original main office was constructed is still the location for the main office today.

dentials impressed the U.S. Steel officials who dominated its board of directors.

The 1929 stock market crash shocked Gary's business elite. However, Gary's 13 banks appeared sound, with deposits totaling $21 million. But, four successive panics within two years toppled them like dominoes until only Gary State remained.

Mr. Gasser directed his corporate enterprise like the patriarch of a large extended family. During the Depression, when politicians, debtors and fellow bankers wanted him to come to their rescue, Mr. Gasser believed that, like a man who could not swim, diving into turbulent waters, to save a drowning friend, would be suicidal to his rigid banking principles. This displeased some persons, but was one of his greatest strengths.

After the Depression waned, the bank grew tremendously. Branches were established in a dozen neighborhoods, beginning with Glen Park in 1937.

Mr. Gasser suffered a heart attack and died on April 24, 1958. He was a sound banker, most of his acquaintances agreed. Although critics claimed that more liberal policies would have spurred even faster growth during the 1940s and 1950s, the fact that Mr. Gasser's fiscal policies kept Gary State afloat during the hard times enhanced the bank's prestige.

In 1983 Gary National Bank became Gainer Bank. Headquartered in Merrillville, it is the fifth-largest Indiana Bank.

W.W. Gasser, Jr., and R.C. Gasser took over where their father left off. Currently chairman and vice chairman of the board, they continue to manage a strong bank. Bruce L. Dahltorp is president and chief operating officer, and two Gasser sons are in management.

Since June 30, 1986, Gainer has acquired three banks: Northern Indiana Bank and Trust Company in Porter County, The Commercial Bank of Crown Point and Hoosier State Bank in Hammond. There are 40 branches in Lake, Porter and LaPorte counties.

In the past three years, the bank's assets have nearly doubled from $700 million to $1.2 billion. Gainer is the dominant financial institution in its Northwest Indiana market.

P.A. Roach taken in 1941.

Roach's Service 1033 Broadway, Gary, Indiana 1934-1940.

Roach's Service 1033 Broadway, Gary, Indiana 1940-1959.

Paris A. Roach, known to his customers as P.A., started in the service station business in late 1928, shortly after his marriage to Edna L. Tucker of rural Dana, Ill. He worked for a short time at the Sinclair Station at 19th and Madison St. for Wade Williams. On 8 Nov 1929 he opened his own Sinclair Station at 15th and Pierce St. This little station, the first Roach's Service, was located just east of the Dixie Dairy Co.

On 1 Oct 1934 Roach's Service was moved to a more central location. As you approached "downtown" Gary from the south you couldn't miss the Sinclair Station at 1033 Broadway, between the Michigan Central Railroad tracks and the I.H.B. Railroad viaduct. P.A. operated the little station there until Aug. 1940 when Monarch Oil Co., from whom he leased the station, built him a larger, white, modern station with the lube rack and wash bay on the inside! He continued to be associated in business with Monarch Oil Co. and Sinclair until 1 Sept when he retired. He received a plaque recognizing his 30 years of business with Sinclair which I now have in my collection.

As a child I recall having "reserved seats" there at every parade that went down Broadway! Every Saturday afternoon my mother took us 4 girls "downtown" on the streetcar and after we finished our shopping we'd get to walk on down Broadway to Daddy's station. He always gave us a bottle of pop and several pennies for a handful of peanuts from the peanut machine!

I remember the "Capacity Day" contests which Dad won several times, thanks to his faithful gasoline customers. He serviced trucks for several neighboring businesses: Reliable Cleaners, House of Muscat, Gary Lime and Cement, Barnes Ice and Coal, Conoco Oil Bulk Plant, Weissbuch's junk yard, and several drivers for Riddle Cartage.

P.A. also won an award of 5 silver dollars in a presentation folder from the Gates Fanbelt Co. because he had noticed the damaged fanbelt in the Gates Mystery Man's car. I remember it because Dad gave them to my son Tom when he was born in 1954 and he still has them!

Paris worked 7 days a week at the station from 7:00 A.M. to 10:00 P.M. until World War II in 1941 when the Federal Government required all stations to close at 7:00 P.M. and on Sundays. Until that time us 4 girls hardly knew our father as he was gone all the time.

I remember the gas rationing during the war and all the problems with those ration stamps! Dad used to buy War Bonds for all his grandchildren, with a percentage from his gasoline sales, and he left each of them a small nest egg from the bonds after they had matured.

Some of the young men who worked for P.A. over the years were: his brother, Bud (Sylvester F.) Roach; Chick and Ross, whose last names I cannot remember; Ray Fulton, who worked for him until P.A. retired; Paul Lepley; Bill Covault, his son-in-law; and several of his nephews.

A few years after he retired the old "Roach's Service" station was demolished during the urban renewal program. Gone too are the old buildings across the street from the station: The Buffalo Lunch, where they always got their coffee bottle refilled; Reliable Cleaners, where 3 of us girls started out working careers after school, and where Jean continued to work for 10 years; Christoff's Confectionary, where we always got to go for a 5 cent bag of candy before we went home on Saturday night; the Silver King Tavern, who had the best barbecued spare rib dinners to go; and the OK Lunch beside the tracks.

We thank all of the faithful customers, friends and relatives for their patronage over those 30 years and for helping to put food on our table!

by Mrs. Erma J. Covault

STORY OF A BUILDING
B13

Gallagher Boat Sales.

I was born in 1919-1920. I was built by C.N. Bunnell for the purpose of selling and storing of automobiles. My address was 502-506 Hohman Ave. In the early thirties, my address was changed to 5036 Hohman; corner of Hohman and Indiana. I was a very unusual building; one of the first in the country so built. I had a foundation for eight stories, although I was only four stories high. My brick walls at ground level were two feet thick and tapered to eighteen inches at my top. I was approximately eighty feet tall. All my floors were about sixteen feet high. One of my unique features was that I had a sprinkler system on each floor that tied directly to the city of Hammond's water main. I also had floors of concrete covered with wood. My original cost was between $125,000 and $150,000. I was a very well built building. I was so strong that in the early 1960's I was one of the few buildings in Hammond to be designated a civil defense air raid shelter.

I started out as home for Bunnell Ford. A short time later, I was owned by Herschback's who also used me for their Ford dealership. Early in the 1939 depression, Herschback's went out of business. I was alone and unused for about fifteen months. Then a young man by the name of Albert Gallagher, who had been driving jitney from downtown Hammond to the South Shore Station for two or three years, saw the opportunity and started to buy the mortgage notes on me. He had a dream and I was part of it. He started the Hammond Yellow and Checker Cab Company around 1930-1931 with three cabs. Since he wanted to give twenty-four hour cab service and to help cover expenses, he made arrangements with Continental Trailways to become their agent and used part of my main floor as a waiting room for buses. His wife, Margaret, started a restaurant to suppliment their income and also to feed the local people.

In all my life, I had only one new addition; a happy time. A baby girl was born on March 21, 1931. Times were difficult and the Gallagher's lived in one of my back rooms and the baby was bedded down in a bottom dresser drawer.

Over the years many changes occurred. For a while there was a tavern in my north corner with the cab and bus business. I was used as a Hertz car and trust rental agency for about eight years from 1947-1955. During this same period, a used car dealer used the upper floors for storage. In 1950, Gallagher Boat Sales began operation and I was used for the boat business until shortly after Mr. Gallagher's death in 1975. I was sold to people who had ideas to make money from me, but I wasn't taken care of as before. My sprinkler system deteriorated; I soon had some fires. I became an eye sore. I was boarded up unused and finally I was blown up because a wrecking ball couldn't knock me down. So on January 15, 1989, I died.

by Marjorie Gallagher Mills

FAGEN-MILLER FUNERAL HOME
B14

Dyer

Mike Fagen of Turkey Creek married Anna Lillig of Iowa on Nov. 24, 1885. They moved to Dyer, but at that time they owned a meat market and slaughtered the animals on the premises. In 1887 they added a bakery to the store.

Anna told her grandchildren that they sold the meat market and ran a restaurant next to the tracks in downtown Griffith in 1893, claiming they made a lot of money serving passengers on their way to and from the Columbian Expo in Chicago. From there they moved to Crown Point and opened a saloon. The same year, in 1894 Nicholas, their second child, was born. Two years later they returned to Dyer and opened the "Funeral Parlor". Undertaker was printed in gold on the "Store" front windows. The adjoining building housed the family, typical of most businesses of that time. Like most "undertakers" they operated a furniture store from the same location. The Parlor was rarely used since most embalming and visitations were done at the family home. This was hard on the Funeral Director since all the equipment had to be carried in and out, including chairs, drapes, candles, bearer, etc.

Besides raising her own family, Anna midwife, often attended to the sick and helped deliver babies. It has been told that she went with her husband on death calls, doing some embalming while Mike talked to the families.

Behind the Funeral Home was a barn which housed the horses and on the rear lot was a garage which the buggy and horse drawn hearse were kept. Also, materials for making coffins were kept there. Anna made several quilts from the velvet material that was left over. They were heavy but soft and warm. The yard had the looks of a farm yard with the "out" house next to the barn. Fruit trees covered the property. After Nick's discharge from the Marines in 1919 he attended Ind. Mortuary School in Indianapolis, graduating and licensed in 1922. Nick came back to Dyer and helped his father (the others were not interested) while working for the railroad as a dispatcher. Monon Depot was located at the crossing of the E.J. & E and Monon tracks. He was later fired when it was learned that he also had a job as deputy coroner and was caught leaving to perform the coroner's duty.

Now it was time to do more around the Funeral Home. Getting rid of the furniture store, remodeling by replacing the "Store" front windows with arched shaped stained glass and lead paneled windows and doors. Also, arched windows were installed on the side of the building. The horses were gone, also the buggy and horse drawn hearse. The only hint of the past were the fly nets (made from heavy yarn) hanging over the rafters in the garage and in the corner were the wooden lanterns. Several years before (in order to modernize the hearse) the lanterns were removed and it was painted a high gloss black paint to cover the previous grey.

About this time Eva Turner moved to Dyer and roomed at the Fagen's. There she met Nick. They married August 14, 1929, four months after the death of Mike Fagen. They bought the home and business from Anna, who at that time moved in with her daughter and her family. Anna remained active in the community and church until her death in 1943.

The first motorized hearse/ambulance I have a picture of is a 1931 Nash. Ambulance services for the small cities and towns were supplied by the funeral homes. One reason was

Fagen Miller Funeral Garden in Dyer.

207

having the manpower (except when on a funeral) and having a vehicle designed to become an ambulance by making a few changes. As an ambulance, shields were placed on the windows, and red lights were added. When a hearse, rollers were put in, for the loading and unloading of caskets, shields were removed and curtains were placed in the windows. Ambulance trips were usually $12 or less, the only area hospitals were in Hammond, Gary, East Chicago, and Chicago Heights. Funeral bills, during the depression, were usually paid but, often with eggs, chickens, or labor.

1932 was the time when one of Al Capone's men was murdered and left in our area. We had his funeral; attended and paid for by Al Capone himself. He and his body guards were very well dressed and well mannered. Mr. Capone arranged to have Nick come to Calumet City for payment. That evening Dad went directly to Calumet City arriving home (by alternate routes) two hours later. He was sure he was set up and was going to be robbed.

I have no information before the 30's about cars. We had a buick limo in the 30's which was traded in on a Packard limo in 1937. That car was modified in the 40's (because of the war) to perform also as a transfer ambulance. This was done by splitting the front seat and making the passenger side removable, the jump seat (fold down) was also made removable. A lever was set locking the frame to the front door when opened. When the seats were removed a carpeted platform was set in place and on that, a cot. This car was stationed at the Dyer funeral home. The combination hearse was in Highland. This car was sold in 1948 when it was replaced by a 1947 Packard limo.

During the 30's and 40's Dyer had telephone switchboard operators who helped us by forwarding calls. If going somewhere we would tell her where, and she would ring that phone. Mrs. Severa was the last person in town to do that before automatic dialing came into use.

In the late 30's or early 40's remodeling was done. The old porch was torn down and the building was extended to the sidewalk, adding a restroom, two closets, plus enlarging the living room. We put double doors in the wall next to the chapel so when he had a service we would open up and double the visiting area. A baby grand piano was placed in the living room so the pianist could see the clergy in the chapel. Grey asbestos shingles were added to the exterior walls.

In 1940 Nick bought a building in downtown Highland and converted it from the IGA store and Post Office into a funeral home. His idea of having a natural rock garden setting was now on its way. He had dreamed of this since the time he spent in France. Viewing the beautiful gardens and grottos brought a feeling of serenity which he felt would be just the background for a casket setting. Up to this time velvet drapes were used at the parlor or in the homes. In 1941 the funeral gardens was open and dedicated to the memory of his parents Michael and Anna Fagen.

In 1951 Maureen married Robert Miller, son of Ralph and Mary Miller. They moved in one of the three apartments above the Highland funeral home. Bob had a death psychosis at this time and had a lot to overcome by this move. In 1955 with the help of Nick and Charles Wells, who was the funeral director managing the Highland branch, Bob decided to attend mortuary school. He took a leave of absence from E.J. & E. Railroad and worked for the funeral home while attending school to support his wife and children, Larry and Jerry. Upon graduation (Chuck had decided to leave and go out on his own) Bob stepped into the manager's spot. Maureen and Bob had two more children, Terri and Gary. Mike Fagen, son of Nick, also became a licensed funeral director around the same time. He married in 1957 and moved into an apartment above the funeral home. He worked a short time and moved to Dyer next door to the funeral home and helped Nick. He left the business to work with his father-in-law in insurance. Also, in the 50's, Highland's funeral home was redecorated with minor changes. Dyer was remodeled, tearing down the old kitchen and adding living quarters to the back, changing the front entrance to the south side, doubling the size. The asbestos shingles were removed and siding was applied.

Nick and Eva started to travel and Bob ran both places with part-time help. In 1969 Ed Mullaney was hired full time. Maureen and Bob bought the business and property from the Fagens in the early 70's. Mrs. Fagen passed away March 20, 1974. Mr. Fagen died July 26, 1977. After graduating from high school, Larry attended mortuary school and became a licensed embalmer and funeral director.

The Miller's bought the Griffith funeral home from Ray Royce in May 1974. Larry Miller and his new bride moved in the apartment above the chapel. Redecorating was done, plans were sent to the town board for approval for adding to the building. After months of deliberation it was found out it was not zoned for a funeral home, although it was a funeral home for thirty years. With another delay and added cost we shelved our plans and added on to the Dyer funeral home. Dyer remodeling, which again doubled its size, was completed in 1980. On January 1, 1981 the ambulance service became a separate corporation owned by the Miller children. On April 23, 1981 Robert Miller died unexpectedly of a heart attack at the age of 50. The operation of the funeral home and ambulance service became the responsibility of Maureen and her children. Terri married William Webb from Schererville in July 1981. Bill enrolled in mortuary school and became a licensed Funeral Director and Embalmer. However, he is more involved with the ambulance service. Larry manages the funeral homes. Jerry, Terri, and Gary are with the ambulance service.

The ambulance service went from two combinations and one straight ambulance to twelve ambulances and three wheelchair vans. Since 1981, Jerry is President, Terri is Office Manager and Gary is Chief Executive Officer.

by Maureen Miller

FAGEN–MILLER FUNERAL GARDENS

Highland

The Fagen family came over from Germany around 1853 and settled in Turkey Creek around 1855. Anthony Foegen (Fagen), born July 18, 1826 died January 1, 1891, married Catherine Fritchen in Frier, Germany in 1853. Their seven children were all born in Turkey Creek.

Anna Mary Bohrofen born March 19, 1832 in Tuensdorf, Germany, died March 25, 1922 in Keota, Iowa. Married John Lillig in Germany. Anna Lillig, daughter, was born in Lendorf, Germany July 19, 1865 and died in Dyer on February 23, 1943.

Michael Fagen married Anna Lillig in Iowa November 24, 1885. They moved to Dyer and operated a meat market and bakery. In 1893 they had a restaurant in Griffith serving train passengers going to and from the World's Columbia Expo in Chicago. They moved to Crown Point where their second son was born, Nicholas in 1894. There they had a saloon. They returned to Dyer in 1896 and operated the original funeral home along with a furniture store. They served the entire Calumet region. After Nick returned from World War I, he brought along a dream of a rock garden casket setting from viewing the beautiful gardens and grottos in France.

Mike Fagen died in 1929 and Nick took over the funeral business in Dyer. He closed the furniture store and went into the ambulance business. The hearse was converted into an ambulance when not needed for a funeral. In 1940 Nick bought the old IGA store and Post Office building in downtown Highland.

Now he would have the garden setting he wanted for years. Up until this time velvet drapes were used as a back ground. First, the floor had to be braced, water added and three and one half ton of rock brought in. Virgle and Clarence Stauffer, designers of the Friendship Gardens in Michigan City, built the garden. Allen Learie, artist from Chicago, did the painting of the mural. Many days Allen would arrive by bus and find he was not motivated and return to Chicago without doing anything. Because of the war we had trouble getting materials; we could build but could not tear down in order to build. So the existing garages across the back of the property had to remain. We built a roof from the main building to the garages and made a new garage so the hearse would fit.

Nick opened the Highland establishment in 1941. Fagen Funeral Gardens became a perpetual memorial to his parents. At the time, the rock garden, was the only such setting in the world. It has since been copied several times.

When Charles Wells, a Highland man, was discharged from the navy, he and his wife moved above the funeral home and managed it for Mr. Fagen. In 1951 when Maureen (Nick and Eva's daughter) married Robert Miller, son of Ralph and Mary (Rutledge) Miller, they moved into the front apartment. Bob worked full time for the EJ&E Railroad and part time on the ambulance. Bob had a death psychosis he had to overcome and did so within the year. He joined the police association as a volunteer policeman for a night or two a month. After five years and two children (Larry and Jerry) he took a year leave of absence from the railroad to attend mortuary school in Chicago. Just as he was being licensed, Chuck left to go out on his own. Bob was offered and accepted a full time job at the funeral home. They had two more children (Terri and Gary). Bob was active in the Lions Club, Emergency Fund, Our Lady of Grace church board, Holy Name and also was a charter member of the Jaycees and the first Governor of the Calumet Ridge Moose Lodge. He was president of the Lake County Funeral Directors, Jaycees Man of the Year in 1964 and associated with the Heart Association. Bob was given many awards in several fields.

Fagen-Miller Funeral Garden in Highland.

Maureen and Bob purchased the funeral home from her parents in 1970. They remodeled the funeral home by tearing down the garages and building three levels out to the alley, more than doubling the size of the funeral home.

This included additional living quarters in which the Miller's moved into. The exterior was changed to a Mansard. The garden remained the same but was refurbished.

In 1974 they bought the Royce Funeral Home in Griffith when their son Larry married. He was a funeral director and managed that location. They had plans to add on to the Griffith place but after a year of going before the town board it was put on hold and an addition was added to the Dyer place.

In 1980 Bob and Maureen decided to separate the ambulance business from the funeral home. A bid was placed and accepted in Griffith for ambulance service starting 1981. The children took over the equipment and opened the business on their own in 1981. From 2 combinations and 1 ambulance there are now eleven and three wheelchair vans.

Terri, who is in charge of the office, married Bill Webb from Schererville. Bill is a licensed funeral director and a paramedic.

Jerry is a paramedic and coordinator of the ambulance, and Gary is an EMT and CEO. Larry, a licensed funeral director, was an EMT and ran on the ambulance but when Bob died suddenly in 1981, he had to devote full time to the funeral business. Maureen is still active in both businesses besides her involvement in community organizations.

by Maureen Miller

OWENS FUNERAL HOME
B16

History of the Owens Funeral Home in Whiting

Grandfather Dominic P. Owens was licensed in Illinois in the early 1890's and located on the east side of Chicago. His first Whiting location was at 414 119th Street around 1905; and within three years the business moved to 426 119th Street. After five years at that location Owens swapped locations with the Helwig Funeral Home which then became Hayden and Helwig Funeral Home. Owens' business address was then 406 119th Street. Sometime after 1910 Owens bought out Hayden and Helwig and in March 1927 the Owens Funeral Home which was then located at 1540 119th Street was razed by fire. D.P. Owens was ill with pneumonia at the time and police officer Ted Bramer carried Mr. Owens across the street to a neighbor's home. After residing with his daughter Mae Emerson on Roosevelt Drive Mr. D.P. Owens died July 28 of the same year.

In 1923 Thomas Sr. had joined the business and together with his mother Theresa continued the business in a temporary location in the Telephone Building on Indianapolis Boulevard owned by Mr. Sullivan. In 1928 the Owens' located their business at 439 119th Street which had been Mrs. Jones Childrens Nursery. The building was between the present location of the Elks Club and the Post Office. About 1932 the government acquired the Owens' property for the Post Office and the next business location was the Sturnburg Building 1231 119th Street where they remained until 1936. For the next 26 years the Owens Funeral Home was located on the corner of 119th Street and Indianapolis Boulevard. It was in 1962 that the funeral home moved to its present location at 816 119th Street.

The Owens Funeral Home is the oldest continuously licensed funeral home in the Whiting-Robertsdale area. There were other undertaking businesses in the early years but Mr. D.P. Owens did the embalming for those firms until 1919.

by Tom Owens

GRANT'S DEPARTMENT STORE
B17

After 76 years of service to the community, Grant's Department Store closed.

The store was among the oldest businesses in Lowell. It had been owned and operated by three generations of the Grant family.

Built by Perry Clark in 1899, the store was one of the first buildings rebuilt after the terrible fire of 1898, which completely destroyed stores along a block of the downtown.

In 1900, the building was taken over by Thomas and James Grant, the present owner's grandfather and great-uncle. Long counters with stools and built-in shelves extending from the floor to the ceiling designed the interior of the store.

Besides selling groceries and household items, the store sold shoes, and clothes for farmers. Since women made their own clothes in bygone eras, they would sit on the stools and examine the bolts of material.

After the first owners died, the store was managed by Byrl Grant and Thomas Purchase, the latter related to the Grant family on his maternal side.

Robert Grant later ran the store with his father, Byrl. In 1969, Robert bought the store from his father and has managed it with his wife, Marlis. His daughter, Roberta, also worked in the store.

The grocery department was removed in 1961. The store then contained clothing, dry goods, and footwear.

(Information taken from the *Times* 6-24-76)

by Karen Hadders

GARD GENERAL STORE
B18

The Gard General Store building is over 100 years old.

It is now the Landmark Country Store and Antique Ye Strippit Shop, 1619 Junction.

The store, built in 1881 by John Stumer, is one of Schererville's oldest buildings.

The George Gard family owned the store from 1908 until 1959. During this time the building was at the corner of Junction and Joliet. It faced Joliet.

After Gard died in 1959, the family sold the store. Martin Porter, who owned the feed store next door, bought the building.

In 1968 Porter wanted a parking lot for the feed store and moved the general store building to the back of the lot. The store then faced Junction.

The building sat vacant for several years. Windows were broken and the place looked run down. An antique business was in there for a while. In 1966 it served as headquarters for Schererville's centennial.

The store has new owners who've done a lot. They have cleaned up the building and tried to give it some of the original atmosphere.

The new owners have been trying to get the building registered as a national historical landmark. They were told it couldn't be registered because it wasn't on its original site.

The upstairs still is used as a home. The present owners live there. They sell antiques and repair them. The wife has learned to cane chairs.

Their son, Timothy, was born in the basement of the store. He's the first child born in the store in 70 years and maybe the only one.

Mrs. Theresa Gard Kuhn lived in the store as a child and again after she was married.

Gard bought the building in 1908 from his wife's sister, Mary, widow of John Weis. The Gards had lived on a farm in St. John Township. Mrs. Kuhn was four when they moved to the store.

The building also served as the Post Office. Weis had been postmaster in 1903. His wife took over in 1908 and Gard became postmaster in 1913 serving until 1928.

Many of the supplies came to the store by train.

Originally the store was half the size it is now which is about 90 feet by 40 feet. Gard enlarged it in 1918.

WEINER FOODS INC.
B19

Herb Weiner, owner of Weiner Foods Inc., has been in business since 1919.

Partner and brother-in-law Jack Kaplan said it is harder to manage a chain store because day-to-day decisions have to be handed down through a corporation bureaucracy.

Weiner's grandparents started the business by selling fruits and vegetables off a horse-drawn cart. With Prohibition, they purchased a tavern and turned it into a grocery store.

During the Depression, many people paid for their groceries not with money but with county script which was similar to food stamps.

Weiner said that it took anywhere from three months to two years for the county to convert the script into cash.

After World War II, Weiner and Kaplan took the business over from Weiner's father but the store was too small to support both of them. They built a new store across the street and now there is a parking lot where the old store once stood.

Weiner Foods has always been a family business. Weiner said that will change because his children are doing other things and will not take over the store.

(Information taken from the Hammond Times 2-5-84)

by Daniel Helpingstine

KAPLAN'S SHOES
B20

Samuel Kaplan, a Russian immigrant, married Sally Biyarski of Chicago Heights.

Her father, who owned a department store, helped set them up in the shoe business, as did Col. Walter J. Riley, founder of the First National Bank of East Chicago. Riley gave Samuel a $3,000 loan.

Samuel Kaplan was the first discount shoe merchant in Northwest Indiana. He would buy shoes in big lots, then sell some of them off to other stores.

Kaplan was a good promoter.

By 1935 Kaplan was sponsoring 16 bowling teams. And in 1939 he was advertising an X-ray machine that could be used to help analyze the foot problems of customers.

He was the first in the area to use one of the machines in a shoe store. The machines, which were used to show customers the shape of the bones in their feet, were quite popular until people realized X-rays could be dangerous.

Son, Melvin Kaplan said his father had a strong temper and when he got old enough to join the business, he went to California instead, where he worked with a friend of his father's at Vogue Shoe Company.

But he returned in 1955 to lead the firm's expansion, opening the firm's first branch at 7005 Indianapolis Blvd. in Hammond. The following year, Kaplan added a store in Griffith.

Now those stores, along with two in Merrillville, will carry on the family name. The original store, which closed in 1985, is rented out.

(Information taken from Hammond Times 2/1/85)

RUDOLF'S HOUSE OF BEAUTY
B21

It was 1936 and Rudolf Wunder had just opened his own beauty shop in Whiting, Indiana.

Wunder and his business remained in that little town and in March of 1986 he celebrated his 50th anniversary as owner and stylist of Rudolf's House of Beauty.

In 1936 the shop originally opened in Whiting's Central Bank Building.

Throughout the years Wunder has prided himself on "being the first to try new things." In 1950 his shop was featured in "Modern Beauty Shop" magazine for being the first salon to have air-conditioning.

Wunder had appeared on Chicago television shows demonstrating styling techniques and through the years many of his articles have been published in trade magazines.

After 50 years Wunder has seen three generations of customers come through his door and after age 75, he still has his own weekly standing appointments.

(Information taken from the *Times* 3-30-86)

by Gayle Kosalko

AUSTGEN HARDWARE STORE
B22

Since 1902 when the late Nicholaus Austgen purchased the hardware store next to his harness shop the Austgen family has been selling hardware in Dyer.

Nicholaus and his wife Theresa lived for 14 years over the store at a time when there were dirt roads and a few buildings and homes in what is now a sprawling suburb.

Mr. Austgen died in 1971 at 93.

The couple's five children helped when they were old enough.

Robert and Donald stuck with the business and were partners until 11 years ago when Robert became sole owner. The store closed in 1974.

(Information taken from the Times of 2-8-74)

BECK'S CROWN BAKERY
B23

The Beck's have owned and operated Beck's Crown Bakery since 1969. In the past two years, they have changed the business from a small, retail bake shop to a wholesale operation employing 52 people.

While they still maintain a store where their baked goods are sold, by far the large proportion of the products is destined for institutional customers.

Beck first began his wholesale business by supplying sweet rolls to the National Baking Co., a national institutional supplier. National makes rolls and bread for hospitals and restaurants, but needed a smaller baker to produce sweet rolls. Recently, National asked Beck to make croissants because of their growing popularity.

Getting into the wholesale business was not part of Beck's original plan. But a series of events thrust him into the larger, more efficient operation that he now has.

When a group of businessmen bought the First National Bank of Crown Point in 1981, they found that a large loan had been made to Frank Beck's bakery. The terms were somewhat questionable, and the payments were becoming difficult for the Becks to make.

Then in 1982, when the First Bank of Whiting took over the Crown Point bank, they asked the businessmen to buy back the Beck loan.

While some in the group advocated selling the bakery and taking what they could from it, one member, Phil Graziani championed Beck's cause.

With Graziani's guidance, the Becks were able to successfully switch from a retail to wholesale business.

(From the Hammond Times of 12-30-84)

by Ann Bochnowski

HUGH McLAUGHLIN AND SONS
B24

Hugh McLaughlin & Sons started over 40 years ago as a reconditioning plant for golf balls. The company has moved once and had two owners since then and during the peak a couple of years ago had about 90 employees. Last year they were down to about 40.

Although it is one of only nine companies manufacturing golf balls in the nation, it is almost totally unknown because it has specialized in making golf balls for others.

Owner Bill Wampler said of the 2,000 or so dozen balls that roll out of the plant each day, all of them have been produced for other major brand name companies, sporting goods chains, smaller mass market merchandisers, driving ranges, or specialty shops.

A significant portion of their business is catalog sales for such items as personalized golf balls that can carry a person's name, company name or personal portrait. McLaughlin also makes balls for country clubs.

After years of making a name for others, Wampler has at last begun a drive to make McLaughlin a name of its own. He plans to sell a new style of golf ball and under the company name.

The ball was introduced last month at the national meeting of the Professional Golf Association in Orlando. The ball, developed over the past five years, is of molded rubber construction with no cover. It has the durability of the cut-proof balls with the performance of the softer balata-covered balls preferred by the pros.

Wampler said the ball has not been submitted to the United States Golf Association for testing to be approved for tournament play because he has not come up with a name to use for marketing it.

(from the Times of 2-16-86)

by Phillip Wieland

SMITH PAINT AND SUPPLY
B25

Founded in 1920 by Leo and Herbert Smith, the Smith Decorating Co. once painted houses all over the city.

The painting and decorating service was discontinued in 1945 when Herbert died, but Dick Smith still remembers spending hours after school and on weekends in the shop.

While Dick was in the service during World War II, his parents bought Herbert's share of the business. Dick came home on December 31, 1945, and two days later he went back to work at the shop and, according to family legend, hasn't stopped working since.

In 1961, Dick and Eileen bought the business from his parents and changed the name to Smith Paint and Supply.

In 1981, their son Daniel joined the company as vice-president in charge of accounting and outside sales.

Two other sons came on board last year. Michael, a graduate of the Harrington Institute of Design, runs an interior design business from the shop, while Tim manages the company's Griffith store.

The Hohman Avenue building, next door to the old Paramount Theater, has been around for 80 years and has always been a paint store. Originally, it was located 20 feet farther west, but when Hohman Avenue was widened, the store had to be moved back.

The family cherishes pictures of the old days showing the company truck that Leo also used to pick up the children from school at lunch time.

The most recent addition to the family business is Triad Design Associates. From his second-floor studio, Michael Smith is running commercial interior design projects both in Northwest Indiana and Chicago.

Including all the family members, 10 people are employed in the business.

(Information taken from *The Times*)

by Cynthia Oborek

DILLABAUGH MOVING ENGINEERS
B26

Bicentennial Profile

Dillabaugh Moving Engineers may not be able to move "heaven and earth," but they can come close.

Charles Dillabaugh started the third generation business as a part-time occupation along with operation of a cider mill. They had moved the mill to their property on Indiana Avenue from Lowell, where they had a 100-tree cherry orchards.

Cider mill customers were said to have come from as far away as Michigan, but milling, being seasonal, gave the Dillabaughs an opportunity to engage in the house moving business.

Charles and wife, the former Emma Wemple, had earlier maintained the Robinson Prairie place, Orchard Grove, Route 55 and Highway 2. It was settled by her parents, who regarded it as an opportunity to have a piece of Robinson Prairie to farm, and with it came the privilege of cutting logs on the Kankakee River bottom land, which they hauled 13 miles to build a cabin for their family.

Leaving the farm after several years, Charles rented Kaiser's blacksmith shop in Crown Point, and 10 years later ventured into the moving business. The housemoving business later was turned over to son Ellis, when the Dillabaughs opened the grocery store they operated until George Cilek bought it.

Other children of their family were Louise (Belinsky) of South East Grove, Nellie (Whitehead), Walter and Ruby (Shay) of Hammond and California.

Moving methods in those early days were carried out mainly by the use of loose rollers and planks, wood beams, rope for power instead of cable, and lever jacks. Power to start a building into motion was generated by means of a large spool mounted in a frame with a reach horse hooked on that went around and around, winding up the rope that went back through pulley blocks.

Mud roads made transportation of equipment difficult. It was a self-assembly business, with tools made from their own resources. Moving was restricted in grandfather's day to homes and small buildings, usually only within a 10-15 mile radius. Jobs accepted were close to a railroad where possible, so equipment could be shipped by rail and the taken to the job. Many times they lived in with the family, or in the town until the job was completed.

Ellis was first married to Hazel Fisher, Denver, Colo. Their children were Grant of Hebron, daughter Shirley Magnar, Detroit, and from a later marriage to Lora Shay, Crown Point, there was Donald, Boston, Mass; Joyce Stoner, Valparaiso; Ellison, Phyllis Ross and Howard Hebron.

Ellis remained to head the business until 1955 when sons Ellison and Howard, and son-in-law Don Ross formed a partnership, to which son Grant was added in 1957. In December, 1959, after the father's retirement, the partnership was dissolved, and Howard and Ellison formed a new corporation with Howard as president, and their wives as stockholders. Howard's sons Donald and Dan work in the business.

Both brothers have learned from experience that moving is the business for them. It is one in which they can combine their individual abilities. Howard, a graduate from Indiana University in business management, with his trained mind for mathematical details, handles job bidding, all legal aspects, gives financial assistance where a customer needs aid, and obtains the numerous permits that have to be obtained before a move can be made.

Each job requires state highway permit, railway permit, county highway permit, public utility permits where electrical and telephone wiring is involved. "One town had six different wire companies to be dealt with," Ellison said. "Each city requires performance bonds for protection against possible damage and often a contractor's license is required.

"Highway departments are cooperative. They have a lot of headaches, because of the business and they want to know that safety devices are adequate. House movers could create a lot of problems, damage to roads and inconvenience to the public if the laws were not enforced," Ellison said.

Ellison has the more mechanical mind that is required in solving many challenging dilemmas.

One of the tightest squeezes came in maneuvering a 100-foot-wide storage tank for Standard Oil through a 99 and one-half foot opening. "We dropped the bottom from the tank and pushed it through," he said. "Watching one man pull a 50-to-60-foot tank with a rope is one of the biggest thrills we encounter.

We sometimes dam up the area and flood it with one to one-and-a-half feet of water, then float the tanks to their new site."

The Dillabaughs now move barns, commercial buildings, water towers, tanks, machinery, store buildings and two- to three-story apartment buildings. Much of their work now is brick, stone and masonry buildings, residential and commercial.

The longest single span bridge, constructed solely of wood, was moved by them. The covered bridge was moved across the Salamonie River south of Wabash for the Dora-New England Holland Historical Village, Inc.

"We moved the bridge for $5,500 and showed a profit," Ellison said. "The next lowest bid was $25,000. We used a different method — putting pontoons under the bridge and floating it across."

"One of our biggest jobs was literally moving the entire village of Somerset to a new hillside location after it had been flooded many times by the Mississinewa River, and the town of Dora that was inundated by the Salamonie River, which was relocated in the rural areas."

"We do turn down some jobs," Ellison admitted, "for various reasons. Some are just not practical or feasible to undertake because of the problems involved. Sometimes tree limbs, streets with heavy traffic, narrow streets or inadequate bridges the movers would have to cross, make the job impossible, or too costly.

"You never know exactly what is underneath you. Such as a washed out sewer under streets which could cave in, and unknown underground tanks which might cause the street to collapse as the heavy building are moved over them," Ellison said.

Such an emergency was a recent call from

the University of Chicago, where an inside four-story brick wall in the Cancer Research building had dropped 14 inches. Water from the street had washed out sand footing around the building, undermining the foundation and causing the drop. Fortunately no one was in the building," Ellison said.

"With the volume of business we do today," he said, "grandfather and Dad would have required as many as 35 men. Today, we have a crew of only seven. Equipment does most of the work. A new hydraulic jack system lifts automatically and evenly. The newest equipment will lift cranes, industrial equipment and machines.

"Steel beams are used to support the hydraulic unit, dollies are set under the building, which is pulled by truck to the new location. Dollies give more even distribution on the road, than placing such a large structure on a truck," Ellison said.

One breath-taking experience recalled by Ellison was while going down a steep hill in southern Indiana with a new house. The truck driver locked the brakes and the house started over a cliff. "We sat in a precarious location for several hours until we could get it back on the road," Ellison said.

"Each moving project is unique and a new challenge of its own. There are days when you would like to just throw in your coat and head for home — but you tie into it and feel a real sense of joy when the job is done," he said.

"Moving is a going business with so many houses being moved, because of road construction, commercial development, flood control, school and business expansion. It has been my life, and I love it. No other occupation could be so rewarding. There is no place in it for a coward. We allow no drinking on the job — only the finest crew," Ellison said.

Cost of re-locating the average house would be 35 to 40 percent of the cost of building a comparable house. Today, most of the houses moved are the better ones. Today, very few homes that need extensive remodeling are moved, because the homeowner must have permission of the new neighbors before he can move a house into a neighborhood.

"I would rather have an old house that has been moved," Dillabaugh said, "than one that hasn't. It will have a better foundation, better plumbing, new heating system and improved landscaping.

"Some days we are not so busy — again so busy we hardly know in which direction to move. There is never a definite pattern. Dull days are made useful with maintenance work on equipment. The business is also expanding into real estate, buying, remodeling and renting commercial and residential buildings, to take up the slack.

Ellison and wife, the former Louise Alexander, Merrillville, were married after his three years with the U.S. Army in World War II. Their children are Peggy, married to Donald Andrietta, carpenter for First National Bank, Gary, and its branches; Harry, married to Sheila Stephen, a jeweler in Taylorville, Ill.; and Sally at home, a dental assistant in Merrillville.

He at an earlier time was active in the American Legion. The past six years have been concentrated in active Christian work in the Emmanuel Baptist Church in Crown Point, where his wife is also a member and involved.

He makes frequent prison visits working toward rehabilitation.

by Violet Irvin

SCHEDDELL AND WENDT BROS. DRUGS, INC.
B27

Scheddell and Wendt Bros. Drugs, Inc., is an institution in downtown Crown Point.

The business was founded at 101 W. Joliet St. by W.A. Scheddell in the late 1870s. He moved the store to its present location around September of 1882.

Scheddell was a pharmacist, doctor and optometrist.

In 1917, Wendt's father, John L. Sr., and his uncle, Walter, were graduated as pharmacists from Purdue University. They both worked for Scheddell.

At the onset of World war I, both Wendts enlisted.

After the war, around 1919, John and Walter bought out Scheddell, whose health was failing. In 1920, Scheddell died.

Prior to the 1950s, most stores specialized in clerk service. Customers had to ask for items. In the late 1950s, open shelves were stocked so that customers could serve themselves.

The store is two and a half times as large today as it was in the 1950s.

The north half of the present store was the original drugstore. In 1966, the Wendt Bros. moved into the south half of the store which originally was Crown Point Savings and Loan. In 1967 they began remodeling the original store, expanding the building to its present size.

Scheddell and Wendt Bros. was a Walgreen agency store from 1923 to 1980. It is now associated with the Zahn Drug Co. as a "Family Drug Center."

The Wendt Bros. business expanded in the 1970s with the addition of a Hebron pharmacy and later a Kouts drugstore. Computerization has changed the drugstore business.

John L. Wendt, Jr. has operated the business since his father died and his uncle, who is now 85, retired.

(from the Post Tribune of 2/7/82)

JACOBSENS INC.
B28

Jacobsens Inc. grew from an insolvent art supply store in Gary to one of the 50 largest office supply dealers in the nation. It celebrated its 50th anniversary in 1979.

The family business was established in 1929 by the late H.W. Jacobsen, Sr.

The business, run by Al Jacobsen, succeeding his father, now has five separate divisions and three stores as it serves four Northwest Indiana counties.

The senior Jacobsen, who died three years ago, was a commercial artist with the Miller Wool Co. during the 1920s. Early in 1929, he bought the small supply store on the second floor of a building in downtown Gary.

His wife, Frieda, still very active in the family business, recalled that display poster signs – painted by the merchants themselves – were popular during those days. Jacobsens stocked them with the needed supplies: paint, posterboards, brushes, canvas and easels.

Professional artists also found Jacobsens an ideal store for their supplies, and the business grew rapidly.

In 1953, a Chicago newspaper reported that "Jacobsens brought the art hobby movement within the reach of the average working person by stocking a wide selection of supplies and selling those quality supplies at very reasonable prices."

The senior Jacobsen himself was a reputable artist. A graduate of the American Academy of Art, Chicago, he often painted showcards while customers and passersby watched.

The showcards with "the Jacobsen touch" became popular throughout Northwest Indiana, and as the numbers of customers increased, Jacobsen was encouraged to expand his lines of merchandise.

That he did, adding office supplies, equipment, furniture, machines, and stationery.

Jacobsens became a dealer of Royal typewriters and Shaw-Walker office supplies, and a representative for other manufacturers.

During World War II, Jacobsens was selected as a procurement agent for the U.S. Government and handled truckloads of typewriters. The service department, reconditioning used typewriters, also expanded.

After the war, the family business continued its growth, branching out to the adjoining counties and developing the five divisions.

Al Jacobsen shares leadership in the firm with James Retseck, business partner and vice president. Major stockholders are Jacobsen, Freida Jacobsen, Dorothy Jacobsen and Retseck.

(from the Post Tribune of 6/10/79)

UNITY SHOE STORE
B29

Spase and Depina Atseff have seemed as they are for the past 20 years, since a young man first entered their shop to purchase a pair of black engineer boots, with a buckle on the side, to be among the elite of the kids at school.

Depina Atseff, who has always worn glasses and worn her dark, black hair pulled back, has always waited on customers while Spase repairs shoes in the back.

Spase moved to this country from Yugoslavia, though born in Macedonia, as a boy of 16. He arrived in Chicago and took a job making 15 cents an hour in a chemical factory, though he apprenticed as a shoemaker in Yugoslavia.

Drafted in 1917, he served in the Army for 18 months and then moved to Hobart and opened his shop, after buying the business and store.

The Atseff's have been married since 1935, when Spase met Depina in Yugoslavia while on vacation. She returned to this country with him and they did not take a vacation together again until four years ago when they just "got tired" and took their two sons and Spase's daughter to Europe on a two-month vacation.

They have operated their business six days a week, week in and week out, for close to 60 years, with the exception of just those two months and he doesn't plan to leave soon.

by Anthony Seed

CROWN MEAT MARKET
B30

Dave Bucholz is in the service.

Bucholz owns the Crown Meat Market, 110 S. Main Street.

His service is providing custom-cut meats to regiments of Crown Point area housewives who parade into the small shop on the square.

To help in his constant battle against inflation and supermarket meats, Bucholz has enlisted the aid of Harry Steinmann, 66.

The well-known Steinmann is very familiar with the shop and many of its customers.

He served two previous tours of duty, first helping his parents who opened the shop around 1920 and then as the owner of the meat market from 1948 to January, 1974.

When he was in command, Steinmann ran the shop as a full-line, service meat market. There were several product and service changes by new owners between early 1974, when Steinmann sold out, and a bit over a year ago when Bucholz bought the shop. The new owner, however, has returned to the full-line, personal service market concept.

Despite his youthful appearance, Bucholz is a veteran of the meat business wars.

He started working part-time in a butcher shop in 1955. Later, he was a regional manager with the Jimmy Dean Sausage Co.

Bucholz has always wanted to run his own little store. He has always liked the Crown Point area and he thinks it's a good idea for meat sales.

The shop specializes in pork sausages, all mixed using fresh meat, spices and herbs. Top sellers are Polish, Italian, bratwurst and garlic sausages.

The shop also cooks its own smoked sausage in a smokehouse built in the basement in the 1920s.

The store, and its operation, has undergone many changes.

It originally was a tavern. Prohibition turned it into a butcher shop, run by Alwin and Bertha Steinmann.

The old counter had a marble top, blocks of ice were brought in each day at 6 a.m. and there was sawdust on the floor. All meat was cut to order as customers waited on stools.

Alwin Steinmann installed the city's first "refrigerated" meat case in 1924. It had bunkers at each end filled with chipped ice with pipes through it to cool meats.

In 1948, the sold chickens whole. There was a lot of resistance to pre-cut meats.

Frozen meats began to be sold about 1955.

Bucholz is winning the battle to regain that reputation for the small meat market.

(Information taken from the Post Tribune 5-13-82)

SCHLEMMER STORE BUILDING
B31

Those more familiar with the Crown Point square in earlier years will have a memory of Schlemmer's Dry Goods Store, in operation a long time, in two different locations on the east side.

After John Schlemmer and his wife Margaretha (Schramm) came to the United States from Bavaria, Germany, they chose Chicago as their first home. John opened his first dry goods store in Chicago. According to family hearsay, their business was affected by the big Chicago fire of 1871, and they began looking for a new home.

No doubt Crown Point had a special appeal because they possibly had friends here from the "old country". The family came to Crown Point around 1872. John soon set up Schlemmer's Dry Goods Store, first at the corner of Main and Joliet Streets, then a two-story frame building that eventually burned down. When rebuilt, it became the People's State Bank Building. Buildings around the square in the 1800's were mostly of frame and brick, and the scene hasn't changed too much today, except for the addition of new fronts.

Son William worked with his father in the business that was in time moved to the corner of Main and Clark Streets. The Schlemmers bought the property and built a new two-story brick building. Designed by a chicago architect, it was put up by local contractors, Rudolph and Crowell, at the cost of only $4,775.

Merchandise included all-around family needs for clothing, down to shoes and boots and some ready-made clothing items, although back then mother sewed for the entire family. At the dry goods counter she found yard goods, laces and trims, accessories, along with many other so-called "notions" to stretch the imagination. The ribbon and thread cases were features to behold. The umbrella stand was popular then.

There wasn't much packaging in those days, and many articles, such as handkerchiefs, ties and gloves, were hung on bars suspended from the ceiling. Even shoes were hung at eye level, in some instances, to conserve space.

One convenience popular in the Schlemmer store, which many remember, was a row of bar-type stools by the yard goods section, which the ladies enjoyed while selecting materials, patterns, and accessories. Of course, the kids liked them too for a few quick twirls before leaving the store.

After John's death in 1899, the business became Schlemmer Brothers Dry Goods Store, operated by William, Frank, and George J. (the name Johann Georg chose to go by). Following William's death on September 1, 1921, Frank and George J. continued the business, with George J. becoming the head buyer. A part of their business was measuring prisoners at the Lake County jail for clothing before they were sent on to Pendleton or other houses of correction. Frank died in 1941 and George J. continued the operation of the store until his death in 1943. Frank's wife Paulina (Fraas) maintained the store briefly to clear out the inventory. Paulina died November 28, 1947.

Gertrude Mulhern and her sister, Mrs. J. Irl Rockwell, then started the Eastgate Dress Shop, later selling out to Olga Chmielewski in 1948. In 1980 Olga Chmielewski sold the business to Toni Rieder. Outfitters, Ltd., operated by the Pause brothers, became the new tenants in 1982, and in 1984 Hobbyland, owned by Bill Wirtz, opened the doors for business. Dan Ver Meulen became the new owner of Hobbyland in 1985. The building remained the property of Mrs. George E. Schlemmer and her four daughters following George E.'s death in 1981 until May 1989 when it was sold to Mr. and Mrs. Peter M. Hernandez and the business is now Peter Martin Jewelers.

by Margaret V. Schlemmer

FAGEN-MILLER AMBULANCE INC.
B32

In 1929 Michael Fagen passed away and left the job of running the business to his son, Nicholas. Nicholas married Eva Turner and bought the home and business from this mother, Anna. Nicholas made a few changes one was to discontinue the furniture store and start an ambulance service.

Ambulance service for small cities and towns were supplied by the funeral homes. One reason for this was having the man power (except during funerals) and having a vehicle designed to become an ambulance by making a few changes. The first motorized hearse/ambulance I have a picture of is a 1931 Nash. As an ambulance shields were placed on the windows, red lights with sirens were added.

Ambulance trips were normally $12 or less during the forties and between $18 and $20 in the fifties. Often emergency calls were responded with only one man relying on getting help at the scene of the call. The only hospitals were in Hammond, Gary, East Chicago and Chicago Heights. Later Mercy Hospital became Our Lady of Mercy with Medical floors and an emergency room. Also, Hobart, Merrillville, Crown Point and Munster built hospitals.

In the 1940s we modified our 37 Packard Limousine to perform also as a transfer ambulance (because of WWII). This was done by splitting the front seat and making the passenger side removable, the jump seat (fold down) was also made removable. The cot fit into that space. No red lights or sirens were needed. This car was stationed at the Dyer Funeral Home. The combination was stationed at the Highland Funeral Home.

A lot of part time help was used with little more than first aid knowledge. All being paid by the trips made. By 1980 Fagen Miller had an ambulance also stationed at the Griffith Funeral Home making 3 combinations and 1 regular ambulance. December 31, 1980 the funeral home ended the ambulance service and the Miller children, (Lawrence, Jerry, Terri and Gary) started Fagen Miller Inc. Ambulance Service January 1, 1981. As of this writing the ambulance service has a fleet of 12 ambulances and 3 wheelchair vans. They are primary responders to Highland, Dyer, St. John and Lake Hills. Giving mutual aid to Schererville and surrounding communities. Providing Basic and Advanced Life Support ambulances. The basic life support is manned by at least one EMT and is equipped with splints, spineboards, oxygen and bandaging supplies and are in radio contact with all hospitals. The advanced life support ambulances have to be manned by one paramedic and one EMT. These ambulances have the basic equipment plus heart monitors, defibulators and IV drugs. We provide the medics for air ambulances.

Fagen's provides credited inservice training monthly to all the area medics and Fire departments. With the wheelchair vans, we offer what we call Home for the Holidays. This is where we transfer people in wheelchairs home for a few hours on a holiday and then take them back to the nursing homes without cost. (Limit to people who could not get home by any other means and are from nursing homes we serve).

Fagen Miller is a total medical transportation network. Ranging from wheelchair transportation to air transportation with a complete medical team.

Fagen Miller is a registered training institution for the American Heart Association C.P.R. We stand-by at special events such as football games and town events.

by Maureen Miller

W.R. DIAMOND STORES CO.
B33

East Chicago, IN.

William R. (Will) Diamond established one of the first grocery stores and meat markets in East Chicago, In. The first store was located at 709 Chicago Avenue.

W.R. Diamond was born ca. 1868 in Byron, In. His wife, Elsie Maxey, was born in September of 1869 in Plymouth, In. They were married in Coles County, Il. on 22 Aug. 1901. After their marriage, they came to East Chicago where the grocery store was established.

Mr. Diamond's store was the traditional one of that era. A customer could come to the store,

Some employees of the W.R. Diamond Stores Co. at a picnic at Long Lake, IN. Standing from (L to R) W.R. (Will) Diamond, Bert Burch, Mrs. Art Schaller, Andy Nancy, and Mrs. Artman, the store's bookkeeper. On the running board: Art Schaller with son Don, on his lap, Mrs. Bert (May) Burch and Mrs. W.R. (Elsie) Diamond.

order groceries and a cut of meat, and have it all delivered to their home. A customer could also call in an order or have the delivery man take an order at their home and have it delivered. There was no charge for this service. Customers could also charge their purchases and be billed at the end of the month.

Both Mr. and Mrs. Diamond participated in community affairs. Mrs. Diamond became interested in establishing a chapter of the Daughters of the American Revolution in East Chicago. She was the organizing regent and founder of the Calumet Chapter of the D.A.R. The founding date was 10 Feb 1911.

In 1914, Will Diamond opened an economy store at 711 Chicago Avenue next to his grocery store.

In that same year, East Chicago had a large parade on Disease Prevention Day. The Diamond Stores Company participated by entering a float in the parade. The float emphasized the cleanliness of the store.

By 1918, this enterprising man had opened a 10¢ store at 526 119th St. in Whiting, Indiana.

Will Diamond employed H.T. Powers as general manager in 1923 to assist him in his growing business.

The store moved to 718-20 Chicago Avenue in 1925. It now had a manager, Lewis B. Caraher, and retained Mr. Power as general manager.

Will Diamond and his wife, Elsie, lived at 709 Chicago Ave. throughout their years in East Chicago. They never had any children. They sold their various enterprises in the late 1920's. They retired to a summer home in Long Beach, In. and a winter home in Orlando, Fl. They continued to visit East Chicago over the years seeing friends and relatives.

by Margaret Burch Kelly

JOHN F. RAHN, INC.
B34

John F. Rahn (left) and Reinhardt P. Rahn in front of John F. Rahn, Inc. office building, 500 W. 150th Street, East Chicago, 1944.

John F. Rahn, Inc. was a vital part of the construction industry of East Chicago for more than 50 years. The company was established by John Frederick Rahn in the early 1900s.

John F. Rahn was an orphan who came to this country from Germany at the turn of the century. He was sponsored by an aunt in Chicago Heights, IL. He knew no English when he came to America but had some training as a carpenter.

Rahn entered the building trade as a carpenter. After a number of years, he went into business for himself building small houses. Soon after that small start, he went into commercial and industrial construction. He did this same work until the end of his career.

He moved his business to East Chicago at the time of the first World War, renting offices in the Calumet Building. As the war progressed, his company grew, because there was much industrial construction in the area. He supervised the work himself and did all the paper work. He had so much work that, at times, he slept only every other night.

Float in Disease Prevention Day Parade in 1914. The float is from the W.R. Diamond Grocery Store in E. Chicago. The people on the float are employees, but names are unknown. The driver of the float is Nathan Albertus (Bert) Burch.

After the war, his son Reinhardt P. Rahn joined him in the business. Reinhardt had studied engineering at the University of Illinois and had served as a lieutenant in the U.S. Army at the Aberdeen Proving Ground. His father welcomed his return and his assistance in the growing business.

In the early 20s, Rahn built the First National Bank Building at the corner of Indianapolis Blvd. and Chicago Avenue. Ever after, the owner, Col. Walter J. Riley, and he were good friends. Rahn moved his office to the new bank building, which had offices on the second floor, and stayed there for a few years.

Col. Riley often called upon Rahn to carry out repairs and remodeling at the Carmelite Orphanage in the Calumet area of East Chicago. Rahn did this work at cost as a favor to the Colonel and because he himself had been orphaned at an early age.

In the late 1920s, the Rahns built their own shops and 2-story office building on a acre plot at 500 West 150th St.

John F. Rahn, Inc. did work for all the large industrial plants in the area — Inland Steel, Youngstown Sheet & Tube, Metal Thermit, Continental Steel, and many, many more. The firm also did some non-industrial work including St. Thomas More school in Munster and an addition to Bishop Noll high school in Hammond.

Rahn worked with all the well-known architects in the Calumet area including Hutton & Hutton of Hammond.

Rahn was called upon over and over by many companies, because they knew he and his company could be relied upon to provide high quality work done with integrity. In fact, the Superheater company (later Combustion Engineering) had Rahn do all their work on a cost plus basis without asking for a bid. They knew John F. Rahn, Inc. would do the work well and submit an honest cost figure for payment.

John F. Rahn and Reinhardt were clever and inventive when it came to building methods and producing high quality work. For example, John F. devised a system of double flooring that he could guarantee would prevent any water seepage into basements of buildings that needed dry floors for storage of flour or similar uses.

John F. Rahn retired in his late 70s or early 80s, and his son Reinhardt carried on the business until the late 1960s.

I began working for the Rahns as secretary and bookkeeper in the summer of 1941 and worked there until 1949. My sister Betty Ann took over the job when I left and worked for the Rahns until 1964. We always made a very good salary, more than secretaries and bookkeepers made in other companies, and were given generous bonuses at Christmas. The Rahns supervised our bookkeeping in the most unobtrusive way not with questions of reprimands, but with a small pencilled question mark next to an entry they thought might be in error.

The Rahns adhered strictly to union rules and were safety conscious on behalf of their workers. They were conscientious about paying their bills for materials and for subcontractors. We always sent out checks before the 10th of the month following submission of an invoice. Just as the persons in charge of construction projects at large and small companies respected the Rahns for their work and their integrity, my sister and I respected them and were proud to work for these 2 highly capable, kind, and honest men.

by Margaret Burch Kelly

KREITZBURG, INDIANA
B35

The Kreitzburg Store – Tavern – Home Circa 1908

Kreitzburg was a small settlement located approximately four miles south of Dyer, Indiana in Hanover Township, Lake County, Indiana. The earliest records show that in 1880 Carl (Mrs. Heisterberg) Hummel owned the property; in 1886, Gustave Klemme; 1895, Elizabeth and Ernest Hauber.

Adolph Russel and his wife owned the store and tavern he established in 1901 in Kreitzburg. The store was located just at the end of Sheffield Avenue and Exchange Road. Among other things, the store had yard goods, and at holiday time special items such as "fancy" gifts and dishes were stocked. The south wall of the store was lined with egg cases. The customers traded eggs, at $.20 a dozen, for merchandise. The north wall of the store held two telephones when they first became available. One telephone was for Illinois, the other for Indiana. The store also had the well known pickle barrel.

A blacksmith shop, operated by the Joe Reichert Sr. family, stood just east of the store. Homes were clustered around both sides of the road.

It was a family affair for dad to take the family to Kreitzburg in those days. (These were still considered horse and buggy days.) The fellas entered and stayed in the tavern, which was located on the front of the building, while mom walked through the living quarters to put the baby on the bed and then entered the store to do her shopping. When she was finished she picked up the baby and the family returned home again. (Sleeping rooms for the owner's family were located upstairs; and a living room downstairs off to the side.) A plank walk on the east side of the store led to the main door entrance.

The Seehausen farm, located in Section One, was just west of the store. In 1948, Mrs. Harry (Alma Rinne) Seehausen purchased the old Zion Evangelical and Reformed Church schoolhouse that stood just northeast of the parsonage, and moved it to the northeast corner of the Seehausen farm homesite, close to the road and made it her home. (The church is referred to now as the Zion United Church of Christ.) To the east, between Mrs. Harry Seehausen's home and the store lived Christ and Emma (Seehausen) Russell in a home built previously by Fred and Mary (Seegers) Seehausen after they retired from the farm. The farm is still owned by Seehausen family.

Across the street from the Seehausens, lived the Grothaus family. The property adjoining the Grothaus property was owned by Jacob and Katherine Herman in 1851. The home was built in 1869 (on what was the Herman property) and owned by Joseph and Regina Scheidt and later owned in 1909 by Henry and Anna (Seegers) Seehausen. In 1938, Theodore and Dora (Piepho) Klemme bought it; and resided quite a few years in this home across the street from the store, as well as other families who have long since moved away. Over the years it saw several more owners including Fred Bremer, Ed Kasper, and Clyde and Marge (Jergon) Parris. At present it is owned by Claude and Marge's son Harold and Dorothy (Briggs) Parris.

After 13 years later, the Adolph Russell family sold the store and tavern and purchased a farm approximately one mile west. Henry Reichert and his family were living on the farm at the time. Henry Reichert bought the tavern and store. In essence, the two families just switched property. Those that helped the two families move had quite a time making sure they got the right belongings to each family.

After getting settled, Henry, removed the partition between the store and store room and made the store into a dance hall. Many gala evenings were spent there from 1920 to the 1940's.

After the dancing faded out, it was remodeled into a store again. Over the years the store had many keepers. Ownership of the store changed many times. These were the Meiers, the Piras and the Duda's. Then the Lashbrook's, who only resided there. It was later purchased by Anton and Agnette Jensen. After Anton died, Agnette, who was of Danish descent, continued the business with their son, Dennis, who graduated from law school. In spite of being robbed several times, she managed there quite a few years. Then she sold it to Mr. and Mrs. Tarrant, who remodeled it and maintained it for several years. It retained the Jensen name until its demise. Tragically, the historic landmark was destroyed by fire early one morning in the early part of 1987.

by Mrs. Ralph Oldendorf

CHARLES W. FRIEDRICH AND THE DYER FLOUR MILL
B36

Charles W. Friedrich, the miller at Dyer, Indiana, was born in Germany on December 24, 1846; and reared and educated in his native country. He attended the public schools during the required limit — up to his fourteenth year, and then became a miller's apprentice. Continuing his trade, he followed his chosen occupation in Germany until 1872, when he embarked and crossed the ocean to America.

For some time Charles was engaged in the express, grocery and saloon business in Oak Park, Illinois. In 1881, he moved to North Judson in Starke County, Indiana, and bought a mill, which he operated until 1883. He then sold the mill and in the following year came north and bought the flouring mill in Dyer,

A familiar scene around the mill site was Henry Friedrich in his Model T. He was most likely seen around town making deliveries; and out of town mainly, bakeries in the area. As far as Chicago Heights, IL. A lot of townsmen would drive the team and wagons for them and later when it became truck deliveries Circa 1920.

Indiana.

The mill had been built in 1856, operated by two French brothers, August and John Du Brueil. They decided to go into the grain business, and so they sold the mill to two men named Scheidt and Davis, who later sold it to Charles.

After Charles improved the mill in many ways, he increased its production capacity to 50 barrels a day. Besides adding to the quality of its output, he built up an extensive trade and demand for all his products.

The mill stood south of the Sheffield Avenue railroad crossing, just off to Matteson Street, the railroad tracks curved away from the main track up to the mill and could still be seen until 1986; the area is now occupied with a used car lot. The depot stood a little northeast of the mill. The Friedrich home still stands, a yellow home, adjacent to the used car lot.

Charles married Mary H. Ness, also a native of Germany, in 1870. They were the parents of William H., who married Ida Ross of North Judson (William took over the mill after Charles retired, and later moved to Chicago, Illinois); Carl, who remained single, worked with his father at the mill and later moved to Chicago; Dr. Louis M., who married Wilhelmina Batterman, of this area, and settled in Hobart, Indiana; Jacob O., who settled in Berwyn, Illinois; Caroline, who "caught" the mail bag from the moving train at the Dyer depot and later resided in Griffith, Indiana; and Johanna who married Gilbert Rowe of Brookston, Indiana.

Mr. Friedrich had been a Democrat ever since entering the ranks of American citizenship, was loyal and public-spirited in his attachment to his adopted land. He was a member of the Lutheran Church, and affiliated with the Masonic Fraternity of Hammond, Indiana.

Mrs. Ralph Oldendorf

THE WILLIAM PAUL FAMILY AND THE BRUNSWICK TAVERN
B37

William Paul was born on February 24, 1870 to Otto and Mary (Russel). He married Amanda Bauermeister on February 2, 1893. She was born on July 4, 1873 to William Sr. and Dorothea (Rohe). William and Amanda made their home on a farm located on the south side of 125th, one half mile east of Calumet Avenue. Their children were: Erwin, William A., Harold, Elmer and Alma. Three of the children died within 1893 and 1897; Alma was one year old, Harold was two and Elmer three years old.

On October 10, 1901, William and Amanda moved out of the farm home and purchased property and buildings including the Brunswick Tavern, which also served as a home, from Mary (Schmal) Gerbing, widow of Fred. John Borger, a friend of William and Amanda, served as a part time bartender. He was their neighbor on a farm to the south; and he was an engineer for the steam tractor that moved from farm to farm during July, August, and possibly September, for the oat harvest. (Threshing the bundles through the machine; the grain separated into a wagon to haul to storage in a nearby upper-story crib.)

Dances were held in the loft of William and Amanda's barn located to the east of the home. Many folks from far away attended these dances "in its day". (The Gerbings also held dances in the loft.) On May 28, 1907, William and Amanda bought additional land from Maria Echterling and her son, Julius. (A dance hall was later built on this land.)

William died on September 23, 1911 at age 41. Amanda was not well enough to carry on with the tavern herself, so through a guardianship the sons Erwin and William Jr. not yet of legal age, continued to run the tavern until it was sold to Charles Stadt on May 15, 1915. (He owned it for a few months, until he moved to Chicago, Illinois.)

Erwin and William Jr. moved to Hammond, Indiana. Amanda went to live for a while in Crown Point, Indiana in 1916. She then made her home in Gary, Indiana. On August 5, 1934, Amanda passed away. She and her husband William are buried on the Zion United Church of Christ Cemetery.

The Brunswick Tavern thrived through the years. In 1915, Bernard ("Ben") Reichert and his wife Clara (Russel) took over the ownership, which lasted for many years. Somewhere between 1923 and 1924, Ben and Clara built the dance hall and held dances there well up in the 1950's. Their children included: Ruby, Della and Elroy. The dance hall was later used as an Auction House and later converted into a garage.

In 1962, Ben and Clara's son Elroy Reichert and his wife Helen (Wornhoff) took over. Their children include: Kay, Sandra and Bernard. The Reichert family continued the business until May 1987 when Robert Allen and his daughter Elizabeth purchased it. The tavern is

Charles W. Friedrich's Dyer Flour Mill he owned in 1893. William Friedrich on the left, a customer in the horse and buggy, Henry, and Carl.

The Brunswick Tavern in 1901 under William and Amanda Paul ownership, with their children on the steps. John Borger stands to the front of the building; a Hotel in early days. Their barn is to the left; where dances were held in the loft, until a dance hall was built south of the living quarters.

still there and is operating under the "Reichert Tavern" name.

by Mrs. Ralph Oldendorf

INDEX

SURNAME INDEX

Index is by story number NOT page number

T - Topical Section   B - Business Section   F - Family Section

A

Abasta, F35
Abdill, T64
Ackemann, F198
Ackerman, F72, F170
Adams, F132
Adank, F102, T60
Adler, F90, F200
Ahles, F231
Ailes, F250
Aken, F1
Akey, T53
Albers, F88
Albright, F268, F270
Aldrich, F305
Alexander, F61
Allen, F47, F52, F141, F268
Allison, F6
Alsman, F190
Alton, F70
Alyce, F11
Anderson, F56, F155, F168, T22
Andrews, F300
Anduski, F93
Ansbro, F2
Antrim, F298
Antusak, F140
Archibald, F313
Arkenburg, F189
Armantrout, T53
Arnold, F141, F308
Arsenault, F135
Ashby, F175
Ashmer, F204
Atseff, B29
Aubuchon, F176
Augustyn, F168
Ault, F172, F173, T7
Austgen, F110, F125, F129, F233, F239
Averill, F313
Avery, F65, F66
Aylen, F108
Aylesworth, F164

B

Babcock, T22
Bacic, F80
Backes, F179
Bacon, F3, F64, F266
Bahr, F171
Bailey, F249, F303, F304, F308, T22, T58
Baker, F180, F187, F226, T56
Baldner, B6
Baldwin, F93
Bales, F268
Ball, F4, F70, F117, F257
Ballantyne, F5, F41
Balser, F268
Bandura, F72
Bane, F204
Banks, F158, F159, F246
Bannwart, F297
Barber, F250, F303
Barbosa, F156
Barcalow, F42
Barcus, F173
Barfeldt, F228
Barley, F128
Barman, F217
Barmore, T60
Barney, F274
Barr, F180
Barry, F129, F194
Bars, F153
Bartelme, F125
Bartlett, F165
Bartz, F135
Bassett, F6, F23, F101
Baster, F267
Bastin, F203
Bates, F267, T53
Batterman, F19, F90, F236, F309
Bauer, F287
Bauermeister, B37, F7, F185
Baumeister, F145
Baumer, F210

Baumgartner, F244, F259
Bauske, F252
Bayh, F194
Bazin, F8, F288, F289
Beachy, F157
Beal, F266
Beam, F21, F171
Beam/Boehme, F23
Bearby, F316
Beattie, F208, F317
Beaumkamp, F9
Becher, F226, F227
Becker, F100, F180, F181, F189, F233
Beckman, F56, F78, F165
Beckmann, F9
Beckwith, F113
Beffa, F126
Behre, F182
Behrens, F236, F237, F238, F294, F295
Beiriger, F40, F233
Belanger, F149
Bell, F10, F13, F210
Bellinger, F126
Bellingham, F283
Bencie, F8
Bennett, F20
Berens, F257
Berg, F9, F155, F228, F230, T22
Berge, T53
Berger, T22
Bergmann, F196
Bergmeier, F88
Bergweiler, F140
Bernhard, F295
Berquist, F11, F12, F151, F247
Berta, F191
Bertova, F191
Besse, T60
Betham, F282
Betz, F148
Beuer, F290
Bevacqua, F156
Beville, F66
Bibler, F160, F180
Biegel, F264
Bieker, F111
Bielek, F63
Biester, F102
Biggs, F99
Bihr, F298
Binyon, T13
Bishoff, B4
Bishop, F97, F146, T53
Bivens, F44
Bixeman, F181
Bjorkquist, F11
Blachley, T2
Black, F13, F152
Blackburn, F141
Blackham, F119
Blackman, F61
Blackwell, F186
Blake, F275, F298
Blakeman, F273
Blanchar, F2
Blanchard, F262
Blattner, F225
Bleicher, F292
Blizzard, F117
Bloesch, F14
Bloodgood, F274
Blue, F156
Blum, F197
Blume, F7, F44, F100, F185, F195
Boby, F53
Bock, F31, F309
Bocknowski, F135
Bodamer, F148
Boer, F289
Boester, F14
Bohling, F15, F16, F17, F90, F125, F131, F217, F218, F228, F258, F259, F263
Bohn, F19
Bohney, F108, F110, F111
Bohr, F108, F233
Bohrofen, B15, F68
Boice, F283
Bokash, F120
Bokich, T22
Bol, F257
Bonaparte, F87

Bond, T22
Bonko, F72
Bonner, F292
Boone, F18, F95, F298
Booth, F283
Borchers, F19, F181, F182
Borden, F92
Borger, F165
Borges, F100
Born, F20, F21, F22, F23, F171
Bornmann, F102
Borrner, F208
Borsits, F155
Bosch, F221
Bosworth, F95, F302
Bothwell, T53
Bottner, F309
Bouwen, F108
Bower, F166
Bowgreen, T22
Bowser, F24
Box, F233
Boyd, F2, F210
Brack, F156
Brackett, F316
Bradshaw, F173
Brady, F126, F165
Brands, T28
Brandt, T60
Brannock, T53
Brasovan, F72
Bredemeier, F88
Brenneman, F151
Brenning, F240
Brey, F300
Brey(e), F300
Breyfogle, F102, F170
Bridge, F25
Briggs, F313
Bright, F204
Briney, F210
Brink, F14
Brisson, F283
Brittain, F42
Britton, F268
Broer, F137
Brom, F127
Bronson, F161, F164
Broughton, F283
Brovine, F158
Brown, F26, F27, F28, F29, F50, F51, F52, F83, F84, F95, F102, F105, F135, F155, F156, F159, F172, F204, F207, F250, T53
Brueckman, T60
Bruhn, F285
Bruich, F14
Brunton, F268
Brusel, T49
Bryan, F161, F163, F207
Bryant, F169
Bryner, F204
Buchan, F122, F123
Bucholz, B30
Buckley, F30, F231
Budney, F300
Buehler, F89
Buehre, F31
Buikema, F244
Bull, F275
Bunnel, F250
Bunnell, B13
Buras, F286
Burch, F32, F53
Burchfield, F223
Burge, F95, F102, F298, T53
Burger, F28, F250
Burke, F250
Burkhart, F244
Burkholder, F268
Burns, F109, F306
Burroughs, F269
Burski, F268
Burton, F270, F271
Bury, F91
Busselberg, F273
Butler, F29, F95, F275
Buttinger, F135
Butts, F40
Byrnes, F47

C

Cabana, F171
Cadwell, F158, F273, F274
Cain, F141, F240
Calabrese, F34
Caldwel, F305
Camblin, F267
Camp, F204
Campbell, F34, F95, F115, F126, F250, F302
Canale, F316
Canino, F35, F39, F121
Cannon, F50, F316
Carey, F158
Carlascio, F297
Carlson, F316, T22
Carmicheal, F17
Carnes, F204
Carozzo, F148
Carrigan, F2
Carson, F79, F107, F153, F186
Carston, F165
Carus, F283
Cary, F210
Casagranda, F317, F318
Case, F42, F43, F297
Casper, F210
Casselberry, F186
Cassill, F188
Castle, F36
Castrogiovanni, F117
Cedar Lake Poultry Farm, B4
Centanni, F35, F37, F38, F39, F144, F150, F178, F235
Chamberlain, F267
Chapman, F187
Charlemagne, F282
Charleston, F120
Cheever, F249, F250
Christenson, F40, F175
Christianson, F41, F297
Chundoga, F53
Church, F70, F71
Churchyard, F186
Clark, F37, F70, F156, F193, F267, T53
Classen, F91, T53
Claus, F100, F114, F155, F216
Claussen, F146
Clay, F126, F265
Clayhorn, F88
Clayton, F317
Cleaver, F172, F267
Cleavinger, F173
Clegg, F204
Clem, F268
Clements, F174
Clingan, F70, F71
Clymer, F101
Coambs, T49
Cobb, F28
Cochran, B10
Cockburn, F280
Cogley, F72
Cohoun, F83
Colbert, F155
Colby, F162, T49
Coldwell, F304
Cole, F21, F172, F270, F275, F307
Coleman, F17, F66, F82, F130, F283
Colley, F280
Collins, F102, F272, F273
Colwell, F305
Combs, F98
Comer, F192
Concialde, F37
Conelan, F122
Connchie, F122
Connelly, F180
Constanza, F39
Contz/Kunz, F179
Cook, F42, F43, F92, F310, T49
Coonrod, F175
Cooper, F51, F70, F98
Corbin, F313
Core, F83
Cormack, F312
Corwin, F132
Costigan, F63
Cotrill, F268
Covault, F44, F45, F204

220

SURNAME INDEX

Index is by story number NOT page number

T - Topical Section B - Business Section F - Family Section

Cowser, F204
Cox, F46, F171, F270, F271
Craft, F164, T13
Cramer, F47, F63, T22
Craven, F48
Crawford, F44, F93
Creighton, F4
Cremer, F158
Cress, F160, F162, F164
Crider, F84
Crisman, F158, T22
Croker, F283
Cross, F267, F274
Crow, F122
Crown Point Manufacturing Company, B2
Crumpacker, F49
Culver, F50, F51, F52, F73, F76
Culwen, F281
Cummins, T22
Cuney, F126
Cunningham, F97
Curtiss, F157
Cusack, F14
Cutler, T53
Cwick, F204
Czapko, F37, F53, F54, F81, F240

D

Dacey, F54
Dacre, F282
Daescher, F165
Dalton, F283
Dancro, F106, F127
Daniels, F55, F158, F274
Dannenberg, F100
Dart, F203
Daskum, F266, F269
Datema, F220
Davey, F155, F156
Davich, F80
Davis, B3, F13, F14, F21, F23, F42, F56, F57, F82, F123, F143, F225, F283, F313
Day, F28, F268
Dayhuff, F72
De Angelo, F155
Death, T2
de Beaumont, F282
de Berkeley, F282
de Clifford, F282
DeCook, F203
de Corwen, F281
de Culwen, F281
De Curruwenne, F281
de Ferrers, F282
DeFoor, F316
de Grandmesnil, F282
DeGroot, F221
de Jong, F222
de Lascelles, F281
DeLau, B6
deLisle, F193
DeLisles, F194
DeMaria, F35
Demmon, F58, F59, F60, F95, F177, F187, F209, F302
Demon, F67
de Musgrave, F282
Dennison, F152
de Pekering, F281
De Pipe, F117
de Quincy, F282
De Reamer, T53
de Vexin, F282
DeVries, F223
Dewain, F270
DeWald, F125
DeWitt, F267
Dewitt, F30
De Young, F223
Diamond, F33
Dianias, F115
Dibble, F93
Diesslin, F212, F215
Dikert, T53
Dile, F166
Dillabaugh, F61, F211, F215
Dillinger, F202
Dinse, F250
Dinwiddie, F180, T53

Dionne, F268
Dishaw, F105
Ditlow, F158
Divis, F56
Dobson, F98
Dockweiler, F272, F273
Doepping, F298
Doescher, F90
Doffin, F179
Dohmeyer, F89
Dohrman, F294
Dollish, F267
Domberg, T22
Don Bales Inc., B3
Donch, F62
Donley, T60
Donnaha, T53
Doolan, F267
Doolin, F284
Dora, F104
Dorman, F181
Doty, F185, F268
Dow, F265
Dowdle, F63
Downie, F122
Drago, F24
Dranchak, F72
Dregg, F281
Dreiser, F140
Dresbaugh, F148
Driscoll, F30
Drygas, F288
DuBois, F110
Dubs/DuBois, F251
Dumsky, F89
Dunkerson, F186
Dunning, F5
Dunsmore, F204
Dupree, F204
Durovcik, F191
Durovcikova, F191
Dutton, F27
Dwyer, F64
Dye, F42
Dyer, F99, F207
Dykstra, F80

E

Earl, F290
Eaton, F268
Eberhart, F42
Ebert, F173, F231, T2
Ech, F68
Echnter, F203
Echols, F314, F315
Echterling, B9, F218
Eder, F102
Edgerton, F276, F278
Edwards, F119
Efting, F74
Eggebrecht, F44
Eggers, T49
Ehrhardt, F175, F188
Eikelberg, F158
Einspahr, F88
Eiweglelben, F42
Eller, F165
Ellicott, T53
Elliott, F116, F152
Elsworth, F112
Elting, F31
Ely, F278
Emerson, B16
Eng, T22
Engel, F7
Engelking, F294
Engelman, F65, F66
Engelmann, F66
Englebright, F141, F142, T60
Ensign, F148
Ensweiler, T53
Epp, F84
Erdman, F66
Erickson, F100, F124, F148
Erlandson, T22
Erlenbach, F9
Erskine, F283
Ervere, F117
Esboldt, F135

Esch, F93
Eshkol, F194
Espinosa, F262
Estovk, F191
Ethelred, F281, F283
Evans, F54, F259
Everett, F92
Ewer, F117, F274, F276
Ewing, F120

F

Faga, F35
Fagen, B14, B15, F69, F109, F111, F167
Fancher, F70, F71, F316, T13
Farrow, F266
Fedler, F117
Fedorchak, F72, F140
Feeley, F30
Ferestad, F50, F73, F74, F75, F76
Fick, F216
Fiegle, F19, F78, F182
Field, F269, F270
Fields, F150
Fieler, B6, F11, F90, F151, F316
Fiene, F309
Fieres, F261
Fifield, T53
Finck, F149
Finklestein, F257
Finn, F135
Finney, F9
Fischer, F19, F182, F268
Fisher, F61, F218
Fiske, F9
Fitch, F95, F190
Fitzgerald, F314, F315
FitzRoy, F282
Fitzwilliam, F282
Flebbe, F236
Fleming, F30
Fleury, F248
Floyd, F224
Flynn, F296
Foegen, B15
Foley, F262, F268
Forkner, F166
Forsha, F164
Forstner, F248, F250
Forsythe, F93, T60
Foster, F287
Fotre, F233
Fowler, F180
Fox, F92, F283
Foy, F88
Fraas, F227
Frame, B4, F203
Franchimont, F156
Frangella, F146
Franklin, F57, F95, F317
Franks, F66
Franz, F90, T60
Frederick, F88
Fredric, F273
Freeman, F130
Freix, F184
Frick, F155
Frisk, F244
Fritchen, B15, F67
Fritz, F129
Frobose, F88
Frohnen, F233
Frolik, F308
Fry, F172, T2
Fryar, F250
Fuegen, F67
Fuller, F269
Furnier, F126
Furtek, F35
Fusko, F115
Futa, F211

G

Galich, F146
Gallagher, B13, F77
Garber, F146
Garcia, F288

Gard, F91, F143
Garland, F107
Garrett, F83
Garrison, F30
Gartnofuaron, F123
Garven, F186
Garvey, F268
Garza, B10
Gaskell, F143
Gast, F268
Gasvoda, B9
Gates, F155
Geer, F14
Gehring, F108
Geiger, F67, F68
Geis, F2, F126, F137
Geisen, F9, F78
Geiser, T53
Gemmer, F173
George, F34
Gerbing, F231
Gerlach, F90, F129, F137, F239
Germain, F73
Gersack, F8
Getschinger, F234
Gettler, F129
Giannini, F126
Gibbs, F60, F79, F97, F153, F269
Gibson, F105
Giegel, F78
Gifford, F278
Gilbert, F208, F317, T53
Gile, F314
Gilliam, F252
Gillies, F250
Gillogly, T53
Gilmore, F83
Givens, F82
Glassen, F131
Glazier, F187
Gleason, F275
Glivar, F265, F292
Glover, F278, T53
Godfrey, F304
Goetcheus, F42
Golcher, F258, F263
Gold, F80
Goldie, F81
Good, F82, F83, F84
Goodge, F233
Goodknight, F127
Goodman, F250
Goodspeed, F2
Gordon, F21, F23, F171, F310
Goring, F224
Gospatrick, F281
Gotheb, F113
Govert, F85, F111
Gowans, F207
Grabe, F7
Gragg, F267
Graham, F203
Granger, F17, F82, F168, F169
Grant, F72, F86, F123, F315
Granzow, F209, F210
Graper, T53
Grau, F259
Graves, F20, F22, F161, F313
Gray, F2, F215
Green, F66, F159, F176
Greene, F135
Greiving, F110
Grenis, F147
Griese, F294, F310
Griesel, F231
Grieser, F233
Grieving, F295
Griffin, F126, F312
Grimmer, F85, F87, F90, F245
Grisby, F54
Gross, T22
Gruel, F148
Gumbiner, F126
Gunder, T53
Gunschivich, F160
Guritz, F88, F89, F100
Gustafson, F40
Guthrie, T60
Gyerko, F156

221

SURNAME INDEX

Index is by story number NOT page number

T - Topical Section   B - Business Section   F - Family Section

H

Haake, F295
Haan, T13
Haberichter, T60
Hack, F90, F91, F125, F131, F143, F200, F229, F230
Hahn, F181
Hains, F6
Hale, F92
Hales, F176
Hall, F92, F93, F94, F156, F169, F250, F261, F284, F310, T60
Halsted, F30, F95
Haltom, F259
Halton, F252
Ham, F2, F126, F137
Hamann, F88
Hamilton, F2, F172, F264, T22
Hammes, F96
Handel, F97
Handenshield, F21
Handley, F70, F97
Handly, B1, F97
Hanks, F84
Hanler, F97
Hanley, F97, F98
Hanlon, F97
Hanna, F233
Hanner, F4
Hanslik, T53
Hanson, F88
Hard, T53
Harder, F44, F142
Hardesty, F158, F256
Harding, F268
Hardy, F26
Harlan, F51
Harmon, F38, F267
Harriet, F60
Harris, B10
Harrison, F193
Hart, F2, F99, F110, F168, F254
Hartman, F132, F181
Harwood, F308
Haselback, F106
Haseman, F100, F185
Haskell, F268, F270
Haskett, F55
Hatcher, F307
Hatfield, F42, F156
Hathaway, B3
Havens, F6, F101, F307
Hawkins, F313
Hawley, T53
Haxton, F210
Hayes, T22
Hayhurst, F107, F192, F267
Haymond, F26
Haynes, F92, F284
Hayward, T49
Head, F268
Hecht, F19
Heelan, F268
Heidbreder, F102, F287, T53
Heighway, F308
Heintz, F287
Heinze, F207
Heinzman, T60
Heiser, F91, F143
Heiss, F186
Heisterberg, F7
Helbling, F317
Held, F97, F100
Heldt, F232
Helfen, F258
Heller, F7
Helmer, F113
Helms, F28, F250
Henderlong, F67
Henderson, F79, F180
Henning, F102, F103, F287
Henricson, F120
Hepp, F143
Herckle, F267
Hermann, F231
Herndon, F72
Herran, F88
Herrick, F250, F306
Herrin, F304
Herring, F303
Herrman, F131
Herrmann, F201
Hertel, F117
Hess, F104, F105, F106, F127
Hessing, F9
Hessler, F127
Hessling, F9
Hetzler, F126
Heuker, F220, F221
Hewitt, F1
Hiatt, F267
Hickman, F306
Higgins, F107, F192, F234
Hight, F180
Hilbrich, F68, F108, F109, F110, F111, F225
Hill, F155, F259, F305, T13
Hills, F73, F74, F75, T2
Hilton, F54, F283
Hindsley, F98
Hine, F172, F173
Hinkelman, F100
Hinze, F295
Hirlston, F81
Hitchcock, F303
Hitchcock-Barber, F304
Hitzemann, F112, F113, F114, F236
Hlad, F175
Hlatko, F34, F115
Hodges, F126
Hodson, F6, F101, F307
Hoevet, F9
Hoffman, F110, F148, F225, T60
Hogan, F17
Holas, F8
Holborn, F271
Holland, B2, F149
Holley, T53, T60
Holmes, F42, F303, F304
Holms, F67
Holstead, F158
Homfeld, F13, T53
Homfold, B3
Hood, F128
Hootman, F116
Hoover, F166
Horban, F212
Horn, F176
Horner, F117
Horst, T53
Horton, F4
Housty, F105
Howard, F34
Howe, F274
Howes, F186
Howie, F267
Howkinson, F71
Hresko, F191
Huber, F78
Hudelson, F155
Hudgins, F107
Hueper, F309
Huff, T22
Hughes, F2, F42, F155
Hulich, F70
Hulse, F205, F206
Hummel, F212, F225
Hunt, F251
Huntington, F66, F168
Hurlburt, F278
Hurst, F268
Huseman, F78, F254
Hussey, F118, F293
Hutchison, T56
Hutton, F11, F151
Hyde, F269
Hyden, F107
Hyry, F135

I

Iacaboni, F261
Iddings, T53
Ingle, F105, F127
Inscho, F119
International Harvester Agency, B3
Isakson, F120
Itczak, B10
Ittel, F121

J

Jabay, F139
Jackson, F173, F204, F283
Jacqua, F276
Jaik, F32
Jamieson, F122, F123, F139
Janetske, F132
Janiga, F72
Jankovich, F174
Jansen, F308
Jarosak, F72
Jeffers, F203
Jeffery, F115, F290
Jenkins, F104, F209
Jensen, F98
Johnson, F120, F121, F129, F160, F180, F313, T22, T53
Jones, F26, F33, F93, F203, F267
Jonkman, F223
Jordan, F124, F247
Jordening, F19, F181
Joseph, F115
Jourdain, F15, F16, F17, F125, F131, F217, F218
Jovanoski, F176
Jovanovich, F141
Joyce, F316
Judd, F158
Judson, F172
Junglas, B3
Jurgenson, F151

K

Kaas, F222
Kahn, F191
Kaiser, F2, F85, F110, F126, F137, F316, T22, T60
Kallas, F192
Kallies, F210
Kammer, F90
Kane, F156
Kapella, F54
Kapperman, F294
Karr, F105, F127
Karsten, F106
Karstensen, F128
Kathryn, F142
Katz, F309
Kaufman, F139
Kautenburger, F108, F110
Kazda, F215
Kegebein, F210
Keiffer, F230, F231
Keilman, F17, F48, F90, F110, F129, F179, F217, F225
Kelby, T53
Keller, F14
Kelley, B9, F155, F308
Kelly, F2, F21, F32
Kelso, F208
Kendall, F281
Kennedy, F94, F130, F261
Kennett, F183
Kenney, B1
Kent, F84
Ketcham, F6
Keuhl, F316
Keup, F112, F113
Keys, F180
Kiedaisch, F7, F88
Kiger, F192
Kikkert, F221
Kilroy, F78
Kimball, F171
Kinder, F14
King, F132, F266
Kinney, F156
Kitchel, F316
Klaeser, F91
Klassen, F15, F16, F91, F125, F131, F218
Klein, F258
Kleine, F111
Kleiner, F32, F33
Klemme, F132, F216
Kleser, F233
Kloosterboer, F221
Kloss, F89
Knarr, F79
Kneif, F195
Knesek, F17
Knief, F309
Kniesley, F174
Knight, F156
Knopf, T53
Knotts, F133, F308
Knox, F302
Knutsen, F134
Kobelin, F154
Kochmar, F316
Kocur, F135, F250
Koedyker, F155
Koehle, F90
Koerner, F251, F260
Kohlscheen, F216
Koicordakora, F72
Kokinda, F8
Kolling, F113, F237
Komenda, F80
Konopa, F56
Koop, F108
Koppe, F27
Kormendy, F97
Kors, F126
Kos, F148
Koscielniak, F70
Koshnick, F111
Kramer, F14
Krebs, F235
Kreis, F153, F215
Kries, F213, F214
Krieter, T60
Krinbill, F136
Krost, F90, F228
Kruslak, F202
Kucia, F2, F126, F137, T60
Kudasill, F21
Kuehl, B6
Kuemmel, F298
Kuhlman, F100
Kuhn, F23, F123, F139, F165, F170, F275
Kukelka, F72, F140
Kuntzschmann, F171
Kurdelak, F314
Kurth, F100, F183, F184
Kyger, F6, F101
Kyle, T53

L

Lacatesa, F35
Lacy, F82, F83, F84
Lageveen, F158
Lahr, F313
Lail, B4, F141, F142
Lail Bros. Egg Farm, Inc., B4
Lain, F166
Lake, F81
Lamarre, F204
Lamey, F56
Lamphire, F268
Landske, F70
Laney, T60
Lange, F141
Langston, F130
Langtree, F283
Lans, F120
Lantz, F180
Larson, F115, F297
LaSalle, F120
Lascelles, F283
Lasser, F179
Latieak, F54
Latta, F268
Latz, T53, T60
Lauer, F203
Lauerman, F56, F233
Lauermann, F143, F233
Laughlin, F186
Lawbaugh, F267
Lawrence, F246
Lawson, F120
La Zouche, F282
Ledak, F144
Ledman, F21
Ledoux, F110
Lee, F84

SURNAME INDEX

Index is by story number NOT page number
T - Topical Section   B - Business Section   F - Family Section

Lehman, T53
Lehnen, F233
Leinen, F91, F230, F258
Leisrael, F194
Leitner, F287
Lem(c)ke, F300
Lemert, T22
Lemon, T22
Lenburg, F145, F146, F147
Lengleys, F281
Lennertz, F316
Leraas, F134
Leslie, F140
Lesniewski, F34
Leszczynski, F148
Letz, B2, F149, F165, F176
Lewandowski, F150
Lewetta, F27
Lewis, F11, F12, F151, F262, F275
Lewry, F193, F194
Leyburne, F283
Lilley, F278
Lillig, B14, B15, F67, F68, F69, F109
Lindeman, F88
Lindsley, F265
Lindstrom, T22
Linton, F316
Lippart, F145
Lisius, F316
Little, F152, F166, F199
Littleton, F156
Livery Stable, B3
Lobraico, F28
Lockman, F66
Lockwoods, F117
Loehmer, F129
Lofler, F271
Lohman, F100
Lokie, F172
London, F308
Long, F42, F51, F67, F77
Lorain, F283
Lorenzen, F88
Lorenzo, F270
Loscovitch, F80
Loucks, F92, F93, F94, F304
Love, F79, F120, F153, F211, F212, F213, F215, F226
Lowry, F186
Loyce, F179
Luchene, F156
Luckoff, F300
Ludwig, F217, F230
Luebke, F6
Luers, T53
Lueth, F300
Lukmann, F251
Lundstrom, T22
Lurie, F193
Lusso, F233
Luther, F70
Luttrell, F205, F206
Lutz, F148
Lybarger, F35

M

Maack, F154, F231
Maatheus, F284
Mabrey, T53
MacAdoo, F307
MacDermid, F66
Macedo, F98
MacFarland, F119
Machnik, F146
Mack, T53
Mackanos, F316
Mader, T60
Madison, F70
Maginot, F15, F125
Magner, F61
Mahoney, F111
Maier, F139
Maki, T60
Making, F70, T60
Malayter, F126, T60
Malcolm, F281
Maleverer, F283
Malmstone, F221
Maloney, F102

Mangold, F67
Manley, F155
Manning, T2
Mantic, F72
Marabel, F316
Marcinak, F314, F315, F317, F318
Marciniak, F175
Marcoff, F80
Mareness, F158
Marin, F120
Mark, F122, F123
Markee, F180
Marko, F80
Marks, F208, F317, F318
Marquardt, F19
Marsh, F166, F268
Marthinich, F227
Martin, F4, F72, F140, F204, F270
Martiny, F305
Martisovic, F140
Marvel, F120
Mason, F44
Massey, F13
Mathew, F268
Mathias, F206
Mathis, F241
Matson, T22
Matthews, F2, F107
Matthias, F182
Mattis, T22
Matyus, F8
Mauger, F155, F156, F157
Maxey, F33
Maxwell, F27, F158, F159, F246
May, T53
McArdle, F199
McBeth, F27
McBrierty, F141
McCann, F155
McCarthy, F212
McCartney, F66
McCarty, F276
McCauley, F264
McColley, F92, F94
McCormick-Deering International Harvester Co., B3
McCullough, F256
McCurdy, F157
McDermit, F97
McDonald, F267
McDowell, F42
McFarland, T64
McGinley, F158
McGrath, F250
McGuire, F155
McHone, F317
McKeehan, F27
McKindley, F47
McKinley, F113
McKinney, F214
McLaughlin, F42, F304
McLeod, F140
McMichael, F70, F130, T60
McMillin, F130
McNair, F148
McNay, T2
McNutt, F115
McPheeters, F34
McPherson, F115
Meader, F172
Medeiros, F63
Medlin, F248, F250
Medon, F119
Meeker, F160, F161, F162, F163, F164, F207, F209, F280, T53
Meier, F89, F128, F181, F294
Mensching, F114
Mensing, F113, F114
Merrill, F312
Messerschmidt, B2, F149
Metchnikoff, F194
Metz, F126, T53
Meyer, F165, F176, F275
Meynwarin, F281
Michaelis, F118
Micheal, T22
Michyelis, F118
Middleton, F283
Mihal, F37
Mikels, F166
Millard, F174

Miller, B14, B15, F4, F21, F28, F69, F77, F88, F121, F122, F167, F203, F234, F249, F250, F273, F300
Mills, F70, F168, F169
Milner, F158, F317
Minas, F193
Miner, F170
Minninger, F23, F139, F171
Mishrock, F66
Mitchell, F272, F273, F310
Mitchum, F23
Moeller, F181, F182
Monzulla, F80
Moody, F156
Mooney, F92, F284
Moore, F26, F28, F82, F83, F84, F172, F173, F175, F186, F205, T7, T49
Morein, F186
Morgan, F29
Morreau, F271
Morreaux, F270
Morris, F268, F274
Morrison, F204, T53
Morse, F60, F95, F174
Morton, F94
Mosier, B6
Mosney, F175
Mosny, F175
Moss, F158, F257
Moulton, F142
Mower, F275
Mrak, F150
Mudge, F173
Mudrich, F316
Mueller, F149, F176, T60
Mulhern, F207
Muller, F110
Mulvany, F192, F310
Mundell, F58, F59, F153, F177
Murdock, F9
Murphy, F248, F250
Murray, F93, F292, F316
Musgrave, F281, F282, F283
Musielak, F223
Mussack, F112
Musto, F297
Muterspaugh, F153
Myers, F259, F261, F270, T22

N

Nasoloski, F178
Natke, F105, F106, F127
Nave, F268
Neal, F107
Neibling, F129
Nellinger, F204
Nelson, F20, F120, F204, F205, F234, F264, F268, T22
Nepsha, F54
Nestor, F8
Nethery, F79
Netzow, F210
Neudorf, F179, F258, F259
Neuman, F87
Nevin, F209
Newbolds, F250
Newland, F192
Newman, T22
Newton, F149
Nichols, F20, F21, F22, F23, F69, F86, F180, F300, F313, T2, T64
Nicholson, F70, F71, F191
Nielsen, F7
Niemeyer, T56
Niles, F274
Nissen, F10
Nitchman, F35
Nitzer, F70
Nixon, F66
Norambuena-Casey, F148
Nordyke, F165
North, F94, F156
Norton, F99
Nowasadski, F148
Nowfel, F45
Nuella, F197
Nyles, F216

O

Oakley, F156
O'Brien, F38
O'Handley, F97
O'Handly, F97
O'Hanley, F97
Ohlendorf, F89, F181, F182, F189, F190
Ohlenkamp, F88, F185
Ohms, F313
Olander, T22
Oldendorf, F19, F31, F181, F182, F183, F184, F190, F195, F197, F294
O'loughlin, F89
Olson, F156, T60
Oltrogge, F7, F100, F185
Oros, F97
Orr, F13, F186
Orte, F90, F200
Ossowski, F14
Ostermeier, F309
Oswald, F121
Osweiler, F255
Otey, F152
Ott, F259, F262, T53
Owens, B16, F59
Oxman, F65, F66

P

Pace, F27
Packham, F290
Padberg, F191
Paige, F315
Palkovich, F156
Palm, F108, F129
Palmer, F278
Paluch, F97
Pampalone, F72
Papp, F8, F289
Parker, F34
Parks, F304
Parris, F166
Parsley, F261
Partington, F44
Pasteur, F194
Pataki, F288, F289
Paterson, F122
Pattee, F172
Patterson, F14
Paul, B37, F7, F183, F185, F188, F189, F190, F295
Pavelchak, F70
Pavell, F191
Pavlish, T60
Pavlo, F191
Pavlov, F250
Pawlek, F150
Pawula, F135
Pearson, F211
Peat, F283
Peck, F152
Pegg, F107, F192, F310
Peifer, F85, F108, F201
Pelham, F34
Pemble, F267
Pendergast, F2
Pendley, F193, F194
Penning, F40
Pennsylvania Railroad Depot, B2
Perkins, F193
Perry, F74, F97
Peters, F13, F72, F102, F272, F300
Peterson, F98, F203, T22
Petertyl, F135
Petraitis, F38
Pettit, F314, F315
Pfaff, F93
Pfau, F195, F197
Pfeil, F287
Pflugradt, F134
Phalon, F156
Phillip, F267
Phillips, F268, F298, T22
Piat, F283
Picard, F155
Pickart, T49
Pickering, F281

223

SURNAME INDEX

Index is by story number NOT page number

T - Topical Section   B - Business Section   F - Family Section

Piepenbrink, F102
Piepho, F128, F181, F183, F190, F195, F196, F197, F198, F216, F232, F309
Pierce, F42, F166
Pierpoint, F283
Piersma, F221, F222
Piller, F199
Piniak, F135
Piper, F105
Pippin, F240
Place, T53
Platko, F314
Platt, F313
Plietner, F165
Plucinski, F202
Plummer, B3
Pluto, F273
Podanova, F286
Pogue, F33
Polak, F308
Poland, F44
Polhamus, F275
Polite, F250
Pollock, F191, F268
Popa, F205, F240
Popik, F81
Potter, F303
Potts, F313
Powell, F50
Powers, F47, F72, F267, F269, F292
Press, F267
Pressley, F82
Preston, F95
Prevo, F7
Price, F42, F43, F166
Priddy, F83
Prugh, F135
Prus, F175
Pryle, F205
Pugh, F235
Pulver, F267
Purdy, F267
Purkey, F141
Putman, F74
Putti, F8

Q

Quantz, T22
Quigley, F2
Quinn, F156

R

Rauscher, F201
Rabatine, F310
Radi, F294
Radu, T60
Radzwill, T60
Rampke, F210
Ramsey, F83
Randhan, F248, F250
Randolph, F97
Rascher, F69, F108
Rasher, F228, F230
Rassier, F228, F230
Ratliff, F107, F192
Ratsch, F157
Rattazzi, F211
Raymond, F304
Ready, F61
Ream, F45, F204
Redar, F87, F200, F201, F251, F254, F255, F259, F260
Reder, F90
Redmond, F81
Reed, F99, F266, F267, F268, F269, F270
Reeder, F228, T49
Reedstrom, F202
Reel, F93, F141
Regnier, F268
Rehborg, F182
Rehm, T60
Reichard, F215
Reichert, B35, B37, F216, F262
Reickhoff, F245
Reinald, F282
Reinhold, F204

Reiter, F33
Reks, F107
Remick, F141
Rendina, F284
Renyard, F2
Rettig, F217
Reynolds, F141
Rhein, F230
Rhodes, F172
Rhodman, F159
Rice, F99, F269
Richard, F215
Richardson, F305
Richolka, F72
Richter, F298
Riechers, F88
Riechert, F14
Riecker, F158, F203, F298
Rietman, F87
Rigsby, F156
Rimbach, F90
Rinkenberger, F14
Ripple, F98
Rippy, T53
Rispens, F223
Ritchie, F44
Ritter, F210
Roach, F44, F45, F204, F205, F206
Roberts, F84
Robinson, F70, F301, F312
Rockwell, F161, F207, T53
Rodman, F159
Roe, F50
Roeda, F223
Roffman, F149, F182
Rogers, F208, F314, F317, F318
Rohe, B37, F7, F294
Rohrsen, F294
Roos, F282
Root, T53
Rosebrook, F23
Rosenbaum, F59, F207, F209, F210, F280
Rosenbower, F93
Rosenbrock, F100
Rosinko, F68, F109
Rosko, F193
Ross, F9, F61, F91, F153, F211, F212, F213, F214, F215, F226, F316
Rothermel, F126
Roy, F9
Rudasill, F23
Rudolph, F88, T53
Ruffin, F191
Ruhe, F181
Ruhs, F244
Ruley, F268
Rumsey, F172
Runge, F140
Rupe, F42, F43
Rush, F97
Russel, B35, B37, F188, F189, F197, F216
Russell, B3, F7, F107, F195
Rust, F19, F216
Rutledge, B15, F167
Ryan, F2

S

Sackley, F105, F106, F127
Sakeld, F283
Salisbury, T53
Sampson, F267
Sanders, F97, F158, F171, F267, F271
Sanderson, F193, F278
Sandor, F135
Sanstead, F120
Sasse, F90
Satellite Sensations, B4
Sattler, F204
Sauer, F113, F234
Sauerman, F90
Saulters, F44
Sauter, F91
Sawtell, F278
Saylor, T53
Schaefer, F15, F17, F90, F125, F156, F217, F218, F258
Schafer, F115, F217, F219, F239
Schaller, F68, F225
Schaper, F88, F100

Schau, F129
Schaufele, F27
Scheeringa, F220, F221, F222, F223, F224
Scheidt, F109, F129, F225
Schellers, F26
Scherer, F78, F90, F91, F219
Scheuneman, F106
Schiesser, F85
Schiessle, F254
Schilling, F180, F316
Schillo, F15, F16
Schlagel, F19
Schlemmer, F215, F226, F227, T53
Schmal, B37, F15, F16, F17, F90, F91, F109, F110, F111, F131, F200, F228, F229, F231
Schmelter, F9
Schmidt, F7, F111, F201, F228, F231, F300
Schmitke, F118
Schneider, F67, F91, F143
Schnurlein, T53
Schoenbeck, F232
Scholl, F143, F233, F254, F256, F260
Schoon, F221, F222, F223
Schrage, F181
Schramm, F227
Schreek, F236
Schreiber, F234, F254
Schrieber, F117
Schroeder, F181, F300, T7
Schubert, F251
Schulenberg, F226
Schulte, F233
Schulties, F235
Schultze, F165
Schumacher, F201, F257, F260
Schuman, F174
Schuster, F93
Schutz, F7, F108, F218, F225, F234
Schwartz, F13
Schweitzer, F254
Scott, F97
Scroggs, F170
Seamples, F316
Sears, F308
Sebben, F9
Seberger, F91, F143, F179, F257
Seddelmeyer, F66
Seegers, F14, F89, F112, F113, F114, F196, F216, F236, F237
Seehausen, F236, F295, F309
Seeley, F42, F313
Sego, F236
Seigel, T56
Seigneuer, F282
Selk, F88
Semsar, F176
Senne, F181
Sennholz, F89
Seramur, F44, F45, F204
Sertich, F156
Shafer, F137
Shaffer, F94, F284
Shanks, F79
Sharp, F268
Shay, F61, F211
Shays, F278
Sheetz, F156
Shelfo, F257
Shelvock, F112
Sheppard, F82
Sherman, F240, T53
Shewmaker, F120
Shimp, F208, F317
Shisler, F47, F63
Shock, F270
Shortridge, F241, T53
Shoub, F23
Shoup, F21
Siebert, F85
Siebrandt, F47
Siefert, F27
Sigler, F58, F59, F177, F312
Signorini, F35
Sikma, F223, F224
Sikorski, B10
Silberman, F14
Silhavy, F56
Sills, F80
Simmons, F215
Simon, F67, F228, F242
Simonetto, T53

Simpson, F116
Sims, F243, F244, F259
Sininger, F250
Slack, F14
Sloan, T22
Sluiter, F253
Slusser, F313
Small, F250
Smederovac, F178
Smith, F42, F67, F129, F159, F164, F173, F204, F245, F246, F268, F271, F292, F314, F315, T53
Smolinski, F193
Snip, F220
Soelker, F253, F255, F260
Sohl, T49
Solke, F232
Sorensen, B3, F13
Sorenson, T53
Souther, F97
Sowash, F70, F60
Spanier, F201, F260
Speck, F63
Spellman, F42
Spencer, F11, F12, F247
Sperb, F2
Spidler, F228, F229
Spiker, F205, F206
Spitler, F268
Spohn, F26, F28, F66, F248, F249, F250
Sprague, F2, F169
Springs, F57
Sprinkle, F70
Stack, F2
Stacker, F314
Staff, F50
Stanek, F256
Stanley, F158
Stapleton, F282
Stark, F2, F111, F131
Starkey, F107
Stawelle, F266
Stebbins, F94
Stedman, F266
Steeb, F165
Steele, F2, F104
Steffel, F45
Stegmeier, F203
Steiber, F232
Steinard, F104
Steinhilber, F272, F273
Steinmann, B30
Stephan, F251, F260
Stephen, F17, F201, F244, F252, F253, F254, F255, F256, F257, F258, F259, F260, F261, F262, F263, F264
Steuer, F110
Steward, F2
Stewart, F122, F123, F265, F292, F305, T53, T60
Stier, F270, F271
Stillson, F278
Stirling, F33
St. John, F169
Stocker, F120
Stockwell, F126, T60
Stommel, F143, F198
Stoneman, F29
Stoner, F61
Stoops, F130
Storey, F210
Stowell, F20, F22, F23, F171, F266, F267, F268, F269, F270, F271
Strader, F268
Strandberg, F11
Streubig, B6
Strickland, F172, F266, F269
Stringham, F270, F271
Strom, T22
Strong, F158, F159, F272, F273, F274
Stroyeck, F259, F264
Studebaker, F42
Studer, F13
Stuhlmacher, F268
Stull, F42
Sturgess, F139, F275
Sturm, F14
Stuyvesant, F275
Sullivan, F56, F77, F174
Surprenant, F276
Surprise, F117, F267, F268, F276, F277

224

SURNAME INDEX

Index is by story number NOT page number

T - Topical Section   B - Business Section   F - Family Section

Sutter, F179, F244, F252, F258, F259, F260, F261, F262, F264
Sutzer, F23, F171, F269, F270, F271
Swanson, B6, F120
Swearingen, F80
Sweeney, F160, F228
Swinford, F89
Swingendorf, F66
Swisher, T56
Sykes, F298
Szackar, F135
Szyllagi, F240
Szymanski, F55

T

Taillebois, F281
Tailloboiso, F283
Tallady, F141
Tamas, F279
Tanger, F176
Tapajna, F140
Targget, F147
Tarlton, F21
Tarnowski, F105, F127
Tatge, F88, F89, F100, F182, F294
Taylor, B4, F82, F83, F276, F300, T60
Taylor Poultry Farm, B4
Teasdall, F253
Teeter, F313
Tegarden, F6
Templeton, F171
Terry, F141, F142, F190
Teske, F188, F295
Theobald, F309
Thiel, F85, F90, F91
Thielen, F91, F217, F231
Thiemann, F113
Thissius, F114
Tholke, F215
Thomae, F119
Thomas, F4, F71, F152, F172, F173, F206, F234, F267, F279, F314, F315, T53
Thomason, F155
Thomen, F126
Thompson, F59, F161, F207, F209, F210, F248, F250, F280, F298, T53
Thorbury, F283
Thorn, F173
Thornburg, F283
Thornburgh, F281, F282
Thornburghe, F283
Thunherst, F184
Tice, B10
Tikvah, F194
Tilton, B1, F172
Todd, F40
Tompkins, F130
Tonchef, F115
Topping, F180
Torbeson, F272, F273
Torrey, F172
Trager, F297
Tramm, F88
Treece, F268, F269
Treibus, F280
Triebold, F128, F195, F197, F198
Trotter, F75
Trowbridge, F20, F266
Troy, F268
Truax, F284
Trulley, T53, T60
Tucker, B4, F45, F141, F204, F205, F206
Tula, F308
Tuley, F285
Tuma, F204
Turner, B14, F68, F69, F180
Tuttle, F186

U

Uhlenbrock, F239
Umstead, F268
Uncle John's Flea Market, B4
Unruh, F128
Upham, T53
Urbahns, F114

V

Vagner, F286
Vail, F313
Valenti, F97
Vandercar, B1
Vander Lugt, F253, F255
Vander Noord, F221, F223
Vandersee, F103, F287
Van Gorden, F165
Van Gundy, F313
VanHouten, F299
Van Koten, T60
Van Ness, F27
Van Slyke, F117, F137
Van Til, F221
Vargas, F174
Vekasi, F8, F288, F289, F307, F308
Vermilyer, F192
Vician, F121
Vick, F172
Vidler, F115, F290
Vilmer, F291
Vincent, F240
Voeller, F204
Von Hollen, F70, F90
Vorhees, F44, F45, F204
Voshage, F88
Vukin, F265, F292

W

Wachter, F110, F218, F228
Wadle, F14
Wagner, F50, F143, F293
Wagoner, F97
Wahl, F203
Waits, F88
Wakefield, F191
Waldron, F298
Walker, F134, F250, F293
Wallace, F137, F253
Walsh, F141
Walton, F2
Wamsher, T49
Warchus, F93, F94
Ward, F27, F146, F147, F157, T64
Warneke, F256
Warner, F267
Warnock, F106
Wascher, F156
Washington, F102
Wasserman, F194
Wassman, F182
Wassmann, F31, F294, F295
Waters, F270, F271
Watkins, F126, T53
Watson, F207, F280
Watts, F105, F274
Weaver, F136, F296
Webb, B14, B15, F167
Weber, F129, F297
Webster, F14, F158
Wehling, F295
Wehmhoefer, F181
Wehrman, F88, F100
Weiler, F17, F158, F203, F298
Weis, F87
Weiss, F158
Wells, F126, F299
Weltner, F42
Wemple, F61, F117
Wendel, F180, F300
Wente, F309
Wentworth, F313
Westerman, T2
Weston, F253
Whalen, F274
Whalls, F317
Wharton, T56
Wheeler, F70, F117, F276, F287, F301, F303, F304
Whelon, F268
Whiley, F226
Whitaker, F267, T53
White, F119, F280, F303, F304
Whitehouse, T56
Whiting, F156

Wickman, F108
Wilcox, F59, F60, F159, F302
Wilder, F168, F303, F304, F305
Wildermuth, F6, F101, F288, F306, F307, F308
Wildes, F316
Wilds, F308
Wilhelm, F238, T49
Wilkening, F88
Wilkerson, T56
Wilkinson, F193
Willcox, F95
Wille, F88, F181, F183, F195, F197, F198, F216, F309
Willem, F217, F218
Willems, F108
Willey, F203
Williams, F97, F158, F268, F269, F278, T53
Williamson, F248, F250
Willis, F192, F310
Willman, F203
Wilson, F27, F58, F122, F199, F214, F308
Windish, F105
Wingate, F122
Wirkington, F281
Wirt, F308, T22
Wirtz, B6, F17, F179, F218
Wise, F61, T60
Wiseman, F263
Wishtoski, F67
Witt, F268
Witter, F126
Wojtowicz, F135
Wolber, B4, F141
Wolf, F139, F141
Wollenhaupt, F158
Wood, F65, F66, F250, F273, F297, F311, T53, T56
Woodhouse, F95
Woods, B6, F312
Worley, F270
Worthington, F56
Wotkun, F155
Wright, F23, F203, F213, F313
Wukasch, F295

Y

Yacos, F72
Yager, F250
Yankauskas, F244
Yaros, F314, F315, F316, F317, F318
Yates, F254, F256
Yonker, F155
Youkey, F126
Young, F108, F290

Z

Zacharias, F193
Zahora, F184
Zanna, F274
Zapotacky, F53
Zeilenga, F223
Zemke, F294
Ziegler, F88
Ziese, F203
Zimmerman, F73, F98, F171
Ziolo, F148
Zirkle, F94
Zury, T53
Zyp, F190

225

To obtain copies of this book
or for information on how to publish
your own county or community history, contact:

**Curtis Media Corporation
1931 Market Center Boulevard
Suite 105
Dallas, Texas 75207
(214) 651-1025**

John Klasen's Bill for keeping two Stray Colts from Oct 1st 1865 to Sep 1st 1866 Said Colts being taken up by John Klasen on his enclosed premises & were by him duly advertised & appraised by Henry Keilmann, & Mathias Schmitt before George F. Gerlach Justice in St John Township where Said John Klasen resides Said Colts were appraised at two Hundred & Forty Dolls.

Bill

John Klasen paid Clerk $1.00
   "   "   " Printer   1.50
   "   "   " George F Gerlach 2.50
   "   "   "   "   "   "   .50
         Charges for wintering $216.00
            "   " Pasturing   46.00
         Taking the Colts to Crown Point 5.00 $216.00
                        Signed Johann Klasen

State of Indiana }
County of Lake   } ss

Subscribed & Sworn to (before) & approved by George F Gerlach a Justice of the Peace in & for the above County this 5th day of Sep 1866

George F Gerlach
Justice of the Peace